Classical and Contemporary Issues in Indian Studies

Essays in Honour of Trichur S. Rukmani

Classical and Contemporary Issues in Indian Studies

Essays in Honour of Trichur S. Rukmani

Edited by
P. Pratap Kumar
Jonathan Duquette

DK PRINTWORLD
Publishers of Indian Traditions

Cataloging in Publication Data — DK

[Courtesy: D.K. Agencies (P) Ltd. <docinfo@dkagencies.com>]

Classical and contemporary issues in Indian studies :
essays in honour of Trichur S. Rukmani / edited
by P. Pratap Kumar, Jonathan Duquette.
p. cm.

Includes bibliographical references.

ISBN: 9788124606520

1. Yoga. 2. Philosophy, Indic. 3. Vedanta. 4. Hinduism.
I. Rukmani, T. S. II. Kumar, P. Pratap, 1952-
III. Duquette, Jonathan.

DDC 181.45 23

First published in India, 2013

ISBN 13: 978-81-246-0652-0 (HB) ISBN 10: 81-246-0652-8

Printed and published by:

D.K. Printworld (P) Ltd.

Regd. Office : *'Vedaśrī'*, F-395, Sudarshan Park
(Metro Station: Ramesh Nagar), New Delhi - 110 015
Phones : (011) 2545 3975; 2546 6019; *Fax* : (011) 2546 5926
e-mail : indology@dkprintworld.com
Web : www.dkprintworld.com

Preface

THE idea of producing a Festschrift volume in the honour of Prof. T.S. Rukmani occurred informally among the colleagues who are close to her and who sincerely felt it might be an opportune moment to reflect on each others' work with her as the focal point. Several scholars responded enthusiastically to our call for their involvement in the project. The project has taken longer than what we had originally anticipated due to various logistic reasons, but more importantly, in the course of a rigorous editorial process to select and determine the essays that would eventually make it to this volume. The idea behind the volume was not only to reproduce current research works in the field of Yoga, a subject close to Prof. Rukmani's primary research field, but also to look more broadly on the Indian studies so as to include issues of contemporary scholarly significance. Fortunately, Prof. Rukmani's scholarly interests are just as diverse that we could accommodate such diversity of essays as are contained in this volume. We tried to fit these essays within the frameworks of classical and contemporary which we used as the overall theme of this volume. We hope that the essays included in this volume would offer a stimulating reading for both, specialists and generalists alike.

P. Pratap Kumar
Jonathan Duquette
(Editors)

Editorial Disclaimer

THE views expressed by scholars in this volume are their own. The editors are in no way to be held responsible. The essays published here are original, and where an essay has been published in a previous publication, permission to reproduce has been secured.

Acknowledgements

ANY amount of resourcefulness on the part of the editors is not sufficient unless the various contributors of the volume cooperate in the course of its final manifestation. To that end we have been extremely fortunate and privileged to have had the opportunity to work with such a distinguished group of scholars who spent their valuable time and effort to work with us to ensure that the essays published are of the best scholarly standards. We take this opportunity to sincerely thank all of them for their patience and cooperation in this project. Scholars come up with their ideas, but publishers make them available to the larger public by investing their money and resources. We could not have asked for a better publisher than the DK Printworld. The enthusiasm they have shown in this project and the cooperation that they have extended in executing this work is deeply appreciated by us as editors of this volume. We express our sincere gratitude to the publishers in making this volume available in print form for wider readership. Finally, we profusely thank Prof. Rukmani for allowing us to use this opportunity to not only celebrate her life and work through this volume, but also for enabling us to offer to the scholarly world some refreshing ideas from various fields of Indian studies. Prof. Rukmani remains the focal point of the diverse ideas expressed by various scholars in this volume.

P. Pratap Kumar
Jonathan Duquette
(Editors)

Contents

Part Five
Issues of Brāhmanical Intellectuals, Ascetics and Renunciants

Part Six
Issues in Contemporary Hinduism: Environment, Non-violence, Gender, Faith and Syncretism

Prof. Trichur S. Rukmani
— A Biographical Profile —

जयति रुक्मिणी भगिनी संस्कृतसेवाव्रता विवेकधना।
विद्याप्रसारनिरता विद्वन्मानसमरालकुलनेत्री।।

देशे तथा विदेशे शास्त्राध्यापनगुरुत्वम् आदधती।
व्यवहारेऽतिविनम्रा जयति सदा रुक्मिणी विदुषी।।

अध्यापनप्रशासन-कुशला विद्यावतां सततवन्द्या।
पातञ्जलार्णवान्तर्-मणिगणगणनापरमनिगुणा।।

"विद्यासागर" हारा विदितसकलवेदवेद्यकुलसारा।
जयति रुक्मिणी प्राज्ञा भारतविद्याधवलकीर्तिः।।

इति वर्धापयति कश्चिद् अग्रज आशीराशिभिः।
— कृतिरियं रामकरणशर्मणः

Long live Sister Rukmiṇī,
Engaged devoutly in the service of Sanskrit, full of wisdom,
Dedicated to the spread of knowledge
She is a leader of the family of learned swans dwelling in the *mānasarovara* lake.
She bears the difficult task of instructing the Śāstras
Both within her own country and outside it,
In her dealings with the world she is very humble
Thus excels the learned Rukmiṇī.
In the field of teaching as well as in administration
She is an adept and is respected at all times,
She is very skilled at discovering the many jewels
Hidden in the ocean of Pātañjala *Yoga-Sūtra*s.
She is known in the family of scholars
As one adorned with the garland that the title *Vidyāsāgara* is,
Thus excels Rukmiṇī the wise one
With her reputation made resplendent by her knowledge of India.

Thus an elder brother conveys his blessings.
— Rāmakarṇa Sharma

These words by Ram Karan Sharma convey eloquently how truly inspiring Prof. Trichur S. Rukmani's life has been for people who were privileged to know her or to work closely with her in some way or another. It is indeed rare to find together in a single individual, impressive qualities such as knowledge, wisdom, love for teaching and consideration towards others. Prof. Rukmani is a rare instance of such an individual. A scholar, a teacher, a supervisor, a community leader, and also a wife and a mother — all these roles together she has assumed "full of humility" in the world. For the past forty-seven years, Prof. Rukmani has been engaged in teaching and research work in various universities and research institutions around the world, both in India and abroad. All through these years, she has been a mentor and a role model for students and admirers of Indian thought, from different backgrounds and nationalities, young and old. But above all, it is her great scholarship and distinguished academic record in the fields of Hinduism and Indian philosophy that perhaps deserve the greatest recognition, and that is what we wish to honour with the present Festschrift.

Prof. Rukmani had her early schooling in Nemmara, Kerala, where she was born, but moved to University of Delhi for her higher education as her father was employed there. After finishing her B.A. at University of Delhi (1952) with distinction and topping the university, she planned to pursue her graduate studies in mathematics as that was her favourite subject. Mathematics appealed to her sense of precision, clarity and logical rigour. But circumstances were such that Sanskrit, and not mathematics, would become her main field of research during her M.A. In fact, it was the desire of her father who had missed the opportunity of learning Sanskrit but had a great desire to know about the Vedas, Upaniṣads and Sanskrit literature, that eventually prompted her to choose Sanskrit, albeit reluctantly, for her graduate studies. As she once remarked, "in our generation you did not go against the wishes of your parents and so I finally agreed to go into Sanskrit studies for my M.A." But soon the talented young Rukmani felt at ease with this choice and initially specialized in Sanskrit grammar which had a special affinity with mathematics, because it also required precision and logical consistency. She was gratified when she graduated with distinction and secured first position in Sanskrit from University of Delhi (1954). In recognition of her achievement, she was awarded the Convocation Gold Medal which she received from the hands of the late Sarvepalli Radhakrishnan (the then chancellor of the university), whom she still remembers telling her, while giving her the medal, to continue with Sanskrit studies. In the meantime, her fascination for Sanskrit grew steadily, and she also developed a strong liking for Indian philosophical thought. Like some of us, it is therefore through Sanskrit that Prof. Rukmani turned to the study of Indian philosophy and Hinduism at large. On this important phase of her academic studies, she comments: "Although I started as a grammarian, I discovered my heart was in philosophy." In the year 1956, she got married to a young Indian Air Force officer, Flt. Lt. S. Rajamani, who was posted in Delhi at that time. Two years later, in 1958, she obtained the Ph.D. for her thesis, *A Critical Study of the Bhāgavata Purāṇa* from the Department of Sanskrit, University of Delhi. This was a remarkable achievement at the time as she was the first woman, and only the second person, to earn a Ph.D. in Sanskrit from University of Delhi. Soon after, in December 1959, she would give birth to her first child, Ravi.

Prof. Rukmani's academic success would extend to a long distinguished career in the due course. In 1962, she got her first appointment in Jodhpur (Rajasthan) as a Lecturer in Sanskrit at the Kamala Nehru College. In 1964, the year when her second child Parvati was born, she received tenure as a Lecturer in Sanskrit at the Indraprastha College, University of Delhi. She held this post until the early 1980s, a long assignment that was interrupted only during the year 1972-73, when she took study leave to work as a postdoctoral fellow in comparative philosophy at the University of Toronto, Canada. Under the guidance of the late B.K. Matilal, she studied a rather difficult Navya-Nyāya text, called *Pakṣatā* of Jagadīśa. This was a difficult yet a very rewarding academic experience, she recalls, because it enabled her to "get a taste" of Navya-Nyāya, a field of Indian philosophy she had not encountered till that time.

Within a few years of her return from Canada in 1982, she was selected to take over as Principal of Miranda House, the only university college for women of University of Delhi. Very well known for its academic standards, this college had at that time over 2,200 students distributed among 17 departments, about 140 faculty members and also a number of non-academic staff. She occupied this post until 1993 when she left India for South Africa, along with her husband, to take up an assignment as the first Chair in Hindu Studies and Indian Philosophy at the University of Durban-Westville, Durban, South Africa. Three years later, in 1996, she joined the Department of Religion at Concordia University (Montreal, Canada) as Professor and Chair in Hindu Studies where she currently is. Founded in 1989, this Chair is the only Chair in Hindu studies in North America. In addition to these appointments, Prof. Rukmani has also occupied positions in universities such as Oxford University, Jawaharlal Nehru University and University of Montreal, and has chaired numerous editorial boards and committees.

Throughout her career, Prof. Rukmani's scholarly work has spanned a wide range of areas. However, she is particularly well known for her seminal works on Yoga philosophy. Primarily drawn to Advaita Vedānta, she smilingly narrates her encounter with Yoga as an "accident." At some point in her research as a graduate level student, she noticed that the medieval north Indian philosopher Vijñānabhikṣu had not been researched on very well and that most scholars hardly knew about him. Although a pre-eminent philosopher in the Sāṁkhya-Yoga tradition, his sub-commentary on Patañjali's *Yoga-Sūtras*, the *Yogavārttika*, had never been translated in English. Thus, Prof. Rukmani embarked on this huge project of translating for the first time Vijñānabhikṣu's *Yogavārttika* in four volumes (1981-89), a work that has since been acclaimed in scholarly circles as a significant contribution to the furtherance of Yoga philosophical thought. In 1991, she was awarded the D.Litt. degree by University of Delhi for this work, the first and the only one to receive this degree to date in the Department of Sanskrit since its inception in 1924.

Besides numerous articles on Yoga, her other pivotal contribution in this field is a two-volume annotated English translation of the *Yogasūtrabhāṣyavivaraṇa* (2001), a commentary on the *Yoga-Sūtras* ascribed to a Śaṅkara who, Prof. Rukmani believes, lived between the twelfth and fifteenth centuries in Kerala. In a lengthy introduction to this critically annotated translation, she examines the vexed question of the text's authorship which scholars like Paul Hacker et al. had attributed to Ādi Śaṅkara of Advaita fame. Considering the question from all angles, Prof. Rukmani concludes that the work could not have been composed by Ādi Śaṅkara but by another Śaṅkara of a later date. Yoga, according to Prof. Rukmani, is more than a school of philosophy. Frederick Smith, a scholar in his own right, has described her contributions to the Yoga studies as "a guide for thinking about Yoga in a realm in which scholastic and personal practices merge." The *Yoga-Sūtras* are not just the fruit of systematic philosophical reflection but also a frame in which one can integrate different strands of personal experience. She concludes an article on the *Yoga-Sūtras* by saying that "it is best to accept it [Yoga] as a discipline to be followed rather than to be understood intellectually."[1]

1. T.S. Rukmani (1997), "Tension Between *Vyutthāna* and *Nirodha* in the *Yoga-Sūtras*," in *Journal of Indian Philosophy*, vol. 25, no. 6, p. 623.

With this perspective in mind, Prof. Rukmani has helped to make Yoga known not only to academics but also to the larger audience of lay people who have increasingly been getting interested in Yoga as a spiritual and physical discipline in the last few decades, both in India and the West.

Besides her works on the Yoga tradition, Prof. Rukmani has published on topics related to the Upaniṣads, Advaita Vedānta and Sāṁkhya. In trying to understand how ancient and classical philosophers of India were "doing philosophy," she has throughout given a lot of importance to the textual approach. In her view, if the scholar has expertise in the language and a proper understanding of its philosophical vocabulary, "going back to the author's text" can be a rewarding experience and can enable one to understand the intention of the author. According to Prof. Rukmani, the historical development of philosophical and cultural ideas in particular holds an important key to understanding the present. "We are not born in a vacuum," she says, and thus it is one of the scholar's important duties to meticulously study texts of the past to reveal their meaning and relevance for the present. Apart from philosophy, Prof. Rukmani has also contributed widely to the field of Hindu studies in subjects ranging from the Epics, Dharmasūtras and women's studies to aesthetics, folk traditions and Hindu diaspora. Reflecting on the evolution of the field of Hindu studies over the last few decades, she notices that "people have started appreciating that Hinduism is not just Vedānta and have adopted a more holistic approach to the understanding of Hinduism." The focus has shifted from seeing Hinduism purely through "philosophical" lenses to appreciating its multi-faceted nature as a complex social, cultural and religious phenomenon. This goes hand in hand with an increasing inclination, in the postmodern West especially, to accord importance to different methodological approaches to Hinduism, including paths that do not privilege solely Western categories. As she says, referring to Indian philosophy in particular, "a significant change over the last decades has been to stop undermining knowledge systems in other parts of the world and to recognize that it is possible to do philosophy in its own unique way." This hermeneutical understanding features in several of Prof. Rukmani's works, especially those in which she deals with comparative and cross-cultural issues. But most importantly, it also informs her humanistic approach to life. To be really open-minded, not only as an intellectual or academic but also as a human being, living in a vast and culturally diversified world, is an ideal she has tried to fully embody in her life and that has deeply touched and impressed most of her students and colleagues.

Beyond her prolific writing and dedicated teaching, Prof. Rukmani has been active at various levels both within and beyond research institutions. A colleague at Concordia University, Prof. Shaman Hatley, has praised her as "a scholar and colleague of boundless warmth and unfailing enthusiasm, dedicated to the advancement of Hindu studies at Concordia University and within the wider community." She offers free non-credit classes to the community at large, both Hindus and non-Hindus alike, on different aspects of Hindu culture, since 1996 when she joined Concordia University. Sensitive to other people's feelings and concerns, Prof. Rukmani has been engaged since her youth in different kinds of social causes. In particular, she has been active in different women organizations and programmes connected with women. She was President of the Women's Association of University of Delhi for two years and a member of the International Federation of University Women's Fellowship Committee, Geneva (Switzerland) for three years. In recognition of her work, Prof. Rukmani has won several awards during her career. Some of these awards especially given for Sanskrit scholarship are the Delhi Sanskrit Academy award for Sanskrit scholarship (1993); a yearly Fellowship twice at the Indian Institute of Advanced Study (Shimla, 1989/2003); the Award by Mandakini, Sanskrit Research Organization, for excellence in Sanskrit Research (Bangalore, 1997); and the Award for Sanskrit promotion in Foreign land by the First Gita Global Conference (Bangalore, 2003). Prof. Rukmani is also the Chaplain for Hinduism at Concordia University.

Jonathan Duquette
Universität Hamburg, Germany

Introduction

As in other disciplines, Indian studies generally tend to privilege the classical against the contemporary as an idealized past. For this reason, classification of our discourse in Indian studies has generally assumed two important categories: "classical" and "contemporary." Undoubtedly, there is a certain privilege associated with the term "classical," especially in treating India. Obviously, it has something to do with the way in which the orientalist discourse privileged the classical as something that is sought after, something that is the best that India was able to produce and something that perhaps had Indo-European connections. On the other hand, the "contemporary" has always been benchmarked against the standards of the classical and hence its status even though it belongs to a certain lower order nature of the discourse. Perhaps this fits in with the scheme that India itself has produced, viz. a cyclical way of seeing things in which the ancient, the primordial, the beginning of the age was seen as the ideal, and what followed was seen as degeneration of the ideal. This is rooted in the religious cosmology of the Hindus. But what has often gone unnoticed or at least has not been said enough about is that in the typical Hindu cosmology the end is supposed to bring a new beginning once again and hence it is *cyclical*. Therefore, seen as a whole, technically there cannot be anything that is either ideal or degenerate. For it is a process. That is, the simple truth of cyclical way of thinking may be put in the modern cliché — what goes around must come around. That does not mean a value judgement on either classical or modern/contemporary. What is considered classical was once contemporary too. In our enthusiasm to eulogize and idealize the past we lose sight of the present and not realize how different the issues are today. Classical writers on India could not have thought of contemporary issues that we face today. Therefore, what is crucial is not to juxtapose the two as radically separable, but rather to find out continuities between the two.

Understanding Indian society and culture requires taking into account disparate issues. It is not necessary to force a coherent frame to these issues in order to illuminate the unity of Indian culture. Given its diversity of philosophical and religious orientations, such forcibly achieved coherence would only result in missing the point. However, it is useful and pragmatic to find continuity between the seeming disparateness of the Indian world views. The essays in this volume attempt just that and present a variety of issues from classical to contemporary times. Each of the essays in its own way sees the importance of continuity between the seeming dualisms and disparateness. Whether it is Ian Whicher trying to achieve integration between *puruṣa* and *prakṛti* or Ashok Aklujkar seeking to establish the link between Pūrva-Mīmāṁsā and Uttara-Mīmāṁsā *vis-à-vis* the *Saṅkarṣa-kāṇḍa* or Sthaneshwar Timalsina finding continuity between Bhartṛhari and Abhinavagupta, just to cite a few examples in this volume, there is a sense that emerges from the essays presented here that there is a larger universal vision in conceptualizing the Indian world view. Synthesis does not obliterate the diversity rooted in the particular philosophical and scholarly engagements. Furthermore, continuity between the classical and the contemporary, the past and the present, need not always overcome the privilege of the classical and its past authority as it gets reinforced in new ways. Gregory Bailey reminds us of this in his reflections on the *Mahābhārata* (*Mbh*) in this volume —

> Part of the attraction of the *Mbh* is that it looks backwards as well as forwards and this requires it to assert and preserve continuities with the past and perhaps even to justify them.

In general, scholars rooted in the classical texts and traditions tend to be absorbed in the technical and in-depth studies of those materials while those who are concerned with contemporary issues tend to tease out the relevance of those materials for the modern society. The former, therefore, has a technical and specialist readership while the latter is read much more widely. But this way of framing those who are engaged in classical issues and those who are engaged in contemporary issues, is only to widen the gap of their mutual relevance and affinity. What is common to both of them is the materials they rely on. Nevertheless, not all classical sources have come to preoccupy contemporary scholars. Barring a handful of scholars who are still busy with Vedic studies, most contemporary scholars have moved on increasingly to Buddhist and post-Buddhist era materials. Even here, there is a predominance of materials from specially Vedānta and Yoga. This shift could be due to many factors including the nineteenth-century changes that impacted on the Indian heritage. One certainly needs to be conscious of the influence of that period in shaping Indian studies in general. There is also a coalescence of scholarly and lay interest in these two broad areas, an important aspect that cannot be ignored. It does not mean that scholarship moves in the general direction of popular interest. But rather it could mean that scholars are concerned with bringing corrective understanding to the many lay and popular assumptions and hence in some sense it is not entirely problematic to say that the popular interest is in some way the *raison d'être* for scholarly attention to certain areas of study.

But then again, it is not that simple. Now and again a certain virtuoso dominates a particular field of study to the extent that many later generations of scholars follow suit with great dedication, whether they agree with him/her or not. A good example would be none other than Ādi Śaṅkarācārya. Whether subsequent commentators agreed with him or not, Vedānta certainly became the most dominant philosophical preoccupation for many centuries after him. Therefore, a shift in the attention to a certain field/s of study could be influenced by a single scholar's dedicated work. It is in this respect that Prof. T.S. Rukmani occupies an extraordinarily influential position today in generating the kind of interest in the study of Yoga as is evident in the number of essays dedicated to this area of study in the present volume. But unlike the classicists who were committed to a single field of study, she is rooted in her contemporary world of diversity and has extended her interests to a much wider set of issues — ranging from Yoga to Advaita Vedānta, to the Purāṇas, the epics and issues of modern society such as the environment, non-violence, women and above all to the issue of combining critical scholarship with the pursuit of her faith commitment to Hinduism. Not surprisingly, some scholars have dedicated their essays to these contemporary issues in this volume as a testimony to her broader interests.

The present volume therefore reflects this plethora of issues to which Prof. Rukmani has dedicated her scholastic life. Scholars in this volume have addressed these issues from their respective specialized areas of study and have illuminated the complexities in understanding the richness of Indian society and culture. It is the editors' responsibility to tease out the links not only between these diverse set of essays but also between the two generic categories, viz. "classical" and "contemporary" under which these essays have been subsumed. So let me present the plan of the book and the rationale for the plan.

In presenting the plan of the volume the rationale that is used is to do justice to the thinking of Prof. Rukmani in prioritizing the critical issues that preoccupied her work. Undoubtedly she began her work with Yoga and continues to contribute to this field. Therefore it is to this field that we have offered priority without implying any classical superiority to it. For over thirty years she has been at the cutting edge of this vast field that has only now begun to blossom and draw more attention. Some of her eminent colleagues have brought some new insights into this field and have generously allowed us to include their essays in this section of the volume.

Linking the various passages back and forth within the *Yoga-Sūtras* text of Patañjali, Christopher Chapple re-examines the fourth *pāda* of the text. Deploying what has been widely used as method in Biblical Studies scholarship in reading texts in particular, Chapple identifies the related pericopes within the *Yoga-Sūtras* text and finds some compatibility between Patañjali, the Jainas and the Buddhists on the notion of *karma*. However, he points out that unlike Śaṅkara, Patañjali is closer to the Sāṁkhya notion of the physical reality of things than to the Buddhists. Here he (Patañjali) might be closer to the Jainas, as argued by Chapple — "experience within the real world is essential for spiritual maturity and advancement." As a comprehensive summation of Patañjali's philosophy, the fourth *pāda* stands alone, agrees Chapple. However, he hastens to add that "without the fuller descriptions of the afflicted *karma* and the eightfold Yoga practice, it would be difficult to see this culminating chapter as more than a critical review, highlighting and emphasizing key points of Yoga."

In the next essay, Daniel Raveh closely analyses the notion of *prajñā* in Patañjali taking his cue from Prof. Rukmani's seminal essay on the same topic. While Prof. Rukmani's essay covered all the references made to *prajñā* in the *Yoga-Sūtras*, he focuses entirely on a single *sūtra*, *Yoga-Sūtras* 1.49. He reads 1.49 in the light of 1.7 and suggests that the category *pratyakṣa* is present in its absence in the *sūtra* (1.49), for it is against it (*pratyakṣa*) that he thinks the notion of *prajñā* is clarified. Furthermore, he argues that *pratyakṣa* and *prajñā* are similar in the sense that "*prajñā* is implicit in every instance of ordinary *pratyakṣa*; that it is another dimension, a deeper layer of perception, commonly unseen or not put into effect." He points out Vyāsa's threefold distinction of perception — *loka-pratyakṣa*, "external" yogic *pratyakṣa*, and "internal" yogic *pratyakṣa* suggesting that Vyāsa formulated *prajñā* "as valid a *pramāṇa* as sense-perception, inference and reliable testimony, 'working' in areas beyond the scope of the former three." He thus argues that Patañjali's commentators projected *prajñā* as *para-pratyakṣa*. The fact that the commentators have shifted their attention from *samādhi* and concerned themselves mainly with the epistemological status of *prajñā* demonstrates that in their mind it is indeed a valid *pramāṇa* — "a yogic *pramāṇa*."

Alluding to the influences of Jaina and Buddhist ideas on the *Yoga-Sūtras*, Ian Whicher re-examines the relationship between *puruṣa* and *prakṛti* with a view to integrating the two. He is critical of scholars who have viewed Patañjali's Yoga, what he calls, "excessively 'spiritual' or isolationistic to the point of being a world-denying philosophy." His attempt is to offer an alternative to the radical dualism that is generally posited in the Yoga system by many scholars and present it as world-affirming philosophy. By re-examining some key notions in the *Yoga-Sūtras*, such as *pratiprasava* and *kaivalya*, he rejects the more commonly held scholarly views of freedom in Yoga system and argues that

> [T]o confuse (as many interpretations of Yoga have unfortunately done) the underlining purificatory processes involved in the cessation of ignorance/afflicted identity as being the same thing as (or as necessitating the need for) a radical elimination of our psychophysical being — the prakṛtic vehicle through which consciousness discloses itself — is, I suggest, to misunderstand the intent of the *Yoga-Sūtras* itself.

While Whicher is keen to see some integration of *puruṣa* and *prakṛti* at the level of *kaivalya*, Frederick M. Smith re-examines the notion of *kaivalya* from the standpoint of its alleged Vedānticization to the extent that "the term *kaivalya* was unrepentantly replaced by that time in at least some circles in the popular discourse of Yoga by the spiritual vision and terminology of Vedānta." So he begins his investigation of *kaivalya* by closely examining *sūtra*s 18-25 of the second chapter of the *Yoga-Sūtras* which he thinks are the most neglected by the commentators. Arguing for the separability of *puruṣa* and *prakṛti*, unlike Whicher, Smith suggests that "[*k*]*aivalya*, then, is the abandonment (*hānam*) of the *saṁyoga* in which the *buddhi* or active substantive awareness identifies, falsely as it turns out, with both the *puruṣa*, which sees, and the objects seen." He reiterates:

> To repeat: *kaivalya* cannot be the exact equivalent to the Vedāntic state of *mokṣa* or *mukti* because it is brought about by a realization of the separability of *buddhi* (hence of *prakṛti*) and *puruṣa*, rather than of the conjunction of the individual self or *ātman* with the abstract absolute *Brahman*.

Unlike the preoccupation of the above scholars with classical issues of interpretation, Gerald James Larson uses the Yoga notion of god to address a contemporary problem that has besought academics and lay people, viz. the problem of the origin of creation. He argues that the notion of god in the Yoga tradition is unique in that god is neither personal nor is the creator.

Part 2 introduces a shift from the Yoga tradition to the Vedānta tradition. To begin with, John Grimes presents a comprehensive overview of Advaita Vedānta and in the process clarifies some key concepts in understanding its core philosophical import. Most difficult of the issues here is obviously *avidyā*. If *avidyā* is construed as *parameśvarāśraya* then its implications for the understanding of *Brahman* still need further clarification.

Offering a modernist approach to reading Śaṅkara's texts as "documents on a web portal that are hyperlinked together," Vidyasankar Sundaresan attempts to question the generally followed method among scholars, that is, treating Śaṅkara as a commentator of several independent texts, such as the *Brahma-Sūtra*, Upaniṣads and the *Bhagavad-Gītā*. Using this method, he pays attention to some of the generally overlooked portions of the *Brahma-Sūtra Bhāṣya* whereby he draws our attention to the need to understand why Uttara-Mīmāṁsā is constructed differently from Pūrva-Mīmāṁsā. Additionally, he also claims to "have unearthed certain unexpected themes and a *bhāṣya* reference to *parisaṁkhyāna*, thus revealing a hitherto unknown context to the third chapter of *US* [*Upadeśasāhasrī*], namely a meditation at the time of death."

Jonathan Duquette and K. Ramasubramanian focus on clarifying Appaya Dīkṣita's explanation of *avidyā-nivṛtti* by the commentators in the post-Śaṅkara period. The central question that Dīkṣita raises is the place of *avidyā-nivṛtti* in the overall theoretical framework of Advaita. Taking a broad pragmatic view Duquette and Ramasubramanian suggest that diversity of views has generally been appreciated within the post-Śaṅkara period. They see no fundamental discontinuity between the two positions, viz. *avidyā-nivṛtti* as *ātmasvarūpa* and at the same time as *anirvacanīya*, suggesting that the first view may be understood from the standpoint of the result, while the second view is understood as a process in the phenomenal world. They conclude that Appaya Dīkṣita "present[s] different conceptions [of *avidyā-nivṛtti*] with absolute clarity without committing himself to any specific viewpoint. In the pure spirit of Advaita Vedānta, he considers all views as basically speculative and different perspectival approaches to non-dual reality."

In a general treatment of Gauḍīya Vaiṣṇava tradition, Barbara Holdrege contrasts it with the Advaita and Yoga systems and suggests that while the embodied existence and false notions of personal identity are the problems in Advaita and classical Yoga, Gauḍīya Vaiṣṇavism "ascribes central importance to both the body and the person in their constructions of the path as well as the goal of realization."

Part 3 begins with Ashok Aklujkar's valuable contribution to our understanding of the missing link between Pūrva-Mīmāṁsā and Uttara-Mīmāṁsā, viz. the *Saṅkarṣa-kāṇḍa*. Contrary to the view that *Saṅkarṣa-kāṇḍa* is an independent and self-standing work, a view that developed in the post-*Śābarabhāṣya* period, Aklujkar, by examining the various *sūtra*s found in the *Saṅkarṣa-kāṇḍa*, argues that the text in question is a link between the Pūrva Mīmāṁsā-sūtra and the Uttara Mīmāṁsā-sūtra in that the three form a whole. He contends that there is sufficient internal evidence for this inference. He, however, for the sake of helping future research, offers a useful summation of the external evidence as well. He therefore argues:

> [T]hus, it cannot be doubted that the *SK* [*Saṅkarṣa-kāṇḍa*] belongs to the pair that the *MS* [*Mīmāṁsā-sūtra*] and *BS* [*Brahma-sūtra*] form, that it presupposes a position in the middle of the pair and that, in content as well as its perceived mission, it is closer to the *MS* than to the *BS*.

On the matter of confusion between *Saṅkarṣa-kāṇḍa* and *Devatā-kāṇḍa* Aklujkar observes that:

> [A]n easy way to take care of this counter-consideration will be to point out that the references presuming the identity of the *SK* with a *DK* [*Devatā-kāṇḍa*] come from relatively late authors and are, therefore, not as reliable as the other references speaking of the *SK* as a part falling between the *MS* and *BS*.

To those who are interested in Vedānta, the fact that there exists a middle text that links the Pūrva-Mīmāṁsā and Uttara-Mīmāṁsā is indeed a valuable finding that compels them to be wary of generalizations in interpreting either or both philosophies.

The second essay in part 3 by Sthaneshwar Timalsina examines the notions of *śakti* in the philosophies of Bhartṛhari and Abhinavagupta. The central question that he tries to answer is — "how can the supreme reality that is not grasped by other means of knowledge be expressed through language and cognized through linguistic apprehension?" He believes that the answer to this is what finds continuity between the Mīmāṁsā, Bhartṛhari and the Trika philosophers. Emphasizing singularity and universality as the overriding notions in both Bhartṛhari and Abhinavagupta, Timalsina attempts to find continuity between the two, that is, between philosophy of language and the tāntric cosmology.

P. Pratap Kumar's essay in this section deals with finding continuity between the philosophy of the *Gītā* and other Indian philosophical ideas, particularly the *puruṣa* of Sāṁkhya, the *kṣetra* of the Pūrva-Mīmāṁsā and the *Brahman* of the Upaniṣads. In line with the scholarly view that the *Gītā* is a synthetic project, Kumar pays special attention to the concepts of *buddhi* and *sattva* in the *Gītā* against the background of Sāṁkhya system. He argues that the *triguṇa* complex — *sattva, rajas* and *tamas* — which is fundamental to the equilibrium of *prakṛti* is reinterpreted in the *Gītā* with *sattva* receiving a certain priority over the other two. Kumar suggests that there is some continuity between the *Gītā* and Sāṁkhya as far as *buddhi* is understood as the instrument of liberation. However, by closely associating *sattva* with *buddhi, Gītā* attempts to achieve a synthesis between *puruṣa* and *prakṛti.*

In part 4, the first essay by Edeltraut Harzer, using Karṇa-Parva of the *Mahābhārata* epic narrative as the *locus,* highlights the issue of following the technicalities of editing an "authentic" version of the text and following a narrative that has been fluid and dynamic for a very long time. Referring to the divergences between the northern and southern recensions of the *Mahābhārata* text on the one hand, and the different editorial agendas of Vaidya who edited the Karṇa-Parva earlier and Sukthankar, the editor of the Poona critical edition on the other, Harzer raises a pertinent question: "Can the narrative be sacrificed solely for the sake of a more or less mechanical philological agenda?" She bemoans the fact that the critical edition (Poona) has ignored a substantial number of manuscripts from the southern recension and relied too much on the northern recension. It is the normative force that the critical edition has exerted, which worries Harzer. So she agrees with Andreas Bigger that the critical edition be used "for lower textual criticism, not focusing on the search for an Ur-text or best reading."

While Harzer was concerned with scholarly obsession with philological and other such agenda that drives the constitution [perhaps reconstitution] of a text, David P. Lawrence is concerned in his essay with the issues of power and its relationship to truth claims. Sheldon Pollock was perhaps one who has consistently problematized the privileged status of the

Śāstras in the South Asian intellectual discourse. Lawrence begins with Pollock as his initial point of departure. But he avoids relying on the Western philosophies to measure the value of South Asian philosophies. However, combining the idea of "practical reason" of Kant, and Apel's notion of "transcendental pragmatics," he suggests that the South Asian philosophical discourse is transcendental. Distinguishing between *vāda, jalpa,* and *vitaṇḍā,* Lawrence suggests that the Nyāya use of *vāda* has the ideal of establishing the truth on the basis of honesty and civility. Such arguments are not based on hegemonic ethic but "truth-oriented ethic." It is in this sense that the South Asian philosophical discourse is different from the "contemporary culture-power analysis and discursive ethics."

If one of the scholarly preoccupations is to distinguish South Asian philosophical discourse from their counterparts in the West, grammarians are relentlessly analytical about issues of grammatical usages in various Sanskrit texts. John Brockington's essay on the use of past active participle in the *Rāmāyaṇa* is an illustration of the scholarly concern for understanding the texts through grammatical conventions. Often such conventions tell us more about the synchronic and diachronic historical problems in interpreting a text. From a believer's point of view, the text of the *Rāmāyaṇa* might be considered the product of a single author during a single period. But in the hands of grammarians, the *Rāmāyaṇa* is a text that reflects a variety of grammatical conventions. Therefore, Brockington's close analysis of *-vat* suffix indicates three stages during which the use of the said suffix varied increasing in its usage by the third stage, thus implicitly demonstrating that the *Rāmāyaṇa* grew over a period of time. This may not be something that scholars such as Harzer wish to emphasize in dealing with South Asian texts, but it remains a genuine interest of scholarly analysis. Nevertheless, scholarship must press on in the margins of philological analysis, narrative fluidity and coherence.

In Part 5, the first essay by Gregory Bailey provides a sort of sociology of intellectuals in the ancient Indian social milieu. He suggests that the *Mahābhārata* is a text that reflects the Vedic heritage and imposes the same on a larger diverse society envisioning how such a society should be organized along the lines of the *varṇa*s and of different ascetic orders. He points out that while the Brāhmanical authors of the *Mahābhārata* do not often care to identify the opponents when they mount polemics against them, they do take cognizance of the visible success of Buddhism and that their critique of Buddhist monks is to affirm the value of the Vedas and the lifestyle associated with them. Bailey underscores the point that the Brāhmanical intellectuals, by reinforcing the theory of the sacrificial system through the texts such as the *Mahābhārata*, attempted to guarantee "the brāhmaṇas' special status in the emergent caste hierarchy." He also argues that the *Mahābhārata* attempts to reinforce the Vedic ideology even if it had to co-opt the non-brāhmaṇa ascetics to do so. The *Mahābhārata* is perhaps not alone in this rather uncomfortable interface between different ascetic orders and Brāhmanical intellectuals.

Leslie Orr provides an insight into the medieval south by examining the interface between Jaina monks and Śaiva and Vaiṣṇava ascetics between the ninth and sixteenth centuries. Most of the temples built by the Śaivites and Vaiṣṇavites during this period were built against the background of the flourishing Jaina orders. Orr examines their identities and points out that the Jaina ascetics (both men and women) played a significant administrative role in the running of the monastic orders, whereas the Śaiva and Vaiṣṇava ascetics played no significant role in the temples. She suggests that the *saṁnyāsa* life is not reconcilable with the Āgama texts of both Śaiva and Vaiṣṇava backgrounds. However, in the thirteenth century she finds greater inscriptional evidence for ascetics of both the Śaiva and Vaiṣṇava kind, even though the inscriptional evidence during the fourteenth and fifteenth centuries drops. Again in the sixteenth century she finds some evidence in the temple copperplates. She concludes that in the three types of ascetics that she observed — Jaina, Śaiva and Vaiṣṇava — it was difficult to find a coherent model for undertaking ascetic practice. Instead, what she finds is that there was mutual criticism of each other's form of ascetic life. While each one was trying to craft a model that could be reconcilable to their tradition, at the same time they attempted to make use of the various possibilities that were available to them. What they were seeking was a synthesis in the face of competing elements, suggests Orr.

The final section, Part 6, introduces a series of contemporary issues with which scholars have been engaged. In the first essay of this section, Georges A. James suggests that while there are good insights in Hindu tradition towards environmental ethics, the political goals of the Hindu right often have been a disadvantage to implementing Hindu values to foster environmental ethics. He argues that the Gandhian attitude towards other religions as equal can provide space for Hindu religious values in dealing with environmental concerns. According to James:

> [A] critical step towards the implementation of traditional Hindu values

> to issues of environmental concern must be a recognition of the environmental insights that are shared by other religious traditions.

In the following essay, Pankaj Jain provides an insight into the Svādhyāya movement and its relationship with natural resources such as earth, water and trees. He emphasizes the reverential attitude that the members of the movement have towards the earth. By collectively offering their labour freely to build dams in several villages in Gujarat, the Svādhyāya followers have inspired society at large. Jain points out that they do so neither out of an utilitarian outlook, nor to protect ecological resources, but rather "to bring about constructive social manifestation of their spiritual understanding towards the divine that is dwelling in them." As such their goal is to bring about spiritual transformation among the farmers. It is for this reason Jain refers to this phenomenon as "dharmic ecological work."

In contrast to the attitude of devotion and worship toward nature by the followers of Svādhyāya movement, Carl Olson calls attention to the problematic nature of technology which conjures up violence. In the light of Heidegger's distinction of an older meaning of *techne* in the sense of "skilful work of a craftsman" and the modern meaning of technology which is devoid of its poetic sense and conjures up control and exploitation, Olson argues that "[T]he danger to human beings is not technology as such, but it is humans themselves that are problematic and threaten themselves." In the light of Heidegger's analysis, Olson identifies technology as a "complete system of ordering," "epitome of subjectivism," and as a tendency to negate death. If Heidegger viewed technology as something that brings about violence when it becomes a closed system and subjective, Olson points out that Derrida "envisions a primordial violence prior to any form of technology." He elaborates that this violence is not to be confused with the opposite of non-violence. Olson notes that Derrida views violence in a more comprehensive manner. He notes:

> [W]ithin this economy, violence circulates and is exchanged, but most significantly it defers the advent of a menace of an even greater and totally annihilating violence. As the possibility of an even greater violence is deferred, violence distributes itself in acts of lesser violence. By constantly distributing itself and defusing the advent of a primordial form, violence manifests the same non-structure as *différance*.

However, Olson underlines that even though both Heidegger and Derrida come from different metaphysical backgrounds, they both underscored the violence associated with modern technology. While both Heidegger and Derrida are concerned with overcoming violence, Olson suggests that Gandhi's view of violence is grounded in his metaphysics, in that he sees non-violence as a means to liberation. Whether or not the three positions are commensurate with each other is a question that leads Olson to suggest that while Heidegger would agree with Gandhi in principle, Derrida's position that violence precedes technology does not quite sit with it. However, Derrida might be inclined to accept on pragmatic level the idea of any reduction of violence.

Madhav M. Deshpande takes the issue of violence a step further and reflects on it in relation to religion. He links it with the question of free will. He explores this question *vis-à-vis* the problem of evil in many religions. In the context of interreligious conflicts, he raises the question whether religion is a cause of evil or solution to it. From the Hindu perspective, using the *Mahābhārata* and the *Bhagavad-Gītā* in particular, he demonstrates the difficulties in interpreting religious texts and alerts to the dangers of misinterpreting them. Contrasting the characters of Arjuna and Dhṛtarāṣṭra, he asks whether free will really means freedom or simply doing God's will. He remarks that in the context of the Mahābhārata War, both of them had freedom to choose, even though Arjuna in the end chose what Kṛṣṇa advised him to do. It is in this sense that Deshpande thinks there is free will. He therefore suggests that one does not need to blindly follow what the text says, "but to use our god-given intelligence to make sense of the scriptures within a bigger context of one's common sense, rationality, and a personal sense of what is right."

Ramdas Lamb deals with notion of *dharma* in the context of rural education in India, particularly in relation to the scheduled caste Hindus. He explores in detail the difficulties of Satnāmī caste members, especially girls, in accessing higher education. He points out that the academic education offered to them is devoid of any traditional values and does not take advantage of religious education to impart values. Religious education is seen as backward and not relevant to modern society. He points out:

> [T]he lack of any positive discussion of *dharma*, values, character, and associated elements leads a significant number of students to believe that these are not that important or relevant in the world of today.

Lamb argues in favour of education that is relevant to the needs of the rural people using collective learning methods especially in an effort to enable rural girls to access quality education.

The penultimate essay in the volume by V.V. Raman takes us through a personal journey as a Hindu. Through this journey he offers his personal views on various theological and doctrinal points in Hinduism, such as afterlife, *karma*, caste, Hindutva movement, and so on. His reflections combine an enlightened Hindu dimension and a strong affinity to one's religious and cultural tradition. His dialectical view of Hinduism is perhaps captured in these lines:

> Unlike many of my co-religionists, I will not say I am *proud* to be a Hindu, because that word smacks of a cultural high-ground on which I am not comfortable to put myself. However, I consider myself to be extremely fortunate to have been born as a Hindu, and this for several reasons. There is no other religion I am aware of that gives its members as much freedom of thought and practice as modern Hinduism does.

In the following essay, which is the final one in this volume, Afsar Mohammad deals with fluid boundaries that exist between Hinduism and Islam, especially with regard to pilgrimage centres in south India. Constructing the narrative around Gūgūḍu village in Andhra Pradesh, Mohammad demonstrates the significance of a local space, but also its multivalent appeal for more than one religious community. As such in a localized sense, *umma* can include both Muslims and Hindus. Through this local space, he explores the connections between Sūfī and Vaiṣṇava traditions in south India.

The last three essays in particular bring to fore religion in actual practice. While Lamb poignantly recounts the difficulties of Satnāmī Hindu young women in accessing further education, Raman shows what it means to be a Hindu in a modern society, and Mohammad reminds us that at the level of religious practice the boundaries between religions are less singular and monolithic than what the orthodoxy wants to preserve.

Returning to the theme of the volume — classical and the contemporary — the essays presented in this volume represent a wide variety of interests and perspectives. Finding meaningful connections between them is the task of the editors. In offering these essays for the readership, we have endeavored to point out such connections. By composing the particular essays, each author attempted to present us with particular ways of engaging with India and its diversity. Whether they stand on classical materials or contemporary religious practices, they tell us something unique and yet all their ideas can be seen in relation to one another. Our scholarly task, therefore, is one of relating ideas in a meaningful way, not for purposes of synthesis *per se,* nor for syncretistic ideals, but rather for placing them in relation to one another. We hope these connections are as meaningful to the readers as these essays in themselves are. It is through these connections and beyond, that we offer them to the larger readership in celebration of the life and work of Prof. T.S. Rukmani, the person who is the reason for scholars to bringing their ideas together in this volume. The inspiration she has provided to the scholarly community in Indian studies is evident from the many eminent scholars who have offered to be part of this project. As a Telugu-speaking person, I invoke the words of Swami Thyagaraja in saluting all of them:

endarō mahānubhāvulu, andariki mā vandanālu

So many eminent people! Our salutations to all of them.

P. Pratap Kumar
University of KwaZulu-Natal, South Africa

Part One
Issues in Interpreting the Yoga Tradition

1

Reading the Fourth Pāda of Patañjali's Yoga-Sūtras

*Christopher Key Chapple**

THE text of Patañjali's *Yoga-Sūtras* encapsulates spiritual practice for India. It drew from earlier traditions such as Buddhism and Jainism. It also provided a framework through which later scholars were able to reflect and interpret their own paths, particularly as found in the Purāṇas and in the Jaina tradition. Of the four sections or *pāda*s of the *Yoga-Sūtras*, the fourth generally receives the least amount of attention. Titled for the ultimate goal of Yoga, *kaivalya*, it relies upon an understanding of the earlier sections and yet introduces some additional key concepts that help to contextualize the Yoga system. By examining eleven cluster themes of the text, and by relating their concepts to the earlier portions of the text, we can hopefully come to a fuller appreciation of the complexity and subtlety of Patañjali's system.

The fourth *pāda* begins with a seemingly perfunctory dismissal of the significance of the perfections that one can achieve through Yoga practice. These perfections have been the topic of the prior chapter, *vibhūti*, and are said to be accessible through not only Yoga but by drug use and other methods. The third chapter warned that accomplishments such as clairvoyance serve merely as distractions to the ultimate purpose of Yoga, which lies in the cultivation of discernment of the difference between the uninvolved witness consciousness and the realm of transformation and change.

The fourth *pāda* then launches into an explication of the nature of the manifested world of *prakṛti*, contrasting it with the witness consciousness associated with *puruṣa*. *Prakṛti* creates and moves; *puruṣa* merely observes,

---

* Department of Theological Studies, Loyola Marymount University.

neither gathering nor leaving any residue. Patañjali goes on to explicate the nature of *karma.* He explains matter (*vastu*), contrasting it yet again with the singular consciousness of *puruṣa.* Circling back to his earlier discussion of *karma,* Patañjali attributes all manifestations to *saṁskāra*s, urging one to stop compulsive actions driven by the past and enter into the bliss of *kaivalyam.* This must be done through careful, constant discernment. Patañjali urges that just as one has been instructed on how to deal with and overcome the impurities (*avidyā, asmitā, rāga, dveṣa, abhiniveśa*), so one must apply the same techniques to pacify all karmic inclinations. Ultimately, Patañjali asserts that through the experience of *dharma megha samādhi* (a term also employed by the Buddhists), one overcomes all the fetters of *karma* and enters a state of eternal knowledge, regaining one's true form.

In examining the themes and styles of the fourth *pāda,* eleven thematic segments may be discerned. Although this grouping of passages has not been part of the commentarial tradition, this organizational structure may help the reader understand some of the enduring themes set forth in the 34 final *sūtra*s composed by Patañjali.[1]

1. An Abundance of Powers

> Perfections are born due to birth, drugs, *mantra,* austerity, or *samādhi.*
>
> — IV. 1

As noted above, this *sūtra* summarizes various yogic accomplishments. It gives particular emphasis to the importance of *samādhi* by virtue of its position as the last of five avenues to perfection. In fact, these seem to be arranged in order of degree of exertion required. If one is born into a perfect state, then no effort need be applied. If one relies upon drugs to feel moments of perfection (or perhaps bliss), then little change within oneself is required. The recitation of *mantra,* a technique highlighted also in the first *pāda,* requires sustained practice, as does the performance of austerity (*tapas*). The term *samādhi* may include both *mantra* and austerity and also connotes advanced levels of philosophical reflection and psychological introspection. We know from the first *pāda* that the cultivation of *samādhi* can help erode negative influences of past action (I.50). The second *pāda* associates *samādhi* with dedication to *Īśvara* (II.45). The third *pāda,* anticipating the very concluding verse of the *Yoga-Sūtras,* links *samādhi* with radiance and "emptiness of self form" (III.3). Patañjali implies that this would be the highest level of perfection.

1. The translations given are adapted from Chapple 2008.

2. The Abundance of Prakṛti

From the flooding of *prakṛti,* arises *pariṇāma* into other births. — IV.2

The cause [of this flooding that results in experiences] is breakage in the enclosure of the *prakṛtis,* as when a farmer [irrigates his fields]. [Experience] is not caused by the "initiator." — IV.3

The fabricating minds arise only from I-am-ness. — IV.4

Patañjali takes the fascinating step here of referring to *prakṛti* in the plural. This might be an allusion to the Jaina reference to the various manifestations of *karma* (up to 148) as *prakṛtis.* It also serves to particularize *prakṛti.* Rather than appearing as an abstract, universalized principle or theory, this sequence indicates that each moment, each circumstance, may comprise a *prakṛti. Prakṛti* spills forth from one birth to the next. Each birth stems from and depends upon the affliction of self-referentiality, leading the mind to generate and fabricate a narrative rooted in *karma* and productive of more *karma.* Patañjali is careful to point out that these situations arise due to the structures of *karma* and *prakṛti* and, although they provide experience, do not arise from the reason that experiences come forth, referred to here as the "initiator," a term that alludes to the witness, the state of pure consciousness.

3. The Witness

The "initiator" is the one mind among many that is distinct from activity. — IV.5

Therein, what is born of meditation is without residue. — IV.6

These *sūtras* refer back to two segments of the first *pāda.* The phrase "distinct from activity" alludes to the definition of the highest self or *Īśvara* as a distinct *puruṣa* "untouched by afflictions, actions, fruitions, or their residue" (I.24). Though all experiences are presented to consciousness, the highest consciousness remains unaffected. By dwelling in the state of equanimity, one does not accrue or engender new activity. In this state, no further consequence occurs. In the first *pāda,* this accomplishment takes place through the ascent of the stages of meditative equipoise or *samādhi.* Patañjali proclaims that "the *saṁskāra* born of it (spiritual attainment) restricts other *saṁskāras*" (I.50). As one sees the distinction between the realm of change (*prakṛti*) and the changeless (*puruṣa*), a purified way of being in the world emerges.

4. The Nature of Karma

> The action of a *yogī* is neither white nor black; that of others is threefold. —IV.7
>
> Hence, the manifestation of habit patterns corresponds to the fruition of that (*karma*). —IV.8
>
> Because memory and *saṁskāra* are of one form, there is a link even among births, places, and times that are concealed. —IV.9
>
> And there is no beginning of these, due to the perpetuity of desire. —IV.10
>
> Because they are held together by causes, results, correspondences, and supports, when these [go into] non-being, [there is the] non-being of them (*saṁskāras*). —IV.11
>
> In their forms, the past and future exist, due to distinctions between the paths of *dharmas*. —IV.12
>
> These have subtle and manifest *guṇa* natures. —IV.13

This pericope describes the functioning of *karma*, the ontological linchpin of virtually all schools of Indian thought. Both similar to and different from the Jaina world view, Patañjali emphasizes the flow of time in regard to the influences of *karma*. Whereas Jainism articulates *karma* as a mass of viscous, colourful particles that adhere to and occlude the soul's consciousness, Patañjali, while acknowledging its colourful aspect, provides a somewhat more streamlined view of *karma* than that found in the writings of his Jaina counterpart, Umāsvāti. Umāsvāti's *Tattvārtha-Sūtra* specifies the binding nature of *karma*, and the need for its expulsion. Some of the details given by Umāsvāti include a listing of the 25 urges that prompt the inflow of *karma*.[2] Without including specifics, Patañjali emphasizes the time-bound nature of *karma* as well as its aspect of interpenetration.

In characteristically terse language, Patañjali argues for the efficacy of action. He asserts that habit patterns (*vāsanā*) manifest into particular results or fruits. These habit patterns and conditionings exist deep in the memory and they will not always be evident. Assenting to the teaching

2. The list of urges includes those that "lead to deluded world view, murderous activity, urges for visual gratification, possessive clinging," and so forth. For a full account of Jaina *karma* theory, see Tatia 1994, particularly chapters 6-9, "The Inflow of Karma, The Vows, Karmic Bondage, and Inhibiting and Wearing Off Karma" (pp. 147-248).

of rebirth, he states that habit patterns from one life will continue over to another, though he does not describe the process through which this occurs. For the Buddhists, this takes place over the course of 49 days; for the Hindus, the process of re-entry requires at least one agricultural cycle; for the Jainas, this is said to take place instantly, as *karma* committed in the last third part of one's life sets forth an exact trajectory for the *karma*-afflicted soul resulting in a specified outcome. True to his ecumenical approach, Patañjali agrees to the principle of the force of *karma* without setting forth specific doctrines regarding the mechanics of how the human psyche, riddled with memories from past experiences, moves to the next birth existence.

In accord with both the Jainas and the Buddhists, Patañjali states that there is no beginning to the process of *karma*. Alluding to *Ṛgveda* X.129, the Hymn of Creation, he posits that desire, which arises from an indeterminate source, pushes all existence forward, and that to find a place before desire is impossible. Even the gods arose after the moment of desire, when the "one breathed without air, before above was differentiated from below." Rather than ascribing to a theological account of the origins of human life and hence human suffering, Patañjali sets forth the origin of all karmic existence within human ignorance, aligning his philosophy with that of the Buddha.

It is important to see, however, that Patañjali does not teach a simplistic fatalism. By giving details on the web of connection that arises from desire manifesting itself through *karma* (causes, results, correspondences, and supports) and by asserting that all these complexities can be consigned through the practice of Yoga to "non-being," he affirms the second aspect of the Buddhist adage "ignorance has no beginning but it does have an end." At core, both Buddhism and Yoga teach *nirodha*, the blowing out of desire, which also corresponds to the Jaina teaching of *nirjarā*, the expulsion of *karma*.

Buddhism, particularly as articulated by the Mādhyamaka philosopher Nāgārjuna, proclaims that neither the past nor the future truly exists. Nāgārjuna builds on a philosophy of emptiness (*śūnya*) to assert that nothing has an abiding essence. Ultimately, there is no substantial self, nor can substance be found in others. Some scholars place Nāgārjuna (*c.* 100) prior to Patañjali and claim that the fourth *pāda* sets forth Patañjali's objections to the Buddhist view. The Vedānta philosopher Śaṅkara, who lived a few centuries after Patañjali, took issue with Patañjali's position, and in a rather Buddhist fashion dismissed the physical reality of things as *māyā*. Patañjali, following the Sāṁkhya philosophy, insists upon the reality of past and future. His argument is based on simple observation: *dharmas* or circumstances arise from the past, exist in the present, and continue into the future. In order for the doctrine of *karma* to make sense, influences from the past must have bearing on the present and future. Without this flow from moment to the next, no moral imperative would be possible, no purification through the practice of Yoga would be necessary.

To further assert the reality of things, Patañjali states that all things have a manifest (*vyakta*) and subtle (*sūkṣma*) aspect. In order for *vāsanās* or *saṁskāras* to operate, they must have a vehicle through which they may remain latent, to be activated at the appropriate moment. The vehicle that contains their seeds would be *prakṛti*, as explained in the section above on the abundance of *prakṛti*.

5. The Substance of Objects

> From the uniformity of its *pariṇāma*, there is the principle of an object. — IV.14
>
> In the sameness of an object, because of its distinctness from the mind, there is a separate path for each. — IV.15
>
> An object does not depend on one mind; there is no proof of this: how could it be? — IV.16
>
> An object of the mind is known or not known due to the anticipation that colours it (the mind). — IV.17

Patañjali continues to assert the "thingness" of things. For him, the objective world must be real. The process of manifestation follows from precedent to present reality, and from present reality into the future. In what some consider to be an argument against the Yogācāra position of "mind-only," (*citta-mātra*) Patañjali asserts that each object has its own story. It conforms to what came prior, carries similarities to other like objects, and follows its own trajectory. An object remains external to oneself; though one may perceive an object, its existence does not rely upon or require one's perception of it to be real. In response to the question: "Does a tree make a sound if it falls in the forest when no one is there to hear?" Patañjali would retort, yes. Nonetheless, the role of mind in the assessment of and response to situations must be acknowledged. Due to past habituations, the mind is tinged with a particular hue that selects its intentions and predilections. These *vāsanās* or *saṁskāras* predispose an individual to seek out particular objects and experiences to the exclusion of other possibilities.

For instance, children may seek candy or toys, young adults may seek out opportunities for social interaction, older persons may seek out ways to improve their health. This does not mean that adults reject the reality of toys or that children are immune from any concerns regarding friendships or health. It merely suggests that the human being will be selective based on past experience when taking up and engaging objects in the present moment.

At a later time, the Jaina philosopher Haribhadra asserts that the sufferings of the world must exist for the path of freedom to be relevant. Without the sting of *karma* there would be no incentive for improvement. In the *Yogadr̥ṣṭisamuccaya* he writes: "if only a singular essence is proclaimed, then there could never be the two states of life (happiness and misery)" [v. 198] (Chapple 2003: 62). For both Patañjali and the Jaina thinkers, experience within the real world is essential for spiritual maturity and advancement. The world and the karmic realm of cause and effect must be real in order for one to learn the lessons offered by life.

6. Puruṣa Cannot Be Seen or Described

> The fluctuations of the mind are always known due to the changelessness of their master, *Puruṣa*. —IV.18
>
> There is no self-illuminosity of that (*citta-vr̥tti*), because of the nature of the Seen. —IV.19
>
> In one circumstance, there is no ascertainment of both (*vr̥tti* and *puruṣa* together). —IV.20
>
> In trying to see another higher mind there is an overstretching of the intellect from the intellect and a confusion of memory. —IV.21
>
> Due to the non-mixing of higher consciousness, entering into that form is [in fact] the perception of one's own intellect. —IV.22

This sequence of verses emphasizes the distinction between the realm of the manifest and the non-involvement of the witness consciousness. Earlier in the text, Patañjali states that "The nature of the Seen (*prakr̥ti*) is only for the purpose of that (*puruṣa*)" (II.21). This echoes the statements in the *Sāṁkhya Kārikā* that *prakr̥ti* operates and performs "for the purpose of the Spirit" (v. 42) and that "this effort in the activity of Nature (*prakr̥ti*) . . . is for the liberation of each Spirit" (v. 56). Just as in the third *pāda* where Patañjali states that there is a difference between the purified *sattva* or state of elevation achieved through Yoga and the witness consciousness that remains forever untainted (III.49), so in this passage, Patañjali lays great emphasis to make sure that one does not fall into the delusion of claiming the higher awareness of pure consciousness as an epiphenomenon of oneself. No matter how many contortions the mind may attempt to manoeuvre, the mind can never know the luminosity of the pure consciousness for whom all actions are performed. Any attempt to attribute this higher mind to one's own identity will result in delusion.

7. The Seen (Prakṛti) Arises Due to Saṁskāras

> All purposes [are known due to] the mind being tainted with Seer and Seen. —IV.23
>
> From action having been done conjointly for the purpose of another, it is speckled with innumerable habit patterns. —IV.24

Patañjali reiterates that the interaction between witness and activity, Seer and Seen, comprises the experience of life. Earlier referred to as a state of confusion (*saṁyoga*), the task of the *yogī* is to undo the tendency to repeat what has been performed in the past due to past habit patterns (*vāsanās*). The aggregation of past experiences both constitutes the beauty of life and also weaves a web of attachment that Yoga seeks to unravel to set one free.

8. See the Difference, Stop Compulsiveness, and Enter into Kaivalyam

> The one who sees the distinction discontinues the cultivation of self-becoming. —IV.25
>
> Then, inclined towards discrimination, the mind has a propensity for *kaivalyam.* —IV.26

To see the difference between the witness consciousness and the realm of activity and change, signals an epistemological maturity that leads to deliverance from the toils and troubles of the world. Patañjali, in a sense, seems to be summarizing, in these two *sūtras*, the culmination of Sāṁkhya as found in Īśvarakṛṣṇa's *Sāṁkhya Kārikā*:

> From the study of the constituents of manifest reality,
> the knowledge arises that "I do not exist, nothing is mine, I am not."
> This knowledge leaves no residue,
> is free from ignorance, pure and singular (*kevala*) —v. 64.

By negating identity with the realm of the individual self, one disentangles oneself from the bondage of *karma*. The residue of past habitual actions ceases. The mind tends to move toward moments of remove and repose rather than attraction and action.

9. How to Cope with Backsliding

In the intervening spaces of that, there are also other intentions, due to *saṁskāras*. —IV.27

The cessation of them is said to be like that of the afflictions. —IV.28

The Jaina system of 14 *guṇa-sthānas* posits that the quest to purge oneself of all karmic tendencies requires spiralling through 14 different levels of varying degrees of karmic burden. With each ascent, some *karma* falls away. With each descent, new *karmas* occlude the energy, consciousness, and bliss of the soul (*jīva*, a term not used by Patañjali). According to commentaries on the *Tattvārtha-Sūtra*, nine rungs on the *guṇa-sthāna* allow one to climb higher. Three rungs force one to fall deeper into the mire of *karma* (Tatia 1994: 36). According to Patañjali, the force of *saṁskāras* asserts itself, resulting in a fall. To avoid this pitfall, the text advises to counteract the *saṁskāras* in the same manner as one confronts the afflictions (*avidyā, asmitā, rāga, dveṣa, abhiniveśa*) that are described at the beginning of the second *pāda*. The first technique is the cultivation of opposites (*pratipakṣa bhāvanā*), a practice found in the observance of the disciplines and observances; the first two limbs of Patañjali's eightfold Yoga. The second technique is the practice of meditation (*dhyāna*). Patañjali specifies the process as follows:

These subtle [afflictions] are to be avoided by return to the origin. —II.10

The fluctuations [generated by those afflictions] are to be avoided by meditation (*dhyāna*). —II.11

The residue of *karma*, rooted in affliction, is felt both in seen or unseen existence. —II.12

While the root exists there is fruition of it as birth, duration, and experience. —II.13

This synoptic description of *karma* highlights that past *karma* must be understood in order to be purged. By tracing back the root cause of action and by taking corrective action, the influence of the afflicted *karmas* can be diminished. By placing oneself into a state of meditation rather than reacting and responding to impulse, one is able to rebuild the patterning of one's life. In order to avoid backsliding, Patañjali prescribes a regular practice of meditation in order to cleanse the psyche.

10. Discernment

Indeed, in [that state of] reflection, for the one who has discriminative

> discernment and always takes no interest, there is the cloud of *dharma samādhi.* —IV.29
>
> From that, there is the cessation of afflicted action. —IV.30
>
> Then, little is to be known due to the eternality of knowledge which is free from all impure covering. —IV.31

This form of meditation becomes integrated into all aspects of daily life. Two key practices cloak such an individual in a perpetual state of virtue. First, the *yogī* develops the unflagging ability to remember that all the incessant changes of *prakṛti*'s dance within the manifest world are for the benefit of the witness. Second, the practitioner identifies with the state of consciousness that, as defined in the *Sāṁkhya Kārikā,* is the witness, independent, neutral, merely observing, and inactive (v. 19). Patañjali describes this witness consciousness with elegant simplicity: "The Seer only sees" (II.20). By girding oneself with this dispassionate wisdom, the *yogī* remains unflappable. Consequently, the influences of the past no longer hold sway. Knowledge (*jñāna*) becomes the mainstay of one's life, removing all afflictions from the past and avoiding further afflictions in the future.

11. Freedom

> From that, the purpose of the *guṇa*s is done and the succession of *pariṇāma* is concluded. —IV.32
>
> Succession and its correlate, the moment, are terminated by the end of *pariṇāma.* —IV.33
>
> The return to the origin of the *guṇa*s, emptied of their own purpose for *puruṣa,* is *kaivalyam,* the steadfastness in its own form, and the power of higher consciousness. —IV.34

Prakṛti manifests the world through the three *guṇa*s, the constituents of reality that take the form of lightness (*sattva*), activity (*rajas*), and heaviness (*tamas*). All that can be seen arises due to the combinations of these aspects. Each particular object and each narrative event, large or small, has taken shape in order to provide experience for the Seer or *puruṣa.* The emergence from latent *saṁskāra*s into manifest aspects of reality is referred to as *pariṇāma.* When the task has been fulfilled and when the mistaken identity of the seen with the seer ceases, then the momentum for reaching outward, propelled by desire into the realm of the senses, ceases. When *pariṇāma* ends, the string of associated afflicted *karma*s goes to a state of pacification.

The concluding *sūtra* sets forth five aspects through which freedom may be described. First, the *guṇas* of *prakṛti*, having served their function of providing experience for the seer, go into quiescence. Second, Patañjali describes this quiescence as a state of empty fullness; they have danced what seemed to be the dance necessary to bring the *yogī* to a state of purgation. Third, this state is deemed to constitute prime singularity, a state of blessed isolation or aloneness, not of a lonely sort, but of radical independence and freedom from all worldly attachments and identities. Fourth, the individual, having lost her or his attachment to individuality, takes up one's own form (*svarūpa*), a state referred to earlier by Patañjali as the stability (*avasthānam*) that arises from quieting the mind (I.3). Fifth, this freedom delivers one into a state characterized as the power of consciousness (*citi-śakti*), suggesting, as does the metaphor of the *dharma* cloud, that consciousness continues after the afflicted realm has been set aside.

Conclusion

Various scholars have regarded the fourth *pāda* to be an independent text, particularly Paul Deussen and J.W. Hauer who parse Patañjali's compendium into five different texts, and Surendranath Dasgupta, who regards it to be a latter addition.[3] From the survey of the text in this present study, aside from the transitional first *sūtra*, I would agree that although it shares vocabulary from many of the earlier *sūtras*, the text stands on its own. It lays out a reason for the pursuit of Yoga (a wholesome way to gain perfection). It sets out its philosophy of *prakṛti*, *puruṣa*, and *karma*. This metaphysical and physical view of reality becomes a call to action. Patañjali urges the application of meditation to abrogate the influences of past afflicted action. The text culminates in a soteriology, a happy ending wherein the premises of the system apparently result in a state of abiding deliverance from suffering and an abiding freedom. In this regard, it provides all the requirements of a *darśana* text and even exceeds the *Sāṁkhya Kārikā* in its brevity. None the less, without the fuller descriptions of the afflicted *karma* and the eightfold Yoga practice, it would be difficult to see this culminating chapter as more than a critical review, highlighting and emphasizing key points of Yoga.

3. Deussen (1920) divides the first *pāda* into two sections, sets forth *kriyā-yoga* as a separate text including the discussions of afflictions and Sāṁkhya, extends the *aṣṭāṅga-yoga* section all the way through the third *pāda*, and proclaims that the *kaivalya pāda* is a separate book. Hauer (1958) names a similar grouping: *Nirodha* (I.1-22), *Īśvarapraṇidhāna* (I.23-51), *Kriyā* (II.1-27), *Aṣṭāṅga* (II.28 – III.55), and *Nirmāṇa-citta* (IV.1-34). Dasgupta (1951) sees a continuous text in the first three *pādas* and considers the fourth *pāda*, the topic for this study, to be a separate, later addition.

By dividing this chapter into eleven themes, the overall intent of Patañjali's philosophy may be clearly discerned. He begins with a transition verse hearkening back to the prior chapter: every *yogī* seeks success (*siddhi*). He next reminds the reader of the two core principles that underlay Yoga: the abundant manifestations of *prakṛti* and the witness consciousness of the *puruṣa* who neither arises from nor creates residues. Patañjali devotes his largest segment of the chapter to the nature of *karma* and its effects, referred to both as *saṁskāra*s and *vāsanā*s. *Karma* is colourful, it resides in the memory, it bears fruition, it has extensive linkages that implicate a range of associated things and behaviours, it has no fixed point of beginning, it can be pacified. Its subtle aspects flower forth into manifestation. Its past aspects fructify in the present and the future.

Patañjali's fifth theme in the chapter relates to the Yoga and Sāṁkhya (and Jaina) commitment to the reality of *karma* and its consequences. Things and narratives result from the process of *pariṇāma*. Karmic events bear fruit as objective realities (*vastu*). Without the reality of this mechanism, no self could experience suffering. Unlike the Buddhists who proclaim no-self (*anātman*) and the Advaita Vedāntins who proclaim all things to be *māyā*, Patañjali proclaims the reality of multiple things that are distinct from one another and that must exist in order to provide experience. Experience leads to suffering (*duḥkha*) which provides the incentive to seek freedom.

Having reiterated his commitment to the significance of substantiality, albeit an instrumental argument (things, which cause suffering, not only exist in their own right but also serve the purpose of advancing the ultimate goal of freedom), Patañjali again returns to explain a subtle aspect of the witness consciousness. The moment that consciousness becomes objectified, it no longer can be called consciousness. Hence, it becomes impossible for a person to logically proclaim his or her own freedom. One might describe a difference within oneself that will also be apparent to others. This difference would be evident in the fact that binding *karma*s no longer drag an individual into the depths of *tamas* or the excitations and perturbations of *rajas*. But the moment one claims or identifies consciousness, unless done with great metaphorical skill, one merely concretizes an identity that by definition is vulnerable to change and hence suffering. Therefore, even at this higher level of grappling with ultimate meaning as expressed through metaphor, the things of the world still depend upon *karma*. By seeing that one's freedom cannot be found even in the best of metaphors, one can stop compulsive behaviour and enter into a state of blessed solitude. If the *saṁskāras* reassert themselves, Patañjali advises the practice of applied discernment and meditation.

Patañjali's final two themes, discernment and freedom, capture the spirit of the enlightened life. Do not become attached. Do not place investment in the outcomes of *karma*. From this, virtue proceeds, surrounding one like a pure white cloud. Afflicted action ceases. Eternal knowledge dawns. All that needed to have been done has been done. The impulse toward creation and manifestation has been quieted. One settles and stands secure in one's own stance as the witness consciousness. The power of consciousness observes.

References

Baba, Bangali (tr.) (1976), *Yogasūtra of Patañjali with the Commentary of Vyāsa: Translated from the Sanskrit into English with Copious Notes*, Delhi: Motilal Banarsidass.

Chapple, Christopher K. (2003), *Reconciling Yogas: Haribhadra's Collection of Views on Yoga with a New Translation of Haribhadra's Yogadṛṣṭisamuccaya*, Albany: State University of New York Press.

—— (2008), *Yoga and the Luminous: Patañjali's Spiritual Path to Freedom*, Albany: State University of New York Press.

Dasgupta, Surendranath (1951), *Yoga Philosophy in Relation to Other Systems of Indian Thought*, Calcutta: University of Calcutta.

Deussen, Paul (1920), *Allgemeine Geschichte der Philosophie*, vol. I, pt. 3, Leipzig: B.G. Teubner.

Hauer, Jakob W. (1958), *Der Yoga*, Stuttgart: Kohlhammer.

Larson, Gerald J. and R. Shankar Bhattacharya (eds.) (2007), *Yoga: India's Philosophy of Meditation* (*Encyclopedia of Indian Philosophies*, vol. XII), Delhi: Motilal Banarsidass.

Rukmani, Trichur S. (2001), *Yogasūtrabhāṣyavivaraṇa of Śaṅkara: Vivaraṇa Text with English Translation and Critical Notes along with Text and English Translation of Patañjali's Yogasūtras and Vyāsabhāṣya*, vols. I-II, New Delhi: Munshiram Manoharlal.

—— (1981; 1983 1985; 1987), *Yogavārttika of Vijñānabhikṣu: Text with English Translation and Critical Notes along with the Text and English Translation of the Patañjali Yogasūtras and Vyāsabhāṣya*, vols. I-IV, New Delhi: Munshiram Manoharlal.

Tatia, Nathmal (tr.) (1994), *Tattvārtha Sūtra: That Which Is by Umāsvāti with the Combined Commentaries of Umāsvāti, Pūjyapāda, and Siddhasenagaṇi*, San Francisco: HarperCollins.

Woods, James H. (1914), *The Yoga System of Patañjali*, Cambridge: Harvard University Press.

2

Rethinking Prajñā
Yoga-Sūtra 1.49 under a Philosophical Magnifying Glass

*Daniel Raveh**

> A real translation is transparent; it does not cover the original, it does not block its light. — Walter Benjamin, *The Task of the Translator*[1]

It is a pleasure to contribute a paper to a volume in the honour of Prof. Rukmani. I share her deep interest and profound enthusiasm, even if not her remarkable proficiency, in Pātañjala-Yoga. Her articles on Yoga philosophy, appended to her "transparent translations" of Vijñānabhikṣu's *Yogavārttika* and of the *Yogasūtra-Bhāṣya-Vivaraṇa*, are in a sense a translator's note, and a translator — as Gayatri Chakravorty Spivak once said, and anyone who has ever tried his hand in translation knows — is the most intimate of readers. Hence, Rukmani does not just write about, but always with and within the text she works on. In her articles she investigates the meanings of key notions of Yoga philosophy such as *avidyā*, *vikalpa*, *vyutthāna*, *nirodha* and *prajñā*. In the following lines I will take Rukmani's perceptive article "Patañjali's Prajñā and Bhartṛhari's Pratibhā: A Comparative Study" as an open invitation to look further into the notion of *prajñā*, or more precisely *ṛtambharā prajñā*, "truth-bearing yogic discernment," as presented in *Yoga-Sūtra* 1.49. If Rukmani, in her thorough article, follows the notion of *prajñā*, which "the entire system of *rāja-yoga* hinges on," (Rukmani 1989b: 183) in all its five appearances in the *Yoga-Sūtra* text (*YS* 1.20, 1.48, 1.49, 2.27, 3.5), then the following paragraphs are an exercise in close reading of a single *sūtra*, 1.49, within the context of the *samādhi-pāda*, and *vis-à-vis* Patañjali's commentators, including Rukmani's own Vivaraṇakāra and Vijñānabhikṣu.

---

* Department of Philosophy, Tel Aviv University.

1. Benjamin 1999: 79.

Patañjali opens the *YS* with the striking definition of Yoga as "cessation (*nirodha*) of mental activity (*citta-vr̥tti*)."[2] Subsequently, he clarifies what he sees as belonging to the category of "mental activity," enumerating a fivefold mental activity scheme which the process of Yoga aims at stopping or at least suspending. The initial component of Patañjali's *citta-vr̥tti* scheme is *pramāṇa*, or "valid knowledge." In *YS* 1.7, he elucidates that "valid knowledge is based on sense-perception (*pratyakṣa*), inference (*anumāna*) and reliable testimony (*āgama*)."[3] Later, in *YS* 1.49, Patañjali introduces the notion of *r̥tambharā prajñā*, "truth-bearing yogic insight," which replaces or at least supplements *pratyakṣa* as the *yogin* moves forward, or inward, on the yogic path.

According to Patañjali,

> [*r̥tambharā prajñā*] is essentially different from knowledge based on reliable testimony and inference, as it touches on particulars.[4]

The capacity of *r̥tambharā prajñā*, as "yogic knowledge" accomplished through *samādhi*, to illuminate particulars, not just universals, will be explained shortly. But first, I would like to call attention to the fact that in light of *YS* 1.7, "something is missing" in *YS* 1.49. Patañjali suggests that *r̥tambharā prajñā* is different from or has an *anya-viṣaya*, a different object (namely particular instead of universal), than knowledge (*prajñā*) based on reasoning and reliable testimony.[5] He does not say that it is fundamentally different from, or has a different object than knowledge based on *pratyakṣa* or sense-perception. I would like to argue that *pratyakṣa* is "present in its absence" in the *sūtra* under discussion. Moreover, I believe that in the present case, as elsewhere in a synoptic work such as Patañjali's, we should listen carefully not just to the said, but even to the unsaid. By not mentioning *pratyakṣa*, or through its "presence in absence," Patañjali alludes to a common denominator between *prajñā* and *pratyakṣa*. Despite their different scopes — *pratyakṣa* depending on and "working" within

2. *yogaś citta-vr̥tti-nirodhaḥ* (*YS* 1.2). Under Rukmani's softer pen, it is "Yoga is the restriction of the modifications of the mind" (1981: 31).
3. *pratyakṣānumānāgamāḥ pramāṇāni* (*YS* 1.7).
4. *śruta-anumāna-prajñābhyām anya-viṣayā viśeṣa-arthatvāt* (*YS* 1.49). Rukmani translates, "[*r̥tambharā prajñā* or truthful discernment] has a different object from that of the intelligence arising from scriptures and inference; because it has a particular as its object" (1981: 247).
5. Reliable testimony — in *YS* 1.7 Patañjali uses the term *āgama*. In *YS* 1.49 he opts for the term *śruta*. His commentators agree that in the present case, *āgama* and *śruta* are synonyms.

the range of the senses, *prajñā* beyond their reach — both are of the capacity of capturing particulars. The special status of *pratyakṣa* in *sūtra* 1.49, its "presence in absence," enables the sūtrakāra to use it as an illustration of *prajñā*, i.e. to clarify what *prajñā* is through sense-perception as its "conventional parallel," and simultaneously to underscore the profound difference between the two. Patañjali cannot proclaim that *prajñā* and *pratyakṣa* are similar, each belonging to a different consciousness-mode, internal opposite external, or yogic *vs.* mundane, but he nevertheless allows the reader to "feel" the "similarity." Moreover, through the "comparison" of the two, Patañjali introduces *prajñā* as a means of "yogic knowledge." Not just of "insight," "discernment," or any other term lacking an epistemological commitment, but of "knowledge" in the full sense of the word. This is to say that like other *mokṣa*-thinkers, Patañjali attempts, at least in the present instance, to "knowledgify" the meditative experience, in order to maintain its "objectivity," "necessity," and even "reality."

Before turning my magnifying glass to Patañjali's commentators on *YS* 1.49, I would like to further speculate whether *prajñā* resembles *pratyakṣa* not just in essence, i.e. in its immediacy, directness, and capacity to reveal the particular, but also in the sense that both are "present in their absence." *Pratyakṣa* is "present in its absence" in the formal sense that in *YS* 1.49 it is pulled out of the *pramāṇa* triplet formulated in *YS* 1.7 and accepted by almost every *darśana* or philosophical position. *Prajñā*, on the other hand, is "present in its absence" in a more fundamental sense. I will try to explain how.

In *YS* 1.47, Patañjali depicts the meditative setting in which *ṛtambharā prajñā* arises. According to him,

> When [the meditative state called] *nirvicāra* becomes lucid, clarity emanating from the inner-self arises.[6]

According to Vyāsa (in *YSb* 1.47), the clarity (*prasāda*) under discussion reveals things "as they are" (*bhūtārtha*). To elucidate his statement, he quotes a saying which resembles this clarity to the lucid vision from the top of a hill. From the (inner) hilltop, the bhāṣyakāra explains, the *aśocya* (free from suffering) *yogin* is in a position to see those who are still "down there" as suffering (*śocya*). Hence *adhyātma-prasāda* (clarity emanating from the inner-self) is presented as an outlook "from above," or as the gaze of a *yogin* no longer involved in or determined by phenomenal or mundane

6. *nirvicāra-vaiśāradye 'dhyātma-prasādaḥ.*

experience. It is an outlook which reveals the phenomenal realm "as it is," i.e. as intermixed with *śoka* or suffering. Vācaspatimiśra clarifies that *adhyātma-prasāda* does not have the self (*ātman*) as its object (*viṣaya*), but rather as its substrate or base (*ādhāra*).[7] Hence it is not clarity which reveals the self, i.e. *puruṣa*, but clarity which *puruṣa* is the source of. The Vivaraṇakāra and Vijñānabhikṣu suggest that it is the clarity with regard to the distinction between *puruṣa* and *prakṛti*, or *puruṣa-prakṛti-viveka* as the latter puts it. This is to say that to see *prakṛti* "as it is," is to see it as different from, or not essentially entwined with *puruṣa*. *Prajñā*, as the following paragraphs will illustrate, is a special type of knowledge facilitated by the clarity emanating from *puruṣa*. What I am trying to suggest is that since *puruṣa* is always there as the inner core of the human person and as the "origin of awareness,"[8] whether acknowledged or not, covered by clouds of *avidyā* or revealed through the yogic process; the clarity or *prasāda* originating from it, is also there, available, "waiting" to be disclosed. Patañjali himself speaks of the process of Yoga in terms of *Prakāśa-āvaraṇa-kṣaya*, or "removal of the covering of the inner light."[9] Patañjali's commentators, as we shall see below, portray *ṛtambharā prajñā* as *para-pratyakṣa* or "higher perception." My contention is that "truth-bearing" *prajñā* is implicit in every instance of ordinary *pratyakṣa*; that it is another dimension, a deeper layer of perception, commonly unseen or not put into effect. As such, it is "present in its absence," or "silently accompanying" every act of perception, to be unveiled as the clarity or light of the inner-self is "released."

How Do the Commentators Read YS 1.49?

Vyāsa opens with the attempt to explain why reliable testimony (*śrutam āgama-vijñānam*) and inference (*anumāna*) cannot capture the particular.[10] In the former case, he suggests, it derives from reliable testimony being based on and rooted in words (*śabda*). He thus echoes Patañjali's stand

7. *Tattvavaiśāradī* 1.47, in Miśra 1998: 125.
8. The articulation is Ian Whicher's (2000: 144).
9. *YS* 2.52 and 3.44; also see Christopher Chapple's "Luminosity and Yoga" (2008: 71-82), a chapter working with images and metaphors of light in the *Yoga-Sūtras*.
10. Patañjali and his commentators do not question the very possibility of perceiving particulars, even through *pratyakṣa*. Monima Chadha, formulating a "Nyāya-Kantian Approach" (2001) and "drawing inspiration from Navya-Naiyāyikas" (2004), argues that (a) we cannot in effect perceive particulars, and the very idea of perceiving a particular-as-such is incoherent; and (b) we can perceive only universal features. Her contribution in this respect is intriguing, even if it is beyond the scope of the present discussion.

with regard to the "vikalpic" nature of language.[11] "*Vikalpa*," Rukmani explains, "depends on understanding the meaning of words, and does not depend on the words referring to an existent object" (Rukmani 1989c: 167). Language, therefore, is "too far" from its referents, remaining always in the sphere of approximation and generality.

Anumāna, as per Vyāsa's gloss, cannot touch on particulars because of its in-built indirectness. When someone reaches somewhere, he exemplifies, we "calculate" through inference that motion has taken place. Hence *anumāna* is portrayed as a second-order *pramāṇa*, which depends on the first-order *pratyakṣa*.[12]

Vyāsa further argues that *loka-pratyakṣa*, "worldly" or ordinary sense-perception, cannot capture subtle (*sūkṣma*), hidden (*vyavahita*) or distant (*viprakr̥ṣṭa*) objects, and therefore *prajñā* is needed. He employs the exact words of *YS* 3.26, a *sūtra* which discusses the activation of extraordinary senses through yogic meditation.[13] Vyāsa, then, distinguishes *prajñā* not just from *śruta* and *anumāna*, mentioned in *YS* 1.49 explicitly, but even from *pratyakṣa*, interpreted by him as *loka-pratyakṣa*, which is very much a part of the *sūtra* — or so I am trying to argue — even if *via negativa*, in its absence. It is implied (taking into consideration the reference to *YS* 3.26) that *prajñā* is "yogic sense-perception," revealing the subtle, hidden and remote, and "working" not with the ordinary senses but with the sharper, supra-normal senses mentioned in the *vibhūti-pāda*.[14]

Vyāsa further alludes to a debate with a *pūrva-pakṣin*, a philosophical opponent who argues that a particular (*viśeṣa*), the knowledge of which cannot be ascertained through *āgama*, *anumāna* or *loka-pratyakṣa*, does not exist. The bhāṣyakāra firmly answers that such a particular, whether pertaining to a subtle element or to one's own consciousness (*bhūta-sūkṣma-gato vā puruṣa-gato vā*), can definitely be grasped through *prajñā* which

11. See *YS* 1.9, 1.42 and 3.17.

12. Vācaspatimiśra in his commentary of *YS* 1.7 (Miśra 1998: 29) refers to *pratyakṣa* as *mūla-pramāṇa*, i.e. as the root of all other (conventional) *pramāṇa*s.

13. *YS* 3.26: "By focusing the light of (extraordinary) sense-activity, knowledge of the subtle, hidden and remote is attained" (*pravr̥tty-āloka-nyāsāt sūkṣma-vyavahita-viprakr̥ṣṭa-jñānam*).

14. See also *YS* 3.37: "Hence (as a result of obtaining *puruṣa-jñāna*, i.e. "knowledge of *puruṣa*" as fundamentally different from *prakr̥ti*), *prātibha* (yogic illumination) and extraordinary senses of hearing, feeling, seeing, tasting and smelling arise" (*tataḥ prātibha-śrāvaṇa-vedanā-ādarśa-āsvāda-vārtā jāyante*); and *YS* 3.42: "Through *saṁyama* on the relation between ear and space, divine hearing is attained" (*śrotra-ākāśayoḥ saṁbandha-saṁyamād divyaṁ śrotram*).

occurs in the course of *samādhi*. In this respect it should be noted that subtlety exists not merely in objects but also in the subject. Or, in other words, *prakṛti*, the inner details of which *prajñā* reveals, is not just "the world" but even one's "worldly selfhood" consisting of the mental faculty and the psychological substratum (the *citta-vṛtti*s and *saṁskāra*s respectively).[15]

Vyāsa's reply to the *pūrva-pakṣin* reveals yet another dimension of *prajñā* as yogic *pratyakṣa*. Not only does it work with extraordinary senses, and is thus related to the *siddhi*s enumerated by Patañjali in chapter 3 of his treatise; but it also touches on the inner details of human consciousness — hidden, remote and concealed in their own way — within the yogic process which leads to *kaivalya*. *Pratyakṣa* is therefore threefold, consisting of *loka-pratyakṣa* (sense-perception in its common denotation), "external" yogic *pratyakṣa* which works at the same domain as *loka-pratyakṣa* but is more "detail-sensitive," and finally, "internal" yogic *pratyakṣa*, which has the capacity "to perceive" inner subtleties within one's consciousness. If according to the *pūrva-pakṣin*, a "knowable" is merely that which is given through a *pramāṇa*, "means of knowledge," then in Vyāsa's formulation, *prajñā* is as valid a *pramāṇa* as sense-perception, inference and reliable testimony, "working" in areas beyond the scope of the former three.

Vācaspatimiśra follows Vyāsa's line of interpretation. He begins by underscoring the limitedness of the conventional *pramāṇa*s, referring in this respect not just to *śruta* and *anumāna* which provide mere generic knowledge, but also to *loka-pratyakṣa*. Hence even for him, the "present in its absence" *pratyakṣa* has a significant role in *YS* 1.49. The weakness of *śruta* or reliable testimony, Vācaspatimiśra argues, is that it is rooted in words (*śabda*), which are *vyabhicāra*, i.e. of the nature of "too wide pervasion,"[16] or "going away from," or even confusion. The obvious

15. It seems that the term *puruṣa* in Vyāsa's response to the *pūrva-pakṣin* (*bhūta-sūkṣma-gato vā puruṣa-gato vā*) does not refer to *puruṣa* in the Sāṁkhyan sense of the word, denoting one's metaphysical core. Āraṇya (1981: 107), under P.N. Mukerji's pen, translates-interprets the term *puruṣa* here as "the *puruṣa*-like receiver (*mahān*)." And Whicher (2000: 237) explains that "*puruṣa* is not an object in *samādhi*. *Puruṣa* is 'subtle', but is in an entirely different category from *prakṛti* and her evolutes. . . . Since the topic of these *sūtras* [*YS* 1.41-49] is cognitive or object-oriented *samādhi*, and it is not until *asaṁprajñāta* (objectless *samādhi*) that the 'aloneness' (*kaivalya*) of *puruṣa* can occur, the degrees of subtlety (*sūkṣmatā*) mentioned above [in *YS* 1.44-5] only lead up to unmanifest *prakṛti*." Whicher's analysis refers to *YSb* 1.45, but is also applicable, or at least this is my contention, to the term *puruṣa* in Vyāsa's gloss of *YS* 1.49.

16. I am drawing on Woods (1998: 95) who translates *vyabhicāra* as "too wide pervasion."

weakness of ordinary *pratyakṣa* is that it depends on the senses. Moreover, Vācaspatimiśra suggests that phenomenal knowledge, that is, knowledge obtained through any of the conventional *pramāṇas*, is inevitably infected by *rajas* and *tamas*, hence intrinsically unclear.[17] If Vyāsa's *pūrva-pakṣin* has argued that "a particular" beyond the scope of *śruta*, *anumāna* and (*loka-*) *pratyakṣa* is necessarily "non-existent," since there is no *pramāṇa* to capture it; then Vācaspatimiśra replies that a *pramāṇa* (means of knowledge) is not the cause (*kāraṇa*) of the *prameya* (object of knowledge), in the strong sense that when the former ceases, so does the latter. He illustrates: even when the moon is just a single *kalā*, namely one-sixteenth of a full moon, and the deer (*hariṇa*) on the moon cannot be seen, no one doubts his existence (Miśra 1998: 128). The illustration is interesting. First, since a deer replaces the more conventional man or rabbit on the moon. Second, and more significantly, the illustration raises the fundamental question of the interplay between *pramāṇa* and *prameya*, "means of knowledge" and "knowable." Does a *pramāṇa* "objectively" reveal an "independent" object to the perceiver, or does it "actively" shape the object, or even ratify its factuality as hinted by the *pūrva-pakṣin*?

The author of the *Vivaraṇa* opens his commentary with the statement that *ṛtambharā prajñā* has a different object than "knowledge of ordinary people" (*sāmānya-puruṣa-pratyaya*) (Rukmani 2001/1: 198). He replicates Vyāsa's contention that *śruta* and *anumāna* are limited to universals, and cannot touch on particulars. Thereafter, he reformulates and extends the dialogue with the *pūrva-pakṣin*. Under his pen, the opponent again argues that a particular, outer or inner, which is beyond the grasp of *śruta*, *anumāna*, and *loka-pratyakṣa* (the only valid *pramāṇa*s according to the Sāṁkhyan narrative adopted in the *YS*), has to be "non-existent." The Vivaraṇakāra counter-argues that every existing thing is graspable by an appropriate *pramāṇa*, which in the present case is *samādhi-prajñā*, "*prajñā* born of *samādhi*." The *pūrva-pakṣin* further asks: If these particulars are to be known through (*prajñā* as higher) *pratyakṣa* (*pratyakṣena*), does it mean that they are not made known by *Īśvara*? The question is intriguing, as it brings *Īśvara* into the picture. The place and role of *Īśvara* or "god" in the *YS*, and more broadly in Pātañjala-Yoga, is beyond the scope of the present discussion. Is he *puruṣa* or *prakṛti*? Patañjali inaugurates a third,

17. Vācaspatimiśra corresponds with the notion of *vaiśāradya* mentioned by Patañjali in *YS* 1.47, which according to Vyāsa, denotes the steady flow of sattvic *buddhi*, "pure mind" devoid of *rajas* and *tamas*.

intermediate, category for him, that of *puruṣa-viśeṣa*, "special *puruṣa*."[18] In brackets let me say that in my reading, there is an encyclopedic dimension to Patañjali's work, in the sense that he mentions other Yoga-types known to him besides his own. In this respect I include the *videha* (bodiless) and *prakṛti-laya* (merged in *prakṛti*) *yogins* of *YS* 1.19; the different, alternative paths leading to the yogic achievements (*siddhis*) enumerated in *YS* 4.1; and *Īśvara*, introduced in *YS* 1.23 after the particle *vā*, "or." The query of the *pūrva-pakṣin* in *YSbV* 1.49 implies that if subtle elements and even one's own consciousness can be known through *prajñā* as "higher *pratyakṣa*," *Īśvara* becomes redundant. The Vivaraṇakāra replies that they are known as *vastutva*, "substances that exist" (Rukmani 2001/1: 199). Therefore, they can, and moreover, should be perceived directly. *Īśvara*, it is implied, is indeed dispensable, at least in this respect.

The opponent does not give up, and wants to know why subtle elements or one's own consciousness cannot be known through reliable testimony or inference. Why directly? Sometimes, he adds, one cannot even grasp a particular placed on one's palm. His attempt is to secure the threefold conventional *pramāṇa* scheme, arguing that *prajñā* is not necessary. First he suggested *Īśvara* as a substitute of the yogic *pramāṇa*, now he is willing to settle for indirect knowledge. The Vivaraṇakāra, in his reply, sticks to his predecessors' maxim, according to which a particular can only be known through direct means. If one cannot perceive a particular as accessible even when on one's own palm, it does not mean that such perception is impossible. On the contrary, it is not merely possible but even necessary, direct perception being the only suitable *pramāṇa* of a particular.

Like his predecessors, Vijñānabhikṣu opens his commentary of *YS* 1.49 by dismissing *śruta* and *anumāna* as possible *pramāṇas* of particulars. The former, he explains, is based on words, which cannot convey but universals. Each word is of infinite possible particular referents. Therefore, upon hearing a word, there is always a quantum of uncertainty (*viśeṣa-saṁśaya*) about the specific referent.

If such is the case, argues the *pūrva-pakṣin*, whose objections Vijñānabhikṣu rearticulates, i.e. if knowledge of particulars cannot be conveyed through reliable testimony and inference, why not opt for "worldly sense-perception" (*laukika-pratyakṣa*)? Why to postulate "yogic

18. See *YS* 1.24: *kleśa-karma-vipāka-āśayair-aparāmṛṣṭaḥ puruṣa-viśeṣa īśvaraḥ* (*Īśvara* is a special *puruṣa* untouched by the *kleśas* [causes of affliction], action and its fruits, and by "long-term karmic imprints" [*āśaya*]).

perception" (*yoga-ja-pratyakṣa*)? Just like his predecessors, Vijñānabhikṣu focuses on and works with the notion of *pratyakṣa*, the *via negativa* of *YS* 1.49. His response to the opponent's objection echoes what has already been argued from Vyāsa onwards, i.e. that ordinary *pratyakṣa* applies merely to the gross (*sthūla*), whereas the subtle (*sūkṣma*) can only be perceived through a "subtle *pratyakṣa*" such as *samādhi-prajñā*. As per Vyāsa, we have seen, *prajñā* applies to subtle elements both in the world and in one's inner world (*bhūta-sūkṣma-gato vā puruṣa-gato vā*). For Vijñānabhikṣu, the term *puruṣa* does not refer to one's consciousness, as suggested by me drawing on his predecessors, but to the Sāṁkhyan *puruṣa* "himself," "the other" of *prakṛti*. He glosses the segment *puruṣa-gato vā*, as suggesting that "the quality of particularity is there in *puruṣa*s as well" (*etena puruṣeṣvapi viśeṣādi-dharmaḥ svīkṛtaḥ*) (Rukmani 1981: 249-50). And Rukmani notes that "each *puruṣa* has its own particularity" (Rukmani 1981: 250). Vijñānabhikṣu thus echoes the Sāṁkhyan narrative about the multiplicity of *puruṣas*,[19] against, for instance, the oneness of the *ātman* in Advaita philosophy, of which everyone and everything is supposed to be a part of. The multiplicity of *puruṣas*, *Sāṁkhya Kārikā* (*SK*) 18 implies, is inferred from the different circumstances (birth, death, different experiences) of different individuals or embodied selves "here" in the world. In other words, according to the Sāṁkhyans, if one denies difference and plurality at the *puruṣa* level, plurality and difference at the phenomenal level cannot be explained. Interestingly, perhaps the greatest challenge of the Advaita tradition is to justify the discrepancy between plurality at the *vyāvahārika* realm and unity at the *pāramārthika* sphere. Moreover, the plurality of *puruṣa*s is not implied by *SK* 19, which projects *puruṣa* as aloof, remote, enclosed. What, if at all, could be the relationship between liberated *puruṣa*s, each of whom, according to *SK* 19, is a monad in itself?

Another explanation for the plurality of *puruṣa*s is found in *YS* 2.22. Here Patañjali suggests that,

> Even though "she" (*prakṛti*) ceases to exist for "him" (*puruṣa*), for whose sake her purpose has been achieved, she continues to exist for others (i.e. for other *puruṣa*s afflicted by *avidyā*) being as she is of a common nature.[20]

---

19. In *SK* 18, Īśvarakṛṣṇa writes that "The plurality of *puruṣa*s is established because of the diversity of births, deaths, and faculties; because of actions or functions [that take place] at different times; and because of difference in the proportions of the three *guṇa*s [in different entities]" (*jananamaraṇakaraṇānāṁ pratiniyamād ayugapatpravṛtteś ca, puruṣabahutvaṁ siddhaṁ traiguṇyaviparyayāc cai'va*). See Larson 1979: 261.

20. *kṛta-arthaṁ prati naṣṭam-apy-anaṣṭaṁ tad-anya-sādhāraṇatvāt* (*YS* 2.22).

The plurality of *puruṣas*, i.e. the fact that there are always *puruṣas* who are yet seeking liberation, to be achieved through the efforts of *prakṛti*, gives "her" a "reason" to "continue." In other words, the plurality of *puruṣas* sustains the world, and fortifies the status of the "here" alongside the "beyond."

According to Vijñānabhikṣu, every *puruṣa*, whether liberated or not (*muktāmukta*), has its own "individual" *dharmas* or "characteristics." In this respect he mentions the past, present and future reflections of the *upādhis* or "limitations" of the different *puruṣas*. The novelty of Vijñānabhikṣu's gloss is that according to him, alongside its function in revealing subtle elements in "the world," which are beyond the scope of conventional *pratyakṣa*, *prajñā* is of the capacity to illuminate the individuality of each and every *puruṣa*; individuality which remains intact even when a *puruṣa* is no longer involved in *prakṛti*. *Puruṣa*, then, in Vijñānabhikṣu's reading, is indeed a "particular" to be captured by *prajñā* as "yogic perception."

Vijñānabhikṣu's *pūrva-pakṣin* raises yet another objection. An object is "hidden," hence beyond the grasp of *pratyakṣa*, when direct contact between the object and one's sense organs cannot be established. How, then, can a hidden object be perceived through *samādhi-prajñā*? Are we to imagine that in *prajñā*, the contact with the object which was not there in ordinary sense-perception is (somehow, mysteriously) recreated? Vijñānabhikṣu replies that:

1. No, *prajñā* is not based on a contact of sense organ and object.
2. However, if in *pratyakṣa*, the object is the "cause" (*kāraṇa*) of knowledge,[21] it is the same with *prajñā*. This is to say that knowledge of subtle elements, as also knowledge of the particularity of a *puruṣa*, depends primarily on them. Or in other words, the knowledge attained through *prajñā* is *vastu-tantra*, not *puruṣa-tantra*, "objective" rather than "subjective."[22] Consequently, the "objects" of *prajñā* as a *pramāṇa* are not and cannot be "non-existent."
3. How does *prajñā* work, then? It removes the *tamas* or "unclarity"

---

21. See Patañjali's own *YS* 4.17: "An object is known or unknown as much as the *citta* (consciousness) is coloured by it (or acquires its form)" (*tad-uparāga-apekṣitvāc-cittasya vastu jñāta-ajñātam*).
22. I am using the terms *vastu-tantra* and *puruṣa-tantra* as in Śaṅkara's *Brahmasūtra-Bhāṣya* 1.1.4.

inherent in "phenomenal," "unenlightened" consciousness. No longer obscured by *tamas*, Rukmani explains, and "being all-pervading in its natural purity [*sattva*], there are no objects beyond the range of the mind" (Rukmani 1981: 251). If the conventional *pramāṇa*s are directed at a certain object (sense-perception revealing its particularity, inference and reliable testimony its generic character), then *prajñā* is directed at or works to dissolve the *tamas* element, interwoven in every episode of conventional cognition. When *tamas* is dispersed, there is "direct contact" with every object, ordinary, subtle, even with the particularity or "individuality" of *puruṣa*. However this "direct contact" is not the sense organ and object contact on which ordinary *pratyakṣa* is based. We are back to *pratyakṣa* as an illustration of *prajñā*. One can only speak of the latter in terms of the former, despite the essential difference between the two underscored by commentator after commentator. Interestingly, the focus of Patañjali's discussion, within which *prajñā* is introduced, is meditation. According to him, *prajñā* takes place in *nirvicārā samāpatti* (meditation beyond reflectivity), *en route* to *nirbīja* (objectless) *samādhi*. The discussion of his commentators shifts from meditation to epistemology, concerned as they are, primarily with the status of *prajñā* as a *pramāṇa*.

Contemporary interpreters and translators of the *YS* do not add much to the discussion of the commentators of old, or rather each of them picks up a segment of the discussion sketched in detail above. Vivekananda, for example, writes on *YS* 1.49 that,

> The central idea of the *yogī*s is that just as we come in direct contact with objects of the senses, so religion even can be directly perceived in a far more intense sense. The truths of religion, as God and Soul, cannot be perceived by the external senses. I cannot see God with my eyes, nor can I touch Him with my hands. — Vivekananda 2004: 163

In his typical style, consisting of God, Soul and Him,[23] all in capital letters, together with the non-Indian notion of "religion,"[24] Vivekananda reinforces

23. Interestingly, Ramakrishna's famous disciple, who sat at the feet of his *guru* in Goddess Kālī's temple at Dakṣiṇeśvara, prefers "Him" to "Her."

24. In this respect see Paul Hacker's discussion (1995: 238) of the "inverted translation" of the Western, monotheistic term "religion" into "*dharma*." The classic notion of *dharma* with its wide range of meanings (from cosmic order to the ritualistic life, to "duty," "truth," "righteousness" and in the Buddhist context, even the teachings of the Buddha), is further expanded to accommodate the idea of "religion." The

→

the classic commentators' presentation of *prajñā* as *para-pratyakṣa*. Vivekananda, famous for searching as a young man, a *guru* who actually "sees god," comes back to his early quest for "direct contact" with the sublime in the present commentary. *Prajñā* is projected by him as the *pramāṇa* which enables *yogins*, such as Ramakrishna and Vivekananda himself, in his Narendranath days at Dakṣiṇeśvara, to "see god" and to "touch Him," even if not through the senses. Vivekananda works with the analogy between *prajñā* and *pratyakṣa* hinted in *YS* 1.49, and like Patañjali, speaks of the yogic experience (or more universally, of "religious experience"), in terms of the more available experience of the senses.

Ian Whicher dedicates a thorough discussion to the notion of *prajñā* in a chapter titled "A Closer Look at Perception in the Yogasūtra" (Whicher 2000: 143-49). The title itself assumes the interconnection between *pratyakṣa* and *prajñā*. Drawing on Vācaspatimiśra's and Vijñānabhikṣu's commentaries of *YS* 1.7, Whicher suggests that *yogi-pratyakṣa* or yogic perception is a synonym of *sākṣātkāra* (direct yogic perception), a term used by Patañjali in the *Vibhūti-pāda* as again, a synonym (or in Whicher's articulation, "the basis of") *saṁyama* (object-centred yogic meditation), which gives rise to various *siddhis*. In *YS* 3.18, for example, Patañjali writes that "through *sākṣātkaraṇa* of the *saṁskāras*, knowledge of previous births is obtained."[25] Here the *saṁskāras* (the subtle-most layer of what I referred to above as "one's own consciousness") are the object of yogic perception. In *YS* 3.19, Patañjali argues that "[Through *sākṣātkaraṇa*] of mental content (*pratyaya*), knowledge of [the content of] other minds is obtained."[26] "This [knowledge]," he adds in 3.20, "does not include [other factors] which determine [the content of other minds], since they are not the object [of *sākṣātkaraṇa*]."[27] This last clarification is important as it highlights the directness, particularity and "objectivity" of yogic perception, all of which have been discussed above.

Whicher depicts perception in Pātañjala-Yoga as a process of purification, or sattvification as he beautifully puts it, very much in tune with the commentators' discussion. In this respect, he speaks of the

---

→ point is that language does not depict but creates and determines. This is to say that Vivekananda not merely borrows a Western term to depict an Indian phenomenon, but rethinks and reinterprets his own tradition *vis-à-vis* the Christian narrative.

25. *saṁskāra-sākṣāt-karaṇāt pūrva-jāti-jñānam* (*YS* 3.18).

26. *pratyayasya para-citta-jñānam* (*YS* 3.19).

27. *na ca tat-sālambanaṁ tasya-aviṣayī-bhūtatvāt* (*YS* 3.20).

transformation from "ordinary perception, by way of the outward facing power of the mind to perceive objects through the senses" to "yogic perception through the inward facing power of the mind." It is the latter which "eventually leads to the mind's complete purification, sattvification, and liberation" (Whicher 2000: 147).

A significant point raised by Whicher apropos perception as a process of purification is that ordinary perception "is subject to distortion due to various karmic factors in the mind (i.e. *saṁskāras* and *vāsanās*), that affect or colour how we perceive and appropriate the objects we encounter" (Whicher 2000: 145). This is to say that ordinary *pratyakṣa* is limited not merely by the senses, but even by karmic factors, to be cleansed in the process of Yoga alongside the "purification" of perception itself from *loka-pratyakṣa* to *para-pratyakṣa*.

Whicher (2000: 147-48) further alludes to *YS* 4.20, which highlights in his reading the "epistemological limitations of the mind." Here Patañjali suggests that the mind (*citta*) cannot perceive both an object and itself simultaneously. Therefore, it perceives objects and is itself "perceived" by *puruṣa* (and as the next *sūtra* suggests in reply to a Buddhist *pūrva-pakṣin*, not by another *citta* or other *cittas*).[28] I would like to suggest that if in *YS* 1.49, Patañjali draws a parallel between *pratyakṣa* and *prajñā* despite their essential difference. Here the parallel is between the mind as the perceiver of objects, and *puruṣa* as the "perceiver" of the mind as it perceives objects. The "problem" is that *puruṣa* does not "perceive" in the same sense as the mind. "He" is indeed depicted in *SK* 19 as endowed with *sākṣitvam* and *draṣṭṛtvam*, i.e. the "qualities" of being a "witness" and a "spectator,"[29] but as per the Sāṁkhyan narrative, "he" is absolutely passive (or endowed with *akartṛ-bhāva*), hence it is "her" (*prakṛti*) who is perceived by "him," or is illuminated by "his" light, rather than "him"

---

28. *YS* 4.19-21: "It is not (i.e. the *citta* or mind is not) a light-to-itself (namely, the mind perceives objects but not itself), as it is seen (or "perceived" by *puruṣa*). Furthermore, both cannot be "grasped" or perceived simultaneously. Had one mind (*citta*) been perceived by another, it would have led to infinite regression (*atiprasaṅga*) from one mind (*buddhi*) to another, and to intermixture of memories.

   na tat sva-ābhāsaṁ dṛṣyatvāt | *eka-samaye ca-ubhaya-anavadhāraṇam* | *citta-antara-dṛśye buddhi-buddher-atiprasaṅgaḥ smṛti-saṅkaraś-ca*

29. The question is what the difference between *sākṣitvam* and *draṣṭṛtvam* is. What do each of these *prima facie* close (almost synonymous) terms denote? Or, how do the two terms complement, or perhaps even overlap one another? The commentators of the *SK* attempt to clarify this ambiguity in their gloss.

"actively" perceiving "her."[30] Vyāsa dedicates his gloss of *YS* 2.20,[31] to the similarity and difference in the perception of the mind (*buddhi*) and *puruṣa*. The mind perceives objects as long as they come in touch with it through the senses, or "colour" it. In the same way but altogether differently, the *buddhi* is "perceived" by *puruṣa*. In the same way, as Vyāsa puts it in his present gloss and Vācaspatimiśra in his commentary of *YS* 1.7, since "*puruṣa* is the introspector[32] of the *buddhi*" (*buddheḥ pratisaṁvedī puruṣaḥ*). The verb *pratisaṁvedī* conveys the link between *puruṣa* and the *buddhi*. Owing to "his" unchanging presence, the ever-changing *buddhi* is "seen." Moreover, in the light emanating from "him," the *buddhi* is not just "seen" but also perceives objects. When "his" light is reflected in the *buddhi*, the light assumes the latter's shape, just as the *buddhi* itself assumes the form of the objects perceived by it. The *buddhi* is hence depicted as a prism, through which the light of *puruṣa* is refracted and transforms into a *citta-vr̥tti*. Similar as *puruṣa*'s "perception" is to the perception of objects by the mind, Vyāsa also underscores the difference between these two perception types. The *buddhi* as *puruṣa*'s "object," he suggests, is not "perceived or not perceived" (*gr̥hītā 'gr̥hītā*) as the objects of the mind are by the mind, but is rather constantly "perceived," the light of *puruṣa* being ever illuminating. Vyāsa, in his gloss of 2.20, cannot but speak of *puruṣa* in

---

30. In *SK* 66, Īśvarakr̥ṣṇa imagines a "farewell conversation" between *puruṣa* and *prakr̥ti*, on the verge of *kaivalya*:

    dr̥ṣṭā maye 'ty upekṣaka ekaḥ | dr̥ṣṭā 'ham ity uparamaty anyā

    Or,

    "She has been seen by me," says the indifferent one. "I have been seen," the other says as she ceases.

    Passive as "he" is, *puruṣa* speaks in the passive form: "she has been seen by me," rather than "I saw her." The passive form is a common way of speech in Sanskrit, but nevertheless I would like to read *puruṣa*'s words as "representing" his in-built passivity.

31. *YS* 2.20: "The seer (*draṣṭr̥*) consists of pure seeing (*dr̥śi*), and though pure (in essence, i.e. contentless), he 'sees' mental activity" (*draṣṭā dr̥śi-mātraḥ śuddho 'pi pratyaya-anupaśyaḥ*).

32. I am drawing on the compilers of the *Yoga Kośa* (1991: 190), who translate *pratisaṁvedana* as "introspection." They add that "though introspection is not quite the correct word for *puruṣa*'s apprehension of the processes of its *citta* (mind), it is better than "seeing." A similar remark is found in Āraṇya's gloss of *YS* 2.20. Here he notes, apropos Patañjali's use of the word *draṣṭr̥* ("seer"), that "*puruṣa* is not a seer in the usual meaning ascribed to the term, because that would be imputing quality and action to *puruṣa*, who is beyond both" (1981: 179). The compilers of the *Yoga Kośa* and Āraṇya alike convey the "short-handedness" of language with regard to *puruṣa*.

terms of the *buddhi*. Perception is a function of the *buddhi* or the mind. However Patañjali's "soteriological pedagogy," as it is referred to by Whicher (2000: 146), compels him and his commentators to speak of the unspeakable. Their "translation task" is to convey "the other" in familiar language, to hint at *puruṣa* through the language of *prakṛti*.

Conclusion

A philosophical magnifying glass always reveals something new, a seldom noticed angle, a hardly touched on *viśeṣa*, even in a text of which so much has already been said and written such as the *YS*. In the present case, the notion of *prajñā*, or more precisely *ṛtambharā prajñā* as depicted in *YS* 1.49, was the focus of enquiry. Our "grand discoveries" included first, the hinted parallel between *pratyakṣa* and *prajñā* based on the reading of *YS* 1.49 *vis-à-vis* *YS* 1.7; a parallel which results in the projection of *prajñā* as *para-pratyakṣa* by Patañjali's commentators. Hence *prajñā* is reformulated as nothing less than a yogic *pramāṇa* or "means of knowledge." This explains the second "grand discovery," about the shift from meditation to epistemology in the discourse of the commentators, who discuss the notion of *prajñā* within the technical, philosophical context of perception. Another "discovery," at least for me, minor but however intriguing, was the "deer on the moon," whom I catalogue together with the "king-bee" (*madhukara-rāja*) of Vyāsa's commentary of *YS* 2.54 (Rukmani 1983: 234). While the deer is as valid an image as any other to be "seen" on the moon, and while science has since discovered that the bee-king is in fact a queen, these rare examples offer unique historical windows to the minds of thinkers whom we read, with whom we think, with whom we spend hours upon hours, yet of whom we know literally nothing beyond the texts ascribed to them.

Abbreviations

SK	*Sāṁkhya Kārikā*
YS	*Yogasūtra*
YSb	*Yogasūtra-Bhāṣya*
YSbV	*Yogasūtra-Bhāṣya-Vivaraṇa*

References

Āraṇya, Swāmi Hariharānanda (1981), *Yoga Philosophy of Patañjali*, translated from the original Bengali into English by P.N. Mukerji, Calcutta: University of Calcutta.

Benjamin, Walter (1999) [1923], "The Task of the Translator," in his *Illuminations*, London: Pimlico, pp. 70-82.

Chadha, Monima (2001), "Perceptual Cognition: A Nyāya-Kantian Approach," in *Philosophy East and West*, vol. 51, no. 2, pp. 197-209.

—— (2004), "Perceiving Particulars-as-such Is Incoherent: A Reply to Mark Siderits," in *Philosophy East and West*, vol. 54, no. 3, pp. 382-89.

Chapple, Christopher Key (2008), *Yoga and the Luminous*, Albany: State University of New York Press.

Hacker, Paul (1995), "Aspects of Neo-Hinduism as Contrasted with Surviving Traditional Hinduism," in *Philology and Confrontation: Paul Hacker on Traditional and Modern Vedānta*, ed. Wilhelm Halbfass, Albany: State University of New York Press, pp. 229-55.

Larson, Gerald James (1979), *Classical Sāṁkhya: An Interpretation of its History and Meaning*, Delhi: Motilal Banarsidass.

Miśra, Śrī Nārayaṇa (ed.) (1998), *Pātañjalayogadarśanam with Vyāsa's Bhāṣya, Vācasptimiśra's Tattvavaiśāradī and Vijñānabhikṣu's Yogavārttika*, Varanasi and Delhi: Bhāratīya Vidyā Prakāśana.

Philosophico Literary Research Department of Kaivalyadhama S.M.Y.M. Samiti (eds.), (1991), *Yoga Kośa: Yoga Terms Explained with Reference to Context*, Lonvala, Pune: Kaivalyadhama S.M.Y.M. Samiti.

Rukmani, Trichur S. (1981-89), *Yogavārttika of Vijñānabhikṣu: Text with English Translation and Critical Notes along with Text and English Translation of the Pātañjala Yoga-Sūtras and Vyāsabhāṣya*, vol. 1: *Samādhipāda* (1981); vol. 2: *Sādhanapāda* (1983); vol. 3: *Vibhūtipāda* (1987); vol. 4: *Kaivalyapāda* (1989), Delhi: Munshiram Manoharlal.

—— (1989a), "Avidyā in the System of Yoga and an Analysis of the Negation in it," in her *Yogavārttika of Vijñānabhikṣu* (1981-89), Appendix 5, pp. 172-76.

—— (1989b), "Patañjali's Prajñā and Bhartṛhari's Pratibhā: A Comparative Study," in her *Yogavārttika of Vijñānabhikṣu* (1981-89), Appendix 7, pp. 183-89.

—— (1989c), "Vikalpa as defined by Vijñānabhikṣu in the Yogavārttika," in her *Yogavārttika of Vijñānabhikṣu* (1981-89), Appendix 4, pp. 166-71.

—— (1997), "Tension between Vyutthāna and Nirodha in the Yoga-sūtras," in *Journal of Indian Philosophy*, vol. 25, pp. 613-28.

—— (2001), *Yogasūtrabhāṣyavivaraṇa of Śaṅkara*, 2 vols., Delhi: Munshiram Manoharlal.

Vivekananda, Swami (2004) [1899], *Raja Yoga or Conquering the Internal Nature*, Kolkata: Advaita Ashrama.

Whicher, Ian (2000), *The Integrity of the Yoga Darśana: A Reconsideration of Classical Yoga*, Delhi: D.K. Printworld.

Woods, James Haughton (1998) [1914], *The Yoga-System of Patañjali or the Ancient Hindu Doctrine of Concentration of Mind, Embracing the Mnemonic Rules Called Yoga-Sūtras of Patañjali and the Comment Called Yoga-Bhāṣya Attributed to Veda-Vyāsa and the Explanation Called Tattva-Vāiśāradī of Vācaspati Miśra*, Harvard Oriental Series, rpt. Delhi: Motilal Banarsidass.

3

Moving Towards a Non-Dualistic Interpretation of Yoga

The Integration of Spirit (Puruṣa) and Matter (Prakṛti) in the Yoga-Sūtra

*Ian Whicher**

Introduction

THIS paper centres on the thought of Patañjali (*c.* second-third century CE), the great exponent of the authoritative classical Yoga school (*darśana*) of Hinduism and the reputed author of the *Yoga-Sūtra*. I will argue that Patañjali's philosophical perspective has, far too often, been looked upon as excessively "spiritual" or isolationistic to the point of being a world-denying philosophy, indifferent to moral endeavour, neglecting the world of nature and culture, and overlooking the highest potentials for human reality, vitality, and creativity. Contrary to the arguments presented by many scholars, which associate Patañjali's Yoga exclusively with extreme asceticism, mortification, denial, and the renunciation and abandonment of "material existence" (*prakṛti*) in favour of an elevated and isolated "spiritual state" (*puruṣa*) or disembodied state of spiritual liberation, I suggest that Patañjali's Yoga can be seen as a responsible engagement, in various ways, of "spirit" (*puruṣa* = intrinsic identity as Self, pure consciousness) and "matter" (*prakṛti* = the source of psychophysical being, which includes mind, body, nature) resulting in a highly developed, transformed, and participatory human nature and identity, an integrated and embodied state of liberated selfhood (*jīvanmukti*).

The interpretation of Patañjali's Yoga *darśana* presented in this paper — which walks the line between a historical and hermeneutic-praxis (some

* Department of Religion, University of Manitoba

might say theological or "systematic") orientation — counters the radically dualistic, isolationistic, and ontologically oriented interpretations of Yoga[1] presented by many scholars and suggests an open-ended, epistemologically and morally oriented hermeneutic which, I maintain, is more appropriate for arriving at a more balanced assessment of Patañjali's system.

It is often said that, like classical Sāṁkhya, Patañjali's Yoga is a dualistic system, understood in terms of *puruṣa* and *prakṛti*. Yet, I submit, Yoga scholarship has not clarified what "dualistic" means or why Yoga had to be "dualistic." Even in avowedly non-dualistic systems of thought such as Advaita Vedānta we can find numerous examples of basically dualistic modes of description and explanation.[2]

---

1. The system of classical Yoga is often reduced to or fitted into a classical Sāṁkhyan scheme — the interpretations of which generally follow along radically dualistic lines. In their metaphysical ideas classical Sāṁkhya and Yoga are closely akin. However, both systems hold divergent views on important areas of doctrinal structure such as epistemology, ontology, ethics, and psychology, as well as differences pertaining to terminology. These differences derive in part from the different methodologies adopted by the two schools: Sāṁkhya, it has been argued, emphasizes a theoretical or intellectual analysis through inference and reasoning in order to bring out the nature of final emancipation, while Yoga stresses yogic perception and multiple forms of practice that culminate in *samādhi*. Moreover, there is clear evidence throughout all four *pāda*s of the *YS* of an extensive network of terminology that parallels Buddhist teachings and which is absent in the classical Sāṁkhya literature. Patañjali includes several *sūtra*s on the "restraints" or *yama*s (namely, non-violence [*ahiṁsā*], truthfulness [*satya*], non-stealing [*asteya*], chastity [*brahmacarya*], and non-possession/greedlessness [*aparigraha*]) of the "eight-limbed" path of Yoga that are listed in the *Ācārāṅga-Sūtra* of Jainism (the earliest sections of which may date from the third or fourth century BCE) thereby suggesting possible Jaina influences on the Yoga tradition. The topic of Buddhist or Jaina influence on Yoga doctrine (or vice versa) is, however, not the focus of this paper.
2. See, for example, Śaṅkara's (*c.* eighth-ninth century CE) use of *vyāvahārika* (the conventional empirical perspective) in contrast to *pāramārthika* (the ultimate or absolute standpoint). Śaṅkara uses dualistic modes of description/explanation, I would suggest mainly for pedagogical purposes to distinguish between the Oneness of *Brahman* and dualism from the perspective of ignorance (which divides *Brahman* into parts) and in order to lead the student to the clear understanding of *Brahman* and indeed realization of *Brahman* alone. Patañjali adopts the dualism of the seer and the seen, where the "seen" mistakes itself for the seer, in order to lead the *yogī*'s attention beyond afflicted identity and release the power of seeing into awareness; therefore liberation results. The need in Yoga is to discern the difference between *puruṣa* and *prakṛti* in order to liberate both from the afflicted veil of ignorance. So in Advaita as in Yoga the pedagogical context harnesses modes of dualistic discourse in order to point the way and bring about liberation. How the state of liberation in both "systems" is understood is subject to interpretation. I hope I have made it clear that there is no proof that Yoga →

Elsewhere (Whicher 1998) I have suggested the possibility of Patañjali having asserted a provisional, descriptive, and "practical" metaphysics, i.e. in the *Yoga-Sūtra* the metaphysical schematic is abstracted from yogic experience, whereas in classical Sāṁkhya, as set out in Īśvarakṛṣṇa's *Sāṁkhya Kārikā*, "experiences" are fitted into a metaphysical structure. This approach would allow the *Yoga-Sūtra* to be interpreted along more open-ended, epistemologically and morally oriented lines without being held captive by the radical, dualistic metaphysics of Sāṁkhya. Despite intentions to render the experiential dimension of Yoga, purged as far as possible from abstract metaphysical knowledge, many scholars have fallen prey to reading the *Yoga-Sūtra* from the most abstract level of the dualism of *puruṣa* and *prakṛti* down to an understanding of the practices advocated. Then they proceed to impute an experiential foundation to the whole scheme informed not from mystical insight or yogic experience, but from the effort to form a consistent (dualistic) world view, a view that culminates in a radical dualistic finality or closure.[3]

Patañjali's philosophy is not based upon mere theoretical or speculative knowledge. It elicits a practical, pragmatic, experiential/perceptual (not merely inferential/theoretical) approach that Patañjali deems essential in order to deal effectively with our total human situation and provide real freedom, not just a theory of liberation or a metaphysical explanation of life. Yoga is not content with knowledge (*jñāna*) perceived as a state that abstracts away from the world removing us from our human embodiment and activity in the world. Rather, Yoga emphasizes knowledge in the integrity of being and action and as serving the integration of the "person" as a "whole." Edgerton concluded in a study dedicated to the meaning of Yoga that: ". . . Yoga is not a 'system' of belief or of metaphysics. It is always a way, a method of getting something, usually salvation. . . ." (Edgerton 1924) But this does not say enough, does not fully take into account what might be called the integrity of Patañjali's Yoga. Yoga derives its real strength and value through an integration of theory and practice (as argued in Whicher 1998).

→ culminates in a radical metaphysical duality or more positively that Yoga may well result in a non-dualistic state that embraces *puruṣa* and *prakṛti* without naming it; or Yoga can be seen as opening into a co-operative duality of *puruṣa* and *prakṛti*.

3. See in particular: Feuerstein (1980: 14, 56, 108); Eliade (1969: 94-95, 99-100); Koelman (1970: 224, 251); and Larson et al. (1987: 13) where Larson classifies Patañjali's Yoga as a form of Sāṁkhya.

Cessation (Nirodha) and the "Return to the Source" (Pratiprasava): Transformation or Elimination/Negation of the Mind?

In Patañjali's central definition of Yoga, Yoga is defined as "the cessation (*nirodha*) of [the misidentification with] the functioning/transformations (*vṛtti*) of the mind/ordinary awareness (*citta*)."[4] What *kind* of "cessation," we must ask, is Patañjali actually referring to in his classical definition of Yoga? What does the process of cessation actually entail for the *yogī*: ethically, epistemologically, ontologically, psychologically, and so on? I have elsewhere suggested (Whicher 1998) that *nirodha* denotes an epistemological emphasis and refers to the transformation of self-understanding brought about through the purification and illumination of consciousness; *nirodha* is not (for the *yogī*) the ontological cessation of *prakṛti* (i.e., the mind and *vṛttis*). Seen here, *nirodha* thus is not, as is often explained, an inward movement that annihilates or suppresses *vṛttis*, thoughts, intentions, or ideas (*pratyaya*), nor is it the non-existence or absence of *vṛtti*; rather, *nirodha* involves a progressive unfoldment of yogic perception (*yogī-pratyakṣa*) that eventually reveals our authentic identity as being rooted in *puruṣa*. It is the state of affliction (*kleśa*) evidenced *in* the mind and not the mind *itself* that is at issue. *Cittavṛtti* does not stand for all modifications or mental processes (cognitive, affective, emotive), but is the very seed (*bīja*) mechanism of afflicted identity, the

4. *YS* I.2 (p. 4): *yogaś cittavṛttinirodhaḥ*. All references from the Sanskrit text of the *YS* of Patañjali and the *YB* of Vyāsa are from Agashe 1904. The modifications or functions (*vṛtti*) of the mind (*citta*) are said to be fivefold (*YS* I.6), namely "valid cognition" (*pramāṇa*, which includes perception [*pratyakṣa*], inference [*anumāna*] and valid testimony [*āgama*]), "error"/"misconception" (*viparyaya*), "conceptualization" (*vikalpa*), "sleep" (*nidrā*) and "memory" (*smṛti*), and are described as being "afflicted" (*kliṣṭa*) or "non-afflicted" (*akliṣṭa*) (*YS* I.5). *Citta* is an umbrella term that incorporates "intellect" (*buddhi*), "sense of self" (*ahaṁkāra*) and "mind-organ" (*manas*), and can be viewed as the aggregate of the cognitive, conative and affective processes and functions of phenomenal consciousness, i.e. it consists of a grasping, intentional and volitional consciousness. For an in-depth look at the meaning of the terms *citta* and *vṛtti* see Whicher (1998). In the first four *sūtras* of the first chapter (*Samādhi-Pāda*) the subject matter of the *YS* is mentioned, defined and characterized. The *sūtras* run as follows: *YS* I.1: "Now [begins] the discipline of Yoga." *YS* I.2: "Yoga is the cessation of [the misidentification with] the functioning/transformations of the mind." *YS* I.3: "Then [when that cessation has taken place] there is abiding in the seer's own form (i.e., *puruṣa* or intrinsic identity)." *YS* I.4: "Otherwise [there is] conformity to (i.e., misidentification with) the functioning [of the mind]." *YS* I.1-4 (pp. 1-7): *atha yogānuśāsanam; yogaś cittavṛttinirodhaḥ; tadā draṣṭuḥ svarūpe 'vasthānam; vṛttisārūpyam itaratra*. For a more comprehensive study of classical Yoga including issues dealt with in this paper see Whicher (1998).

misidentification of consciousness with *prakṛti* from which all other *vṛttis* and thoughts arise and are (mis)appropriated or self-referenced in the state of ignorance (*avidyā*), that is, the unenlightened state of mind. Spiritual ignorance gives rise to a profound dysfunction or misalignment of *vṛtti* with consciousness that in Yoga can be remedied thereby allowing for a proper alignment or "right" functioning of *vṛtti* (Whicher 1998). It is the *cittavṛtti* as our confused and mistaken identity, not our *vṛttis*, thoughts, and experiences in total that must be brought to a state of definitive cessation. Ordinary awareness consists of our mental patterns that are governed by spiritual ignorance and define our normal sense of self or identity. Patañjali clearly wanted to distinguish that mode of self (= non-self) from pure consciousness (*puruṣa*). Yoga, thus purifies and liberates the *cittavṛtti* dynamic from ignorance and enables, I suggest, one to get beyond afflicted identity (as ordinary awareness masquerading as consciousness). To be sure, there is a suspension and transcendence of all the mental processes as well as any identification with an object (i.e., in *asaṁprajnāta-samādhi*, this being for the final purification of the mind, see chapter 6 in Whicher 1998: 170-71), but it would be misleading to conclude that higher *samādhi* results in a permanent or definitive cessation of the *vṛttis* in total thereby predisposing the *yogī* who has attained purity of mind to exist in an incapacitated, isolated, or mindless state, and therefore, of being incapable of living a balanced, useful, and productive life in various ways.

From the perspective of the discerning *yogī* (*vivekin*) human identity contained within the domain of the three *guṇas* of *prakṛti* (i.e., *sattva*, *rajas*, and *tamas*) amounts to nothing more than sorrow and dissatisfaction (*duḥkha*).[5] The declared goal of classical Yoga, as with Sāṁkhya and Buddhism, is to overcome all dissatisfaction (*duḥkha*, *YS* II.16) by bringing about an inverse movement or counter-flow (*pratiprasava*)[6] understood as a "return to the origin" (Chapple and Kelly 1990: 60) or "process-of-involution" (Feuerstein 1979: 65) of the *guṇas*, a kind of reabsorption into the transcendent purity of being itself. What does this "process-of-involution" — variously referred to as "return to the origin," "dissolution into the source" (Arya 1986: 146, 471) or "withdrawal from manifestation"

5. *YS* II.15 (p. 74): *pariṇāmatāpasaṁskāraduḥkhair guṇavṛttivirodhāc ca duḥkham eva sarvaḥ vivekinaḥ*. "Because of the dissatisfaction and sufferings due to change and anxieties and the latent impressions, and from the conflict of the transformations of the *guṇas*, for the discerning one, all is sorrow alone."

6. Patañjali uses the term *pratiprasava* twice, in *YS* II.10 and IV.34.

— actually mean? Is it a definitive ending to the perceived world of the *yogī* comprising change and transformation, forms and phenomena? Ontologically conceived, *prasava* signifies the "flowing forth" of the primary constituents or qualities of *prakṛti* into the multiple forms of the universe in all its dimensions, i.e., all the processes of manifestation and actualization or "creation" (*sarga, prasarga*). *Pratiprasava*, on the other hand, denotes the process of "dissolution into the source" or "withdrawal from manifestation" of those forms relative to the personal, microcosmic level of the *yogī* who is about to attain freedom (*apavarga*).

Does a "return to the origin" culminate in a state of freedom in which one is stripped of all human identity and void of any association with the world including one's practical livelihood? The ontological emphasis usually given to the meaning of *pratiprasava* — implying for the *yogī* a literal dissolution of *prakṛti*'s manifestation — would seem to support a view, one which is prominent in Yoga scholarship, of spiritual liberation denoting an existence wholly transcendent (and therefore stripped or deprived) of all manifestation including the human relational sphere. Is this the kind of spiritually emancipated state that Patañjali had in mind (pun included)? In *YS* II.3-17 (which set the stage for the remainder of the essay on yogic means or *sādhana*), Patañjali describes *prakṛti*, the "seeable" (including our personhood), in the context of the various afflictions (*kleśas*) that give rise to an afflicted and mistaken identity of self. Afflicted identity is constructed out of and held captive by the root affliction of ignorance (*avidyā*) and its various forms of karmic bondage. Yet, despite the clear association of *prakṛti* with the bondage of ignorance (*avidyā*), there are no real grounds for purporting that *prakṛti* herself is to be equated with or subsumed under the afflictions. To equate *prakṛti* with affliction itself implies that as a product of spiritual ignorance, *prakṛti*, along with the afflictions, is conceived as a reality that the *yogī* should ultimately abandon, condemn, avoid or discard completely. Patañjali leaves much room for understanding "dissolution" or "return to the source" with an epistemological emphasis thereby allowing the whole system of the Yoga *darśana* to be interpreted along more open-ended lines. In other words, what actually "dissolves" or is ended in Yoga is the *yogī*'s misidentification with *prakṛti*, a mistaken identity of self that — contrary to authentic identity, namely *puruṣa* — can be nothing more than a product of the three *guṇa*s under the influence of spiritual ignorance. Understood as such, *pratiprasava* need not denote the definitive ontological dissolution of manifest *prakṛti* for the *yogī*, but rather refers to the process of "subtilization" or "sattvification" of consciousness so necessary for the uprooting of misidentification — the incorrect world view born of *avidyā* — or incapacity of the *yogī* to "see" from the yogic perspective of the seer (*draṣṭṛ*), our authentic identity as *puruṣa*.

The discerning *yogī* sees (*YS* II.15) that this guṇic world or cycle of sāṁsāric identity is in itself dissatisfaction (*duḥkha*). But we must ask, what exactly is the problem being addressed in Yoga? What is at issue in Yoga philosophy? Is our ontological status as a human being involved in day-to-day existence forever in doubt, in fact in need of being negated, dissolved in order for authentic identity (*puruṣa*), immortal consciousness, finally to dawn? Having overcome all ignorance, is it then possible for a human being to live in the world and no longer be in conflict with oneself and the world? Can the *guṇa*s cease to function in a state of ignorance and conflict in the mind? Must the guṇic constitution of the human mind and the whole of prakṛtic existence disappear, dissolve for the *yogī*? Can the ways of spiritual ignorance be replaced by an aware, conscious, nonafflicted identity and activity that transcend the conflict and confusion of ordinary, sāṁsāric life? Can we live, according to Patañjali's Yoga, in an embodied state of freedom?

"Aloneness" (Kaivalya): Implications for an Embodied Freedom

In the classical traditions of Sāṁkhya and Yoga, *kaivalya*, meaning "aloneness,"[7] is generally understood to be the state of the unconditional existence of *puruṣa*. In the *Yoga-Sūtra*, *kaivalya* can refer more precisely to the "aloneness of seeing" (*dṛśeḥ kaivalyam*) which, as Patañjali states, follows from the disappearance of ignorance (*avidyā*) and its creation of *saṁyoga*[8] — the conjunction or apparent conflation of the seer (*puruṣa*) and the seeable (i.e., *citta*, *guṇa*s) — explained by Vyāsa as a mental superimposition (*adhyāropa*, *YB* II.18). "Aloneness" thus can be construed as *puruṣa*'s innate capacity for pure, unbroken, non-attached seeing/perceiving, observing or "knowing" of the content of the mind (*citta*).[9] In an alternative definition, Patañjali explains *kaivalya* as the "return to the origin" (*pratiprasava*) of the *guṇa*s, which have lost all soteriological purpose for the *puruṣa*, the seer, as it were, having recovered its transcendent

7. The term *kaivalya* comes from *kevala*, meaning "alone." Feuerstein (1979: 75) also translates *kaivalya* as "aloneness" but with a metaphysical or ontological emphasis that implies the absolute separation of *puruṣa* and *prakṛti*.

8. *YS* II.25 (p. 96): *tadbhāvāt saṁyogābhāvo hānaṁ taddṛśeḥ kaivalyam*.

9. *YS* II.20 and IV.18.

autonomy.[10] This *sūtra* (*YS* IV.34) also classifies *kaivalya* as the establishment in its "own form/nature" (*svarūpa*), and the power of higher awareness (*citiśakti*). Although the seer's (*draṣṭṛ/puruṣa*) capacity for "seeing" is an unchanging yet dynamic power of consciousness that should not be truncated in any way, nevertheless our karmically distorted or skewed perceptions vitiate against the natural fullness of "seeing."[11] Having removed the "failure-to-see" (*adarśana*), the soteriological purpose of the *guṇas* in the sāṁsāric condition of the mind is fulfilled; the mind is relieved of its former role of being a vehicle for *avidyā*, the locus of egoity and misidentification, and the realization of pure seeing — the nature of the seer alone — takes place.

According to yet another *sūtra* (*YS* III.55), we are told that *kaivalya* is established when the *sattva* of consciousness has reached a state of purity analogous to that of the *puruṣa*.[12] Through the process of subtilization or "return to the origin" (*pratiprasava*) in the *sattva*, the transformation (*pariṇāma*) of the mind (*citta*) takes place at the deepest level bringing about a radical change in perspective: the former impure, fabricated states constituting a fractured identity of self are dissolved resulting in the complete purification of mind. Through knowledge (in *saṁprajñāta-samādhi*) and its transcendence (in *asaṁprajñāta-samādhi*) self-identity overcomes its lack of intrinsic grounding, a lack sustained and exacerbated by the web of afflictions in the form of attachment, aversion, and the compulsive clinging to life based on the fear of extinction. The *yogī* is no longer

---

10. *YS* IV.34 (p. 207): *puruṣārthaśūnyānāḥ guṇānāṁ pratiprasavaḥ kaivalyam svarūpapratiṣṭhā vā citiśakter iti.*

11. Patañjali defines spiritual ignorance (*avidyā*), the root affliction, as: "seeing the non-eternal as eternal, the impure as pure, dissatisfaction as happiness, and the non-self as self" (*YS* II.5).

12. *YS* III.55 (p. 174): *sattvapuruṣayoḥ śuddhisāmye kaivalyam iti.* One must be careful not to characterize the state of *sattva* itself as liberation or *kaivalya*, for without the presence of *puruṣa* the mind (as reflected consciousness) could not function in its most transparent aspect as *sattva*. It is not accurate, according to Yoga philosophy, to say that the *sattva* is equivalent to liberation itself. The question of the nature of the *guṇas* from the enlightened perspective is an interesting one. In the *Bhagavad-Gītā* (*BG* II.45) Kṛṣṇa advises Arjuna to become free from the three *guṇas* and then gives further instructions to be established in eternal *sattva* (beingness, light, goodness, clarity, knowledge), free of dualities, free of acquisition-and-possession, Self-possessed (*nirdvandvo nityasattvastho niryogakṣema ātmavān*). It would appear from the above instructions that the nature of the *sattva* being referred to here transcends the limitations of the nature of *sattva-guṇa* which can still have a binding effect in the form of attachment to joy and knowledge. It is, however, only by first overcoming *rajas* and *tamas* that liberation is possible.

dependent on liberating knowledge (mind-*sattva*),[13] is no longer attached to *vṛtti* as a basis for self-identity. Cessation, it must be emphasized, does not mark a definitive disappearance of the *guṇas* from *puruṣa*'s view.[14] For the liberated *yogī*, the *guṇas* cease to exist in the form of *avidyā* and its mental impressions (*saṁskāras*), *vṛttis*, and false or fixed ideas (*pratyaya*) of selfhood that formerly veiled true identity. The changing guṇic modes cannot alter the *yogī*'s now purified and firmly established consciousness. The mind has been liberated from the egocentric world of attachment to things prakṛtic. Now the *yogī*'s identity (as *puruṣa*), disassociated from ignorance, is untouched, unaffected by qualities of mind,[15] uninfluenced by the *vṛttis* constituted of the three *guṇas*. The mind and *puruṣa* attain to a sameness of purity (*YS* III.55), of harmony, balance, evenness, and a workability together: the mind appearing in the nature of *puruṣa* (*YB* I.41).

Kaivalya, I suggest, in no way destroys or negates the personality of the *yogī*, but is an unconditional state in which all the obstacles or distractions preventing an immanent and purified relationship or engagement of person with nature and spirit (*puruṣa*) have been removed. The mind, which previously functioned under the sway of ignorance colouring and blocking our perception of authentic identity, has now become purified and no longer operates as a locus of misidentification, confusion, and dissatisfaction (*duḥkha*). *Sattva*, the finest quality (*guṇa*) of the mind, has the capacity to be perfectly lucid/transparent, like a dust-free mirror in which the light of *puruṣa* is clearly reflected and the discriminative discernment (*vivekakhyāti*) (*YS* II.26) between *puruṣa* and the *sattva* of the mind (as the finest nature of the seeable) can take place (*YS* III.49).

The crucial (ontological) point to be made here is that in the "aloneness" of *kaivalya*, *prakṛti* ceases to perform an obstructing role. In effect, *prakṛti* herself has become purified, illuminated, and liberated[16]

---

13. *YB* III.55 (p. 175): *nahi dagdhakleśabījasya jñāne punar apekṣā kācid asti.* "When the seeds of afflictions have been scorched there is no longer any dependence at all on further knowledge."

14. Swāmi Hariharānanda Āraṇya writes (1963: 123) that in the state of *nirodha* the *guṇas* "do not die out but their unbalanced activity due to non-equilibrium that was taking place . . . only ceases on account of the cessation of the cause (*avidyā* or nescience) which brought about their contact."

15. *YB* IV.25 (p. 201): *puruṣas tv asatyām avidyāyāṁ śuddhaś cittadharmair aparāmṛṣṭa.*

16. Vijñānabhikṣu insists (*YV* IV.34: 141) that *kaivalya* is a state of liberation for both *puruṣa* and *prakṛti* each reaching its respective natural or intrinsic state. He then cites the *Sāṁkhya Kārikā* (62) where it is stated that no *puruṣa* is bound, liberated or →

from *avidyā*'s grip including the misconceptions, misappropriations, and misguided relations implicit within a world of afflicted identity. The mind has been transformed, liberated from the egocentric world of attachment, its former afflicted nature abolished; and self-identity left alone in its "own form" or true nature as *puruṣa* is never again confused with all the relational acts, intentions, and volitions of empirical existence. There being no power of misidentification remaining in *nirbīja-samādhi*,[17] the mind ceases to operate within the context of the afflictions, karmic accumulations, and consequent cycles of *saṁsāra* implying a mistaken identity of selfhood subject to birth and death.

The *YS* has often been regarded as calling for the severance of *puruṣa* from *prakṛti*; concepts such as liberation, cessation, detachment/dispassion, and so forth have been interpreted in an explicitly negative light. Max Müller, citing Bhoja Rāja's commentary (*RM* I.1, p. 1), refers to Yoga as "separation" (*viyoga*) (Müller 1899: 309). More recently, numerous other scholars[18] have endorsed this interpretation, that is, the absolute separateness of *puruṣa* and *prakṛti*. In asserting the absolute separation of *puruṣa* and *prakṛti*, scholars and non-scholars alike have tended to disregard the possibility for other (fresh) hermeneutical options, and this radical, dualistic metaphysical closure of sorts surrounding the nature and meaning of Patañjali's Yoga has proved detrimental to a fuller understanding of the Yoga *darśana* by continuing a tradition based on an isolationistic, one-sided reading (or perhaps misreading) of the *YS* and Vyāsa's commentary. Accordingly, the absolute separation of *puruṣa* and *prakṛti* can only be interpreted as a disembodied and non-relational state implying death to the physical body. To dislodge the *yogī* from bodily existence is to undermine the integrity of the pedagogical context that lends so much credibility or "weight" to the Yoga system. I am not here implying a simple idealization of Yoga pedagogy thereby overlooking the need to incorporate a healthy critical approach to the *guru-śiṣya* dynamic. Rather, I am suggesting that it need not be assumed that, in Yoga, liberation

→ transmigrates. It is only *prakṛti* abiding in her various forms that transmigrates, is bound and becomes liberated. For references to Vijñānabhikṣu's *YV*, I have consulted Rukmani (1981-89).

17. *YS* I.51 and III.8; the state of *nirbīja* or "seedless" *samādhi* can be understood as the liberated state where no "seed" of ignorance remains, any further potential for affliction (i.e., as mental impressions or *saṁskāras*) having been purified from the mind.

18. See, for example, Eliade (1969), Koelman (1970), Feuerstein (1979), and Larson et al. (1987).

coincides with physical death.[19] This would only allow for a soteriological end state of "disembodied liberation" (*videhamukti*). What is involved in Yoga is the death of the atomistic, egoic identity, the dissolution of the karmic web of *saṁsāra* that generates notions of one being a subject trapped in the prakṛtic constitution of a particular body-mind.

Not being content with mere theoretical knowledge, Yoga is committed to a practical way of life. To this end, Patañjali included in his presentation of Yoga an outline of the "eight-limbed" path (*aṣṭāṅga-yoga*)[20] dealing with the physical, moral, psychological, and spiritual dimensions of the *yogī*, an integral path that emphasizes organic continuity, balance, and integration in contrast to the discontinuity, imbalance, and disintegration inherent in *saṁyoga*. The idea of cosmic balance and of the mutual support and upholding of the various parts of nature and society are not foreign to Yoga thought. Vyāsa deals with the theory of "nine causes" (*navakāraṇāni*) or types of causation according to tradition.[21] The ninth type of cause is termed *dhṛti* — meaning "support" or "sustenance." Based on Vyāsa's explanation of *dhṛti* we can see how mutuality and sustenance are understood as essential conditions for the maintenance of the natural and social world. There is an organic interdependence of all living entities wherein all (i.e., the elements, animals, humans, and divine bodies) work together for the "good" of the whole and for each other.

Far from being misconceived exclusively as an introverted path of withdrawal from life, classical Yoga acknowledges the intrinsic value of "support" and "sustenance" and the interdependence of all living

---

19. I am here echoing some of the points made by Chapple in his paper entitled, "*Cittavṛtti* and Reality in the *Yoga-Sūtra*" (Chapple 1983). See also Chapple and Kelly (1990: 5) where the authors state: ". . . *kaivalyam* . . . is not a catatonic state nor does it require death." *SK* 67 acknowledges that even the "potter's wheel" continues to turn because of the force of past impressions (*saṁskāras*); but in Yoga, higher dispassion and *asaṁprajñāta* eventually exhaust all the impressions or karmic residue. Through a continued programme of ongoing purification Yoga allows for the possibility of an embodied state of freedom utterly unburdened by the effects of past actions. As such Yoga constitutes an advance over the fatalistic perspective in Sāṁkhya where the "wheel of *saṁsāra*" continues (after the initial experience of liberating knowledge) until, in the event of separation from the body, *prakṛti* ceases and unending "isolation" (*kaivalya*) is attained (*SK* 68). In any case, the yogic state of supracognitive *samādhi* or entasy goes beyond the liberating knowledge of *viveka* in the Sāṁkhyan system in that the *yogī* must develop dispassion even toward discriminative discernment itself. For more on an analysis of the notion of liberation in Sāṁkhya and Yoga, see Chapple (1996).
20. *YS* II.29; see the discussion on *aṣṭāṅga-yoga* in chapter 4 of Whicher (1998).
21. *YB* II.28 (pp. 99-101).

(embodied) entities, thus upholding organic continuity, balance, and integration within the natural and social world. Having achieved that level of insight (*prajñā*) that is "truth-bearing" (*ṛtaṁbharā*) (*YS* I.48), the *yogī* perceives the natural order (*ṛta*) of cosmic existence, "unites" with, and embodies that order. To fail to see clearly (*adarśana*) is to fall into disorder, disharmony, and conflict with oneself and the world. In effect, to be ensconced in ignorance implies a disunion with the natural order of life and inextricably results in a failure to embody that order. Through Yoga, one gains proper access to the world, and is therefore, established in right relationship to the world. Far from being denied or renounced, the world, for the *yogī*, has become transformed, properly engaged.

We need not read Patañjali as saying that the culmination of all yogic endeavours — *kaivalya* — is a static finality or inactive, isolated, solipsistic state of being. *Kaivalya* can be seen to incorporate an integrated, psychological consciousness along with the autonomy of pure consciousness, yet pure consciousness to which the realm of the *guṇas* (e.g., psychophysical being) is completely attuned and integrated. On the level of individuality, the *yogī* has found his/her place in the world at large, "fitting into the whole" (Klostermaier 1989).

In the last chapter of the *YS* (Kaivalya-Pāda), "aloneness" (*kaivalya*) is said to ensue upon the attainment of *dharmamegha-samādhi*, the "cloud of *dharma samādhi*." At this level of practice, the *yogī* has abandoned any search for (or attachment to) reward or "profit" from his or her meditational practice; a non-acquisitive attitude (*akusīda*) must take place at the highest level of yogic discipline.[22] Vyāsa emphasizes that the identity of *puruṣa* is not something to be acquired (*upādeya*) or discarded (*heya*).[23] The perspective referred to as *Pātañjala Yoga Darśana* culminates in a permanent state of clear "seeing" brought about through the discipline of Yoga. Yoga thus incorporates both an end state or "goal" and a process.[24]

Dharmamegha-samādhi presupposes that the *yogī* has cultivated higher dispassion (*para-vairāgya*) — the means to the enstatic consciousness realized

22. *YS* IV.29 (p. 202): *prasaṁkhyāne 'pi akusīdasya sarvathā vivekakhyāter dharmameghaḥ samādhiḥ.*

23. *YB* II.15 (p. 78): *tatra hātuḥ svarūpamupādeyaṁ vā heyaṁ vā na bhavitumarhati.* "Here, the true nature/identity of the one who is liberated cannot be something to be acquired or discarded."

24. Thus the term *yoga* (like the terms *nirodha* and *samādhi*) is ambiguous in that it means both the processes of purification and illumination and the final result of liberation or "aloneness."

in *asaṁprajñāta-samādhi* (*YB* I.18). Thus, *dharmamegha-samādhi* is more or less a synonym of *asaṁprajñāta-samādhi* and can even be understood as the consummate phase of the awakening disclosed in ecstasy, the final step on the long and arduous yogic journey to authentic identity and "aloneness" (Feuerstein 1980: 98). A permanent identity shift — from the perspective of the human personality to *puruṣa* — takes place. Now free from any dependence on or subordination to knowledge or *vṛtti*, and detached from the world of misidentification (*saṁyoga*), the *yogī* yet retains the purified guṇic powers of virtue including illuminating "knowledge of all"[25] (due to purified *sattva*), nonafflicted activity[26] (due to purified *rajas*), and a stable body-form (due to purified *tamas*).

YS IV.30 declares: "From that [*dharmamegha-samādhi*] there is the cessation of afflicted action."[27] Hence the binding influence of the *guṇas* in the form of the afflictions, past actions, and misguided relationships is overcome; what remains is a "cloud of *dharma*" which includes an "eternality of knowledge" free from all impure covering (*āvaraṇa-mala*, *YS* IV.31) or veiling affliction and where "little (remains) to be known."[28] The eternality or endlessness of knowledge is better understood metaphorically rather than literally: it is not knowledge expanded to infinity but implies *puruṣa*-realization which transcends the limitations and particulars of knowledge (*vṛtti*).

The culmination of the Yoga system is found when, following from *dharmamegha-samādhi*, the mind and actions are freed from misidentification and affliction and one is no longer deluded/confused with regard to one's true form (*svarūpa*) or intrinsic identity. At this stage of practice the *yogī* is disconnected (*viyoga*) from all patterns of action motivated by egoity. According to both Vyāsa[29] and the sixteenth-century commentator Vijñānabhikṣu,[30] one to whom this high state of purification

25. *YS* III.49 and III.54.

26. *YS* IV.7; see also *YS* IV.30.

27. *YS* IV.30 (p. 202): *tataḥ kleśakarmanivṛttiḥ*. Thus, it may be said that to dwell without defilement in a "cloud of *dharma*" is the culminating description by Patañjali of what tradition later referred to as living liberation (*jīvanmukti*).

28. *YS* IV.31 (p. 203): *tadā sarvāvaraṇamalāpetasya jñānasyānantyājjñeyam alpam*.

29. See *YB* IV.30 (pp. 202-03): *kleśakarmanivṛttau jāvanneva vidvānvimukto bhavati*. "On cessation of afflicted action, the knower is released while yet living."

30. *YV* IV.30 (pp. 123-24). Elsewhere in his *Yoga-Sāra-Saṁgraha* (p. 17) Vijñānabhikṣu tells us that the *yogī* who is "established in the state of *dharmamegha-samādhi* is called a *jīvanmukta*" (. . . *dharmameghaḥ samādhiḥ*. . . *asyāmavasthāyāḥ jīvanmukta ityucyate*). Vijñānabhikṣu is critical of Vedāntins (i.e. Śaṅkara's Advaita Vedānta →

takes place is designated as a *jīvanmukta*: one who is liberated while still alive (i.e., embodied or living liberation).

By transcending the normative conventions and obligations of karmic behaviour, the *yogī* acts morally not as an extrinsic response and out of obedience to an external moral code of conduct, but as an intrinsic response and as a matter of natural, purified inclination. The stainless luminosity of pure consciousness is revealed as one's fundamental nature. The *yogī* does not act saṁsārically and ceases to act from the perspective of a delusive sense of self confined within *prakṛti*'s domain. Relinquishing all obsessive or selfish concerns with the results of activity, the *yogī* remains wholly detached from the egoic fruits of action.[31] This does not imply that the *yogī* loses all orientation for action. Only attachment (and compulsive, inordinate desire), not action itself, sets in motion the law of moral causation (*karma*) by which a person is implicated in *saṁsāra*. The *yogī* is said to be non-attached to either virtue or non-virtue, and is no longer oriented within the ego-logical patterns of thought as in the epistemically distorted condition of *saṁyoga*. This does not mean, as some scholars have misleadingly concluded, that the spiritual adept or *yogī* is free to commit immoral acts (Zaehner 1974: 97-98), or that the *yogī* is motivated by selfish concerns (Scharfstein 1974: 131-32).

Actions must not only be executed in the spirit of unselfishness (i.e., sacrifice) or detachment, they must also be ethically sound, reasonable and justifiable. Moreover, the *yogī*'s spiritual journey — far from being an "a-moral process" (Feuerstein 1979: 81) — is a highly moral process! The *yogī*'s commitment to the sattvification of consciousness, including the cultivation of moral virtues such as compassion (*karuṇā*)[32] and non-violence (*ahiṁsā*),[33] is not an "a-moral" enterprise, nor is it an expression of indifference, aloofness, or an uncaring attitude to others. Moral disciplines are engaged as a natural outgrowth of intelligent (sattvic) self-understanding, insight, and commitment to self-transcendence that takes

→ school) that, he says, associate the *jīvanmukta* with ignorance (*avidyā-kleśa*) — probably because of the liberated being's continued link with the body — despite Yoga's insistence on the complete overcoming of the afflictions.

31. This is the essence of Kṛṣṇa's teaching in the *Bhagavad-Gītā* on *karma-yoga*; see, for example, *BG* IV.20.

32. *YS* I.33 (p. 38): *maitrīkaruṇāmuditopekṣāṇāṁ sukhaduḥkhapuṇyāpuṇyaviṣayāṇāṁ bhāvanātaś cittaprasādanam*. "The mind is made pure and clear from the cultivation of friendliness, compassion, happiness and equanimity in conditions or toward objects of joy, sorrow, merit or demerit respectively."

33. *YS* II.35.

consciousness out of (ec-stasis) its identification with the rigid structure of the monadic ego, thereby reversing the inveterate tendency of this ego to inflate itself at the expense of its responsibility in relation to others.

Having defined the "goal" of Yoga as "aloneness" (*kaivalya*), the question must now be asked: What kind of "aloneness" was Patañjali talking about? "Aloneness," I suggest, is not the isolation of the seer (*draṣṭṛ, puruṣa*) separate from the seeable (*dṛśya, prakṛti*), as is unfortunately far too often maintained as the goal of Yoga, but refers to the "aloneness" of the power of "seeing" (*YS* II.20, 25) in its innate purity and clarity without any epistemological distortion and moral defilement. The cultivation of *nirodha* uproots the compulsive tendency to reify the world and oneself (i.e., that pervading sense of separate ego irrevocably divided from the encompassing world) with an awareness that reveals the transcendent, yet immanent seer (*puruṣa*). Through clear "seeing" (*dṛśi*) the purpose of Yoga is fulfilled, and the *yogī*, free from all misidentification and impure karmic residue (as in the former contextual sphere of *cittavṛtti*), gains full, immediate access to the world. By accessing the world in such an open and direct manner, in effect "uniting" (epistemologically) with the world, the *yogī* ceases to be encumbered by egoism (i.e., *asmitā* and its egoic attitudes and identity patterns), which, enmeshed in conflict and confusion and holding itself as separate from the world, misappropriates the world. The sacrifice of egoity/afflicted identity for the purpose of identifying as *puruṣa* is precisely what renders *prakṛti* sacred and ultimately reveals her intrinsic significance and value. By implication, in "aloneness" (*kaivalya*) sacrifice becomes an effortless, automatic (spontaneous) sanctification of the totality of life. Yoga can be recognized as a highly developed and integrated state of mystical illumination that extends and enhances our self-identity. The *yogī* can dwell in a state of balance and fulfilment serving others while feeling/being at home in the world. Freedom denotes a transformation of our entire way of being or mode of action as embodied within the lived world itself.

Yoga can be seen to unfold — in *samādhi* — states of epistemic oneness that reveal the non-separation of knower, knowing, and the known (*YS* I.41) grounding our identity in a non-afflicted mode of action. *Kaivalya* implies a power of "seeing" in which the dualisms rooted in our egocentric patterns of attachment, aversion, fear, and so forth have been transformed into unselfish ways of being with others (*YS* I.33). The psychological, ethical, and social implications of this kind of identity transformation are, needless to say, immense. I am suggesting that Yoga does not destroy or anaesthetize our feelings and emotions thereby encouraging neglect and indifference toward others. On the contrary, the process of "cessation" (*nirodha*) steadies one for a life of compassion, discernment, and service informed by a "seeing" that is able to understand (literally meaning "to stand among, hence observe") — and is in touch with — the needs of others. What seems especially relevant for our understanding of Yoga ethics is the enhanced capacity generated in Yoga for empathic identification with the object one seeks to understand. This is a far cry from the portrayal of the *yogī* as a disengaged figure, psychologically and physically removed from the human relational sphere, who in an obstinate and obtrusive fashion severs all ties with the world. Such an image of a wise *yogī* merely serves to circumscribe our vision of humanity and, if anything else, stifle the spirit by prejudicing a spiritual, abstract (and disembodied) realm over and against nature and our human embodiment. In Yoga philosophy "seeing" is not only a cognitive term but implies purity of mind, that is, it has moral content and value. Nor is "knowledge" (*jñāna, vidyā*) in the Yoga tradition to be misconstrued as a "bloodless" or "heartless" gnosis.

I wish to argue, therefore, that through the necessary transformation of consciousness brought about through yogic discipline, an authentic and fruitful coherence of self-identity, perception, and activity emerges out of the former fragmented consciousness in *saṁyoga*. If Patañjali's perception of the world of forms and differences had been destroyed or discarded, how could he have had such insight into Yoga and the intricacies and subtle nuances of the unenlightened state?[34] If through *nirodha* the individual form and the whole world had been cancelled for Patañjali, he would more likely have spent the rest of his days in the inactivity and isolation of transcendent oblivion rather than present Yoga philosophy to others! Rather than being handicapped by the exclusion of thinking, perceiving, experiencing, or activity, the liberated *yogī* actualizes the potential to live a fully integrated life in the world. I conclude here that there is no reason why the liberated *yogī* cannot be portrayed as a vital, creative, thoughtful, empathetic, balanced, happy, and wise person. Having adopted an integrative orientation to life, the enlightened being can endeavour to transform, enrich, and ennoble the world. I am therefore suggesting that there is a rich, affective, moral, and cognitive as well as

34. Although the historical identity of Patañjali, the Yoga master, is not known, we are assuming that Patañjali was, as the tradition would have it, an enlightened Yoga adept.

spiritual potential inherent in the realization of *puruṣa*, the "aloneness" of the power of consciousness/seeing.

Yoga presupposes the integration of contemplation and activity; there can be no scission between *theoria* and *praxis*. The *YS* is a philosophical text where *praxis* is deemed to be essential. Without actual practice the theory that informs Yoga would have no authentic meaning. Yet without examination and reflection there would be no meaningful striving for liberation, no "goal," as it were, to set one's sight on. In an original, inspiring, and penetrating style, Patañjali bridges metaphysics and ethics, transcendence and immanence, and contributes to the Indic and global fold a form of philosophical investigation that, to borrow J. Taber's descriptive phrase for another context, can properly be called a "transformative philosophy." That is to say, it is a philosophical perspective which "does not stand as an edifice isolated from experience; it exists only in so far as it is realized in experience" (Taber 1983: 26).

Conclusion

To conclude, it can be said that *puruṣa* indeed has some precedence over *prakṛti* in Patañjali's system, for *puruṣa* is what is ordinarily "missing" or concealed in human life and is ultimately the state of consciousness one must awaken to in Yoga. The liberated state of "aloneness" (*kaivalya*) need not denote either an ontological superiority of *puruṣa* or an exclusion of *prakṛti*. *Kaivalya* can be positively construed as an integration of both principles — an integration that, I have argued, is what is most important for Yoga. I have proposed that the *YS* does not uphold a "path" of liberation that ultimately renders *puruṣa* and *prakṛti* incapable of "co-operating" together. Rather, the *YS* seeks to "unite" these two principles without the presence of any defiled understanding, to bring them "together," properly aligning them in a state of balance, harmony, and a clarity of knowledge in the integrity of being and action.

The purified mind, one that has been transformed through yogic discipline, is certainly no ordinary worldly awareness, nor is it eliminated for the sake of pure consciousness. To confuse (as many interpretations of Yoga have unfortunately done) the underlining purificatory processes involved in the cessation of ignorance/afflicted identity as being the same thing as (or as necessitating the need for) a radical elimination of our psychophysical being — the prakṛtic vehicle through which consciousness discloses itself — is, I suggest, to misunderstand the intent of the *YS* itself. There are strong grounds for arguing (as I have attempted to show) that through "cessation" *prakṛti* herself (in the form of the guṇic constitutional make-up of the *yogī*'s body-mind) is liberated from the grip of ignorance. Vyāsa explicitly states (*YB* II.18) that emancipation happens in the mind and does not literally apply to *puruṣa* — which is by definition already free and therefore has no intrinsic need to be released from the fetters of saṁsāric existence.

Both morality and perception (cognition) are essential channels through which human consciousness, far from being negated or suppressed, is transformed and illuminated. Yoga combines discerning knowledge with an emotional, affective, and moral sensibility allowing for a participatory epistemology that incorporates the moral amplitude for empathic identification with the world, that is, with the objects or persons one seeks to understand. The enhanced perception gained through Yoga must be interwoven with Yoga's rich, affective and moral dimensions to form a spirituality that does not become entangled in a web of antinomianism, but which retains the integrity and vitality to transform our lives and the lives of others in an effective manner. In Yoga proper, there can be no support, ethically or pedagogically, for the misappropriation or abuse of *prakṛti* for the sake of freedom or *puruṣa*-realization. By upholding an integration of the moral and the mystical, Yoga supports a reconciliation of the prevalent tension within Hinduism between (1) spiritual engagement and self-identity within the world (*pravṛtti*) and (2) spiritual disengagement from worldliness and self-identity that transcends the world (*nivṛtti*). Yoga discerns and teaches a balance between these two apparently conflicting orientations.

This paper has attempted to counter the radically dualistic, dissociative and isolationistic interpretations of Yoga presented by many scholars — where the full potentialities of our human embodiment are constrained within a radical, rigid, dualistic metaphysical structure — and propose instead an open-ended, morally and epistemologically oriented hermeneutic that frees Yoga of the long-standing conception of spiritual isolation, disembodiment, self-denial, and world-negation and thus, from its pessimistic image. Our interpretation does not impute that *kaivalya* denotes a final incommensurability between spirit and matter. While Patañjali can be understood as having adopted a provisional, practical, dualistic metaphysics, there is no proof that his system either ends in duality or eliminates the possibility for an ongoing cooperative duality. Yoga is not simply "*puruṣa*-realization"; it equally implies "getting it right with *prakṛti*."

To be sure, the yogic path in all of its knowledge, power and glory must be transcended. One must, as it were, step outside of the vehicle of *prakṛti* and dwell as the consciousness of *puruṣa* in true form (*svarūpa*). Yet I want to suggest that transcendence need not be taken to mean a "static finality": abiding in non-afflicted, disengaged, formless, transcendent bliss. Rather, more elliptically, Patañjali may well have set the stage for an inclusive awakening allowing for a convergence and engagement in life, a "growing up" in life with an integrity and fullness that perhaps knows no bounds. Now that, I would like to suggest, is a matured Yoga, the possibility of which we must not overlook or close the door on.

Abbreviations

BG *Bhagavad-Gītā*

RM *Rāja-Mārtaṇḍa* of Bhoja Rāja (*c.* eleventh century CE)

SK *Sāṁkhya Kārikā* of Īśvarakṛṣṇa (*c.* fourth-fifth century CE)

YB *Yoga-Bhāṣya* of Vyāsa (*c.* fifth-sixth century CE)

YS *Yoga-Sūtra* of Patañjali (*c.* second-third century CE)

YV *Yoga-Vārttika* of Vijñānabhikṣu

References

Agashe, K.S. (ed.) (1904), *Pātañjalayogadarśana with the Vyāsa-Bhāṣya of Vyāsa, the Tattva-Vaiśāradī of Vācaspati Miśra and the Rāja-Mārtaṇḍa of Bhoja Rāja*, Poona: Ānandāśrama Sanskrit Series, vol. 47.

Āraṇya, Swāmi Hariharānanda (1963), *Yoga Philosophy of Patañjali*, Translated into English by Paresh N. Mukerji, Calcutta: University of Calcutta.

Arya, Usharbudh (1986), *Yoga-Sūtras of Patañjali with the Exposition of Vyāsa: A Translation and Commentary*, vol. 1: *Samādhi-Pāda*, Honesdale, PA: Himalayan International Institute.

Chapple, C.K. (1983), "Citta-vṛtti and Reality in the Yoga Sūtra," in *Sāṁkhya-Yoga: Proceedings of the IASWR Conference, 1981*, ed. Christopher K. Chapple, Stoney Brook, New York: The Institute for Advanced Studies of World Religions.

——— (1996), "Living Liberation in Sāṁkhya and Yoga," in *Living Liberation in Hindu Thought*, ed. Andrew O. Fort and Patricia Y. Mumme, Albany: State University of New York Press.

——— (2008), *Yoga and the Luminous*, Albany: State University of New York Press.

Chapple, Christopher K. & Yogi Ananda Viraj (Eugene P. Kelly, Jr.) (1990), *The Yoga-Sūtras of Patañjali: An Analysis of the Sanskrit with Accompanying English Translation*, Delhi: Sri Satguru Publications.

Edgerton, Franklin (1924), "The Meaning of Sāṁkhya and Yoga," in *American Journal of Philology*, vol. 45, pp. 1-46.

Eliade, Mircea (1969), *Yoga: Immortality and Freedom*, Translated by Willard R. Trask, 2nd edn., Bollingen Series no. 56, Princeton: Princeton University Press.

Feuerstein, Georg (1979), *The Yoga-Sūtra of Patañjali: A New Translation and Commentary*, Folkstone, England: Wm. Dawson and Sons, Ltd.

——— (1980), *The Philosophy of Classical Yoga*, Manchester: Manchester University Press.

Halbfass, Wilhelm (1991), *Tradition and Reflection: Explorations in Indian Thought*, Albany: State University of New York Press.

Hauer, Jakob W. (1958), *Der Yoga*, Stuttgart: W. Kohlhammer.

Jha, Ganganath (tr.) (1894), *An English Translation with Sanskrit Text of the Yogasāra-Saṁgraha of Vijñānabhikṣu*, Bombay: Tattva-Vivechaka Press.

Klostermaier, K.K. (1989), "Spirituality and Nature," in *Hindu Spirituality: Vedas through Vedanta*, ed. Krishna Sivaraman, New York: The Crossroad Publishing Company, pp. 319-37.

Koelman, Gaspar M. (1970), *Pātañjala Yoga: From Related Ego to Absolute Self*, Poona, India: Papal Anthenaeum.

Larson, Gerald J. and R. Shankar Bhattacharya. (eds.) (1987), *Sāṁkhya: A Dualist Tradition in Indian Philosophy* (*Encyclopedia of Indian Philosophies*, vol. IV), Princeton, New Jersey: Princeton University Press.

——— (eds.) (2008), *Yoga: India's Philosophy of Meditation* (*Encyclopedia of Indian Philosophies*, vol. XII), Delhi: Motilal Banarsidass.

Müller, Max (1899), *The Six Systems of Indian Philosophy*, London: Longmans, Green and Co.

Oberhammer, Gerhard (1977), *Strukturen Yogischer Meditation*, vol. 13, Vienna: Verlag der Osterreichischen Academie der Wissenschaften.

Radhakrishnan, Sarvepalli (1948), *The Bhagavadgītā*, London: George Allen and Unwin.

Rukmani, Trichur S. (tr.) (1981-89), *Yogavārttika of Vijñānabhikṣu: Text along with English Translation and Critical Notes along with the Text and English Translation of the Pātañjala Yogasūtras and Vyāsabhāṣya* (4 vols.), New Delhi: Munshiram Manoharlal.

Scharfstein, Ben-Ami (1974), *Mystical Experience*, Baltimore, NM: Penguin Books.

Taber, John (1983), *Transformative Philosophy: A Study of Śaṅkara, Fichte and Heidegger*. Honolulu: University of Hawaii Press.

Varenne, Jean (1976), *Yoga and the Hindu Tradition*, Chicago: University of Chicago Press.

Whicher, Ian R. (1998), *The Integrity of the Yoga Darśana*, Albany: State University of New York Press.

Whicher, Ian and David Carpenter (eds.) (2003), *Yoga: The Indian Tradition*, London and New York: Routledge Curzon.

Woods, James Haughton (tr.) (1914), *The Yoga System of Patañjali*, Harvard Oriental Series, vol. 17, Cambridge: Harvard University Press.

Zaehner, Robert C. (1974), *Our Savage God*, London: Collins.

4

Yoga-Sūtras II.25 And the Conundrum of Kaivalya

*Frederick M. Smith**

AMONG the more neglected subdivisions of the *Yoga-Sūtras* (*YS*) is the section containing *sūtra*s 18-27 of the second chapter, the *sādhana-pāda* or chapter (*pāda*) on practice (*sādhana*).[1] These *sūtra*s sequentially and logically (if not formally) complete the section on *kriyā-yoga*, the "yoga of action" (II.1-27).[2] This comparative neglect has troubled me for many years, after reading a number of Sanskrit commentaries and popular works on Yoga, most of which attempt to explain *kaivalya*, the apparent denouement of *kriyā-yoga*, in terms of Vedānta (especially Advaita Vedānta) or attempt to write it out of the text altogether, often through benign neglect. This reflects the appropriation of the *YS* for well over a millennium by individuals and schools for whom the philosophies and soteriologies of unity or non-dualism made (and continue to make) better sense than the philosophies and soteriologies of separation or dualism. The problem has been recognized in both the public sphere of yoga-teaching and in the realm of scholarship. For example, in the former realm the well-known modern Yoga master B.K.S. Iyengar (b. 1918) notes in his discussion of

* Department of Religious Studies, The University of Iowa.

1. See, for example Larson's introduction in Larson and Bhattacharya (2008: 117), where these *sūtra*s are dismissed in a single sentence. Unquestionably the most neglected subsection is the bulk of the third chapter, the *vibhūti-pāda* or chapter on extraordinary perception, especially *sūtra*s III.16-52.

2. *YS* II.1 reads: *tapaḥsvādhyāyeśvarapraṇidhānāni kriyāyogaḥ*, "The Yoga of action includes austerities, study of the knowledge associated with one's own lineage, and devotion to *Īśvara*." One might equally argue that *kriyā-yoga* extends through the entire extent of the second *pāda*, which would include the first five *aṅga*s or limbs of the eight-limbed (*aṣṭāṅga*) path (II.28-55), the final three members of which appear at the beginning of the third chapter (*vibhūti-pāda*). But we cannot discuss this further here.

YS II.25 in his popular book *Light on the Yoga-Sūtras of Patañjali* (which contains a translation better gauged as an explanation) that "[w]ithout doubt, *sūtra*s II.17-25 are terse and many have groped for a precise and clear explanation of them. We must read and re-read them in order to grasp their meaning" (1993: 128). With the goal of partially rectifying this lacuna, I would like to offer a few reflections on these *sūtra*s, especially on *YS* II.25.

The first question that must be asked, then, is what is it about these *sūtra*s that has challenged the classical commentators and forced both modern scholars and modern Yoga masters and enthusiasts to arrive at interpretations that are patently ideological, neglect the history of the text, or follow the classical commentators in sidestepping the distinctive character of *kaivalya*? It is neither practical nor interesting to inventory the many strange or fragmentary interpretations of these *sūtra*s; it is better to cite a few of them that appear to be representative, then to offer my own interpretation.

Practically, since the composition of the *YS* and the commentary by Vyāsa, the bulk of the former probably around the third century CE and the entirety of the latter perhaps a couple of centuries later,[3] *kaivalya* has been rejected as a term of practical value in Yoga traditions, and has consistently (and often unconvincingly) been replaced by other concepts

3. This dating has become current; cf. Bronkhorst (1985), Larson and Bhattacharya (2008: 21f.), Sarbacker (2005), and many others, including recent primers on Hinduism, e.g. Lipner (2010: 190), Michaels (2004: 267). Views of the *YS* as the work of a much earlier period, such as the fourth-second century BCE Mauryan dynasty, should now be discarded. Just as certain, we cannot assume that all the *sūtra*s were composed by a single author or even during the same century. It is not possible to enter into that debate here, but it appears to me that close study of the *sūtra*s will identify different strata of composition. Similarly, Bronkhorst (1985) is right to question the identity of Vyāsa and the intriguing suggestion that he (whoever he was) also composed the *YS*. It is more likely, as just suggested, that the *YS* consists of a floating collection of *sūtra*s that were probably not intended to appear under a single title — there are simply too many repetitions and contradictions — until they were brought together by Vyāsa, the "redactor" whose identity will forever remain unknown. Michaels states the case succinctly: "The system of Yoga is based mainly on a text, the *YS*, which is supposed to have been composed by an author named Patañjali but which is composed of various fragments and traditions of texts stemming from the second or third century. The first commentary, allegedly composed by Vyāsa [. . .] dates from the fifth century CE. In between these two texts, there are considerable gaps in the transmission of the tradition" (2004: 267). This gap in lexical understanding and ideology is largely responsible for the problematic nature of *kaivalya* in the writing of both the commentators and the subsequent Yoga tradition.

and their correlative terms. Nearly all commentators, followed by significant bandwidths of the Yoga tradition, particularly Nāth Yoga and modern Yoga (which I believe we must now regard as a distinct Yoga tradition, even if it has a growing number of branches and manifestations), have tried to wish it away. As a term indicative of the ultimate state realizable through the practice of Yoga, as the *YS* clearly states, most writers on Yoga in English, Hindi, Marathi, and other Indian languages translate or envision *kaivalya* as *mokṣa*, *mukti*, or *apavarga* (which is mentioned in *YS* II.18 but is not equated with *kaivalya*), terms more widely used for or associated with "liberation" as it receives its impetus in various forms of Vedānta. An example of a widely read and highly regarded twentieth-century interpreter is Swami Prabhavananda, the leading translator of classical Sanskrit philosophical texts for the Vedanta Society, one of the earliest (and still most prominent) Anglicized movements that advocated a conjunction of Yoga and Vedānta. Prabhavananda translates *kaivalya* as "independent and free" in *YS* II.25 and as "liberation" in *YS* IV.33.[4] Similarly, he uses the word "liberation" for the name of the fourth chapter, the *kaivalya-pāda*. This is not entirely wrong, but it is taking an easy road through difficult terrain. I need not go into Prabhavananda's other Vedāntic recastings of Yoga terminology except to say that he translates both *puruṣa* in I.16 and *draṣṭā* in II.20 as *ātman* (as an English word with an unquestioned Vedāntic pedigree), and that the word *kaivalya* does not appear in his index of terms discussed.

Similarly, most commentators from antiquity to the twenty-first century are more comfortable discussing the carefully nuanced word *samādhi*, nuanced, that is, in the Yogaśāstra, including in the *YS* itself. Occasionally, not even this word is mentioned, however. A recent study by Som Dev Vasudeva of a late eighteenth-century Sanskrit text called *Haṁsavilāsa* (Transport of the Haṁsas) by a classically educated Gujarātī Śaiva *paṇḍita* named Haṁsamiṭṭhu replaces *kaivalya* as the culmination of Pātañjala Yoga with the comparatively unspecified term *rāja-yoga* (Vasudeva 2011).[5] At

4. See Prabhavananda and Isherwood (1953). Another similar example is the recent popular translation and discussion by Bryant (2009: 234), a work that strongly reflects the positions of Bengali Vaiṣṇava non-dualism. Bryant translates the word *hānam* in II.25 (no doubt a difficult word here) as "freedom." See Hatcher 2008, esp. pp. 99ff., for a description of the intellectual beginnings of modernism in Bengal, including the antecedents of the neo-Advaita of the Vedanta Society and elsewhere, in what Hatcher calls "bourgeois Hinduism."

5. On *rāja-yoga*, see Larson and Bhattacharya 2008: 137f. In that volume, Bhattacharya describes a late text (probably nineteenth century) called *Rājayoga-Bhāṣya* (wishfully

→

the very least this is testimony that the term *kaivalya* was unrepentantly replaced by that time in at least some circles in the popular discourse of Yoga by the spiritual vision and terminology of Vedānta.

It is not within the scope of the present study to discuss the crucial question of the viability of interpretations of *samādhi*, which is prominently discussed in both the text of the *YS* and its commentaries and which is curiously detached from the regularly sidestepped or misunderstood *kaivalya* except when the latter is defined by classical or modern interpreters in terms of the former (which misses the intent of the *YS*). The term *kaivalya* is murkier when reviewing the literature of both classical Yoga and modern Yoga and realizing that no one (to the best of my knowledge) has (ever?) used the word *kaivalya* as a descriptor of their own or another's spiritual state. Nevertheless, most classical and modern authors have been forced by the language of their own religious or spiritual predilections and lineages to understand *kaivalya* as "absolute freedom, emancipation, absorption in the supreme soul," as Iyengar does (1993: 128). This is implicitly defining *kaivalya* as *samādhi*. Another ready example of defining *kaivalya* in terms of *samādhi* appears in the analysis of Patañjali's teachings by Swami Kuvalayananda, who established Kaivalyadhāma, one of the early centres of modern "scientific" Yoga, in Lonavla, between Pune and Bombay, in 1924. Joseph Alter writes appositely:

> [W]hen *samādhi* is described as a state of bliss, it is the bliss of *mokṣa* or final liberation from bondage to the material world, as that bondage is manifest in the cycle of births. It is the bliss of absolute nothingness reflected in the synonymous term *kaivalya*, from which Swami Kuvalayananda derived the name for his ashram laboratory.
>
> — 2004: 101

Is *kaivalya* synonymous with *samādhi* rather than (or as well as) its practical result? Was it intended to indicate "the bliss of absolute nothingness" (rather than absolute fullness or clarity of cosmological vision)? This is not to say that Kuvalayananda or Alter misused or misunderstood the term, given the culture of Yoga out of which the term *kaivalya* was

→ attributed to Śaṅkarācārya) that is characteristic of the recent amalgamation of a few Sāṁkhya principles with a number of relatively well-known tāntrically inspired Yoga practices, cloaked in a veneer of Vedānta (ibid: 361-66; see also Buhnemann 2007 for notes on the antiquity of the term *rāja-yoga*). Consistent with this, the term *rāja-yoga* is used rather amorphously in modernity to indicate any kind of Vedānta-based meditation practice.

interpreted in the second millennium.[6] Because the origins of *kaivalya* and the way it is conceived in the *YS* as a teleological possibility of Sāṁkhya ontology were disrupted by its subjugation to the hegemonic spiritual culture of Vedānta, it will be the best way to review its domain through a discussion of the entire subsection, *YS* II.18-26. It will be best, however, to begin with notes on *YS* 11.25.

Yoga-Sūtras II.25 reads: *tadbhāvāt saṁyogābhāvo hānaṁ taddṛśeḥ kaivalyam.* It may be translated,

> The absence of [the perception of] union (*saṁyoga*) [between *puruṣa* and *buddhi* as an aspect of *prakṛti*] occurs after the disappearance of ignorance (*tad*). This negation or rejection (*hānam*) is the absolute singularity (*kaivalya*) of the seer.

Several problems arise in the interpretations of the dualism expressed in this *sūtra*. First of all we must inquire into the dualisms or polarities presented in a number of the *sūtras*, specifically *sattva/puruṣa* (*YS* III.35, 49, 55), *sva/svāmī* (*YS* II.23), and *dṛś/darśana* (*YS* II.6), keeping in mind that the final *sūtra* of the third *pāda* (III.55) informs us that *kaivalya* is, in addition to what is stated in II.25, a state in which purity is equalized and maximized in both positively perceived being-as-existence (*sattva*), which is a step away from primordial materiality (*prakṛti*, Larson's term) or substantiality, and the unchanging and pervasive, yet unsubstantial, absolute (*sattvapuruṣayoḥ śuddhisāmye kaivalyam*). Most of the commentators and translators understand all of these polarities as expressive of *buddhi* and *puruṣa*, *buddhi* as an explicable gloss for *sattva* (pure awareness as the finest level of individuation), *dṛś* (the observer) and *sva* (that which is one's own). One might question this by asking why the distinction to be realized is between *puruṣa* and *buddhi*, rather than *puruṣa* and *prakṛti*, and whether *prakṛti* and *buddhi* (or *sattva*) are here equivalent? We must assume *buddhi* is operative here because it represents the aspect of awareness within the realm of *prakṛti*, and is therefore regarded as in some way substantial; awareness or individual consciousness is to be understood as a substance. Most importantly, however, *buddhi* must be recognized as part of this *saṁyoga* because its power to overlap the boundary between

---

6. See, for example, the eighteenth-century commentary by Sadāśivendra Sarasvatī, a Tamilian advocate of Advaita Vedānta, called Yogasudhākara (cf. Bhattacharya in Larson and Bhattacharya 2008: 356-59 for a summary). He comments on I.25: *dṛśer nityamuktāyāś citiśakteḥ kaivalyam ity arthaḥ*, viz. that *kaivalya* is equivalent to permanent liberation.

puruṣa and *prakṛti* is mentioned in *YS* II.6 and III.49.[7] If we accept this, then we must conclude that *sattva* as used here is not the same as *sattva* as one of the three *guṇas*, but is equivalent with *buddhi* in the sense of pure unmodified awareness-as-substance, synonymous with *mahat* in the Sāṁkhya cosmology. Why, then, we might wonder, is this *sūtra* found in the second chapter rather than in the fourth chapter where *kaivalya* is otherwise discussed? In fact, like this series of *sūtras*, the fourth chapter is also often disregarded; it appears, at first glance at least, to be problematically out of place.

Before we address this problem more definitively, however, the *sūtra* itself should be discussed. The word *saṁyoga*, "conjunction," must be understood in the context of *YS* II.23, another difficult *sūtra*. That *sūtra* reads: *svasvāmiśaktyoḥ svarūpopalabdhihetuḥ saṁyogaḥ*. This can be rendered as follows: "What is called *saṁyoga* or conjunction is the cause (*śakti*) of the cognition (*upalabdhi*) of the true nature (*svarūpa*) of the owned (*sva*) with its lord or master (*svāmī*)." Many commentators are drawn into a Vedāntic backreading of this *sūtra*, understanding it to say that *sva* (property, that which is "one's own") and *svāmī* (its owner, lord, or master) are in fact *buddhi* and *puruṣa*, the individual and the absolute, *ātman* and *Brahman*, respectively. This, however, is not a necessary inference. It is true that according to this *sūtra*, *saṁyoga* is defined as the underlying force behind the cognition of the true nature of an individual, in terms of its materiality and its ownership. This force, a kind of magnetic or symbiotic necessity, is constituted of individuality and universality that are conjoined in a composite whole which is impossible to disentangle without yogic insight. They reflect and recognize each other, but they are not identical. This is the dualism that must be recognized in order to fulfil the goals of Yoga. One might regard the *svarūpa* of an individual, in the context of Yoga, as purely spiritual in the sense of a body imbued with different fundamentally balanced energies (*prakṛti*) that is thoroughly pervaded by an absolute unchanging *puruṣa*. But this is not the case; the *YS* here

---

7. II.6: *dṛg-darśana-śaktyor ekātmatevāsmitā*, indicating that one's sense of individuality is due to an inseparable unity of the energies of the seer or experiencer with the power inherent in the seeing, which is to say in the experience, III.49: *sattva-puruṣānyatā-khyāti-mātrasya sarva-bhāvādhiṣṭhātṛtvaṁ sarva-jñātṛtvaḥ ca*, "Supremacy of all conditions and mastery of all knowledge is reserved only for one who is able to perceive the distinction between pure intellect (*sattva*) and the experiencer (*puruṣa*)." This distinction is realized through the processes involved in *saṁyama*, the power of the three highest states of Patañjali's eightfold Yoga taken together, namely *dhāraṇā*, *dhyāna*, and *samādhi* (*YS* III.1-5).

carefully considers the fact that anything possessing appearance or form (*rūpa*) must be constituted of elements which confer aspects of this form within the material world in order to produce discreet degrees of individuation, but which never loses contact with the all-pervasive element of consciousness animating that form. However, that consciousness is regarded as substantial within the realm of *prakṛti*. It is not *puruṣa*, which does not appear to be regarded here as pure consciousness. Rather, it appears to be a force that lies beyond consciousness, which, as Sāṁkhya and Yoga see it, has mass and energy; it is a substance. Even if *puruṣa* pervades an individual, it does not appear to be part of this equation, even if we want it to be.

This, unfortunately, is bad news for Vedāntins. This is the unattainable aspect of Sāṁkhya, the heart of the conundrum of *kaivalya*: even if it references *puruṣa*, it can "exist" only within the realm of the many subtle layers of *prakṛti*, which is to say of *buddhi* (or *sattva*), the finest or the most subtle stratum of awareness. The connection between this realm and the more defined or constructed realms of the individual constitute the context in which the word *saṁyoga* must be understood in II.23 and II.25.

The *sūtra* II.24 informs us that the cause of this conjunction is ignorance (*tasya hetur avidyā*), understood as ignorance of the separability of *prakṛti* and *puruṣa*, of *sva* and *svāmī*, of the relative world of cognitively accessible awareness, substance, and energy, and the uncognizable absolute (which, however, cannot be surrendered to a conceptualization of "nothingness"). Although we cannot actively distinguish these two, or even passively separate them, we must understand that from the perspective of Sāṁkhya-Yoga they are the two fundamental, if separable, aspects of universal wholeness, and that it is ignorance, a lack of vision or understanding, which obstructs our apprehension of this separability. *Sūtra* 25 informs us that we have the capacity to gain an active cognition of this separability, but that this capacity arises only after ignorance is eradicated. This newfound clarity that arises when ignorance is eliminated encompasses an understanding that the conjunction of the perceiver with an object of perception is inherent in the construction of the universe, but that *svarūpa*, the true nature or essential form of a person, object, idea, or entity, lies within the domain of *prakṛti* but is apprehended only by understanding the relationship between *prakṛti* and *puruṣa*. Patañjali calls this realization *hānam*, "abandonment." Although Patañjali employs this rather ordinary and deceptively simple word as a technical term, he quickly adds that what this means is that once we realize that this conjunction is, in the final analysis, an error in our perception, we abide in a state of *kaivalya*. What is abandoned is our lifelong habit of misrecognition of the fundamental constituent elements of the universe.

The very foundation of our grip on the world in which we live is our ability to create identity structures and relations between them. In other words, our sense of who we are is grounded in our ability to construct *saṁyogas* or conjunctions between and within ourselves and the world. But according to Yoga philosophy, as we can see here, these conjunctions, which are nothing other than false identifications of the seer with the seen, obscure the dual nature of ourselves, as well as the dual nature of any ideas, entities, or objects with which we might feel connected or identified. It is assumed in the *YS* that these links or conjunctions are forged as a result of unexamined psychophysical and mental processes. But once we subject ourselves to protracted discriminative and absorptive practices that give rise to different states of *samādhi* which are beyond the vicissitudes of ordinary thought (these states are described in the first chapter of the *YS*), we can bring back into our lives in the world a cognitive or apperceptive state called *kaivalya*. *Kaivalya*, then, is the abandonment (*hānam*) of the *saṁyoga* in which the *buddhi* or active substantive awareness identifies, falsely as it turns out, with both the *puruṣa*, which sees, and the objects seen; it is the abandonment of the identification of the absolute person with the constructed individual.[8] Delinking *buddhi* from both of these becomes the expression of the absolute independence of *kaivalya*. To repeat: *kaivalya* cannot be the exact equivalent to the Vedāntic state of *mokṣa* or *mukti* because it is brought about by a realization of the separability of *buddhi* (hence of *prakṛti*) and *puruṣa*, rather than of the conjunction of the individual self or *ātman* with the abstract absolute *Brahman*. It is, thus, a state of liberation engendered by seeing through the ultimate erroneousness of conjunctions rather than through the ultimate truth of any conjunction, including the conjunction of *Brahman* and *ātman*. Operating from within this understanding, within this field of *kaivalya*, the *yogin*'s actions are imbued with the power of *dharmamegha-samādhi* (*YS* IV.29), the *samādhi* in which a cloud (*megha*) of *dharma* or righteous action pours forth effortlessly.

The reason *sūtras* 18-25 of the second chapter are placed where they are rather than in the fourth chapter, in which *kaivalya* is more clearly the focus, is because it is understood as the epitome or perfection of *kriyā*-

8. I am grateful to long discussions with Lloyd Pflueger of Truman State University while thinking this through.

yoga. In spite of the fact that approximately half of the second chapter discusses the first five of the eight limbs of the eightfold path of Yoga (II.28-54), *kriyā-yoga* is the primary context of this chapter of the *YS*; it is in this context that Patañjali wants us to understand his discussion of *kleśa*s or fundamental afflictions, the way to resolve them, the discussion leading up to this *sūtra* defining *kaivalya*, and the first five limbs of the eightfold path. Recalling the first *sūtra* of the second chapter, we see that *kriyā-yoga* includes (1) *tapas* — enthusiastic spiritual practice; (2) *svādhyāya* — the study, memorization, and practice of the Vedic recitation of one's own ancestral lineage; and (3) *īśvarapraṇidhāna* — dedication or surrender to God (*īśvara*), which Patañjali identifies as a special *puruṣa* (*puruṣaviśeṣa*, *YS* I.24). By employing a neutral term (*īśvara*) that avoids mention of any sectarian deity, he suggests that this is the inner self of the *yogin*. Regardless of what he had in mind, however, it is certain that the mention of *kaivalya* in II.25 expresses the final result of the practice of *kriyā-yoga*. *Kaivalya*, in great measure engendered by almost innumerable practices that are possible under these three categories, is the final state of realization of *kriyā-yoga*.

Let us now briefly return to the earlier *sūtra*s in this section. *YS* II.17, which concludes the earlier section on *kleśa*s or afflictions, states that their cause, which it to be avoided, is the conjunction between the observer and the observable (*draṣṭṛdṛśyayoḥ saṁyogo heyahetuḥ*).[9] This presages the sense of *saṁyoga* in II.25. *YS* II.18 describes the trajectory of the observable, what is seen or "apprehended" through the senses (*prakāśakriyāsthitiśālaṁ bhūtendriyātmakaṁ bhogāpavargārthaṁ dṛśyam*). Anything experienced through the senses is accomplished (in part) because of the object's qualities of light, action, or stability (*prakāśa*, *kriyā*, and *sthiti*, the apprehensible manifestations of the three *guṇa*s: *sattva*, *rajas*, and *tamas*, respectively), which appear to operate independently of the experiencer. Any such apprehension may be used for either sensual pleasure (*bhoga*) or liberation literal sense of grasping the separation of *puruṣa* from materiality (*apavarga*). The next *sūtra*, II.19, emphasizes that objects of perception are specified or non-specified, and that they may or may not reflect their provenance. In all cases they are aspects of the three *guṇa*s (*viśeṣāviśeṣaliṅgamātrāliṅgāni guṇaparvāṇi*). The text continues that the seer is exclusively a witness. Although it is pure, it observes all cognitive activity (*draṣṭā dṛśimātraḥ śuddho 'pi pratyayānupaśyaḥ*, II.20). This highlights the absence of involvement of *puruṣa* in the created world, inclusive of the material

9. The clearest summary of the commentaries views on the first two *pāda*s of the *YS* is Arya/Veda Bharati 1986, 2001.

constructions of the three *guṇa*s and the discriminative powers of the *buddhi*. Nevertheless, the following *sūtra* indicates that what is seen or cognized must perforce be subordinate to the *puruṣa*. It must serve the purpose of *puruṣa* or have *puruṣa* as its goal (*tadartha eva dṛśyātmā*, II.21). This appears to weaken the absolute independence or separation of *puruṣa* and *prakṛti* or *sattva*. In fact, however, the recognition of *puruṣa* by the *yogin* and of the perceptible by the *puruṣa* demonstrates that individual awareness, not to mention all created form, is framed or given meaning by the very fact of the eternality, permanence, and unchanging nature of *puruṣa*, just as *puruṣa* is conferred meaning because of its recognition of *prakṛti*. In spite of their separateness, then, the *puruṣa* and the *buddhi* recognize each other even if it is not stated that the *puruṣa* guides any particular action or process. Predestination cannot be part of Patañjali's system. The following *sūtra*, II.22, argues that a cognition disappears for the individual cognizer once it has served this purpose, but it does not disappear as common property, so to speak, because it can be picked up by others and used for the same purpose (*kṛtārthaṁ prati naṣṭam apy anaṣṭaṁ tadanyasādhāraṇatvāt*). This sets the scene for the understanding of *saṁyoga* and its rejection as *kaivalya* in II.23-25, as discussed above. *Sūtra*s II.26 and 27, which we cannot unpack here, describe the clarity and wisdom of one who has attained *kaivalya*, having seen and deconstructed this *saṁyoga*.

Finally, working our way back to the earlier discussion of the transmission of this understanding in both the Śāstric tradition of *YS* commentary, which was always minor compared with the widespread study of Vedānta, Nyāya, Mīmāṁsā, and, before the end of the first millennium, Buddhism, and the public domain of what is taught as adjunct to Yoga practice, it is important to remember that until the twentieth century the Yoga traditions were strictly housed in India, and that they operated entirely within the domain of a few renunciates and fewer scholars.[10] There was no history of Yoga as a householder practice until around the year 1900. This does not mean that until then Yoga was never practised by householders; it is certain that occasional householders did practise postural or meditative Yoga. But until approximately that date it was not so widespread that it could be labelled a householder *tradition*. I mention this because *kaivalya*, as discussed here, was first and foremost a deep intellectual or cognitive realization. It was based on the experience and understanding of *samādhi* and on the actualization of the three areas of practice that constituted *kriyā-yoga* as described in *YS* II.1. Patañjali is

10. This will be demonstrated forcefully by David Gordon White, forthcoming 2012.

careful not to state that *kaivalya* is the result of a single specified practice or regime of practices. This is also why he leaves the specifics of *aṣṭāṅga-yoga* practice completely open-ended.

Kaivalya, then, the state of liberation achieved as a result of the realization of the distinction between *prakṛti* and *puruṣa*, required, above all, great powers of discrimination. The means to achieve this lay comfortably within the domain of *kriyā-yoga*, even if they are not described in detail. The reasons, then, why *sūtra*s II.18-25 are rarely studied, and are not treated at length in many of the Sanskrit commentaries, is because the Brāhmanical spiritual traditions grounded in Sanskrit culture became, shortly after Patañjali's time, so thoroughly imbued with the discourse of the dominant, indeed hegemonic, Vedānta that the very word *kaivalya* all but disappeared, except as a relic to be subsumed within other categories. What it appears to mean, based on these *sūtra*s, is that the false identity structures that we habitually adopt must be broken down into their most fundamental and isolated components, replacing the recognition of the ever-present unity of *ātman* and *Brahman* with the ever-present separation of *prakṛti* and *puruṣa*. And for various cultural reasons, this was the work of mendicant *yogin*s and, more particularly perhaps, Sanskritically trained scholars who held the intellectual keys, and perhaps the practical knowledge, to master the deep reflection that this required.

References

Alter, Joseph S. (2004), *Yoga in Modern India: The Body between Science and Philosophy*, Princeton: Princeton University Press.

Arya, Usharbudh (1986), *Yoga-Sūtras of Patañjali with the Exposition of Vyāsa: A Translation and Commentary: Samādhi-pāda*, Honesdale, PA: Himalayan Institute Press.

Bronkhorst, Johannes (1985), "Patañjali and the Yoga Sūtras," in *Studien zur Indologie und Iranistik*, vol. 10, pp. 191-212.

Bryant, Edwin (2009), *The Yoga-Sūtras of Patañjali, A New Edition, Translation, and Commentary*, New York: North Point Press.

Buhnemann, Gudrun (2007), *Eighty-four Āsanas in Yoga: A Survey of Traditions*, New Delhi: D. K. Printworld.

Hatcher, Brian A. (2008), *Bourgeois Hinduism, or the Faith of the Modern Vedantists, Rare Discourses from Early Modern Bengal*, Oxford, New York: Oxford University Press.

Iyengar, B.K.S. (1993), *Light on the Yoga-Sūtras of Patañjali*, London: Acquarian Press; New Delhi: HarperCollins.

Larson, Gerald J. and R. Shankar Bhattacharya (eds.) (2008), *Yoga: India's Philosophy of Meditation, Encyclopedia of Indian Philosophies*, vol. XII. Gen. ed. Karl Potter, Delhi: Motilal Banarsidass.

Lipner, Julius (2010), *Hindus: Their Beliefs and Practices*, London & New York: Routledge.

Michaels, Axel (2004), *Hinduism, Past and Present*, Princeton: Princeton University Press.

Prabhavananda, Swami & Christopher Isherwood (tr.) (1953), *How to Know God: The Yoga Aphorisms of Patanjali*, New York: Harper.

Rukmani, T.S. (1983), *Yogavārttika of Vijñānabhikṣu*, vol. II: *Sādhanapāda*, New Delhi: Munshiram Manoharlal.

Sadāśivendra Sarasvatī (ed. J.K. Balasubrahmanyam) (1911), *Yogasudhākaro nāma Yogasūtravṛttiḥ*, Srirangam: Srīvāṇīvilāsa Press.

Sarbacker, Stuart (2005), *Samādhi: The Numinous and Cessative in Indo-Tibetan Yoga*, Albany: State University of New York Press.

Vasudeva, Som Dev (2011), "Haṁsamiṭṭhu: 'Pātañjalayoga is Nonsense'," in *Journal of Indian Philosophy*, vol. 39, no. 2, pp. xxx-xxx.

Veda Bharati, Swami (2001), *Yoga-Sūtras of Patañjali with the Exposition of Vyāsa, A Translation and Commentary*, vol. II, *Sādhana-Pāda*, Delhi: Motilal Banarsidass.

White, David Gordon, 2012 (forthcoming), *The Yoga-Sūtras of Patañjali: A Biography*. Princeton: Princeton University Press.

5

Yoga's Theism
A New Way of Understanding God

*Gerald James Larson**

Introduction

LET me begin my presentation with a simple thought experiment. John Cottingham in his book, *The Spiritual Dimension*, mentions what C. S. Peirce calls "abductive inference," or "inference to the best explanation" (Cottingham 2005: 19). He then comments:

> A scientific hypothesis may reasonably be adopted if it provides the most comprehensive and plausible account available of a given range of observable data. Now religious claims have sometimes been interpreted as inferences to the best explanation in this sense. . . . Invoking God is, for example, taken to be the best way of explaining the order in the world, or the apparent emergence of the cosmos out of nothing at the big bang.
>
> — ibid.

He then asks, "[But] is the hypothesis of an all-powerful and surpassingly benevolent creator really the best explanation for the existence of the world as we find it — the world that contains so much terrible suffering?" He then quotes an intriguing thought experiment passage as set forth by the British analytic philosopher, Simon Blackburn, in his book, *Think*. Says Blackburn:

> Suppose you found yourself at school or university in a dormitory. Things are not too good. The roof leaks, there are rats about, the food is almost inedible, some students in fact starve to death. There is a closed door, behind which is the management, but the management never comes out. You get to speculate what the management must be like. Can you infer

* Department of Religious Studies, University of California, Santa Barbara, India Studies Program, Indiana University, Bloomington

> from the dormitory as you find it that the management, first, knows exactly what conditions are like, second, cares intensely for your welfare, and third, possesses unlimited resources for fixing things? *The inference is crazy*. You would be almost certain to infer that either the management doesn't know, doesn't care, or cannot do anything about it. Nor does it make things any better if occasionally you come across a student who declaims that he has become privy to the mind of the management, and is assured that the management indeed knows, cares and has resources and ability to do what it wants. The overwhelming inference is not that the management is like that, but that this student is deluded.
>
> — Blackburn 1999: 20

Cottingham then concludes,

> Blackburn is arguing that if we start from the observed facts — the balance of evidence around us — then to draw the conclusion that it is created by an omniscient, supremely benevolent, and omnipotent God is a vastly implausible, indeed, a crazy, inference. — Cottingham 2005: 20

Some Recent Attacks on God and Religion

As we are all aware, there have been several books of late that attack not only the notion of god but the very notion of religion itself. Moreover, many of these recent books attack not only Jewish, Muslim and Christian conceptions of god and religion — the so-called Abrahamic traditions — but notions about god and religion in South Asian and East Asian religious traditions as well. The first such frontal attack on god and religion was Sam Harris' *The End of Faith: Religion, Terror and the Future of Reason* (2004). Harris, however, is at least sympathetic to Buddhist meditation. After Harris came Daniel C. Dennett's, *Breaking the Spell: Religion as a Natural Phenomenon* (2006). Shortly thereafter came Richard Dawkins' *The God Delusion* (2006), a sequel to an earlier series of essays of his entitled, *A Devil's Chaplain* (2003). Finally, there is the *coup de grace* in this recent sequence, namely Christopher Hitchens' *God Is Not Great: How Religion Poisons Everything* (2007).

The primary reason for this recent series of attack-books is not difficult to identify. The books taken together are responding to the perceived growing influence of strident exclusivist religious behaviour among certain Christian evangelical proselytizing groups, Islamist extremists who traffic in suicide bombing, right-wing Zionist groups whose violent rhetoric denigrates Palestinian Arabs, extremist "Hindutva" groups who have encouraged on occasion violence against Muslims and Muslim monuments such as the Babri Masjid, and on and on and on. Strident exclusivist religiosity appears to be alive and well almost everywhere — the dark underside, as it were, of the process of globalization.

The books taken together criticize such mindless religiosity and argue, instead, for the life of reason in place of unquestioning faith, serious acceptance and continuing research into Darwinian evolution in place of simplistic notions of Intelligent Design, and the recovery, or renaissance, of the values of the Enlightenment. These books all put special emphasis on the Enlightenment's commitment to rationality and the crucial importance of adequate evidence in any serious research or theorizing.

While I am sympathetic to the work of Harris, Dennett, Dawkins and Hitchens in regard to their critiques of mindless religiosity, I am also deeply troubled by their own propensity to be more than a little strident, exclusivist and mindless in their own work. Their work often borders on an arrogant and narrow-minded "scientism" in many ways as unattractive as the traditions they are criticizing, and their knowledge of the history of religions appears to be confined to what they learned in some mandatory Sunday School from which they are still engaged in adolescent rebellion. Even the titles of their work are troubling, for example, *The God Delusion* or *God Is Not Great: How Religion Poisons Everything*. Dawkins and Hitchens are especially inclined towards a prose that combines half-truths with deeply insulting ridicule. To cite only one glaring example, this is how Dawkins opens the discussion of his second chapter regarding "The God Hypothesis":

> The god of the Old Testament is arguably the most unpleasant character in all fictions: jealous and proud of it; a petty, unjust, unforgiving control-freak; a vindictive, bloodthirsty ethnic cleanser; a misogynistic, homophobic, racist, infanticidal, genocidal, filicidal, pestilential, megalomaniacal, sadomasochistic, capriciously malevolent bully.
>
> —Dawkins 2006: 31

Whatever else one might wish to say about such a passage, that it represents an open-minded invitation to discuss "the god hypothesis" is surely not one of the things. Clearly the author is signalling that "The God Hypothesis" will not fare very well in the sequel!

The Notion of "God" in Yoga

Be that as it may, the title for my presentation is *Yoga's Atheistic-Theism: A Unique Answer to the Never-Ending Problem of God in Comparative Philosophy of Religion*. As most scholars know, the systems of Classical Sāṁkhya and

Classical Yoga are usually taken together as a twin-pair or a "common tradition" (*samāna-tantra*) in Indian philosophy. The two other orthodox or *āstika* common pairs are Nyāya and Vaiśeṣika, and Mīmāṁsā and Vedānta. The pair Nyāya and Vaiśeṣika has to do primarily with Logic and Physics or Atomism. Mīmāṁsā and Vedānta have to do primarily with scriptural interpretation, either in terms of ritual meaning (the Mīmāṁsā) or the knowledge portion of the Vedic scriptures (the Vedānta). The pair Sāṁkhya and Yoga has to do primarily with meditation, with Sāṁkhya said to be the theory of meditation, and Yoga usually described as the practical working out of the theory. The main difference between Sāṁkhya and Yoga, according to almost all the books on Indian philosophy, is that Sāṁkhya is atheistic, or perhaps better, non-theistic, whereas Yoga is theistic, or, in other words, accepts some sort of notion about god. No one says very much more about Yoga's accepting the notion of god, however, and most interpreters have assumed that Yoga's theism is typical of other types of theism in Indian religious thought.

In fact, however, the Yoga notion of god is peculiar, even eccentric, not only in terms of Indian thought but, rather, in terms of any of the standard conceptualizations regarding god. Moreover, I want to argue in this presentation that the manner in which classical Yoga philosophy deals with the notion of god may offer some new perspectives for thinking about the problem of god in contemporary discussions of the issue.

Patañjali's Yoga-Sūtras, Book One (The Samādhi-Pāda)

I shall proceed in the following manner. First, I want to summarize briefly what Patañjali's *Yoga-sūtras* (hereafter *YS*) says about god.[1] Second, I want to discuss four sorts of "de-constructions" and/or "re-conceptualizations" that the notion of god in Yoga entails. Finally, I want to conclude by highlighting what we might learn from classical Yoga philosophy regarding a unique approach to the problem of theism.

First, then, what do we learn about the notion of god in Patañjali's *YS*? The issue is discussed primarily in the first book, the *Samādhi-Pāda*. The first six *sūtras* set the stage for the discussion of Yoga overall, providing the definition of Yoga, the nature of ordinary awareness (that is, the *citta-vr̥ttis*), and the ultimate goal of Yoga (that is, the attainment of pure consciousness or *puruṣa*).

Sūtras 7 through 11 then define each of the five functions of ordinary

1. The version of the *YS* used for this essay is Larson and Bhattacharya 2008: 161-83.

awareness. *Sūtras* 12 through 16 describe the principal means for attaining the cessation of the functioning of ordinary awareness, namely Yogic praxis (*abhyāsa*) and renunciation (*vairāgya*). *Sūtras* 17 through 22 then describe the four levels of "concentration" (*samādhi*) that have some sort of object (*saṁprajñāta-samādhi*), namely an empirical object (*vitarka*), a rational or intellectual object (*vicāra*), an aesthetic object (*ānanda*) and ordinary subjective or self-awareness (*asmitā*).

Thereafter, from *sūtras* 23 through 29, Patañjali introduces the discussion of god (*Īśvara*). Says Patañjali:

> Or, concentration having an object (*saṁprajñāta-samādhi*) can also be attained through focusing on God (as the object of meditation).
> (*īśvara-praṇidhānād vā*) — I.23
>
> God is a particular or unique consciousness (*puruṣa*) among consciousness-es (*puruṣas*), untouched by the afflictions, karmic tendencies, karmic fruits and long-term karmic predispositions (that are characteristic of all other sentient beings associated with *puruṣas*).
> (*kleśa-karma-vipāka-āśayair a-parāmṛṣṭaḥ puruṣa-viśeṣaḥ īśvaraḥ*) — I.24
>
> In God the pinnacle of omniscience has been attained.
> (*tatra nir-atiśayaṁ sarva-jña-bījam*) — I.25
>
> (God is) the teacher even of all preceding teachers inasmuch as God is not limited by time.
> (*pūrveṣām api guruḥ kālena anavacchedāt*) — I.26
>
> The verbal expression for god is the sacred syllable (*praṇava*) (or, in other words, the syllable *OṀ*).
> (*tasya vācakaḥ praṇavaḥ*) — I.27
>
> Repetition of it (the sacred syllable) (and) meditation on the object of the expression (namely, god) (should be practised in order to achieve *samādhi*).
> (*taj-japas tad-artha-bhāvanam*) — I.28
>
> Then (when concentration has been properly cultivated) there is a going over into one's own pure consciousness and the disappearance of the obstacles as well.
> (*tataḥ pratyakcetanadhigamo 'py antarāyābhāvaś ca*) — I.29

The description of god in these *sūtras*, in my judgement, is absolutely unique in the general history of religions, both in terms of the great Abrahamic religions (Judaism, Christianity and Islam) as well as the notions of god in South Asian and East Asian traditions; and in order to understand this unique yogic notion of god, one is required to re-think, or, to "re-construct," or, if you prefer, to "de-construct" one's usual ways of thinking about god. To grasp the unique yogic view of god requires four kinds of "de-constructive" and/or "re-constructive" thinking, namely:

(a) An act of **de-personalization**;

(b) An act of **de-humanization**;

(c) An act of **de-mythologization**; and, finally

(d) An act of **re-conceptualization**.

Alternatively, one might put the matter simply in the following way:

(a) For Yoga, the notion of god is never personal;

(b) For Yoga, there is no notion of god as creator;

(c) For Yoga, the notion of god cannot be reduced to any one of the conventional religions of the world;

(d) Finally, the notion of god requires re-conceptualizing what is usually meant by the term "unity" and the usual way of construing the distinction between the One and the Many.

Let me comment on each one of these four.

(I) AN ACT OF DE-PERSONALIZATION OR, FOR YOGA, THE NOTION OF GOD IS NEVER PERSONAL

The idea of the person or ego, called *asmitā* in Yoga (or *ahaṁkāra* in Sāṁkhya), is a fundamental "affliction" (*kleśa*) that must be overcome. Of course, each of us has our personal identity, or even a variety of personal identities, that make possible our everyday functioning, or what C.G. Jung called our "ego-masks" — for example, our "mask" as parent, or our mask as spouse or lover, our mask as personal friend, or whatever. The concept of the person or ego is basically a flawed notion, however, and who and what we are — that is, our deeper selfhood — is much broader and complex than our everyday notion of "person" would allow. To then project the notion of "person" on to the notion of god is to compound our confusion, both in regard to our own authentic selfhood, as well as any understanding of the nature of god.

Since the beginning of the last century, in the work of Jung and, perhaps especially, Freud, it has become commonplace to recognize that the notion of "ego" or "person" is only a superficial characterization. There are vast depths of unconscious processes, both physical and psychological, that take place apart from our personal awareness. More recently in the fields of cognitive psychology and philosophy of mind, the notion of "person" or what philosophers of mind call "folk psychology," or, in other words, our ordinary self-awareness has been found to be seriously incorrect. Our traditional understanding of the "person" or the "self-conscious mind" as "having" certain sensations or being the subject of certain attitudes, may be so fundamentally naïve and simplistic as to be flat out wrong or false.

Paul Churchland, the well-known philosopher of science and philosopher of mind, has commented that the traditional notion of the "person" or "folk psychology" fails to give an adequate account of reasoning. It is inadequate in understanding learning theory. It is vague and superficial in its account of perception. It is murky and unsatisfactory in understanding the dynamics of emotion. It is inadequate in understanding language acquisition. Perhaps, most importantly, it is nearly useless in understanding the nature or adequate treatment of memory disorders, depression or the various types of mental illness (Churchland 1986: 114).

In this regard, I want to share a story told to me by Dr P.N. Tandon, President of the National Brain Research Centre, based in Gurgaon, Haryana. Dr Tandon is a brain surgeon (neurosurgeon). On a certain occasion, a woman was brought to his hospital suffering from a brain haemorrhage. Following surgery to stop the bleeding, the woman became comatose and was not expected to live. Dr Tandon and another doctor were discussing her case while in the patient's room, but then they decided not to discuss anything further about her, since there was no way of knowing whether the woman was able to hear or understand their conversation. Shortly thereafter, another doctor was in the woman's room and started reciting a Bengali poem of Tagore to a nurse in the room. The doctor could not remember the last line in the poem, at which point the comatose woman then proceeded to recite the final line in clear and correct Bengali. The woman died some two days later, and when her brain was opened during the autopsy, Dr Tandon described the woman's brain as being little more than "porridge," in other words, completely dysfunctional. Presumably, there was some sort of memory residue deep in her awareness, possibly associated with some powerful emotional experience in her life, to which she was somehow able to respond even while in a deep coma. There is no satisfactory scientific explanation, although cases such as this suggest that cognitive and linguistic functioning operate within a larger brain system that transcends our conventional understanding of personal awareness.

In terms of the classical philosophy of Yoga, the point here is that to take our problematic and deeply flawed notion of the "person" and to project that flawed notion onto god is to miss the point of what god could possibly be. Surely our notion of the personal, or egoity, the notion of *asmitā* or *ahaṁkāra*, cannot be the case in terms of understanding the nature or essence of god. For Yoga, god is "untouched" by the "affliction" known as egoity — god, in other words, is never personal.

(II) AN ACT OF DE-HUMANIZATION OR, FOR YOGA, THERE IS NO NOTION OF GOD AS CREATOR

The world has no beginning in time. It is, according to Yoga, beginningless (*an-ādi*), although there are periods of dissolution (*pralaya* and *mahāpralaya*), when the world dissolves back into its primordial condition, after which other periods of manifestation will take place. This is a sort of theory, as it were, to use a contemporary idiom, of multiple universes in which a sequence of "big bangs" occur after periods of entropy burn-outs — endless in that sense!

The point, however, is that our human species is hardly central in the scheme of things, and it is certainly not the case, according to Yoga, that the universe was created for human beings to be sovereign. Any philosophy of humanism (that is, the centrality of the human) whether religious or secular, is like the notion of the "ego" or "person." The human species is only one rather minor species in the great hierarchies of sentient beings. More than that, because of the Yoga notion of *karma* and rebirth that is beginningless, hence infinite, at one time or another, we have cycled into every conceivable form of sentient existence.

For Yoga, the human is hardly central and the notion of god as creator is as incoherent as the notion of god as person. Regarding the insignificance of the human in the larger framework of nature, E.O. Wilson in his fascinating recent book, *Creation,* offers two contrasting comments about the vast expanse of nature. From one perspective we are becoming increasingly aware that there are vast numbers of species all around us. Says Wilson, "In one gram of soil, far less than a handful, live at an average 10 billion bacteria belonging to as many as 6000 species" (Wilson 2006: 29). At the same time, however, Wilson also comments that in the context of Nature as a whole,

> . . . our [human] biomass is almost invisibly small. It is mathematically possible to log-stack all the people on Earth into a single block of one cubic mile and lower them out of sight in a remote part of the Grand Canyon. [. . .]
>
> . . . [yet] the destructive power of Homo sapiens has no limit . . . humanity

> is already the first species in the history of life to become a geophysical force.
> — ibid.

Thus, there is the interesting paradox that an insignificant amount of biomass (that is, the human portion of the hierarchies of life) nevertheless by its destructive excesses and misuse of resources threatens the ecology of the entire planet. Ours is surely a predator species in this regard. Clearly, it is becoming increasingly essential to see our human place within the hierarchies of life in a much more realistic and mature manner. The notion of a personal god, whether the Father God of the great Abrahamic religions or the *bhakti*-saviours of Hindu and Buddhist piety, who create the world for the sake of human well-being and worldly order, is seriously in need of reformulation. According to the philosophy of Yoga, the very notion of god as creator is fundamentally incoherent and remarkably naïve. Gordon Kaufman makes a comparable point from his perspective as a contemporary theologian:

> What could we possibly be imagining when we attempt to think of god as an all-powerful personal creator existing somehow before and independent of what we today call the universe? As far as we know, personal (agent) beings did not exist, and could not have existed, before billions of years of cosmic evolution of a very specific sort and then further billions of years of biological evolution also of a very specific sort had transpired. . . . What possible content can this more or less traditional idea of god have . . .?
> — Kaufman 2004: 1004

The answer, of course, is: not much!

(III) AN ACT OF DE-MYTHOLOGIZATION OR, FOR YOGA, THE NOTION OF GOD CANNOT BE REDUCED TO ANY ONE OF THE CONVENTIONAL RELIGIONS OF THE WORLD

In *YS* III.26, the detailed cosmology of Yoga is described, ranging from the seven cosmic regions (*Satya-loka*, and so forth) down through the lowest hells. The locations of the *videha*s and *prakṛti-laya*s and the released *yogin*s are described, and in *YS* I.26 (mainly in the commentaries) the various traditional religious traditions are discussed, including the Buddhist, Jaina, Śaiva, Vaiṣṇava, and so forth. One could easily add the great Abrahamic religions, namely the Jewish, Christian and Islamic traditions as well. God or *Īśvara*, however, according to Yoga, has nothing to do with any of these. He is totally outside all such networks, since god cannot be encompassed by any temporal framework. Again, as *YS* I.26 puts it, "(God is) the teacher even of all preceding teachers inasmuch as god is not limited by time."

Here, one thinks, of course, of the great Meister Eckhart (1260-1327), who in his Latin essays and German sermons, introduces the notion of "Gottheit" or "Godness" behind the god of the Christian Trinity — God the Father, God the Son and God the Holy Spirit. Eckhart was accused and convicted of heresy, and specifically the heresy of atheism, since he suggested that the Christian doctrine of god must be subsumed under the greater notion of "Gottheit," or god-ness.

Or, again, one thinks of the twentieth-century theologian, Paul Tillich, who likewise rejected the traditional Abrahamic notion of god, whether Jewish, Christian or Islamic. The notion of god, says Tillich, is only a symbolic formulation. What is more basic is what Tillich called, the "ground of Being," or "Being itself." Like Eckhart, Tillich also was often called an atheist.

And, of course, there is the great Śaṅkara, who in the famous *Adhyāsa-bhāṣya*, his brilliant introduction to the commentary on the *Brahma-Sūtra*, argues that even the contents of the Vedic corpus, including all of the utterances in the Upaniṣads are, finally, only *avidyā* and *māyā*. God is only *saguṇa*, a lower symbolic formulation. Only the attributeless or *nirguṇa* Absolute (*Brahman*) truly is! Like Eckhart in the medieval period and Tillich in the modern period, so the great Śaṅkara in his time was attacked by non-Advaitins for his atheism.

Regarding this notion of de-mythologization, of course, Yoga would concur with Śaṅkara and the Advaitins, and, for that matter, with Meister Eckhart and Paul Tillich as well. God, according to the philosophy of Yoga, transcends all cultural and religious traditions. He is outside or beyond the Cosmic Egg, as it were. It is almost as if one must become an atheist in terms of conventional religion if one is properly to understand the notion of the divine.

(IV) AN ACT OF RE-CONCEPTUALIZATION OR, FOR YOGA, THE DISTINCTION BETWEEN "UNITY" AND "PLURALITY" OR THE DISTINCTION BETWEEN THE "ONE AND THE MANY" IS RE-CONFIGURED

At this point, however, an interesting twist occurs in the Yoga analysis that takes a seemingly paradoxical conceptual turn that is oddly counterintuitive, whether in regard to Indian philosophy or European philosophy. For the sake of simplicity of exposition I shall confine myself to the Indian tradition, although what I am suggesting holds, likewise, in my view, for much of Western thought as well.

Whereas Vedānta and Yoga appear initially to be moving in the same direction in their joint quest for a contentless, non-intentional consciousness, early along each takes an interestingly different turn in their structuring of the problem of the One and the Many. It is not simply a distinction between dualism *versus* monism, although to be sure that is a true enough distinction as far as it goes. What is more interesting by way of contrast, however, is what might be called the "double reflection" antithesis between Vedānta and Yoga regarding their interpretations of the One and the Many and the meaning of the term "unity."

Śaṅkara's One and the Many is the exact antithesis, or perhaps better by way of using a "reflection" metaphor, the mirror reversal of Yoga's One and the Many. For Śaṅkara and the Vedānta generally, contentless consciousness (*ātman*) is always One, whereas the multiplicity of the phenomenal, empirical everyday world is a bewildering and, finally, highly suspect and non-rational Many (*māyā, avidyā*). For Yoga, the exact opposite or the mirror reversal is the case. Contentless consciousness (*puruṣa*) reveals itself as Many, whereas the multiplicity of the phenomenal, empirical world is a completely intelligible, rational One (*prakṛti* as *traiguṇya*). For Śaṅkara, a single cosmic consciousness disperses itself into a random and finally unintelligible multiplicity. For Yoga, many consciousnesses reside in a single, rational world. For Śaṅkara, contentless consciousness (*ātman*) can never be particular or individual; it can only be general or universal. For Yoga, contentless consciousness (*puruṣa*) can never be general or universal; it can only be particular or individual. For Śaṅkara, what truly is and what is truly intelligible and what is ultimately satisfying (that is, *sat, cit* and *ānanda*) can only be the sheer transparency of contentless consciousness (*ātman*); anything else is an unintelligible, mysterious otherness. For Yoga, the world is truly intelligible and rational; what is unintelligible and mysterious is my particular or individual presence in it.

In trying to explain why Vedānta and Yoga should have structured the problem of the One and the Many in the manner in which the traditions developed, it appears that it had to do largely with the way in which the notion of the "unity" of consciousness was construed. Milton Munitz, an ontologist and philosopher of science, in his interesting book, *Cosmic Understanding: Philosophy and Science of the Universe*, expresses the issue as follows:

> The notion of unity, in general, contains at least two separate meanings. According to one of these meanings, to speak of "unity" is another way of referring to identity. We express this notion of unity by saying that what we might otherwise think are two distinct entities are in fact identical:

> they are one and the same. . . . There is, however, another meaning of unity besides that of identity; "Unity" can also stand for uniqueness.
>
> — Munitz 1986: 207

The two separate meanings of "unity" are nicely portrayed in European thought in the dialectical theology of the great medieval theologian, Meister Eckhart. Bernard McGinn, one of the important interpreters of Eckhart, puts the matter as follows:

> The predicate *unum* ["unity" or "one"] has special advantages from a dialectical point of view. "We must understand [says Eckhart] that the term 'one' is the same as 'indistinct' [i.e., not-to-be-distinguished], for all distinct things are two or more, but all indistinct things are one." Since indistinction is the distinguishing mark of *unum*, what sets it off from everything else, to conceive of God as *unum*, or Absolute Unity, is to conceive of him as simultaneously distinct and indistinct, indeed, the more distinct insofar as he is indistinct. — McGinn 1981: 34

Śaṅkara and the Vedāntins in their attempt to fashion a notion of contentless consciousness obviously followed the path of identity. The followers of Yoga, perhaps not so obviously, appear to have followed the path of uniqueness, and then oddly enough, to have argued for a "plurality of *puruṣa*s" (*puruṣa-bahutva*) or, in other words, for a "plurality of uniqueness-es." Remember, the notion of God in Yoga:

> God is a particular or unique consciousness (*puruṣa*) among consciousness-es (*puruṣa*s), untouched by the afflictions, karmic tendencies, karmic fruits and long-term karmic predispositions (that are characteristic of all other sentient beings associated with *puruṣa*s).
>
> — YS I.24

Clearly there is some sort of equivocation operating, since the notion of "plurality" among absolutely unique *puruṣa*s cannot possibly mean "plurality" as it is meant within the realm of *prakṛti*. In other words, just as there is more than one meaning of the notion of "unity," so there must surely be more than one meaning in the notion of "plurality" (*bahutva*). Plurality as a general notion (*sāmānya*) within the realm of *prakṛti* would mean such common groupings as "cows" sharing in the qualities of "cowness," or the various *tattva*s of Sāṁkhya and Yoga making up the structure of the single *mūlaprakṛti*, and so forth. To say that the grouping (or "plurality") of *puruṣa*s shares the quality of "*puruṣa*-ness" (*puruṣa-sāmānya*) is to reduce the notion of consciousness to the realm of prakṛtic entities. On the other hand, to say that the *puruṣa*s are totally "distinct" in their "indistinctness," that is, in their contentlessness, is to move in the direction of Vedāntic identity (or, if you prefer, Leibnitz's "identity of indiscernibles").

K.C. Bhattacharya, to my knowledge, is the only important modern philosopher in India to have tried seriously to think through this issue of a different meaning of the notion of "plurality." He argues that the general notion of *puruṣa*, or, if you will, the "universal" of *puruṣa* (*puruṣa-sāmānya*), such that there can be a "plurality" of *puruṣas*, must be construed in a most eccentric fashion. Says Bhattacharya:

> It is an abstraction in the sense that it cannot be represented like a universal or a substance as really or apparently comprising individuals (or modes) under it, being intelligible only as the *svarūpa* (or character of being itself) of the individual. The subject is manifest as what has no character (*nirdharmaka*), but this characterlessness is itself taken as its character of self-manifestness. . . . *Puruṣa-sāmānya* or selfhood is this necessary universality of a singular, being universal only if uniqueness or the unique-in-general is universal. Unique-in-general means **any** unique, not **all** unique-s. 'All A is B' indeed means 'any A is B' but 'any A is B' need not mean 'All A is B', for even the distributive all has an implied collective character. As applied to the object, any and all may be regarded as equivalents but not as applied to the subject. . . . In point of being, each subject is absolute. . . . In this sense we may say that the self is known in *buddhi* as having with it a community of selves.[2]

Puruṣa, in other words, is the singular universal or the universal singular in the sense that its very individuality requires "plurality" in this unusual sense of the "unique-in-general" that means "**any** unique, not **all** uniques." *Puruṣa-bahutva*, therefore, rather than begging the question, shows itself instead as the only intelligible way of formulating the question of contentless consciousness within *buddhi*-awareness. Instead, therefore, of Leibnitz's "identity of indiscernibles," Yoga's "plurality of *puruṣas*" becomes the paradoxical obverse, namely the "discernibility of non-identicals." Consciousness, in other words, becomes the warrant for the absolute uniqueness or irreducible singularity of any sentient being.

In the history of Western thought, it is, of course, Hegel who treats in depth the problem of the "concrete universal" or the "singular universal" in his discussion of the Notion (*der Begriff*) in *Wissenschaft der Logik* (Hegel 1989: 620-22). For Hegel, however, the singular universal or the concrete

2. Bhattacharya 1956: 195-96. See also, Larson 1992.

universal is finally the most completely determinate. It is that which has the most content, the most character. It is the most completely intelligible, the fully rational and the fully real. Substance is finally Subject as Absolute *Geist*, and the rational is the real. Such, however, is hardly the "singular universal" of the Yoga or Sāṁkhya *puruṣa-bahutva*. The Hegelian formulation of Absolute *Geist* is perhaps closer to the Vedānta notion of the Absolute *Brahman*, so long as one recognizes that Hegel's notion of the completely determinate is reduced in Vedānta to *māyā* and *avidyā*. Interestingly enough, the Hegelian formulation is the mirror reversal of the Yoga conceptualization of *prakṛti*. In other words, for Yoga, Hegel's "Substance is finally Subject" is precisely reversed: Subject (*citta*, and so forth) is finally revealed as Substance!

A better locus for the Yoga equivalent to *puruṣa-bahutva* in the history of European thought would be Hegel's *Gegenspieler*, namely the great Kierkegaard, who refused to be reduced to Hegel's system. I have in mind here the famous essay on Kierkegaard by Jean-Paul Sartre, first presented at the UNESCO Conference on Kierkegaard in April 1964, and later published in *Situations* with the title "Kierkegaard: The Singular Universal" (Sartre 1974). Kierkegaard's "lived experience" in its sheer singularity becomes a "non-knowledge" in the very heart of knowledge, or put somewhat differently, Kierkegaard's simple presence ". . . constitutes itself within knowledge as irreducible non-knowledge" (ibid.: 147, 152). Says Sartre about Kierkegaard: ". . . the anchorage of the individual made this universal into an irreducible singularity" (ibid.: 156). Or again: "Kierkegaard . . . wanted to designate himself as a transhistorical absolute. . . . The subjective has to be what it is — a singular realization of each singularity" (ibid.: 145, 147). Hegelian "knowledge" knows everything that can possibly be known about Kierkegaard but, finally, really knows nothing about Kierkegaard" (ibid.: 157). Sartre concludes: "Kierkegaard lives on because, by rejecting knowledge, he reveals the contemporaneity of the dead and the living." In other words, contra the absolute determinism of the Hegelian project, Kierkegaard shows us ". . . the inaccessible secret of interiority," "the human singularity of the concrete universal," and the remarkable revelation that ". . . each of us is an incomparable absolute."

I am inclined to think that the Yoga conceptualization of a non-intentional contentless consciousness that focuses on "unity" and "plurality" in the sense of the "**unique-in-general**" as "**any** unique, not **all** uniques," to use K.C. Bhattacharya's idiom, or in the sense of an "irreducible singularity," to use the idiom of a Kierkegaard or Sartre, could prove to be an innovative way of re-thinking the problem of theism. On one level, it preserves an irreducible formulation of the value and importance of the spiritual life of "any" sentient being without falling into the trap of a vacuous identity wherein all distinctions are obliterated and one is left with what Hegel called the "night in which all cows are black." On another level, it preserves the notion of an intelligible, rational world and the possibility of a rigorous scientific realism "from Brahmā down to a blade of grass," that is, the realm of *prakr̥ti* and *traiguṇya*.

Conclusion

Who or what, then, is this God of Yoga, this *puruṣa-viśeṣa*, this "particular *puruṣa* among *puruṣas*"? And what sort of formulation of the problem of theism does classical Yoga present to us? (*kleśa-karma-vipāka-āśayair a-parāmr̥ṣṭaḥ puruṣa-viśeṣaḥ īśvaraḥ*). If, according to Yoga, God is not touched by afflictions, actions, the consequences of actions, and the resulting traces and/or predispositions, then obviously God cannot be personal in any intelligible sense. God cannot be a creator in any meaningful sense. God as consciousness cannot be a thing or entity, and because consciousness (*puruṣa* and *īśvara* as *puruṣa-viśeṣa*) is contentless or objectless, it can only appear as what it is not. What distinguishes God can only be what consciousness, untouched by afflictions, actions, consequences and predispositions, appears not to be. What appears not to be in such an environment can only be "perfect *sattva*" (*prakr̥ṣṭa-sattva* or *prakr̥ṣṭa-cittasattva*) in which *rajas* and *tamas*, though present, are inoperative (and see Vyāsa on *YS* I.24). The environment of "perfect *citta-sattva*," in turn, which pure consciousness appears not to be, functions by way of making possible a non-intentional awareness (*nirbīja-samādhi*) of the presence of pure consciousness, as being distinct from itself. God, then, is the "eternal excellence" (*śāśvatika-utkarṣa*) of the presence of "perfect *sattva*" and contentless or objectless consciousness (*puruṣa*).

God's "office" or "role" (*adhikāra*) can only be to appear as what it is not. Or, to put the matter somewhat differently, the capacity of consciousness (*citi-śakti*) can only be to illumine what is distinct from itself. Thus, it is in this sense that the *YS*, the Vyāsa *Bhāṣya* and the *Tattvavaiśāradī* use the terms "profound longing" (*praṇidhāna*), "inclination" (*āvarjita*), "unique sort of devotion" (*bhakti-viśeṣa*) and a "moving towards" (*anugraha*). These terms are apparently "verbal constructions" (*vikalpas*) or symbolic portrayals for the purpose of highlighting the inherent tendency within each of the two ultimate *tattvas* (*puruṣa* and *prakrti*). That is, it is the inherent tendency of *puruṣa* to appear as what it is not, thereby illuminating the presence of "perfect *sattva*," and it is the inherent tendency of "perfect *sattva*" to appear as what it is not, thereby illuminating the presence of pure consciousness. This "eternal excellence" of God, unlike all other embodied forms of sentience, is beginningless and is always present throughout the ongoing cycles of manifestation and dissolution (*pralaya* and *mahāpralaya*). In each subsequent unfolding world period, God is present as the exemplum of permanent spiritual liberation (*kaivalya*), and there is always also the inherent longing (*praṇidhāna, abhidhyāna*) within *citta-sattva* for complete freedom. In other words, there is always an inherent urge in *citta-sattva* to break free from the afflictions and karmic bonds of "ordinary awareness" (*citta-vr̥ttis*). God, thus, is never the creator. Only sentient beings through their *karma* create the multi-verse. God, rather, is the enabler of the unfolding processes of creative becoming and dissolution by virtue of the non-intentional, pre-reflective presence that enables all manifest Beings (*sattā-mātra*) to be reflexively aware.

The *Vyāsa Bhāṣya* (*YS* I.24), then, poses the question as to whether there is some sort of proof or warrant for the "eternal excellence" of such a God. The answer is that the proof is to be found in the Śāstra. According to Vācaspatimiśra, Śāstra means in Śruti, Smr̥ti, Itihāsa and Purāṇa. But what, then, is the proof or warrant for the validity of the Śāstra, asks the *Vyāsa Bhāṣya*? The answer is that the warrant is in "perfect *sattva*." The truth in Śāstra, in other words, is the content illuminated by *citta-sattva* when *rajas* and *tamas* have become inoperative. God is the "eternal excellence" in which pure consciousness and "perfect *sattva*" are present to one another, a dyadic substantive transcendence in which the "pinnacle of omniscience" (*niratiśayam sarvajña-bījam*) has been attained (*YS* I.25).

God for Yoga, then, serves both as a regulative idea and as an interesting ontological argument. God is a regulative idea in the sense that even at the height or pinnacle of what can be known, God always has a body distinct from pure consciousness, namely perfect *sattva*. Even when the entire manifest world dissolves in the *mahāpralaya*, God as the "seed of the omniscient" (*sarvajña-bīja*) continues to abide inasmuch as God is the "eternal excellence" which must always be! God for Yoga is also an interesting ontological argument in the sense that "than which nothing greater can be conceived," namely pure, contentless consciousness, can only show itself, or, if you will, reveal itself, as the eternal presence in the reflective discernment (*adhyavasāya*) of "perfect *sattva*" (*prakṛṣṇa-citta-sattva*). In this sense, God for Yoga is a mediating position between the theology of Advaita Vedānta and the "theology" of Buddhist thought. In Vedānta, *citta-sattva* dissolves as an ontological principle in *māyā*, and there is, finally, only *Brahman*. In Buddhist thought, *citta* as temporal becoming is ultimate, and beyond *citta* there is no substantive transcendence.

It should be stressed again, as discussed earlier, that God in Yoga, therefore, cannot be reduced to any identifiable personal deity or highly achieved *yogin*, whether Śiva, Viṣṇu, the *buddha*s, the *jina*s or *tīrthaṁkara*s, or figures such as Kapila, and so forth. To be sure, God as the "eternal excellence" or exemplum of the presence of *puruṣa* and *citta-sattva* in any and all realms of becoming is the "teacher" of all of these (*YS* I.26), but God cannot be identified with any one of them without compromising God's transcendence of temporal becoming (*kālena anavacchedāt*) (*YS* I.26). For followers of Sāṁkhya and Yoga, of course, Kapila is the "primal knower" (*ādi-vidvān*), but, says Vācaspatimiśra (on *YS* I.25), the "primal knower" can never equal the "eternal excellence" of God. Likewise, the particular kind of *bhakti* (*bhakti-viśeṣa*, the *Vyāsa Bhāṣya* at I.23-24, II.1, II.32 and II.45), can only be a turning towards God by way of dedicating all one's actions towards the goal of the "eternal excellence" that God embodies. That "eternal excellence," of course, is pure consciousness (*puruṣa*) and "perfect *sattva*" (*prakṛti*) eternally present to one another, and, thus, God's token or representation can only be the sacred syllable (*praṇava*), *OṀ* (*YS* I.27). Access to God can only occur through continuous meditation on the token symbol, which is God's intentional content (*YS* I.28). The notion of "worship" or "prayer" in classical Yoga, therefore, is an *ekāgra* or one-pointed, intentional *samādhi*, a profound meditation and longing (*bhakti-viśeṣa*) for the "eternal excellence" (*śāśvatika-utkarṣa*) of that "perfect embodiment" (*prakṛṣṭa-sattva*) of what truly is!

Finally, of course, as the *Vyāsa Bhāṣya* has clearly indicated (see comment on *YS* I.2), our halting attempt at theological discourse reaches the point beyond which ordinary words cannot take us, and we can only say with Wittgenstein:

Die Grenzen der Sprache . . . die Grenzen meiner Welt bedeuten;
Wovon man nicht sprechen kann, daruber muss man schweigen.

The limits of language . . . inform the limits of my world;
What we cannot speak of we must pass over in silence.[3]

---

3. Cited in Cottingham 2005: 120, from Ludwig Wittgenstein, *Tractatus Logico-Philosophicus* [1921], propositions 5.62 and 7.

References

Bhattacharya, K.C. (1956), "Studies in Sāṁkhya," in *Studies in Philosophy*, vol. I, ed. Gopinath Bhattacharya, Calcutta: Progressive Publishers.

Blackburn, Simon (1999), *Think*, Oxford: Oxford University Press.

Churchland, Paul (1986), *Scientific Realism and the Plasticity of Mind*, Cambridge: Cambridge University Press.

Cottingham, John (2005), *The Spiritual Dimension: Religion, Philosophy and Human Value*, Cambridge: Cambridge University Press.

Dawkins, Richard (2006), *The God Delusion*, New York: Houghton Mifflin.

Hegel, G.W.F. (1989), "Wissenschaft der Logik," in *Hegel's Science of Logic*, tr. A.V. Miller, Foreword by J.N. Findlay, Atlantic Highlands, NJ: Humanities Press International, Translation based on George Allen and Unwin edition of 1969.

Kaufman, Gordon (2004), "Presidential Address," in *Journal of the American Academy of Religion*, vol. 72, no. 4 (December).

Larson, Gerald J. (1992), "K.C. Bhattacharya and the Plurality of Puruṣas (puruṣa-bahutva) in Sāṁkhya," in *Journal of the Indian Council for Philosophical Research*, vol. 10, no. 1, pp. 93-104.

Larson, Gerald J. and R. Shankar Bhattacharya (eds.), (2008), *Yoga: India's Philosophy of Meditation*, vol. XII, Encyclopedia of Indian Philosophies, General Editor: Karl H. Potter, Delhi: Motilal Banarsidass.

McGinn, B. (1981), "Theological Summary," in *Meister Eckhart: The Essential Sermons, Commentaries, Treatises and Defence*, ed. and tr. Edmund Colledge and Bernard McGinn, New York: Paulist Press, pp. 24-61.

Munitz, Milton (1986), *Cosmic Understanding: Philosophy and Science of the Universe*, Princeton: Princeton University Press.

Sartre, J.P. (1974), "Kierkegaard: The Singular Universal," in *Between Existentialism and Marxism*, tr. John Mathews, New York: Pantheon Books, pp. 141-69.

Wilson, E.O. (2006), *Creation*, New York: W.W. Norton.

Part Two
Issues in Interpreting the Vedānta Tradition

6

Advaita Vedānta Insights

*John Grimes**

THE earliest known occurrence of the word *vedānta* refers to that part of the Vedas known as the Upaniṣads.[1] The term *vedānta* = *veda* (wisdom) + *anta* (end/essence), was used as a synonym for the Upaniṣads for two reasons, one literal/physical, the other conceptual/philosophical: (1) Because the Upaniṣads are literally, physically, found at the back of the Vedas (i.e. at the end of the book), they are said to form the concluding portion or end of the Vedas; (2) besides literally expressing the fact that the Upaniṣads form the concluding part of the Vedas, the term also expresses the idea that the Upaniṣads represent the *essence* of the Vedas. As such, the Upaniṣads as Vedānta, are spoken of as the crown or summit of the Vedic wisdom. Thus, the term *vedānta* is the most apt synonym for the Upaniṣads. Like most Sanskrit terms, there is a *śleṣa* or multivalent element involved. The Sanskrit *anta*, like the English word "end," means both "end" and "essence" (e.g., "the end/essence of practice is proficiency"). This transparent multiplicity of meanings permeates the philosophy of Vedānta. Multiple meanings from multiple standpoints coexist, and each possesses both a truth and a use from a given perspective.

The word *veda* (wisdom) traditionally has three different referents (which need not necessarily be exclusive).[2] One meaning refers to a "direct inner intuitive knowledge." This is most dramatically reflected in the great sayings (*mahāvākya*) of the Upaniṣads. It is testimony to the experience of the oneness of the Self with the Absolute. Śaṅkara remarked: "The

* Department of Religious Studies, Michigan State University

1. The word *vedānta* first makes its appearance as a synonym for the Upaniṣads in two places: *Muṇḍaka Upaniṣad* 3.2.6-8 and *Śvetāśvatara Upaniṣad* 6.22.
2. The Vedas declare that three levels of scriptural interpretation happen simultaneously: the transcendent or spiritual (*ādhyātmika*); the intrinsic or cosmic (*ādhidaivika*); and the extrinsic or physical (*ādhibhautika*).

essential aim of the Vedas is to teach us the nature of the imperishable *ātman* and show us that we are That."[3] Latent within it is the insight that one is what one always is. One is the Self, here and now. To attain the unattained, action is necessary. But to attain the already attained, no action is required. To bring out the full implication of this particular usage, for the seer, the Vedic statement declares, "Veda is no longer Veda." The Upaniṣad itself claims that Veda-as-a-direct-inner-intuitive-wisdom is merely a contextual expression:

> Where verily there is, as it were, a duality, there one smells, sees, thinks, knows another. But when to the Knower of the Self, where everything has become the Self, then by what and whom should one smell, see, think, and know? Through what should one know That owing to which all this is known? Through what, O Maitreyī, should one know the Knower?[4]

Secondly, the word *veda* refers to revealed knowledge which has been divided into four collections: *Ṛgveda, Yajurveda, Sāmaveda,* and *Atharvaveda* (along with their numerous recensions) and divisions into Mantra, Brāhmaṇa, Āraṇyaka, and Upaniṣad. Thirdly, the word *veda* refers to "the entire body of Vedic revelation." This usage refers not only to the content or subject matter of the *mantras*, but also the form of expression that they assume. The later schools of Vedānta will draw upon this usage to present a body of teachings, which will be used as external and internal aids for self-realization. This standpoint represents "practice based upon theory."

Therefore, depending upon one's point of view, this threefold schema permeates the Vedas. We shall see that the Advaita tradition employs this insight as it speaks of: (1) the "thunderous silence" which "speaks" about the unspeakable; (2) "words to live by" for the spiritual aspirant who is seeking personal experience; and (3) a "philosophy" for the seeker/scholar who desires a theory with conceptual consistency. In other words, there are seemingly different perspectives, viz. (i) one could say that Reality may be approached from a position of radical non-duality; (ii) a position of qualified non-duality; or (iii) a position of multiplicity. For instance: A man may be viewed from the perspective of himself; from the perspective of father and child; and from the perspective of an employee. In other words, one person is viewed from three perspectives, with each succeeding perspective involving a greater degree of separation from oneself: At first, one feels one is in the light (the world is external to

3. Excerpt from Venkataramiah 1978, Talk 30 (4 February 1935).

4. *Bṛhadāraṇyaka Upaniṣad,* 2.4.14. The sage Yājñavalkya to Maitreyī.

you); secondly, the light is in you (the world is within you); thirdly, you are the light. Advaitins often adopted these three different standpoints (sometimes calling them *ajāti-vāda*, *dṛṣṭi-sṛṣṭi-vāda*, and *sṛṣṭi-dṛṣṭi-vāda*, and sometimes as *pāramārthika*, *vyāvahārika*, and *prātibhāsika*) when they speak about the nature of the physical world. One should note that one or the other of them is applicable to whatever they speak about. It cannot be stressed enough that it behoves the reader to be consciously aware of from what/whose perspective they are speaking.

Indeed, Advaitins never get tired nor wearied in asserting that, from the viewpoint of a sage, a *mukta*, there is only the one indivisible Self; there is neither a knower, nor known, nor any process of knowing; neither a *guru*, nor disciples, nor teachings; neither a liberated individual, nor any bound individual. The essence of Advaita's teachings is that there is a single, immanent, partless, indivisible Reality, directly experienced by everyone, that is simultaneously the source, the substance, and real nature of all that is. In an attempt to speak of this non-relational, ineffable, indivisible Reality, Advaitins refer to it by various names: the fourth (*turīya*), Existence, Consciousness, Bliss (*sat-cit-ānanda*), That (*tat*), the Self (*ātman*), the Absolute (*Brahman*), to name but a few. One should not misunderstand this and think that Reality has attributes, names, or forms, but only that each name signifies the one non-dual Reality. "Truth (ultimate Reality) is One; sages call it by different names."[5]

Though there exists a plethora of source material as well as thousands of secondary works on Advaita Vedānta, it is extremely difficult to convey exactly what "absolute non-duality" (Advaita Vedānta) is, apart from an intellectual understanding of it. This is because Advaita is described in three different, interrelated ways. First and the foremost, it primarily points to a direct inner intuitive experience. At this level, silence is the only adequate "description" of pure non-duality; and silence is a woefully inadequate communicator for most people. Historically, when Gautama the Buddha was asked, "What is the Truth?" he remained silent. When Pilate asked Jesus, "What is the Truth?" he remained silent. An Upaniṣadic sage, Vāskalin when asked by a seeker Bhava, "What is the Truth?" the former remained silent. Interestingly, when I am asked, "what is the Truth," I, too, remain silent. On the surface, all the four answers appear similar, and yet the first three persons remained silent out of wisdom, while I remain silent out of ignorance. Such is the difficulty before us.

---

5. *Ṛgveda*, 1.164.46.

At another level, Advaita Vedānta connotes a body of words to live by. At this level, it is a system of spiritual instructions or indicators for "obtaining the already obtained," i.e. self-realization. Śaṅkara said:

> When the knowledge of *Brahman* is firmly grasped, it is conducive to one's own beatitude and to the continuity of the knowledge of *Brahman*. And the continuity of knowledge of *Brahman* is helpful to people as a boat is helpful to one wishing to get across a river.[6]

Finally, and what is by far the most commonly used designation, Advaita Vedānta is a system of philosophy, a conceptual theory, one among many, and for many individuals, a rather distasteful, dry, and absurd theory at that. Philosophy is for the scholar who desires conceptual consistency. In other words, there are seemingly several Advaitas; however, it would be more accurate to say that Advaita has often been approached from three perspectives, though it should never be forgotten that the final word in Advaita is always the one, non-dual self or *Brahman/ātman*.

Advaita Vedānta, as a philosophical system, derives its name "Vedānta" from the fact that it is based on the teachings found in the Upaniṣads. The Upaniṣads constitute the foundation for all Vedānta (philosophical) systems, and the qualifier "Advaita" was later applied to this original school in order to distinguish it from other Vedāntic systems which subsequently arose.[7] The sourcebooks foundational to all Vedāntic systems alike are: the Upaniṣads, the *Bhagavad-Gītā*, and the *Brahma-Sūtra*. Together these three are known as the *prasthāna-traya*, the triple canon of Vedānta. *Prasthāna* means "foundation" and thus, these three constitute the three foundations. They are known as: Primary Scripture, the Śruti-*prasthāna* (i.e. Upaniṣads); Remembered Tradition, the Smṛti-*prasthāna* (i.e. *Bhagavad-Gītā*); and Reason, the Nyāya-*prasthāna* (i.e. *Brahma-Sūtra*).

The central question for Vedānta concerns the nature of *Brahman*. Thus, the *Brahma-Sūtra*, which philosophically strings together the central concepts of the Upaniṣads in an orderly manner begins: "Now, therefore, the enquiry into *Brahman*."[8] And this enquiry is not only intellectual, but

6. *Upadeśasāhasrī*, 2.1.3.
7. Vedānta is a commonly used name by many schools of philosophy that have all based their teachings upon the Upaniṣads. Because Advaita was the first philosophical school to do so, it is very often referred to as "the Vedānta."
8. *athāto brahma jijñāsā* (*Brahma-Sūtra* 1.1.1). Every *sūtra* of the *Brahma-Sūtra* is based upon an Upaniṣadic passage. The verse upon which *Brahma-Sūtra* 1.1.1 is based comes from the *Bṛhadāraṇyaka Upaniṣad* wherein Yājñavalkya tells Maitreyī, "The self ought to be known."

also practical. Like Advaitic thought which circles around the theme, "*ātman* is *Brahman*."[9]

Advaita's approach is primarily self-enquiry. Advaita's concern is for individuals, here and now. Advaita's goal is that which is eternally present, immediate, and accessible. Therefore, one should note that Advaita is concerned about *Brahman*, about the self, not because *Brahman* is great, but because the self is *Brahman*. The spiritual quest begins with enquiry, an enquiry into the self, into who one really is, not because the Upaniṣads, the *Brahma-Sūtra* or the Advaita tradition advocate such a view, but because it is the fruit of sages' direct experience of the self. Why should self-enquiry alone be the direct means to liberation? Because every kind of spiritual discipline except that of self-enquiry presupposes the retention of the mind as the instrument for carrying on the spiritual discipline, and without the mind it cannot be practised.

Is it not a fact that every individual, in some way or other, must partake of the Reality? If this is granted, and it does appear to be a logical necessity, then each individual, in the final analysis, must investigate to find out who it is that does so. When push comes to shove, it is just not good enough that an ancient sage or the *buddha* or whatever great individual is enlightened, peaceful, blissful, and so on. Each individual wants a "piece of the action" too. Thus, one should begin an enquiry into who one really is. "Who am I" is where the quest begins, as well as ends.

To reveal the self is the be-all and end-all of Advaita. This experience, Advaita further claims, is within the reach of all. The same method of approach may not suit everyone. The average person can have no knowledge of the particular combination of factors that is necessary to bring to completion the hitherto neglected factors of one's being. Thus, it is not really theory that Advaita advocates, so much as experience. "Philosophy is not his (Śaṅkara's) aim, but is rather a vital weapon with which to fulfil this aim, which is to rescue people out of transmigratory existence."[10]

Advaita means "non-duality." The prefix "non" applies not only to duality, but also to "isms" and "systems of thought." The goal of Advaita is not so much to "know about" the self, as it is to "personally experience" the Self. If "knowing about" is helpful, or conducive to this goal, so much the better. But Advaita never loses sight of the fact that "I am the Absolute" is an experiential statement, not a theory. Gauḍapāda explained: "This

9. *ayam ātma brahma* (*Māṇḍūkya Upaniṣad* 2.7).
10. *Upadeśasāhasrī*, pp. 11-12.

view (that there is duality) is only for the sake of instruction. When the truth is known, all duality disappears."[11]

The "Absolute alone is real" for Advaitins because Advaita defines the Real as that which is always real, which never changes. Anything that comes and goes is, in the ultimate scheme of things, not worth pursuing or obtaining. Anything that changes is declared to be "other than the Real." The world is defined as non-real (not unreal), as illusory (in a particular definition of illusoriness), *in relation to* the Absolute. Everything in the universe changes, and thus it can't be ultimately Real. But the world is not totally unreal, i.e. like a square-circle or a married-bachelor, because it *does* appear. Thus it has a strange status known as "neither real nor unreal," as illusory. Finally, the self is not other than the Absolute. This does not mean that the finite individual human being as comprised of name and form is the Absolute, but that the true nature of an individual is not other than the Absolute. Hiriyanna said:

> Śaṅkara regards all diversity as being an illusion. But it is very important to grasp correctly the significance of so describing it. Śaṅkara's conception of the real (*sat*) is that of the eternal Being, and *Brahman* is the sole reality of that type. Similarly, his conception of the unreal (*asat*) is that of absolute nothing. The world, in all its variety, is neither of the one type nor of the other. It is not real in this sense, for it is anything but eternal. Nor is it unreal in the sense defined, for it clearly appears to us as no non-entity can. Nobody, as it is stated in Advaitic works, has ever seen or is ever going to see a hare's horn or a barren woman's son. They are totally non-existent. Further, it possesses, unlike non-entities, practical efficiency or has value, being serviceable in life. This is the reason why the world is described in Advaita as other than the real and the unreal (*sad-asad-vilakṣaṇa*) or as an illusory appearance. The serpent that appears where there was only a rope is neither existent nor non-existent. It is psychologically given, but cannot be logically established. In other words, the things of the world, though not ultimately real, are yet of a certain order of reality. They are appearances in the sense that they depend for their being upon some higher reality. The "serpent," for example, points to the existence of the rope, and the dependence is one-sided, for while the disappearance of the rope necessarily means the disappearance of the serpent, the reverse does not hold good.
>
> — Hiriyanna 1978: 155-58

The quintessence of Advaita is its doctrine that the individual human

11. *Māṇḍūkya Kārikā* 1.80.

being is non-different from the Absolute. This essential identity is most directly and eloquently expressed in the four "Great Sayings" (*mahāvākyas*) of the Upaniṣads: "The Absolute is Consciousness,"[12] "The Self is the Absolute,"[13] "That thou art,"[14] and "I am the Absolute."[15] The inner meaning of these great sayings directly reveals, "All this is only One" (*ekam eva advitīyam*).[16] In other words, That (Absolute) alone am I in which there is no form or formlessness, it is beyond name and form, transcending even the beyond. It does not imply, as some interpreters seem to think, that *ātman/Brahman* is a "bare nothing." Śaṅkara foresaw this possible misinterpretation, for he said,

> *Brahman*, free from space, attributes, motion, fruition, and difference, being in the highest sense and without a second, seems to the slow of mind no more than non-being.[17]

This identity of an individual with *Brahman* needs clarification. It is the individual in its true essential nature, as *ātman*, which is identical with *Brahman* and not the individual as is empirically encountered. In the ordinary world, an individual thinks of oneself as an egotistic mind-body complex. This is an illusion, a delusion, an expression of ignorance caused by ignorance.

The essence of Advaita is persistently declared again and again, "You are That, here and now." To the person who objects, "But is not my search proof of my having become lost?" the reply comes, "No, it only shows that you *believe* you are lost." For, what are you in search of? How can you find that which you already are? A sage once said,

> Let me tell you a simple fact. If you set aside your ego for a moment, you will realize that you, the traveller, are that which you are seeking. Everything is within you. The supreme inner stillness is your destination.

Or, to word it another way, "Any seeking is a denial of the presence of the sought." To paraphrase Śaṅkara,

> Why are you looking for the Self or God in city after city, temple after temple? God dwells in the heart within. Why look in the East and in the

12. *Aitareya Upaniṣad* 3.1.3 of *Ṛgveda — prajñānam brahma.*
13. *Māṇḍūkya Upaniṣad* 2.7 of *Atharvaveda — ayam ātma brahma.*
14. *Chāndogya Upaniṣad* 6.8.7 of *Sāmaveda — tat tvam asi.*
15. *Bṛhadāraṇyaka Upaniṣad* 1.4.10 of *Yajurveda — aham brahmāsmi.*
16. *Chāndogya Upaniṣad* 2.1.
17. *Chāndogya Upaniṣad Bhāṣya* 8.1.1 and *Brahma-Sūtra-Bhāṣya* 2.2.22.

West? Don't look for God, look for the *guru*. God dwells within you; in truth, you are God. You don't need to find God, you need to find a *guru* who will guide you to yourself.

The word "liberation" (*mukti*) is so provoking. Why should one seek it? One believes that there is bondage and therefore seeks liberation. But the fact is that there is no bondage, but only liberation. Why call it by a name and seek it? The seeker replies, True, but I am ignorant. Reply: Only remove ignorance. That is all there is to be done. All questions relating to *mukti* are inadmissible. *Mukti* means release from bondage that implies the present existence of bondage. There is no bondage and therefore no *mukti* either.

Throughout history, individuals have found themselves tossed between the twin banks of pleasure and pain, gain and loss. They are seemingly alienated from themselves, alienated from others, and alienated from the Absolute. From such a perspective it makes sense to ask, "How is it possible for a finite, relative, mortal individual human being to be identical with an infinite, immortal Absolute?"[18] Each of the Great Sayings of the Upaniṣads imparts a threefold knowledge that Advaita seizes upon to provide an answer to this question. First of all, the *mahāvākyas* remove the deep-seated misconception that the individuals are finite, bound, imperfect, and mortal beings; and conversely, they reveal that the true self of each individual is infinite, ever-free, ever-perfect, immortal. Secondly, they remove the wrong notion that the supreme Reality is remote, hidden, unattainable, and declare that It is immediate, direct, the innermost self of all. Thirdly, they reveal that there are not separate individuals and an Absolute. Instead, they declare unequivocally, "You are That," without an iota of difference. In other words, Advaita rejects all the three types of difference: "There is nothing similar to *Brahman*; there is nothing dissimilar to *Brahman*; and there is no internal variety."[19]

When individuals mistakenly superimpose various qualities (e.g. mortality, imperfection, gender distinction, and so on) upon themselves and the opposite qualities (e.g. immortality, perfection, omniscience, distance) upon the Absolute, Advaita resorts to a series of negations (*neti-neti*) to correct this misunderstanding.[20] Śaṅkara, commenting on this, says,

18. This is a frequently asked question in independent Advaita manuals.
19. *Pañcadaśī* 2.20.
20. See *Bṛhadāraṇyaka Upaniṣad* 3.3.6 and 3.8.8; *Kaṭha Upaniṣad* 1.3.15; *Upadeśasāhasrī* 17.70.

"The Absolute can never be properly denoted by any words, including the word 'Absolute' (*ātman/Brahman*)."[21]

Hence, in the Advaita tradition, though there are passages like "Everything is *Brahman*,"[22] "the Self is all this,"[23] "the world is an unbroken series of perceptions of *Brahman* and hence nothing else but *Brahman*,"[24] until one's ignorance is destroyed, such statements will neither be correctly understood nor experienced as true.

Any personal effort necessarily comes from the very same illusory separate individual from which one is seeking escape. It should seem obvious that the ego cannot understand that which it is not. The self is not an "object" to be seen, felt, or obtained. Though there is nothing that It is not, to look for It is to lose it. The seeker is the sought. One cannot "hold" It, but then one cannot get rid of It. An individual person can only be concerned with the process of "becoming." Yet the self is, and therefore cannot be attained or achieved.

Thus, for spiritual aspirants, Advaita speaks of "not-this, not-this," which is given, not so much as to say that appearances are not applicable to the Absolute, as to indicate the impossibility of attributing any conceptualization to It. The self is beyond description, beyond what the finite mind can fathom. The self is called *a-dvaita* to point to the fact that there is nothing that it may be compared.

It is the thesis of Advaita that the self is ever-present and yet, one does not realize it. With Vedānta there is actually nothing to be done. Though the self's nature is inexpressible, it cannot be denied. "A man may doubt of many things, of anything else; but he can never doubt his own being."[25]

The purpose of Advaita, of the *guru*, and of spiritual disciplines, is to kindle an awakening to this ever-present, already established self. This it does by drawing one's attention to the fact that appearances cannot appear independent of a reality that upholds them. To realize that one is the self, one must make an enquiry into the nature of the self, the content of the notion "I." Advaita declares that the self is not a hypothetical postulate.

---

21. *Bṛhadāraṇyaka Upaniṣad Bhāṣya* 2.3.6, "There is no other and more appropriate description than this 'not-this'."
22. *Chāndogya Upaniṣad* 3.14.1 — *sarvam khalvidam brahman.*
23. *Chāndogya Upaniṣad* 7.25.2.
24. *Vivekacūḍāmaṇi* 521.
25. *Brahma-Sūtra-Bhāṣya* 2.3.7.

It is the most immediate, direct, and certain perception of all. Because one believes in oneself, the thinker, seer, hearer, and so forth, one has faith that what one thinks, sees, and hears is "real." Instead, why not doubt the things which come and go, for example, thoughts, sights, and sounds, and hold onto that which is always there and is foundational to it all, one's Self. The "I am" can never be changed into an "I am not." To say "I do not exist" is to affirm the "I" who will do the doubting.[26] *What* is experienced, as well as its meaning, is always open to doubt. But that *someone* experienced is certain.

Advaita asks one to enquire into exactly who this "I" is. It is seeking the ultimate unity that pervades the universe of multiplicity. To discover this essence, Advaita employs numerous methods. It employs the "time-honoured" method of prior superimposition and subsequent denial.[27] Because individuals find themselves superimposing qualities upon themselves, and upon the Absolute, one is led from the familiar to the unknown. Gradually, attributes are negated as a deeper and deeper analysis is performed. One's attachment becomes detachment, and the self finally stands revealed. Hand in hand with this method is "not-this, not-this." According to Advaita, the well-known final discipline for self-realization is to hear the liberating word (*śravaṇa*), reflect upon it (*manana*), and digest and experience its purport (*nididhyāsana*).[28]

Advaita traditionally commences with an enquiry into the Self. How does one refer to oneself? Only as "I." It is one single syllable. Every person says "I," but who is making an effort to know what this "I" exactly is? One usually refers to the physical body when one speaks of "I," but a little reflection will reveal that the "I" cannot be the physical body. The body itself cannot say "I," for it is inert.[29] One says, "this is *my* coat, this is *my* hair, this is *my* body." What is "mine" belongs to me. "My" is a personal possessive pronoun implying ownership. What belongs to me is not me. I am separate from it; I possess it. Whatever I possess, I can dispense with, and still remain who I am. On a deeper level, when one says "I," one is referring to the faculties of thinking, feeling, and willing. Yet the same analysis applies. These are *my* thoughts, *my* feelings, *my* emotions — they come and go. I know them. I am the knower, and they are the known. No one says, "I am this shirt" or "I am this house."

26. *Vivekacūḍāmaṇi* 240; *Upadeśasāhasrī* 1.2.1.

27. *Bhagavad-Gītā Bhāṣya* 8.12.

28. *Bṛhadāraṇyaka Upaniṣad* 4.4.22.

29. *Vivekacūḍāmaṇi* 87-92; *Ātmabodha* 10-11.

Likewise, it is a mistake to superimpose one's body, one's thoughts, and one's feelings, upon the "I."[30]

What is this "I"? In the body arises a sense of awareness. As a collection this is usually called the mind. What is the mind but a collection of thoughts? And this collection is where the "I" functions as their basis. Every thought relates to you, the "I," either directly about you or connected with you as individuals, objects, things, events, opinions. In other words, every thought is rooted in your "I." So what is this "I" — where is it rooted? Track it to its source. This process is called *ātma-vicāra* or an enquiry into the Self.

Advaitins propose that the "I" (*jīva*) performs two searches: one outwards and empirical and the other inwards and spiritual. When the *jīva* identifies with the mind-body complex, there arise the notions of "I" and "mine." This association is the result of an interaction among the self, ignorance, the internal organ, and external objects. The self which is one and non-dual is non-relational. When the self associates with ignorance, it develops numerous relations with objects.

There is a pseudo "I," the empirical "I," and there is the real "I," the *ātman* or self. Between the ever-luminous self (which neither rises nor sets) and the non-real, not-self, the insentient body (which cannot of its own accord say, "I"), arises a false "I" which is limited to the body, the ego, and this meeting place is known as *cit-acit-granthi,* the knot between the sentient self and the insentient body. The term "I," when used by the not-self is but a convenient label.

Then, what is the "I"? Advaita avers that a little reflection will reveal that upon awakening from sleep, the first thought that arises is the "I"-thought. One thinks, "*I* slept well last night" or "*I* am still tired" or "*I* am going to the bathroom." First, the "I" and then the drama of one's life. Further, there is not a single thought anytime, which does not first invoke this "I." One has never, and will never have, a thought or experience without this "I" being present. It is the pillar around which each and every thought clings. Every thought relates to the "I," either directly or in connection with other individuals, objects, things, events, opinions, and so on. The "I" is the basis for everything else — the entire myriad universe of second and third persons, the universe of he, she, and it. Everything, inclusive, is rooted in one's "I."

Before anything can come into existence, there must be someone to

30. *Vivekacūḍāmaṇi* 93-96; *Ātmabodha* 12.

whom it comes. All appearance and disappearance presuppose a change against some changeless background. The "I" is that support. One is not "what happens" to oneself, but to whom things happen. Who am I? Advaita avers that it is enough to know what you are not. The "I" is not an object to be known. Truly, all one can say is that "I am not this, not that." The "this" and "that" of the world come and go. But the "I" persists. If one can point to something, one cannot meaningfully say, "I am (only) that." If one can point to something, one is obviously more than that. One is not "something else" and yet, without you, nothing can be perceived, nor imagined either.

To understand, let alone appreciate, any philosophical system demands that one comprehend its particular perspective. In Advaita Vedānta, it is crucial that one understands the distinction made between the absolute (*pāramārthika*) and the relative (*vyāvahārika*) points of view.[31] This distinction pervades the entire system, and what is true from one point of view is not so from another. Without being absolutely clear regarding this distinction, it is likely that one will not only misinterpret Advaita's doctrine, but further accuse the Advaitin of inconsistencies, contradictions, and absurdities. One must be absolutely clear that these two "levels" distinction is but a pragmatic device and does not mean that there are *really* two levels.

To illustrate the Advaita doctrine of perspectives with a simple analogy: From the sun's perspective, the sun neither rises nor sets; there is neither darkness nor concealment nor varying shades of light. By definition, darkness cannot be where light is. However, from the perspective of an individual upon the earth, the sun rises and sets; there are both light and darkness and varying shades in between, and it is valid to label the sun's light an enemy of darkness. Two seemingly contradictory propositions, both equally valid, and true, once their particular perspectives are correctly understood. Nevertheless, note that what is valid from one perspective *is not* from another. From the sun's perspective, "all is light." From darkness' perspective, there is relative light and relative darkness, and every shade in between. The question is, "Which do you identify with; are you the physical body, or are you the Self?"

While Advaita acknowledges that distinctions *appear* individual at the empirical level, all distinctions lose their distinct individuality from the Absolute point of view. That is, "All this is *Brahman*" is absolutely true

---

31. *Māṇḍūkya Kārikā* 4.25; *Brahma-Sūtra-Bhāṣya* 1.1.11.

while "all this is individually separate and distinct" is relatively true. What is true from one point of view or level of reality is not from another. However, this does *not* mean that there are two realities, two truths. There is one Reality, as seen from two different perspectives. Śaṅkara avers that one perspective is from the point of view of ignorance; it is relatively true (the sun seemingly rises and sets), while the other point of view is from the perspective of wisdom (I am the Light). The sun is *seen* to traverse across the sky, and yet everyone knows that it does not move! Water is *seen* in a mirage, and yet there is no water there. I see my body and yours, and a myriad others, and yet I may be mistaken as to the validity of what I see. *That* I see something is not in question; *what* that something is, is the question.

The Advaita position is that there are not two types of being, nor two truths, but one reality, one truth, as seen from two different perspectives. This is the entire crux of the matter and precisely the point that is most easily misunderstood.

> *Brahman* is known in two forms as qualified by limiting conditions owing to the distinction of name and form, and also as the opposite of this, i.e. as what is free from all limiting conditions whatever . . . thus many texts show *Brahman* in two forms according as it is known from the standpoint of knowledge or from that of ignorance.[32]

From the point of view of ignorance of the self, Advaita admits of numerous distinctions, while from the absolute perspective of wisdom, there is only *Brahman*, one and non-dual. Because it acknowledges these two perspectives, it is able to address and make sense of the metaphysical riddle of the one and the many; of how individuals are seemingly different from one another, and of the existence of a seeming plurality of things. Epistemologically, there is the problem of the subject-object dichotomy, of the problem of truth and error. Ethically, there is the problem of bondage, freedom, and the means thereto. Without these two perspectives, all such problems are philosophical enigmas.

Either a person is bewitched by multiplicity (to be under the sway of ignorance) or one experiences the all-pervading Consciousness. The pluralism that is experienced at the empirical level, and with which philosophical enquiry, and spiritual disciplines commence, is what is in question. Merely because one imagines that one is a distinct, limited physical being, a finite entity in a universe of infinite entities, does not make it so. Advaita avers

32. *Brahma-Sūtra-Bhāṣya* 1.1.11.

that there is the self, one and non-dual, not "my self," "his self," "her self." Because an individual is misled by the seeming diversity of names and forms, minds and bodies, one imagines multiple selves. However, that does not mean that multiplicity is the only vision possible.

Advaitins speak of three modes of approach or standpoints to the metaphysical problem of creation. They speak about all of them at different times, but it is clear from their comments that only the first one is always true and that the second mode is useful for spiritual aspirants.

The highest and supreme mode is the theory of non-origination (*ajāti-vāda*) as expounded by Gauḍapāda[33] (however, even this perspective is but an approximation to the truth). Gauḍapāda said, "*Ajāti* is meaningful only so long as *jāti* (birth) carries meaning. The absolute truth is that no word can designate or describe the self."[34] From this level there is no creation, no birth, no death, no dissolution, no bondage, no liberation, and no one striving for liberation. It is a sage's experience that nothing has ever happened, because the self alone exists as the sole unchanging reality. From this perspective, the (relative) reality of the world is not denied. A sage perceives appearances like anyone else. However, the sage does not perceive the world as comprised of separate objects. An appearance is not unreal merely because it is an appearance. The real nature of an appearance is inseparable from the self and partakes of its reality. What is not real is to mentally construct an illusory world of separate, interacting objects.

The next mode, which is a middling concession to the absolute truth for seekers who find the *ajāti-vāda* impossible to digest, posits that creation is simultaneous with perception (*sr̥ṣṭi-dr̥ṣṭi-vāda*). According to this perspective, the world arises like a dream on account of a person's own thoughts induced by the defect of not knowing oneself as the non-dual self. With the arising of the "I"-thought, the world simultaneously comes into existence and ceases to exist when the "I"-thought ceases. The world only exists when it is perceived. Upon awakening from sleep, the first thought a person has is the "I"-thought and upon its emergence, the entire universe consisting of objects other than oneself springs into existence. Once the "I"-thought, mistakenly taken as meaning "me" (male, father,

33. See *Māṇḍūkya Kārikā*; also *Kaṭha Upaniṣad* 1.2.18, "The knowing self is never born; nor does it die at any time"; *Br̥hadāraṇyaka Upaniṣad* 4.4.20; *Bhagavad-Gītā* 2.20, "The self is neither born nor does it die"; *Vivekacūḍāmaṇi* 111, "It is not born; it does not die; it does not grow; it does not decline; it does not change. It is eternal."

34. *Māṇḍūkya Kārikā* 4.74.

thin, healthy, etc.) arises as the subject, then everything other than me becomes an object. In deep sleep, when the "I"-thought is absent, so is the universe. This is everyone's personal experience, though they refuse to admit so. Some Advaitins encourage followers to accept this theory as a working hypothesis because, if one is constantly regarding the world as an unreal creation of one's mind, then it will lose its attraction, its seductiveness, and it will be easier for that person to then maintain an undistracted awareness of the "I"-thought. Thus, this theory is "true" in so far as the mind of an unenlightened person does create an imaginary world for itself. At the same time, from the standpoint of the Self, an imaginary "I" creating an imaginary world is no creation at all and thus does not contradict *ajāti-vāda*.

Finally, there is the "what has been created is perceived theory" which is the ordinary common sense view that believes that the world is an objective reality governed by laws of cause and effect which can be traced back to an act of creation by a creator. This theory states that the world exists prior to anyone's perception of it and that it is external to oneself. Advaitins only invoked this theory when the person they are speaking with is unwilling to accept either of the other two theories. The idea being that the theory of "what is created is seen" should not be taken too seriously, as all it does is to satisfy one's intellectual curiosity. There may be any number of theories of creation. All of them extend outwardly. There will be no limit to them because time and space are unlimited. They are, however, only in the mind . . . creation is explained scientifically or logically to one's own satisfaction. But is there any finality about it? Such explanations are called gradual creation. On the other hand, simultaneous creation is instantaneous creation. Without the seer, no objects are seen. Find the seer and the creation is comprised in him. Why look outward and go on explaining the phenomena that are endless?

Critics sometimes label Advaita Vedānta as "illusion-theory" (*māyā-vāda*), and Advaitins are called "illusionists" (*māyā-vādins*). These terms are used disparagingly, and yet there is a grain of truth in the matter. *Avidyā/māyā* cannot exist, or function, independent of *Brahman*, and it ceases to bewitch a person once *Brahman* is realized. However, strictly speaking, *Brahman* is the be-all and end-all of Advaita, and if anything, Advaita should be called *Brahma-vāda*. This is so because Advaita never loses sight of its central doctrine that *Brahman* is real, the world is non-real, and the individual is non-different from *Brahman*.

It would appear that ignorance (*avidyā*) is a term that is fundamentally and basically a description of an affliction of the psyche, an existential description of a state of being, an experiential realm of ignorance. It is not a metaphysical entity, a full-blown philosophical concept, so much as it is a useful tool and a description.

Śaṅkara defined ignorance (*avidyā*) as: "the mutual superimposition of subject and object, the mutual transposing of the Self and the non-Self, the unacceptable combining of true and false."[35] In the same place, he also said that "learned men regard this superimposition (*adhyāsa*) thus defined as *avidyā*,"[36] and that superimposition is the imposition of a thing on what is not that thing. As well, he said:

> *Avidyā* is *parameśvarāśraya*, that is, ignorance depends upon *Brahman*. And in it (*avidyā*) individuals, having lost their identity with *Brahman*, rest.[37]

As a philosophical term, *avidyā/māyā* is crucial to the understanding of Advaita. Since Śaṅkara did not differentiate between *avidyā* and *māyā*, as post-Śaṅkarite Advaitins did, I present the two terms as one key concept here.

Avidyā/māyā is the means, not the end. It is an explanatory concept. Within Advaita, any "means" exists only at the relative level. From the absolute perspective, one is the self, one does not become the self. When the rope is seen, there is no question about a snake. When the self is realized, there are no questions about *māyā*. Thus, *māyā* is a provisional explanation as to how the eternally all-pervasive self appears otherwise to deluded individuals. Though *avidyā/māyā* is not ultimately real, its importance cannot be exaggerated for the role that it plays. No one can deny that individuals seemingly *perceive* multiplicity and distinctions. How does this happen?

According to Advaita, the real is that which is eternal, which suffers no sublation, while the unreal is that which never is. Advaita contends the unreal can *never* appear, not even in one's wildest dreams, e.g. a square-circle or the child of a barren woman. Because appearances are *perceived*, they cannot be said to be unreal (*asat*). Similarly, because the real (*sat*) never changes, appearances, which change, cannot be called *sat*. Therefore, appearances are indeterminable. How miraculous, mysterious, inscrutable!

---

35. *Brahma-Sūtra-Bhāṣya* 1.1.1.

36. Ibid.

37. Ibid.; also see *Upadeśasāhasrī* 2.2.51.

All that is perceived as "other than you" is neither real nor unreal! There never has been, nor is, nor will be, water in a mirage and yet, somehow, it is perceived. Thus, Advaita calls all appearances, *sad-asad-vilakṣaṇa*, "what is other than the real or the unreal." It is only in this sense that the seeming plurality of the universe is called "illusory" (*māyā*). Any enquiry into *māyā* is not to make the concept intelligible, but to enable one to go beyond it. Once one has destroyed ignorance, there remains no problem to be solved, no questioner to enquire whether appearances are real or not.

By the criterion of completeness, the self alone is absolutely real. All else will be called "real" only by courtesy. The distinction between one individual and another, the existence of a plurality of things, the superimposition of attributes on the Absolute are all concessions to the truth made from the relative point of view. By this criterion, *avidyā/māyā* is not a second entity. Only a person under the spell of ignorance perceives its effects. The sun does not ask, "Where is this darkness you speak about?" Because one denies what one is, the self, and superimposes upon the self what it is not, the not-self, does not therefore make the not-self real.

Finally, Advaita is primarily an enquiry into the self, the reality that is involved in, and is the basis of an individual's every experience, the self that is everyone's birthright. The self is here and now; not something to be obtained from outside, at a later time. The Absolute is not a God, above and beyond. "That thou art" declares the Upaniṣad. Thus, according to Advaita, *ātman* and liberation (*mokṣa*) have the same meaning. This leads us to the nature of spiritual disciplines, and ultimately to the concept of liberation-while-living (*jīvan-mukti*).

In the Advaita tradition, all manifestations are considered but name (*nāma*) and form (*rūpa*). According to Advaita, so long as the seeker regards him/herself as a separate individual human being, then spiritual disciplines are absolutely essential. The final position (*siddhānta*) of Advaita is that there is no teacher, no taught, no teachings. "All this is *Brahman* only." But until that vision becomes an experienced realization, Advaita advocates a series of preliminary disciplines, i.e. righteous behaviour consisting of external remote aids which help purify the mind, the fourfold proximate aids to spiritual discipline,[38] and the principal proximate aids

38. I.e., the ability to discriminate between the transient and the eternal; the absence of any desire for securing pleasures or avoiding pain, either here or elsewhere; the attainment of the virtues, calmness, temperance, spirit of renunciation, fortitude, power of concentration of the mind, faith; a burning desire for liberation (*mumukṣutva*).

of hearing the truth, reflecting upon the truth, and digesting the truth.[39] Obviously, all of these disciplines presuppose and demand the presence of a teacher, an aspirant, and teachings as well as a place in which to practise the teachings. Advaita is not averse to spiritual disciplines such as the various *yoga*s and all the myriad *sādhana*s, but considers them as being but preliminaries to liberation.

Another way in which the "means to liberation" can be analysed is to analyse the nature of the aspirant. When an individual's sense of duality is very strong and their practices are predominantly external, then their spiritual disciplines fall under the category of "remote aids." When an individual's sense of distinctness is middling and their practices are predominantly internal, then their spiritual disciplines may be subsumed under the category of "proximate aids." Finally, when an aspirant's direct awareness of reality is awakened within through the grace of the preceptor (*guru*), and only a subtle distinction exists between the goal and the path, then such a one's disciplines are called the "principal proximate aids."

Hence, Advaita envisions a series of spiritual disciplines ranging from the grossest, most external, remote disciplines, all the way to liberation itself, about which, at the highest level, nothing can be said. There is no disciple, nor is any discipline rejected. Whichever means is adopted depends upon the nature and understanding of the disciple. Developing in different ways, from differing initial states, each disciple's practice leads to greater states of awareness, eventually culminating in the self. Indeed, Śaṅkarācārya said:

> Until a person awakens to the knowledge of their identity with the Self, liberation can never be achieved. . . . Therefore, let the wise person give up craving for pleasure in external things, and struggle hard for liberation. Let such a one seek out a noble and high-souled teacher, and become absorbed wholeheartedly in the truth that is taught by him.[40]

Though the transcendental self is radically personal, individuals are not

39. The principal proximate aids obviously involve a *guru* who conveys the sacred text, a student who listens to the text, and a place where this knowledge is conveyed. Hearing involves removing any doubts one may have as to what one should know (the self). Reflection removes any doubts one may have as to what one should know as to what the self is like. Digestion is for removing any remaining thoughts that one is not the self. Of the principal proximate aids, there are two types: those statements (*avāntara vākya*) which indirectly convey wisdom and those statements (*mahāvākya*) which directly illumine the disciple.

40. *Vivekacūḍāmaṇi* 6.8.

consciously aware of it in the way that they are aware of sense-objects. Human beings, with their outward turning sense organs, have been fascinated with an external world consisting of innumerable persons, places, things, and events. But in dealing with something that is not an object, and is totally unrelated to space-time concepts, their attention has been inadequate. Instead of directing one's attention outwards to the world of "others," one should learn to direct one's attention inwards, towards the indwelling self.

In other words, to seek the self, an individual must make an earnest enquiry into the self through discrimination. Though the self is not something to be gained afresh, it does need to be discriminated from the not-self. Such a search is not divorced from, nor outside of, one's personal experience. This means that, at any given time, an aspirant's qualifications and readiness determine how seriously, earnestly, and completely one seeks the self.

Vedānta teaches that one is the self, here and now. Why one does not realize this ever-present fact and suffers, is due to ignorance.[41] Individuals aver, "I am deficient, inadequate, incomplete, right now." The evidence for this appears overwhelming. "Isn't it a fact that I am a male or female, who is compulsively pursuing pleasure and security? I am full of desires, wants, and needs." Further, the fulfilment of these desires is so incredibly important precisely because they are going to be the means of one's fulfilment. The logic of separation is easy to understand: "What one doesn't have, one must obtain to thereby become complete." However, what is usually overlooked is that sense enjoyment has a double sting: it takes off the edge of the sense organs by making them blunt, and it sets the mind afire by making the mind desire for more of the same enjoyment. The mind wants enjoyment, but the body can't take it. One burns the candle at both ends.

But the self is not another "object," even the greatest of objects, to be obtained. The self is the seeker as well as the sought, even though the seeker does not know this due to ignorance. Since the individual, as the not-self, is neither real nor unreal, the very question of an individual self seeking union with the Absolute is ludicrous. And yet, if one does not seek, one will not find. As the *Gītā* says:

> Though quite self-evident, easily knowable, quite near and forming the very self, *Brahman* appears to the unenlightened, to those whose

41. *Brahma-Sūtra-Bhāṣya* 1.1. Preamble; *Vivekacūḍāmaṇi* 55; 137; 192.

understanding is carried away by the differentiated phenomena of names and forms created by ignorance, as unknown, difficult to know, very remote, as though he were a separate thing.[42]

The idea that the individual, as individual, is a mere fiction and its corollary, that the individual is really here and now, the self, is the purest Advaita. Generally, this is too difficult a teaching for one to digest immediately and thus arises the need for a gradual awakening. One is led from the unreal to the real, from darkness to light, from death to immortality, step by step. This is the general teaching of Advaita philosophy. Any, and every "other," be it an experience or an object, is, by definition, going to be ultimately inadequate. Experiences and objects come and go. Since they have a beginning, and they will have an end. The "other" must ultimately disappoint one. Thus, if there is truly something called the self, something called completeness, it must be present, here and now, or it cannot be at all.

> The real teaching of Vedānta is that the ignorance that is destroyed never really existed. To destroy ignorance and attain bliss is to destroy what never was and to attain what we have always had.
>
> — Muktananda 1994: 169

The final teaching of Advaita, from the absolute perspective, is that there is not incompleteness during *sādhanā* and completeness upon liberation; there is no duality during spiritual practices and non-duality during liberation.[43] There is only the ocean of the self, before, during, and after. This leads us to Advaita's conception of the nature of achievement. There are said to be two types of attainment: attainment of the not-yet-attained and attainment of the already attained. What has not-yet-been-attained, the attainment of a new automobile, is achieved in space and time. It may be attained by a limited effort and will produce a limited result, i.e. a new car. This type of attainment always involves both gain and loss. One gains a new condition and loses one's old condition.

However, Vedānta also talks about another type of attainment, "obtaining the already obtained."[44] To obtain the already obtained, neither space nor time is involved. One can only obtain that which one does not already have. Since there never was a time when one was not the self, the

42. *Bhagavad-Gītā* 18.50.
43. *Vivekacūḍāmaṇi* 569-72.
44. *Ātmabodha* 44.

Upaniṣads say: "And being already released, he is released; being already *Brahman*, he attains *Brahman*."[45]

Since Advaita declares that liberation can be "attained" here and now, provided a person makes oneself fit, one need not wait until death overtakes the physical body. Such a person is called a *jīvan-mukta*, liberated even while living in a body.[46] The continuance of the body is in no way incompatible with the state of self-realization. What happens is merely a change of perspective; ignorance has been destroyed. Right knowledge of the self puts an end to ignorance. If the body were real, then liberation could come only after the destruction of the body. But since one is not the physical body, its continued appearance or disappearance is of no consequence. From the standpoint of the *jīvan-mukta*, there is only *Brahman/ātman*. It is to the ignorant that the *jīvan-mukta* appears to tenant a body. Even to refer to such a one as "him" or "her" is due to one's ignorance. The self alone exists.

Gauḍapāda (*c.* fifth century CE) was one of the most venerated sages of Indian philosophy and the first historical person whose teachings on the Upaniṣadic wisdom of Advaita have survived. He analysed the three states of existence (waking, dream, and deep sleep) and showed that the self (which is referred to as the "fourth" or "transcendent" (*turīya*)), underlies and transcends these changing states.[47] The self is constant, not subject to change, the ground of the other three, and the one reality of which the other three states are appearances. It alone is Real, being permanent, while the other states come and go. Then, employing reason, Gauḍapāda established logically this absolute non-duality (the self alone is truly Real) and the illusory nature of the phenomenal world (though it appears, it is not Real inasmuch as it changes). His central doctrine was that "nothing has ever been born, nothing has ever happened."[48] Using impeccable and remarkable reasoning, Gauḍapāda advanced the doctrine which he is best known for, "nothing is ever born" or the theory of non-origination (*ajāti-vāda*) — nothing is ever born, not because "nothing" is the ultimate truth, but because the self is the only unchanging reality. This is the pinnacle of Advaita thought. There is no dissolution or creation, no one in bondage, nor anyone pursuing spiritual practices. There is no

45. *Kaṭha Upaniṣad* 5.1; *Bṛhadāraṇyaka Upaniṣad* 4.4.6.

46. *Brahma-Sūtra* 3.4.51; *Bṛhadāraṇyaka Upaniṣad Bhāṣya* 4.4.6; *Vivekacūḍāmaṇi* 425-42; 551-54.

47. See the *Māṇḍūkya Kārikā*.

48. *Māṇḍūkya Kārikā* 3.48; 4.71.

one desiring liberation nor anyone liberated. This is the absolute truth. One who is established in the self sees this by his knowledge of reality (Venkataramiah 1978: 25).

In summation, for a person to enquire, "from where did ignorance or the empirical ego arise," *ajāti* Advaitins answer, "from nowhere," as it is as much an ontological fiction/non-reality as a mirage, a hallucination, or a dream. In actuality, there is no water in a mirage now, never has been and never will be. A dreamer did not go to Los Angeles last night, though he dreamed he did. Appearances happen; reality they are not. This is obvious with regard to the contents of dreams and hallucinations. While they are being experienced, they are taken as real. But once a person awakens from the dream or stops hallucinating, one knows that their contents were not real. Advaita contends that the same fictional ontological status pertains to the subjects and objects of empirical knowledge and the proof of such is the words of the enlightened sages. The only person who enquires as to why there is empirical consciousness is one who is deluded. What comes and goes is not real. If a person has had an experience that came and went, it was not an experience of the self because the self never comes and goes. If this is true, it means that all empirical experiences and most waking-up experiences are merely new states of mind. It is only when the mind dies completely, never to rise again, that the self really shines as one's own natural state.

References

PRIMARY SOURCES

Ātmabodha (1989), *Self-Knowledge*, Translated from the Sanskrit with Notes, Comments, and Introduction by Swami Nikhilananda, New York: Ramakrishna-Vivekananda Center.

Bhagavad-Gītā/ Bhagavad-Gītā Bhāṣya (1977), *The Bhagavad-Gītā with the Commentary of Śrī Śaṅkarācārya*, tr. Alladi Mahadeva Sastry, Chennai: Samata Books.

Brahma-Sūtra/Brahma-Sūtra-Bhāṣya (1954), *Brahma-Sūtra Bhāṣya of Śaṅkarācārya*, tr. Swami Gambhirananda, Calcutta: Advaita Ashrama.

Māṇḍūkya Upaniṣad/Kārikā (1936), *Māṇḍūkyopaniṣad with Gauḍapāda's Kārikā and Śaṅkarācārya's Commentary*, tr. Swami Nikhilananda, Mysore: Sri Ramakrishna Ashrama.

Pañcadaśī (1975), *Pañcadaśī of Vidyāraṇya*, tr. Swami Swahananda, Madras: Ramakrishna Math.

Upadeśasāhasrī (1992), *A Thousand Teachings: The Upadeśasāhasrī of Śaṅkara*, tr. and ed. Sengaku Mayeda, New York: SUNY Press.

Upaniṣads (1963), *The Principal Upanishads*, tr. Sarvepalli Radhakrishnan, London: Allen & Unwin Ltd.

Vivekacūḍāmaṇi (2004), *Vivekacūḍāmaṇi of Śaṅkarācārya Bhagavatpāda*, Introduction and tr. John Grimes, London: Ashgate Press.

SECONDARY SOURCES

Hiriyanna, Mysore (1978), *The Essentials of Indian Philosophy*, Bombay: Blackie and Son Publishers Ltd.

Muktananda, Swami (1994), *Secret of the Siddhas*, Siddha Yoga Publication, 3rd edn.

Venkataramiah, Mungala (ed.), (1978) *Talks with Sri Ramana Maharshi*, Tiruvannamalai: Sri Ramanasramam.

7

Śāṅkara Granthāḥ Katham Otāḥ Protāś Ca?

*Vidyasankar Sundaresan**

THIS essay is based on a talk presented in a session chaired by Prof. Rukmani at the 17th International Congress of Vedanta in 2007. My own studies of Śaṅkara have been outside a formal academic environment and have increasingly led me in a direction that seeks to better understand how Śaṅkara construes the philosophical and doctrinal relationships between Advaita Vedānta and other streams of Indian philosophical thought. Yoga and Sāṁkhya necessarily lay claim to a significant portion of one's attention in such an enterprise. It is a privilege to contribute this essay in honour of a scholar who has researched extensively on these Indian *darśana*s. With all that has already been written about Advaita Vedānta, and by so many, a reader might wonder whether there is possibly anything original left to say. Therefore, I would like to begin with two major assertions and leave it to the reader to judge how well I succeed in substantiating them. My first assertion is that the full gamut of Śaṅkara's thought cannot be understood properly unless his texts are read in a fundamentally different fashion from what most academic scholars normally do. My second assertion is that the new methodology proposed in this paper towards this end will significantly challenge a number of currently accepted academic scholarly assumptions and conclusions about Śaṅkara's thought.

It has become *de rigueur* to narrowly define Śaṅkara first and foremost as the author of a commentary (*bhāṣya*) on the *Brahma-Sūtra*s. It is then assumed that the same author also wrote commentaries on the *Bhagavad-Gītā* and ten major Upaniṣads, in addition to an independent text (*prakaraṇa grantha*) called *Upadeśasāhasrī*. This approach necessarily privileges the *Brahma-Sūtra-Bhāṣya* over the other Śaṅkaran texts and the parameters set thereby have more or less been accorded the status of a scholarly consensus. The other major commentaries are used minimally, if at all, in

* Lead Technologist, GE Water & Process Technologies

defining key positions adopted by Śaṅkara. In my opinion, regarding Śaṅkara's commentaries as independent books and reading them comparatively only with respect to specific points hinders a fuller and broader understanding of these texts. To be sure, this self-imposed scholarly limitation is partly determined by genuine scepticism about authorship and textual attribution, but it has also led to a lack of clarity on a number of issues that are fundamental to Advaita Vedānta. These have then been addressed via speculation about the order in which Śaṅkara may have written his texts, about changes in his interpretative intent and content over time, about his compromising philosophical consistency for the purpose of pedagogy and about his misconstruing the stance of some opponent, deliberately or otherwise, while delineating his own positions.[1] Scholars also often draw conclusions about a particular word-usage or position being forced by Śaṅkara's source text. This not only begs the question why Śaṅkara would have chosen the said source text to comment upon or cite in the first place, but also implies that he may have written differently if he had written independent treatises, unconstrained by source texts. Of course, the authenticity of almost all the independent texts traditionally attributed to Śaṅkara is doubted, precisely because they seem different, unconstrained by any one source text.[2] What we have, is therefore, a widely accepted self-certifying attitude towards a study of Śaṅkara. On the contrary, it seems to me that this exhibits a basic failure to come to terms adequately with some of Śaṅkara's assumptions and conclusions. They also seem to be based upon expectations that Śaṅkara must have written his texts in some sequential order, that each text can be defined page-by-page, bound between covers, and that we can explain seemingly variant interpretations as indicative of changes in his thought over time.[3] They ignore the fact that Śaṅkara is known to provide two different but equivalently valid interpretations of the same text in quick

1. I refer here to (a) Hacker's view that Śaṅkara converted from Yoga to Advaita, via exposure to Gauḍapāda (Halbfass 1995: 101-34), (b) Mayeda's view that Śaṅkara compromises consistency for pedagogy, when advocating *parisaṁkhyāna* in a prose chapter of *Upadeśasāhasrī* after criticizing *prasaṁkhyānavāda* (Mayeda 1992: 88-94, 254), and (c) the often repeated view (e.g. Suthren Hirst 2005: 91) that Śaṅkara's criticism of *śūnyatā* in Mādhyamaka Buddhism misconstrues that school's position.

2. For example, see discussions on Śaṅkara's attitude towards *ānanda* and *Brahman* (Potter (1981) and references therein), as also a brief critique of what has become scholarly consensus on this issue (Sundaresan 2000).

3. I don't intend to debate what constitutes a text and what defines its boundaries, but it seems to me that the idea of a book bound between cover pages is a very

→

succession, even if they may not be quite compatible with each other.[4] To sum up, in my opinion, reading Śaṅkara's texts separately and linearly often misses the forest for the trees, as it were, on numerous issues in Vedānta.

How should one read Śaṅkara's texts in their totality then? And how should one decide what constitutes the totality of Śaṅkara's texts? To address this issue, I look towards another publishing model that has come to stay in the world, namely the Internet. I propose that Śaṅkara's texts must be read together and understood as if they constitute a set of documents on a web portal that are hyperlinked together. The approach outlined in the rest of this essay makes no assumptions about textual authenticity at all and therefore does not attempt to answer the second question above.[5] Rather, I intend to focus only on examining how the major Śaṅkaran texts are interwoven together and how one should understand the content of any given text in relation to other texts. The other texts are chosen purely by the internal logic and cross-references of the starting text. This is based upon the fact that Śaṅkara quite often justifies one of his conclusions by pointing to an earlier or later reference within the same text, or to another source text, or by citing a number of

→ poor model to apply to the Veda and its derivative traditions that are well known for the central importance of orality in their transmissions. How did the first manuscripts of Śaṅkara's texts come into being? Did he ever sit down with ink, stylus and leaf/bark/cloth to write down his commentaries? Did one or more of his disciples take down notes in the course of oral instruction and compile them later? Were professional scribes employed? Whatever that process may have been, did Śaṅkara take up one source text at a time to comment upon or did he interpret a number of them in parallel? Did he learn in the traditional manner to recite every one of his numerous source texts? Did he ever rely on manuscripts and if yes, did he use them sparingly or moderately or extensively? I believe that while such questions can never be answered to anyone's satisfaction, they are nevertheless *not* the questions that scholarship on Śaṅkara is hitherto accustomed to asking.

4. See *BSBh* 1.1.3 (pp. 13-15), where Śaṅkara interprets the term *śāstra-yoni* in two ways: the first describes *Brahman* as the source (*yoni*) of scripture (*śāstra*), while the second describes scripture (*śāstra*) as the source (*yoni*) of valid knowledge (*pramāṇa*) of *Brahman*. Also see his explanations of *brahmaṇo hi pratiṣṭhā aham* in *BGBh* 14.27 (pp. 427-28). In the first explanation, the word *Brahman* is the highest *ātman* (*paramātmā*) and the word *aham* refers to the individual self (*pratyagātmā*). In the second, *Brahman* is the lower, *savikalpakaṁ brahma*, while *aham* is the higher, *nirvikalpaka brahma*.

5. In Sundaresan (2000), I have re-examined the authorship question and pointed to the need for rigorous text-critical scholarly work to be done on the numerous works attributed to Śaṅkara.

source texts in quick succession. I will use these textual citations as hyperlinks to connect to the independent commentaries on the cited texts, whenever possible. In theory, one could pick any random place in any of the major texts and use the citation of another sentence therein as a hyperlink to navigate to that text. In turn, the citations made in the second text become hyperlinks to those references and so on. Reading what Śaṅkara says in one text, noting the internal and external textual citations made therein and navigating to his commentaries on those citations would be akin to how one is accustomed to reading Internet websites. In addition to citational references, another set of internal hyperlinks can be made within each text, by virtue of the corresponding material being bracketed within the same section, e.g. *adhikaraṇa* in *BS* or chapter in an Upaniṣad or *BG*. A third way of hyperlinking the texts would be to follow specific phrases or themes with high terminological or doctrinal significance. However, I do not intend to use words like *ātman*, *Brahman*, *avidyā* or *māyā* as hyperlinks interconnecting these texts, because such an exercise will result in a massively dense interweaving, making it impossible to discern any thematic trends in them. One possible danger of this approach is that as with browsing the Internet, one could follow irrelevant or inconsequential sequences of hyperlinks, ending up somewhere very far removed from one's starting point. To counteract this, I will demonstrate how one can stay within the boundaries dictated by a theme or pattern of common citations and navigate through a number of texts in loops, frequently returning to one's starting text.

Let me start this voyage through Śaṅkara's texts at the beginning of *BSBh*, without necessarily privileging the authenticity of this text over that of all the others. After introducing mutual superimposition (*adhyāsa*) of the self and not-self as the root cause of bondage, Śaṅkara discusses the how and why of seeking to know *Brahman*. *BSBh* 1.1.1 sets the ground for separating the Uttara-Mīmāṁsā inquiry into *Brahman* and *mokṣa* from action (including Vedic rituals such as the *Agnihotra*) and the Pūrva-Mīmāṁsā inquiry into *dharma*. This passage also lists the well-known qualifications necessary for embarking upon the inquiry into *Brahman*.[6] The external texts cited here are *CU* 8.1.6, *TU* 2.1 and 3.1, along with a reference to *BS* 1.1.2.[7] These provide an internal hyperlink to *BSBh* 1.1.2 and external hyperlinks to the corresponding portions of *CUBh* and *TUBh*.

6. . . . *nitya-anitya vastu viveka iha-amutra-artha bhoga virāgaś śama-damādi sādhana saṁpat mumukṣutvaṁ ca* (*BSBh* 1.1.1, p. 6).
7. *darśayati, "tad yathā iha karmacito lokaḥ kṣīyata evam eva amutra puṇyacito lokaḥ kṣīyate"* →

Note that *BSBh* 1.1.1 specifies only *śama* and *dama* among the qualities of the seeker, leaving the rest under a general *et cetera*. This is an implicit reference to *BU* 4.4.23, serving as an indirect hyperlink to the corresponding portion of *BUBh*. The expression *śama-damādi* in *BSBh* 1.1.1 also serves as a direct internal hyperlink to *BS* 3.4.27 and the commentary thereon.[8]

Following the first internal hyperlink to *BSBh* 1.1.2, we notice that Śaṅkara cites all of *TU* 3.1 to 3.6, *BU* 2.4.5 (or 4.5.6) and *CU* 6.14.2,[9] which serve as direct external hyperlinks to the corresponding commentaries. In the process, within the space of two *sūtras*, he has set out some of his major themes — knowledge of *Brahman*, the self, is the highest goal; the nature of *Brahman* is taught in the Vedic canon, especially the Upaniṣad texts, mediated by the *ācārya*, who instructs and guides the seeker who has the prerequisite qualifications for self-knowledge; this knowledge is independent and imperishable, unlike results of actions and negates the Pūrva-Mīmāṁsā premise that injunctions (*vidhi*) and prohibitions (*pratiṣedha*) for actions are the primary intent of the Vedas. In the process, he has drawn our attention to some very significant Upaniṣad sources.

Following the next internal hyperlink from *BSBh* 1.1.1 to 3.4.27, we see that Śaṅkara explicitly cites *BU* 4.4.23,[10] thereby confirming an indirect hyperlink to *BUBh* from *BSBh* 1.1.1. In this passage, Śaṅkara emphatically interprets *BU* 4.4.23 as an injunction for the seeker to develop the qualities beginning with *śama*. He notes that the Mādhyandina text of *BU* reads as an explicit injunction and then cites *BS* 3.4.20. Following this hyperlink to *BSBh* 3.4.20, we see that after examining the case for renunciation and wandering mendicanthood (*saṁnyāsa, pārivrājya*) from various angles,

---

→ (*CU* 8.1.6) *ityādiḥ. tathā brahma-vijñānād api paraṁ puruṣārthaṁ darśayati – "brahmavid āpnoti param"* (*TU* 2.1) *ityādiḥ. tasmād yathokta sādhana-sampatty anantaraṁ brahma-jijñāsā kartavyā, brahmaṇo jijñāsā brahma-jijñāsā. brahma ca vakṣyamāṇa lakṣaṇaṁ "janmādy asya yataḥ"* (*BS* 1.1.2) *iti . . . "yato vā imāni bhūtāni jāyante" ity ādyāḥ śrutayaḥ "tad vijijñāsasva tad brahma"* (*TU* 3.1) *iti pratyakṣam eva . . .* (*BSBh* 1.1.1, p. 7)

8. *śama-damādy upetas syāt tathā api tu tad vidhes tad aṅgatayā teṣām avaśya-anuṣṭheyatvāt* (*BS* 3.4.27, p. 738).

9. *tathā hi, "śrotavyo mantavyaḥ"* (*BU* 2.4.5, 4.5.6) *iti śrutiḥ "paṇḍito medhāvī gandhārān eva upasaṁpadyeta evam eva iha ācāryavān puruṣo veda"* (*CU* 6.14.2) *iti ca . . . "bhṛgur vai vāruṇiḥ . . ." ity upakramya āha, "yato vā imāni bhūtāni jāyante . . . tad brahmeti." tasya ca nirṇaya vākyam "ānandāddhy eva khalv imāni bhūtāni jāyante . . . abhisaṁviśanti" iti.* (*TU* 3.1-3.6) *anyān apy evaṁjātīyakāni vākyāni . . .* (*BSBh* 1.1.2, pp. 11-12)

10. *śama-damādy upetas syād vidyārthī "tasmād evaṁvic chānto dānta uparatas titikṣus samāhito bhūtvā ātmany eva ātmānaṁ paśyati"* (*BU* 4.4.23) *iti vidyā-sādhanatvena śama-damādīnāṁ vidhānād, vihitānāṁ ca avaśya-anuṣṭheyatvāt. . . . "paśyed" iti ca mādhyandinā vispaṣṭam eva vidhim adhīyate* (*BSBh* 3.4.27, p. 739).

Śaṅkara strongly states that the Veda imparts an original injunction (*apūrva vidhi*) to enter into the fourth *āśrama*. He holds that this is because the state of being established in *Brahman* is only possible for the renouncer and that complete renunciation is an integral part of the final fruition of *Brahman*-knowledge.[11] Thus, Śaṅkara still finds room for an original injunction to operate on the seeker of knowledge, although the said injunction impels one not to perform any action, but to renounce all action! *Brahman*-knowledge is not the result of any action and scripture therefore enjoins neither the knowledge of *Brahman* nor meditation on *Brahman*, at least in the Pūrva-Mīmāṁsā sense of an injunction (*vidhi*). However, Śaṅkara also has clear and complex views on what scriptures enjoin, and how, with respect to what needs to be done prior to the rise of *Brahman*-knowledge and for entry into renunciation, in order for that knowledge to be firmly established and reach its final fruition. Is it Bādarāyaṇa's use of the word *vidhi* in *BS* 3.4.20 and 3.4.27 that forces these injunctive interpretations upon Śaṅkara? Or, is Śaṅkara making a concession to Pūrva-Mīmāṁsā or sacrificing logical consistency to compromise for the sake of pedagogy or Brāhmanical orthopraxy?[12] If we follow some of the external hyperlinks already listed from *BSBh* to the corresponding Upaniṣad commentaries, we will see that such is not the case and that this is indeed Śaṅkara's primary understanding of his source texts.

The first hyperlink out of *BSBh* 1.1.1 takes us to *CU* 8.1.6. Śaṅkara provides only a simple and straightforward explanation of this sentence in the corresponding portion of *CUBh*. He also provides a short introduction to the eighth chapter of *CU* and states that *sādhana*s like *brahmacarya* are enjoined upon the seeker of knowledge, in order to counter the thirst for sense objects, born out of numerous prior lifetimes of

11. *tathā ca uktaṁ "vidhir vā dhāraṇavat"* (*BS* 3.4.20) *iti.* (*BSBh* 3.4.27, p. 739) *vidhir vā ayam āśrama-antarasya . . . vidhir eva abhyupagantavya apūrvatvād vidhy-antarasya adarśanāt vispaṣṭaś ca āśrama-antara-pratyayāt. . . . parivrāḍ eva brahma-saṁstha iti setsyati. . . . atra ucyate, brahma-saṁstha iti hi brahmaṇi parisamāptir ananya-vyāpāratā-rūpaṁ tan niṣṭhatvam abhidhīyate. . . . brahma-jñāna paripāka-aṅgatvāc ca pārivrājyasya . . .* (*BSBh* 3.4.20, pp. 730-33).

12. In fact, Śaṅkara's orthoprax Brāhmanical opponent in *BSBh* 3.4.20 takes the view that the Vedas can contain no injunction to renounce action, because the performance of ordained action such as the *Agnihotra* can never be stopped without incurring sin. Śaṅkara's response is that the sin of not performing enjoined action pertains only to the student, householder and forest-dweller. Renunciation of action is indeed enjoined upon the seeker of self-knowledge and once this injunction is obeyed, nothing remains to be achieved except attaining self-knowledge and being established in it.

indulging in desires for objects.[13] *CU* 8.1.1 and 8.7.1 both state that *Brahman* is to be sought (*anveṣṭavya*) and known (*vijijñāsitavya*). Śaṅkara states in *CUBh* 8.7.1 that this is a restrictive injunction (*niyama vidhi*), not an original one (*apūrva vidhi*).[14] The next hyperlink from *BSBh* to *CU* takes us to *CUBh* 6.14.2. In this passage, Śaṅkara provides the key arguments for the state of liberation while yet embodied, or what is called *jīvan-mukti* in the later tradition. These are well known and often repeated explanations in Advaita Vedānta and I will not dwell on them here. What is more interesting to note here is that Śaṅkara concludes his commentary on *CU* 6.14.2 with an internal hyperlink to *CUBh* 2.23.1, and reiterates that although the *Brahman*-knower continues to be embodied, no action is incumbent upon him.[15] *CUBh* 2.23.1 is a fairly lengthy passage, with numerous citations from other Upaniṣad and Smṛti texts, including *BG*. Rather than enumerating all the hyperlinks to these other texts, I would like to point out that Śaṅkara utilizes *CU* 2.23.1 to emphasize the Vedic basis of the fourth *āśrama*, which he labels as *pārivrājya* here. He states that this *CU* sentence is meant to praise, but not to enjoin, meditation on the *praṇava* as a symbol of *Brahman* and to praise immortality, the result of being established in *Brahman*.[16] *CU* 2.23.1 is cited in *BSBh* 3.4.19 and the bulk of the discussion in *CUBh* 2.23.1 is entirely reminiscent of *BSBh* 3.4.20. This allows us to navigate in a loop back to our starting point. *BSBh* 1.1.2 cites *CU* 6.14.2, the commentary on which cites *CU* 2.23.1, which is cited in *BSBh* 3.4.19, which is in the same *adhikaraṇa* as *BS* 3.4.20, which is cited in *BSBh* 3.4.27, which is linked by the phrase *śama-damādi* to *BSBh* 1.1.1,

13. . . . *aneka-janma-viṣaya-sevā-abhyāsa-janitā viṣaya-viṣayā tṛṣṇā na sahasā nivartayituṁ śakyata iti brahmacaryādi sādhana-viśeṣo vidhātavyaḥ* (*CUBh* 8.1.1, p, 471).

14. . . . *dahare 'smin yad antas tad anveṣṭavyaṁ tad vāva vijijñāsitavyam iti* (*CU* 8.1.1). *gurv-āśraya-śravaṇādy upāyair anviṣya ca sākṣātkaraṇīyam ity arthaḥ* (*CUBh* 8.1.1, pp. 472-73). . . . *satyakāmas satyasaṁkalpas sa anveṣṭavyas sa vijijñāsitavyas sa sarvāṁś ca lokān āpnoti* . . . (*CU* 8.7.1) *śāstra-ācāryopadeśair jñātavyas sa viśeṣeṇa jñātum eṣṭavyaḥ vijijñāsitavyas sva-saṁvedyatām āpādayitavyaḥ*. . . . *anveṣṭavya vijijñāsitavya iti ca eṣa niyama vidhir eva, na apūrva vidhiḥ*. . . . *niyamārthatā eva asya vidher yuktā, na tv agnihotrāḍīnām iva apūrva-vidhitvam iha saṁbhavati* (*CUBh* 8.7.1, pp. 506-07).

15. *jñāna-utpatter ūrdhvaṁ ca brahmavidaḥ karma-abhāvam avocāma "brahma-saṁstho 'mṛtatvam eti"* (*CU* 2.23.1) *ity atra. tac ca smartum arhasi* (*CUBh* 6.14.2, p. 403).

16. *parivrāḍ turīyo brahma-saṁstho brahmaṇi samyak-sthitas, so 'mṛtatvaṁ puṇya-loka-vilakṣaṇam amaraṇa-bhāvam ātyantikam eti, na āpekṣikaṁ devādy amṛtatvavat, puṇyalokāt pṛthag amṛtatvasya vibhāga karaṇāt*. . . . *atra ca āśrama-dharma-phala upanyāsaḥ praṇava-sevā-stuty arthaḥ, na tat-phala-vidhy arthaḥ* . . . *nivṛtta-karmā brahma-saṁstha ucyate, sa ca parivrāḍ eva, anyasya asaṁbhavāt*. . . . *ataś ca idam eva ekaṁ vedoktaṁ pārivrājyam*. . . . *vedānta pramāṇa janita ekatva-pratyayavata eva karma-nivṛtti lakṣaṇaṁ pārivrājyaṁ brahma-saṁsthatvaṁ ca iti siddham* (*CUBh* 2.23.1, pp. 122-24).

which cites *BS* 1.1.2. Thus, having stepped out of *BSBh* 1.1.2, we return to the same passage by going through portions of *CUBh* and some later portions of *BSBh*. This is perhaps best understood in a diagrammatic fashion and is shown as Loop 1 in *fig*. 7.1. Numerous other hyperlinks out of this loop exist, from each of the commentary passages named therein, but are not shown in this figure. I will now move to a second loop, consisting primarily of hyperlinks out of *BSBh* 1.1.1-2 to *TUBh*.

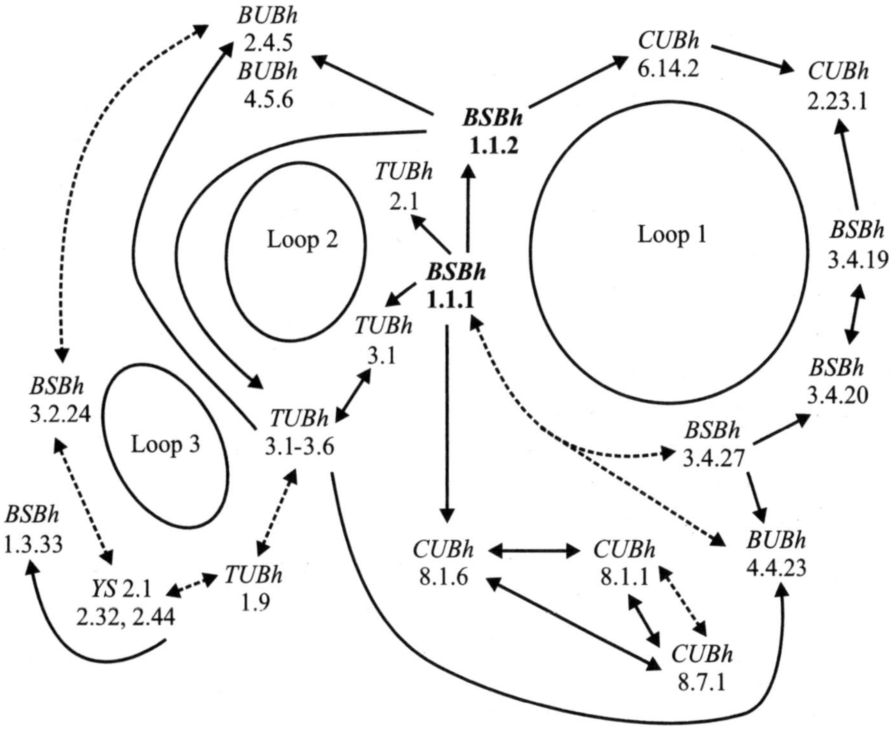

fig. 7.1. Diagrammatic representation of hyperlinks connecting texts: unidirectional arrows are hyperlinks pointing to direct textual citations. Thin solid lines, bidirectional arrows are a priori internal hyperlinks within a source text, e.g. same *adhyāya, prapāṭhaka* or *brāhmaṇa* of a given Upaniṣad or same *adhikaraṇa* within *BS*. Dotted bidirectional arrows represent a thematic link between texts, e.g. the expression *śama-damādi* between *BSBh* 1.1.1 and 3.4.27 or *BUBh* 4.4.23 and the terms *anveṣṭavya-vijijñāsitavya* connecting *CUBh* 8.1.1 and *CUBh* 8.7.1. The loops defined by textual hyperlinking are shown as ellipses and numbered.

A number of Śaṅkara's fundamental ontological positions are found in his extensive comments on *TU* 2.1, with his citations providing a very rich set of hyperlinks to numerous other texts. Śaṅkara introduces *TUBh* 2.1 with a statement that while the first chapter of *TU* points to a vision of the self in association with limiting adjuncts, the second chapter conveys the highest knowledge of the self, devoid of any limiting adjuncts whatsoever. He mentions some of the same points made in *BSBh* 1.1.1 and as in *BSBh* 1.1.2, cites *BU* 2.4.5 (4.5.6).[17] *TUBh* 2.1 also cites *TU* 2.9, while *TUBh* 2.9 easily connects to the third chapter of *TU*. Śaṅkara begins *TUBh* 3.1 with a statement of the purpose of this chapter, which is to describe *upāsanās* concerning *anna* and highlight *tapas* as the *sādhana* to obtain *Brahman*-knowledge.[18] In *TUBh* 3.1, he notes that Bhr̥gu practices *tapas* even before Varuṇa instructs him to do so, because *tapas* is well known to be the best means to accomplish any goal. *TUBh* 3.6 concludes that the purpose of *TU* 3.1-3.6 is to teach the seeker of *Brahman* to practise *tapas*, controlling the external and internal organs. *Brahmavarcas*, a quality of the *Brahman*-knower in *TU* 3.6, is interpreted as being characterized by *śama*, *dama* and *jñāna*.[19]

In the concluding portion of the third chapter of *TU*, Śaṅkara's view is that the only purpose of the meditations on *anna* is to lead to the praise of *Brahman*-knowledge in the concluding passage, where he who knows *Brahman* conveys the wonder of this knowledge by exclaiming that he is food, the eater of food and the eater of the eater of food. Śaṅkara concludes *TUBh* by reiterating that like Bhr̥gu, the seeker of *Brahman* should practise *tapas* and develop the qualities of *śama*, *dama*, etc. These lessons that Śaṅkara draws from *TUBh* are not explicitly stated in *TU* itself, but his

---

17. *saṁhitādi viṣayāṇi karmabhir aviruddhāny upāsanāny uktāni. anantaraṁ ca antaḥ-sopādhikam ātma-darśanam uktaṁ . . . . . . vidhūta-sarva-upādhi-viśeṣa-ātma-darśanārtham idam ārabhyate "brahmavid āpnoti param"* (*TU* 2.1) *ityādi. . . . vakṣyati ca, "vidvān na bibheti kutaścana"* (*TU* 2.9) *iti. . . . śravaṇādi-pūrvakaṁ hi vidyā-phalam "śrotavyo mantavyo nididhyāsitavya" ityādi śruty antarebhyaḥ* (*TUBh* 2.1, p. 663).

18. . . . *ānanda-vallyāḥ vivakṣito 'rthaḥ. parisamāptā ca brahma-vidyā. ataḥ paraṁ brahma-vidyā-sādhanaṁ tapo vaktavyam, annādi viṣayāṇi ca upāsanāny anuktāni ity ata idam ārabhyate* (*TUBh* 3.1, p. 729).

19. . . . *tapa eva sādhaka-tamaṁ sādhanam iti hi prasiddhaṁ loke. tasmāt pitrā anupadiṣṭam api brahma-vijñāna-sādhanatvena tapaḥ pratipede bhr̥guḥ. tac ca tapo bāhyāntaḥkaraṇa-samādhānam . . . brahma vijñātavān tapasā eva sādhanena bhr̥guḥ. tasmād brahma-vijijñāsunā bāhyāntaḥkaraṇa-samādhāna-lakṣaṇaṁ paramaṁ tapas sādhanam anuṣṭheyam iti prakaraṇārthaḥ. . . . brahmavarcasena śama-dama-jñānādi nimittena tejasā* (*TUBh* 3.1-3.6, pp. 731-39). See Sundaresan (2003) for a discussion of the connections that Śaṅkara draws between the practice of Yoga and *samādhāna* of the organs, external and internal, and for citations of numerous statements in *BGBh* that the seeker ought to cultivate, as part of the means to *Brahman*-knowledge, the very same personal qualities that are characteristic of the *Brahman*-knower.

focus throughout is on what a seeker of knowledge has to do and the qualities he needs to develop. *TUBh* concludes with an explicit reference to *BU* 4.4.23,[20] which is implicitly cited in *BSBh* 1.1.1 and explicitly in *BSBh* 3.4.27, thereby completing the loop on this excursion to *TUBh* (Loop 2 in *fig*. 7.1) and connecting it to the earlier excursion to *CUBh*.

Śaṅkara's emphasis on *tapas, śama* and *dama* in the third chapter of *TUBh* also provides an internal hyperlink to *TU* 1.9, which lists *tapas, śama* and *dama* along with *svādhyāya* and *pravacana*. This, in turn, allows an external hyperlink to the second chapter of *YS*, where *tapas, svādhyāya* and *Īśvara-praṇidhāna* are grouped together.[21] This secondary voyage out to Yoga texts can also be connected back to at least two different unexpected *BSBh* passages. Śaṅkara quotes *YS* 2.44 in *BSBh* 1.3.33, while in *BSBh* 3.2.24, he refers to *praṇidhāna* as one of the means by which *yogins* see the self. These independent references to Yoga and *yogins* in *BSBh* are certainly not forced by source text or discussion context. In *BS* 1.3.33, the discussion is on whether the gods are entitled to *Brahman*-knowledge. It is Śaṅkara's own contribution to this issue, when he quotes *YS* 2.44 and reinforces it with a reference to *ŚU* 2.12, a verse praising Yoga. The discussion in *BSBh* 3.2.22-23 is focused on the *via negativa* definition of the self (*neti neti*) in *BU* 2.3.6, while *BSBh* 3.2.24 affirms that *yogins* see the self through *bhakti, dhyāna* and *praṇidhāna*. Śaṅkara backs this up with verse citations from the fifth and twelfth *parvans* of *MBh*. Of the numerous verses that he could have cited, to say that the self is seen, although it cannot be positively described, Śaṅkara has chosen two that refer to *yogins* seeing the luminous Self. He also cites *KaU* 4.1 and *MU* 3.8, which pertain to withdrawal of the senses from objects and *dhyāna*.[22] The seeing of the

20. *yo 'yam anna-annāda-ādi lakṣaṇaṁ saṁvyavahāraḥ kārya-bhūtas sa saṁvyavahāra-mātram eva, na paramārtha vastu. sa evaṁbhūto 'pi brahma-nimitto brahma-vyatirekeṇa asann iti kṛtvā brahma-vidyā-kāryasya brahma-bhāvasya stuty-artham ucyate. . . . iti vallī-dvaya-vihitā upaniṣat paramātma-jñānam. tām etāṁ yathoktām upaniṣadaṁ "śānto dānta uparatas titikṣus samāhito bhūtva"* (*BU* 4.4.23) *bhṛguvat tapo mahad āsthāya ya evaṁ veda, tasya idaṁ phalaṁ yathokta-mokṣa iti* (*TUBh* 3.10, pp. 753-54).

21. *tapaś ca svādhyāya-pravacane ca. damaś ca svādhyāya-pravacane ca. śamaś ca svādhyāya-pravacane ca. . . . svādhyāya-pravacane eva . . . taddhi tapas taddhi tapaḥ* (*TU* 1.9). *tapaḥ kṛcchrādi. damo bāhya-karaṇa upaśamaḥ. śama antaḥkaraṇa upaśamaḥ . . .* (*TUBh* p. 641) *tapas svādhyāya īśvara-praṇidhānāni kriyā yogaḥ* (*YS* 2.1), *śauca santoṣa tapas svādhyāya īśvara-praṇidhānāni niyamāḥ* (*YS* 2.32), *svādhyāyād iṣṭa-devatā saṁprayogaḥ* (*YS* 2.44).

22. *api ca smaranti "svādhyāyād iṣṭa-devatā saṁprayoga"* (*YS* 2.44) *ityādi. yogo 'py aṇimādy aiśvarya-prāpti-phalakas smaryamāṇo na śakyate sāhasa-mātreṇa pratyākhyātum. śrutiś ca yoga-māhātmyaṁ prakhyāpayati, "pṛthiv-ap-tejo-'nila-khe samutthite pañcātmake yogaguṇe pravṛtte, na tasya rogo na jarā na mṛtyuḥ prāptasya yogāgni-mayaṁ śarīram"* (*ŚU* 2.12) *iti* (*BSBh* 1.3.33, p. 208). . . . *enam ātmānaṁ nirasta-samasta-prapañcam*

→

self also links us to the word *draṣṭavyaḥ* in *BU* 2.4.5 (4.5.6), thus connecting back to *BSBh* 1.1.2 (Loop 3 in *fig.* 7.1).

I emphasize the looping back to *BSBh* 1.1.1-2 merely because I chose to start this discussion at the beginning of *BSBh*. Notice that in each case above, the re-entry to *BSBh* 1.1.1-2 is through its citations of *BU* sentences. I could have equally well begun the entire discussion at *BUBh* 2.4.5 (4.5.6) or 4.4.23 and hyperlinked to other commentaries from those passages. The same loops of textual interconnections would have emerged out of that analysis, which is why I hold that when reading the texts in a hyperlinked fashion, one could possibly start at any random place in any commentary to work one's way through other texts and that one's starting point does not necessarily privilege that text over all others.

I will now take up another circuit of hyperlinks from *BUBh* to a number of important passages from other texts. In *fig.* 7.2, note the citational and thematic hyperlinks from *BUBh* 4.4.23 to *CUBh* 8.7.1, *BSBh* 3.4.19-20 and 3.4.27. We have already seen that *BSBh* 3.4.27 interprets *BU* 4.4.23 as an injunction for the seeker of self-knowledge to develop prerequisite qualities of *śama, dama*, etc. Śaṅkara's explanations of each of these qualities in *BUBh* 4.4.23 provide thematic hyperlinks from this passage to *BSBh* 4.1.9-11. This uncovers another general hyperlink to Yoga texts, because *BSBh* 4.1.10 says that various postures are taught in the Yoga-Śāstra as aids to meditation on *Brahman*.[23] Natural hyperlinks exist from *BUBh* 4.4.23 to 4.4.21 and 4.4.22, where Śaṅkara again argues for an original injunction for renunciation,[24] just as in *BSBh* 3.4.19-20. *BUBh* 4.4.21 provides another link to *BUBh* 1.4.7,[25] where Śaṅkara strongly denies an original injunction

→ *avyaktaṁ saṁrādhana kāle paśyanti yoginaḥ. saṁrādhanaṁ ca bhakti-dhyāna-praṇidhānādy anuṣṭhānam. . . . smṛtir api ". . . jyotiḥ paśyanti yuñjānas tasmai yogātmane namaḥ"* (*MBh* 12.47.35) *"yoginas taṁ prapaśyanti bhagavantaṁ sanātanam"* (*MBh* 5.45.1-21) *iti ca evam ādyā* (*BSBh* 3.2.24, pp. 601-02).

23. *śānta bāhyendriya-vyāpārata upaśāntas, tathā dānta antaḥkaraṇa-tṛṣṇāto nivṛtta, uparatas sarva-eṣaṇā-vinirmuktas saṁnyāsī, titikṣur dvandva-sahiṣṇus, samāhita indriya-antaḥkaraṇa-calana-rūpād vyāvṛttya aikāgrya-rūpeṇa samāhito bhūtva . . .* (*BUBh* 4.4.22, p. 655) *acalatvaṁ ca āpekṣya, smaranti ca, yatra ekāgratā tatra aviśeṣāt* (*BS* 4.1.9-11). *ata eva padmakādīnām āsana-viśeṣāṇām upadeśo yoga-śāstre* (*BSBh* 4.1.10, pp. 783-84).

24. *. . . tasmād ātmānaṁ lokam icchantaḥ pravrajanti pravrajeyur ity eṣa vidhir arthavādena saṁgacchate . . . yasmāt pūrve vidvāṁsaḥ prajādi karmabhyo nivṛttāḥ pravrajitavanta eva, tasmād adhunātanā api pravrajanti pravrajeyuḥ . . .* (*BUBh* 4.4.22, pp. 650-51) *. . . tathā "etam eva pravrājino lokam icchantaḥ pravrajanti"* (*BU* 4.4.22) *ity asya veda-anuvacanādibhis samabhivyāhāraḥ* (*BSBh* 3.4.20, p. 729).

25. *. . . vijñāya upadeśataś śāstrataś ca prajñāṁ śāstra-ācārya-upadiṣṭa viṣayāṁ jijñāsā-parisamāptikarīṁ kurvīta brāhmaṇaḥ. evaṁ prajñā-kāraṇa sādhanāni saṁnyāsa-śama-* →

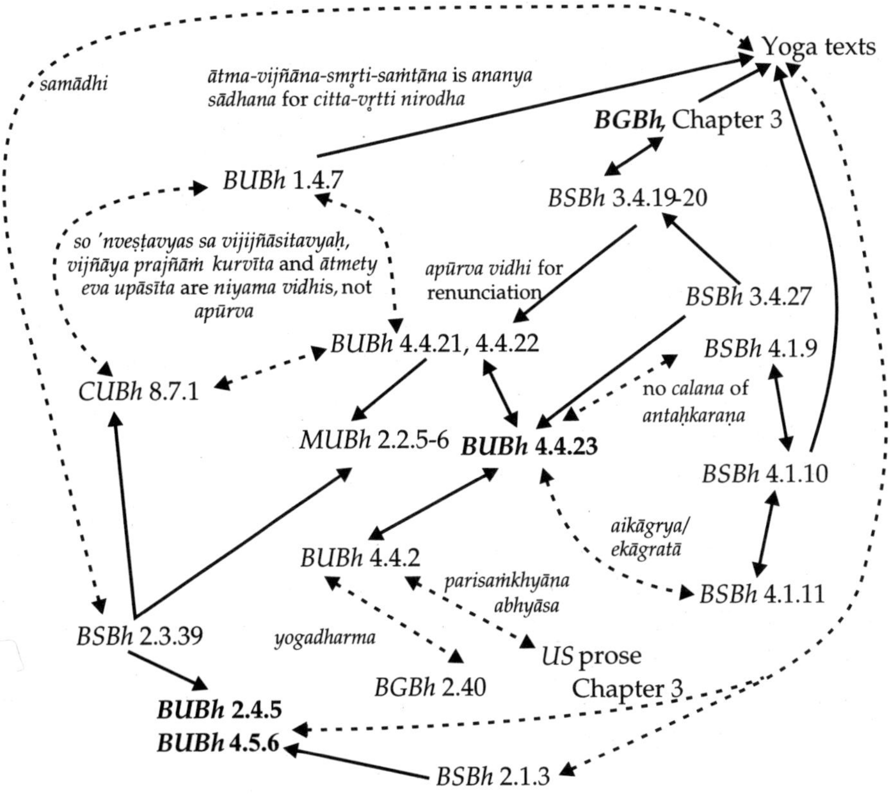

fig. 7.2. The hyperlinked interconnectivity of texts from *BUBh* is depicted using the same convention of arrow styles as in *fig.* 7.1. Some of the key themes that hyperlink other texts to *BUBh* passages are shown alongside the corresponding arrows. A general placeholder category called "Yoga texts" is shown here, because Śaṅkara's references to Yoga in passages like *BSBh* 2.1.3, 2.3.39, 4.1.10 and *BGBh*, chapter 3, are not necessarily to *YS* and derivative texts. Notice the number of hyperlinks that point to "Yoga texts" from the major commentaries, both thematically and in terms of citations.

for self-knowledge, but interprets *BU* 1.4.7 and 4.4.21 as restrictive injunctions (*niyama vidhis*), consistent with *CUBh* 8.7.1. The content of this restrictive injunction pertains to the steady recollection of self-

→ *dama-uparama-titikṣā-samādhānāni kuryād ity arthaḥ . . . kevala-ātma-aikatva-pratipādakās svalpāś śabdā anujñāyante "aum ity evaṁ dhyāyatha ātmānam"* (*MU* 2.2.6) *"anyā vāco vimuñcatha"* (*MU* 2.2.5) *iti ca ātharvaṇe* (*BUBh* 4.4.21, p. 640). *tyāga-vairāgyādi sādhana-balāvalambena ātma-vijñāna-smṛti-saṁtatir niyantavyā bhavati, na tv apūrvā kartavyā, prāptatvād ity avocāma. tasmāt prāpta-vijñāna-smṛti-saṁtāna niyama-vidhy arthāni "vijñāya prajñāṁ kurvīta"* (*BU* 4.4.21) *ityādi vākyāni* (*BUBh* 1.4.7, p. 113).

knowledge, which is also described as the only sure means to *citta-vṛtti nirodha*. This provides yet another external hyperlink to Yoga texts.[26] Another passage is naturally hyperlinked to *BUBh* 4.4.23, namely *BUBh* 4.4.2, by virtue of being within the same section in the source text. Here, Śaṅkara states that one should practise *yoga-dharma* and *parisaṁkhyāna* meditation at the time of death, in order to achieve independence. This lesson is not particularly forced by *BU* 4.4.2, and in turn allows us to hyperlink to *BGBh* 2.40 and the third prose chapter of *US*.[27]

MU 2.2.6, one of the texts cited in *BUBh* 4.4.21, is also cited in *BSBh* 2.3.39, which says that *samādhi* is taught in the Upaniṣads as the means to self-knowledge.[28] As Śaṅkara also cites *CU* 8.7.1 and *BU* 2.4.5 (4.5.6) in *BSBh* 2.3.39, I have drawn thematic hyperlinks from these texts to the general category of Yoga texts in *fig.* 7.2. This will likely be unacceptable to those scholars who hold that the word *samādhi* in *BS* 2.3.39 has a different intent from that in Yoga. I beg to differ, precisely because the methodology of hyperlinking of the texts shows otherwise. In *BSBh* 2.1.3, where Śaṅkara examines Yoga, he cites the same *BU* sentence as an instance of the Upaniṣad enjoining Yoga,[29] and further cites *ŚU* and *KaU* verses that more explicitly refer to Yoga. What he refutes in *BSBh* 2.1.3 is the Sāṁkhya-based dualism of the Yoga school, but he does not deny the proposition that the *BU* 2.4.5 statement about *śravaṇa*, *manana* and *nididhyāsana* is related to Yoga. The citation of the same *BU* sentence in

26. *ananya-sādhanatvāc ca nirodhasya. na hy ātma-vijñāna-tat-smṛti-saṁtāna vyatirekeṇa citta-vṛtti-nirodhasya sādhanam asti. abhyupagamya idam uktaṁ, na tu brahma-vijñāna vyatirekeṇa anyan mokṣa-sādhanam avagamyate* (*BUBh* 1.4.7, p. 111).

27. *tasmāt tat-kāle svātantryārthaṁ yoga-dharma-anusevanaṁ parisaṁkhyāna-abhyāsaś ca viśiṣṭa-puṇyopacayaś ca śraddadhānaiḥ paralokārthibhir apramattaiḥ kartavya iti* (*BUBh* 4.4.2, p. 606). . . . *svalpam apy asya dharmasya yoga-dharmasya anuṣṭhitaṁ trāyate rakṣati mahato bhayāt saṁsāra-bhayāt janma-maraṇādi lakṣaṇāt* (*BGBh* 2.40, p. 50). *mumukṣūṇām upātta-puṇyāpuṇya-kṣapaṇa-parāṇām apūrva-anupacaya-arthināṁ parisaṁkhyānam idam ucyate . . . iṣṭa-aniṣṭa-miśra-phalāni karmāṇy upacīyanta iti tan mokṣārtham* (*US* prose chapter 3, p. 147).

28. *samādhy abhāvāc ca* (*BS* 2.3.39) *yo 'py ayam aupaniṣad-ātma-pratipatti-prayojanas samādhir upadiṣṭo vedānteṣu, "ātmā vā are draṣṭavyaḥ śrotavyo mantavyo nididhyāsitavyaḥ"* (*BU* 2.4.5, 4.5.6), *"so 'nveṣṭavyas sa vijijñāsitavyaḥ"* (*CU* 8.7.1), *"oṁ ity evaṁ dhyāyatha ātmānam"* (*MU* 2.2.6) *ity evaṁ lakṣaṇaṁ* . . . (*BSBh* 2.3.39, p. 469).

29. *etena yogaḥ pratyuktaḥ* (*BS* 2.1.3) . . . *samyag-darśana-abhyupāyo hi yogo vede vihitaḥ, "śrotavyo mantavyo nididhyāsitavya" iti. "trir unnataḥ sthāpya samaṁ śarīram"* (*ŚU* 2.8) *ityādinā ca āsanādi-kalpanā puraḥsaraṁ bahu-prapañcaḥ yoga-vidhānaṁ śvetāśvataropaniṣadi dṛśyate. liṅgāni ca vaidikāni yoga-viṣayāṇi sahasraśa upalabhyante, "tāṁ yogam iti manyante sthirām indriya dhāraṇām"* (*KaU* 6.11) *iti, "vidyām etāṁ yoga-vidhiḥ ca kṛtsnam"* (*KaU* 6.18) *iti ca evamādīni. yoga-śāstre 'pi "atha tad darśana-abhyupāyo yoga" iti samyag-darśana-abhyupāyatvena eva yogo 'ṅgīkriyate* (*BSBh* 2.1.3, p. 287).

BSBh 2.3.39 under the word *samādhi* cannot therefore be quite divorced from Yoga. Note also that what is cited in *BSBh* 2.1.3 as Yoga-Śāstra is not the currently available *YS* text, which is cited elsewhere in *BSBh*. We have also already seen Śaṅkara's positive references to Yoga and *yogins* in *BSBh* 1.3.33 and 3.2.24, showing that his attitude towards Yoga is not one of simple refutation. *BUBh* 1.4.7 shows another aspect of where the Advaitic conception of being established in self-knowledge agrees with the goal of Yoga. Note also that the introduction to the third chapter of *BGBh* includes Yoga-Śāstra and Itihāsa-Purāṇa among the texts that enjoin renunciation upon the seeker of liberation.[30] I have examined this in greater detail elsewhere (Sundaresan 2003) and will not expand much upon it here. Suffice it to say that Śaṅkara relates Yoga to the process of seeking self-knowledge, obtaining it and being established in it, thereby moving Yoga away from its dualistic Sāṁkhya history and realigning it with non-dualistic Vedānta.

Many scholars, including the redoubtable Paul Hacker, see *BUBh* 1.4.7 as a refutation or devaluing of Yoga. However, the way these important texts are interconnected also compels our attention towards the heavily Mīmāṁsā-oriented background of this discussion. Śaṅkara accepts an original injunction only for renouncing action, but categorically denies one for *Brahman*-knowledge and for *citta-vr̥tti nirodha* as a means to it. However, in the same breath, he accepts a restrictive injunction instead, for the steady recollection of self-knowledge, and states that this recollection is the only means to *citta-vr̥tti nirodha*. This complicated Mīmāṁsā argument, with its rejection of original injunctions for self-knowledge, often gets mistaken as being against Yoga. Self-knowledge is not and cannot be enjoined, but this does not mean that self-knowledge is itself thereby refuted. This is well understood by all. However, when it comes to *citta-vr̥tti nirodha*, its not being enjoined is mistakenly seen as a refutation of Yoga and Śaṅkara's subsequent statement about it gets ignored. Śaṅkara's acceptance of restrictive injunctions with respect to the ancillaries of self-knowledge, which are in turn intimately connected to Yoga, also often gets ignored, while his reasons for holding to an original injunction for renunciation do not seem to be well understood at all. The consistent twining together of themes from Yoga and Pūrva-Mīmāṁsā in Śaṅkara's thought stands out in stark relief only when the

30. *sarva-upaniṣatsv-itihāsa-purāṇa-yoga-śāstreṣu ca jñānāṅgatvena mumukṣos sarva-karma-saṁnyāsa-vidhānāt, āśrama-vikalpa-samuccaya-vidhānāc ca śruti-smr̥tyoḥ* (*BGBh*, chapter 3, p. 77).

major commentaries are read together in a hyperlinked fashion. This feature cannot be explained away by supposing that an enthusiastic young Śaṅkara was influenced by dualistic Yoga thinking and only the mature Śaṅkara became a thorough non-dualist Vedāntin. Nor can Śaṅkara's acceptance of an original injunction to renounce action be seen as a sacrifice of theoretical consistency for the sake of pedagogy or for accommodating his Pūrva-Mīmāṁsaka opponents. In fact, Śaṅkara's insistence that the Upaniṣads carry an original injunction to renounce action is a remarkably novel application of Pūrva-Mīmāṁsā principles in the service of Uttara-Mīmāṁsā, which turns the Pūrva-Mīmāṁsā argument about action and injunctions on its head. The hyperlinking methodology also immediately calls our attention to passages where Śaṅkara shows that even though self-knowledge is non-enjoinable, it is quite compatible with an original injunction to renounce all action. Furthermore, the currently accepted scholarly near-consensus on how post-Śaṅkaran authors have been influenced by Yoga, notwithstanding Śaṅkara's "supposedly complete" rejection of that school, will need to be thoroughly revisited in light of this fresh perspective on Śaṅkara's thought.

To conclude, I realize that the hyperlinking methodology may appear to some as being old wine in a new bottle, being merely a description of something that a thorough student of the texts already would do implicitly. I would like to point out that setting out this principle explicitly and applying the methodology to Śaṅkara's commentaries without any preconceptions allows the texts to speak for themselves. The concept of hyperlinking can also be extended to other authors in the long history of Indian philosophy, to gain insights that are probably still waiting to be discovered. For numerous reasons, the world of academia is increasingly embracing the usage of online publishing and the e-text is becoming a very attractive option. Viewing ancient texts in a hyperlinked fashion may well become the norm for future generations of scholars. The research tasks of future scholars will certainly turn in important ways upon the availability, searchability and I might add, hyperlinkability, of electronic texts. As seen in this discussion, the thematic and citational interconnections among various passages that are far-flung from one another within the Śaṅkaran corpus cannot be appreciated if these texts are read separately and linearly, whether on a printed page or on an electronic device. Hyperlinking has drawn our attention to easily overlooked or little understood portions of *BSBh* and the other commentaries. The close intertwining of Yoga and Pūrva-Mīmāṁsā concerns in these texts has also highlighted the need to understand Pūrva-Mīmāṁsā well, in order to understand how Uttara-Mīmāṁsā is constructed differently. In the process, we have unearthed certain unexpected themes and a *bhāṣya* reference to *parisaṁkhyāna*, thus revealing a hitherto unknown context to the third chapter of *US*, namely a meditation at the time of death.[31] We might discover more detail about other less understood issues in Advaita Vedānta if we apply this hyperlinking methodology consistently and more extensively to these texts. Halbfass (1983) had cautioned against "seeing inconsistencies and contradictions that would be illegitimate in Śaṅkara's own horizon."[32] Hyperlinking Śaṅkara's texts rigorously and studying them together might just help clarify and refine where that horizon lies.

Abbreviations

BG — Bhagavad-Gītā; BGBh — Bhagavad-Gītā-Bhāṣya; BS — Brahma-Sūtra; BSBh — Brahma-Sūtra-Bhāṣya; BU — Bṛhadāraṇyaka Upaniṣad; BUBh — Bṛhadāraṇyaka Upaniṣad Bhāṣya; CU — Chāndogya Upaniṣad; CUBh — Chāndogya Upaniṣad Bhāṣya; KaU — Kaṭha Upaniṣad; MBh — Mahābhārata; MU — Muṇḍaka Upaniṣad; MUBh — Muṇḍaka Upaniṣad Bhāṣya; ŚU — Śvetāśvatara Upaniṣad; TU — Taittirīya Upaniṣad; TUBh — Taittirīya Upaniṣad Bhāṣya; US — Upadeśasāhasrī; YS — Yoga-Sūtra

References

PRIMARY SOURCES

Upadeśasāhasrī (1983), *Śrī-śāṁkara-granthāvaliḥ: Upadeśaracanāvaliḥ*, vol. 3, pp. 113-246, Chennai: Samata Books.

Bṛhadāraṇyakopaniṣadbhāṣyam (1983), *Śrī-śāṁkara-granthāvaliḥ*, vol. 10, Chennai: Samata Books.

Brahmasūtrabhāṣyam (1983), *Śrī-śāṁkara-granthāvaliḥ*, vol. 7, Chennai: Samata Books.

Chāndogyopaniṣadbhāṣyam (1983), *Śrī-śāṁkara-granthāvaliḥ*, vol. 9, Chennai: Samata Books.

Bhagavadgītābhāṣyam (1983), *Śrī-śāṁkara-granthāvaliḥ*, vol. 6, Chennai: Samata Books.

Taittirīyopaniṣadbhāṣyam (1983), *Śrī-śāṁkara-granthāvaliḥ:Upaniṣadbhāṣyaṇi*, vol. 8, pp. 615-756, Chennai: Samata Books.

---

31. I find no mention of the *BU* 4.4.2 reference to *parisaṁkhyāna* in Bader (1990) or in Mayeda's in-depth study and translation of *US* (1992). Consequently, there is no comparison found in these studies to other meditations recommended especially for the moment of death, e.g. in the eighth chapter of *BGBh*.

32. I can do no better than quote Halbfass (1983: 39) *verbatim*, "It requires extreme caution to identify 'inconsistencies' and 'contradictions' which would be illegitimate in Śaṅkara's own horizon and which would provide reliable, unambiguous clues for actual *changes* in his thought and for a development from earlier to later positions."

SECONDARY SOURCES

Bader, Jonathan (1990), *Meditation in Śaṅkara's Vedānta*, New Delhi: Aditya Prakashan.

Halbfass, Wilhelm (1983), *Studies in Kumārila and Śaṅkara*, Reinbek: Inge Wezler.

—— (ed.) (1995), *Philology and Confrontation: Paul Hacker on Traditional and Modern Vedanta*, Albany: State University of New York Press.

Mayeda, Sengaku (1992), *A Thousand Teachings: The Upadeśasāhasrī of Śaṅkara*, Albany: State University of New York Press.

Potter, Karl H. (1981), *Advaita Vedānta up to Śaṅkara and His Pupils*, vol. 3, Encyclopedia of Indian Philosophies, Delhi: Motilal Banarsidass.

Sundaresan, Vidyasankar (2000), "What Determines Śaṅkara's Authorship?: The case of the Pañcīkaraṇa," in *Philosophy East and West*, vol. 52, no. 1, pp. 1-35, Honolulu: University of Hawai'i Press.

—— (2003), "Yoga in Śaṅkaran Advaita Vedānta: A Reappraisal," in *Yoga: The Indian Tradition*, ed. Ian Whicher and David Carpenter, London: Routledge Curzon, pp. 99-129.

Suthren Hirst, Jacqueline G. (2005), *Śaṅkara's Advaita Vedānta: A Way of Teaching*, London: Routledge Curzon.

8

Appaya Dīkṣita on Avidyānivṛtti
A Critique in Siddhāntaleśasaṁgraha

Jonathan Duquette, K. Ramasubramanian***

Introduction

WAY back in the sixteenth century, on the banks of river Pālār in the North Arcot district (South India), Appaya Dīkṣita — one of the pre-eminent Sanskrit intellectuals of pre-modern India — engaged himself with the monumental task of producing more than hundred works on a variety of subjects, including hymns in praise of gods and goddesses as well as classical treatises in literature, religion and philosophy. One of the highly acclaimed works by Dīkṣita is the *Siddhāntaleśasaṁgraha* (*SLS*). Being a compendium (*saṁgraha*) of the major views held by post-Śaṅkara philosophers up to his time on a variety of topics pertaining to Advaita Vedānta, *SLS* also includes a detailed treatment on the concept of *avidyānivṛtti* (cessation of ignorance). This concept is of utmost importance in Advaita Vedānta, as it proclaims time and again that it is only through the cessation (*nivṛtti*) of ignorance (*avidyā*) about the true nature of oneself that a person obtains liberation (*mokṣa*) from all the bondages, once and for all.

The nature of *avidyānivṛtti* has been discussed at great length by Advaitins starting at least from Maṇḍana Miśra, contemporary of Śaṅkara, to Madhusūdana Sarasvatī, a towering giant among Advaitins who lived towards the end of the sixteenth century. Dīkṣita's discussion on this topic in his *SLS* provides a succinct account of the different conceptions of *avidyānivṛtti* held by different *ācārya*s (great teachers) in the Advaita tradition. The aim of the present paper is to closely examine these

---

* Abteilung für Kultur und Geschichte Indiens and Tibets, Universität Hamburg

** Department of Humanities and Social Sciences, IIT, Bombay conceptions as presented by Dīkṣita as well as to shed some light on his distinctive style of philosophizing.

Liberation, Avidyā and Three Views of Avidyānivṛtti

In Advaita Vedānta, liberation (*mokṣa*) is considered to be a state in which a person is free from desire, despondency, delusion and so on, and in general from all kinds of bondages of the world. As the root cause of bondage is conceived to be ignorance (*avidyā*), knowledge (*vidyā*) is the only means for liberation. Liberation comes with fully realizing the identity of one's own self (*ātman*) with *Brahman*, the absolute, non-dual and all-comprehensive reality. The "liberated state" is not something acquired from outside but the very essence of one's being, self-revealed when ignorance about oneself is removed or destroyed. Hence, freedom from the grip of *avidyā*, or *avidyānivṛtti*, is what constitutes the very essence of liberation and the supreme end of human endeavour.[1]

According to Advaitins, *Brahman-ātman* is the highest truth and reality, one without a second (*advaita*), changeless (*kūṭastha*), eternal (*nitya*) and of the nature of pure consciousness (*caitanya*). This being the case, the task of reconciling this concept of reality with the perceived manifold, material and changing world is something that is onerous on the Advaitins. It is precisely in this context that the concept of ignorance (*avidyā*) is invoked as a theoretical construct, and the explanation offered is as follows: *ātman* does not change and is not manifold; it is our own ignorance that makes it appear so. However, there have been debates among Advaitins as well as between their opponents with regard to the fundamental nature of *avidyā*, its ontological status and in particular its relation to *Brahman-ātman*. As Kaplan notices, if "Advaitins have continuously tried to present *avidyā* in intelligible ways . . . these efforts may be said to [have raised] at least as many questions as they answer" (Kaplan 2007: 178). This remark essentially conveys the complexity involved in theorising *avidyā* within the framework of Advaita Vedānta; it certainly applies to the case of *avidyānivṛtti* too.

As noted earlier, all agree that it is through the cessation of ignorance about the true nature of one's self that a person is liberated. In his *Laghucandrikā*, Brahmānanda, the commentator of Madhusūdana

1. See Śaṅkara's commentary on *Bṛhadāraṇyaka Upaniṣad* I.1.7: "the result [sought after] is liberation or cessation of ignorance" (*phalaṁ ca mokṣo 'vidyānivṛttir vā*). In *Upadeśasāhasrī* I.1.5: "Since the root cause of this [transmigratory existence] is ignorance, its destruction is desired. Knowledge of *Brahman* therefore is entered on. Final beatitude results from this knowledge"(*ajñānaṁ tasya mūlaṁ syād iti taddhānam iṣyate | brahmavidyāta ārabdhā tato niḥśreyasaṁ bhavet | |*)

Sarasvatī's *Advaitasiddhi*, cites a *kārikā* that conveys how *avidyā* relates to *mokṣa*: *avidyāstamayo mokṣaḥ sā ca bandha udāhṛtaḥ* (*Advaitasiddhi* : 2).[2] In short, *mokṣa* consists in the disappearance of ignorance (*avidyāstamaya*) as the latter is the cause of bondage (*bandha*). While discussing the nature of *mokṣa* in the fourth chapter (*caturtha-pariccheda*) of his *SLS*, Dīkṣita raises a pertinent question: what place does *avidyānivṛtti* have within the framework of Advaita Vedānta, in which self (*ātman*) or *Brahman* is the only real/ eternal entity? If we assume *avidyānivṛtti* to have some positive existence, then what is its exact relationship with *ātman*? Should it be perceived as an entity that is not different from *ātman* or envisaged as an entity that is different from it? If *avidyānivṛtti* is identified with *ātman*, which is already free and eternal, the pursuit of liberation through removing ignorance about oneself seems to be a futile enterprise. On the other hand, if *avidyānivṛtti* is taken to be an entity or process other than *ātman* then we land ourselves in a situation where we have to accept two fundamental entities — *ātman* and *avidyānivṛtti* — which goes against the non-dualistic stand of Advaita Vedānta.

The difficulty in coming to terms with the ontological status of *avidyānivṛtti* is also entailed by the fact that *avidyā* is characterized by indefinability (*anirvacanīyatva* = *sad-asad-vilakṣaṇatva*) in Advaita. By "indefinable" what is meant is that *avidyā* is neither existent (*sat*) nor non-existent (*asat*). Since *avidyā* is destroyed in the wake of right knowledge about an object, it cannot be *sat* or absolutely real. But since it manifests itself until then, it cannot be *asat* (like hare's horns, or the son of a barren woman). Obviously, it cannot be both *sat* and *asat* since it would involve a contradiction. Being different from both the existent and the non-existent, we have to declare *avidyā* as *sad-asad-vilakṣaṇa* or *anirvacanīya*. Then, if *avidyā* is *anirvacanīya* the question of defining the status of its *nivṛtti* arises as well, i.e. is *avidyānivṛtti* definable or not?

In order to understand the context in which Dīkṣita develops his own reflections we need to present the three main conceptions of *avidyānivṛtti* held by Advaitins after Śaṅkara. As far as Śaṅkara is concerned, one notes that he did not extensively discuss the nature of *avidyānivṛtti* either in his commentarial or independent works. However, his conception

---

2. In his commentary, Brahmānanda mentions that he is citing from a *vārttika*. However, efforts to trace this passage from a *vārttika* have been futile so far. It may be that some section of the *vārttika* is not available. An almost identical *kārikā* is found in the *Brahmasiddhi* of Maṇḍana Miśra — *avidyāstamayo mokṣaḥ sā saṁsāra udāhṛtā* (*Brahmasiddhi* 1999: 569).

seems to have been that *avidyānivṛtti* is identical with *Brahman-ātman* (Veezhinathan 1994: 104-05).

Avidyānivṛtti is Identical with Brahman or Knowledge of Brahman

The view that equates *avidyānivṛtti* with *Brahman*-knowledge (*brahma-vidyā*) is ascribed to Śaṅkara's contemporary Maṇḍana Miśra (*c.* eighth century), the author of *Brahmasiddhi*, by Dīkṣita in his *SLS* (*ātmaiveti brahmasiddhikārāḥ*).[3] In Maṇḍana's *Brahmasiddhi*, the disappearance of ignorance is equated with liberation itself: *avidyāstamayo mokṣaḥ*. Also, according to Maṇḍana, the wake of right knowledge itself is the removal of *avidyā*. As he says in the *Brahmasiddhi*: *avidyā hi bandhahetuḥ, tattvajñānodaya eva ca tannivṛttiḥ* (*Brahmasiddhi* 1937: 78). Thus, according to Maṇḍana, getting enlightened about the true nature of the self is equivalent to cessation of ignorance (*avidyānivṛtti*) which is equivalent to *mokṣa*, which in turn is none other than being one with *Brahman*. Along the lines of Śaṅkara and Maṇḍana, Citsukha (*c.* thirteenth century) supports the view that *avidyānivṛtti* is identical with the Absolute. In his *Tattvapradīpikā*, Citsukha is engaged in refuting various objections raised by followers of rival systems against the doctrines of Advaita. His views on *avidyānivṛtti* come while replying to Naiyāyikas who argue against the very existence of such a thing as removal of ignorance. Like Naiyāyikas, he sets aside all conceptions of *avidyānivṛtti* but in the end argues that the only significant thesis seems to be the one that equates *avidyānivṛtti* with *Brahman-ātman*. He bases his reasoning on an analogy with the nacre-silver illusion where nacre appears as silver. His point is that the removal of a superimposed entity is but its being reduced to its substratum. Just as the contradiction of the knowledge of silver in nacre is nothing but nacre itself, the removal or cessation of ignorance — which is superimposed upon *Brahman* — must necessarily be of the nature of its substratum, namely *Brahman* (Sharma 1974: 217).[4]

Since *nivṛtti* and *Brahman* are identical for Citsukha, there is no ambiguity for him as to whether *avidyānivṛtti* should be indeterminable

3. The passages quoted from *SLS* are taken from 1973: 366-73, reproduced in the Appendix of this paper.

4. This idea is expressed by the following well-known principle, namely that "any theoretical construct and/or entity having illusory (*kalpita*) reality, when it gets annihilated, simply merges with the substratum" (*adhiṣṭhānāvaśeṣo hi naśaḥ kalpitavastunaḥ*). Though this has been cited by several reputed Advaitins including Dharmarājādhvarīndra, the original source, to our knowledge, remains unknown.

or of a different nature than *Brahman*. However, this view leads to a serious objection: since *Brahman* is ever-existent, *avidyānivṛtti* must also be ever-existent and so no attempt needs to be made to "achieve" removal of ignorance by knowing *Brahman*. Deferring the reply to this objection to the next section, we now proceed to outline the theory ascribing a "fifth form" (*pañcamaprakārā*) of reality to *avidyānivṛtti*.

Avidyānivṛtti as a "Fifth Form" (pañcamaprakārā) of Reality

The *pañcamaprakārā* conception, as the term indicates, is that the state of *nivṛtti* is different from the four usual predicables: *sat* (real), *asat* (unreal), *sad-asad-ubhaya* (both real and unreal) and *sad-asad-anubhaya* (neither real nor unreal, i.e. *anirvacanīya*). It is not real because the introduction of a second real different from *Brahman-ātman* means admission of duality. It is not unreal because it would then have no relation to knowledge and could not be attained through knowledge of *Brahman*. We can neither consider this state as both real and unreal because it would involve a logical contradiction. It is also not *anirvacanīya* because the existence of an indeterminable necessarily presupposes the existence of *avidyā*. If *avidyānivṛtti* were *anirvacanīya*, its existence would depend upon *avidyā*, which is impossible because *avidyā* and *avidyānivṛtti* cannot coexist together. Therefore, some argue that *avidyānivṛtti* has to be given a special status — a reality of a fifth kind — other than the four usual ones.

Who proposed this fifth form (*pañcamaprakārā*) first? In Dīkṣita's *SLS*, the *pañcamaprakārā* conception is ascribed to Ānandabodha, a well-known Advaitin of the twelfth century (*pañcamaprakārāvidyānivṛttir iti ānandabodhācāryāḥ*). Ānandabodha indeed discusses and favours this view in his *Nyāyamakaranda*.[5] But Advaitins prior to him, like Vimuktātman (*c.* eleventh century) and Sarvajñātman (*c.* eleventh century), have also discussed *pañcamaprakārā*. So, for sure, the originator of this view cannot be Ānandabodha. According to Panda (1992: 112) and Sundaram (1968: 397), Vimuktātman was the first to propose the *pañcamaprakārā* view, and it is quite probable that Sarvajñātman[6] and Ānandabodha (of whom Vimuktātman was probably the *guru*) only followed him in enunciating their own conception of *avidyānivṛtti*.

5. *na san nāsan na sadasat nānirvācyo 'pi tatkṣayaḥ* (*Nyāyamakaranda*: 355).
6. *sadasatsadasadvikalpitapratipakṣaikavapurnivartanam | tamaso 'bhyupagamyate 'nyathānupapattyāpatanaikahetutā* (*Saṁkṣepaśārīraka*, IV.12). In IV.14, Sarvajñātman refers to the "expert in liberation" (*muktikovidāḥ*), which most probably denotes Vimuktātman, the author of the *Iṣṭasiddhi*.

Vimuktātman's position about *avidyānivṛtti* seems ambiguous since he upholds the *pañcamaprakārā* view in the first chapter of his *Iṣṭasiddhi*,[7] whereas in the eighth chapter he describes *avidyānivṛtti* as *anirvacanīya* or *mithyā*. In his commentary on *Iṣṭasiddhi*, called *Iṣṭasiddhi-Vivaraṇam*, Anubhūtisvarūpa takes note of this apparent contradiction and attempts to resolve it. He points out that the source of the problem lies in the interpretation of *mithyātva*. Its most commonly accepted definition, which can be easily related to one's own experience, is *jñānanivartyatvam*, i.e. something is *mithyā* if it gets sublated in the wake of right knowledge. Since this is obviously not the case with *avidyānivṛtti* as it only rises in the wake of right knowledge and does not get sublated, it indeed cannot be called *mithyā* in this sense. This is perhaps one of the reasons as to why Vimuktātman propounds the *pañcamaprakārā* view. However, *avidyānivṛtti* is also *mithyā* considering the general principle upheld by Advaitins that "something different from *Brahman*, the pure consciousness (*śuddha caitanya*), is *mithyā*."[8]

Though categorization of cessation of ignorance as a fifth form of reality is well known as the original idea of Vimuktātman, it seems he only proposed this view as a rebuttal in the context of argumentation with some other schools. As a detailed discussion on this is out of the scope of the present paper we leave it here by merely mentioning that the commentator Anubhūtisvarūpa pointed out that the *pañcamaprakārā* view, though proposed by Vimuktātman, was not dear to his heart: ". . . since *anirvacanīyatva* has been accepted in the eighth chapter and *nivṛtti* needs necessarily to being accompanied by the material cause (*upādāna*) . . . the purport is that the fifth form of *nivṛtti* is only *mithyā*."[9]

Avidyānivṛtti is Anirvacanīya

Besides these views on *avidyānivṛtti*, Dīkṣita in his *SLS* mentions another view which would have been advocated by Advaitavidyācārya, a less known exponent of Advaita Vedānta (Revathy 1990). Interestingly, to

7. *sadasatsadasadanirvacanīyaprakārebhyo hi anyaprakāraiva ajñānasya nivṛttir yuktā* (*Iṣṭasiddhi*: 85).

8. What is here paraphrased is the following inference (*anumāna*) from the *Advaitasiddhi*: *vimataṁ mithyā, dṛśyatvāt, jaḍatvāt, paricchinnatvāt, śuktirūpyavat*. Here the word *vimataḥ* denotes all those entities on whose status of reality we have doubt; it includes the aggregate of all manifest things (except the substratum *Brahman*, which is by definition unmanifest) (*Advaitasiddhi*: 30-31).

9. *aṣṭamādhyāye ca anirvācyatāṅgīkārāt, nivṛtteḥ nirupādānatvena upādānasthityaprasaṅgāc ca . . . pañcamaprakārā nivṛttiḥ mithyā ity eva rahasyam* (*Iṣṭasiddhi-Vivaraṇam*: 78).

our knowledge, the only reference to the thought of this author is found in the *SLS*. Suryanarayana Sastri is of the view that Advaitavidyācārya may have been the father of Dīkṣita (who was Dīkṣita's *guru*), Raṅgarāja Makhin, the author of works like *Advaitavidyāmukura* and *Vivaraṇadarpaṇa* (*SLS* 1935: 31). According to Advaitavidyācārya, *avidyānivṛtti* is neither identical with the Absolute nor its knowledge, nor is it a fifth kind of reality; it is *anirvacanīya*.

Dīkṣita's Discussion on Avidyānivṛtti in SLS

Beginning the fourth chapter (*caturtha-pariccheda*) of his *SLS* with the question "what is this *avidyā-nivṛttiḥ*" (*atha keyam avidyānivṛttiḥ*), Dīkṣita succinctly presents the viewpoints of different *acāryā*s on the nature of *avidyānivṛtti*. For lack of space, in what follows we present Dīkṣita's incisive analysis of two of the three views stated above:

1. *avidyānivṛtti* is identical with *ātman/Brahman*, a view which he ascribes to Maṇḍana Miśra;
2. *avidyānivṛtti* is *anirvacanīya*, which is the stand taken by Advaitavidyācārya.

AVIDYĀNIVṚTTI IS OF THE NATURE OF THE SELF (ĀTMASVARŪPA)

In his commentary on *SLS*, called *Kṛṣṇālaṁkāra*, the commentator Acyutakṛṣṇānanda-Tīrtha raises two objections against the view that *avidyānivṛtti* differs from the self (*ātman*). Firstly, if we admit *avidyānivṛtti* is a real and eternal entity (*sat*)[10] that is different from the self, we must accept the existence of a second eternal entity besides *ātman*, which amounts to admission of duality. Secondly, if *avidyānivṛtti* were to be a non-existing entity (*asat*), thus also different from the self, then it becomes meaningless to have pursuit towards knowledge, as no sane person makes any pursuit towards acquiring a non-existing entity. Starting from these considerations, the *ātmasvarūpa* stand is taken and demonstrated to be a tenable one in the view of Advaita Vedānta tenets.

10. An objection that could be raised here is that since *avidyā* is an entity having transactional/empirical reality, *avidyānivṛtti* as the "removal" or "cessation" of ignorance should also be conceived of having empirical reality. How, then, can it be identified with *ātman* (*sat-padārtha*) having an absolute/eternal reality? This objection can be handled as follows: it is not necessarily the case that both the entity (*padārtha*) and its negation/absence (*nivṛtti/abhāva*) should have the same state of reality. In technical jargon, it is described as *anyūnasattakāḥ abhāvaḥ*. In the illusion of shell taken as silver, for instance, both the entity "silver" and its knowledge have illusory reality (*prātibhāsika*) whereas the absence of silver and its knowledge have empirical reality (*vyāvahārika*, one level "up").

As is customary in the Indian philosophical tradition, objections to a given position are first raised and shown to be untenable in order to uphold one's position. Against the view that *avidyānivṛtti* is of the nature of the self (*ātmasvarūpa*), Dīkṣita states that since the self is eternal and already "achieved," it appears that any effort towards its realization can only be futile. Since *avidyānivṛtti* is ever-existent, being equated with the self, there is no ignorance to be "removed." This argument is not a new one. Other Advaitins prior to Dīkṣita, such as Sarvajñātman (in his *Saṁkṣepaśārīraka*) and later Nṛsiṁhāśrama (in his *Tattvabodhinī*, a commentary on Sarvajñātman's *Saṁkṣepaśārīraka*) also raised and addressed this objection (Veezhinathan 1994: 102). However, in this context Dīkṣita analyses the objection from a different perspective.

What is at stake in Dīkṣita's argumentation is the very pursuit of self-knowledge: since it has the ever-existent *avidyānivṛtti* as a result, this pursuit does not seem an achievable and meaningful endeavour (*sādhyatvāyogāt*). Here, Dīkṣita's commentator Acyutakṛṣṇānanda-Tīrtha mentions two instances where the pursuit of knowledge can be considered futile (*tattvajñānasya vaiyarthyam*): (1) A specific knowledge is futile because there is no *useful purpose* in gaining this knowledge; and (2) A specific knowledge is futile because the goal it seeks to achieve (*sādhya*), in this case absence of ignorance, through certain means (*sādhana*), is already achieved. In response to the first instance, Dīkṣita holds that ignorance (*avidyā*) being the main cause of undesirable ends (*anarthahetu*), it is always useful, if not essential, to aim at a better and ever refined knowledge of things. It is known from experience that knowledge comes as a handy tool in avoiding/resolving particular problems and overcoming difficult situations. Thus, the pursuit of knowledge (and more specifically, self-knowledge) certainly cannot be damned as a futile enterprise.

In order to rebut the second type of futility, Dīkṣita has recourse to a semantic analysis of the goal/result to be achieved, called *sādhya*. As detailed by the commentator, two different definitions of *sādhya* can be given, a restricted and a general one:

(a) The restricted definition (*janyatvarūpam*) is applicable only to those entities that come into existence at a certain point of time when all the required means (*sādhana*) are present together;

(b) The general definition is formulated in such a way that it includes all entities, i.e. even those *sādhya*s that exist *before* the required means (*sādhana*) are present together. This is formulated by Dīkṣita in the following manner:

yasmin sati agrimakṣaṇe yasya sattvaṁ yadvyatireke ca abhāvaḥ tat tatsādhyam,

which might be translated as follows:

> That is [also conceived to be] *sādhya* (*y*) of that (*x*), in the presence of which (*x*) that (*y*) would be present and in the absence of which (*x*) it (*y*) would be absent.[11]

In the above definition, *x* refers to the aggregate of all means (*sādhanasāmagrī*) necessary to produce the *sādhya* (*y*). We may illustrate this definition with a situation that most of us are familiar with. We all know that if a subordinate commits a mistake and comes to his boss seeking apology, then anger does not arise in the boss. Here the act of apologizing is to be conceived as the *sādhana* (*x*), and the absence of anger as the *sādhya* (*y*). In the case where there is no seeking apology, it is quite likely that the subordinate will be the victim of the anger of the boss. Hence, the act of apology (*x*) — which merely contributes to the maintenance of the absence of anger, *which was already existing before* — though it really does not produce *y*, is considered to be the *sādhana* (*x*) of the *sādhya* (*y*), i.e. the absence of anger.

Given this extended definition of *sādhya*, it seems reasonable to take *avidyānivṛtti* as a proper *sādhya*. Like apology being a means to absence of anger (which was already there), *jñāna* is a means to *avidyānivṛtti* (= *ātmasvarūpa*, which is already there). If apology were not to be tendered, absence of anger would not be maintained and anger would become manifest. Similarly, in absence of *jñāna* it is impossible to maintain absence of ignorance. Both absence of anger and absence of ignorance are appropriate *sādhya*s because in the absence of specific means, their opposite (i.e., anger and ignorance) arises. Hence, efforts to acquire knowledge are not futile as they help in shedding ignorance, indeed a very meaningful *sādhya*. Through this ingenious definition of *sādhya* that can accommodate the existing *sādhya*s as well as the ones that would be coming to existence, Dīkṣita is able to maintain that *avidyānivṛtti* is of the nature of the self.

AVIDYĀNIVṚTTI IS A PHENOMENAL ENTITY (ANIRVACANĪYA-PADĀRTHA)

Some preceptors of Advaita argue that *avidyānivṛtti* cannot be *anirvacanīya*. According to them, any entity that is *anirvacanīya* necessarily owes its existence to *avidyā* (*anirvacanīyanām avidyopādānakatvam*). Thus, if

11. The letters *x* and *y* were added by the authors for the sake of clarity.

avidyānivṛtti were to be *anirvacanīya* it would presuppose the existence of *avidyā* too. But this proves impossible because the state of liberation, characterized by *avidyānivṛtti*, would also be characterized by *avidyā*. In this case, as Dīkṣita notices, there would be contingency of non-release.[12] As noted earlier, this problem led some Advaitins to hold that *avidyānivṛtti* is a fifth form of reality. However, it is possible to avoid contingency of non-release while admitting that *avidyānivṛtti* is *anirvacanīya*, for contingency can arise only if *avidyānivṛtti continues to exist* as an indeterminable entity in the state of liberation. But this is not necessarily the case if we admit that the process of removing ignorance is *instantaneous*. In this case, *avidyānivṛtti* would not exist in the state of liberation and so also *avidyā*.

In his discussion, Dīkṣita presents the viewpoint of *avidyā* as *anirvacanīya* as that of Advaitavidyācārya. The objection raised against this view, probably worked out by Advaitavidyācārya himself and expounded here by Dīkṣita, introduces the cause-effect relationship linking *avidyā* to *avidyānivṛtti*. According to Advaita, every phenomenon is related to *avidyā* in some sense or another. Insofar as our ignorance of the true nature of reality is responsible for presenting the world as something different from *Brahman*, each and every phenomenon is said to emerge out of ignorance (*avidyā-janya*). As a phenomenal entity, *avidyānivṛtti* must have a cause and naturally its material cause (*upādānakāraṇa*) can only be *avidyā*. In this regard, two facts are noteworthy:

(a) In accordance with the conception of causation advocated by Advaitins (*satkāryavāda*), the effect pre-exists in the material cause and is thus not independent from it. As a consequence, *avidyā* and *avidyānivṛtti* are ontologically inseparable from each other;

(b) *Avidyānivṛtti*, as the process by which ignorance is *removed* at a certain point of time, is analogically equivalent to the process of destruction (*dhvaṁsa*) (say, of an entity like a pot). What is common to both is that once it occurs, it "occurs" for ever: destruction or removal does not end in time. It has to be taken to be eternal. Otherwise, we may land into trouble; that is, by accepting destruction of destruction, which is equivalent to the emergence of the entity, we may have to logically accept the birth of the same entity that was already destroyed. Since this is not tenable, we have to accept that *nivṛtti* is eternal.

---

12. *anirvācyasya sādeḥ ajñānopādānakatvaniyamena muktāv api tadupādānājñānānuvṛttyāpatteḥ* (*Siddhāntaleśasaṁgraha* 1973: 368).

From these considerations, it is argued that *avidyā*, which is inseparable from *avidyānivṛtti*, must co-exist eternally with the latter. But this everlasting state in which there is absence of ignorance is defined by Advaitins as the state of liberation, or *mokṣa*. But then the objection is that the state of liberation cannot be characterized by *avidyā*.

Against this objection, Advaitavidyācārya tries to show that *avidyānivṛtti* is an *instantaneous* process which does not perpetuate itself in the state of liberation. He does that by analysing the concept of *nivṛtti* (or *dhvaṁsa*) as analogous to that of origination (*utpatti*). According to him, origination is *instantaneous* as shown by the verbal usage commonly used with respect to origination. In the origination of a pot (*ghaṭaḥ*), for instance, three different verbs are used depending on whether we refer to its past, present or future state. At the first instant of its origination, we say that "the pot is originated" (*ghaṭaḥ utpadyate*); after its origination, we say "the pot was originated" (*ghaṭaḥ utpannaḥ*); and similarly, when we want to refer to the future origination of the pot, we say "the pot will be originated" (*ghaṭaḥ utpatsyate*). As is evident, the use of the present tense only corresponds to the first instant of the origination of the pot. This shows that origination itself is an *instantaneous* process. Otherwise, the verb *utpadyate* would continue to be used long after the pot originated, and this is not the case.[13] Consequently, what is referred to by the word *utpatti* (origination) cannot be an everlasting state but only an *instantaneous* one. The same reasoning can be applied to destruction or *nivṛtti*. A pot which is being destroyed is referred to by the expression "the pot is being destroyed" (*ghaṭaḥ nivartate*); but a pot already destroyed is referred to by "the pot was destroyed" (*ghaṭaḥ nivṛttaṁ*); and for a pot that is going to be destroyed, we say "the pot will be destroyed" (*ghaṭaḥ nivartiṣyate*). Destruction (*nivṛtti*) exists only during the last moment of existence of an object and is thus instantaneous. Otherwise, if origination and destruction were permanent, we would find usages like "the pot is now originated" (*ghaṭaḥ idānīm utpadyate*) or "the pot is now destroyed" (*ghaṭaḥ idānīm nivartate*) long after origination or destruction.[14]

---

13. *utpatteḥ prathamasamayamātra-saṁsargibhāvavikāratvavat nivṛtter api caramasamayamātra-saṁsargibhāvavikāratvopapatteḥ | ata eva yathā pūrvaṁ paścāc ca "utpatsyate" "utpannaḥ" iti bhāvibhūtabhāvena vyavahriyamāṇāyā utpatteḥ prathamasamayamātre "utpadyate" iti vartamānatvavyavahāraḥ* (*Siddhāntaleśasaṁgraha* 1973: 368).

14. *tathā pūrvaṁ paścāc ca "nivartiṣyate" "nivṛttaḥ" iti bhāvibhūtabhāvena vyavahriyamāṇāyā nivṛtteḥ caramasamayamātre "nivartate" "naśyati" "dhvaṁsate" iti vartamānatvavyapadeśaḥ | nivṛtter anuvṛttau tu ciraśakalite 'pi ghaṭe "idānīṁ nivartate" ityādi vyavahāraḥ syāt* (*Siddhāntaleśasaṁgraha* 1973: 368-69).

Dīkṣita follows this with more detailed arguments involving grammar and hermeneutics which are not covered in this paper.[15] The main point is that this argument based on a semantic analysis of verbal usage aims to show that *nivṛtti*, and by extension *avidyānivṛtti*, cannot be permanent. Consequently, *avidyānivṛtti* cannot co-exist eternally with *mokṣa* and the objection that *avidyā* co-exists with the state of liberation simply evaporates. The concept of *mokṣa* defined before remains meaningful even when the *anirvacanīya* stand is taken.

Now, given that *avidyānivṛtti* is here considered an *instantaneous* phenomenon, should we not conclude that *mokṣa* itself — which is characterized by *avidyānivṛtti* — is also an "event" taking place in time? How then can we reconcile this statement with the recognized permanent nature of *mokṣa*? This question is raised by Dīkṣita after his presentation of Advaitavidyācārya's views. He argues that though *avidyānivṛtti* is generated through right knowledge (*jñāna*), it cannot be taken as a human goal (*puruṣārtha*) in the same sense as *mokṣa*. This is because *avidyānivṛtti* differs from happiness and absence of misery. It is more appropriate to consider *avidyānivṛtti* as a *means* towards *mokṣa* rather than an end in itself (*na hy avidyānivṛttiḥ svayam eva puruṣārtha iti tasyā jñānasādhyatvam upeyate*). In turn, this implies that *mokṣa* cannot be envisaged as an "event" in time in the sense in which *avidyānivṛtti* is. Through removal of ignorance, that ignorance which is construed as obscuring the infinite bliss (*akhaṇḍānanda*) and as the root cause of all the ailments, *akhaṇḍānanda* manifests itself. Thus, Dīkṣita ends this discussion with a rather elegant description of *avidyānivṛtti* as the process by which *avidyā* is removed in the manner of a veil hiding the limitless bliss (*akhaṇḍānandāvāraka*). When the veil is removed the blissful self shines by itself, thus putting an end to all suffering. Therefore, *mokṣa* is not something to be "achieved" in some other world or "produced" through certain means: absolute reality being eternal and ever existent, liberation is the experience of the already available bliss that eternally exists beyond ignorance.[16]

Conclusion

At first sight, the two stands just discussed — *avidyānivṛtti* as *ātmasvarūpa* and *avidyānivṛtti* as *anirvacanīya* — would seem to be in stark contradiction

15. For a detailed exposition of these arguments, see Revathy 1990: 225-29.

16. In the *Vedāntaparibhāṣā* (2003: 155), liberation is described as the "attainment even of the already attained bliss and the removal even of the already removed misery. . . ." (*evaṁ prāptasyāpy ānandasya prāptiḥ, parihṛtasyāpy anarthasya nivṛttir mokṣaḥ prayojanam*)

to each other. How can *avidyānivṛtti* be identified to *ātman* while being characterized as *anirvacanīya* at the same time? However, it seems possible to resolve this apparent contradiction by way of interpreting these stands as two different and yet valid ways of understanding the nature of *avidyānivṛtti*. The first view obviously considers *avidyānivṛtti* from the viewpoint of its *result*, i.e. as absence of ignorance. Considering such absence as an entity (*vastu*), *avidyānivṛtti* can only be equated with *ātman*, which is the locus where *avidyānivṛtti* is sought and the reality underlying each and every phenomenon. The second view, transactional in nature, looks upon *avidyānivṛtti* as a *process* happening at a particular point of time leading to the discovery of the true nature of *ātman*. As a process taking place in time, it is necessarily phenomenal and thus *anirvacanīya*. As far as the essential teachings of Advaita are concerned, both standpoints are valid in their own domain because *ātman* is taken as the absolute reality in both cases.

It is well known that the corpus generated in Advaita Vedānta, particularly post-Śaṅkara, as in any other philosophical tradition, has not been without dissension and conflicts. On many theoretical issues, Advaitins among themselves have adopted different — and sometimes apparently contradictory — stands. The different conceptions of *avidyānivṛtti* held by Advaitins as discussed above, amply illustrate this point. However, there have also been attempts to clarify as to why there has been dissent, and how to appreciate the dissenting views by drawing appropriate boundaries within which a certain explanation is valid. This perhaps finds its most refined expression in works from the medieval period like Dharmarājādhvarīndra's *Vedāntaparibhāṣā*, Madhusūdana Sarasvatī's *Advaitasiddhi* and Appaya Dīkṣita's *Siddhāntaleśasaṁgraha*. In all these works, there is no attempt to promote a particular view as opposed to others. On the contrary, diversity and variety in terms of views and approaches seem to be appreciated and even encouraged. However, it must also be mentioned that in presenting diverse views, the authors have been extremely scrupulous not to compromise the basic tenets of Advaita.

What is remarkable of Appaya Dīkṣita is his extraordinary ability to present different conceptions with absolute clarity without committing himself to any specific viewpoint. In the pure spirit of Advaita Vedānta, he considers all views as basically speculative and different perspectival approaches to non-dual reality. In fact, this has been amply made clear by Dīkṣita in his preamble to *SLS* wherein he declares that "different models have been proposed by the ancients with a clear understanding that much importance need not be given to the theoretical formulations (that are essentially human constructs, and thereby bound to differ) so long as the primary purpose of recognizing the oneness of the self is achieved."[17] This comprehensive approach adopted by Dīkṣita throughout his *SLS* gets mirrored in his treatment of *avidyānivṛtti*.

17. *prācīnair vyavahārasiddhaviṣayeṣu ātmaikyasiddhau paraṁ sannahyadbhir anādarāt-saraṇayo nānāvidhā darśitāḥ* (*Siddhāntaleśasaṁgraha* 1973: 3).

Appendix

We reproduce here the section of the *Siddhāntaleśasaṁgraha* discussed in this paper (1973: 366-73):

atha keyam avidyānivṛttiḥ
ātmaiveti brahmasiddhikārāḥ | na ca tasya nitya(tvena) siddhatvāt jñānavaiyarthyam | asati jñāne anarthahetvavidyāyā vidyamānatayā anartham api tiṣṭhed iti tadanveṣaṇāt, "yasmin sati agrimakṣaṇe yasya sattvaṁ yadvyatireke ca abhāvaḥ tat tatsādhyam" iti lakṣaṇānurodhena ātmarūpāyā apy avidyānivṛtteḥ jñānasādhyatvāc ca | jñāne sati agrimakṣaṇe ātmarūpāvidyānivṛttisattvaṁ tadvyatireke tatpratiyogyavidyārūpaḥ tadabhāva iti uktalakṣaṇāsattvāt |
ātmānyaiva avidyānivṛttiḥ | sā ca na satī | advaitahāneḥ | nāpy asatī | jñānasādhyatvāyogāt | nāpi sadasadrūpā | virodhāt | nāpy anirvācyā, anirvācyasya sādeḥ ajñānopādānakatvaniyamena muktāv api tadupādānājñānānuvṛttyāpatteḥ, jñānanirvartyatvāpatteś ca | kiṁtu uktaprakāracatuṣṭayottīrṇā pañcamaprakārā iti ānandabodhācāryāḥ | avidyāvat tannivṛttir apy anirvācyaiva | na ca tadanuvṛttau tadupādānājñānasyāpy anuvṛttiniyamāt anirmokṣaprasaṁgaḥ | tadanuvṛttau pramāṇābhāvāt | utpatteḥ prathamasamayamātra-saṁsargibhāvavikāratvavat nivṛtter api caramasamayamātra-saṁsargibhāvavikāratvopapatteḥ | ata eva yathā pūrvaṁ paścāc ca "utpatsyate" "utpannaḥ" iti bhāvibhūtabhāvena vyavahriyamāṇāyā utpatteḥ prathamasamayamātre "utpadyate" iti vartamānatvavyavahāraḥ, tathā pūrvaṁ paścāc ca "nivartiṣyate" "nivṛttaḥ" iti bhāvibhūtabhāvena vyavahriyamāṇāyā nivṛtteḥ caramasamayamātre "nivartate" "naśyati" "dhvaṁsate" iti vartamānatvavyapadeśaḥ | nivṛtter anuvṛttau tu ciraśakalite 'pi ghaṭe "idānīṁ nivartate" ityādi vyavahāraḥ syāt | ākhyātānāṁ prakṛtyarthagatavartamānatvādyarthābhidhāyitvāt |
[...]
nanv evam avidyānivṛtteḥ kṣaṇikatve mokṣaḥ sthirapuruṣārtho na syād iti cet, bhrānto 'si | na hy avidyānivṛttiḥ svayam eva puruṣārtha iti tasyā jñānasādhyatvam upeyate | tasyāḥ sukhaduḥkhābhāvetaratvāt | kiṁ tu akhaṇḍānandāvārakasaṁsāra-duḥkhahetv avidyocchede akhaṇḍānandas-phuraṇaṁ saṁsāraduḥkhocchedaś ca bhavatīti tadupayogitayā tasyās tattvajñānasādhyatvam upeyate.

References

PRIMARY SOURCES

Advaitasiddhi (1997), *Advaitasiddhi of Madhusūdanasarasvatī*, ed. N.S. Ananta Krishna Sastri, New Delhi: Parimal Publications.

Brahmasiddhi (1937), *Brahmasiddhi of Maṇḍanamiśra with Commentary by Śaṅkhapāṇi*, ed. S. Kuppuswami Sastri, Chennai: Madras Government Oriental Manuscript Series.

Iṣṭasiddhi (1933), *Iṣṭasiddhi of Vimuktātman (with Jñānottama's Vivaraṇa)*, Gaekwad's Oriental Series, no. LXV, Baroda: Oriental Institute.

Iṣṭasiddhi-Vivaraṇam (2006), [1982] *A Commentary on the Iṣṭasiddhi of Vimuktātman*, Doctoral Dissertation of R. Krishnamurti Sastri, Chennai: University of Madras, Published with English translation by Adi Sankara Advaita Research Centre, Chennai.

Nyāyamakaranda (1907), *Nyāyamakaranda of Ānandabodha*, Benares: Chowkhamba Sanskrit Series, no. 38.

Saṁkṣepaśārīraka (1972), *The Saṁkṣepaśārīraka of Sarvajñātman*, ed. N. Veezhinathan, Chennai: University of Madras.

Siddhāntaleśasaṁgraha (1935), *The Siddhantaleśasaṁgraha of Appaya Dīkṣita*, Translated in English by S.S. Suryanarayana Sastri, Chennai: University of Madras.

Siddhāntaleśasaṁgraha (1973), *Śāstra-Siddhānta-Leśa-Saṁgrahaḥ of Śrīmad-Appaya-Dīkṣitendra with the Commentary Kṛṣṇālaṁkāra of Acyutakṛṣṇānanda-Tīrtha*, ed. S.R. Krishnamurti Sastri and N. Veezhinathan, Secunderabad: Prakāśana-Samiti.

Upaniṣads (1998), *The Early Upaniṣads*, Annotated text and translation by P. Olivelle, New Delhi: Munshiram Manoharlal.

Upadeśasāhasrī (2006), *A Thousand Teachings: The Upadeśasāhasrī of Śaṅkara*, tr. and ed. S. Mayeda, New Delhi: Motilal Banarsidass.

Vedāntaparibhāṣā (2003), *Vedāntaparibhāṣā of Dharmarāja Adhvarin*, ed. by S.S. Suryanarayana Sastri, Chennai: Adyar Library and Research Centre.

SECONDARY SOURCES

Kaplan, Stephen (2007), "Vidyā and Avidyā: Simultaneous and Coterminous? : A Holographic Model to Illuminate the Advaita Debate," in *Philosophy East and West*, vol. 57, no. 2, pp. 178-203.

Panda, Rabindra Kumar (1992), "Cessation of Nescience as Fifth Kind of Reality in Advaita Vedānta: An Appraisal," in *Sri Venkateswara University Oriental Journal*, vol. 35, pp. 109-17.

Revathy, S. (1990), *Three Little Known Advaitins*, Chennai: University of Madras.

Sharma, V. Anjaneya (1974), *Citsukha's Contribution to Advaita (with special reference to the Tattva-pradīpikā)*, Mysore: Kavyalaya Publishers.

Sundaram, P.K. (1968), *Advaita Epistemology with Special Reference to Iṣṭasiddhi*, Chennai: University of Madras.

Veezhinathan, N. (1994), "The Locus, Content, and Removal of Avidyā," in *The Tradition of Advaita: Essays in Honour of Bhāṣyabhāvajña V.R. Kalyāṇasundara Śāstrī*, ed. R. Balasubramanian, New Delhi: Munshiram Manoharlal.

9

The Gauḍīya Challenge to Advaita Vedānta and Classical Yoga
Re-figuring Models of Embodiment and Personhood

*Barbara A. Holdrege**

THE Gauḍīya Sampradāya, an important Vaiṣṇava *bhakti* (devotional) school inspired by the Bengali leader Caitanya (1486-1533 CE) in the sixteenth century, developed a hierarchical taxonomy of religious experience that critically assessed and ranked contending philosophical schools and *bhakti* traditions in the Indian cultural landscape in light of its own distinctive path of Kṛṣṇa *bhakti*. Caitanya himself did not leave a legacy of devotional poetry or other literary expression beyond eight verses, termed *Śikṣāṣṭaka*, that are traditionally ascribed to him. The Gauḍīya Vaiṣṇavas claim that he charged a group of his disciples known as the "six Gosvāmins of Vṛndāvana" with the task of developing a formal system of theology and practice to perpetuate the *bhakti* movement inspired by him.[1] This theology, together with the associated regimen of practices termed *sādhana-bhakti*, is articulated in five of the most important works of the Gauḍīya Sampradāya: Rūpa Gosvāmin's (*c.* 1489-1564 CE) *Bhaktirasāmṛtasindhu*,[2] *Ujjvalanīlamaṇi*, and *Laghubhāgavatāmṛta*;[3] Jīva Gosvāmin's (*c.* 1513-1608 CE) *Bhāgavata Sandarbha*, which comprises six

* Department of Religious Studies, University of California, Santa Barbara

1. For an overview of the history and works of the six Gosvāmins, see De 1961: 111-165.
2. According to Haberman (2003: xxxiii), the *Bhaktirasāmṛtasindhu* was completed in 1541. The *Bhaktirasāmṛtasindhu*, "The Ocean of the Nectar of *Bhakti-Rasa*", is divided into four quarters (*vibhāgas*) — Eastern, Southern, Western, and Northern — each of which is subdivided into chapters called "waves" (*laharīs*). References in the Notes to the *Bhaktirasāmṛtasindhu* indicate quarter (*vibhāga*), chapter (*laharī*), and verse(s).
3. References in the Notes to the *Laghubhāgavatāmṛta* indicate section (*khaṇḍa*), chapter (*pariccheda*), and verse(s).

sandarbhas;[4] and Kṛṣṇadāsa Kavirāja's (*c*. 1517-1620 CE) *Caitanya Caritāmṛta*,[5] the Bengali compendium by one of the Gosvāmins' most acclaimed disciples.[6]

The Gauḍīyas' analysis of religious experience interweaves three categories — *bhakti* (devotion); *rūpa* or *deha* (body); and *rasa* (aesthetic enjoyment) — in order to generate a distinctive new theology that I term an "embodied aesthetics of *bhakti*" in which both divine bodies and human bodies are ascribed pivotal roles not only on the path but also as integral parts of the goal of spiritual realization. In his *Bhaktirasāmṛtasindhu* and *Ujjvalanīlamaṇi*, Rūpa Gosvāmin reframes the authoritative devotional teachings of the *Bhāgavata Purāṇa* in light of Indian theories of aesthetics and produces a new form of embodied aesthetics founded on the category of *bhakti-rasa*. In Rūpa's theory of *bhakti-rasa* the aesthetic experience of *rasa* is reimagined as a transcendent religious experience and the religious experience of *bhakti* is reimagined as a transcendent aesthetic experience, and it is this transcendent aesthetic-religious experience of *bhakti-rasa* that is the culmination of the Gauḍīya path. This theory of *bhakti-rasa* is elaborated by Jīva Gosvāmin in his commentaries on Rūpa's works and in his *Bhakti Sandarbha* and *Prīti Sandarbha*. Kṛṣṇadāsa Kavirāja provides an encapsulation of the key elements of the theory in his *Caitanya Caritāmṛta*.

In his recent study of Jīva Gosvāmin's contributions to Indian philosophy, Ravi Gupta argues that Jīva, as one of the principal architects of the Gauḍīya Vaiṣṇava theological edifice, helped to construct a distinctly "Caitanya Vaiṣṇava Vedānta system of theology" by bringing into dialogue "four powerful streams of classical Hinduism: (1) the various systems of Vedānta; (2) the ecstatic *bhakti* movements; (3) the Purāṇic commentarial tradition; and (4) the aesthetic theory of Sanskrit poetics" (2007: 5). I

4. According to Brzezinski (1992: 20), the *Bhāgavata Sandarbha* was composed between 1555 and 1561. The *Bhāgavata Sandarbha* is also called *Ṣaṭ Sandarbha*, since it comprises six *sandarbhas*: *Tattva Sandarbha*, *Bhāgavat Sandarbha*, *Paramātma Sandarbha*, *Kṛṣṇa Sandarbha*, *Bhakti Sandarbha*, and *Prīti Sandarbha*. References in the Notes to the *sandarbhas* indicate section (*anuccheda*).

5. According to Dimock (1999: 31-32), the *Caitanya Caritāmṛta* was most likely completed around 1615 and Kṛṣṇadāsa Kavirāja died between 1615 and 1620. References in the Notes to the *Caitanya Caritāmṛta* indicate section (*līlā*), chapter (*pariccheda*), and verse(s) and follow the numbering convention adopted in Dimock's (1999) translation, *Caitanya Caritāmṛta of Kṛṣṇadāsa Kavirāja*, which is based on the Bengali edition of the *Caitanya Caritāmṛta* edited by Rādhāgovinda Nātha (1948–1952). All translations of the *Caitanya Caritāmṛta* are from Dimock 1999.

6. Among scholarly studies of the works of Rūpa Gosvāmin, Jīva Gosvāmin, and Kṛṣṇadāsa Kavirāja, see De 1961; Haberman 1988, 2003; Delmonico 1990; Brzezinski 1992; Dimock 1999; Gupta 2007; Stewart 2010.

would contend that this integrative tendency is evident in the Gauḍīya theology of religious experience as articulated not only by Jīva Gosvāmin but also by Rūpa Gosvāmin and Kṛṣṇadāsa Kavirāja. Moreover, I would argue that this integrative tendency is itself at times used in the service of a broader principle, which I term the principle of "superordination". Through this principle the Gauḍīyas appropriate, domesticate, and subordinate elements of the teachings propounded by competing philosophical schools and *bhakti* traditions and establish a multidimensional hierarchy of ontologies, paths, and goals in which their own distinctive form of embodied Kṛṣṇa *bhakti* is represented as the pinnacle of spiritual realization. First, they develop a *bhakti-śāstra*, a formal discourse of *bhakti*, to establish the supremacy of the *bhakti-mārga*, path of devotion, over competing paths: in particular, the *jñāna-mārga*, path of knowledge, advocated by exponents of the Advaita Vedānta of Śaṅkara (*c.* 788-820 CE), and the *yoga-mārga*, path of *yoga*, advocated by the exponents of the classical Yoga of Patañjali (*c.* 400-500 CE). Second, they deploy the rhetoric of *rasa* from Indian aesthetic theories to reimagine the *bhakti-mārga* and establish a hierarchy of modes of devotional relationship that distinguishes the Gauḍīya path of embodied aesthetics from other forms of *bhakti* propounded by competing Vaiṣṇava schools.[7]

In the following analysis, I will seek to illuminate how the early Gauḍīya authorities deploy the embodied aesthetics of *bhakti* in the service of their "theology of superordination" in order to articulate a distinctive model of embodiment and personhood and secure their claims to supremacy over the contending paths of Advaita Vedānta and classical Yoga.

Kṛṣṇa Bhakti and Contending Models of Realization

CONTENDING ONTOLOGIES

The Gauḍīya theology of religious experience is founded on an ontological hierarchy that includes a ranked assessment of the three aspects of the supreme Godhead, from lowest to highest: Brahman, Paramātman, and Bhagavān.[8] In Gauḍīya formulations these three aspects of the Godhead

7. The early Gauḍīya authorities are concerned in particular to establish a distinctive tradition-identity for the Gauḍīya *bhakta-saṅgha* in relation to the Śrī Vaiṣṇava Sampradāya founded by Rāmānuja (1017-1137 CE), the Brahma Sampradāya established by Madhva (1238-1317 CE), and the Vallabha Sampradāya founded by Vallabha (1479-1531 CE).

8. To provide a scriptural basis for their hierarchical assessment of the three aspects of the Godhead, the Gauḍīyas invoke *Bhāgavata Purāṇa* 1.2.11 and interpret the order of terms in the verse as indicating increasing ontological importance: "The →

are associated with different dimensions of embodiment. Brahman, the lowest aspect of the Godhead, is the impersonal, formless, attributeless, and undifferentiated ground of existence that is beyond the material realm of *prakṛti* and is the radiant effulgence of the absolute body of Bhagavān. Paramātman, the intermediary aspect of the Godhead, is the indwelling Self who on the macrocosmic level animates the innumerable universes, or cosmos bodies, and on the microcosmic level resides in the hearts of all *jīvas*, embodied beings. Bhagavān, the highest aspect of the Godhead, is transcosmic — beyond both the macrocosmos and the microcosmos — and is personal, possessed of infinite qualities (*guṇas*), and endowed with an absolute body (*vigraha*) that is non-material and self-luminous.[9]

The early Gauḍīya authorities invoke the declaration in *Bhāgavata Purāṇa* 1.3.28 that "Kṛṣṇa is Bhagavān himself (Bhagavān *svayam*)" in order to establish Kṛṣṇa's supreme status as *pūrṇa* Bhagavān, the full and complete Godhead, who encompasses within himself Brahman and Paramātman and is at the same time beyond both.[10] The ultimate goal of human existence is represented as the attainment of a state of realization in which the *jīva* awakens to the reality of Kṛṣṇa as *svayaṁ* Bhagavān, the supreme personal Godhead beyond Brahman, and realizes its true identity as a part (*aṁśa*) of Bhagavān. Liberated from the bondage of material

→ knowers of reality declare the ultimate reality to be that which is non-dual knowledge. It is called Brahman, Paramātman, and Bhagavān." All translations of Sanskrit texts are my own.

9. In the first seven sections (*anucchedas*) of the *Bhāgavat Sandarbha*, Jīva Gosvāmin introduces the three aspects of the Godhead, Brahman, Paramātman, and Bhagavān. He then provides an extended analysis of the nature of Bhagavān in the remaining sections of the *Bhāgavat Sandarbha* and an extended analysis of the nature of Paramātman in the *Paramātma Sandarbha*. He insists that it is not necessary to devote a separate *sandarbha* to an analysis of Brahman because the *Bhāgavat Sandarbha*, by providing a full explication of the nature of Bhagavān, simultaneously serves to clarify the nature of Brahman as an incomplete manifestation (*asamyag-āvirbhāva*) of Bhagavān. Kṛṣṇadāsa Kavirāja provides an overview of the three aspects of the Godhead — Brahman, Paramātman, and Bhagavān — in *Caitanya Caritāmṛta* 1.2.2-18; 2.20.134-137; 2.24.57-60.

10. After expounding the three aspects of the Godhead in the *Bhāgavat Sandarbha* and *Paramātma Sandarbha*, Jīva Gosvāmin's principal concern in the *Kṛṣṇa Sandarbha* is to establish Kṛṣṇa's supreme status as *pūrṇa* Bhagavān, the full and complete Godhead. For an analysis of the arguments used by Jīva Gosvāmin in the *Kṛṣṇa Sandarbha* to establish the indisputable authority of *Bhāgavata Purāṇa* 1.3.28 as the *mahā-vākya*, authoritative scriptural utterance, at the basis of all the *śāstras*, see De 1961: 316-325. *Bhāgavata Purāṇa* 1.3.28 appears at the end of the *Bhāgavata*'s account of twenty-two *avatāras* and is invoked not only by Jīva but also by Rūpa Gosvāmin and Kṛṣṇadāsa Kavirāja to establish that Kṛṣṇa, as *svayaṁ* Bhagavān, is not himself an *avatāra* but is rather the *avatārin* who is the source and container of all *avatāras*.

existence, the *jīva* enjoys the bliss of *preman*, all-consuming love for Kṛṣṇa, in an eternal relationship of *acintya-bhedābheda*, inconceivable difference-in-nondifference, with Bhagavān.

The early Gauḍīya authorities, by assigning Bhagavān, the transcosmic personal Godhead, the highest place in the ontological hierarchy and relegating Brahman and Paramātman to subordinate positions as partial aspects of Bhagavān, engage in a polemic that is aimed both implicitly and explicitly at challenging the ontologies, paths, and goals advocated by the Advaita Vedānta of Śaṅkara and the classical Yoga of Patañjali.[11]

The Advaita Vedānta of Śaṅkara is based on a monistic ontology that identifies the ultimate reality with Brahman, an impersonal unitary reality that in its essential nature is *nirguṇa*, completely devoid of attributes, and as such is described as undifferentiated (*nirviśeṣa*), non-active (*niṣkriya*), and formless (*nirākāra*). As *saguṇa* (with attributes), Brahman assumes the form of Īśvara, the personal God who manifests the phenomenal world of forms as *māyā*, an illusory appearance. Deluded by ignorance (*avidyā*), the *jīva*, empirical self, becomes enchanted by the cosmic play and mistakenly identifies with the psychophysical complex, becoming bound in *saṁsāra*, the cycle of birth and death. The goal of human existence is *mokṣa* or *mukti*, liberation from the bondage of *saṁsāra* and the fetters of embodiment, which is attained through knowledge (*jñāna* or *vidyā*) alone. When knowledge dawns the *jīva* awakens to its true nature as Ātman, the eternal, universal Self, and realizes its identity with Brahman. In this state of embodied liberation, *jīvanmukti*, the liberated sage enjoys a unitary vision of the all-pervasive effulgence of Brahman in which he sees the Self in all beings and all beings in the Self.

11. In the *Caitanya Caritāmṛta* Kṛṣṇadāsa Kavirāja recasts this polemic in the form of explicit debates in which Caitanya is portrayed as disputing and refuting exponents of Advaita Vedānta, Sāṁkhya, Pātañjala Yoga, and other philosophical schools.

> The philosophers and Mīmāṁsakas and followers of the Māyāvāda [Advaitins], and Sāṁkhyas and Pātañjalas, and followers of *smṛti* and the *purāṇas* and *āgamas* — all were vastly learned in their own *śāstras*. Prabhu [Caitanya] examined them critically and faulted the opinions of all of them. Everywhere Prabhu established the Vaiṣṇava doctrines, and no one was able to fault the doctrines of Prabhu. Being defeated one after the other, they accepted Prabhu's opinions (*Caitanya Caritāmṛta* 2.9.36-39; cf. 2.25.42-47).

Among the critiques of Advaitin doctrines in the *Caitanya Caritāmṛta*, see in particular 1.7.38-145, which portrays Caitanya engaging in a debate with a group of Advaitin *saṁnyāsins* (renunciants) in Kāśī (Benares) in which he refutes Śaṅkara's interpretation of the *Brahma-Sūtras*. For an analysis of the critiques of Śaṅkara's teachings in this passage, see Chilcott 2006: 75-79.

In refutation of the Advaitins' characterization of the ultimate reality as an impersonal, undifferentiated unitary reality that in its essential nature is without attributes, without form, and devoid of activity, the Gauḍīyas assert that, on the contrary, the highest aspect of the Godhead is personal, replete with infinite qualities (*saguṇa*), differentiated (*saviśeṣa*), possessed of innumerable energies or *śakti*s (*śaktimat*), and endowed with an absolute body (*vigraha*) that is non-material (*aprākṛta*). Moreover, in opposition to the Advaitin ontological hierarchy in which the personal God is identified with *saguṇa* Brahman and is associated with the domain of *māyā* as a lower manifestation of the impersonal *nirguṇa* Brahman, the Gauḍīyas maintain that the impersonal Brahman is itself subsumed within the supreme personal Godhead as an incomplete manifestation (*asamyag-āvirbhāva*) of Bhagavān. In the Gauḍīya perspective Brahman is simply the effulgence that shines forth from the self-luminous absolute body of Bhagavān (*tanu-bhā* or *aṅga-prabhā*). Moreover, they assert that the joy that arises from realization of the impersonal Brahman is as insignificant as a tiny puddle of water contained in a cow's hoofprint when compared to the pure ocean of bliss (*āhlāda-viśuddhābdhi*) that arises from direct visionary experience (*sākṣāt-kāra*) of Bhagavān's absolute body.[12]

The Gauḍīyas also provide a critical assessment of the dualistic ontology advanced by the classical Yoga of Patañjali, which builds upon the ontology of Sāṁkhya and posits a plurality of *puruṣa*s that are eternally distinct from *prakṛti*, primordial matter. *Puruṣa* is pure consciousness, which is the eternal, non-changing Self that is the silent, uninvolved witness of the ever-changing transformations of *prakṛti*. Bondage is caused by ignorance (*avidyā*) of *puruṣa* as distinct from *prakṛti*. The *jīva*, empirical self, mistakenly identifies with the activities of the ego, intellect, and mind, which are subtle forms of materiality, and is thereby subject to the binding influence of *prakṛti*. Liberation from bondage is attained through an eight-limbed programme of Yoga termed *aṣṭāṅga-yoga*, which includes physical and mental disciplines aimed at purifying the psychophysiology and attenuating the afflictions (*kleśa*s) and the residual karmic impressions (*saṁskāra*s) that perpetuate the cycle of rebirth. The eight-limbed programme centres on a meditation practice that culminates in *samādhi*, an enstatic experience of absorption in the Self, *puruṣa*. Through sustained practice of *aṣṭāṅga-yoga* the *yogin* ceases to identify with the fluctuations of ordinary empirical awareness (*citta-vṛtti*) and attains direct experiential

12. *Bhaktirasāmṛtasindhu* 1.1.39, citing *Haribhaktisudhodaya* 14.36; *Caitanya Caritāmṛta* 2.24.29, with *śloka* 9; 3.3.184, with *śloka* 13.

knowledge (*viveka-khyāti*) of the true nature of *puruṣa* as separate from the realm of *prakṛti* and from other *puruṣa*s. The liberated *yogin*, having become permanently established in the non-changing Self, *puruṣa*, enjoys eternal freedom in *kaivalya*, a state of absolute isolation in which identification with the dance of *prakṛti*, the ever-changing realm of embodiment, ceases.

In their hierarchical assessment of contending ontologies, the Gauḍīyas allot a higher place to the dualistic ontology of classical Yoga than to the monistic ontology of Advaita Vedānta. In the Gauḍīya perspective the Yoga school's goal of *kaivalya*, in which the *yogin* awakens to the reality of the non-changing Self, *puruṣa*, as distinct from *prakṛti* and from other *puruṣa*s, is a higher state of realization than the Advaitins' goal of *mokṣa*, in which the *jīvanmukta* awakens to the reality of the universal Self, Ātman, as identical with the distinctionless unitary reality, Brahman. The Gauḍīyas understand the Yoga school's goal of realization of *puruṣa* as pointing to the realization of *saviśeṣa* (differentiated) Paramātman, which they assert is a higher state than the realization of *nirviśeṣa* (undifferentiated) Brahman. However, while the advocates of classical Yoga are viewed as avoiding the Advaitin extreme of absolute unity, they are critiqued for indulging in the opposite extreme of absolute separation. While they are applauded for maintaining the distinctions among the plurality of *puruṣa*s — which the Gauḍīyas term *jīva*s — they are chided for failing to recognize that the individual *jīva*s are themselves parts (*aṁśa*s) of a greater all-encompassing totality: Bhagavān, who is Puruṣottama, the supreme *puruṣa*, and who subsumes within himself both differentiated Paramātman and undifferentiated Brahman as partial aspects of his totality.

CONTENDING PATHS

The Gauḍīya critiques of Advaita Vedānta and Yoga are articulated as a contestation among paths (*mārga*s) to realization in which the *bhakti-mārga* emerges victorious as the supreme path that surpasses both the *jñāna-mārga* advocated by the Advaitins and the *yoga-mārga* advocated by the exponents of classical Yoga. The early Gauḍīya authorities maintain that although those who follow the *jñāna-mārga* may realize their identity with Brahman, the lowest aspect of Kṛṣṇa, and those who follow the *yoga-mārga* may experience Paramātman, the intermediary aspect of Kṛṣṇa, neither the *jñānin* nor the *yogin* realizes the highest aspect of Kṛṣṇa as Bhagavān, the supreme personal Godhead, who is attained through the *bhakti-mārga* alone.[13] Invoking the canonical authority of the *Bhāgavata Purāṇa*, the Gauḍīyas declare that *jñāna* and *yoga*, when devoid of *bhakti*, are barren paths that cannot yield the highest fruit of realization in which one awakens to Kṛṣṇa as *svayaṁ* Bhagavān.

> The *śāstras* say: abandon *karma* and *jñāna* and *yoga*. Kṛṣṇa is controlled by *bhakti*, and by *bhakti* he should be worshiped. . . . "Only that very powerful *bhakti* toward me [Kṛṣṇa] is able to compel me; I am not [compelled by] *yoga*, *sāṁkhya*, *dharma*, Vedic study, *tapas*, or renunciation."[14]

The Gauḍīyas' hierarchical analysis of religious experience provides a striking example of what I term the "theology of superordination" in that, in contrast to a theology of supersessionism, the Gauḍīyas do not claim to *exclude* or *replace* the contending models of realization propounded by the exponents of Advaita Vedānta and classical Yoga, but rather they posit a model of realization that *incorporates* and *domesticates* the Advaitin and Yoga models by recasting them as lower levels of realization of their own all-encompassing Godhead.

CONTENDING GOALS

The Gauḍīya critiques of Advaita Vedānta and Yoga thus encompass not only the nature of their respective paths but also their formulations of the goal of human existence. The Gauḍīyas, in upholding the ideal of *acintya-bhedābheda*, inconceivable difference-in-nondifference, relegate to subordinate positions as lower levels of realization both the goal of absolute unity or identity with Brahman advanced by the Advaitins and the goal of absolute separation or isolation (*kaivalya*) advanced by the exponents of Yoga. In this context they provide a critique of the formulations of liberation, *mokṣa* or *mukti*, propounded by both schools.

Invoking the *Bhāgavata Purāṇa* as their scriptural authority, the Gauḍīyas assert that true *bhakta*s do not desire any form of liberation but rather cherish *bhakti*, selfless devotion to Kṛṣṇa, as the highest end of

13. See, for example, *Caitanya Caritāmṛta* 2.20.134-137; 2.24.57-60; 1.2.2-18. In the *Bhakti Sandarbha* Jīva Gosvāmin discusses at length the defining characteristics and practices of *bhakti* and its relationship to other paths such as the *jñāna-mārga* and the *yoga-mārga*. See, for example, *Bhakti Sandarbha* 326-328.

14. *Caitanya Caritāmṛta* 2.20.121, with *śloka* 13, which cites *Bhāgavata Purāṇa* 11.14.20. See also *Caitanya Caritāmṛta* 1.17.71, with *śloka* 5; 2.22.14-16. Jīva Gosvāmin invokes *Bhāgavata Purāṇa* 11.14.20 in *Bhakti Sandarbha* 327 in support of his arguments regarding the supremacy of the path of *bhakti* over the paths of *jñāna* and *yoga*.

human existence.[15] Among the various types of *mukti*, they disparage in particular *sāyujya*, in which one attains undifferentiated unity with the deity, for they consider it to be synonymous with the Advaitin goal of absolute unity in which one merges with the impersonal Brahman like a drop merging with the ocean.[16] In the Gauḍīya hierarchy of models of realization, the ultimate goal is not non-duality but rather union-in-difference in which some distinction between the subject (*āśraya*) and the divine object of devotion (*viṣaya*) is maintained so that the *bhakta* may enjoy eternally the bliss of *preman*, the fully mature state of supreme love for Kṛṣṇa. Having realized its true identity as an *aṁśa* of the supreme Godhead, the *jīva* savours the exhilarating sweetness of *preman* in eternal relationship with Bhagavān. Consistent with the principle of superordination, the Gauḍīyas assert that the realized *bhakta* who has attained Kṛṣṇa-*preman* is the "crest-jewel of *muktas*",[17] for although liberation is not the goal of the *bhakta*, it is the natural by-product of the perfected state of *preman*.

Bhakti-Rasa and Modes of Devotional Relationship

The Gauḍīya theology of religious experience includes a hierarchical assessment of the various modes of devotional relationship (*bhāvas*) that are cultivated

---

15. The Gauḍīyas' critical assessment of *mukti* includes an analysis of five types of liberation, which they recast from a theistic perspective as five modes of realization of the deity: *sālokya*, in which one resides in the world (*loka*) of the deity; *sārṣṭi*, in which one enjoys the powers of the deity; *sāmīpya*, in which one lives near the deity; *sārūpya*, in which one assumes a form (*rūpa*) like that of the deity; and *sāyujya*, in which one attains a state of undifferentiated unity with the deity. In support of their position the Gauḍīya authorities invoke the following verses from the *Bhāgavata Purāṇa*: "The distinguishing characteristic of unqualified *bhakti-yoga* is declared to be that devotion (*bhakti*) to the supreme Puruṣa [Kṛṣṇa] which is without motive and ceaseless. Even if *sālokya, sārṣṭi, sāmīpya, sārūpya*, and *ekatva* (unity) are offered, devotees do not accept anything except worship (*sevana*) of me. This very thing called *bhakti-yoga* is declared to be the highest end" (*Bhāgavata Purāṇa* 3.29.12-14; cf. 9.4.67). These verses are invoked by Rūpa Gosvāmin as part of his extended discussion of the glories of *bhakti* over the quest for *mukti* in *Bhaktirasāmṛtasindhu* 1.1.13-17; 1.2.22-57. Regarding the five types of *mukti*, see *Bhaktirasāmṛtasindhu* 1.1.13-15; 1.2.28; 1.2.38; 1.2.55-57; *Bhakti Sandarbha* 234; *Prīti Sandarbha* 10; *Caitanya Caritāmṛta* 2.6.236-242, with *śloka* 23; 2.9.243, with *ślokas* 24-26; 1.4.172, with *ślokas* 34-37; 2.19.149-150, with *ślokas* 22-25; 2.24.119, with *śloka* 66; 3.3.177, with *śloka* 12; 1.3.15-16. In the opening sections of the *Prīti Sandarbha*, Jīva Gosvāmin provides a critical assessment of the various types of *mukti* in relation to the ultimate goal (*prayojana*) of human existence: *prīti*, or *preman*, all-consuming love for Kṛṣṇa.
16. See, for example, *Caitanya Caritāmṛta* 2.6.236-242; 1.3.15-16; 1.5.27.
17. *Caitanya Caritāmṛta* 2.8.203.

in the *bhakti-mārga* and that find fruition in the various "flavours" through which the *bhakti-rasa* of *preman* is expressed. This conception of *bhakti-rasa* is developed by Rūpa Gosvāmin as part of his creative appropriation of the rhetoric of *rasa* derived from Indian aesthetic theories.

FROM AESTHETIC TASTE TO FLAVOURS OF BHAKTI-RASA

In Indian aesthetics the Sanskrit term *rasa*, which means "essence", "juice", "taste", or "flavour", is ascribed central importance as the pivotal term that designates aesthetic enjoyment. The aesthetic theory of *rasa* first appeared in the *Nāṭya-Śāstra* (*c.* fourth or fifth century CE), an authoritative treatise on drama attributed to Bharata. One tradition of reflection on *rasa* celebrates Abhinavagupta (tenth century CE), the eminent exponent of Kashmir Śaiva traditions, as its principal spokesman and became the dominant school of Indian aesthetics. A radically different theory of *rasa* was advanced by a second influential school of Indian aesthetics whose principal exponent was Bhoja, an eleventh-century king of Malwa (Rajasthan). It appears that Bhoja's school may have exerted a more profound influence on Rūpa Gosvāmin's theory of *bhakti-rasa* than Abhinavagupta's school.[18]

The theory of *rasa*, as originally laid out in the *Nāṭya-Śāstra*, classifies human emotions into eight fundamental types termed *sthāyi-bhāvas*, or abiding emotions — *rati* (love), *hāsa* (humour), *śoka* (sorrow), *krodha* (anger), *utsāha* (courage), *bhaya* (fear), *jugupsā* (disgust), and *vismaya* (wonder) — and elucidates the dramaturgic principles through which each of the *sthāyi-bhāvas* can be reproduced on stage and elicit the corresponding *rasa*, which will be relished by the audience as aesthetic enjoyment. The eight types of *rasa* are *śṛṅgāra* (erotic), *hāsya* (comic), *karuṇa* (tragic), *raudra* (furious), *vīra* (heroic), *bhayānaka* (terrifying), *bībhatsa* (disgusting), and *adbhuta* (wondrous). Some recensions of the *Nāṭya-Śāstra*, as well as Abhinavagupta's commentary the *Abhinavabhāratī*, add a ninth *rasa*, *śānta* (tranquil), which corresponds to a ninth *sthāyi-bhāva* called *śama* (tranquillity).

In Rūpa's theory of *bhakti-rasa*, the aesthetic experience of *rasa* is reimagined as a transcendent (*alaukika*) religious experience that is the culmination of the path of *bhakti*. The components of classical Indian aesthetics are reformulated as critical components of the divine play,

18. Among studies of the various traditions of reflection on *rasa* in classical Indian aesthetics, see De 1960; Gerow 1977; Masson and Patwardhan 1970; Ingalls, Masson, and Patwardhan 1990. For analyses of Rūpa Gosvāmin's theory of *bhakti-rasa* and its relationship to the theories of *rasa* propounded by the dominant schools of Indian aesthetics, see Delmonico 1990, 1998; Haberman 2003: xxxvi-lxvii.

Kṛṣṇa's *līlā*, that is recorded in literary form in the *Bhāgavata Purāṇa*.[19] The tenth book of the *Bhāgavata Purāṇa* recounts the divine drama through which Kṛṣṇa, the supreme Bhagavān, descends to earth and appears in the form of a cowherd boy in the area of Vraja in north India, where he unfolds his *līlā* with his fellow cowherds (*gopa*s) and cowmaidens (*gopī*s). In the Gauḍīya interpretation, this earthly *līlā*, which is represented in the *Bhāgavata* as occurring at a particular time and place in history, is understood as the manifest *līlā* (*prakaṭa līlā*) that is the terrestrial counterpart of the unmanifest *līlā* (*aprakaṭa līlā*) that goes on eternally within Bhagavān in the transcendent Vraja beyond the material realm of *prakṛti* and beyond Brahman. The various companions of Kṛṣṇa in Vraja are understood in this perspective to be his eternal associates (*parikara*s or *pārṣada*s), who participate in his essential nature and revel with him for all eternity in the unmanifest *līlā*.

In Rūpa's appropriation of *rasa* theory, the *Bhāgavata Purāṇa*'s account of Kṛṣṇa's *līlā* is recast as an aesthetic-religious drama in which Kṛṣṇa and his eternal associates in Vraja assume the roles of the central characters and the *bhakta*, the devotee of Kṛṣṇa, assumes the role of the religious aesthete (*sahṛdaya*) who relishes the divine play. This theory gives precedence to *rati*, love — and more specifically to Kṛṣṇa-*rati*, love for Kṛṣṇa — as the principal *sthāyi-bhāva*, which is savoured in the heart of the *bhakta* as the *bhakti-rasa* of *preman*, the pure transcendent enjoyment of supreme love.

According to the theory of *bhakti-rasa*, the *sthāyi-bhāva* of Kṛṣṇa-*rati* manifests in five distinct modes of devotional relationship (*bhāva*s), which find fruition in five corresponding flavours of the *bhakti-rasa* of *preman* that are ranked hierarchically, from the lowest to the highest, according to increasing degrees of intimacy: (1) *śānta*, tranquil; (2) *dāsya*, serviceful affection; (3) *sakhya*, friendship; (4) *vātsalya*, parental love; and (5) *mādhurya*, erotic love.[20] The theory of *bhakti-rasa* thus incorporates two of the nine

---

19. For an analysis of Rūpa Gosvāmin's reformulation of the components of Indian aesthetics as components of Kṛṣṇa's *līlā*, see Holdrege [2012], chapter 2.

20. Rūpa Gosvāmin discusses the five forms of primary Kṛṣṇa-*rati* in *Bhaktirasāmṛtasindhu* 2.5.6-38. He enumerates the five primary *rasa*s in *Bhaktirasāmṛtasindhu* 2.5.115. He then devotes the five chapters of the Western Quarter of the *Bhaktirasāmṛtasindhu* (3.1-3.5) to a discussion of each of these five *rasa*s. Rūpa's *Ujjvalanīlamaṇi* is devoted entirely to *mādhurya-rasa*, which he ranks as the highest in the hierarchy of primary *rasa*s. Jīva Gosvāmin, elaborating on Rūpa's aesthetics of devotion, provides an extended exposition of the five primary *rasa*s in the *Prīti Sandarbha*.

*rasa*s of classical Indian aesthetics in its hierarchy of five primary *rasas*: *śānta-rasa*, the tranquil *rasa*, which is positioned at the bottom of the hierarchy, and *śṛṅgāra-rasa* or *mādhurya-rasa*, the erotic *rasa*, which is ranked at the top of the hierarchy.[21]

The Gauḍīyas' hierarchy of *rasa*s accommodates and domesticates the contending path of the *yoga-mārga* by recasting the *yogin*'s practice of *aṣṭāṅga-yoga* and quest for experience of the non-changing Self (*puruṣa*) as a form of *śānta-rasa*, a meditative form of *bhakti* that culminates in a direct visionary experience (*sākṣāt-kāra*) of Kṛṣṇa in his four-armed form as Viṣṇu.[22] *Śānta-rasa* is relegated to the lowest rung of the hierarchy because it is devoid of any form of intimate emotional relationship with Bhagavān. The paradigmatic exemplars of the other four forms of *rasa* are the eternally perfected associates of Kṛṣṇa in Vraja: *dāsya-rasa*, the *rasa* of serviceful affection, is exemplified by Kṛṣṇa's attendants in Vraja; *sakhya-rasa*, the *rasa* of friendship, is exemplified by the *gopa*s, Kṛṣṇa's cowherd companions; *vātsalya-rasa*, the *rasa* of parental love, is exemplified by Kṛṣṇa's foster parents, Nanda and Yaśodā; and *mādhurya-rasa*, the *rasa* of erotic love, is exemplified by the *gopīs*, Kṛṣṇa's cowmaiden lovers, who are represented as the consummate embodiments of erotic-ecstatic *bhakti*. As the highest in the hierarchy of *rasas*, *mādhurya-rasa* is celebrated as the most intimate, refined, and sublime expression of *preman*.[23]

---

21. The other seven *rasa*s of Indian aesthetics are relegated to the status of secondary *rasa*s, for they are based on seven corresponding emotions (*bhāva*s) that are nourished by a contracted form of Kṛṣṇa-*rati*. Rūpa Gosvāmin discusses the seven forms of secondary Kṛṣṇa-*rati* on which the seven secondary *rasa*s are based in *Bhaktirasāmṛtasindhu* 2.5.39-72. He enumerates the seven secondary *rasa*s in *Bhaktirasāmṛtasindhu* 2.5.116 and then devotes the first seven chapters of the Northern Quarter of the *Bhaktirasāmṛtasindhu* (4.1-4.7) to a discussion of each of these seven *rasa*s. An analysis of the seven secondary *rasa*s is also included in Jīva Gosvāmin's *Prīti Sandarbha*.
22. *Bhaktirasāmṛtasindhu* 3.1.4-10; 3.1.36-42. See in particular *Bhaktirasāmṛtasindhu* 3.1.37: "That bliss (*ānanda*) which, due to the complete destruction of all ignorance, manifested in the meditative state of distinctionless (*nirvikalpa*) *samādhi* became concentrated and increased ten-millionfold when the Lord of the Yādavas [Vāsudeva Kṛṣṇa] appeared directly (*sākṣāt*) to me."
23. For references regarding the five primary *rasas*, see n. 20. For a brief discussion by Rūpa Gosvāmin of the unrivalled status of the *gopīs* as the highest in the hierarchy of *bhakta*s, see *Laghubhāgavatāmṛta* 2.1.29-46. For a recent translation and study of the *rāsa-pañcādhyāyī*, the five chapters of the tenth book of the *Bhāgavata Purāṇa* pertaining to Kṛṣṇa's *rāsa-līlā* (circle dance) with the *gopīs*, see Schweig 2005. Schweig's illuminating study draws on the works of Rūpa Gosvāmin, Jīva Gosvāmin, and Kṛṣṇadāsa Kavirāja, as well as later Gauḍīya commentators such as Viśvanātha Cakravartin (seventeenth century CE).

THE EMBODIED AESTHETICS OF BHAKTI

In the final analysis *bhakti-rasa* functions in Gauḍīya theology not simply as a *theory* of religious aesthetics but above all as a *path* to realization. In contrast to the secular aesthete, the goal of the *bhakta* is not simply to attain a temporary state of pure aesthetic enjoyment through listening to recitations of *līlā* narratives or witnessing dramatic re-enactments of *līlā* episodes on the manifest plane of human existence. Rather, the ultimate goal of the *bhakta* is to attain an eternal state of pure transcendent enjoyment through direct experiential realization of Kṛṣṇa's unmanifest *līlā* in the transcendent Vraja in which he or she enters into the divine play as an eternal protagonist. While the early Gauḍīya authorities maintain that all *jīvas* share in the essential nature of Bhagavān, at the same time they insist that each *jīva* is unique, possessing a unique inherent nature, or *svarūpa*, and a correspondingly unique *non-material* body, or *siddha-rūpa*, by means of which the *jīva* assumes a distinctive role as an eternal participant in the unmanifest *līlā*. They delimit the roles that the *jīva* may assume in the unmanifest *līlā* to the four principal modes of devotional relationship — the four flavours of *prema-rasa* — that are embodied by the paradigmatic eternally perfected associates of Kṛṣṇa who reside with him in the transcendent Vraja.

The aesthetics of *bhakti*, as formulated by Rūpa Gosvāmin and elaborated by Jīva Gosvāmin, is a path of *embodied* aesthetics that engages both the external (*aṅga*) and internal (*antar-aṅga*) aspects of the psychophysiology.[24] This path involves the fashioning of a devotional body by means of *sādhana-bhakti*, an elaborate system of embodied practices that comprises two forms of devotional discipline: *vaidhī-bhakti*, in which the *bhakta* performs external bodily practices with the *sādhaka-rūpa*, the material psychophysical complex, in order to transform the body of bondage into a body of devotion; and *rāgānugā-bhakti*, an advanced form of *sādhana-bhakti* in which the *bhakta* engages in internal meditative practices and seeks to realize the *rasa* that accords with his or her *svarūpa* — whether that of a servant, friend, elder, or lover — by becoming identified with the corresponding eternal associate. Gauḍīya formulations of the embodied aesthetics of *bhakti* culminate in the vision of an embodied state of realization in which the *bhakta* attains a *siddha-rūpa*, a perfected devotional body that is non-material (*aprākṛta*), eternal (*nitya*), and made of bliss (*ānanda*).[25]

---

24. *Bhaktirasāmṛtasindhu* 1.4.4-5.

25. The two forms of *sādhana-bhakti*, *vaidhī-bhakti* and *rāgānugā-bhakti*, are discussed in *Bhaktirasāmṛtasindhu* 1.2-1.4; *Bhakti Sandarbha* 235-340; *Caitanya Caritāmṛta* 2.22.55-96.

In Gauḍīya formulations of the embodied aesthetics of *bhakti*, the perfected *bhakta*'s internal state of enraptured devotion, *prema-rasa*, is marked on the external body in a panoply of physical signs, which in the rhetoric of *bhakti-rasa* theory are termed *sāttvika-bhāva*s. The internal ecstatic state saturates all the senses and the organs of action and erupts in spontaneous bodily manifestations such as perspiration, trembling, bristling of body hair, tears, faltering voice, and change of colour.

> It is the nature of *prema* to agitate the body and mind. . . . By the nature of *prema* the *bhakta* laughs, and cries, and sings and being mad he dances and runs here and there. Sweat, trembling, thrilling, tears, choking, pallor, madness, sadness, composure, pride, happiness, humility — in all these *bhāva*s does *prema* cause the *bhakta* to dance; he floats in the sea of the nectar of *ānanda* of Kṛṣṇa.[26]

The Gauḍīyas emphasize that while the realized *bhakta*'s consciousness, immersed in the ocean of Kṛṣṇa's *ānanda*, reverberates with the exhilarating waves of the nectar of *prema-rasa*, the *bhakta*'s physical body also thrills with the intoxicating "divine madness" (*divyonmāda*) of devotion. The transformed material body, infused with bliss, manifests an array of involuntary physical symptoms, *sāttvika-bhāva*s, that are considered the externalized manifestations of the internal ecstatic state.[27]

Re-figuring Models of Embodiment and Personhood

In the Gauḍīya Sampradāya the human body is thus a site of central significance that is ascribed a pivotal role on three levels: first, as the material psychophysical complex that is to be cultivated on the path to realization; second, as the eternal, non-material body that is to be attained in the highest state of realization; and third, as the transformed material body that is the external counterpart of the eternal body of bliss. As we have seen, the Gauḍīya theology of religious experience challenges, both implicitly and explicitly, the ontologies, paths, and goals advocated by Advaita Vedānta and classical Yoga. This theology poses additional challenges to the perspectives on embodiment and personhood promulgated by the exponents of these two philosophical schools by ascribing a critical role to the human body at every phase of the path and also, more importantly, as part of the goal of realization.

---

26. *Caitanya Caritāmṛta* 1.7.84-87; cf. *Bhaktirasāmṛtasindhu* 1.2.241.
27. For a study of the role of *divyonmāda*, the divine madness of *bhakti*, in the Gauḍīya Vaiṣṇava tradition, see McDaniel 1989: 29-85.

In both the Advaita Vedānta of Śaṅkara and the classical Yoga of Patañjali, the human body is regarded as a fundamental problem intrinsic to the human condition because it is inextricably implicated in the bondage of the material realm. The root cause of bondage is not the human body in itself but rather ignorance (*avidyā*), which causes the empirical self to assume a false notion of atomistic personal identity by mistakenly identifying with a particular material psychophysical organism. In both schools the goal of human existence is to attain a state of liberation in which the empirical self casts off false notions of personal identity and realizes its true nature as the eternal Self — Ātman-Brahman in Advaita Vedānta or *puruṣa* in classical Yoga — that in its essential nature is beyond the material realm and the fetters of embodiment associated with *saṁsāra*, the endless cycle of birth and death. The Gauḍīya Sampradāya, in contrast, ascribes central importance to both the body and the person in its constructions of the path as well as the goal of realization.

In order to highlight the distinctive approaches of the three schools — Advaita Vedānta, classical Yoga, and the Gauḍīya Sampradāya — and elucidate the relative importance ascribed to the body and the person in their respective models of realization, I will present each school's model in terms of a comparative framework that distinguishes four phases in the progression from bondage to the state of liberation or realization.

ADVAITA VEDĀNTA

Bondage. The *jīva*, empirical self, deluded by ignorance (*avidyā*), becomes bound in *saṁsāra* through its infatuated absorption in the illusory world of *māyā* and its mistaken notion of personal identity based on attachment to the psychophysical complex.

Path. The aspirant embarks on the path to liberation, *mokṣa* or *mukti*, which, as laid out by Śaṅkara, involves abandoning the accoutrements of worldly life — home, family, sexuality, food production, ritual practices, and social duties — and adopting the lifestyle of a lifelong renunciant (*saṁnyāsin*) whose sole focus is the attainment of knowledge (*jñāna* or *vidyā*) of Brahman. The renunciant adopts a regimen of practices that is designed to reconstitute the body of bondage as an ascetic body, including disciplines of celibacy aimed at restraining the sexual impulse; practices of begging and fasting aimed at minimizing food production and consumption; and meditation techniques, breathing exercises, and physical austerities aimed at disciplining the mind, senses, and bodily appetites and uprooting attachment to the psychophysical complex.

Embodied Liberation. The renunciant attains the state of embodied liberation, *jīvanmukti*, which is represented as a state of unity in which he or she awakens to his or her true nature as the universal Self, Ātman, that is identical with the undifferentiated unitary reality, Brahman. The liberated sage, established in the unitary vision of the all-pervasive Brahman, continues to maintain the body and the associated vestiges of personal identity as *leśāvidyā*, the remnant of ignorance, until the time of death.

Liberation beyond Death. At the time of death the liberated sage's body and all other vestiges of personal identity cease and the impersonal, formless, distinctionless Brahman alone remains.[28]

CLASSICAL YOGA

Bondage. The empirical self becomes ensnared in the web of afflictions, *kleśa*s, that perpetuate the bondage of *saṁsāra* — ignorance (*avidyā*), egoism (*asmitā*), attachment (*rāga*), aversion (*dveṣa*), and clinging to life (*abhiniveśa*) — and mistakenly identifies with the ever-changing material realm of *prakṛti* and the fluctuations of ordinary empirical awareness (*citta-vṛtti*).

Path. The aspirant embarks on the path to liberation, *kaivalya*, which, as laid out in Patañjali's eight-limbed programme, *aṣṭāṅga-yoga*, centres on the purification and transformation of the psychophysiology in order to attenuate the *kleśa*s and the residual karmic impressions (*saṁskāra*s) that are the root causes of bondage. The *yogin* engages in sustained practice of the eight-limbed programme of yogic practices that is designed to transform the body of bondage into a yogic body, a perfected body (*kāya-sampad*) that manifests *siddhi*s, psychophysical powers. The first four limbs involve external practices, including a series of vows of abstinence (*yama*), psychophysical disciplines (*niyama*), bodily postures (*āsana*), and breathing exercises (*prāṇāyāma*). The fifth limb involves withdrawal of the mind from external sense objects (*pratyāhāra*) in preparation for the internal practice of *saṁyama*, the threefold meditation technique that encompasses the final three limbs, comprising two phases of meditation (*dhāraṇā* and *dhyāna*) and culminating in *samādhi*, experiential absorption in the Self, *puruṣa*, which is pure consciousness.

Embodied Liberation. The *yogin* attains the state of embodied liberation, which is represented as a dualistic state of isolation, *kaivalya*, in which the *yogin* becomes permanently established in his or her essential nature

28. For analyses of Śaṅkara's perspectives on liberation and renunciation, see Fort 1998: 31-46; Nelson 1996; Sawai 1986. Among studies of Śaṅkara and classical Advaita Vedānta, see Potter 1981; Halbfass 1995; Timalsina 2009.

(*svarūpa*) as the Self, *puruṣa*, in eternal separation from *prakṛti* and from other *puruṣa*s. The liberated *yogin*, having become established in the non-changing *puruṣa*, remains eternally non-attached as the uninvolved witness of the ever-changing transformations of *prakṛti*, while at the same time he or she continues to maintain his or her perfected body until the time of death.

Liberation beyond Death. At the time of death the perfected body ceases along with all remnants of personal identity, and in this bodiless state of liberation (*videha-mukti*) the *puruṣa* alone remains as pure luminous consciousness.[29]

GAUḌĪYA SAMPRADĀYA

Advaita Vedānta and classical Yoga thus both ascribe negative valences to embodiment and personhood as inextricable parts of the "baggage" of bondage. Although the human body is ascribed a provisional role as an instrument to be disciplined or transformed on the path to realization, this instrument is dispensed with once the goal is reached. In Gauḍīya constructions, in contrast, both the body and the person are ascribed critical roles not only on the *path* but also as part of the *goal* of realization.

Bondage. The *jīva* forgets its true identity as an *aṁśa* of Bhagavān and, turning its face away from Kṛṣṇa, mistakenly identifies with the material psychophysical complex and becomes enslaved by the binding influence of Kṛṣṇa's *māyā-śakti* that governs the material realm of *prakṛti*.

Path. The aspirant turns his or her face towards Kṛṣṇa and embarks on the path to realization, becoming a *sādhaka* who follows the twofold discipline of *sādhana-bhakti*. In *vaidhī-bhakti* the *sādhaka* engages in a regimen of external bodily practices with the *sādhaka-rūpa* that is designed to reconstitute the body of bondage as a body of devotion, transforming all aspects of the material psychophysical complex — mental faculties, sense organs, and organs of action — into instruments of devotion to Bhagavān. In *rāgānugā-bhakti* the *sādhaka* engages in an advanced regimen of internal meditative practices that is designed to catalyze the realization of a *siddha-rūpa*, a perfected devotional body that is an eternal, non-material body of bliss.

---

29. Whereas earlier scholarship on the *Yoga-Sūtras* tended to interpret *kaivalya* as a bodiless state of liberation that implies death of the physical body, more recent scholars such as Chapple (1996) and Whicher (1998, 2003) have argued that the *Yoga-Sūtras* support the notion of liberation while living as an embodied being. Among T.S. Rukmani's many contributions to the study of classical Yoga, see Rukmani 1981–1989; 2001. Among other extended studies, see Whicher 1998; Larson and Bhattacharya 2008; Bryant 2009.

Embodied Realization. The *sādhaka* becomes a *samprāpta-siddha*, a perfected *bhakta* who has attained embodied realization in which the *jīva* awakens to its *svarūpa*, unique inherent nature, and *siddha-rūpa*, the unique form of its non-material body, and reclaims its role as a participant in the unmanifest *līlā* in the transcendent Vraja in eternal relationship with Bhagavān. While inwardly the realized *bhakta* remains absorbed in savouring the exhilarating nectar of *prema-rasa* with the *siddha-rūpa*, outwardly he or she continues to perform external bodily practices with the *sādhaka-rūpa*, the transformed material body, which thrills with the bliss of devotion.

Realization beyond Death. Even when the material body ceases at the time of death, the realized *jīva* maintains its non-material *personal* and *bodily* identity in the form of its unique *svarūpa* and *siddha-rūpa* in the transcendent Vraja and relishes the intoxicating streams of *prema-rasa* for all eternity in a relationship of inconceivable difference-in-nondifference with the supreme personal Godhead, Kṛṣṇa, *pūrṇa* Bhagavān.

The early Gauḍīya authorities thus engage in a critical comparative enterprise through which they generate a nuanced hierarchical taxonomy of models of realization. They begin with a threefold ranking, from the lowest to the highest — (1) absolute unity without distinction (Advaita Vedānta); (2) absolute separation in eternal distinction (classical Yoga); and (3) inconceivable difference-in-nondifference (Gauḍīya Sampradāya) — and then within the latter category they further distinguish four different flavours of devotional relationship through which one may savour union-in-difference with the deity. This theology of superordination serves as a means through which the Gauḍīyas accommodate, domesticate, and subordinate the contending models of realization promulgated by the exponents of Advaita Vedānta and classical Yoga and position their own ideal of *acintya-bhedābheda*, inconceivable difference-in-nondifference, as the pinnacle of realization. They thereby radically re-figure prevailing notions of the relationship between embodiment, personhood, and materiality on both the divine and human planes. On the one hand, they assert the existence of a supreme Godhead, Bhagavān, who is beyond the impersonal, formless Brahman and is supremely personal and possessed of an absolute non-material body. On the other hand, they maintain that the goal of human existence is for the *jīva* to awaken to its *svarūpa*, its unique inherent nature, and to realize the particular form of its *siddha-rūpa*, its eternal, non-material body made of bliss. The highest state of realization is thus represented as an eternal relationship between two *persons* — the supreme Bhagavān and the individual *jīva* — each of whom possesses an eternal, non-material *body*.

References

PRIMARY SOURCES

Bhāgavata Purāṇa (1983), *Bhāgavata Purāṇa of Kṛṣṇa Dvaipāyana Vyāsa*, ed. J.L. Shastri. Delhi: Motilal Banarsidass.

Bhāgavata Sandarbha of Jīva Gosvāmin (1951), *Śrīśrībhāgavatasandarbha*, ed. Purīdāsa Mahāśaya, 6 books in 2 vols. Vrindavan: Haridāsa Śarma.

Bhāgavata Sandarbha of Jīva Gosvāmin (1982-1986), *Śrībhāgavatasandarbha*, ed. and trans. (Hindi) Haridāsa Śāstrī, 6 vols. Vrindavan: Śrīgadādharagaurahari Press.

Bhaktirasāmṛtasindhu of Rūpa Gosvāmin (1946), *Śrīśrībhaktirasāmṛtasindhu*, ed. Purīdāsa Mahāśaya. Vrindavan: Haridāsa Śarma.

Bhaktirasāmṛtasindhu of Rūpa Gosvāmin (1981), *Śrībhaktirasāmṛtasindhu*, ed. and trans. (Hindi) Śyāmadāsa. Includes the commentaries of Jīva Gosvāmin and Viśvanātha Cakravartin. Vrindavan: Harināma Press.

Brahma-Sūtra Bhāṣya of Śaṅkara (1948), *The Brahmasūtrabhāṣya*, ed. Nārāyan Rām Ācārya, 3rd ed. Bombay: Nirṇaya Sāgar Press.

Caitanya Caritāmṛta of Kṛṣṇadāsa Kavirāja (1948–1952), *Caitanya Caritāmṛta*, ed., Rādhāgovinda Nātha, 3rd ed., 6 vols. Calcutta: Sādhanā Prakāśanī.

Kṛṣṇa Sandarbha of Jīva Gosvāmin (1986), *Śrīkṛṣṇasandarbha and Its Critical Study*, ed. Chinmayi Chatterjee. Calcutta: Jadavpur University.

Laghubhāgavatāmṛta of Rūpa Gosvāmin (1995), *Śrī Laghubhāgavatāmṛtam*, ed. and trans. (Bengali) Bhakti Vilāsa Tīrtha. Mayapur: Caitanya Maṭha.

Ujjvalanīlamaṇi of Rūpa Gosvāmin (1954), *Ujjvalanīlamaṇi*, ed. Purīdāsa Mahāśaya. Vrindavan: Haridāsa Śarma.

Ujjvalanīlamaṇi of Rūpa Gosvāmin (1985 [1932]), *Ujjvalanīlamaṇi*, ed. Durgāprasāda Dvivedi. Includes the commentaries of Jīva Gosvāmin and Viśvanātha Cakravartin. Delhi: Chaukhamba Sanskrit Pratishthan.

Yoga-Sūtras of Patañjali (1963), *Pātañjala-Yogadarśanam with Vyāsabhāṣya and Tattvavaiśāradī of Vācaspati Miśra*. Varanasi: Bharatiya Vidya Prakasana.

SECONDARY SOURCES AND ENGLISH TRANSLATIONS

Bryant, Edwin F., trans. (2009), *The Yoga-Sūtras of Patañjali*, New York: North Point Press.

Brzezinski, J.K. (1992), "Jīva Gosvāmin's Gopālacampū", Ph.D. dissertation, University of London, School of Oriental and African Studies.

Chapple, Christopher (1996), "Living Liberation in Sāṁkhya and Yoga", in *Living Liberation in Hindu Thought*, eds. Andrew O. Fort and Patricia Y. Mumme, 115-134, Albany: State University of New York Press.

Chilcott, Travis (2006), "Appropriation and Subordination of Vedic Authority in the Gauḍīya Vaiṣṇava Tradition", *Journal of Vaishnava Studies* 15, no. 1: 71-86.

De, Sushil Kumar (1960 [1923–1925]), *History of Sanskrit Poetics*, 2 vols. in 1, 2nd rev. ed., Calcutta: K.L. Mukhopadhyaya.

De, Sushil Kumar (1961 [1942]), *Early History of the Vaisnava Faith and Movement in Bengal*, 2nd ed., Calcutta: K.L. Mukhopadhyaya.

Delmonico, Neal Gorton (1990), "Sacred Rapture: A Study of the Religious Aesthetic of Rupa Gosvamin", Ph.D. dissertation, University of Chicago.

Delmonico, Neal (1998), "Sacred Rapture: The Bhakti-Rasa Theory of Rūpa Gosvāmin", *Journal of Vaiṣṇava Studies* 6, no. 1: 75-98.

Dimock, Edward C., Jr., trans. (1999), *Caitanya Caritāmṛta of Kṛṣṇadāsa Kavirāja*, ed. Tony K. Stewart, Cambridge: Harvard University Press.

Fort, Andrew O. (1998), *Jīvanmukti in Transformation: Embodied Liberation in Advaita and Neo-Vedanta*, Albany: State University of New York Press.

Gerow, Edwin (1977), *Indian Poetics*, Wiesbaden: Otto Harrassowitz.

Gupta, Ravi M. (2007), *The Caitanya Vaiṣṇava Vedānta of Jīva Gosvāmī: When Knowledge Meets Devotion*, New York: Routledge.

Haberman, David L. (1988), *Acting as a Way of Salvation: A Study of Rāgānugā Bhakti Sādhana*, New York: Oxford University Press.

Haberman, David L., trans. (2003), *The Bhaktirasāmṛtasindhu of Rūpa Gosvāmin*, New Delhi: Indira Gandhi National Centre for the Arts; Delhi: Motilal Banarsidass.

Halbfass, Wilhelm, ed. (1995), *Philology and Confrontation: Paul Hacker on Traditional and Modern Vedanta*, Albany: State University of New York Press.

Holdrege, Barbara A. ([2012]), *Bhakti and Embodiment: Fashioning Divine Bodies and Devotional Bodies in Kṛṣṇa Bhakti*, New York: Routledge.

Ingalls, Daniel H.H., Jeffrey Moussaieff Masson, and M.V. Patwardhan, trans. (1990), *The Dhvanyāloka of Ānandavardhana with the Locana of Abhinavagupta*, Cambridge: Harvard University Press.

Larson, Gerald James, and Ram Shankar Bhattacharya, eds. (2008), *Encyclopedia of Indian Philosophies*, vol. 12, *Yoga: India's Philosophy of Meditation*, Delhi: Motilal Banarsidass.

Masson, J.L., and M.V. Patwardhan (1970), *Aesthetic Rapture: The Rasādhyāya of the Nāṭyaśāstra*, 2 vols., Pune: Deccan College.

McDaniel, June (1989), *The Madness of the Saints: Ecstatic Religion in Bengal*, Chicago: University of Chicago Press.

Nelson, Lance E. (1996), "Living Liberation in Śaṅkara and Classical Advaita: Sharing the Holy Waiting of God", in *Living Liberation in Hindu Thought*, eds. Andrew O. Fort and Patricia Y. Mumme, 17-62, Albany: State University of New York Press.

Potter, Karl H., ed. (1981), *Encyclopedia of Indian Philosophies*, vol. 3, *Advaita Vedānta up to Śaṃkara and His Pupils*, Princeton: Princeton University Press.

Rukmani, T.S., trans. (1981-1989), *Yogavārttika of Vijñānabhikṣu*, 4 vols., New Delhi: Munshiram Manoharlal.

Rukmani, T.S., trans. (2001), *Yogasūtrabhāṣyavivaraṇa of Śaṅkara*, 2 vols., New Delhi: Munshiram Manoharlal.

Sawai, Yoshitsugu (1986), "Śaṅkara's Theory of Saṁnyāsa", *Journal of Indian Philosophy* 14, no. 4: 371-387.

Schweig, Graham M., trans. (2005), *Dance of Divine Love: The Rāsa-Līlā of Krishna from the Bhāgavata Purāṇa, India's Classic Sacred Love Story*, Princeton: Princeton University Press.

Stewart, Tony K. (2010), *The Final Word: The Caitanya Caritāmṛta and the Grammar of Religious Tradition*, New York: Oxford University Press.

Timalsina, Sthaneshwar (2009), *Consciousness in Indian Philosophy: The Advaita Doctrine of 'Awareness Only'*, New York: Routledge.

Whicher, Ian (1998), *The Integrity of the Yoga Darśana: A Reconsideration of Classical Yoga*, Albany: State University of New York Press.

Whicher, Ian (2003), "The Integration of Spirit (*Puruṣa*) and Matter (*Prakṛti*) in the *Yoga-Sūtra*", in *Yoga: The Indian Tradition*, eds. Ian Whicher and David Carpenter, 51-69, New York: Routledge–Curzon.

Part Three

Issues of Continuity and Compatibility

10

Saṅkarṣa-kāṇḍa
A Victim in Mīmāṁsā Madhyama-vyāyoga*

*Ashok Aklujkar***

§1.1 STORIES in which a middle brother has to face hardship or even the risk of losing life are found in Indian traditions and possibly in a few other traditions of the world. Generally, the set-up for his less than desirable lot in life is some extremely dangerous situation that befalls his family — a situation in which the family would not survive unless it accepts the wisdom of the proverb *sarva-nāśe samutpanne ardhaṁ tyajati paṇḍitaḥ* ("When everything is likely to be lost, a wise man settles for losing a part")[1] and agrees to sacrifice one of its members in order to save the

* My articles pertaining to the early history of the Mīmāṁsā, written for various Festschrifts, have not appeared in the expected sequence. The references given with '2009a,' '2009b' and '2009c' in 'Aklujkar 2009,' should, therefore, no longer contain the year specification.

My way of using hyphenation and italic typeface is explained in Aklujkar 2011: first asterisked fn.

I distinguish A. Subrahmanya Sastri and S. Subrahmanya Sastri by using the full form of the name in the case of the former and the abbreviation 'SSS' in the case of the latter. Similarly, Thangaswami Sarma and K.V. Sarma are distinguished below by employing the last name with the personal name in the case of the former and 'Sarma' without the initials in the case of the latter.

A part of the essay was presented at the 220th meeting of the American Oriental Society held at St. Louis in March 2010.

** Professor Emeritus, Department of Asian Studies, University of British Columbia

1. The intention behind this remark is unlikely to have been to say that a wise man agrees to give up control of exactly a half. First, in the specified circumstance, that man will not be in a position to dictate the terms of settlement. Secondly, if he is really wise, he will not proceed on the assumption that he must sacrifice at least a half; he will first check if the other party can be satisfied with as little a personal loss as possible.

others.[2] He is obliged to accept hardship or death in order to discharge his duty toward his family. The father, being close to the eldest brother, does not wish to lose him. The mother, being especially soft-hearted toward the youngest, does not wish to lose him. This kind of trying situation has been handled with an extraordinary mix of pathos and humor in the playlet Madhyama-vyāyoga 'Adversarial encounter or altercation[3] with the Middle One' said (by modern scholars) to have been written by Bhāsa. A Brahmin named Keśava-dāsa is going through a forest with his wife and three sons to meet Yudhiṣṭhira, the eldest of the five Pāṇḍava brothers, who have been forced by the villain Duryodhana to give up their kingdom and live in the same forest. Ghaṭotkaca, the son of the middle Pāṇḍava Bhīma and Hiḍimbā, a demoness, stops the Brahmin family and demands that one member of the family should be handed over to him for his mother's meal, subsequent to a vow involving fasting that she had just

---

2. Another proverb similar in intent is: *tyajed ekaṁ kulasyārthe grāmasyārthe kulaṁ tyajet | grāmaṁ jana-padasyārtha ātmārthe pṛthivīṁ tyajet ||* 'For the sake of the family, a person should give up one member (that is, if one's family can be saved only by sacrificing a family member, one should resign oneself to doing that). For the sake of the village, one should give up a family. For the sake of the country, one should give up a village. For the sake of the self (i.e., for self-realization), one should give up the earth.'
3. The essential characteristics of vyāyoga listed in Sanskrit texts dealing with dramaturgy are given in the following note of Janvier (1921: 35): 'A kind of dramatic representation or composition in one act, with a fictitious plot, describing some military or heroic exploit, from which the sentiment of love is excluded.' The characteristics have been serially presented in Hindi in Soma Śarmā 1992: 3-9. The same book sums them up and compares them with the characteristics attributed to other Sanskrit-Prakrit drama forms on pp. 9-18. However, neither it nor the annotated edns of the Madhyama-vyāyoga that I have been able to consult so far offer an explanation of what *vyāyoga* would mean in ordinary Sanskrit or even what the specific nature of the action, state or phenomenon meant by *vyāyoga* as a technical term of dramaturgy is. The same is the case in standard Sanskrit-English dictionaries commonly used. In the translations (=trs) of the title *Madhyama-vyāyoga,* as far as the latter member is concerned, we do not go beyond 'military spectacle play', 'a play with intense and manifold action', 'heroic play' and so on. I have tried to rectify the situation with my tr 'altercation, adversarial encounter' above. In translating thus, I have tried to remain close to the literal meanings of the constituent morphemes *vi, ā* and *yuj*. The noun *āyoga* means 'joining forth, engagement, entanglement'. With *vi,* it would mean 'a specific kind of entanglement'. The following line in the Nāṭya-śāstra (18.92) definition of vyāyoga also refers to actions and states of which the common denominator is 'forceful and competitive coming together': *yuddha-niyuddhādharṣaṇa-saṅgharṣa-kṛtaś ca kartavyaḥ.* 'The vyāyoga should be composed (as a play) associated with multi-person conflict, boxing, physical abuse or friction (in proving one's superiority).'

completed. Partly for the kind of reasoning I have already indicated and also because he is mindful of the greater good of the family, the middle son offers himself to Ghaṭotkaca and asks for a little time to purify himself in the nearby river. After a little while, Ghaṭotkaca thinks that the son is taking too long a time to finish his ablutions and repeatedly calls him to return, addressing him with the word *madhyama*. Bhīma, who is exercising nearby, thinks that someone is calling him and approaches Ghaṭotkaca and the fear-frozen Brahmin family. After he figures out what the situation is, he offers himself in the place of the Brahmin's middle son, without revealing his own identity in order to play a joke upon his son Ghaṭotkaca. When Ghaṭotkaca takes him as a captive to Hiḍimbā, she points out to him that he has brought his own father as a prospective victim. A possible tragedy is averted and the Brahmin continues his journey without losing any member of his family.

§1.2 The Saṅkarṣa-kāṇḍa (= SK), printed in the 1965 edn by S. Subrahmanya Sastri (= SSS), once occupied a position in the middle of the MS and BS (as argued in §§2.1-7 below). As in Bhāsa's (?) playlet, this madhyama too had a doublet. This doublet, called Devatā-kāṇḍa (= DK), took the position of the SK in the minds of several scholars active in the Mīmāṁsā field, approximately from the eleventh century AD to the first half of the twentieth century. The only significant doubt was whether once there really was a DK or whether one was only expected to interpret a part of the SK as a hermeneutic of deities figuring in ritual-related Vedic literature. However, regardless of how the DK was viewed, as something real or as a phantom, it was assigned to a position between the MS and the BS in several sources. Two contenders to the middle position certainly existed.

§1.3 V.A. Ramaswami Sastri (1933: 207; 1936: 102) demonstrated that the text he found in certain mss was the original SK and it was old. K.V. Sarma (1963: ix-xiv) and SSS (1965), who edited, respectively, a sūtra-pāṭha and a sūtra-pāṭha accompanied by a bhāṣya commentary (= comm), arrived at the same conclusion. Richard Lariviere (1981) further buttressed the conclusion, mainly on the basis of the texts printed by Sarma and SSS.

The evidence used by these scholars primarily consisted in the references made by Śabara and later authors in the Indian tradition. Although some 'cracks' or cases of lack of full agreement existed in the references,[4] they were rightly held to be, on the whole, accurate and

4. Under BS 3.3.42/43, Śaṅkara, Rāmānuja and Śrī-kaṇṭha cite a Saṅkarṣa or Sāṅkarṣaṇa (sūtra) with minor variation. The reading of Śaṅkara and Śrī-kaṇṭha is *nānā vā devatā, pṛthag-jñānāt*, that of Rāmānuja °*tā-pṛthaktvāt*. The sūtra was not found in the mss on →

adequate pointers to a historical truth.[5] In support of this judgment about the evidence, I would add the following: There exists an impressive agreement in the authorities named by Jaimini and Bādarāyaṇa, on the one hand, and the authorities named in the SK, on the other. The teacher convergence found in the case of the MS and BS (Aklujkar 2011: §2.15h) is not disturbed when we place SK in the middle of the pair. This fact or test strengthens the suggestion of the previously collected evidence that there is a shared intellectual milieu and a shared plan in the creation of the MS, SK and BS. It should be noted in particular that the engagement of Kāśakr̥tsna with the infrequently mentioned ācāryas Āśmarathya and Auḍulomi found in BS 1.4.20-22 is also found in SK 2.4.42, 4.2.2 and 3.1.12.

§1.4 Ramaswami Sastri was the first scholar to argue that the SK had

---

→ which SSS based his edn. This fact may be viewed as a 'crack' in the evidence.

In the particular instance, the reasons given or indicated by SSS for including the sūtra in the SK (as sūtra number 2.2.36: *nānā vā devatā pr̥thaktvāt*) are good. The pūrva-pakṣa sūtra is found in the mss. The beginning of the uttara-pakṣa sūtra (the one quoted by Śaṅkara et al.), *nānā vā*, is found in the corresponding part of Bhāskara-rāya's supplementation of the Bhāṭṭa-dīpikā. As Sarma (1963: xix) observes, the supplementation is based on the SK and D-S's comm on the SK. Further, Appayya-dīkṣita has named the adhikaraṇa *pradānādhikaraṇa*, of which name the crucial word *pradāna* exists in the Pūrva-pakṣa sūtra, recovered though it may be from D-S's comm in SSS's edn.

SSS should have considered the possibility that the part he marked as unclear, namely *buddhistho vā na ha veda* at the end of D-S's comm on the Pūrva-pakṣa sūtra, could be a remnant of D-S's comm on the reinstated uttara-pakṣa-sūtra. The content of that part, to the extent it is clear, corresponds to that of *jñāna* in Śaṅkara's and Śrī-kaṇṭha's citation of the sūtra. The particle *vā* frequently marks transition from one view to the other in the sūtra style, particularly as it is found in the MS, SK and BS. It is also present in the citation of the sūtra by Śaṅkara et al.

Such a change in SSS's presentation of the text found in the mss of D-S's comm will also take care of a possible objection along the following line: 'Could the sūtra and its D-S bhāṣya be so cleanly lost in the SK mss? Are such losses usually not accidental, leaving rough edges in the remaining text?' The suggested re-arrangement of the text matter will show that the loss is indeed accidental.

The point of the preceding paragraph further suggests that SSS would have been more justified in reconstructing the sūtra wording presumed by D-S in conformity with how Śaṅkara and Śrī-kaṇṭha cite the sūtra, as against how Rāmānuja cites it, that is, with *jñāna*. In the centuries between Śaṅkara and Rāmānuja, a word might have been lost in the copies of Śaṅkara's BS-bhāṣya available to Rāmānuja. (It is not certain that copies of the SK were available to Rāmānuja.)

5. In addition to Śabara and Śaṅkara, we have Someśvara, Hemādri, Appayya-dīkṣita and Vāsudeva-dīkṣita who quote sūtras that agree with the text found in the mss utilized by SSS. Cf. SSS 1965: 258-59. See also Sarma 1963: 16-17; Kevalānanda-sarasvatī, Mīmāṁsā-koṣa p. VII.4074.

not been irretrievably lost. This he did in 1933. He was reacting to Mohan Lal Sandal's 1925 thesis that a new middle book was being passed under the name of Jaimini by Khaṇḍa-deva and Bhāskara-rāya (approximately AD 1640-1759). Ramaswami Sastri's arguments were repeated by Sarma with minor additions. The debate has deservedly died in favor of Sastri and Sarma.

The trend to treat the SK as a separate, self-standing work seems to have begun some time after Śabara's bhāṣya was composed (not later than the fifth century AD). By the eighth-ninth century AD, the first twelve adhyāyas of Karma-, Dharma- or Pūrva-mīmāṁsā were probably being referred to with the name Dvādaśa-lakṣaṇī. When Alberuni and Abul Fazal speak of this Mīmāṁsā in the eleventh and early sixteenth century AD, respectively, they show awareness only of the contents of the first twelve adhyāyas. However, the SK was lost only in certain parts of north and south India.

SK's position in the middle

§2.1 In Aklujkar "2011: §2.1, §2.15f-h, §3.1, and §3.4," there are a few arguments, offered as the focus of the essay required, that point in the direction of why one should view the MS, SK and BS as forming a continuum. Below, I will add a few more arguments:

(a) At least in fifteen but probably in twenty-five, sūtras, the SK connects itself with the MS. Because the SK and its bhāṣya by Deva-svāmin (= D-S) have come down to us as texts damaged in transmission and because the MS with its oldest accessible comm, the one by Śabara, is yet to be critically edited, one cannot be certain in each instance that the expectation created by an SK reference is met by an MS passage. But, even when the doubtful cases are set aside, a substantial number of valid references remain. These are:[6]

SK 1.3.11 : MS 3.5.13

SK 1.3.48 : MS 10.4.14 → 10.4.25; 9.3.1?

6. SSS is inconsistent in tracing as well as specifying the references. I have made up for the deficiencies as far as I could. A few details may change when we have critical edns of the texts involved (I have indicated the relatively high probability of change in the case of the sūtra specified immediately before by using a question mark). However, the general picture presented here will not be affected.

In some cases, the sūtra numbers given by SSS do not match with the numbers in the edns accessible to me. I have indicated this fact by putting an arrow between his number and my number.

SK 1.4.6	:	MS 2.2.9 → 2.2.23
SK 2.1.31	:	MS 3.2.21
SK 2.1.65	:	MS 3.5.26
SK 2.1.80	:	MS 3.3.13
SK 2.3.37	:	MS 3.5.33, 3.7.51, or 3.8.32?
SK 3.1.4	:	MS 6.8.23?
SK 3.2.55	:	MS 4.2.2 → 4.2.17? 7.3.21
SK 3.3.1	:	MS 3.6.33
SK 3.3.13	:	MS 4.4.1
SK 3.3.21	:	MS 2.3.12 → 2.3.25
SK 3.4.20	:	MS 5.1.4
SK 4.2.15	:	MS 5.1.9 → 5.1.16
SK 4.3.8	:	MS 4.3.3

In addition to these fifteen, the probable ones are:

SK 1.3.35	:	MS 4.2.20? MS 7.3.19?
SK 2.1.58	:	MS 2.1.31; see under SK 2.1.31 above
SK 2.1.69	:	See SK 2.1.59 and SSS 1965: 250 for reasons of uncertainty.
SK 2.4.31/32	:	Should correspond to an MS discussion of direction to face in avabhr̥tha, pitr̥-yajña, etc.
SK 3.1.7	:	MS 11.3.37?
SK 3.3.28	:	Should correspond to an MS discussion of aupānuvākya or paśu-śiras.
SK 3.3.30	:	MS 2.2.28? 3.6.43? 6.2.6? 6.6.38? 10.5.65?
SK 3.3.38	:	MS 1.4.10? 3.1.5? 7.3.33?
SK 4.3.16	:	Should correspond to an MS discussion of amātva and prava[t?]tva.
SK 4.3.20	:	MS 2.1.13? 4.2.27? 12.4.3?

(b) When the passages listed in (a) are analyzed, it becomes evident that there is a deeper pattern that strengthens the case for regarding MS, SK and BS as a continuity. The last-named text uses the sentence *tad uktam* to refer to earlier sūtras (Aklujkar 2011: §2.15h). The first one also does the same in MS 5.3.9 and perhaps in MS 9.2.2. The SK, too, uses a sentence consisting of *tad* and *vyākhyāta* with a similar aim in mind. The retention of *tad* in an expression that is syntactically independent of the preceding sūtra, that is, is a sentence by itself, in all three works indicates that there was a convention to be observed in the composition of the three texts. Since this convention is insignificant in itself — the message of back-reference could have been conveyed even with some other pronoun or with a phrase like *iti uktam/vyākhyātam*, its uniform presence suggests that it is an outcome of joint planning.

(c) MS and BS use *vyākhyāta* in the following sentences:

MS 11.1.67/68 *vyākhyātaṁ tulyānāṁ yaugapadyam agr̥hyamāṇa-viśeṣāṇām,*

MS 11.4.42 *eka-dravye saṁskārāṇāṁ vyākhyātam eka karmatvam,*

BS 1.4.17-18 *jīva-mukhya-prāṇa-liṅgān neti cet tad vyākhyātam. . .,*

BS 1.4.28 *etena sarve vyākhyātā vyākhyātāḥ,*

BS 2.1.12 *etena śiṣṭāḥ parigrahā api vyākhyātāḥ,*

BS 2.3.7/8 *etena mātariśvā vyākhyātaḥ.*

In all these, *vi+ā+khyā* has the sense 'dispose of, render unfit for specific/individual treatment, be covered through some other item's coverage.'[7] The same form and sense is found in about sixty-one SK sūtras — the twenty-five mentioned above in references to the MS plus the thirty-five or thirty-six references to those statements within SK itself which occur earlier.

When the corresponding statement is found outside of the SK itself, that is, in what is viewed as someone else's work, the wording used is *tad vyākhyātam* as in BS 1.4.17-18 quoted a few lines above.

When the back-reference is internal, the form accompanying *vyākhyāta* is the instrumental singular of the pronoun *etad*, that is,

---

7. The sense is close to one of the two probable etymological meanings of the composition *vi+ā+khyā* (with *khyā* 'to notice,' *ā* + *khyā* 'to convey,' *vi* + *ākhyā* (a) 'to convey specifically' or (b) 'not to convey' (cp. *smr̥* : *vi* + *smr̥* etc.) → 'to speak off' → 'not to deem necessary for communication.'

In the past participle *vyākhyāta*, with which alone we are concerned in the present context, the final sense in (b) could have resulted also from (a): '(something) conveyed specifically' → 'something no longer needing a statement of its own.'

My point is not that there is something unexpected or unusual about the sense of *vyākhyāta* found in the MS, SK or BS. It is that a particular sense and form are found uniformly.

etena (as in BS 1.4.28, 2.1.12 and 2.3.7/8). This *etena* may be preceded by *iti* coming at the end of the sūtra proper, that is, that part of the sūtra which expresses the new proposition, thought or detail in the given context. Occasionally, *etena* is replaced by the instrumental of a stem expressing the relevant concept or action. This is evident in the following 35/36 SK sūtras: 1.1.25, 1.1.29, 1.2.15, 1.2.33, 1.3.12, 1.3.44, 1.3.46, 1.3.58, 1.4.13, 1.4.24, 1.4.30, 1.4.42, 2.1.74, 2.2.6, 2.2.28, 2.2.31, 2.4.4, 2.4.26, 2.4.28, 2.4.36, 2.4.38, 2.4.47, 2.4.50, 2.4.53,[8] 3.1.8, 3.3.21, 3.2.9, 3.2.13, 3.2.19, 3.2.46, 3.3.46, 3.4.14, 3.4.19, 4.2.29, 4.3.23, 4.4.5.[9] Again, one gets the impression that sūtra composition is being done according to a convention accepted before or during the MS-SK-BS composition.[10]

(d) Our impression is confirmed by a remark of D-S. Under SK 2.2.10, he, with respect to MS 9.3.1, asks: *nanu punar-uktam idaṁ navame vicāritatvād asya nyāyasya.* 'Is this not a repetition, since the same principle has been subjected to consideration in the ninth (adhyāya)?' The question would be uncalled for, unless D-S's perception is that there is nothing unusual in thinking of the SK as a continuation of the MS.

(e) If Kāśakr̥tsna is accepted as the author of the SK as argued in Aklujkar 2012, his chronological and/or authorial relationship with Bādarāyaṇa, under the continuum thesis, should be similar to Jaimini's. Just as the latter two refer to each other, Kāśakr̥tsna and Bādarāyaṇa should refer to each other. This expectation is met by SK 2.1.52,[11] 2.3.21, and 3.2.38 on the one hand and BS 1.4.22,

8. It seems from D-S's comm that the reading in sūtra 2.4.53 should be *vyākhyānam*. If this reading is accepted, the sūtra should not count as an instance in the present context.

9. One case with *enena* and two or three cases with *anena* are found. It is, however, possible that these minor variant readings will be replaced by *etena* when a truly critical edn is prepared.

10. In the MS, no need is likely to have been felt to distinguish between *vyākhyātam* and 'instrumental + *vyākhyātam*', because it was the first text in the triad. Just as its *uktam* cannot refer to what is going to come in the SK or BS, its *vyākhyātam* (occurring in 11.1.67/68, 11.4.42 and possibly 11.1.51) cannot refer to a sūtra work other than itself.

11. The *manyate sma* part included in the sūtra here should be transferred to the bhāṣya. Secondly, the editor should not have marked the sūtra as a Pūrva-pakṣa sūtra. The following sūtra only gives an additional reason in support of the uttara-pakṣa, and the adhikaraṇa concludes.

on the other. Furthermore, like Jaimini, the SK author, does not ever put Bādarāyaṇa in the place of a pūrva-pakṣin (Aklujkar 2011: §5.5a).

Thus, the SK text can justifiably be viewed as a participant in a schematic progression and its author as carrying out a role in the middle of a scheme adopted to present a team's views on issues in the hermeneutic of Vedic literature.[12]

§2.2 In view of the internal evidence adduced above, there is really no need of external evidence to ascertain if the SK available in SSS's edition is a part of the MS-BS complex — is a text that turns the 'MS : BS' pair into a trilogy. Nevertheless, I will summarize the external evidence here in order to facilitate the work of future researchers and to blow away any cobwebs of doubt that may still be there in the minds of some scholars.

(a) The Prapañca-hṛdaya (= PH) explicitly puts the SK between the MS and the BS.

(b) As noted in Aklujkar 2011: §2.15k, an inscription of AD 999 brought to bear on the issue by S.K. Aiyangar (1940) situates the SK after the MS and before the BS.[13]

(c) A Vṛttikāra statement cited by Rāmānuja uses the phrase *jaiminīyena ṣoḍaśakena*, which can make a sense consistent with that of other similar expressions (*ṣoḍaśa-lakṣaṇī* etc.) only if the SK is associated with the MS of Jaimini.

(d) As Lariviere (1981: 180 fns 3 and 5) reports, the designation *madhyama-mīmāṁsā* is used for the SK/DK in Sarva-mata-saṅgraha (p. 10). Vedānta-deśika's Mīmāṁsā-pādukā verse 37 and the comm Mīmāṁsā-pādukā-paritrāṇa (pp. 299-300) thereon by Varadācārya or Kumāra Vedānta-deśika employ the word *madhya-kāṇḍa* to the same effect.[14]

12. As suggested in Aklujkar 2011: §2.11 and §5.12k, we should bear in mind the possibility that the thinkers involved were not expressing their personal or real-life views but only the presuppositions needed for the specific discussion they had undertaken. These presuppositions could have become conventions or axioms because of the work carried out by their predecessors and hence may be a part of their inheritance rather than invention.

13. To judge from Lariviere 1981: 179 fn 4, the content of the following publication seems to be the same as the article I have mentioned here: Aiyangar, S.K. 1936. 'Editorial.' *Journal of Indian History* 15, pt. 2: 261-64.

14. (a) For simplicity of statement, I assume here that even when the DK is mentioned in some of these texts it is really the SK that is meant. A logically independent justification for my assumption ('untenability of the view that a separate DK text →

(e) The sixteenth-century work Prasthāna-bheda (p. 11) authored by Madhu-sūdana-sarasvatī puts the SK in the middle as a part of the Karma-mīmāṁsā; cf. Lariviere 1981: 182.

(f) Bhāskara-rāya's seventeenth-eighteenth century comm, completing Khaṇḍa-deva's comm on the MS, deals with the SK as the concluding section of the MS, consisting of twelve adhyāyas, and accordingly numbers the four SK adhyāyas as MS 13-16.[15]

Thus, it cannot be doubted that the SK belongs to the pair that the MS and BS form, that it presupposes a position in the middle of the pair and that, in content as well as its perceived mission, it is closer to the MS than to the BS (cf. the evidence above in this section and in §3.11 and §3.14 below, although I have mentioned the evidence there for other purposes).

§2.3 As my use of 'SK/DK' in §2.2d indicates, a small part of the preceding evidence may be viewed as compromised — as losing its force, because of the confusion or ambiguity created by the talk of another claimant to the middle position or by the description of the SK as DK. The use is an admission of the fact, discussed at length in the 1981 and 1989 articles of Lariviere and Kanazawa, respectively, that we cannot easily reconcile all the references that have been made to the SK or to Madhyama-mīmāṁsā. Some seem to make sense only if the SK's identity with a DK is presumed or a DK different from the SK but capable of fitting between the MS and BS is thought to have existed at one time.[16]

An easy way to take care of this counter-consideration will be to point out that the references presuming the identity of the SK with a DK come from relatively late authors and are, therefore, not as reliable as the

→ going beyond 3-4 sūtras once circulated') is given in §§ 2.4-7.

(b) *Pūrva-mīmāṁsā, Madhyama-mīmāṁsā* and *Uttara-mīmāṁsā* would form one way in which the text continuum with which we are concerned can be described.

If Parpola's (1981) proposal that the terms *PM* and *UM* owe their origin to the fact that the Mīmāṁsā-sūtras were originally thought to be a continuous text having two major divisions is accepted, then *Madhyama-mīmāṁsā* would fit even better. The situation will be comparable to that of the Brahmāṇḍa-purāṇa, which has a Pūrva-bhāga, Madhyama-bhāga and Uttara-bhāga.

15. This alternative way of numbering the adhyāyas could have predated Bhāskara-rāya, since the usage *jaiminīya ṣoḍaśaka* probably goes back to Upavarṣa's time. The SK sūtra-pāṭha mss used by Sarma and SSS and the D-S bhāṣya mss used by SSS, however, number the SK adhyāyas from 1 to 4. Preferring Bhāskara-rāya's numbering, A. Subrahmanya Sastri (1961: Preface p. ii), on the other hand, employs the clause: '. . . SK, which forms chapters 13 to 16 of Mīmāṁsā . . .'

16. Recall also the possible objection arising out of how Śaṅkara, Śrī-kaṇṭha and Rāmānuja cite an SK sūtra. This objection is dealt with in my note 4 above.

other references speaking of the SK as a part falling between the MS and BS. This way implies a confusion or lack of accurate knowledge on the part of the later authors, which confusion or lack is generally more likely than a confusion or lack on the part of authors close in time to the subject. 'Sources of our information usually become less numerous, thinner or more contaminated as time passes by' is what we normally (and in most cases justifiably) presuppose.

As for sources becoming less numerous, we have evidence of scarcity of copies of the SK text. The author of the PH does not speak about the work as one having access to it would. Vedānta-deśika leaves no doubt that the work had not come to his sight. Almost certainly Madhu-sūdana-sarasvatī, too, did not ever see it, for he indicates his inability to specify its contents. Rāja-cūḍā-maṇi-dīkṣita probably managed to study only the first adhyāya (cf. Sarma 1963: xix-xx).

The nature of the later references is also worth noting. A slipped-in identification is found in the PH (surmised to have been composed in the eleventh century AD or a little later). An explicitly acknowledged problem regarding identity is raised in the time of Vedānta-deśika (*c.* AD 1268-1369). A serious effort to make sense of the identification is made in the time of Appayya-dīkṣita (sixteenth century AD).[17] Therefore, we can justifiably hold that we have evidence of the gradual spread of a wrong view.

§2.4 Ordinarily, such a commonsensical hypothesis, namely that the later sources of our information are confused or are under-informed, should be adequate to account for the (mistaken) identification of the SK with the DK. However, the hypothesis has so far not been advanced as far as I know. In its place, we find pronouncements like the following (A. Subrahmanya Sastri 1961: Preface, p. ii): 'This [= SK] is also called DK in view of the discussions regarding deities conducted herein in many adhikaraṇas' and (corresponding section of the same scholar's Sanskrit introduction, Bhūmikā, p. 5): . . . *kvacid devatā-vicāreṇa devatā-kāṇḍam iti cābhiyuktānāṁ vyavahāraḥ prāvartiṣṭa.* SSS, who edited the SK, also arrives at the same solution.

The preceding half-hearted solution has its origin in Appayya-dīkṣita's Brahma-sūtra-kalpa-taru-parimala (Aklujkar 2012: §2.2). It is understandable in Appayya-dīkṣita's time, since he could not have pieced together the indications as I have above because of the modern facilities

17. The relevant PH passage is cited in full and translated in Aklujkar 2009: §2.1. Vedānta-deśika's and Appayya-dīkṣita's remarks are specified in Aklujkar 2012: §§1.2-6, §2.2.

available to me. However, modern paṇḍitas like the two Subrahmanya Sastris were aware of most of the evidence. They could have gone to the full extent involved in saying that the DK tradition is not or does not seem original or authentic. If I may articulate an 'educated guess', they have tried to accommodate the later DK or DK/SK tradition formed by the statements of later authors, fewer in number, for the following three reasons:

(a) There exist some references to the DK where a few short texts in sūtra style, which could plausibly be its parts, are cited.[18] No scholar has so far been able to trace those sūtras to any known work. If a work with a distinctive name existed and what seem like its parts are not found in the present SK, then that work with the distinctive name must have been different from the SK. It too must have been eligible for a place between the MS and BS. We cannot arbitrarily privilege one over the other.

(b) The difference of view about the reality or physicality of devatās between Jaimini and Bādarāyaṇa is well-recorded in the Mīmāṁsā-Vedānta literature. On the other hand, there is the tradition that the two Mīmāṁsās — Karma- (or Tantra-)mīmāṁsā and Brahma-mīmāṁsā (or Vedānta) or Pūrva-mīmāṁsā and Uttara-mīmāṁsā — form one śāstra. A third text that discusses deities or upāsanās directed to a deity would serve to effect a transition from the PM to the UM and would fit well between the MS and BS.[19]

(c) Those who make references to the DK or view the SK as devoting a significant space to the deities were scholars of high stature known for their moral integrity and/or spiritual achievements. They could not have informed us wrongly.

§2.5 Of these, the first alone is an objective reason. However, it turns out to be not so strong when we take into consideration the fact that the references to the DK come from later authors and the passages cited as

---

18. Kanazawa 1989: 35: 'a work from which *sa viṣṇur āha hi* is quoted together with the designation Deva-śāstra in Madhva's Anuvyākhyāna . . . this Deva-śāstra would seem to begin according to the commentator Jaya-tīrtha . . . with *athāto daivī (jijñāsa?)* and, following *sa viṣṇur āha hi*, to end with *tam brahemty ācakṣate*. . . . According to Sarma, these [latter] two were preceded by a sūtra reading *ante harau tad-darśanāt*.'

19. See Kanazawa 1989: 36-37 for passages from Vedānta-deśika and Rāghava-bhaṭṭa indicating analogous reasoning and Aklujkar 2012: §1.8 notes 31-33 for a discussion of the textual problems associated with the passage from Vedānta-deśika.

coming from the DK have a connection with the Mādhva tradition, which is known to carry within itself passages that find no corroboration in the mainstream versions of the specified texts (e.g., the *Mahābhārata*) mentioned as sources in the passages (cf. Mesquita 1997). This particular tradition has consequently been accused of uncritical acceptance of contemporary or near-contemporary sources and even of generation of self-serving testimony.[20] Even if the accusation is set aside, one cannot be certain that if a gap of the kind specified in (b) was perceived, an attempt to fill it was not made in some theistic schools. An uncritical acceptance could have occurred, especially at a time when the means for locating all relevant mss and determining their relative reliability were quite limited.

§2.6 Whatever be the origin of the sūtras said to come from the DK or the Madhyama-mīmāṁsā, there is no reason why a person venerable in one area should not be fallible in another — could not have made a mistake in a domain of learning with which he was only casually, temporarily or superficially engaged. Even while having great respect for the reference makers concerned, one should be willing to follow the maxim 'No one knows everything.' This should all the more be the case when even a great scholar and spiritual figure like Vedānta-deśika does not hesitate to show his uncertainty about the Vṛttikāra meant by Rāmānuja, about the authorship of the SK or about the contents of the SK. We should also be mindful of the reality that an inaccurate judgment can result from various causes. It need not necessarily come from inferiority of intelligence, absence of honesty or a less-than-noble motive. The sheer fact that pre-

20. (a) In contrast to what I have advocated here, Kanazawa (1989: 34) takes the following position: 'Even on the basis of the material that has been made available to date, the present writer is of the opinion that it should be considered that there definitely did exist a work called the SK, Saṅkarṣaṇa-k[āṇḍa], Devatā-k[āṇḍa] or Upāsanā-k[āṇḍa] other than the present SK.' I wonder if he would have taken this position if he would have been aware of the points made in §§2.3-5. One should also note the 'Hari : Viṣṇu' variation in the paltry evidence of four sūtras coming from more than one source.

(b) There could have been more than one attempt to bridge the distance that was perceived to exist between the MS and the BS or to meet the needs of the Bhakti communities. The attempt may not always have been in the form of writing a new text. Pre-existing texts like the Nārada-bhakti-sūtra or Śāṇḍilya-bhakti-sūtra could also have been simply recognized with different names or adapted to new needs with some changes.

(c) We need to bear in mind that particularly the authors who speak of a text like Saṅkarṣaṇa-kāṇḍa/sūtra or Upāsanā-kāṇḍa/sūtra without giving any indication of first-hand acquaintance with it could have been misled by ms corruption or by what they learned from their source.

modern scholars did not have access to as many far-flung sources as we have suffices as a reason if we get the impression, on solid objective grounds, that a particular piece of information coming from them does not seem right. There should, therefore, be no hesitation in saying that those reference makers who wavered between the SK and the DK or unequivocally accepted the DK as a book between the MS and the BS went wrong or that, if an attempt was made to introduce a link between the MS and BS by writing a new text, it was just that, not a recovery of an earlier historical entity. Such a statement would not imply that the reference makers were not worthy of trust or reverence in other respects.

§2.7 To proceed further, an attempt like Appayya-dīkṣita's, which tries to reconcile two names for the same text, is not convincing. It is understandable in its time and must be commended for the effort it makes to collect evidence from the text itself (which is what a good historian tries to do), but ultimately it does not succeed.

In its engagement with the devatās, the SK is not much different from the MS. It has 27 sūtras in which the word *devatā* appears: 1.1.5, 1.2.33, 1.3.2, 1.3.45, 1.3.50, 1.3.58, 2.1.18, 2.1.21, 2.2.36, 2.3.3, 2.3.5, 2.3.19, 2.3.23, 2.4.1, 2.4.3, 2.4.39, 3.2.20, 3.3.7, 3.3.11, 4.2.14, 4.2.16, 4.3.9, 4.3.16, 4.4.5, 4.4.11, 4.4.13, 4.4.16. The MS has 49 sūtras mentioning the devatā concept: 2.1.13, 2.1.14, 3.2.13, 3.2.28, 3.2.40, 3.2.41, 3.3.41, 4.2.27, 5.4.19, 5.4.21, 6.3.18, 6.3.19, 6.4.29, 6.5.17, 8.1.34, 8.2.10, 8.3.2, 9.1.4, 9.1.6, 9.1.9, 9.3.32, 9.3.34, 9.3.35, 9.3.37, 9.3.41, 9.3.43, 9.4.60, 10.1.17, 10.1.29, 10.1.33, 10.4.31, 10.4.34, 10.4.48, 10.4.49, 10.7.46, 10.8.43, 10.8.49, 10.8.52, 11.1.51, 11.2.9, 11.2.24, 11.2.32, 11.3.54, 11.4.30, 12.2.9, 12.2.18, 12.2.19, 12.4.3, 12.4.18. Even if allowance were made for the larger size of the MS, it would remain justifiable to hold that the MS has not left a vacuum for the filling of which an SK devoted to devatās was needed.

Nor is any difference of the expected kind detected between the SK treatment of the devatās and the MS treatment of the same. Both treatments remain particularistic (concerned with specific rites and passages) and occasional. The SK contains nothing that addresses the devatā concept in general, let alone advance a concept that would take Jaimini's (real-life or theoretically adopted) view closer to Bādarāyaṇa's — would link or harmonize the thinking of the two munis regarding the devatās.[21] In the SK chapters 1.4, 3.1, 3.4 and 4.1, the word *devatā* does not

21. Bādarāyaṇa uses *devatā* only in BS 1.2.27/28 and *deva* in 2.1.25.

even appear. The sūtras in which it appears are almost never followed by sūtras continuing the discussion.[22]

§2.8 The middle son in the Madhyama-vyāyoga, although not unloved by his parents, does not get such love as the elder son gets from the father or the younger son from the mother. The SK, occupying a middle position in the scheme of ancient India's two most well-known hermeneutical texts, does not receive whole-hearted acceptance from the Karma-mīmāṁsā camp or the Vaiṣṇava-bhakti camp. Yet, the connection between the MS and the SK edited by SSS is so integral and so widely based (all across the four adhyāyas of the latter as shown in §2.1 above) that we should not hesitate to accept it as the original and genuine link between the MS and the BS — closer to the former, and hence a part of Karma-mīmāṁsā, but not without attachment to the latter and the Brahma-mīmāṁsā in it.

Endangered existence of the SK and its comms

§3.1 The middle brother takes too long a time to come back from his ablutions according to Ghaṭotkaca in the Madhyama-vyāyoga. The SK has resurfaced after being inaccessible or being only partially accessible for at least seven hundred years. Why did it not enjoy as good a life as the other Mīmāṁsā texts?

Before I attempt an answer, I should clarify that among the śāstra texts the Pūrva-mīmāṁsā seems to have faired particularly badly. The SK is not the only text that went out of common currency. Seminal texts that we know were available to scholars approximately until about AD 1000 (Kumārila's Bṛhaṭ-ṭīkā, Prabhākara's Vivaraṇa etc.) have gone into oblivion. It does not seem likely at all at present that they will ever come to our hand. On this background, perhaps the SK and its bhāṣya by D-S should be said to be fortunate.

The main reason of loss or near loss must be common to all the texts I have mentioned. As the entry of Islam in India changed the extent and nature of support for Brahmanical learning, approximately in the second

22. The following wording of Belvalkar (1927: 166) gives too much prominence to the devatās: '. . . the Saṅkarṣa-kāṇḍa which deals with the devatās and kindred topics . . .' The text edited by SSS is not known to have been accessible to Belvalkar. Bhāskara-rāya's complementation of the Bhāṭṭa-dīpikā, which was available to Belvalkar does not come across as primarily concerned with the devatās. If the devatā prominence was as easy to arrive at as Belvalkar's comment may lead one to believe, scholars like Appayya-dīkṣita would not have made the effort they made to demonstrate the SK's concern with devatās.

millennium AD, the ritual and public or communal side of Brahmanism lost more ground than the basic educational (Vyākaraṇa etc.) and practical (Āyur-veda etc.) side. The PM, which might not ever have been as widely studied a subject as Vyākaraṇa, Āyur-veda etc. had to give up more ground than the other branches of systematic knowledge. In the unfolding of this main causal factor, a text like the SK was particularly vulnerable. It did not have the same utility range and hence the same potential for survival as the MS and BS (particularly the latter). Being more like a set of notes added to the MS, it could only be studied if the MS was studied.[23]

To speak of these plausible reasons is not to deny the possibility of other reasons for loss and damage, such as chance, absence of adequate care extended to mss etc. One cannot prove that they did not have a part to play.

§3.2 In addition to D-S, whom I have mentioned above as occasions arose, we get the names of Bodhāyana, Upavarṣa, Bhava-dāsa, Śabara, Govinda or Govindopādhyāya, Rāja-cūḍāmaṇi-dīkṣita and Bhāskara-rāya (or Bhāskarārya, Bhāskara-rāya-makhin) as the names of SK commentators in our sources. Their relative chronology is reflected in the order I have adopted in mentioning the names. As will be pointed out in §§3.8-10 below, there should be no hesitation to place D-S between Upavarṣa and Bhava-dāsa.

§3.3 Saṅkarṣaṇa is mentioned as a commentator in the PH (see Aklujkar 2009: §2.1 for the relevant passage and its tr). According to Lariviere (1981: 184 fn 24; 190), the Sarva-mata-saṅgraha does the same, and Narasiṁhācārya (1945: lxii-lxiii), whose work is not accessible to me, even uses the attestation of Saṅkarṣaṇa as a commentator to explain the name *SK*. Lariviere rightly rejects Narasiṁhācārya's explanation as 'pure conjecture' and attaches the label 'conjecture' also to the mention of Saṅkarṣaṇa in the PH and the Sarva-mata-saṅgraha. It would have been better if he had added that there are no known instances of a commentator giving his name to a commentandum (inadvertently an error in attribution may occur in ms transmission or cataloguing). Whether the reference to Saṅkarṣaṇa (through the secondary form *sāṅkarṣaṇa* in some edns) in Rāmānuja's Śrī-bhāṣya (3.3.42) is a corruption of *saṅkarṣa* needs to be made

23. The description of the BS, which consists of four adhyāyas, as a part of an eight-adhyāya text — as an aṣṭādhyāyī, consisting of four adhyāyas of the Devatā-kāṇḍa (= SK) and four adhyāyas of the Jñāna-kāṇḍa — that is given in the Sarva-siddhānta-saṅgraha verses 20-21 (discussed in §3.12 below) has very little, if any, support in other texts.

definite through a genuine critical edn.[24] My view is that a corruption has indeed occurred. The obscure *saṅkarṣa* is very likely to be mistaken for the well-known *saṅkarṣaṇa*, especially in Viśiṣṭādvaita, in which the latter word occurs many times as that of a vyūha personality.

§3.4 Another ghost commentator is Bhava-svāmin. He may be a historically verifiable commentator in the case of other texts, but in the case of the SK his name has arisen out of a conflation of *bhava-dāsa* and *deva-svāmin* in Appayya-dīkṣita's Kalpa-taru-parimala. The passage Appayya cites under the name of Bhava-svāmin is actually found in D-S's work under SK 2.2.37 (cf. SSS 1965: iii).

§3.5 The PH speaks of the comms of Bodhāyana and Upavarṣa as extending from the MS to BS, with the SK in between. That of the MS is said to have been increasingly shortened by Upavarṣa, D-S, and Śabara. Upavarṣa may have given a similar treatment to the BS, but there is no articulation of this possibility in the surviving literature explored for the history of the Mīmāṁsās. His successors — we are informed by the PH — did not comment on the BS. D-S stopped with the SK, and Śabara probably planned to do the same. The PH associates Bhava-dāsa, too, with the Jaiminīya only, which adjective contextually includes the MS and SK. However, it seems from the way the PH statement is placed and worded (see Aklujkar 2009: §2.1) that Bhava-dāsa did not participate in the process of making abridgements of Bodhāyana, although Aiyangar (1940: 2) thinks that he did.

§3.6 Bodhāyana's comm seems to have gone out of currency even before the time of Śaṅkara (Śaṅkarācārya or Ādiśaṅkara, not later than the early ninth century AD). Upavarṣa's is likely to have survived at least in parts up to Rāmānuja's time (Aklujkar 2009: §§3.3-4). He (i.e., Upavarṣa) may have acquired the epithet *kr̥ta-koṭi* in recognition of his achievement of creating a shorter recast of Bodhāyana's massive work from 'end-to-end',[25] probably with some significant contribution of original thought in

24. The Melkote edn. is better and more useful but not exactly critical. It does not classify the relatively few mss it uses or ascertain their relative reliability. It does not consistently try to determine the readings presupposed by the commentators nearer to Rāmānuja in time.

25. The PH (eleventh century AD or later) applies the designation *kr̥ta-koṭi* to Bodhāyana's comm. This conflicts with the application of that designation to Upavarṣa in the Saṁyami-nāma-mālā (*hāla-bhūtis tūpavarṣaḥ kr̥ta-koṭi-kaviś ca saḥ*) and Yādava-prakāśa's Vaijayantī lexicon (*upavarṣo hāla-bhūtiḥ kr̥ta-koṭir ayācitaṁ.* We should rely on the latter sources, since they corroborate each other. Also, the context in which a view is attributed to Kr̥ta-koṭi in Sucarita-miśra's Kāśikā on →

between. When the terms *vṛttikāra* and *vṛtti* are used without any qualification in the relatively early Pūrva- and Uttara-mīmāṁsā texts, they almost invariably stand for Upavarṣa and his comm. Bhava-dāsa's work has been referred to as *vṛtty-antara* in the few references that are made to it. He and Śabara probably made original contributions while commenting on certain parts of the MS, since some of their views have attracted critical comment.

§3.7 There is no reason to doubt that the SK comm SSS has edited is D-S's work. The colophons of pādas 1.3, 2.4, 3.1, 3.2, 3.3 and 4.4 contain D-S's name. A reference by Hemādri (SSS 1965: 260) contains the words *saṅkarṣa* and *deva-svāmin* and can be related to the comm printed under SK 3.1.7. Appayya-dīkṣita's reference with *saṅkarṣa* and *bhava-svāmin*, which must be an oversight on Appayya's part or a ms corruption for *deva-svāmin* (cf. SSS 1965: iii), tallies with the comm on SK 2.2.37.

We learn from the PH that Śabara followed D-S. If this indeed is the case, there should be some reflection of D-S in Śabara's work. This expectation is fulfilled by the printed D-S bhāṣya. It shows affinities of expression with Śabara's bhāṣya. These go beyond the technical and other expected vocabulary of the śāstra under discussion. In other words, they are not due only to the force of the context. For example, use of only the verbal form *manyate* or *manyate sma* when a sūtra contains an ācārya name is found in D-S 1.1.11, 2.1.52, 2.3.21, 2.4.41 etc. as well as in Śabara 6.3.4 etc. In such instances, Śabara can be thought of as retaining sentences from D-S, without ruling out the possibility that elsewhere he changed them when necessary.

§3.8 An early dating of D-S necessitates a reconsideration of the statements of researchers that identify the SK D-S with the D-S who commented on the Āśvalāyana-gṛhya-sūtra and is also said to have commented on the Āśvalāyana-śrauta-sūtra and Baudhāyana-śrauta-sūtra and to have composed a digest of Smṛtis.[26] P.V. Kane (1975: p. I.2: 281) and the scholars who have followed him place this other D-S at the close

→ Kumārila-bhaṭṭa's Śloka-vārttika is similar to the one in which a view is attributed to Vṛttikāra or Upavarṣa in other texts (see Aiyangar 1928: 65 for the evidence; his conclusion should have been different).

26. Ramaswami Sastri (1933: 294) proposes the identity of our D-S with the Āśvalāyana-gṛhya-sūtra commentator. In his later publication (1936: Introduction pp. 58-59), he speaks of the identity of our D-S with the D-S who commented on both the Āśvalāyana-gṛhya-sūtra and the Āśvalāyana-śrauta-sūtra. In the following remark of Thangaswami Sarma (1996: 210) Baudhāyana-śrauta-sūtra comes in the place of Āśvalāyana-śrauta-sūtra: *baudhāyana-śrauta-sūtra-āśvalāyana-gṛhya-sūtrāṇāṁ vyākhyātrā dvādaśa-lakṣaṇyā api alabdha-bhāṣyakāra iti prasiddhena* →

of the tenth century or the first half of the eleventh century AD. On the other hand, the SK commentator D-S must be earlier than the fifth century AD, the latest possible date for Śabara. From the discussion in Aithal 1982: 106-18 and the language and style of the citations collected therein, I have a feeling that it *may* be possible to push back the date of the D-S who commented on the Āśvalāyana-gṛhya-sūtra, and perhaps on the Āśvalāyana-śrauta-sūtra and Baudhāyana-śrauta-sūtra. However, even before my feeling can be turned into a hypothesis, two steps need to be taken: (a) a comprehensive comparison of the SK bhāṣya with the published Āśvalāyana-gṛhya-sūtra-bhāṣya; (b) establishment of the identity or difference of the D-Ss associated with the other two texts, namely the comms on the Āśvalāyana- and Baudhāyana-śrauta-sūtras, with either the SK-bhāṣya author or the Āśvalāyana-gṛhya-sūtra-bhāṣya author. Step (a) is now relatively easy to carry out, especially because an edn of the Āśvalāyana-gṛhya-sūtra-bhāṣya has been expertly made available by Parameswara K. Aithat (Madras: Adyar Library and Research Centre, *c.* 1969).

However, making the texts of the D-S comms on the Āśvalāyana-śrauta-sūtra and the Baudhāyana-śrauta-sūtra available is anything but certain. We learn from Aithal (1982: 106 fn 1) that the comm on the Āśvalāyana-śrauta-sūtra ascribed to a D-S was expected to be published by the Vishveshvaranand Vedic Research Institute. It does not seem to have been published during the past eighteen years. It is possible that Deva-trāta has been mistaken as D-S,[27] and there is, in fact, no Āśvalāyana-śrauta-sūtra-bhāṣya by a D-S.

Further, no ms of the comm by a D-S on the Baudhāyana-śrauta-sūtra seems to have been accessed since the nineteenth century. Theodor Aufrecht's *Catalogus Catalogorum* (p. 260) refers to 'NP. VII, 6' as a source for the information that such a comm exists. Here, 'NP' stands for *A Catalogue of Sanskrit Manuscripts in Private Libraries of the North-Western Provinces, Allahabad: 1877-86*, and 'VII' specifies the vol. number (the catalogue is said to have ten vols. in all). As the ms was in a private collection, as more than 115 years have passed since the publication of the catalogue and as the area in which the ms was likely to be found has been

→ *deva-svāmina* (AD 1050) *ekādaśa-śatakāt pūrvatanena kṛtaṁ saṅkarṣa-kāṇḍa-bhāṣyam* [reference to SSS's edn follows].

27. The institute to which Aithal refers has published an Āśvalāyana-śrauta-sūtra comm within a few years of 1982, the date of Aithal's article. The publication details are: *The Āśvalāyana Śrauta Sūtra. With the Commentary of Deva-trāta,* Edited Critically and Annotated with Comparative Data from Original Manuscripts and Other Available Material by Ranbir Singh Bawa, Hoshiarpur: V.V.R.I. Press, vol. 1: 1986, vol. II: 1990, vol. 3: 1996.

subjected to political upheavals leading to large changes of population, it is unlikely that the ms will ever come to the purview of a researcher. Let us hope that it has miraculously survived and/or a copy of it was made for safekeeping at another place.

§3.9 My placing of D-S between Upavarṣa and Bhava-dāsa (cf. Kane 1929: 153-54) conflicts with Sarma's (1963: xviii) remark, 'Bhava-dāsa is earlier to [→ than] D-S since his comm is found quoted by D-S [under SK 3.2.1]' and Lariviere's remark (1981: 188), 'Deva-svāmin mentions Bhava-dāsa in his comm.' Both remarks are based on Ramaswami Sastri (1933: 294): 'D-S . . . in his bhāṣya on 15.II.1 [= SK 3.2.1; see note 15] says *asmin pāde 'apūrvāt tathā somaḥ' ity ārabhyā pāda-parisamāpter bhāvadāsam eva bhāṣyam iti.* ["In this pāda, only the bhāṣya authored by Bhava-dāsa (exists) from (the sūtra) *apūrvāt tathā somaḥ* to the end of the pāda."] The same attribution is repeated in Ramaswami Sastri 1936: Introduction pp. 19-20, 58.

However, as SSS points on p. 5 of his English introduction and pp. ii-iii of his Sanskrit introduction, the attribution of the ms line quoted above to D-S is incorrect. The line should be attributed to a copyist of D-S's SK bhāṣya.[28] Obviously, a significant gap had occurred in the exemplar of the copyist from whose copy all of our SK bhāṣya mss used so far have come down (except *perhaps* one of the two mentioned by Ramaswami Sastri in 1950: 103 fn 5 and Sarma 1963: xviii fn 22). When the copyist noticed the gap and could not fill it with other mss of D-S's comm, he filled it with the corresponding part of another commentary on the same work and indicated the extent of this imported material.

Similar cases are found in the mss of some other texts. SSS refers in this connection to the mss of *Rāmāyaṇa* and *Mahābhārata*. I do not know whether the parallels are exact to the extent of giving the beginning and ending with precise author specifications. From that point of view and also as a parallel coming from a śāstra text, I would draw attention to what is seen in the mss of Helā-rāja's comm on Bhartṛ-hari's Vākyapadīya or Trikāṇḍī. There we find two fillings with the specification that they come from Phullarāja's comm and extend from such and such place to such and such place in the text. See the edn by K.A. Subramania Iyer 1963: xiii, 261-68, 280-83.

28. I would add, 'or possibly but not very probably, to D-S's 'MS + SK' bhāṣya', since we learn from the PH that D-S commented on the first two texts of the 'MS : SK : BS' triplet. As the MS is an extensive text, the mss of D-S's comm on it are unlikely to have included the comm also on the SK, even if D-S aimed at writing a shorter comm than Bodhāyana and Upavarṣa. Śabara's MS comm, which should not be at least longer than D-S's comm according to the indications in the PH statement, is usually not found in its entirety in a single mss.

§3.10 As Devasthali (1967: 44-45) has pointed out, SSS has not correctly specified the extent of the part imported from Bhava-dāsa's comm. SSS puts the copyist's remark *asmin pāde* . . . (see §3.9) at the beginning of the comm on 3.2.1. This creates the impression that the remark applies to pāda 3.2. But the sūtra *apūrvatvāt tathā somaḥ* is printed in pāda 3.1, after sūtra 29. The bhāṣya of Bhava-dāsa must then begin after sūtra 3.1.29 and end with the end of pāda 3.1 at sūtra 44. Accordingly, the remark should be printed at the end of the bhāṣya on sūtra 44 or before the beginning of sūtra 3.1.29, depending on where it actually occurs in the mss.[29]

Another possibility not entertained by Devasthali, namely that, originally, the second pāda of the third adhyāya began with the sūtra *apūrvāt tathā somaḥ* also needs to be explored.

The discussion in §3.9 and the present section suggests that we need (a) to have a truly critical edn of the SK, based preferably on more ms material, (b) to compare more consistently and minutely the SSS-established text with Bhāskararāya's adaptation of the D-S bhāṣya text and (c) to ascertain if the diction and style are different in the part ascribed to Bhava-dāsa.

§3.11 Śabara's references to SK recorded by scholars are two: (a) MS 10.4.32: *sviṣṭakr̥d-vikāraś ca vanaspatir iti saṅkarṣe vakṣyate.* (b) 12.2.11: *auṣadhārthā avahananārthā vā. yathā patnī tulyavac.chrūyata iti saṅkarṣe vakṣyati.*[30] The first reference agrees with SK 2.4.39 (*sviṣṭakr̥d-vikāre yājyāyāṁ devatā-nigamāḥ syuḥ prakr̥ty-upabandhāt*), and the second with SK 1.1.36 (*avahananārthaḥ vā yathā patnī tulyā śrūyate*).

As a passive construction, the former leads us to believe that the expected statement will be made by Śabara when his commenting reaches the SK 2.4.39 part of the MS-SK text — that Śabara thought of himself as one who would comment on the SK as well (see Aklujkar 2011: note 34; 2009: §3.3 and note 28). Probably based on this observation is the tradition

29. From the way SSS has reported the remark, the first alternative, namely printing at the end of sūtra 44, is more likely to be supported by the mss. However, it seems advisable to consult once again the mss used by SSS, as well as any other mss or mss fragments that may become available. Secondly, the remark should be printed in a fn or in the parentheses that are usually adopted for signaling text matter not belonging to the main text or text proper. The remark under consideration could not have been written by D-S and hence should not be presented as a part of his bhāṣya.

30. The text in the Bibliotheca Indica edn should be corrected, as in Sarma 1963: xv fn 16, at this point; *auṣadhārthā* should be a part of the preceding sentence, and a new sentence should begin with *avahananārthā*. Note also that this text does not contain *vat* after *patnī*, which is found in Ratna-gopāla-bhaṭṭa's edn.

to which the following remark of Ramaswami Sastri (1933: 293-94) refers: 'Tradition holds that Śabara-svāmin's bhāṣya covers also the SK.' But then in his fn 8 at this point, Ramaswami Sastri calls our attention to the following sentence from the PH (Gaṇapati Śāstrī's edn p. 39) as going against the tradition:

> *punar dvi-kāṇḍe dharma-mīmāṁsā-śāstre pūrvasya tantra-kāṇḍasyācārya-śabara-svāminātisaṅkṣepeṇa saṅkarṣa-kāṇḍaṁ dvitīyam upekṣya kṛtaṁ bhāṣyam.*
>
> In turn, Ācārya Śabara-svāmin, prepared a highly abridged bhāṣya of the first Tantra part (= the first twelve adhyāyas only), playing down the existence of the second (part), namely the SK, from among the two-part Dharma-mīmāṁsā-śāstra.[31]

How this sentence can be understood as conflicting with the tradition or the evidence in Śabara's comm baffles me. The PH passage simply conveys that its author was not aware of the existence of any comm on the SK by Śabara, while the wording in Śabara's comm does not go beyond suggesting that Śabara expected himself to be able to comment on the SK. There can be many a slip between intending to do something and actually being able to do it. Besides, the content of the MS and SK is not such that Śabara would need a very different kind of expertise to comment on the latter. The correct inference, therefore, would be that Śabara intended or planned to comment on the SK but did not manage to do so (and that the PH author did not wish to convey anything more than his non-awareness of a Śabara-authored comm on the SK).

§3.12 The little we know about Govinda as a commentator of the SK can be found in Lariviere 1981: 190-91 and Thangaswami Sarma 1996: 211: *govindopādhyāyena kṛtā anyā vyākhyā hemādri-pariśeṣa-khaṇḍe nirdiṣṭā . . . idānīṁ na labhyate.* It has been speculated that this Govinda may be the same as the Govinda who is mentioned as the teacher of Śaṅkara, the well-known Advaita philosopher. The speculation may turn out to be

---

31. The tr offered here is mine. Ramaswami Sastri did not offer any tr, which makes it difficult to determine how he arrived at the interpretation of the passage given above.

    Justification for taking *upekṣya* in the sense 'playing down the existence' can be found in Aklujkar 2009: fn 11.

    Further, Ramaswami Sastri does not specify the source of what he calls 'tradition''. It is possible that the source was none other than the passage cited from Śabara and some clarification necessitated by it regarding how the commentators use active and passive voices in making back- or forward-references.

correct, but some problems with the evidence used in support of the speculation have not been noticed.

The relevant Sarva-siddhānta-saṅgraha passage (1.20-22) reads thus:

bhavaty uttara-mīmāṁsā tv aṣṭādhyāyī dvidhā ca sā ।
devatā-jñāna-kāṇḍābhyāṁ. vyāsa-sūtraṁ dvayoḥ samam ॥20॥
pūrvādhyāya-catuṣkeṇa mantra-vācyātra devatā ।
saṅkarṣaṇoditā. tad.dhi devatā-kāṇḍam ucyate ॥21॥
bhāṣyaṁ caturbhir adhyāyair bhagavat-pāda-nirmitam ।
cakre vivaraṇaṁ tasya. tad vedāntaṁ pracakṣate ॥22॥

Tr: The Uttara-mīmāṁsā, consisting of eight adhyāyas, is twofold on account of the DK and the Jñāna-kāṇḍa. The sūtra of Vyāsa is the same in both (→ the sūtra of Vyāsa is common to both → Vyāsa composed the sūtras of both).[32]

"With the first four adhyāyas, Saṅkarṣaṇa stated the deity expressed in the mantras.[33] That (collectivity of four adhyāyas) is called DK."

"The comm for advanced learners composed by Bhagavat-pāda explained it in four adhyāyas. People call it Vedānta."[34]

What the passage expresses is not expressed in any other traditional text that researchers exploring the present area of inquiry have used: (a) The middle four adhyāyas form a companionship with the last four adhyāyas, not with the first twelve adhyāyas. (b) Saṅkarṣaṇa authored the middle four adhyāyas or a comm on the middle four adhyāyas.[35]

32. As my tr indicates, the sentence *vyāsa-sūtraṁ dvayoḥ samam* does not immediately fit the context. However, if it is not taken in the sense I extract, the obviously intended parallelism with *asyāṁ sūtraṁ jaiminīyam,* in verse 18 will be lost. As for the possible conflict with the next verse, which can be understood as declaring Saṅkarṣaṇa to be the author of the first four adhyāyas called DK, see the discussion to follow.

33. That 'stated' is not the only possible tr of *uditā* will be clear below. Though uncertain and problematic, the tr needs to be entertained at this point in the interest of the discussion to follow.

34. The tr or paraphrase of these verses by M. Raṅgācārya, as it is quoted by Lariviere (1981: 183), reads thus: 'The Uttara-mīmāṁsā on the other hand consists of eight chapters; and it is also divided into two parts under the head dealing (respectively) with deities and with the wisdom (of true philosophy). Both these divisions of the Uttara-mīmāṁsā have alike had their sūtras (aphorisms) composed by Vyāsa. In the first four chapters here (in the Uttara-mīmāṁsā) the deities referred to in the mantras are (given as) described by Saṅkarṣaṇa. For this reason it is called devatā-kāṇḍa (i.e., the part dealing with deities).'

35. Proposition (b) can at the most be inferred from the questionable epithet *sāṅkarṣaṇa* →

The passage's equating of Vedānta with one bhāṣya of four adhyāyas is also problematic.

None of these propositions finds any support in the BS comm of Śaṅkara, which cannot be credited with any more knowledge of the SK than as a book occurring before the BS and having occasional concern with offering (pradāna) and devatās. Therefore, it is not incumbent upon us to assume that the author of the Sarva-siddhānta-saṅgraha is the same as the author of the BS bhāṣya, that is, the well-known Śaṅkarācārya.

The explanation offered by the author of the unpublished comm quoted by the first editor of the Sarva-siddhānta-saṅgraha, M. Raṅgācārya, and, following him, by Lariviere (1981: 191) poses further problems. It goes thus:

> ***bhagavat-pādaḥ*** *śrīmān śaṅkarācārya-guru-govinda-bhagavata-pūjyaḥ* [→ *śrīmac.chaṅka°? °gurur go°? °vat-pū°? °pūjya-pādaḥ?*].[36] *asya devatā-kāṇḍasya* ***bhāṣyaṁ*** *sūtrāṇāṁ vyākhyānaṁ* ***bhagavat-pāda-nirmitam*** *ity āha. uttara-kāṇḍasyāpi bhāṣyam ācārya-praṇītam ity āha.* ***tasy****ottara-catuṣkasya vedānta-sūtrasya* ***vivaraṇaṁ*** *śārīraka-bhāṣyaṁ yac* ***cakre tad*** *lokaḥ [→ lokāḥ]* ***vedāntam*** *iti* ***pra****vadantīty arthaḥ*

For a short text, this raises too many textual queries as my arrows pointing to expected readings would indicate. Since there are other mistakes in the printing of Sanskrit words in Lariviere's article, it could be the case that at least some of the readings I have questioned do not come from Raṅgācārya. However, even if one sets aside the question of the source of mistakes, there remains ambiguity about how the author is construing *bhagavat-pāda-nirmitam*. If he has taken it as a part of the sentence in verse 21, that sentence is complete as it is and does not need *bhagavat-pāda-nirmitam* as a verbal complement. Besides, the pāda *bhāṣyaṁ caturbhir*

→ found in some mss of Rāmānuja's Śrī-bhāṣya on BS 3.3.42. As far as I can check, it has not found explicit articulation in any other text.

36. The first emendation is not absolutely necessary. A phrase like *śrīmān/śrīmāñ śaṅkarācārya-gurur govinda-bhagavat-pujya-pādaḥ* is as grammatical as *śrīmac.chaṅka° . . . pādaṁ*. However, it does not seem likely that the author would speak of Śaṅkarācārya without an honorific. The colophons of works thought to be Śaṅkarācārya's always contain *śrīmac.chaṅka°*. . . . The second emendation does not make too great a semantic difference. It just reflects my instinct that a pre-modern Sanskrit author is unlikely, at this point, to put *guru* in a compound and thereby de-emphasize it, even though it is a part of the predicate and a detail to which attention is to be directed. The third emendation (change of *bhagavata* to *bhagavat*) would probably amount only to a correction of a typographical error. The fourth is supported by the fact that the compound *govinda-bhagavat-pūjya-pāda-śiṣya* is found in the colophons of all the works that are usually ascribed to Śaṅkara.

adhyāyaiḥ, coming in between, will make the joining of *bhagavat-pāda-nirmitam* with verse 21 very unnatural. On the other hand, if the author is understood as confining *bhagavat-pāda-nirmitam* to verse 22, where it occurs, his explanation (*asya...vyākhyānam*) of verse 21 would remain syntactically incomplete. A verb like *akarot, aracayat, praṇināya* or a verb substitute like *kr̥tavān* or *praṇītavān* is missing after *vyākhyānam*. If, to avoid this predicament, we take *bhagavat-pāda-nirmitam* not as a citation for the sake of explanation but as the commentator's own word that just happens to be identical with what is used in verse 22 and *uttara-kāṇḍasyāpi bhāṣyam ācārya-praṇītam ity āha* as a sentence introducing the explanation of verse 22 (the best alternative under the circumstances in my view), the word *api* seems appropriate, the nature of a gloss that the following sentence (***tasy****ottara-catuṣkasya vedānta-sūtrasya* ***vivaraṇaṁ*** *śārīraka-bhāṣyaṁ* . . .) has makes sense, and the repeated use of *ity āha* does not seem very odd. But a question arises as to who the ācārya now is. Is it Śrīmac.chaṅkarācārya-guru Govinda-bhagavat-pūjya-pāda or Śaṅkara himself (since the title *śārīraka-bhāṣya* is so strongly associated with his BS comm)?

In verse 21, there is no word that clearly means 'commentary.' It would be odd if the verse were to speak of the comm or of the ' sūtra + comm' text as DK, the word by which it has spoken just a verse before only of the sūtra text.

If this point is admitted, there must once have been at least one verse between the present 21 and 22 that brought about a transition from the talk of sūtra text(s) to the talk of comm(s). After the statement about the DK, one expects a statement about the Jñāna-kāṇḍa or BS. Instead, in the present form of the text, the verse author directly comes to a comm on the Jñāna-kāṇḍa or BS. There is no antecedent for his *tasya* in the text actually present. It is the commentator who enlightens us that *tasya* stands for uttara-catuṣka or Vedānta-sūtra.[37]

The commentator seems to have brought in Govinda only because he thought of the work Sarva-siddhānta-saṅgraha as Śaṅkara's composition. He seems to have reasoned that if a verse in this work speaks of a bhāṣya on four adhyāyas, having Vedāntic content, as coming from Bhagavat-pāda, that cannot be a bhāṣya of Śaṅkara. How could Śaṅkara describe

37. An awareness of this problem may have led Narasiṁhācārya (mentioned in Lariviere 1981: 190) to take Saṅkarṣaṇa as a commentator of the DK (→ SK) rather than as the author of the DK or as the source of a specific devatā concept and to propose that the work got its name *SK* because of the name of the commentator — a solution worse than the problem.

himself with such a glory-bestowing term as *bhagavat-pāda?* On the other hand, how could the well-known Śārīraka-bhāṣya be declared to be a work of someone other than Śaṅkara? Therefore, there must be two bhāṣyas, one the well-known one of Śaṅkara and the other of Śaṅkara's teacher. This teacher was the only other person broadly known as the referent of *bhagavat-pāda*. The colophons of Śaṅkara's own works referred to him with that epithet.[38] While we can thus understand why the commentator has interpreted the way he has, the fact remains that verse 22 can apply to Śaṅkara himself without any strain even if we do not make the authorship presupposition that commentator has made.

We need to ascertain if a more extensive consultation of Sarva-siddhānta-saṅgraha mss would enable us to recover the missing verse. We also need to go beyond the 'excerpts' (cf. Lariviere 1981: 191) of the unpublished comm if it is possible to do so. Without these two steps, the investigation will face a handicap, but even in the present unsatisfactory textual state it should be clear that the talk of a comm by Saṅkarṣaṇa and the talk of a comm by Govinda identical with the teacher of Śaṅkarācārya have uncertain support and deserve to be suspended until further textual work is done.

§3.13 Whether there is any realistic hope of finding Rāja-cūḍāmaṇi-dīkṣita's (AD 1580-1650) comm Saṅkarṣa-nyāya-muktāvalī, mentioned by him in his Kāvya-darpaṇa, is not clear. We learn only the following from Ramaswami Sastri (1933: 294, fn 11): 'The work is noticed by Dr. Hultzsch in his *Reports of South Indian Mss.*, vol. II, no. 1489.' If the ms/mss listed by Hultzsch about one hundred years ago stayed in private collections, it would be nearly impossible to locate it/them now. According to Thangaswami Sarma (1996: 210), who does not indicate that he is aware of Ramaswami Sastri's remark, the work is not available.

Sarma (1963: xix-xx) observes that an extract from Rāja-cūḍā-maṇi's comm indicates that he commented only on the first adhyāya. This raises the possibility that only a ms like Sarma's and SSS's sūtra-pāṭha ms was available to Rāja-cūḍā-maṇi. It could even be the same ms as the one now available at Madras/Chennai but in a time-ravaged form, with most of its later parts lost. That Rāja-cūḍā-maṇi's comm was not left incomplete

38. Several Govindas were known and respected as commentators in various branches of Sanskrit literature (e.g., the Govinda who commented on the Rāmāyaṇa). If a Govinda was known as an SK commentator even by hearsay, he was very likely to be viewed on a background of respect and unlikely to be denied the respect that was associated with Śaṅkara's teacher.

because of any reason such as the author's impairment or death is indicated by the fact that, in the Kāvya-darpaṇa, he refers to the comm as if it was complete. Also, according to Sarma, a reference by a commentator of his Rukmiṇī-kalyāṇa indicates that the comm was complete. Did this commentator mean only completeness as far as the first adhyāya went?

§3.14 Sarma (1963: xix) has already provided the corrective that what the editor of Bhāskara-rāya's SK comm thought of as quotations from Śabara are actually quotations from D-S. A further corrective provided by him deserves elaboration and greater reception. The name of the comm has been given as Bhāṭṭa-candrikā by such Mīmāṁsā specialists as Ramaswami Sastri (1933: 294, 1936: 140) and Thangaswami Sarma (1996: 211). However, Bhāṭṭa-candrikā is not the title under which the text has been published in the *Pandit*, New Series vols. 14-16. It has rightly been treated there as a completion and extension of Khaṇḍa-deva's Bhāṭṭa-dīpikā.[39] Nor do the library catalogues list any matching work with Bhāṭṭa-candrikā as the title. Bhāskara-rāya's actual wording is:

adyāvadhi kr̥tir eṣādyanta-vihīneti [→ eṣā hy anta°?] dīpikākhyāsīt[40] ||
ṣoḍaśa-kalābhir adhunā paripūrṇā bhāṭṭa-candrikātvam agāt ||

Until now, this work (of Khaṇḍa-deva), which lacked a beginning and an end,[41] was called (Bhāṭṭa-)dīpikā ('a little lamp illuminating the views of Kumārila-bhaṭṭa's school'). It is now, being complete with sixteen parts (digits), has become Bhāṭṭa-candrikā ('moonlight illuminating the views of Kumārila-bhaṭṭa's school').

39. Khaṇḍa-deva could have planned to cover the SK in his comm. His Bhāṭṭa-dīpikā on MS 4.3.11 has the phrase *saṅkarṣe vakṣyamāṇatvāt* according to SSS p. 258. But I have not yet been able to determine if the phrase refers to the SK or Khaṇḍa-deva's own (planned but obviously unwritten or unfinished) comm.

40. The syntax of this otherwise simple verse half is made problematic by the place at which *iti* occurs. If *iti* is taken in the sense of 'since, because,' the meaning would be 'because it does not have a beginning or an end, it was known as a dīpikā ('little lamp'),' which does not make a congruent sentence. It seems better, therefore, to take the *iti* as bhinna-krama 'occurring outside of the expected order' and imagine it after *dīpikā*.

41. If *ādy-anta-* is the correct reading, it will follow that Bhāskara-rāya provided a beginning as he provided the end. Bhāskara (latter half of the seventeenth and first half of the eighteenth century AD) was close in time to Khaṇḍa-deva (around AD 1640). He may have known the latter personally and provided the title, maṅgala verse, etc. according to the latter's wish. However, it is also possible that Bhāskara did not employ *ādi* in a strict sense; 'filling the gaps in some pre-SK parts' may have been his intended meaning.

This only conveys that Bhāskara-rāya turned the Bhāṭṭa-dīpikā into a Bhāṭṭa-candrikā by giving it four additional chapters and bringing the total to sixteen, reminiscent of the sixteen digits of the Moon. It does not convey that Bhāskara-rāya employed any distinctive title for what he achieved. Such an understanding also agrees with his statement that he presented the work as a supplementation and as a saṅgraha.[42]

Ramaswami Sastri (1933: 294-95) observes:

> If we take the opening verse in the Bhāṭṭa-candrikā [?] of the SK, *praṇamya jaimini-munim̐ khaṇḍa-deva-kr̥tāv iha* | *anugrahāya mandānāḥ saṅgraho 'yam̐ vidhīyate* || [as] authentic, then it is clear that Khaṇḍa-deva has written a comm on this kāṇḍa, a summary of which has been afterwards written by Bhāskara-rāya. But the concluding verses in the Bhāṭṭa-candrikā[43] [?] give us a different idea. . . . We have got no tangible evidence as yet to prove Khaṇḍa-deva's authorship of any works on this kāṇḍa.

Ramaswami Sastri's concluding sentence is correct (although what I observe in note 39 needs to be borne in mind). What puzzles me is this: why should he have drawn the initial inference from Bhāskara-rāya's verse and raised the possibility that Khaṇḍa-deva actually authored an SK comm in the first place? The basis for Bhāskara-rāya's Saṅgraha could not have

42. It is also not likely that Bhāskara-rāya intends to suggest here that, at his hands, Khaṇḍa-deva's work moved from being a small illuminator to being a big illuminator. The metaphor he employs is not to be extended to convey anything more than the thought that the lacking parts were supplied and the original was enabled to realize its full potential.

43. (a) These verses are: *khaṇḍa-deva-kr̥ta-bhāṭṭa-dīpikā lakṣaṇaiḥ katipayair asambhr̥tā* | *ity udīkṣya budha-bhāskarāgnicit [→ °skaro 'gnicid?] bhāratī varibharām-bhabhūva tām* ||2|| 'The Bhāṭṭa-dīpikā authored by Khaṇḍa-deva lacked some sūtras. On noticing this, Bhāskara, a Brahmin, who maintained the sacred fire and had (the title) Bhāratī (after his name), very much made up all the deficiencies.' *adyāvadhi kr̥tir eṣādyanta-vihīneti dīpikākhyāsīt* | *ṣoḍaśa-kalābhir adhunā paripūrṇā bhāṭṭa-candrikātvam agāt* ||3|| [see §3.14 for tr] *āsīt ṣoḍaśa-lakṣaṇī śruti-padā yā dharma-mīmām̐sikā* | *saṅkarṣākhya-caturtha-bhāga-vidhurā kālena sājāyata* || *gāyatrī tri-padātmikeva vibudhair adyāpi pāpaṭhyate tām̐ pūrṇām atanoc.chrameṣa mahatā gambhīrajo bhāskaraḥ* ||4|| 'There was (at one time) a Dharma-Mīmām̐sā (= PM + SK) concerned with Śruti words (and having four feet, that is, fully stable) and consisting of sixteen adhyāyas. In the course of time, it lost one-fourth of itself (i.e., the last four adhyāyas) called *Saṅkarṣa*. It is very much studied even now by scholars (in its incomplete three-part form) like the Gāyatrī (mantra) consisting of three (metrical) quarters. Bhāskara, the son of Gambhīra, completed it (i.e., brought it back to its original four-feet form) with great effort (or hardship).'

(b) *śruti-padā* involves a play on words that my tr in parentheses tries to capture. Since the Śruti, the Veda, primarily consists of four books, *śruti* also has the meaning 'four'; *pada* commonly means either 'foot' or 'word, expression.'

been a comm by Khaṇḍa-deva. If such a comm had existed, he would not have been required to undertake the great effort of which he speaks in his last verse. He would have simply produced a better or (by taking out the problematic parts) a shorter version of Khaṇḍa-deva's work. Also, *saṅgraha* is not a word that naturally means 'comm.' Recovering, that is, collecting, as much of the surviving SK and its explanation as was possible is a concern writ large over Bhāskara-rāya's work, and his use of the word *saṅgraha* to convey what he planned to accomplish is in keeping with this concern. Ramaswami Sastri himself seems to have realized this, for, in 1936: p. 140, he emphatically rejects the proposal that Khaṇḍa-deva commented on the SK. As my note 39 indicates, Khaṇḍa-deva, like Śabara, could have envisioned the possibility of writing a SK comm, but he had to leave it to Bhāskara to actualize what he envisioned.

§3.15 In the Madhyama-vyāyoga, while the middle brother was preparing to face what then must have seemed inevitable death, his relations, too, suffered smothered helpless pain. As can be seen from the preceding account of the SK comms, they too have withered in various ways. A 'rescue' of the SK based on a wider collection of mss, will reinvigorate the study of its comms. Let us hope that a gifted and determined scholar will make a timely entrance in this research field and pull back the SK family of texts from the brink of extinction just as the great Pāṇḍava hero Bhīma saves the Brahmin family in Bhāsa's (?) charming little play.

Abbreviations

BS = Brahma-sūtra, Vedānta-sūtra, Uttara-mīmāṁsā-sūtra.

Comm = commentary, commentator.

D-S = Deva-svāmin.

Ed/ed = editor, edited by.

Edn/edn = edition.

Fn/fn = footnote.

Ms/ms = manuscript.

MS = Mīmāṁsā-sūtra, Pūrva-mīmāṁsā-sūtra. PM.

PH = Prapañca-hr̥daya.

PM: see MS.

SK = *Saṅkarṣa-kāṇḍa / Saṁkarṣa-kāṇḍa.*

SSS = S. Subrahmanya Sastri.

Tr/tr = Translation/translator.

UM: see BS.

Vol./vol. = volume.

References

Aithal, P.K., 1982, 'Deva-svāmin: a forgotten jurist?' in *Indology and Law, Studies in Honour of Professor J. Duncan M. Derrett*, pp. 106-19, (eds.), Günther-Dietz Sontheimer; Parameswara Kota Aithal, Wiesbaden: Steiner Verlag.

Aiyangar, S.K., 1928, *Manimekhalai in Its Historical Setting*, London: Luzac & Co.

———, 1940, 'Viṁśaty-adhyāya-nibaddhaṁ Mīmāṁsā-śāstram', in *Woolner Commemoration Volume: In Memory of the Late Dr. A.C. Woolner*, pp. 1-6, (ed.), Mohammad Shah, Lahore: Mehar Chand Lachhman Das. Sanskrit and Prakrit Series 8.

Aklujkar, Ashok, 2009, 'Vr̥tti and Vr̥ttikāra in Rāmānuja's Śrī-bhāṣya', *Studia Orientalia* 108: 3-20.

———, 2011, 'Unity of the Mīmāṁsās: how history hides historiography', in *Vācaspati-vaibhavam*, a Volume in Felicitation of Professor Vachaspati Upadhyaya, pp. 821-900 (eds.), Radhavallabh Tripathi, Shashiprabha Kumar et al., New Delhi: D.K. Printworld.

———, 2012, 'Authorship of the Saṅkarṣa-kāṇḍa', in *Devadattīyam. Johannes Bronkhorst Felicitation Volume*, pp. 191-227 (eds.), François Voegli, et al. Bern etc.: Peter Lang.

Appayya-dīkṣita, *The Brahma-sūtra Śāṅkara Bhāṣya with the Commentaries Bhāmatī, Kalpa-taru and Parimala*, (eds.), N. Anantha Krishna Śāstri, and Vāsudev Laxman Shāstrī Paṇśīkar, Bombay: Nirnaya Sagar Press, 1917.

Belvalkar, S.K., 1927, 'Jaimini's Śārīraka-sūtra', in *Aus Indiens Kultur. Festgabe Richard von Garbe dem Forscher und Lehrer zu seiner 70. Geburtstag*, pp. 163-70, Erlangen: Verlag von Palm & Enke.

Bhartr̥-hari. *Trikāṇḍī* or *Vākyapadīya*. (a) *Vākyapadīya of Bhartr̥-hari with the Commentary of Helā-rāja. Kāṇḍa III, Part 1 [Samudeśas 1-7]*. (ed.) K.A. Subramania Iyer, Poona: Deccan College Postgraduate and Research Institute, 1963. Deccan College Monograph Series 21. (b) *Vākyapadīya of Bhartr̥-hari with the Prakīrṇaka-prakāśa of Helā-rāja, Kānda III, Part II [Samudeśas 8-14]*. (ed.) K.A. Subramania Iyer, Poona: Deccan College, 1973. [Continuation of Deccan College Monograph Series no. 21?].

Bhāsa (?), *Madhyama-vyāyoga*, tr. Ernst Paxron Janvier, [Philadelphia?]: Printed at the Wesleyan Mission Press. Probably published by the author as a part of his Ph.D. degree requirement at the University of Pennsylvania, 1921, several more recent trs are available.

Bhāskara-rāya, A comm completing Khaṇḍa-deva's *Bhāṭṭa-dīpikā*, first published in installments in the periodical *Paṇḍita*, published from Varanasi. Details of this serial publication are available in Lariviere 1981: 182 fn 13. The publication details of the book in which the serialized parts were published together are: (ed.), Rāma Miśra Śāstrī (same as that of the serialized version). Benares Sanskrit Series 1894.

Devasthali, G.V., 1967, "Review of Subrahmanya Sastri 1965", *Indian Antiquary* (New Series) II.3: 43-45.

Helā-rāja: see Bhartṛ-hari.

Jaimini, (a) *The Aphorisms of the Mīmāṁsā . . . with the Commentary of Śabara-svāmin,* (ed.), Maheśachandra Nyāya-ratna, Calcutta: The Asiatic Society of Bengal, 1873- Bibliotheca Indica, New series nos. 44, 85, 95, 101, 115, 142, 154, 174 & 208. (b) *Mīmāṁsā-darśanam Śrī-Śabara-svāmi-viracita-bhāṣya-sahitam,* (ed.), Ratna-gopāla-bhaṭṭa. Benares City: Harikrishna Dāsa Gupt, Chowkhambha-Saṁskṛta-pustakālaya, 1910, 4 vols. (c) *Pūrva-mīmāṁsā-darśanam with Khaṇḍa-deva's Bhāṭṭa-dīpikā Commentary,* (ed.), A. Mahadeva Sastri, Mysore: Oriental Library, Government Oriental Library Series, Bibliotheca Sanskrita no. 35, vol. 1, 1908.

Janvier: see Bhāsa.

Kanazawa, Atsushi, 1989, 'Notes on the Saṅkarṣa-kāṇḍa: under stimulus from the article by Lariviere', *Acta Asiatica* 57: 31-44.

Kane, Pandurang Vaman, 1929, 'Bhava-dāsa and Śabara-svāmin', *Annals of the Bhandarkar Oriental Research Institute* 10: 153-54.

———, 1975, *History of Dharmaśāstra: Ancient and Medieval Religious and Civil Law.* See the details of vol. 1.2 below. First edn.: 1930-58/1962. 5 thematic vols. divided into 7 physical vols. Second edn.: 1968-77. Physical vols. 8 (vol. I was expanded and hence needed two parts). Poona/Pune: Bhandarkar Oriental Research Institute. Government Oriental Series. Class B, no. 6. Vol. I.1 First edn: 1930. Second edn. revised and enlarged: 1968. Vol. I.2: First edn: 1930. Second edn. revised and enlarged 1975. Vol. II.1. First edn.: 1941. Second edn.: 1974. Vol. II. 2. First edn.: 1941. Second edn: 1974. Vol. III: First edn.: 1946. Second edn: 1973. Vol. IV: First edn.: 1953. Second edn.: 1973. Vol. V.1: First edn.: 1958. Second edn.: 1974. Vol. V.2: First edn.: 1958. Second edn.: 1977. Third edn. or a photo reprint of the second edn.: 1990/91-1997.

Kevalānanda-sarasvatī, 1952-1966 (ed.), *Mīmāṁsā-koṣa,* 7 vols. Wai: Prājña Pāṭha-śālā. Prājña Pāṭha-śālā Maṇḍala Grantha Mālā.

Khaṇḍa-deva: see Bhāskara-rāya and Jaimini.

Lariviere, Richard W. 1981, 'Madhyama-mīmāṁsā: The Saṅkarṣa-kāṇḍa', *Wiener Zeitschrift für die Kunde Südasiens* 25: 179-94.

Mesquita, Roque, 1997, *Madhva und seine unbekannten literarischen Quellen: einige Beobachtungen,* Wien 1997.

Parpola, Asko. 1981, 'On the formation of the Mīmāṁsā and the problems concerning Jaimini with particular reference to the teacher quotations and the Vedic schools [Part I].' *Wiener Zeitschrift für die Kunde Südasiens* 25: 145-77.

Prapañca-hṛdaya, Author unknown, (a) 1915. (ed.), T. Gaṇapati Śāstrī, Trivandrum: Government of His Highness the Maharajah of Travancore, Trivandrum Sanskrit Series XLV. (b) 1987, non-photographic reprint of the preceding edn with Madhu-sūdana-sarasvatī's *Prasthāna-bheda* added, (ed.), Yudhiṣṭhira Māmāṁsaka. Bahālagaḍha (Sonīpata, Harayāṇā): Yudhiṣṭhira Māmāṁsaka. Sole distributor: Ramlal Kapoor Trust, Bahālagaḍha.

Prasthāna-bheda: see under *Prapañca-hṛdaya.*

Rāmānuja, *Śrī-bhāṣya.* (a) (ed and annotator) N.S. Rāma-bhadrācārya, (General ed). M.A. Lakshmithathachar, Melukoṭe/Melkote: Saṁskṛta-saṁśodhana-saṁsat/ The Academy of Sanskrit Research, 4 vols . 1985, 1987, 1990, 1991. As far as I could determine, a clear statement regarding the annotator is available only at the end of the annotation in vol. 4 on p. 423. (b) With Sudarśanācārya's *Śruta-prakāśikā* and Vedānta-deśika's *Tattva-ṭīkā,* (ed.), Dharaṇīdhara Śāstrī, Śrīdharācārya-śāstrī.

Vrindāvan: Śrīnivāsa-yantrālaya. 1916. (c) With Vedānta-deśika's *Tattva-ṭīkā* (ed.), Śrīvaṇ Śaṭhakopa, Śrī-vaiṣṇava-siddhānta-grantha-ratna-mālā 2, Madras: Śrī-vaiṣṇava-siddhānta-pracāra-sabhā, 1938. (d) With Vedānta-deśika's *Tattva-ṭīkā* and Vīra-rāghavācārya's Tattvārpaṇa thereto, (ed) Uttamur T. Vīra-rāghavācārya, Madras, Ubhaya-Vedānta-grantha-mālā, 1974.

Ramaswami Sastri, V.A. 1933, 'The Saṅkarṣa Kāṇḍa: a genuine supplement to the Pūrva-Mīmāṁsā Śāstra', *Indian Historical Quarterly* 9 (= M.M. Haraprasāda Śāstrī Commemoration Volume): 290-99.

———, 1936 (ed.), *Tattva-bindu by Vācaspati-miśra with Tattva-vibhāvanā by Ṛṣi-putra Parameśvara,* Annamalai: Annamalai University, Annamalai University Sanskrit Series 3.

———, 1950, 'Further light on Saṅkarsa-kāṇḍa', in *Siddha-Bhāratī,* or, *The Rosary of Indology* [in Honour of Siddheshwar Varma], part 2, pp. 102-05, (ed.), Viśvabandhu Śāstrī, Hoshiarpur: Vishveshvaranand Vedic Research Institute.

Ratna-gopāla-bhaṭṭa: see Jaimini.

Śabara: see Jaimini.

Śālika-nātha-miśra, *Prakaraṇa Pañcikā of Śālika-nātha Miśra with the Nyāya-siddhi of Jaipuri Nārāyaṇa Bhaṭṭa* (ed.), A. Subrahmanya Sastri, Varanasi: Banaras Hindu University, 1961, Kāśī-hindū-viśvavidyālayīya-darśana-grantha-mālā 4.

Sandal, Mohan Lal, 1925, Introduction to his English tr of the MS, Allahabad: Sacred Books of the Hindus series, reprint: Cosmo, 2007.

Saṅkarṣa-kāṇḍa: see Subrahmanya Sastri, S.

Sarma, K.V. 1963 (ed.), *Saṅkarṣa Kāṇḍa Sūtras of Jaimini,* Hoshiarpur: Vishveshvaranand Vedic Research Institute, Vishveshvaranand Indological Series 18.

Śarmā, Soma, 1992, *Saṁskṛta meṁ vyāyoga* = Vyayogas in Sanskrit, Dillī [= Delhi]: Nirmāṇa Prakāśana.

Sarva-mata-saṅgraha, Author said to be Śaṅkara, (ed.), T. Gaṇapati Śāstrī, Trivandrum: Government Press, 1918, Trivandrum Sanskrit series no. 62.

Sarva-siddhānta-saṅgraha, Author said to be Śaṅkara, who is probably a different historical person from Śaṅkarācārya or Ādiśaṅkara the famous Kevalādvaitin philosopher, (ed.), M. Raṅgācāya, Madras: Government Press, 1909.

Subrahmanya Sastri, A.: see Śālika-nātha-miśra.

Subrahmanya Sastri, S., 1965 (ed.), *Saṅkarṣa Kāṇḍa of Sage Jaimini with the Bhāṣya of Deva-svāmin,* Madras: University of Madras, Jaimini's authorship is refuted in favor of Kāśakṛtsna's in A. Aklujkar, 2012.

Thangaswami Sarma, R., 1996, *Mīmāṁsā-mañjarī,* New Delhi: Indian Council of Philosophical Research (= Bhāratīya-dārśanikānusandhāna Pariṣat) and Munshiram Manoharlal.

Vedānta-deśika (sometimes also referred to as Vedāntācārya and Veṅkaṭa-nātha): see Rāmānuja.

11

Linguistic and Cosmic Powers
The Concept of Śakti in the Philosophies of Bhartṛhari and Abhinavagupta

*Sthaneshwar Timalsina**

Śakti: The Power of Language

In general, the term *śakti* means force: the power of words to signify their referents, or the cosmic power or powers pertinent to gods in general, or to *Brahman*.[1] The concept of linguistic power is central to Bhartṛhari's philosophy of language. At its apogee in the Trika tradition, the cosmic nature of *śakti* refers to the procreative cosmic force identified by the term *vimarśa* (reflection) that is inseparable from *prakāśa,* or awareness. In Trika philosophy, these two aspects are identified with the primordial couple, Śiva and Śakti, and are addressed as inseparable. This divine Śakti embodies all that exists, gives rise to sequence, and thus is instrumental for causing events to occur. Tāntric Kaula tradition elaborates upon the personal and embodied nature of this energy. Although these linguistic, cosmic, and embodied aspects of *śakti* appear distinct and similar in terms, a close examination of the philosophies of Bhartṛhari and Abhinavagupta allows us to establish a nuanced relation of these concepts.

Contrary to theological schools, Indian philosophical systems consistently use the term *śakti* to refer to linguistic power. The central debate between Mīmāṁsā and Nyāya concerning the expressive power of language can be synthesized as the positions regarding the universal, the particular, or their combination as what is expressed by language. Although Bhartṛhari's concept of *śakti* is still related to the signifying

* Department of Religious Studies, San Diego State University

1. For treatment on *śakti,* see Larson 1974, Cefalu 1973, and Padoux 1990. For the concept of *pratibhā,* see Kaviraj 1924, Joshi 1977, Rukmani 1987, Dragonetti and Tola 1990, Kuanpoonpol 1991.

power of language, it is much wider, and Bhartṛhari is aware of these positions while promulgating his own theory of language. It does not take time to notice that linguistic expression in Bhartṛhari's philosophy does not merely describe the phenomenal reality: his *śabda* is identical to *Brahman*, and is also the means to reveal the highest truth. This self-revealing aspect of language is what particularly links Bhartṛhari with subsequent Trika philosophers.[2] The Vedic Mīmāṁsā philosophers, Bhartṛhari, and the Trika philosophers all present their response to the metaphysical question, how can the supreme reality that is not grasped by other means of knowledge be expressed through language and cognized through linguistic apprehension?

Two concepts found in the expressive power of language are crucial to the current discussion. The Nyāya position appears secularized while emerging from a theological foundation, as the early concept of expressive power is distinctively the "Will of God" (*īśvarecchā*), while this becomes merely the will of the user of a word to signify a specific object.[3] This will in the Trika paradigm is both the dormant will among the individuals, and the Will of Śiva that is manifest in the form of the world. Next, the scope of linguistic expression, both as universal and particular, demonstrates the expressive power of language to embody the totality in its subsequent theological twist, while still referring to the particulars.[4]

Bhartṛhari analyses the two different positions that words describe the particular or the universal in two separate chapters of the *Vākyapadīya* (*VP*). In the *Jāti-Samuddeśa,* Bhartṛhari asserts that when a speaker uses a word, it is his intention that determines whether it is a universal or a particular that is meant. He identifies the "superimposition of conception" (*adhyāropa-kalpanā*) as what occurs in the process of knowing particulars

2. Besides conceptual connections, there are also historical links between Bhartṛhari and the Trika philosophers. Bhartṛhari has remained popular among the Kāśmīrī scholars. Both Helārāja and Puṇyarāja, the commentators on Bhartṛhari's texts, hail from Kashmir. Trika philosophers such as Somānanda prominently engage the philosophy of Bhartṛhari, even when they are rejecting his view. The most compelling reason, however, is that Helārāja is one of the teachers of Abhinava. Abhinava is noticeably respectful to Bhartṛhari, as he often cites from Bhartṛhari's *Vākyapadīya*.

3. It is Vātsyāyana to first bring "desire" (*icchā*) to the discussion of the designating power of words, and for him, the primacy of universal or particular relies on the desire of the speaker. See the commentary of Vātsyāyana on *NS* 2.2.63.

4. For universal as the significance of language, see the *Bhāṣya* of Śabara on the *Mīmāṁsāsūtra* 1.3.30-35. For Kumārila's defense of universal as the signified, see the *Ākṛtivāda* section in the *Ślokavārttika*.

after comprehending the universal directly signified by word. This discussion favours "universal" as the meaning, defining the universal property as something common to all members of a class that distinguishes the particular members of that class from other classes.[5] In the next chapter, Dravya-Samuddeśa, Bhartṛhari identifies "substance" as the essential nature (*ātman*), an entity (*vastu*), and the intrinsic nature (*svabhāva*) or reality (*tattva*). In this discussion, the generic form (*ākāra*) is referred to as something that helps one to know the intrinsic nature of the entity. The *dravya* discussed in this section is not the particular that is born or is perishable, but rather, it is the essential nature, the true nature of the substance that is free from origin or destruction.[6] What is noteworthy in Bhartṛhari's discussion is the way he understands "universal," where *sattā* is the highest universal, which is identical to *pratibhā*, and is understood as what is essentially referred to by words. The description that the very *ātman* is the referent of a word or that the very essential being is the meaning, transcends the dichotomy of the phenomenal and the real; his neutral terminology embraces both meanings. This also helps to establish a link between linguistic power expressed in terms of "fitness" (*yogyatā*)[7] and metaphysical power. Although various aspects of linguistic power are absent in the cosmic depiction of Śakti, nuances shared by Bhartṛhari and the Trika philosophers such as Abhinava allow us to establish a link between these two systems.

Śakti as the Causal Factor

The concept of *śakti* in Bhartṛhari's philosophy is wider than the mere signifying power of language in the common sense. Identified in plurality (*VP* 1.2), these *śakti*s located in *Brahman* are of a mutually exclusive character.[8] While remaining the power of the word principle,[9] their existence does not contradict the singularity of *Brahman*, as these are described as the very self-nature of the *Brahman*. Since the word principle is the essence of all these powers, having multiple *śakti*s does not connote

5. This discussion comes from the Jāti-Samuddeśa of *VP*. See Coward and Raja 1990: 154.
6. This topic is elaborated in the exposition of the *sūtra "siddhe sabdārthasambandhe"* on *MB* 1.1.1. *"evam hi dṛśyate loke . . . ākṛtyupamardanena dravyameva śiṣyate."* — Ibid.
7. *indriyāṇām svaviṣayasvanādir yogyatā yathā* I *anādirarthaiḥ sabdānām sambandho yogyatā tathā* I I — *VP*.3.3.29.
8. *ekatvasyāvirodhena śabdatattve brahmaṇi samuccitā virodhinya ātmabhūtāḥ śaktaya?* I — *VPvṛ* 1.2. Iyer 1966, p. 16, lines 1-2.
9. *brahmedaṁ śabdanirmāṇam śabdaśaktinibandhanam* I— Cited in *VPvṛ* on *VP* 1.1. Iyer 1966, p. 14, line 3.

duality.[10] Of the various powers of *śabda*, Bhartṛhari identifies two among them, direction (*dik*) and time (*kāla*), with terminology similar to that applied to consciousness (*caitanya*).[11] This similarity is particularly crucial in comparing Bhartṛhari's philosophy with the Trika system.

Crucial to a comparison of the linguistic power discussed in *VP* with the concept of Śakti in Trika philosophy, consciousness in Trika system is identified as the "light" (*prakāśa*) that is never devoid of self-reflection (*vimarśa*). Relying on the concept that awareness is always self-aware, Trika philosophers propound that these two aspects of consciousness are inseparable. The early terminology of neuter gender *caitanya* shifts to feminine *citi* to describe consciousness, and this is linked with this relationship of cosmic power with the power of linguistic expression.[12]

The issue of the number of energies is central to both the Trika categorization of divine energies and Bhartṛhari's philosophy of expressive power. While Bhartṛhari lists four pertinent powers of language, he also cites a position that holds six different powers (*VP* 3.7.35). This identification is noteworthy, because the energies that give rise to plurality are described as beyond distinctness and identity,[13] and the entity that is the substrate for these energies is described as free from all mental constructions.[14] Just like *kāla* and *deśa* are two central categories within which all Śaivite categories are found, these two powers are pertinent to Bhartṛhari's discourse on language. Allowing us to identify a further link, the *śakti*s in Bhartṛhari's philosophy allow the word principle to manifest successively through the power of sequence (*krama-śakti*) in the forms of word and sentence.[15] Following this presentation, word-meaning can be cognized only in sequence (*kramagrāhya*), and it does not transcend the conditions of subject and object in the sequence of manifestation.[16] Through

10. *sarvaśaktyātmabhūtatvam ekasyaiveti nirṇayaḥ* | — *VP* 3.1.22.

11. *caitanyavat sthitā loke dikkālaparikalpanā* |— *VP* 3.6.18.

12. For instance, see the terminology of Utpala in *ĪP* 1.5.13 that addresses *parā vāc* and *citi* in the same breath.

13. . . . *bhedasaṁsargasamatikrameṣa samāviṣṭam sarvābhiḥ śaktibhir vidyāvidyāpravibhāga-rūpam apravibhāgam* . . . — *VPvṛ* on *VP* 1.1. Iyer 1966, p. 1, line 3 – p. 2, line 1.

    tad evaṁ apṛthaktvaṁ pṛthakpratyavabhāsānām api mithaḥ sarvaśaktīnām | — *VPvṛ* on *VP* 1.2. Iyer 1966, p. 17, line 2.

14. . . . *sarvavikalpātīta ekasminn arthe sarvaśaktiyogād draṣṭṛṇāṁ darśanavikalpāḥ* . . . — *VPvṛ* in *VP* 1.9. Iyer 1966, p. 35, lines 4-5.

15. *VP* 1.86. See also: *sa tv evaṁ pratilīnaḥ* . . . *kramaśaktiṁ pratigṛhṇāti* | — *VPvṛ* in *VP* 1.51. Iyer 1966, p. 110, line 5 – p. 111, line 2.

16. *VP* 1.52 and the *Vṛtti* (*VPvṛ*) thereon.

the association of interacting powers, this word principle becomes many, just as the earth element transforms into the form of plants.[17] The aspects of "sequence" addressed while addressing linguistic power is contextual for reading the Tāntric Krama system, as it adopts the same premise while addressing the sequence of Kālīs. This philosophy of sequence not only describes the soteriological order, but it also grounds the ontological and epistemic orders.

Bhartr̥hari identifies entities as the constellation of *śakti*s.[18] Since the *śakti*s, to which he refers, are the powers of the word principle, the objects of cognition, following this line, are merely the fusion of various powers inherent to the word principle. The commentary on *VP* 3.7.2 further confirms this position by stating that, "pot, etc. are merely the constellation of powers."[19] Just like specific energies in a *maṇḍala* embody further energies within, Bhartr̥hari asserts that there are further *śakti*s within *śakti*s. In other words, a *śakti* can simultaneously be the power of one entity and also endowed with further powers.[20] Bhartr̥hari's discourse on power paves the path for refining Trika notion of Śakti, as can be seen in Abhinava's definition of *śakti*, that it is the essential form of the entities assumed by the subject (*Tantrāloka*, hereafter *TĀ*, 1.69). The *śakti*s in Bhartr̥hari's cosmology are neither one nor many (*VP* 3.7.39).[21] Paralleling the depiction above, Abhinava, with the example that there is no distinction between fire and its powers of burning and cooking, confirms that there is no real difference among the powers inherent to Śiva (*TĀ* 1.70). On the same ground, he also confirms that there is no distinction between power itself and that which is endowed with power (*TĀ* 1.71-72). Relating further to Bhartr̥hari's discussion on *śakti*, Abhinava maintains that the absolute appears in plurality due to its power of autonomy (*svātantrya*, *TĀ* 1.73).

Śaktis in Plurality

The role of *śakti* in the mechanism of linguistic apprehension in the

17. *sa ca saṁsr̥ṣṭaprāptaśaktir vivarttaṁ pr̥thivīkalalanyagrodhadhānādivad bhedam upagr̥hṇāti* | — *VPvr̥* 1.119. Iyer 1966, p. 180, lines 1-2.
18. *śaktimātrāsamūhasya viśvasyānekadharmaṇaḥ* | *sarvadā sarvathā bhāvāt kvacit kiñcid vivakṣate* || — *VP* 3.7.2.
19. *ata eva tāḥ śaktayas tatra mātrā bhāgā iti śaktisamāhāramātraṁ ghaṭādayaḥ* | — commentary on ibid.
20. *parasparaśaktimanto bhāvāḥ*, commentary on *VP* 3.7.11. Bhartr̥hari gives the example of taste to describe that something that is in itself power can embody further powers (see, *VP* 3.7.11). The position that energies can hold further energies within is identified by Bhartr̥hari as that of the *saṁsargavādin* (see *VP* 3.7.9).
21. For the issue concerning singularity or plurality of powers, see *VP* 3.6.24-27.

philosophy of Bhartṛhari is as crucial as it is in the cosmic manifestation and self-realization in the philosophy of Abhinava. According to Bhartṛhari, the multiple powers inherent to *śabda* that relate word to meaning also allow the single principle to manifest as many. *Śakti,* in this paradigm, plays the role of both the signifying linguistic power and the cosmic forces that give rise to duality. The metaphysical aspect of these powers is explicit in descriptions wherein the entities in their latent form become fully manifest in their external form by their intrinsic powers (Iyer 1992: 109). Bhartṛhari describes the powers such as time (*kāla*), direction or space (*dig*), means (*sādhana*), or action (*kriyā*) in such a way that these simultaneously identify the linguistic process and the cosmic manifestation. Bhartṛhari asserts that while these powers are inherent to the word principle, these are also endowed with further powers, such as the powers of "obstruction" (*pratibandha*) and "permission" (*abhyanujñā*) inherent to time (*VP* 3.9.4, 30). Along the same lines, relation (*sambandha*) is considered to be the power even of powers.[22]

Bhartṛhari identifies direction or space as a separate power for the reason that it is distinct from substances and foundational for their transformation. Since the cognition of an entity presupposes both space and time, these are therefore considered as powers. Space is also considered as the power for qualifying objects that are located within it while never being revealed on its own.[23] In this discussion, Bhartṛhari points out that powers inherent to entities are known through their effect (*VP* 3.6.6), and also that it is through these powers that division is conceived of even the entity that is devoid of it (*VP* 3.6.13). Bhartṛhari relies on the argument that consciousness is confirmed by itself when he argues that the confirmation of *śakti*s, such as time and direction, in the same way, does not rely on any other means of knowledge (*VP* 3.6.18). Some of these arguments are borrowed in the subsequent development of the Trika concept of Śakti and also its treatment of consciousness.

When addressing another power, namely *sādhana,* Bhartṛhari explains that concrete entities are merely the materialization of powers (*VP* 3.7.2) and the plurality of powers relies on different cognitive functions (*VP* 3.7.6). Crucial to this discussion is the identification that entities are powers in essence is the philosophy of the Saṁsargavādins (*VP* 3.7.9). This is to suggest that a similar concept must have existed prior to Bhartṛhari himself

22. *śaktīnām api sā śaktir guṇānām apy asau guṇaḥ* | — *VP* 3.3.5.

23. Significant to this discussion are the passages in *VP* 3.6. 3, 6, 13, 14, 20, 24, and 27.

and he is merely synthesizing one strand of the philosophy of power. While addressing the issue of whether the energies are distinct from their substrate entity, Bhartṛhari argues that neither the view that power and the entity that is endowed with it are identical, nor the view that these are distinct, is real in the absolute sense. In his opinion, it is the very essence (*tattva*) that manifests as identical or distinct from each other (*VP* 3.7.39-40). Also noteworthy is Bhartṛhari's presentation of three views in this discussion of the nature of *śakti*. According to the first view, power is produced in an entity before action through other causes. Following the second view, this *śakti* is inborn in an entity. The third view says that action occurs prior to the rise of powers, holding that the cause of action is not the same as that of the power (*VP* 3.7.32). Parallel to these positions, the power inherent to Śiva is defined in different ways by the dualistic Siddhānta and monistic Trika Śaiva traditions. Congruent with Bhartṛhari's opinion that *śakti* is ultimately singular, Abhinava asserts that the powers identified in various forms are essentially one, as they cannot be distinguished in their essential Khecarī form.[24] Similar to the doctrine of Saṁsargavādins, Tāntrics maintain that "there exist two categories, power and that what is endowed with power."[25] The concept that a singular power appears as many (*VP* 3.7.37, 146) tallies with the Śākta understanding of power.

As understood by Bhartṛhari, action (*kriyā*) is the power that brings about transformation,[26] and is explained as the successive process that is presented as to be accomplished, whether finished or unfinished (*VP* 3.8.1). Bhartṛhari defines action as a collection of activities produced in a sequence that is mentally conceived of as one (*VP* 3.8.4). Each part of the action appears to occur in sequence due to the *śakti*s inherent in its parts (*VP* 3.8.14). Following this depiction, action in reality is one and without sequence but is presented in parts (*VP* 3.8.18). Being (*sattā*), in Bhartṛhari's understanding, is autonomous in its power to assume forms, whether as an entity or process (*VP* 3.8.35). Here, an entity is considered to be the accomplished form of action. Bhartṛhari presents the view of other philosophers, according to whom action is the eternal creative force (*VP* 3.8.36). Many of these arguments are seminal to the development of the

24. *Parātrīśikā*. Singh 1988, p. 13, lines 22-23.

25. *śaktiś ca śaktimāṁś caiva padārthadvayam ucyate | śaktayo 'sya jagat kṛtsnaṁ śaktimāṁs tu maheśvaraḥ | | Sarvavīrabhaṭṭāraka*. — Cited in *Mahārthamañjarī* 80:19-20.

26. This view is presented by Yāska as *bhāvapradhānamākhyātam sattvapradhānāni nāmāni* (*Nirukta* 1.1). Durgācārya has elaborated upon this in his commentary.

Śākta philosophy of Krama that explains cosmic and epistemic processes in terms of the sequence of Kālī, the power inherent to time.

Bhartṛhari's characterization that action in reality is one and without sequence is comparable to Utpala's segmentation of action into the phenomenal and eternal, the second belonging to the Lord (*ĪP* 2.1.2). Utpala defines time in this context as nothing but sequence (*ĪP* 2.1.3), which parallels the description of time and action found in *VP*. Similar to Bhartṛhari's depiction that action is mentally conceived of as one, Utpala proposes that the mind produces mental constructs such as action (*ĪP* 2.2.3). As found in *VP* 3.8.30 — that a single time attains sequence due to its powers — Utpala asserts that action, while remaining one, involves succession (*ĪP* 2.4.5). The autonomy of *sattā* in assuming manifoldness parallels the autonomy of Śiva that gives rise to external entities. Just as Śiva in the Trika system transcends sequence, Bhartṛhari posits that there is no sequence in reality, as sequence is not possible of something that does not exist and something that exists does not render a sequence (*VP* 3.8.36).

Bhartṛhari identifies "relation" (*sambandha*) as the factor that unites all other powers. Since it binds all other powers while itself being power, it is defined as the *śakti* of all *śakti*s and the attribute of all attributes.[27] This power is identified as inherence (*samavāya*) and is addressed as the power that motivates other powers. Similar to the description of *paśyantī* found in the *Vṛtti* upon *VP* (*VPvṛ*), relation (*sambandha*) is identified as beyond identity and difference.[28] Bhartṛhari's characterization of the attributes of *śakti* also parallels the position of those adopting *Brahman* as the singular reality that gives rise to sequence (*krama*, *VP* 3.3.83). Arguably, this is the position of the Advaitins prior to Bhartṛhari and it is likely that they were the Saṁsargavādins. Helārāja's commentary upon *VP* 3.3.83 that identifies this power of *Brahman* to be the power of autonomy (*svātantrya*) further allows us to bridge the grammarian's concept of *śakti* with that of the Trika philosophers.

Based on these select examples, it can be concluded that Bhartṛhari's philosophy of language is a source text for the discussion on *śakti* and its nuanced treatment in subsequent literature. It is also explicit that several categories in Bhartṛhari's cosmology parallel Tāntric cosmology. The

27. *śaktīnām api sā śaktir guṇānām apy asau guṇaḥ* | — *VP* 3.3.5.

28. *tāṁ śaktiṁ samavāyākhyāṁ śaktīnām upakariṇīm | bhedābhedavyatikrāntām anyathaiva vyavasthitām* || — *VP* 3.3.10. Helārāja elucidates *śaktīnām upakārāṇi* as *sādhanadiśaktīnām cāśrayavasthānena upakārīṇi*; which connects this inherent *śakti* with the other *śakti*s like *sādhana*, etc. by word.

argument here is not to reduce the Tāntric Śākta paradigm to the linguistic philosophy of Bhartṛhari, as the theological elements of Śakti, such as devotion to Śakti or her iconic visualization, are unique to Tāntric traditions. Based on the above discussion of linguistic and cosmic powers, we can further explore the concepts of *vāc*, *pratibhā*, or *kāla*, crucial to Trika perspective.

Vāc: Linguistic and Cosmic

Bhartṛhari asserts that *vāc* or speech manifests in the three levels of *vaikharī*, *madhyamā*, and *paśyantī* (*VP* 134 [142]). Trika philosophers beginning with Somānanda criticize him for accepting *paśyantī* as the highest speech.[29] The Trika system introduces *parā* or transcendent speech, surpassing the three other levels of speech. This categorization becomes standard even among subsequent grammarians. If the division of speech into four categories is considered unique to Trika Śaivas, then even in this case, the credit goes to Bhartṛhari for providing the framework. The addition of *parā*, however, needs to be read in light of the deity Parā, central to the Trika system.[30] What is not explained is, is this *parā* speech distinct from the Goddess Parā? Or, is there a separate deity, such as Kālī, always in the Trika Maṇḍala placing the Goddess Parā as subordinate?

While the very concept of the stratification of speech is relevant to our discussion on *śakti*, two internal modes, "seeing" (*paśyantī*) and the "middle" (*madhyamā*), are quintessential. The *VPvṛ* describes the "middle" as abiding inside, "as if assuming sequence" (*parigṛhītakrameva*). This position is congruent with sequentiality and the transcendence of consciousness that is found in the Trika depiction. Resembling the depiction of Kālasaṅkarṣiṇī in Tāntric liturgy and the essential nature of consciousness in Trika philosophy, the "seeing" aspect of speech is described as "where the sequence is absorbed" (*pratisaṁhṛtakramā*), and "endowed with the power of sequence" (*samāviṣṭakramaśakti*) while being non-dual in nature. Just like Trikas depict consciousness as subsuming paradoxicality, *paśyantī* is depicted as being "motionless while moving" (*calācalā*), "pure while remaining covered" (*āvṛtā ca viśuddhā ca*), and

29. Somānanda endeavours to refute the *paśyantī* of the grammarians. See *Śivadṛṣṭi* (*ŚD*), Chapter 2, and Chapter 3, verses 85-87.

30. In the Trika system, three goddesses constitute the essential cognitive and cosmic triad. In this paradigm, Parā relates to will (*icchā*), Parāparā is linked with cognition (*jñāna*), and Aparā is associated with action (*kriyā*). These deities are viewed as sitting atop a trident in the most common *Triśūlābjamaṇḍala*. Tripurā system relates three aspects of *icchā*, *jñāna*, and *kriyā* with the deities of the central triangle, Kāmeśvarī, Vajreśvarī, and Bhagamālinī.

"associated with the forms of the objects of cognition while being formless and having forms hidden."[31] The *VPvr̥* also introduces the transcendent (*parā*) form of *paśyantī* that is beyond all conventions in the world (*lokavyavahārātīta*). This introduction of the transcendent form of *paśyantī* can be identified as the foundation for the depiction of *parā* speech found in later traditions.

Further research uncovers reasons that allow comparison of the divinity Parā identified by Trika philosophers with the fourth state of speech, *parā*. First of all, Utpala identifies *paśyantī* as the Goddess Parāparā,[32] with this identity further confirmed by Abhinava.[33] When making this identification, he also addresses Parā by saying that *paśyantī* is of the character of Parāparā which is the essential energy of Parā, giving an example of counter-image.[34] In *ĪP* 1.5.13, *parā* is described as awareness of the character of self-reflection and identified as *parā* speech. While elaborating upon this linguistic *parā* (*ĪP* 1.5.14), Utpala cites a verse from the *Parātriṁśikā* that describes the Goddess Parā and not the *parā* speech. Evidently, Utpala is comfortable with this identification. The identification of speech with awareness, as found in *ĪP* 1.5.13, is commonplace in the philosophy of Bhartr̥hari. Abhinava identifies Aparā with the "middle" speech.[35] This identity is not only crucial to Trika cosmology, since establishing the parallels between speech and the deities opens up a soteriological domain of Trika that is grounded on the divination of speech.

Pratibhā: Meeting Point of the Powers of Śabda and the Powers of Śiva

The concept of *pratibhā* is very broad, and it is not necessary to repeat

31. *sanniviṣṭajñeyākārā pratilīnākārā nirākārā ca.* This commentary comes in the verse, "*vaikharyā . . .*" that is listed as 1.142 in Biardeau's and Raghunātha Śarmā's editions. Abhyankar and Limaye (1965) list this as 1.143.

32. Pandey 1963: 634. See *ĪP* 1.5.13-14. See also *ŚD* 2.1-2 and Utpala's commentary thereon.

33. *Parātrīśikā*. Singh 1988, p. 22, lines 7-11.

34. *paśyantī ca parāparābhaṭṭārikāsatattvā paraśakter eva sātmaśaktir darpaṇakalpā* —*PTV*. Singh 1988, p. 49, lines 8-9; . . . *paśyantyādiviniviṣṭaparāparābhaṭṭārikādiprasarā* . . . —*PTV*. Singh 1988, p. 38, lines 17-18; *parāparādipaśyantyādiprasara* . . . —*PTV*. Singh 1988, p. 30, line 12; . . . *paśyantyādikāḥ parāparābhaṭṭārikādisphārarūpāḥ*. . . . —*PTV*. Singh 1988, p. 35, lines 24-25; see also Singh 1988, p. 38, lines 17-18. Abhinava also relates the deity *parā* with *paśyantī* identifying the second as the expression of the first: *parābhaṭṭārikāyāś ca paśyantyāditādātmyaḥ nirṇītam prāg eva* | —*PTV*. Singh 1988, p. 19, line 15. . . *paśyantyāpi parābhaṭṭārikāyāḥ prathamaprasaratvāt* | —*PTV*. Singh 1988, p. 28, line 20.

35. . . . *madhyamākr̥tim aparātmakaśaktinālikā*. . . —*PTV*. Singh 1988, p. 17, lines 13-14.

many of the arguments of the early scholars.[36] This term is used in mystical, metaphysical, religious, aesthetic, and psychological contexts with different meanings (Pandey 1963: 693), and so it is not possible to address all these aspects in this brief paper. The scope of this essay is to establish a link between linguistic *pratibhā* with cosmic Pratibhā. According to Bhartṛhari, *pratibhā* is the meaning of language itself; it is the intuitive power of the yogins; it is the spontaneous surge of specific qualities such as the particular voice of the cuckoos in the spring; and it is poetic ability. In these applications, the cosmic aspect of *pratibhā* that grounds the Trika philosophy of Abhinava is not explicitly identified.

The yogic intuition that can be found in Nyāya-Vaiśeṣika and the Yoga system of Patañjali appears in the treatment of *pratibhā*, both in the philosophy of Bhartṛhari and the Trika system. Just like the concept of the autonomy of *śakti*, the intuitive power that surges in *yogī*s, sometimes even automatically, appears to be an earlier concept expanded upon by both Bhartṛhari and the Trika masters. *VPvṛ* identifies this *pratibhā* as the power through which *yogin*s become aware of another's intention.[37] Not only that, even the power of goblins and demons to "enter into another being's body" (*parāveśa*) and to be invisible are identified as the same *pratibhā*.[38] The intuitive knowledge or *pratibhā* of the seers, in the same way, is revealed through their knowledge of the Vedas (*VP* 1.30). This description makes explicit that the *pratibhā* of Bhartṛhari is not only the meaning of a sentence, as it covers varied concepts.

The application of *pratibhā* as the meaning of sentence, where the "meaning" itself is referring to non-dual awareness, binds Bhartṛhari's linguistics with soteriology. This dual application of the term, on one hand the meaning in the phenomenal sense, and on the other hand, the essential meaning, the very being (*sattā*) that governs all that exists, is paving the way for further expansion, as is evident in the subsequent Trika application. Making the linguistic application in describing reality contextual, the *pratibhā* of Bhartṛhari is directly revealed by word, or by its impression in its absence.[39] The inner awareness, the inspiration that

36. The most noteworthy of the treatments of *pratibhā* is in Gonda 1963: 318-48. For a detailed treatment of *pratibhā*, see Pandey 1963: 678-732.

37. *yoganimittā kācit | tad yathā yogināṁ avyabhicāreṣa parābhiprāyajñānādiṣu* | —*Vṛtti* on *VP* 2.152.

38. *tathā kācidadṛṣṭanimittā | tadyathā rakṣaḥpiśācādīnāṁ parāveśāntardhānādiṣu* | — *Vṛtti* on *VP* 2.152.

39. *vicchedagrahaṇe 'rthānāṁ pratibhānyaiva jāyate* | — *VP* 2.145.

one has by hearing sentences, is free from object and is understood as the very *pratibhā*. The rise of this awareness is identified as non-sequential, since the surge of sudden awareness does not depend upon understanding meaning in any specific mode of time.

As mentioned above, the *pratibhā* of Bhartṛhari is not merely the meaning of a sentence, because in his cosmology, the power embodied within *śabda* constitutes the world and this is identified as of the essence of *pratibhā*.[40] The rise of cognition in this paradigm is through the process wherein the powers of objects retract to the sense organs, the powers sense organs retract to cognitions, and the powers of cognition remain at the core of speech through the retraction of sequence.[41] This power of word described by Bhartṛhari is not simply the signifying power of language. Bhartṛhari asserts that, besides their power to refer to something, words have powers to carry out magical effects such as removing poison (*VP* 1.130 (138). The inclusion of the power of *mantra* within the discussion of the signifying power of language facilitates an alignment of Bhartṛhari's *śakti* with the expanded concept of *pratibhā* that includes intuitive and divine powers. His understanding of *pratibhā* as meaning needs to be read in this light. For Bhartṛhari, it is not interconnection (*saṁsarga*), action (*kriyā*), or purpose (*prayojana*) that is the meaning of a sentence, but the intuition (*pratibhā*) that arises immediately upon hearing the sentence. It is this collective and indivisible entity (*akhaṇḍa*), the meaning understood in a flash that is identified by *pratibhā*. This is considered to be distinct from the meaning derived from words.[42] This *pratibhā* cannot be grasped as "this" or "that"; it is established as self-evident to each and every subject; and it is not determined even by the subject.[43] This *pratibhā* is supposed to arise spontaneously, like the intoxicating power that arises in specific time in some substances.[44] For Bhartṛhari, this *pratibhā* is common to all sentient beings. It is through the

40. *śabdeṣv evāśritā śaktir viśvasyāsya nibandhanī* | *yannetraḥ pratibhātmāyaṁ bhedarūpaṁ pratāyate* || — *VP* 1.110 (118) in the Iyer edition (1966).

41. *yathāpareṣām indriyeṣu viṣayamātrāśaktayaḥ pratilayaṁ gacchanti tathendriyamātrāśaktayo buddhiṣu buddhi-mātrāśaktayaḥ pratisaṁhṛtakrame vāgātmani* | — *VPvṛ* 1.110 (118).

42. *vicchedagrahaṇe 'rthānāṁ pratibhānyaivopajāyate* | *vākyārtha iti tam āhuḥ*. . . — *VP* 2.143.

43. *idaṁ tad iti sānyeṣām anākhyeyā kathañcana* | *pratyātmavṛttisiddhā sā kartrāpi na nirūpyate* || — *VP* 2.144.

44. *yathā dravyaviśeṣāṇāṁ paripākair ayatnajāḥ* | *madādiśaktayo dṛṣṭāḥ pratibhās tadvatām tathā* || — *VP* 2.148.

same *pratibhā* that even birds such as cuckoos have a distinct voice during the spring (*VP* 2.149).

Abhinavagupta identifies *pratibhā* as awareness (*cit*).[45] This, however, is not simply awareness in a generic sense. This is the consort of Bhairava and the Supreme Deity Parā. What is explicit is that Abhinava has incorporated the concept of time found in Bhartṛhari's writing into the deified *pratibhā*, as this deity is synonymous with the "power of autonomy" (*svātantryaśakti*) in Abhinava's depiction, whereas *VPvṛ* describes time in terms of *svātantrya*.[46] To further buttress this argument, it is evident that *pratibhā* is foundational to the concept of powers in Abhinavagupta's Trika doctrine. Among the powers of autonomy (*svātantryaśakti*), the desire to manifest in succession (*kramasaṁsisṛkṣā*), and to have succession (*kramātmatā*), the first, or the power of autonomy, appears identical to this *pratibhā*, which is also identified with Parā, the central deity of the Trika doctrine.[47] Although not deified and not visualized in iconic form, *pratibhā* is also at the centre of the powers of language, as propounded by Bhartṛhari.

The linguistic aspect of *pratibhā* is incorporated within the wider application of this term in Abhinava's philosophy, where he describes it in terms of *parā-pratibhā* that not only holds *paśyantī* within, but also the endless varieties of objects (Pandey 1963: 679). The application of *pratibhā* as awareness that embodies all that exists adds a layer to the *paśyantī* that plays the same role in Bhartṛhari's metaphysics. The linguistic character of *pratibhā* in Bhartṛhari's writings can be fruitfully compared to the application of this term found in the Pratyabhijñā system of Utpala and Abhinava. In his commentary on Utpala's statement,

> that what is identified as *pratibhā* is coloured in the sequence of distinct objects, the self, that is the supreme Lord, is beyond sequence and of the character of unbound consciousness. —ĪP 1.7.1

Abhinava identifies two different etymologies of the term *pratibhā*: (1) *pratibhāti*, or "appears," in the sense of the appearance of entities to awareness, and (2) *prati bhāti*, or "appears with regard to the self," which

---

45. . . . *citpratibhāṁ*. . . — *TĀ* 1.2. Jayaratha interprets this phrase as *cidrūpā cāsau pratibhā prajñā*, further identifying *cit* and *prajñā* with *pratibhā*.

46. *kālākhyena hi svātantryeṣa sarvāḥ paratantrā śaktayaḥ samāviṣṭāḥ kālaśaktivṛttim anupatanti* | — *VPvṛ*, p. 18, lines 3-4.

47. *svātantryaśaktiḥ kramasaṁsisṛkṣā* | *kramātmatā ceti vibhor vibhūtiḥ* | | *tad eva devītrayam antarāstām* | *anuttaraṁ me prathayatsvarūpam* | | — *TĀ* 1.5.

refers to consciousness that is given to the self, or to itself.[48] The first meaning refers to the knowing of objects whereas the second meaning refers to the self-aware nature of consciousness. While the first meaning confirms the appearance of an object, the second meaning reinforces the concept that it does not manifest independent of the conscious subject. In this sense, both subject and object are within the domain of *pratibhā*.

With the identification of *pratibhā* as awareness, the argument that *pratibhā* cannot be denied in any mode of cognition since it envelops all concepts, is an extension of the premise that consciousness is self-aware. Abhinava can none the less be credited for establishing the meaning of *pratibhā* as awareness. His interpretation of the suffix *śatr̥* that follows the root √*bhās* in the term *pratibhā* as relation is interpreted in terms of autonomy (*svātantrya*), the term identified with Parā and also with Pratibhā.[49] This *pratibhā* has the appearance of sequence (*kramāvabhāsa*) when linked with external objects.[50] In the context of explaining *pratibhā*, Abhinava identifies autonomy (*svātantrya*) as the power of time (*kālaśakti*), a further nexus between himself and Bhartr̥hari.[51] He describes this *pratibhā* in its essential form as beyond sequence (*akramā*), due to its real nature of awareness itself.[52] This description of *pratibhā* embodying both the cognitive modes while remaining pure in its essential nature, occurring in sequence and still remaining transcendent to the sequence, tallies with the description of *paśyantī* found in *VPvr̥*. The identity of *pratibhā* as *paśyantī* is made in the *VPvr̥*.[53]

The Kāla-Śakti of Bhartr̥hari and the Goddess Kālī

There is no unanimity among classical Indian philosophers regarding the concept of time. The Vaiśeṣikas viewed time as a substance (*dravya*) while the Advaita Vedāntins depicted time as identical to ignorance (*avidyā*), and time was shown as the power of the word principle in Bhartr̥hari's literature. To apply *kāla* in its widest sense to the concept of Kālī found in

48. *pratibhāti ghaṭa iti yady api viṣayopaśliṣṭam eva pratibhānaṁ bhāti tathāpi na tadviṣayasya svakaṁ vapur api tu saṁvedanam eva tat tathā cakāsti māṁ prati bhātīti pramātr̥lagnatvāt* | — *Vimarśinī* on *ĪP* 1.7.1.

49. *Vimarśinī* on *ĪP* 1.7.1. Iyer 1986, p. 350, lines 3-4.

50. Ibid. p. 351, line 1.

51. Ibid. p. 352, lines 1-3.

52. *paramārthataś ca antarmukhatvena prakāśamātraparamārthatayā bhedābhāvād akramā* | — *Vimarśinī* on *ĪP* 1.7.1. Iyer 1986, p. 352, lines 5-6.

53. *vāgvikārāṇāṁ prakr̥tīṁ paśyantyākhyāṁ pratibhām*. . . — *VPvr̥* on *VP* 1.14. Iyer 1966, p. 48, line 1.

Krama philosophy, thus, can be misleading and inaccurate. However, just as Trika philosophers adopted the framework of Bhartṛhari and added new categories like the levels of speech identified above, so also did they expand upon the concept of deified time. There is also a historical link, Helārāja being the main figure that bridges the soteriology of Kālī found in Krama system with the linguistic philosophy of Bhartṛhari. To initiate the discussion, *Pañcaśatikā*, a liturgical text on Krama, asserts that Kālī is transcendent to *Śabda-Brahman*.[54]

Bhartṛhari identifies three different philosophies concerning time (*VP* 3.9.62). The first view considers it as *śakti* where *śakti* stands for instrumental cause. This view differs from the Vaiśeṣika understanding that instrumental cause is not an independent category and comes closer to the Mīmāṁsakas. However, Mīmāṁsakas do not acknowledge time as belonging to the category of independent cause. Thus, this view of considering time as power in the sense of instrumental cause and as an independent category depicts a distinct school of thought. The second view considers time as the *ātman* or the individual self. The third view, most likely the view held by Bhartṛhari himself,[55] considers time as the divinity, the power of *Brahman* having the character of awareness.[56] In other words, the linguistic philosophy of Bhartṛhari considered time as divine. Helārāja's terminology to describe this, such as "the gulp that devours the entire world" (*sakalajagadgrāsaghasmarā*), and that the awareness (*saṁvit*) that in itself is devoid of sequence (*akramā*) manifests as if in sequence (*parigṛhītakrameva*), are similar to Abhinava's language to describe the Goddess Kālī. In Abhinava's words, awareness (*saṁvid*) reveals as both inside and outside and while revealing itself, it appears as if revealing the other, the external entity.[57] Abhinava identifies this very

---

54. *śabdabrahmapadātītā ṣaṭtriṁśāntanavāntagā* | — Cited by Jayaratha in *TĀ*, *Viveka* 4.163.

55. *anye tu vigrahavatīṁ mahāprabhāvāṁ devatāṁ kālatvena pratipadyante* | *atrāpi cidrūpasya brahmaṇaḥ śaktir devataiva sakalajagadgrāsaghasmarety etad ānuguṇyam eveti* | *idam evātra siddhāntarūpaṁ darśanam* | *ata evaitat kāladarśanam avidyāyāṁ saṁsārahetubhūtāyāṁ prathamam, bhedāvabhāsamayo hi saṁsāro bhedaś ca deśakālābhyāṁ tatra kālabhedo jagatsṛṣṭer ādyaḥ* | *akramā hi paśyantīrūpā saṁvit prāṇavṛttim upārūḍā kālātmanā parigṛhītakrameva cakāsti* | — Helārāja on *VP* 3.9.62.

56. Although Bhartṛhari is not explicit in assigning this position to himself, classical Indian scholars generally presented their opinion at the end, after presenting other viewpoints. At least, this is what Helārāja thinks.

57. *ata eṣā sthitā saṁvid antarbāhyobhayātmanā* | *svayaṁ nirbhāsya tatrānyad bhāsayantīva bhāsate* || — *TĀ* 4.147.

awareness, pure and eager to manifest external entities, as Sṛṣṭikālī (*TĀ* 4.148). Helārāja's terminology is also comparable to the one found in the *Kramastotra*.[58] In the philosophy of Bhartṛhari, time in itself is devoid of sequence wherein the sequence of entities is grasped.[59] Abhinava's depiction that Mahākāla is where the duality in terms of subject and object is dissolved (*TĀ* 4.168) parallels the concept of the word principle that is beyond the dyad. Abhinava's depiction of Kālī as transcending sequence while also manifesting in sequence (*TĀ* 4.179) tallies with Bhartṛhari's depiction of time as beyond sequence and transcending differences (*VP* 3.9.30-31). Abhinava establishes awareness as the entity beyond description in terms of sequence and non-sequence.[60] Furthermore, time as depicted by Bhartṛhari is not itself in sequence, as time is shown as obtaining sequence through its power of obstruction (*pratibandha*) and permission (*abhyanujñā*).[61] He also confirms that the world, which in reality is the very *Brahman*, is devoid of sequence, but appears as if in sequence due to time (*VP* 3.9.46). This position can be compared with Abhinava's, for whom time is the pulsation (*kalanā*) present both in sequence and beyond sequence.[62]

Among the powers of *śabda* that are identical to *Brahman*, time is the most prominent one for Bhartṛhari.[63] What is significant for this discussion is that this power is identified in the *VPvṛ* as the power of autonomy (*svātantrya*).[64] Following the *Vṛtti*, it is due to the support of this power of autonomy that the cognition of the appearance of sequence is possible.[65] The small measurements (*mātrā*) of this time that are found in sequence, following this depiction, give rise to transformations such as origination,

---

58. *sarvārthasaṅkarṣaṇasaṁyamasya* | *yamasya yantur jagato yamāya* || *vapur mahāgrāsavilāsarāgāt* | *saṅkarṣayantīṁ praṇamāmi kālīm* || — *Kramastotra*, cited by Jayaratha in his commentary *Viveka* on *TĀ* 4.151. See also, . . . *ghasmarasaṁvidām*. . . *Kramastotra*, cited by Jayaratha on *TĀ*, *Viveka* 4.154.

59. *tamaṁprakāśavat tv ete trayo'dhvāno vyavasthitāḥ* | *akramās teṣu bhāvānāṁ kramaḥ samupalabhyate* || — *VP* 3.9.52.

60. *kramākramakathātītaṁ saṁvittattvaṁ sunirmalam* | — *TĀ* 4.180.

61. *pratibandhābhyanujñābhyāṁ vṛttir yā tasya śāśvatī* | *tayā vibhajyamāno 'sau bhajate kramarūpatāṁ* || — *VP* 3.9.30.

62. *kramākramakalanaiva kālaḥ* | — *Tantrasāra* (*TS*), Ch. 6. Chakravarty 1986, 50:3.

63. He addresses this power in the very beginning of his text (*VP* 1.3).

64. *kālākhyena hi svātantryeṣa sarvāḥ paratantrā śaktayaḥ samāviṣṭāḥ kālaśaktivṛttim anupatanti* | — *VPvṛ*, Iyer 1966, p. 18, lines 3-4.

65. . . . *śaktyavacchedena kramavānivābhāsopagamo lakṛate* | — *VPvṛ*, Iyer 1966, p. 18, line 4 – p. 19, line 1.

growth, and destruction. In the philosophy of Bhartṛhari, the power of time (*kāla-śakti*) is the dynamic creative force and its functioning is identified as the power of autonomy. The word principle is the material cause of the rise of the world and time is presented here as the auxiliary cause. Since creation, sustenance, and dissolution are dependent upon time, it is considered a foundational requisite for change. Time, therefore, is addressed as the architect of the world which functions by limiting some entities and activating others (*VP* 3.9.3-4). The three aspects of time are described as its powers that are differentiated into further categories (*VP* 3.9.37-38). When time is perceived in its own form without being relative to existence or non-existence and is reflected in a sudden awareness, this is defined as the present time (*VP* 3.9.89-90). It is noteworthy that Utpala identifies awareness not only in terms of Parā speech, he also calls it "autonomy" (*svātantrya*, *ĪP* 1.5.13). The autonomy of awareness, identical to the self or to Śiva, is one of the central elements of the Trika doctrine that makes it distinct from the Advaita of Śaṅkara.[66] This autonomy is one of the key concepts that links Bhartṛhari's concept of time with the Goddess Kālī.

This power of *śabda* identified as time is endowed with two powers of obstruction (*pratibandha*), and permission (*abhyanujñā*) (*VP* 3.9.4, 30). The origin and continuity of entities is due to the permission aspect of time, whereas the inability of entities to continue or to accomplish their purpose is due to the aspect of obstruction. Depiction of three modes of time as consisting of three distinct powers, and the presentation of present time as the play of permission and the other two modes of time as that of obstruction also confirms the autonomy of *śakti* in this paradigm. Abhinava's depiction that time is a limiting factor (*TĀ* 4.166) tallies with Bhartṛhari's depiction of time endowed with the power of obstruction.

Abhinava assigns meaning to the term Kālī according to its derivation from four different verbal roots. With the root √*kala kṣepe*, he interprets Kālī as the force that establishes difference or that reveals external reality. From the next root, √*kala gatau*, he identifies Kālī as the power to recognize entities that are perceived as "outside" as the very self. With the same root, he derives another meaning of Kālī as acknowledging the essential

66. See *Pratyabhijñāhṛdaya* 1 (Singh 1963); *ātmā prakāśavapur eṣa śivaḥ svatantraḥ svātantryanarmarabhasena nijaṁ svarūpam* . . . — *TS* 1.5. As Abhinava argues: *sa ca prakāśo na paratantraḥ prakāśyataiva hi pāratantryam* | — *TS*, Ch. 1. Chakravarty 1986, 5: 10-11. Abhinava explains the first aphorism form the Śivasūtra, *caitanyam ātmā*, as: *caitanyam iti byāvāntaṁ śabdaḥ svātantryamātrakam* | — *TĀ* 1.28. See also *TĀ* 1.31, 1.73.

nature of the self, as in the case of a counter-image, which, although not distinct from the image, is cognized as different. From the root √*kala saṅkhyāne*, he derives the meaning of Kālī as referring to the actual manifestation outside. From the root √*kala nāde,* he interprets Kālī as the awareness of the self (*TĀ* 4.173-175). Kālī, then, constitutes a range of subtle, yet distinct and overlapping, meanings.

The *kāla* of Bhartr̥hari reveals and conceals entities with its two powers. The terms he uses to describe it, *unmīlana* and *nimīlana* (*VP* 3.9.56), are noteworthy for this comparison. Bhartr̥hari also describes this in terms of "seeing" (*darśana*) and "not seeing" (*adarśana*) (*VP* 3.9.61). The functions of *unmīlana* and *nimīlana* inherent to Śiva, following Kṣemarāja's interpretation, are the powers that give rise to the world and reabsorb it.[67] These two terms also describe two different modes of absorption in his soteriology.[68]

Similar to Bhartr̥hari's identification of *kāla* as the action in which the form enters into cognition and which in turn coalesces into awareness without any other action occurring,[69] Abhinava identifies Kālī as being of the character of awareness.[70] The description of the sequence of Kālīs, where the objects of cognition (*prameya*) dissolve into cognition and that in turn into the subject (*pramātr̥*) and that to the awareness free from limitations is comparable to this understanding of time. While the ontological and epistemological nuances of the concept of time in these two systems are closely comparable, the Krama system of Kālī, while exploiting early philosophies on time, expands upon the concept and amplifies its meaning.

Conclusion

Based on the above discussion, a number of conclusions can be drawn. Spanning all the arguments is the point that the secular notion of power, predominantly found in the discussion on the scope of language, overlaps the theological *śakti*, the divine power. The initial point of discussion, the concept of *śakti* as the divine will that has been dropped in the later Nyāya

---

67. *Nirṇaya* commentary on *Spandakārika* 1.1. Singh 1980, p. 8, line 30.
68. *nimīlanonmīlanasamādhidvaye 'pi*... —Singh 1980, p. 26, line 15; *nimīlanasamādhi*. . . *vaiśvātmyam unmīlanasamādhi*. . . — Singh 1980, p. 108, lines 28-30; *nimīlanonmīlanasamādhidvaya*. . . — Singh 1980, p. 127, line 6.
69. *jñāne rūpasya saṁkrāntir jñānenaivānusaṁhr̥tiḥ* | *ataḥ kriyāntarābhāve sā kriyā kāla ucyate* | | — *VP* 3.9.78.
70. *parāmarśasvabhāvatvād etasyā*. . . | — *TĀ* 4.181.

writings and identified as merely the will of the user, demonstrates the cosmic aspect of language. Simply put, if language is of the divine origin, it has the potential to reveal the divine, and if it is merely a human enterprise, it cannot be instrumental to revealing the divine. Along the same lines, both the particular and universal as defined by Bhartṛhari embrace cosmological nuances, with the highest universal being (*sattā*), as identical to *Brahman* and the particular defined in terms of "essential being" and the "self."

More important than the specific *śakti*s identified by Bhartṛhari is the nature and function of *śakti*s as defined in *VP* to the comparison of *śakti* as depicted in the Trika system. For both Bhartṛhari and Abhinava, *śakti*s are found in plurality; they are inherent to the absolute within their own system; they depict the autonomy of consciousness; and are the power that embraces sequence while transcending it. As Bhartṛhari rejects the existence of concept in the absence of language, Abhinava finds *prakāśa* and *vimarśa* to be inseparable. Both hold a monistic world view, accepting that the highest principle manifests in plurality due to its own inherent powers.

For both Bhartṛhari and Abhinava, *śakti*s can embody further *śakti*s. Tāntric *maṇḍala*s rely on this assumption. Bhartṛhari states that these *śakti*s are born together (*sahaja*), a concept crucial to subsequent Tāntric traditions. Two central categories found in Bhartṛhari's discussion of the philosophy of language that are crucial to the development of Trika system are the concepts of *pratibhā* and *parā*. For both, Bhartṛhari and Abhinava, *pratibhā* stands for the intuitive power that transcends sequence. Many nuances of the concept of *parā* as the highest speech, found in terms of *parā-paśyantī* in Bhartṛhari's system, parallel the description of the divine Parā in Abhinava's writings. In the cases of both *pratibhā* and *parā*, what is missing from Bhartṛhari's writings is the deified *pratibhā* or *parā*, their iconic form, and accompanying rituals that are found in Abhinava's Tantrism.

Among the number of powers identified by Bhartṛhari, the depiction of the powers of time is very close to the description of Kālī in the Krama system. The exposition of time as the autonomous power (*svātantrya*) found in Bhartṛhari's depiction further confirms this identification. The two powers intrinsic to time, the power to reveal and to conceal entities, *unmīlana* and *nimīlana* in Bhartṛhari's terminology, can be compared with the two functions of *unmeṣa* and *nimeṣa*, the two modes of Śiva of emanating and retrieving the world. Although many of the other powers of Bhartṛhari are not crucial to the Trika system, the description of the powers such as *sādhana* or *dik* resonates with the description of *śakti* in the Tāntric Krama system. Finally, the description of *kriyā-śakti*, the power of action, suggests this power in the Trika system.

Abbreviations

ĪP	*Īśvarapratyabhijñā Kārikā* of Utpala
MB	*Mahābhāṣya* of Patañjali
MS	*Mīmāṃsā-Sūtra* of Jaiminī
NS	*Nyāya-Sūtra* of Vātsyāyana
PTV	*Parātrīśikāvivaraṇa* of Abhinavagupta. See Singh 1988.
ŚD	*Śivadṛṣṭi* of Somānanda
TĀ	*Tantrāloka* of Abhinavagupta
TS	*Tantrasāra* of Abhinavagupta
VP	*Vākyapadīya* of Bhartṛhari
VPvṛ	*Vākyapadīya-Vṛtti*. See Iyer 1966.

References

PRIMARY SOURCES

Mahābhāṣya (1987), *The Mahābhāṣya of Patañjali: With Kaiyaṭa's Bhāṣyapradīpa and Nāgeśa's Bhāṣyapradīpodyota* (vol. 1), ed. Bhargava Sastri Bhikaji Josi, Delhi: Chaukhamba Sanskrit Pratishthan.

Mahārthamañjarī (1992), *Mahārthamañjarī of Maheśvarānanda: With Auto-commentary 'Parimala'*, Varanasi: Sampurnand Sanskrit University.

Nirukta (1920-27, rpt. 1984), *The Nighaṇṭu and Nirukta*, ed. Lakshman Sarup. Delhi: Motilal Banarsidass.

Nyāyasūtra (1986), *The Nyāyasūtra of Gautama with the Nyāyabhāṣya of Vātsyāyana. With the Prasannapadā Commentary of Sudarśanācārya*, ed. Dwarikadas Shastri, Varanasi: Sudhi Prakashana.

Śābarabhāṣya (1987), *The Mīmāṃsā-Śābara-Bhāṣya*, Hindi Commentary by Yudhisthira Mimamsaka, Haryana: Yudhiṣṭhira Mīmāṁsaka.

Śivadṛṣṭi (1986), *The Śivadṛṣṭi of Somānanda Nātha: With the Vṛtti of Śrī Utpaladeva*, ed. with Hindi Translation by Radheshyam Chaturvedi, Varanasi: Varanaseya Sanskrit Sansthan.

Ślokavārttika (1978), *The Ślokavārttika of Kumārilabhaṭṭa: With the commentary Nyāyaratnākara* by Pārthasārathi Miśra, Varanasi: Ratna Publications.

Tantrāloka (1987), *The Tantrāloka of Abhinavagupta: With the Commentary of Jayaratha* (vols. 1-8), ed. R.C. Dwivedi and Navjivan Rastogi, Delhi: Motilal Banarsidass.

Vākyapadīya (a), (1964) *Vākyapadīya Brahmakāṇḍa. Avecla Vṛtti de Harivṛṣabha*, ed. and tr. Madeleine Biardeau, Paris: òditions E. De Boccard.

Vākyapadīya (b), (1979) *The Vākyapadīya of Bhartṛhari (Part III Vol. II), With Prakāśa*

Commentary by Helārāja, ed. with Ambākartr̥ commentary by Raghunātha Śarmā, Varanasi: Sampurnand Sanskrit University.

SECONDARY SOURCES

Abhyankar, K.V. & V.P. Limaye (1965), *Vākyapadīya of Śrī Bhartr̥hari*, Poona: University of Poona.

Cefalu, Richard Francis (1973), *Shakti in Abhinavagupta's Concept of Mokṣa*, Doctoral Dissertation, Fordham University.

Chakravarty, Hemendra Nath (1986), *Tantrasāra*, Varanasi: Varanaseya Sanskrit Sansthan.

Coward, Harold G. and K. Kunjunni Raja (eds.), (1990), *The Philosophy of the Grammarians* (*Encyclopedia of Indian Philosophies*, vol. V), Delhi: Motilal Banarsidass.

Dragonetti, Carmen & Fernando Tola (1990), "Some Remarks on Bhartr̥hari's Concept of Pratibhā," in *Journal of Indian Philosophy*, vol. 18, pp. 95-112.

Gonda, Jan (1963), *The Vision of the Vedic Poets*, The Hague: Mouton.

Iyer, K.A. Subramania (1966), *Vākyapadīya of Bhartr̥hari: With the Vr̥tti and the Paddhati of Vr̥ṣabhadeva*, Poona: Deccan College.

———, (1971) *The Vākyapadīya of Bhartr̥hari*, Chapter III, Pt. I, English tr., Poona: Deccan College.

———, (1974) *The Vākyapadīya of Bhartr̥hari*, Chapter III, Pt. II, English tr., Delhi: Motilal Banarsidass.

———, (1992) *Bhartr̥hari: A Study of the Vākyapadīya in the Light of the Ancient Commentaries*, Pune: Deccan College.

Iyer, K.A.S. and K.C. Pandey (eds.), (1986), *Īśvarapratyabhijñā of Utpala with the Vimarśinī of Abhinavagupta*, with the commentary Bhāskarī (vols. 1-3), Delhi: Motilal Banarsidass.

Joshi, S.D. (1977), "Bhartr̥hari's Concept of Pratibhā: A Theory on the Nature of Language Acquisition," in *Some Aspects of Indo-Iranian Literary and Cultural Traditions* (*Commemoration Volume of Dr. V.G. Paranjpe*), ed. Suniti Kumar Chatterji et al., Delhi: Ajanta Publications, pp. 71-76.

Kaviraj, Gopinath (1924), "The Doctrine of Pratibhā in Indian Philosophy," in *Annals of Bhandarkar Oriental Research Institute*, no. 5, pp. 1-18 and 113-32.

Kuanpoonpol, Priyawat (1991), *Pratibhā: The Concept of Intuition in the Philosophy of Abhinavagupta*, Doctoral dissertation, Harvard University.

Larson, Gerald James (1974), "The Sources for Śakti in Abhinavagupta's Kashmir Śaivism: A Linguistic and Aesthetic Category," in *Philosophy East and West*, vol. 24, pp. 41-56.

Padoux, André (1990), *Vāc: The Concept of the Word in Selected Hindu Tantras*, Albany: State University of New York Press.

Pandey, Kanti Chandra (1963), *Abhinavagupta: A Historical and Philosophical Study*, Varanasi: Chowkhamba Sanskrit Series.

Rukmani, Trichur S. (1987), "Patañjali's Prajñā and Bhartr̥hari's Pratibhā: A Comparative Study," in *Indian Philosophical Quarterly*, vol. 14, no. 1, pp. 81-90.

Sharma, Peri Sarveswara (1972), *The Kālasamuddeśa of Bhartr̥hari's Vākyapadīya*, Delhi: Motilal Banarsidass.

Singh, Jaideva (1963), *Pratyabhijñāhṛdaya: The Secret of Self-Recognition*, Sanskrit Text with English Translation, Notes, and Introduction, Delhi: Motilal Banarsidass.

———, (1980) *Spandakārika: The Divine Creative Pulsation: The Kārikās and the Spanda-nirnaya*, translated into English, Delhi: Motilal Banarsidass.

———, (1988) *Parātrīśikāvivaraṇa: The Secret of Tantric Mysticism*, Delhi: Motilal Banarsidass.

12

Freedom in the Bhagavad-Gītā

An Analysis of Buddhi and Sattva Categories

*P. Pratap Kumar**

Introduction

THE *Bhagavad-Gītā*, of the many Hindu sacred texts, occupies a singularly significant place among both Hindus as well as among the Western intellectual community. The West came to know of the text first through the translation of it by Charles Wilkins in 1775 into English and thereafter scores of translations became available in many European languages. Exactly 100 years later, in 1885, Edwin Arnold rendered the text into poetic version and titled it "the Song Celestial." Incidentally, it was this translation of the *Gītā* that Gandhi (Koppendrayer 2002) is said to have read and became influenced by its philosophical simplicity and beauty and used it as a daily guide. In the late nineteenth century the text became an important tool in the struggle for freedom, deployed by many reformers and political commentators and activists, the most significant among them being Bal Gangadhar Tilak (Brown 1958) and Aurobindo Ghosh (1970). While Tilak produced a commentary (*Gītārahasya*) of political activism playing on its philosophy of *karma*, Aurobindo produced a commentary on it with an emphasis on transcendentalism.[1] Many Western intellectuals, such as Tolstoy and Robert Oppenheimer, were deeply affected by the text. Oppenheimer is said to have become so deeply affected by its philosophy of *karma* as detached action, that he is claimed to have defended his scientific activities in producing the atomic bomb through what he believed as *Gītā*'s philosophy to perform one's duty without regard to its effects (Hijiya 2000).

---

* University of KwaZulu-Natal, South Africa

1. For a substantial comment on the influence that *Gītā* had on various Indian intellectuals, see Kosambi 1961.

The *Gītā*, of course, first has to be understood as part of its traditional place within the corpus of Hindu sacred texts. It stands as a part of the epic text known as the *Mahābhārata*. It is a philosophical dialogue between the warrior hero Arjuna and his mentor and friend, Kṛṣṇa, on the eve of the war between the feuding cousins, the Pāṇḍavas and the Kauravas, in which the former were considered the heroes being led by Arjuna, and the latter led by Duryodhana were considered the villains. Whether or not the *Gītā* was originally part of the epic text has been debated in Western scholarship. Reviewing the translation of Nārāyaṇīya-Parvan of the *Mahābhārata* by Anne-Marie Esnoul, Carlo Coppola makes reference to the idea that Nārāyaṇīya-Parvan was a later interpolation into the *Mahābhārata* than the *Gītā* (Coppola 1981: 171). However, van Buitenen (1968) argued, in general agreement with the traditional Indian scholarly position that it does belong to the epic text as an organic whole. Be that as it may, for my purpose here it is a secondary issue. The key issue that needs to be clarified at this stage is that it belongs to the epic tradition and hence belongs to what is distinguished as Smṛti part of the sacred texts of the Hindus. The Hindu texts as we know are separated as Śruti, meaning those that are revealed and hence occupy higher position, and the Smṛti texts which are generally attributed to the human authorship. The key issue, therefore, is that the *Gītā* being part of the corpus of texts that are attributed to human agency, in fact, occupies the position of the Śruti texts. In traditional context, the *Gītā* is also called *Gītopaniṣad*, thereby alluding to its position being on a par with those of the Upaniṣadic texts which are placed in the category of Śruti. When and how this elevation of the *Gītā* to the position of Śruti occurred is hard to speculate. But certainly by the time of Śaṅkara (ninth century CE) we are able to say that it has already been elevated to this extraordinary status. Van Buitenen (1965: 109) says,

> [T]he very fact that Śaṅkara felt impelled to comment on the *Gītā*, a text far from congenial to his central doctrines, should sufficiently show in how high an esteem the *Gītā* was held as a quasi-philosophical, moralistic and religious discourse.

Right at the beginning of his commentary on the *Gītā*, in his introduction, Śaṅkara alludes to the fact that the text had been commented upon before him by a number of commentators. Arvind Sharma points out that the *Anugītā*, perhaps composed around third century CE, may have been the first commentary on the *Gītā* (Sharma 1978: 262). It is therefore understandable that Śaṅkara reinforces its status by placing alongside the two other corpus of texts that enjoyed the higher status, viz.

Bādarāyaṇa's *Brahma-Sūtras* and the Upaniṣads. Thus, together with the *Brahma-Sūtras* and the Upaniṣadic texts, the *Gītā* is declared as part of the triad that needed to be commented upon if a traditional scholar wanted to engage in Vedānta philosophical debates and establish one's own position on it. Śaṅkara was probably following an established tradition in recognizing the *Gītā* as being on a par with the texts that are classified under the Śruti category. However, he certainly must be credited for being the first known traditional scholar who commented on the three texts in an attempt to develop his particular view of Vedānta that has come to be identified as non-dual philosophy. Ever since Śaṅkara, every major and minor Vedānta scholar who came afterwards, had to comment on the triad. Thus, it would be safe to say that the establishment of the triad for the proper understanding of the Vedānta philosophy was achieved first by Śaṅkara without a doubt. As per the *Gītā*, Śaṅkara's commentary is the only extant one before others, such as Rāmānuja, followed him with his commentary, unless we accept *Anugītā* as its first known commentary, as Sharma (1978) argues.

What perhaps makes the *Gītā* specially suitable to be in such a distinguished position is that it takes the same content that is discussed in the *Brahma-Sūtras* and the Upaniṣads about the nature of Self/*Brahman*, the individual and the world, and presents it in a dialogical format with its own emphasis on the idea of *karma* as action without attachment to the fruits of it. It is here that it makes a special connection with the Pūrva-Mīmāṁsā philosophical tradition, and hence, with the old ritual tradition of the Vedas.[2] It is perhaps this fundamental reinterpretation of the ancient ritual tradition as action without attachment to the consequent fruits that might give the *Gītā* its unique place in the exposition of the Vedānta philosophy. Additionally, in its method unlike the Upaniṣadic texts that contain often several different dialogues between several different characters the *Gītā* is a single and continuous dialogue from the beginning to the end. Nevertheless, much like the Upaniṣads it is also very open and amenable to different interpretations and hence carries the characteristics of the Śruti type texts. It is, therefore, not strange that both Śaṅkara and his rival commentators that came later, could find appropriate passages in it to support their respective points of view.

Gītā in Relation to other Indian Systems

In order for us to understand the distinct way in which the *Gītā* develops

2. Christopher Chapple had shown the relationship of *karman* in the *Gītā* and the idea of sacrifice in the Vedas (see Chapple 1986).

its notion of freedom *vis-à-vis buddhi* and *sattva*, we need to understand the proximity between the *Gītā* and Sāṁkhya. Notwithstanding its openness to different interpretations, the *Gītā* is known to be a synthetic text that brings together different philosophical ideas in the form of easily readable verses, hence the name *Gītā*. The philosophical tradition of Sāṁkhya is identified with what is known as the religion of renunciation (*nivr̥tti dharma*) followed by the sages such as Śaunaka, Sanandana et al., whereas, the religion of works (*pravr̥tti dharma*) is followed by sages such as Marīci. The ultimate goal of the Upaniṣadic religion is the realization of *Brahman*. The *Gītā*, by its emphasis on *dharma*, attempts to bring synthesis of these three philosophical traditions. Simply put, the *puruṣa* of Sāṁkhya, the *kṣātra* of the Pūrva-Mīmāṁsā, or what Śaṅkara calls "earthly *Brahman*" (referring to the Vedas, Brāhmaṇas and the sacrifices) and the *Brahman* of the Upaniṣadic texts are synthesized into one coherent whole. While there is wider scholarly consensus on the relationship between the *Gītā* and Sāṁkhya of an earlier version, points of contention might be in some details of the relationship between the two. One of the contentious points on the relationship between the *Gītā* and Sāṁkhya may depend on which manuscript one is consulting. Schrader argued that Kāśmīrī recension contained the more ancient version of the text than the Vulgate text of the *Gītā* (Schrader 1930). However, Edgerton (1932: 75) finds Schrader's findings less convincing, while van Buitenen argues that the Kāśmīrī recension is later than that of Bhāskara (van Buitenen 1965: 104f). Commenting on one of the two manuscripts lodged in the library of the Trinity College, Dublin, Denis Crofton was convinced that the philosophy of the Sāṁkhya of Kapila is the same as that of the *Gītā* (Crofton 1867: 4). Mircea Eliade pointed out generally that the *Gītā* is "an amalgamation of Sāṁkhya-Yoga and Vedānta" (Eliade 1954: 394). Among recent scholars, David White has pointed out well the synthetic project of the *Gītā*. He argues that the *Gītā* attempts to synthesize the "the Upaniṣadic Vedānta and the proto-Sāṁkhya" (White 1979: 501). The point that the *Gītā* author/s bring together three distinct philosophical traditions, viz. the Sāṁkhya, the Pūrva-Mīmāṁsā and the Upaniṣadic ideas of *Brahman*, has also been made by, *inter alia*, Larson (1975: 660).

White (1979) mainly takes into account the chapter nine of the *Gītā* in examining the synthetic project of the *Gītā*. I will return to White's comments later in the essay in dealing with the category of *buddhi*. However, R.C. Zaehner (1969) thought that chapter thirteen of the *Gītā* was perhaps the best illustration of the synthesis between proto-Sāṁkhya and the *Gītā*, and of course, White does take cognizance of it (White 1979: 501). Much debate had occurred in the earlier scholarship on the *Gītā* that dealt with the question whether or not the text of the *Gītā* is to be viewed as a single whole or "patchwork." However, it is useful to point out that Zaehner (1969) viewed *Gītā* as a unified text making use of different philosophical ideas from Sāṁkhya, Buddhism and the Upaniṣads in contrast to the view expressed by Richard Garbe and Rudolf Otto that the *Gītā* is, as Wendy O'Flaherty puts it, a "patchwork of various strands of philosophies current in India between the fifth and second centuries BCE." (O'Flaherty 1971: 78). O'Flaherty agrees with Zaehner that it is a "jigsaw puzzle to be pieced together rather than as a tangle to be unravelled" (O'Flaherty 1971: 78).

Edgerton further points out that while the *Gītā* distinguishes between Sāṁkhya and Yoga as methods, in the *Mahābhārata* the teachings of Sāṁkhya and Yoga are considered same — "the same teaching (as to truth; Śāstra) that is declared by Sāṁkhya is also the view (*darśana*) of Yoga" (Edgerton 1924: 21). The *Gītā* spends a substantial part of its deliberations on the Sāṁkhya categories and concepts in an attempt to illuminate its own distinctive philosophical view. However, most scholars are of the view that the Sāṁkhya ideas that one finds in the *Gītā* are from an earlier form of Sāṁkhya and in the view of Edgerton what one finds in the *Gītā* regarding Sāṁkhya need not be thought of as a system, but rather simply "the opinion that man could gain salvation by knowing the supreme truth, however formulated" (Edgerton 1924: 6, 14). In his view this usage of the term Sāṁkhya is consistent with the earlier usages in the early Upaniṣads and does not take seriously the reference to Sāṁkhya as *anvīkṣī* (philosophy) in Kauṭilya's *Arthaśāstra* (Edgerton 1924: 17).

Buddhi and Sattva in Gītā and Sāṁkhya

Let us now consider the importance of *buddhi* and *sattva* for the notion of freedom in the *Gītā*. Edgerton suggested that early Sāṁkhya was not atheistic (Edgerton 1924: 7). In the same vein Robinson (1972) finds that the early Sāṁkhya that is present in the *Kaṭha Upaniṣad* (*KU*) and the *Bhagavad-Gītā*, which appears after it, is very similar. That is to say, unlike Buddhism which denied the existence of Self, the early Sāṁkhya separates the material and the ultimate Selves. He says:

> [T]his formula follows the procedure of the *yogin* who first withdraws from material objects, then from the lower forms of mental activity, and finally from the higher forms of thought. — Robinson 1972: 300

And he further notes that this formula of the early Sāṁkhya is found in the *KU*. Referring to *KU* 1.3.10-11, he identifies this progression from the sense-powers (*indriya*) to subtle objects (*artha*) to thought-organ (*manas*) to intellect/consciousness (*buddhi*) and from *buddhi* to the great soul (*mahān ātmā*) and beyond the *mahān ātmā* to the unmanifest (*avyakta*), and then beyond the unmanifest to the spirit (*puruṣa*). He says that the ultimate goal is to realize the "highest self" and in this process *buddhi* is the "instrument for realization." This is according to the *Kaṭha Upaniṣad* (Robinson 1972: 300). He then finds the same structure in the *Gītā*, in that *buddhi* is placed below *puruṣa* and *prakṛti* but above *manas* (Robinson 1972: 302). However, Robinson shows that although *buddhi* in the *KU* is understood as the instrument of realization, it is also synonymous with the Buddhist notion of *vijñāna* (Robinson 1972: 310). In both cases, it is understood as the "driver of the *manas*" (Robinson 1972: 300). Thus both in the early Upaniṣadic tradition as well as in the *Gītā*, *buddhi* is not to be understood as consciousness, according to Robinson. While comparing the early Sāṁkhya and *Buddhacarita*, Stephen Kent points out that the *Buddhacarita* of Aśvaghoṣa describes the metaphysical system of sage Arāḍa which contains twenty-five principles. He then goes on to show that the system of Arāḍa, and the early Upaniṣads, especially the *Kaṭha* and *Śvetāśvatara Upaniṣad* are "referred to as forms of 'early Sāṁkhya'" (Kent 1982: 259). The important point for us is that Arāḍa distinguishes between the twenty-four *tattva*s and the *tattva* called *ātman* (Kent 1982: 260). Together the twenty-four *tattva*s constitute what is known as the field (*kṣetra*) and the *ātman* is known as the knower. This dualism between the knower and the field is emphasized in the classical Sāṁkhya (Kent 1982: 260). Furthermore, Kent also points out that although in some earlier Sāṁkhya systems *buddhi* is referred to as consciousness (*cetana*) or intellect (*vijñāna*), in the classical Sāṁkhya it comes to be devalued "as simply "ascertainment" or 'determination' (*adyavasāya*)."[3] He suggests that this devaluation has to do with the transcendence of *puruṣa* in the classical Sāṁkhya (Kent 1982: 265). Explaining the difference between *ātman* and *kṣetrajña* in Arāḍa's Sāṁkhya system, Kent points out that the best way to understand the difference is to view the former in cosmic terms and the latter in individual person's sense. Furthermore, the *ātman* is understood as "unknowing" (*ajña*) and *kṣetrajña* as "knowing" (*jña*). In other words, *kṣetrajña* is the name given to the one who is the liberated *ātman* (Kent 1982: 269). He then points out the significance of this for the classical notion of *puruṣa*. He says:

---

3. *Sāṁkhya Kārikā* 23.

> [O]f significance for the later doctrine of the classical *puruṣa* is that the difference between *kṣetra* and *kṣetrajña* explicitly foreshadows the classical dualism. Furthermore, the unknowing *ātman* and the knowing *kṣetrajña* are reflected in the classical doctrines of the deluded *puruṣa* "apparently" entangled in matter and the witnessing *puruṣa* conscious of its separate nature from it.
> — Kent 1982: 270

In the Sāṁkhya system — both early and classical — *sattva, rajas* and *tamas* form the core categories that characterize the nature of *prakṛti.* For *prakṛti* to remain in equilibrium the three categories of *sattva, rajas* and *tamas* must be in perfect balance. Neither of the three can remain in balance without the other. However, in the early Sāṁkhya system, at least found in the *Buddhacarita* of Aśvaghoṣa, the *avyakta* (unmanifest *prakṛti*) is devoid of attributes (*guṇa*s), whereas, in the classical system, the *avyakta* consists of the *guṇa*s (Kent 1982: 261). Emphasizing that in classical Sāṁkhya the *sattva, rajas* and *tamas guṇa*s are the functional energies of *prakṛti,* Rao (1963: 69) argues, "[T]hey cannot be taken in isolation, for each involves the other, not only ontologically but also functionally, and any individual consideration of them is purely academic and not real." This is in stark contrast to the role of *guṇa*s understood in the early Sāṁkhya, as per the presentation of Aśvaghoṣa. Kent, however, points out that Aśvaghoṣa in presenting the early Sāṁkhya system of Arāḍa associates the three roots of good[4] with *sattva* and the three roots of evil (*rāga* — passion, *dveṣa* — hatred and *moha* — delusion) with the *guṇa*s of *rajas* and *tamas*. In ultimate liberation terms, it means that the *guṇa*s of *rajas* and *tamas* must be destroyed by the increase of *sattva* (Kent 1982: 262).

Thus, the early Sāṁkhya implies a gradation of the three *guṇa*s, whereas in the classical system the triad is not necessarily placed in hierarchical relation to one another, notwithstanding their unique characteristics, and although it does speak of the predominance of one or the other (*Kārika* 54). It is the cumulative balance of the three that is fundamental to the equilibrium of *prakṛti,* in the classical system. However, in the conception of the *Gītā, sattva* emerges as a superior category to the other two. Thus, in the *Gītā* 2.45, Kṛṣṇa says to Arjuna "Vedas are about the three *guṇa*s. O Arjuna, be free from the three *guṇa*s. Be free from dualities and be permanently seated in the *sattva* being free from both attachment and protection" (translation mine). Unpacking this verse can perhaps provide us with some clue as to how the author(s) of the *Gītā*

4. Kent notes that Aśvaghoṣa does not mention what the three roots of good are. See Kent 1982: fn 35.

text has/have come to incorporate the early Sāṁkhya ideas into their own philosophical scheme. Firstly, it is now clear that the *Gītā* and the early Upaniṣadic texts seem to draw from commonly known Sāṁkhya ideas of the time. The older tradition of the Vedas, viz. the ritual tradition, dealt with the more mundane aspects, hence their nature being described as *traiguṇya* in the verse above. Secondly, whereas in classical Sāṁkhya scheme the *triguṇa* complex is fundamental to the equilibrium of the *prakṛti*, the *Gītā* sees *rajas* and *tamas* as an impediment and wants them to be overcome by *sattva*. However, it selectively accepts the *sattva* as a positive element in the progressive development of one's spirituality and hence the call for Arjuna to be "seated in the *sattva*." By thus prioritizing *sattva*, the *Gītā* by necessity creates a hierarchy between the three *guṇas*. This is a fundamental difference between the *Gītā* and the classical Sāṁkhya scheme.

The *Gītā* then provides a redefinition of *yoga* in 2.48 — "Having abandoned attachment, perform actions with equilibrium (*yogasthaḥ*) and by becoming equal in success and failure. [Such] equilibrium is called *yoga*" (translation mine). In this redefinition, *yoga* is seen in the context of the ritual tradition of the Vedic sacrificial system as something that enables individuals to perform their ritual actions with a sense of evenness about the results of ritual actions. In this, the meaning of the sacrifice itself is fundamentally changed. The sacrifice is now no longer for the personal achievement of material wealth and prosperity, but it is with the intention of relinquishing the fruits of those rituals. The text then goes on to the next level, viz. *buddhi* — "Be far away from undesirable action by the attachment to *buddhi*, O Danañjaya! Seek shelter in *buddhi*, [for] the seekers of fruits are miserable" (2.49). Firstly, it must be noted that the *Gītā*'s philosophical framework must be understood against the background of the ritual system of the Vedas within which seeking after the fruits of ritual, viz. wealth is the normative activity. It is not accidental that the author chooses to use the epithet "Danañjaya" (conqueror of wealth) to address Arjuna. From the point of view of Sāṁkhya, what is significant is that the author now takes the key concept of Sāṁkhya and places it within the broader Upaniṣadic philosophical framework. In classical Sāṁkhya, *buddhi* (intellect) is where liberation of the individual must occur. The apprehension of objects takes place in *buddhi* (*Sāṁkhya Kārikā* 35), and because it is *buddhi* which brings together the whole enjoyment of objects, it is therefore, the very same *buddhi* (intellect) that discriminates the difference between *puruṣa* (Spirit) and *prakṛti* (Nature) (*Sāṁkhya Kārikā* 37) and hence liberation truly must occur in the *buddhi*.[5] It is not surprising therefore, that the text of the *Gītā* suggests that one should take shelter in the *buddhi*. Be "seated in the *sattva*" (*Gītā* 2.45) and "take shelter in *buddhi*" (*Gītā* 2.49) are significant instructions to Arjuna in the context of his freedom from the attachment to the fruits of action. Here, there seems to be no fundamental difference between the *Gītā* view of liberation and the classical Sāṁkhya view. Of course, this does not mean the nature of liberation is the same in both. It is the one who is attached to *buddhi* (*buddhiyuktaṁ*) that overcomes both good and bad in this world (*Gītā* 2.50).

The *Gītā*'s radical departure from the Vedic ritual tradition is underlined when it says that "[W]hen your *buddhi* (intellect) overcomes the forest of illusion, then you become indifferent to that which is to be heard and that which has been heard" (*Gītā* 2.52, translation mine). It reinforces this stance in the next verse — "When your *buddhi* (intellect) remains firm and unperturbed by what is heard (*śrutivipratipannāḥ*)[6] fixed in trance (*samādhi*), then you will attain *yoga*" (*Gītā* 2.53, translation mine). Moving away from the Vedic revelation that prioritized the ritual system on the one hand, and by drawing closely from the Sāṁkhya conceptualizations, the *Gītā* lays the foundation for a new doctrine of desireless action. The terms *yogasthaḥ* (*Gītā* 2.48), *buddhiyuktaṁ* (*Gītā* 2.51) and *sthitaprajñaḥ* (*Gītā* 2.55) must then be seen in relation to each other. The one who is seated in *Yoga*, attached to *buddhi* is the one who overcomes all desires produced by the mind and is called the one who is seated in knowledge (*sthitaprajñaḥ*) (*Gītā* 2.55). By closely analysing the relationship between the senses and the objects of senses and the mind, *Gītā* underlines the idea of the state of *Brahman* (*brahmasthitiḥ*) at which stage one's delusion is completely overcome (*Gītā* 2.72).

Here it is worthwhile taking a look at David White's interpretation of *buddhi*, especially in relation to liberation. White brings out an interesting interpretation of *buddhi* from a Western point of view. He points out, first that "actions are accomplished entirely by the *guṇas* of *prakṛti*" (*Gītā* 3.27); second, "there is nothing on earth or even among the deities in heaven, no being whatever, that could ever be free of these three *guṇas* originating from *prakṛti*" (*Gītā* 18.40); third, "We must conclude, therefore, that the *Bhagavad-Gītā* conceives of human action as completely caused, and there is no freedom of action whatever if by "freedom" we mean action that is not caused by other action." He then points out that

5. In the classical Sāṁkhya *buddhi* is associated with the predominance of *sattva guṇa* (see Rao 1963: 68). In this regard, the early Sāṁkhya, the classical Sāṁkhya.

the *Gītā* (2.45) also speaks of becoming free of the *guṇa*s (White 1984: 295-96). In an attempt to overcome these mutually exclusive doctrines, White refers to the passage in *Gītā* 9.28 — "be free from the bonds [*bandhana*] of that action which produces good and evil fruits." He explains this passage suggesting that "[L]iterally, then, in the view of the *Gītā*, human freedom consists of freedom from bondage to actions, not freedom from the causative operation of actions themselves" (White 1984: 296). He distinguishes two kinds of freedom — the highest freedom and instrumental freedom. Being free from dualities of human experience constitutes instrumental freedom. In other words, one does not overcome the pairs of opposites, such as pleasure and pain, but rather the *Gītā* calls for one to remain in equanimity:

> Freedom from bondage to the dualities, therefore, means that human beings must continually practise a discipline which the *Gītā* defines as "evenness of mind" (*samatva*) in all circumstances of pleasure and pain, success and failure (11.48), for it is the *Gītā*'s contention that such equanimity is the very foundation of human freedom in the midst of activities of all kinds. — White 1984: 298

From a Western perspective this freedom from dualities is what he calls, "attitudinal freedom" which in the Western discourse is not considered freedom in any serious sense. However, he argues that this attitudinal freedom is an important aspect, as it fundamentally affects our mental activities, and because they constitute the actions of the mind. He therefore argues, that:

> [F]reedom from the delusion of the *guṇa*s and their dualities thus constitutes a very important kind of human freedom indeed, since in this view attitudes are perceived as significant elements of the causal complex resulting in other kinds of actions. — White 1984: 298

He further points out that this freedom, in the *Gītā* view, is possible because of the *sattva guṇa* which is understood in the *Gītā* (14.6) as pure and having the nature of illumination. Referring to the idea of *sāttvikī buddhiḥ* (*Gītā* 18.30) White points out,

> [I]t is therefore the sāttvic, integrated *buddhi* or intellect that is capable of discerning and understanding the basic dualities, and it is this kind of discrimination which makes possible that evenness of mind which is the act of freedom from bondage to those dualities. — White 1984: 299

Thus, White interprets *Gītā*'s view of *buddhi* as the "highest function of human consciousness" that serves to develop the necessary evenness of mind that is essential for ultimate human freedom (White 1984: 301).

From this close analysis it becomes clear that the *Gītā* brings together the notions of Sāṁkhya-Yoga and the Upaniṣadic notion of *Brahman*. In this synthesis, the notion of *buddhi* in Sāṁkhya obtains the meaning of *prajñā* because of its association with the idea of *sattva*. In other words, the *Gītā* sees *sattva* as of superior nature to its counterparts, viz. *rajas* and *tamas* and encourages the aspirant of freedom to cultivate *sattva* kind of *buddhi*. The ultimate liberation of the individual is, therefore, no longer through an endless pursuit of ritual actions and their fruits, but rather by steady contemplation (*samādhi*).

In order to illuminate the meaning of freedom in the *Gītā* sense, it would be useful now to offer a brief comment on the relationship between *puruṣa* and *prakṛti* in the *Gītā*. It is not the distinguishing the subtle difference between Spirit (*puruṣa*) and Nature (*prakṛti*) as in the classical system of Sāṁkhya, but rather a radical synthesis of the two that is the final goal in the *Gītā*. While classical Sāṁkhya leaves the relationship between *puruṣa* and *prakṛti* in mystery by not clarifying why *prakṛti* evolves itself into material universe, the *Gītā* unequivocally states in the following way: "Under my direction *prakṛti* produces the moving and the non-moving. Because of it, O son of Kuntī, this universe is operating" (*Gītā* 9.10, translation mine). The primordial nature (*prakṛti*) is now clearly brought under the supervision of Kṛṣṇa. Furthermore, the primordial nature is now considered the divine nature (*daivīm prakṛtim*) of Kṛṣṇa (*Gītā* 9.13). As the embodiment of the universe, Kṛṣṇa thus becomes the singular object of devotion of the great souls (*mahātmān*) (*Gītā* 9.14). However, such devotion is rooted in knowledge (*jñāna*). It thus returns to the idea of sacrifice but characterizes it as *jñānayajña* — "By offering the sacrifice of knowledge others worship me as one, as dual, as many and as the universal form" (*Gītā* 9.15, translation mine). The text goes even further by identifying the very sacrifice and everything around it with Kṛṣṇa:

> I am the ritual (*kratuḥ*), I am the sacrifice (*yajñaḥ*), I am the oblation (*svadhāḥ*), I am the medicine (*auṣadam*), I am the chanting (*mantra*), I am the melted butter (*ājyam*), I am the fire (*agni*), I am the offering (*hutam*).
>
> — *Gītā* 9.16, translation mine

It is with this identification of Kṛṣṇa as the *Rik-*, *Sāma-* and *Yajurveda* (*Gītā* 9.17) that the authors of the text come full circle in bringing into its synthetic scheme what it has initially rejected, viz. the Vedic ritual system, but in doing so, it fundamentally transforms it.

Returning to the *Gītā* view of liberation *vis-à-vis buddhi* and *sattva*, three fundamental points need to be made: (1) the *Gītā* sees *buddhi* as the method (*buddhi yoga*) in achieving the ultimate freedom; (2) The *Gītā* sees *buddhi* being intrinsically influenced by the *sattva guṇa* which is considered pure and hence superior to the other two *guṇas*; (3) in the method of *buddhi* (*buddhi yoga*), the state of *sthitaprajña* is a prelude to the state of *brahmasthitiḥ*. It is here the *Gītā* fundamentally differs from the classical Sāṁkhya but conjures up an earlier Sāṁkhya notion of liberation which is the realization of the ultimate Self (*puruṣa*) as we noted above with reference to *Kaṭha Upaniṣad*.

Conclusion

Given the substantial consensus that exists among scholars that the *Gītā* belongs to a period when an earlier form of Sāṁkhya was common to both the early Upaniṣadic texts as well as the author(s) of the *Gītā*, the two important ideas that the *Gītā* must be credited with are the *buddhi* and *sattva*. There is some continuity between the *Gītā* and the classical Sāṁkhya, in the sense that both acknowledge the necessity of *buddhi* being the chief instrument of liberation. However, in the *Gītā*, *sattva* emerges as a superior category in line with the earlier Sāṁkhya view, and the aspirant of freedom needs to cultivate the sāttvic *buddhi* in order to develop equanimity in the face of the polarities of pleasure and pain. Therefore, what the *Gītā* presents is a *buddhi yoga* characterized by *sattva*. This is different from the three paths identified in the Vedānta — path of knowledge, path of action and path of devotion.

References

Bhagavad Gītā as it is (1983), Translated and commented by A.C. Bhakti Vedānta Swami Prabhupada, Los Angeles: Bhakti Vedānta Book Trust International Inc.

Brown, Mackenzie D. (1958), "The Philosophy of Bal Gangadhar Tilak: Karma vs. Jñāna in the Gītā Rahasya," in *The Journal of Asian Studies*, vol. 17, no. 2, pp. 197-206.

Chapple, Christopher (1986), *Karma and Creativity*, Albany, New York: SUNY Press.

Coppola, Carlo (1981), Review: *Nārāyaṇīya Parvan du Mahābhārata*, tr. and ed. Anne-Marie Esnoul (Paris: Les Belles Lettres, 1979). Published in *World Literature Today*, vol. 55, no. 1.

Crofton, Denis (1867), "On the Collation of a MS. of the Bhagavad-Gītā," in *The Transactions of the Royal Irish Academy*, vol. 24, Polite Literature, pp. 3-12.

Edgerton, Franklin (1924), "The Meaning of Sankhya and Yoga," in *The American Journal of Philology*, vol. 45, no. 1, pp. 1-46.

———, (1932) Review: *The Kashmir Recension of the Bhagavad Gītā*, by F. Otto Schrader (Beiträge zur Indischen Sprachwissenschaft und Religionsgeschichte, herausgegeben von J.W. Hauer. Drittes Heft. Stuttgart: Kohlhammer, 1930). Published in *Journal of the American Oriental Society*, vol. 52, no. 1, pp. 68-75.

———, (tr.) (1944), *Bhagavad-Gītā* (2 vols.), Cambridge, Mass.: Harvard University Press.

Eliade, Mircea (1954), *Yoga, Immortality and Freedom*, New York: Pantheon Books.

Esnoul, Anne-Marie (tr.) (1979), *Nārāyaṇīya Parvan du Mahābhārata*, Paris: Les Belles Lettres.

Ghosh, Aurobindo (1970), *Essays on the Gītā*, Pondicherry: Sri Aurobindo Ashram.

Gotshalk, Richard (tr.) (1985), *Bhagavad-Gītā*, Delhi: Motilal Banarsidass.

Hijiya, James A. (2000), "The Gītā of J. Robert Oppenheimer," in *Proceedings of the American Philosophical Society*, vol. 144, no. 2, pp. 123-67.

Hill, W. Douglas P. (tr.) (1928), *The Bhagavad-Gītā*, London: Oxford University Press.

Kent, Stephen A. (1982), "Early Sāṁkhya in the 'Buddhacarita'," in *Philosophy East and West*, vol. 32, no. 3, pp. 259-78.

Koppendrayer, Kay (2002), "Gandhi's 'Autobiography' as Commentary on the Bhagavad-Gītā," in *International Journal of Hindu Studies*, vol. 6, no. 1, pp. 47-73.

Kosambi, Damodar D. (1961), "Social and Economic Aspects of the Bhagavad-Gītā," in *Journal of the Economic and Social History of the Orient*, vol. 4, no. 2, pp. 198-224.

Larson, Gerald James (1975), "The 'Bhagavad-Gītā' as Cross-Cultural Process: Toward an Analysis of the Social Locations of a Religious Text," in *Journal of the American Academy of Religion*, vol. 43, no. 4, pp. 651-69.

O'Flaherty, Wendy (1971), Review: *The Bhagavad-Gītā, with a Commentary Based on the Original Sources*, by R.C. Zaehner (London: Oxford University Press, 1969), published in *Journal of the Royal Asiatic Society*, vol. 103, no. 1, pp. 77-78.

Randle, H.N. (1929), Review: *The Bhagavad-Gītā*, by W. Douglas P. Hill (London: Oxford University Press, 1928), published in *Bulletin of the School of Oriental Studies*. vol. 5, no. 3, pp. 638-41.

Rao, K.B. Ramakrishna (1963), "The Guṇas of Prakṛti according to the Sāṁkhya Philosophy," in *Philosophy East and West*, vol. 13, no. 1, pp. 61-71.

Robinson, Richard H. (1972), "Some Buddhist and Hindu Concepts of Intellect-Will," in *Philosophy East and West*, vol. 22, no. 3, pp. 299-307.

Schrader, F. Otto. (1930), *The Kashmir Recension of the Bhagavad Gītā* (Beiträge zur Indischen Sprachwissenschaft und Religionsgeschichte, herausgegeben von J.W. Hauer. Drittes Heft.), Stuttgart: Kohlhammer.

Sharma, Arvind (1978), "The Role of the Anugītā in the Understanding of the Bhagavad-Gītā," in *Religious Studies*, vol. 14, no. 2, pp. 261-67.

Sharma, Har Dutt (ed.) (1933), *Sāṁkhya Kārika: with the Commentary of Gauḍapāda*, Cawnpore: Oriental Book Agency.

The Bhagavad-Gītā (1979), (with the commentary of Sri Śaṅkaracharya), tr. Alladi Mahadeva Sastry, Madras: Samata Books.

Theodor, Ithamar (2010), *Exploring the Gītā: Philosophy, Structure and Meaning*, Surrey, UK: Ashgate Publishing Limited.

van Buitenen, Johannes A.B. (1965), "Contribution to the Critical Edition of the Bhagavad-Gītā," in *Journal of the American Oriental Society*, vol. 85, no. 1, pp. 99-109.

——— (1968), *Rāmānuja on the Bhagavad-Gītā*, Delhi: Motilal Banarsidass.

White, David (1979), "Proto-Sāṁkhya and Advaita Vedānta in the Bhagavad-Gītā," in *Philosophy East and West*, vol. 29, no. 4, pp. 501-07.

———, (1984) "The Bhagavad-Gītā's Conception of Human Freedom," in *Philosophy East and West*, vol. 34, no. 3, pp. 295-302.

Zaehner, Robert C. (1969), *The Bhagavad-Gītā, with a Commentary Based on the Original Sources*. London: Oxford University Press.

Part Four

Issues of Narrative, Philosophical Discourse and Grammar

13

Forging the Fate of Karṇa
Observations on the Critical Edition of the Mahābhārata

*Edeltraud Harzer**

A RECURRING challenge facing scholars of the *Mahābhārata* is the need to consult frequently the critical apparatus and appendices while reading the critical edition of the text, in order to find connecting and tacitly understood passages omitted from the text.

Vishnu S. Sukthankar, the editor-in-chief of the critical edition of the *Mahābhārata*, operated on the general principle of accepting as original a reading which is documented uniformly by all manuscripts (Sukthankar 1933: xxxvii). Compliant with text critical practices, for the resolution of doubts and conflicts, he took as his guide the Śāradā manuscript along with a couple of Kāśmīrī manuscripts which represented the shortest text. Apparent lacunae in the critical edition's text are probably attributable to these editorial practices.

Recently, Aditya Adarkar addressed the problem in the context of an academic discussion about orality and literacy and other issues of South Asian canonical literature, as part of an attempt to create a fixed version of the *Mahābhārata*, the Poona critical edition (Adarkar 2007). In his study "Turning a Tradition into a Text: Critical Problems in Editing the Mahābhārata," he outlined two "veins of criticism," the first evoking Sylvain Lévi and Madeleine Biardeau. These scholars preferred using as their base an established text, such as the edition of Nīlakaṇṭha, of the seventeenth-century commentator and editor of the *Mahābhārata*. This text is considered representative of the tradition. Lévi and Biardeau would have preferred such an approach to the futile search for an archetype.

---

* Department of Asian Studies, The University of Texas at Austin

The second "vein of criticism" that Adarkar highlights is Tamar Reich's distinction between omission and insertion. Reich challenges the principles of critical editing to which Sukthankar was committed, as she says: "we must begin to think of expansion as a practice constitutive to the *Mahābhārata*, and not as an aberration of the tradition" (Reich 1998: 50).

Andreas Bigger considers what he calls "the normative redaction of the *Mahābhārata*" (Bigger 2002: 30). He discusses how different manuscripts give varied narrations of the same incidents, after having commented previously how useful it is to examine different recensions of the *Mahābhārata*, as each is a version of the *Mahābhārata*. He says: "To the redactor or scribe it was a text that to him — more or less — made sense" (Bigger 2002: 29). Bigger points to various crucial passages missing in the critical edition, to start, the one in which Draupadī dismisses Karṇa at the marriage contest. The cause for Karṇa's scorn toward Draupadī in the rest of the text is never explicitly known from reading the critical edition. Adding insult to injury, Arjuna, archival of Karṇa, wins Draupadī after she had disqualified Karṇa from competing for her hand because of his low social status.

In this study, I'll address some issues that pose a concern in using the critical edition of the *Mahābhārata*. The focus will be on the impact to the narrative of some of the pertinent points missing in the critical edition text, particularly impact on the narrative's flow, and most importantly impact on the eighth book, the Karṇa-Parvan, section 67.

Text of Karṇa-Parvan

Parashuram Lakshman Vaidya, the editor of the critical edition of the Karṇa-Parvan, the eighth book of the *Mahābhārata*, hypothesized that there are two heroic events (Vaidya 1954 (10): xxx) underlying the text of the Karṇa-Parvan. One is the death of Duḥśāsana, while the other is the duel between Karṇa and Arjuna, which culminates in the death of Karṇa. This latter death also signals the end of the war between the Kauravas and the Pāṇḍavas.

The Karṇa-Parvan exhibits some features that are not shared with other books, namely that there are no sub-divisions (sub-*parvans*) of the book as are found elsewhere. Many have aptly commented on the substantial divergence between the northern and southern recensions. Considering the difference between the two recensions, Vaidya postulated that *adhyāyas* 1-5 were added later to fashion a description of the *parvan* in order to help integrate it with the other books (Vaidya 1954 (10): 676-

77).[1] Vaidya observed that, unlike the Karṇa-Parvan, the structure of the Northern and Southern versions is identical in the Droṇa-Parvan and Śalya-Parvan, the two *parvans* surrounding the Karṇa-Parvan. He also observed that the northern and southern recensions are vastly divergent in terms of text, but not content (ibid. as above).

Problems with the Critically Edited Text

In examining the duel between Karṇa and Arjuna, reflecting a reverse relationship to friendship, first pointed out by W. Ruben,[2] the text often appears incongruous, jumbled and re-arranged in comparison with other editions and manuscripts [see comparison between the critical edition or constituted text and the Vulgate (Bombay/Poona) edition below]. Vaidya in his introduction avowed the same editorial policies as outlined by Sukthankar in the first critically edited volume, the Ādi-Parvan.[3]

John Brockington observes that Vaidya, also editor of *Harivaṁśa*, was unaware of the research by Kirfel and Ruben pointing to the relationship

1. Furthermore, Mary Carroll Smith in her study *The Warrior Code of India's Sacred Song* proposes a kernel of the warrior epic on the basis of extracting 2000 "non-regular" verses (*triṣṭubh*). She also claims that by excising (her word) the *triṣṭubh* verses, it is possible to postulate the warrior class without the intervening filter of a Brāhmaṇic commentary. Mary Carroll Smith's method of uncovering and intent are different from Vaidya's. She still may be entertaining the possibility of an Ur-text as she adopts E.W. Hopkins' idea of a nucleus buried in the intangible collection of "strings," that is the nucleus that Hopkins declares to be a story. See, Smith 1992: 14-15.
2. See Ruben 1943: 221, n. 11. Ruben likened the exchange between Karṇa and his charioteer a reverse (a kind of parody) of the exchange between Kṛṣṇa and Arjuna in the *Bhagavad-Gītā*. Alf Hiltebeitel (2007: 25) pointed out the similarity of the combat between Karṇa and Arjuna to the combat of Cúchulainn with Fer Diad in Táin Bó Cuailnge, tracing them both to a common Indo-European source. Hiltebeitel already discussed this in his *The Ritual of Battle: Kṛṣṇa in the Mahābhārata* (1990: 256) and elsewhere. Hiltebeitel refers to Ruben's comparison of the two. Among the many topics that Alf Hiltebeitel extrapolated from the *Mahābhārata*, a recent one (Hiltebeitel 2007: 48ff.) is a discussion and translation of the last battle of Karṇa in the Karṇa-Parvan, the 8th book of the critical edition of the *Mahābhārata*.
3. Questions arise regarding his application of these policies by recalling another instance in which he took great liberties and deviated from the editorial practices. It was the "critical" edition of the *Harivaṁśa*, 1969-71. As Brockington pointed out, the text is radically shorter than that of the Vulgate of the *Harivaṁśa*. According to Brinkhaus, the 318 *adhyāya*s and *c*. 16,000 *śloka*s of the Vulgate seem expansive in comparison to the 118 *adhyāya*s and 6,073 *śloka*s of Vaidya's edition. Vaidya considered the Vulgate an expanded text and not the oldest text at all. Vaidya's greatest deviation from the critical editorial practices was his decision to include evidence from the four printed editions alongside the 36 manuscripts.

between the *Harivaṁśa* and the Purāṇas (Brockington 1998: 319). Vaidya in fact claims, without considering other possibilities, that the scribes of some manuscripts deliberately incorporated material from the *Bhāgavata Purāṇa*. In the introduction he says:

> I, therefore, feel compelled to draw the conclusion that copyists of [manuscripts] K3, K4, and D2 were themselves Pandits well-versed in the *Bhāgavata Purāṇa*, and thought that the *Harivaṁśa* might have been in its narration of the life of Lord Kṛṣṇa a lacuna and it was their duty to fill it up. — Brockington referring here to *Harivaṁśa* 1969-71: xxv

Thus, Vaidya relegated more than two-third of the text of the *Harivaṁśa* to Appendix I (Brockington 1998: 320). This observation leads me to suspect a parallel in Vaidya's work on the Karṇa-Parvan. Perhaps it was with rougher results and less finesse — Vaidya completed the Karṇa-Parvan edition fifteen years before completing the *Harivaṁśa*.

In editing the Karṇa-Parvan of the *Mahābhārata*, Vaidya did not include, among others, most of the sections in which Karṇa is accused of trespassing *dharma*. He says in Critical Notes, under Karṇa-Parvan 67.2-3:

> In the midst of a large number of incidents found in manuscripts, some of which had no reference to Karṇa, we have selected only the four incidents mentioned above, because they are preserved in Ś[ārdā] & K[ashmir] 1,2, though they lack universal support.
>
> — Vaidya 1954 (10): 696

The four incidents that Vaidya included among Karṇa's transgressions are: (1) dragging Draupadī to the assembly; (2) vanquishing Yudhiṣṭhira, who did not know how to play dice, at the hands of Śakuni, an expert at dice; (3) laughing at Draupadī when she was dragged to the assembly and insulting her husbands; (4) suggesting a second round of dice at the instigation of Śakuni (ibid.).

Vaidya, in adhering strictly to the rules of the critical editing, expunged many other of Karṇa's roles, such as his role in burning down the wax house in Vāraṇāvata, intending to burn the five Pāṇḍavas but killing instead some innocent people, Karṇa's role in Abhimanyu's death, and so on. Vaidya seemed to be focused on incidents bearing on the main storyline, while treating as superfluous the rest of the accusations against Karṇa.[4]

4. Curiously enough, Sukthankar can be chastised for similar choices in I.178.15-17, the passage in which Draupadī insults Karṇa, prior to his aggressive and hostile behaviour toward her, in fact retaliation, as we have seen above in the discussion of A. Bigger.

Many manuscripts and editions do not reduce the number of cases prejudicial to Karṇa, nor leave out the Pāṇḍavas' rejoicing over Karṇa's death (Vulgate 91.56ff., see below). Vaidya included only one verse that truly expresses, in a subdued fashion, joy over Karṇa's death — the *pāda* (*b*) of verse 8.67.28, *tam somakāḥ prekṣya hataḥ śayānaṁ prītā nādaṁ saha sainyair akurvan.* (The Pañcālas (Somakas) seeing him lying down dead, were pleased and gave out a roar along with the troops). In the Vulgate,[5] the verse preceding this one relates how Kṛṣṇa and Arjuna rejoiced over the slaying of Karṇa.

Vaidya's detection of obscure and difficult passages led him to discuss them in an article, "The so-called *kūṭaśloka*s in the Karṇa-Parvan" (Vaidya 1960: 209-18). Traditionally, *kūṭaśloka*s were employed to slow down Gaṇeśa in writing down the *Mahābhārata*. One of particular interest is 8.67.33. I cannot reproduce the whole of Vaidya's discussion, but he concluded, after comparing different commentators, that *aparāhṇe parāhṇasya sūtaputrasya māriṣa, chinnam añjalikenājau sotsedham apatac śiraḥ* should be rendered:

> The head together with the body of the son of the Sūta (i.e., Karṇa), cut off by an arrow of the Añjalika type, fell down, sir, on the afternoon (*aparāhṇe*) of the second day (*parāhṇasya*) (of Karṇa's generalship).

Vaidya proposes that the so-called *kūṭaśloka*s are not to be attributed to Vyāsa, "but are fabricated by ingenious commentators or interpreters or reciters of the *Mahābhārata*" (Vaidya 1960: 218). This claim actually would deserve a separate inquiry, at another time.

Vaidya maintains that the text has been fluid since early times (Vaidya 1954 (10): xxiv). This fluidity accounts for transposition of passages, to which Vaidya himself seems to have contributed. Vaidya points to several places of difficulty where, in my opinion, he has not made the best choices. These are verses 3-5 and 11-12 in the constituted text.[6] I shall use these two cases for my investigation.

First, I would like to take verses 3-5 as a unit; they are the only accusations directed toward Karṇa by Kṛṣṇa that Vaidya included in the text. Various other accusations are missing, such as Karṇa's suggestion to Draupadī that she choose another husband since the Pāṇḍavas are enslaved, or Karṇa's killing of Abhimanyu. Karṇa did not respond —

5. Nowadays "Vulgate" is a reference primarily to the Bombay edition, whereas in the past, the term incorporated other printed editions as well, such as Calcutta.

6. Vaidya also despaired over verse 8.67.35. I will discuss this problem in my expanded version of the paper.

only hung his head and raised his bow to strike Arjuna. Kr̥ṣṇa's command to Arjuna to strike Karṇa with the divine weapon is omitted as well in Vaidya's edition. It is as if Vaidya is playing down some of the implications for the characters involved. Crucial developments in the plot are found in the Vulgate (Bombay/Poona) edition:

> *yodhayāmāsa vai pārthaṁ mahāvegaparākramaḥ*
> *tato 'bravīd vāsudevaḥ phālgunaṁ puruṣārṣabham.*
> *divyāstreṇaiva nirbhidya pātayasva mahābala,*
> *evam uktas tu devena krodham āgāt tadārjunaḥ.*
> — *Mbh.*, Pt.IV., Poona (1931): 8.91.17-18

> [Karṇa] of great energy and valor fought Arjuna;
> Then Kr̥ṣṇa said to Arjuna, the best of men:
> Strike him with your divine weapon, fell him, oh, mighty one;
> Arjuna, being addressed by the lord in this way, rose to anger.

With this and similar verses absent, the audience remains unaware that both Karṇa and Arjuna were angered by Kr̥ṣṇa's baiting (Smith 1992: 99).[7] If it is the case, as Vaidya proposes, that 64-67 may be the kernel of the Karṇa-Parvan (Vaidya 1954 (10): xxiii),[8] why would he want to omit a crucial interaction between the two warriors whose chariot duel (*dvairatha*) was ultimately the turning point in the war? When I compare the other editions, I observe many more accusations directed at Karṇa, which together amplify the dramatic effect.[9] Notably, several accusations directed toward Karṇa by Kr̥ṣṇa are diminished to two in the constituted text: (1) Karṇa's smirking at Draupadī in the assembly when she is brought there against her will, and (2) Karṇa's challenging Yudhiṣṭhira to another round of dice at Śakuni's bidding. Vaidya claims that only these two incidents are attested by text critical-means in the manuscripts (Vaidya 1954 (10): xxxix).[10]

7. Mary Carroll Smith (1992: 99): "The theme of goading a warrior to hot fury before a battle is found in chapters 45 through 49 when Yudhiṣṭhira and Arjuna trade insults. Chapter 48 of the Karṇa-Parvan is one of the liveliest exchanges in the *Mahābhārata*."

8. Karṇa appeals to the rules of war, as Karṇa, unarmed, is on the ground trying to release the stuck wheel of his vehicle and is thus caught without a weapon.

9. Inquiry in other parts of the constituted text of Duryodhana's accusations against Kr̥ṣṇa and Gāndharī's against Kr̥ṣṇa should support or counter this idea.

10. It may be observed that redactors and scribes had their own idiosyncracies. See, Bigger (2002: 29), where he comments about the attitude of the scribe to whom the text made sense. He further discusses how different manuscripts give varied narrations of the same incidents, having just previously pointed out how useful it is to examine different recensions of the *Mahābhārata*, as each is a version of the *Mahābhārata*.

In his description of the manuscripts, Vaidya frequently complains about their condition. For example he says of 8.67.4-5:

> The entire text narrating Kṛṣṇa's reply to the appeal of Karṇa is engulfed in a bewildering mass of material where not only recensions and versions, but even individual manuscripts present their respective text in utter confusion. — Vaidya 1954 (10): xxxviii.[11]

Between verses 5 and 6 of the constituted text, there are eight verses present in the Vulgate.

Similarly, the material absent between verses 11 and 12 drew my attention. Reading verse 11 of the critical edition, it seems there is no connection to the preceding verse. I could make sense of the verse only somewhat after I had continued on for another two verses. Still it was obvious that there was something amiss. Initially, it was this part that led me to consult other editions, the Vulgate in particular. After consulting the Vulgate editions, i.e. the Bombay/Poona and the Calcutta editions, the context became clear.[12]

Verse 11 in the constituted text corresponds to verse 25ab in the Vulgate. The Vulgate has almost ten additional verses. Particularly two of the preceding verses, 33 and 34 (of the Vulgate) would be helpful, verse 12 in the constituted text would have made better sense. Vaidya has deposited the "missing" verses to Appendix I, no. 42, where he claims that manuscripts K4, V1,[13] B, D (except D2, 3), and T2 (Vaidya 1954 (10): 668) have "inserted" these verses.

Now, we lose the context that Karṇa's banner has been struck by Arjuna. Leaving out the word "banner," *ketum*, in the verse 12 (verse 35 in the Vulgate, where the word is duly in place) makes the verse confusing.[14] The manuscripts listed in the critical apparatus have a variety of words instead of *-pravaram*. Among them manuscripts Dn1, T2 have *ca ketum*, T1,

---

11. The Vulgate gives a number of other verses that make perfectly good sense, even though the narrative is protracted.
12. With the exception of the *Harivaṁśa* as duly noted, all other textual references pertain to the *Mahābhārata*.
13. V1 refers to Maithilī version, the oldest manuscript for Karṇa-Parvan, *c.* CE 1447.
14. As Patrick Olivelle reminded me, the rule in critical editing is *lectio difficilior* and not *lectio facilior*. Vaidya seemed to follow doggedly the rules, without considering first the general rule that Sukthankar himself used as a criterion, namely, that the Śāradā manuscript and/or the two Kāśmīrī manuscripts be employed in conditions of confusion and lack of clarity, but not for reducing the text and obscuring it.

G, and M[15] *hi ketum* (for *ca bāṇaiḥ*). Manuscripts Ś1, K1,3, V1, B, D (Vaidya 1954 (10): 594) provide Vaidya with his adopted reading because these have been a guiding force for Vaidya throughout his work. He has not worked with the southern recension manuscripts like Sukthankar did. Similarly, the two verses preceding the "banner" verse relate clearly that Kṛṣṇa commands Arjuna to cut off Karṇa's head while Karṇa is off his chariot attending to a wheel stuck in the mud (Vulgate 8.91.33). I did not translate verse 12 but can provide Alf Hiltebeitel's translation of the same, based on the constituted text. He too felt the absence of the banner in the verse but endnoted the place, as he drew help for it from the appendix, which made him understand that the word "banner" is missing in the constituted text (Hiltebeitel 2007: 48, with n. 156):

> and with arrows, the best of the elephant girth-cords [Hiltebeitel's fn 156]
> adorned with gold, pearls, gems, and diamonds, very beautiful,
> highly exempt from the quality of darkness,
> made with care by the best craftsmen with time and effort.
> (See Sanskrit text below.)

The footnote 156 on p. 70: The emblem on Karṇa's chariot flag; as in the passage in the previous note.

A table of comparison of these verses in the constituted text and the Vulgate (Bombay/Poona edition) is given on the next page. Verses given in the right hand column in smaller point size are verses that exist in the Vulgate, but not in the constituted text.

Karṇa and the Karṇa-Parvan

It is beyond the scope of the present paper to discuss the feasibility of Adolf Holtzmann's (nephew)[16] interpretation that Karṇa is the original protagonist. There is an obvious yet inexplicable concern and even obsession with Karṇa in the *Mahābhārata*. If we observe the rivalry between Karṇa and Arjuna, clashing from their very first encounter, we can see that they are on an equal footing as warriors as well as in terms of their respective integrity. Karṇa in popular sentiment became and is still much

15. Vaidya must have not been aware that Sukthankar was also consulting closely the M (Malayalam) manuscripts, as a crosscheck with the Śāradā, as they seem to be very close.

16. Two scholars of this same name were Indologists. In the scholarly literature they are distinguished by the younger one being called "the nephew."

Critical edition 8.67.	Vulgate 8.91.
taṃ samīkṣya tataḥ karṇo *brahmāstreṇa dhanaṃjayam,* *abhyavarṣat punar yatnam akarod* *rathasarjane,* *tad astram astreṇāvārya* *prajahārāsya pāṇḍavaḥ*. 8	*tat samīṣkya* ..20c *tad astram astreṇāvārya prajaḥāra* *ca pāṇḍavaḥ*. 22ab
tato 'nyad astram kaunteyo dayitaṃ *jātavedasaḥ,* *mumoca karṇam uddiśya tat* *prajajvāla vai bhṛśam*. 9	= 22cd = 23a (instead *vai bhṛśam* = *tejasā*)
vāruṇena tataḥ karṇaḥ śamayāmāsa *pāvakam,* *jīmūtaiś ca diśaḥ sarvāś cakre* *timiradurdināḥ*. 10	= 23c = 23d = 24ab-
pāṇḍaveyas tv asaṁbhrānto *vāyavyāstreṇa vīryavān,* *apovāha tadā abhrāṇi rādheyasya* *prapaśyataḥ*. 11	= 24c = 24d = 25ab-
	tato 'rjunaḥ prāñjalikaṃ mahātmā tato *'bravīt vāsudevo 'pi pārtham, chindhyasya* *mūrdhānam areḥ śareṇa na yāvad ārohati* *vai rathaṃ vṛṣaḥ*. 33
	tathaiva sampūjya sa tad vacaḥ prabhos *tataḥ śaraṃ prajvalitaṃ pragṛhya, jaghāna* *kakṣām amalārkavarṇāṃ mahārathe* *rathacakre vimagne*. 34
taṃ hastikakṣyāpravaraṃ ca bāṇaiḥ *suvarṇamuktāmaṇivajramṛṣṭam,* *kālaprayatnottamaśilpiyatnaiḥ.* *kṛtaṃ surūpaṃ vitamaskam uccaiḥ*. 12	*taṃ hastikakṣāpravaraṃ ca ketuṃ* *suvarṇamuktāmaṇivajrapṛṣṭham* *jñānaprakarṣottamaśilpiyuktaiḥ* *kṛtaṃ surūpaṃ tapanīyacitram*. 35
ūrjaskaraṃ tava sainyasya nityam *amitravitrāsanam īḍyarūpam,* *vikhyātam ādityasamasya loke tviṣā* *samaṃ pāvakabhānucandraiḥ*. 13	*jayāspadaṃ tava sainyasya nityam* *amitravitrāsanam īḍyarūpam,* *vikhyātam ādityasamaṃ sma loke* *tviṣā samaṃ pāvaka-bhānu-candraiḥ*. 36
tataḥ kṣureṇādhiratheḥ kirīṭī *suvarṇapuṇkhena śitena yattaḥ.* *śriyā jvalantaṃ dhvajam unmamātha* *mahārathasymādhirather mahātmā*. 14	*tataḥ kṣurapreṇa susaṃśitena* *suvarṇapuṇkhena hutāgnivarcasā.* *śriyā jvalantaṃ dhvajam unmamātha* *mahārathasyādhiratheḥ kirīṭī*. 37.

Critical edition 8.67.	CE translation
taṃ samīkṣya tataḥ karṇo brahmāstreṇa dhanaṃjayam, *abhyavarṣat punar yatnam akarod rathasarjane,* *tad astram astreṇāvārya prajahārāsya pāṇḍavaḥ.* 8	Then Karṇa looked at Arjuna and showered him with his *brahmāstra* missile, once again he made an effort at releasing his chariot. The Pāṇḍava covered that missile with his own and attacked him. 8
tato 'nyad astraṃ kaunteyo dayitaṃ jātavedasaḥ, *mumoca karṇam uddiśya tat prajajvāla vai bhṛśam.* 9	Then Arjuna released another missile of fire, a favourite one, aiming it at Karṇa; it blazed up profusely. 9
vāruṇena tataḥ karṇaḥ śamayāmāsa pāvakam, *jīmūtaiś ca diśaḥ sarvāś cakre timiradurdināḥ.* 10	Then Karṇa quenched the fire with the missile of water; He made all the directions as dark gloomy days with the clouds (of his arrows). 10
pāṇḍaveyas tv asaṃbhrānto vāyavyāstreṇa vīryavān, *apovāha tadā abhrāṇi rādheyasya prapaśyataḥ.* 11	But the powerful Pāṇḍava persevering (*asaṃbhrānta*) dispersed the clouds, even while Karṇa was watching. 11
taṃ hastikakṣyāpravaraṃ ca bāṇaiḥ *suvarṇamuktāmaṇivajramṛṣṭam,* *kālaprayatnottamaśilpiyatnaiḥ.* *kṛtaṃ surūpaṃ vitamaskam uccaiḥ.* 12	
ūrjaskaraṃ tava sainyasya nityam *amitravitrāsanam īḍyarūpam.* *vikhyātam ādityasamasya loke tviṣā* *samaṃ pāvakabhānucandraiḥ.* 13	It always invigorated your soldiers, praiseworthy as a scare to the enemy, famous in the world by its splendour for the similarity to the sun, compared to fire, sun, and the moon. 13
tataḥ kṣureṇādhiratheḥ kirīṭī *suvarṇapuṇkhena śitena yattaḥ.* *śriyā jvalantaṃ dhvajam unmamātha* *mahārathasyādhirather mahātmā.* 14	Then with a gold-shafted and barbed arrow the magnanimous crown-wearing Arjuna tore down the chariot warrior's banner which was blazing with radiance. 14
Vulgate 8.91.	
tat samīkṣya ..20c	
tad astram astreṇāvārya prajaḥāra ca pāṇḍavaḥ. 22ab	
= 22cd = 23a (instead *vai bhṛśam* = *tejasā*)	

= 23c = 23d = 24ab- = 24c = 24d = 25 ab-	
tato 'rjunaḥ prāñjalikaṃ mahātmā *tato 'bravīt vāsudevo 'pi pārtham,* *chindhyasya mūrdhānam areḥ śareṇa* *na yāvad ārohati vai rathaṃ vṛṣaḥ.* 33	
tathaiva sampūjya sa tad vacaḥ *prabhos tataḥ śaraṃ prajvalitaṃ* *pragṛhya, jaghāna kakṣām* *amalārkavarṇāṃ mahārathe* *rathacakre vimagne.* 34	Praising the words of the Lord, he [Arjuna] picked an effulgent arrow and struck the girth [of the elephant] coloured as the spotless sun, while the wheel of the chariot of the great chariot warrior was sunk. 34
taṃ hastikakṣāpravaraṃ ca ketuṃ *suvarṇamuktāmaṇivajrapṛṣṭham* *jñānaprakarṣottamaśilpiyuktaiḥ* *kṛtaṃ surūpaṃ tapanīyacitram.* 35	The banner distinguished by the elephant's girth, its surface with gold, pearls, rubies, and diamonds, painted with gold was made attractive by the capable superior craftsmen of knowledge and excellence. 35
jayāspadaṃ tava sainyasya nityam *amitravitrāsanam īḍyarūpam,* *vikhyātam ādityasamaṃ sma loke* *tviṣā samaṃ pāvakabhānucandraiḥ.* 36	

favoured and very beloved. In the hearts of the Indian people, he is treated affectionately and with respect. I cannot propose an explanation for this phenomenon as I have not researched it. Instead, I will advance some thoughts for consideration.

It is obvious that Karṇa is important enough to become an army general, to have a whole *parvan* named after him, and to fight the combat with Arjuna, the very one that is decisive for the outcome of the war. In addition to these points, thought needs to be given to the mirror-images of the warriors and their charioteers, namely Arjuna and Kṛṣṇa and Karṇa and Śalya, positive and negative, respectively.[17]

17. Cf. Ruben (1943: 284) and Hiltebeitel (1990: 267). We can observe that all four contenders are in one way or another on the side of the Pāṇḍavas, even though they may not be fighting on the Pāṇḍava side. Śalya agrees to Yudhiṣṭhira's ploy of goading Karṇa in the battle. Then when Śalya is the last general of the Kauravas, Yudhiṣṭhira kills Śalya on Krishna's advice. In some respect this encapsulates and underscores the discord within the one family, the Pāṇḍava branch, more than is generally accepted. So there is a feud within a feud, apart from the main discord.

In all the difficult relations of Karṇa, the main point seems to be that he does not belong, whether on account of his being born to an unwed mother, or his upbringing as a lower-caste person, but most poignantly on account of his being the son of the sun. This may point to Karṇa's origins in the solar lineage, which indeed is different from the rest of the Bharatas, who presumably are of the lunar dynasty. In view of Karṇa's importance in various respects, the Karṇa-Parvan, named after him, is not satisfactorily edited in the critical edition.

I am convinced that one of the principles set out for the critical edition, namely abbreviating whenever possible the material, is not unequivocal, especially since the Śāradā and Kashmir manuscripts are considered more prototypical than any of the others. The hallmarks of these manuscripts are their brevity, which was applied more mercilessly by Vaidya than by Sukthankar. I do not want to deconstruct the narrative, or see what the "best" reading might be,[18] but rather see an edition based on both northern and southern recensions, and not primarily based on the northern recension. The texts of the southern recension are in general hardly represented. Also the *testimonia* deserve to be explored. Can the narrative be sacrificed solely for the sake of a more or less mechanical philological agenda? Possibly Vaidya did not accord the narrative sufficient priority.

The almost deliberate omission of Kr̥ṣṇa's baiting Arjuna to kill Karṇa after Karṇa has dismounted from his chariot, leaving behind his weapon, would be an example (Vulgate 8.91.33). Is Vaidya sparing Karṇa and Kr̥ṣṇa because of some bias? Is this a cultural or religious bias to "protect" favourite heroes or reduce slander directed at them?

In approaches to reconstituting a text, the *Mahābhārata* in particular, Vaidya is on the opposite end of the spectrum from the scholars and poets who looked for the best story while preparing their editions, as was common in the nineteenth century and the beginning of the twentieth. In contrast, the critical edition was governed by the principles of critical

18. Likewise in his many publications, Hiltebeitel discusses the text of the critical edition, reading it closely. One such case is his examination of the scene just before Draupadī's disrobing. The usher comes to take her to the court. Upon hearing the summons, Draupadī reflects. The text of her reflection brings up some confusing matter (MBH 2.60.13). Hiltebeitel exclaims that "At this point the Critical Edition text itself becomes contestable" (Hiltebeitel 2001: 244). Considering the decisions of the editor of the *Sabhāparvan*, Franklin Edgerton, he says that he could be convinced that the text is corrupt here. Hiltebeitel could see why a couple of verses as documented in the Northern recension could be taken out for the text to make a better sense, but then he acquiesces to the "more difficult reading" (Hiltebeitel 2001: 245).

editing used with Western classics and thus the principle of *lectio difficilior*. Consequently, concern for the best story did not necessarily play a role in the choices made since the choices were constrained by the manuscripts selected for the purpose of editing.

A Discussion of Archetype

I would now like to move on to a larger question, namely what the nature of a critical edition should be in view of the discussion about an archetypal text. On this topic, Andreas Bigger claims:

> The assumption that there is an archetype, a single text from which all the manuscripts available descended, is a *condition sine qua non* for any critical edition. It forms the basis of the critical edition of the *Mahābhārata*. In taking the critical edition for what it is meant to be, we are accepting (silently or openly) the historical existence of an archetype. — Bigger 2002: 19

Early estimates of the authorship and issues of composition vacillated from one extreme to another. For example, Joseph Dahlmann responded to the view of Adolf Holtzmann, "nephew" of the scholar Adolf Holtzmann, with the result that Dahlmann can be considered Alf Hiltebeitel's precursor, postulating a single author for the *Mahābhārata*.

In the discussions of the *Mahābhārata* over the past 110 years, there is an obvious tension between the proponents of the multifarious tradition and unwieldy compilations of the text versus the few who proclaim the *Mahābhārata* to be a single text, especially the product of a single time period, from Holtzman to Hiltebeitel, inclusive of Fitzgerald (Fitzgerald 1991).

Alf Hiltebeitel, the stalwart of contemporary American scholarship regarding the *Mahābhārata*, argues that as a whole, the work is a composition by a single author at a particular point in time. Hiltebeitel in his Karṇa article (2007) disagrees strongly with Mary Carroll Smith for suggesting that a kernel or nucleus (after Washburn Hopkins) of the *Mahābhārata* can be traced to certain parts of the Karṇa-Parvan on the basis of metrical analysis. To Washburn Hopkins, the nucleus was the story, not an "Ur"-text (Smith 1992: 15). Hiltebeitel ridicules the idea that a pristine core could be traceable from the oral tradition. He argues for a written work by a single author and in a certain time period (Hiltebeitel 2007: 24).

Hiltebeitel is deeply immersed in the reading of the text over and over. His immersion informs his position, which is supported by the traditional views. R.G. Bhandarkar, who collected data from literary works, concluded that "the *Mahābhārata* existed in a form complete, so far as the story concerning the principal character goes, in Bāṇa's time, i.e. the first half of the seventh century" (Bhandarkar 1933/1872: 87). Furthermore, Bhandarkar shows that the *Mahābhārata* used to be read in temples for the edification of worshippers, finding support in the Kādambarī. He then comments: "just as is done in our days" (Buehler and Kirste 1892: 2).[19] Hiltebeitel has made the choice to read the *Mahābhārata* as a single text, as was and is done at the temples. He begs to differ with other scholars in that he considers the epic as the tradition does — as one thing. His position rejects much scholarship that has attempted to examine the *Mahābhārata* using precise linguistic or literary analysis.

Among Hiltebeitel's major claims are the two, we mention here; namely that the *Mahābhārata* was written to move people and mainly that Kr̥ṣṇa's divinity is not a literary after-effect (Hiltebeitel 2007: 24), but vital to the authorial motivation. The idea of an initial absence of Kr̥ṣṇa in the *Mahābhārata* was propagated by scholars such as Walter Ruben (Ruben 1943: 283). Already, before the inception of the work on the critical edition of the *Mahābhārata*, there were differing opinions as to authorship, dating, and recensions. A.C. Burnell (Burnell 1875; 1880) had shown that the southern recension (Grantha and Malayalam, named after the scripts used to write down the Sanskrit text) differed greatly from the Devanāgarī editions (Winternitz 1898: 68).[20]

Andreas Bigger observes that Madeleine Biardeau on the one hand rejects the idea of an archetype and on the other discusses hypothetically the case of an archetype in an article forming part of her conversation with Bedekar. Bigger accuses her (Bigger 2002: 2) of being inconsistent: in one article proclaiming the impossibility of an archetype and in the other discussing it conditionally or hypothetically. I believe Bigger's reading of Biardeau here is too literal. There is a contextual difference which Bigger wrongly ignores. Be that as it may, we have a long list of names representing the orality camp, often supporting their views with a multiplicity of sources for the *Mahābhārata*.[21]

The methods applied in creating the monumental critical edition, the methods employed by Sukthankar, the editor-in-chief, and his team, are

19. They describe actually the findings in the article by Bhandarkar (Bhandarkar 1933/1872).

20. Nīlakaṇṭha's, but also others, such as from Madras in Telugu script, based on the Calcutta edition, with Nīlakaṇṭha's text, cf. Winternitz 1898.

21. It is generally true that when a text is committed to writing there seems to be a need to preserve it. This must have been true in all different parts of India where these texts were inscribed on palm leaves, in a variety of scripts.

questionable according to some. These methods excluded large parts of the manuscripts on which the edition was based and excluded other manuscripts altogether. It is possible to say that the critical edition is rather representative of the northern recensions. Sukthankar voices his concern about applying the methods of classical philology to an unwieldy, fluid body of texts. Still he claims, "Indeed our ideal is the same as that of the classical philologist: restoration of the text, as far as possible, to its original form" (Sukthankar 1933: lxxvii). The critical edition has made its mark and is here to stay. But my concern is with the critical edition's normative force,[22] not unlike the normative force exerted by the Indian TV serials of the epics at the end of the last century.

In the history of the critical edition, Winternitz and Lüders, who initiated the work, were naturally responsible for some of the conceptual errors and misunderstandings that ensued. Sukthankar, a pupil of the above scholars, became the editor-in-chief of the critical edition. The project took forty-one years, spanning 1927-66. Although Sukthankar adopted Winternitz' recommendations and followed methods from Western classical philology, the entire project has been a product of Indian scholars with one exception: Franklin Edgerton edited the Sabhā-Parvan, after Winternitz declined (Lüders declined to edit the Karṇa-Parvan).

What of the place of the southern recension, of which large numbers of manuscripts were excluded from consideration in constituting the text of the critical edition? These southern manuscripts have been faulted for being repetitive and too ornate. Reducing this type of literature to a text by methods that were developed for written works in a different cultural context and time period does the southern manuscripts an injustice. As Bigger discusses in his article "The Normative Redaction of the Mahābhārata," examining different recensions of the *Mahābhārata* amounts to examining different texts. Bigger suggests using the critical edition as a basis for lower textual criticism, not focusing on the search for an Ur-text or best reading (Bigger 2002: 31).

The voices of dissatisfaction with the critical edition come from scholars who themselves have not worked on critically editing a text. I do share in many points of the dissatisfaction. At the same time, I also realize, especially after my discussion with Patrick Olivelle, that the critique does not keep the procedures that govern unequivocally the processes of critically editing a text as the deciding factor. So we really have not arrived at a proper conversation between two parties intent on studying the

22. See also Bigger 2002.

Mahābhārata. Rather we have a collection of valid but one-sided views. Having said this, it is necessary to keep in mind that so many diverse complaints are rooted in a sincere concern for the fate of the *Mahābhārata*. We can ask why this is not the case with other Sanskrit texts' critical editions. The answer can be manifold, but two issues can be construed as the main causes in the case of the *Mahābhārata*. One is that the text is so voluminous. Two is that it attracts scholars with different goals. Mainly it attracts those who are interested in the contents of the text and have very little thought for the procedures of critical editing.

Adarkar points out that Sukthankar was aware that he could not satisfy both scholarly and popular expectations with the critical edition. Sukthankar wrote in the *Prolegomena* (1933: ciii) that the constituted text would probably not be the best text or a good one. He responded to the repeated urgings of Moriz Winternitz to prepare a critical edition so as to have a "sound basis for all *Mahābhārata* studies" (Winternitz 1929: 58). Sukthankar modestly said that it would be prudent to claim not too much for the first critical edition (1933: ciii-civ).

Therefore, we can agree with Bigger and in a way with Winternitz that the textual history of the *Mahābhārata* does not end with the critical edition. Rather it should become the source for a discussion of the cultural development inside a text that has never stopped changing.

tadudyatādityasamānavarcasaḥ śarannabhomadhyagabhāskaropamam |
varāṅgam ūrvyām apatac camūpater[23] *divākaro astād iva raktamaṇḍalaḥ* | |

With its splendour resembling the rising sun,
like the sun moving in the autumnal sky,
the head of the army general fell on the wide earth,
as if from the setting horizon (*astāt*), the sun rolled off, an orb blood-red.

— *Karṇa-Parvan* 8.67.24

References

Adarkar, Aditya (2007), "Turning a Tradition into a Text: Critical Problems in Editing the Mahabharata," in *Theoretical Approaches to the Transmission and Edition of Oriental Manuscripts*, ed. Judith Pfeiffer and Manfred Kropp, Würzburg: Ergon Verlag (Beiruter Texte and Studien 111), pp. 133-46.

Anonymous (1966), "The Completion of the Critical Edition of the Mahābhārata," in *Annals of the Bhandarkar Oriental Research Institute*, vol. XLVII (i-xiv).

Bedekar, V.M. (1969), "Principles of Mahābhārata Textual Criticism: A Need for a Restatement," in *Purāṇa*, vol. 11, no. 2, pp. 210-28.

23. Several manuscripts read *bhūpater*. I adopted Vaidya's choice here. Translation mine.

Bhandarkar, R.G. (1933/1872), "Consideration of the Date of the Mahābhārata: In Connection with the Correspondence from Col. Ellis," in *Collected Works of Sir R.G. Bhandarkar*, vol. I. Government Oriental Series Class B, no. 1. Originally appeared in *Journal Bombay Branch Royal Asiatic Society*, 1872, vol. X, pp. 79-93.

Biardeau, Madeleine (1968), "Some more Considerations about Textual Criticism," in *Purāṇa*, vol. 10, no. 2, pp. 115-23.

——— (1970), "The Story of Arjuna Kārtavīrya without Reconstruction," in *Purāṇa*, vol. 12, no. 2, pp. 286-302.

——— (2002), *Le Mahābhārata : un récit fondateur du brahmanisme et son interprétation*, Paris: Éditions du Seuil.

Bigger, Andreas (2002), "The Normative Redaction of the Mahābhārata: Possibilities and Limitations of a Working Hypothesis," in *Stages and Transitions* (Proceedings of the Second Dubrovnik International Conference on the Sanskrit Epics and Purāṇas. August 1999), pp. 17-33.

Brinkhaus, Horst (2002), "The Division into Parvans and the Bhaviṣya-Parvan of the Harivaṁśa," in *Stages and Transitions* (Proceedings of the Second Dubrovnik International Conference on the Sanskrit Epics and Purāṇas. August 1999), pp. 157-76.

Brockington, John (1998), *The Sanskrit Epics*, Leiden: Brill.

——— (1999), "Issues Involved in the Shift from Oral to Written Transmission of the Epics: A Workshop Report," in *Composing a Tradition: Concepts, Techniques and Relationships* (Proceedings of the First Dubrovnik International Conference on the Sanskrit Epics and Purāṇas. August 1997), pp. 131-38.

Buehler, Georg & J. Kirste (1892), "Contributions to the History of the Mahābhārata (Indian Studies II)," in *Sitzungsberichte der phil.-hist. Klasse der kaiserlichen Akademie der Wissenschaften*, vol. 127, pp. 1-58.

Burnell, Arthur Coke (1875), *On the Aindra School of Sanskrit Grammarians*, Mangalore: Basel Mission Book.

——— (1880), *A Classified Index to the Sanskrit Mss. in the Palace at Tanjore*, London: Trübner & Co.

Dunham, J. (1991), "Manuscripts used in the Critical Edition of the Mahābhārata: A Survey and Discussion," in *Essays on the Mahābhārata*, ed. Arvind Sharma, Leiden: Brill, pp. 1-18.

Edgerton, Franklin (1928), "Review of *The Mahābhārata*, for the first time critically edited by Vishnu S. Sukthankar," in *the Journal of the American Oriental Society*, vol. 48: 186-90.

Fitzgerald, James (1991), "India's Fifth Veda: The Mahābhārata's Presentation of Itself," reprinted in *Essays on the Mahābhārata*, ed. Arvind Sharma, Leiden: Brill, pp. 150-71.

——— (2004), "Mahābhārata," in *The Hindu World*, ed. Gene Thursby and Sushil Mittal, New York: Routledge, pp. 52-74.

Gruenendahl, Reinhold (1993), "Zur Klassifizierung von Mahābhārata-Handschriften," in *Indica et Tibetica*, vol. 22, pp. 101-30.

——— (1997), "Zur Stellung des Nārāyaṇīya im Mahābhārata," in *Nārāyaṇīya Studien*, Wiesbaden: Harrassowitz Verlag, pp. 197-240.

Hiltebeitel, Alf (1982), "Brothers, Friends, and Charioteers: Parallel Episodes in the Irish and Indian Epics," in *Homage to George Dumezil. Journal of Indo-European Studies* Monographs, 3.

——— (1990), *Ritual of Battle: Kṛṣṇa in the Mahābhārata*, Albany: SUNY.

——— (2001), *Rethinking the Mahābhārata: A Reader's Guide to the Education of the Dharma King*, Chicago: The University of Chicago Press.

——— (2007), "Kṛṣṇa in the Mahābhārata: The Death of Karṇa," in *Kṛṣṇa: A Sourcebook*. ed. Edwin F. Bryant, Oxford: Oxford University Press.

Hopkins, Edward Washburn (1901), *The Great Epic of India*, New York.

Jacobi, Hermann, H. Lüders and M. Winternitz (1904), *Promemoria über den Plan einer kritischen Ausgabe des Mahābhārata*, Wien.

Lévi, Sylvain (1917), "Tato Jayam Udīrayet," in *Annals of the Bhandarkar Oriental Research Institute*, I, 1918-20, pp. 13-20.

Mahābhārata, The. (1933-1966) Critically ed. Vishnu S. Sukthankar and others, 19 vols. Poona: Bhandarkar Oriental Research Institute.

Mahābhārata, The, Karṇa-Parvan (1954), Eighth Book. Critically ed. Parashuram Lakshman Vaidya, Poona: Bhandarkar Oriental Research Institute.

Mahābhārata, Book Eight, Karṇa, vol. 1 (2006) & vol. 2 (2008), tr. Adam Bowles, New York: JJC Foundation.

Mahābhāratam (1837), *The Mahābhārata:* An Epic Poem Written by the celebrated Veda Vyasa Rishi, ed. the learned pandits attached to the establishment of the Education Committee, vol. III, Calcutta: Asiatic Society of Bengal.

Mahābhāratam (1931), [Vulgate, Bombay/Poona edition] Shriman Mahābhāratam Part IV with Bharata Bhawadeepa by Nīlakaṇṭha, ed. Ramchandrashastri Kinjawadekar Poona City.

Mehta, Mahesh (1976), *The Mahābhārata: A Study of the Critical Edition*, Bombay: Bhāratīya Vidyā Bhavan.

Raychaudhuri, H. (1922), "The Mahābhārata and the Besnagar Inscription of Heliodoros," in *Journal and Proceedings of the Asiatic Society of Bengal*, vol. 18, pp. 269-71.

Reich, Tamar (1998), "A Battlefield of a Text: Inner Textual Interpretation in the Sanskrit Mahabharata," Doctoral dissertation, University of Chicago.

Ruben, Walter (1930), "Schwierigkeiten der Textkritik des Mahābhārata," in *Acta Orientalia*, vol. 8, pp. 240-56.

——— (1943), *Kṛṣṇa, Konkordanz und Kommentar der Motive seines Heldenlebens*, Istanbul.

Shulman, David (1985), *The King and the Clown in South Indian Myth and Poetry*, Princeton: Princeton University Press.

Sivadatta, Mahamahopadhyaya P. and K. Pandurang Parag (eds.) (1984), *The Bhāratamañjarī of Kṣemendra*, Delhi: Motilal Banarsidass.

Slaje, Walter (1998), "Nāsti Daive Prabhutvam: Traces of Demythologisation in the Indian Epic Thought," in *Journal of Indian Philosophy*, vol. 26, no. 1, pp. 27-50.

Smith, Mary Carroll (1975), "The Mahābhārata's Core," in *Journal of the American Oriental Society*, vol. 95, no. 3, pp. 479-82.

——— (1992), *The Warrior Code of India's Sacred Song*, New York: Garland Publishing.

Sukthankar, Vishnu S. (1933), *Prolegomena, Mahābhārata, Ādiparvan*, Introduction and apparatus, Poona: Bhandarkar Oriental Research Institute.

——— (1934-35), "More text-critical notes (Epic Studies IV)," in *Annals of the Bhandarkar Oriental Research Institute*, vol. 16, pp. 90-113.

——— (1936), "The Bhṛgus and the Bhārata: A Text-historical Study," in *Annals of the*

Bhandarkar Oriental Research Institute, vol. 18, pp. 1-76.

——— (1998), *On the Meaning of the Mahābhārata*, Delhi.

Vaidya, Parashuram L. (ed.) (1954), "The Karṇa-Parvan," in *The Mahabharata for the First Time Critically Edited*, ed. Vishnu S. Sukthankar and S.K. Belvalkar, Poona: Bhandarkar Oriental Research Institute.

——— (1960), "The so-called *kūṭaślokas* in the Karṇa-Parvan," in *Professor P.K. Gode Commemoration Volume*, ed. H.L. Hariyappa and M.M. Patkar, Poona: Oriental Book Agency ed., pp. 209-218.

Vassilkov, Yaroslav (1995), "The Mahābhārata Typological Definition Reconsidered," in *Indo-Iranian Journal*, vol. 38, no. 3, pp. 249-56.

von Schroeder, Leopold (1910), *Bericht über die Verhandlung der Mahābhārata-Angelegenheit auf der Generalversammlung der Internationalen Assoziation der Akademien zu Rom, 9. bis 15. Mai 1910.* Wien.

Winternitz, Moriz (1898), "On the South-Indian Recension of the Mahābhārata," in *The Indian Antiquary*, vol. 27, pp. 67-81; 92-104; 122-36.

——— (1929), "The Critical Edition of the Mahābhārata," in *Indologica Pragensia*, vol. 1, pp. 58-68.

——— (1934), "The Critical Edition of the Mahābhārata: Ādiparvan," in *Annals of the Bhandarkar Oriental Research Institute*, vol. 15, pp. 159-75.

——— (1991), *Kleine Schriften. Hrsg. von Horst Brinkhaus.* Glasenapp-Stiftung, Bd. 30. vols. XXVI: 464; XVII: 465-968. Stuttgart: Franz Steiner Verlag.

14

Truth and Power in Sanskrit Philosophical Discourse

*David Peter Lawrence**

I AM honoured and delighted by the invitation to contribute to this felicitation volume for Prof. T.S. Rukmani. She is recognized as one of the leading scholars of Indian philosophy of our time, on the basis of her wide-ranging and learned studies and translations of Sanskrit texts — from the *śāstras* of Sāṁkhya-Yoga and Advaita Vedānta through the Purāṇas and *Mahābhārata* — and her engagements of Indian thought with contemporary issues as diverse as the Hindu diaspora, religious ethics, women and religion, hermeneutics and consciousness studies. I have had the good fortune of developing a friendship with Prof. Rukmani at a number of conferences over the years, and of working with her as a colleague at Concordia University in 2002-03. In 2008 we invited her to the North Dakota Diversity Conference, held at the University of North Dakota, to participate in a panel on interreligious understanding. The audience was fascinated by her engagement of Hinduism in dialogue with representatives of Islam, Christianity, Judaism and Native American religion.

As long as I have known Prof. Rukmani, I have been as much impressed by her personal qualities, such as her friendliness, help for others, modesty, and enthusiasm for intellectual exchange. As those who have known her will agree, she is exceptionally eager to engage in dialogue, not to defend any of her own positions, but rather for the sake of learning from one another. She is truly an exemplary representative of the "discourse ethics" of cooperative inquiry, oriented towards intellectual and existential advancement, which has inspired the greatest thinkers of South Asia and other civilizations of the world.

* Philosophy and Religion Department, University of North Dakota

Introduction

The present essay[1] reflects on ways in which scholars of South Asian religions and philosophies may endeavour to think beyond the analysis of culture and power predominant in the contemporary academy. That mode of analysis plays an invaluable role in critiquing and counteracting various kinds of hegemony and oppression — including colonial and neocolonial "Orientialist" thought. However, among its pitfalls is an insidious perpetuation of the very problems it criticizes.

Important roots of such analysis may be found in the Western Renaissance and enlightenment, in explicit and implicit agendas in the emerging fields of the humanities and social sciences to implement the instrumental, cause-effect rationality of the physical sciences. As people became increasingly aware of the historical and geographical diversity of ways of experiencing, knowing and acting — cultures and societies — scholars endeavoured to find broadly empirical "causes" of this diversity. There has been great variety in the ostensible causes identified up to the present — linguistic and other semiotic systems of meaning, narratives, paradigms, metaphors, kinship, ethnicity, race, and various other social, political, economic systems and processes.

There are a number of reasons why scholars of culture and society have become especially preoccupied with relationships of power. Thinking about power developed in the transitions between feudal and modern democratic, capitalist and communist political-economic systems, in systematic programmes of cultural and social engineering, as well as in an increasing realization of the contradictions between egalitarian ideals and hegemonic facts. Of course, such thinking was given distinct and highly consequential methodological formulations in the nineteenth century by Karl Marx and Friedrich Nietzsche. It was further elaborated in the later twentieth century by scholars such as Michel Foucault and Edward Said, and continues in numerous varieties of colonial, post-colonial, subaltern and cultural studies. In South Asian studies, the analysis of power has been applied to issues including caste, ethnicity, gender, empire building and maintenance, syncretism and hybridity, religious communalism and nationalism, as well as academic neocolonialism.

The most sophisticated culture-power analysis that has been applied to traditional South Asian philosophical works along with other Sanskrit

1. An earlier version of this paper was presented at the Annual Meeting of the Dharma Association of North America, Montreal, November 2009.

academic texts, *śāstras*, is probably that of Sheldon Pollock. In a series of influential articles, Pollock characterizes *śāstra*s as efforts to define eternal models of knowledge with prescriptive force for all cultural practices:

> We may, in fact, characterize the ideological effects of the shastric paradigm as follows: First, all contradiction between the model of cultural knowledge and actual cultural change is thereby at once transmuted and denied; creation is re-creation, as the future is, in a sense, the past. Second, the living, social, historical, contingent tradition is naturalized, becoming as much a part of the order of things as the laws of nature themselves: Just as the social, historical phenomenon of language is viewed by Mīmāṁsā as natural and eternal, so the social dimension and historicality of all cultural practices are eliminated in the shastric paradigm. And finally, through such denial of contradiction and reification of tradition, the sectional interests of pre-modern India are universalized and valorized. The theoretical discourse of *śāstra* becomes in essence a practical discourse of power. — Pollock 1985: 516[2]

In his grand opus, *The Language of the Gods in the World of Men* (2006), Pollock situates *śāstra* within a broader interpretation of all Sanskrit literature, and comparative theories of cosmopolitanism, in which he eschews crude conceptions of "legitimation." More recently, he has also acknowledged limited innovativeness in Sanskritic philosophies immediately preceding modernization.[3] Nevertheless his basic position about how *śāstras* universalize and valorize various kinds of privilege remains the same.

The scholar of Tantra, David Gordon White is more candid. White describes the philosophical writings of monistic Kāśmīrī Śaiva writers — my own specialty — as a distortion of tantric traditions, "generated in an effort to win a certain support base of high-caste householders in Kashmir and, later, in Tamil Nadu" (White 2003: 14).[4] He likewise claims that the great philosopher

> Abhinavagupta's "packaging" of Tantra as a path to ecstatic, exalted god-consciousness was pitched at a leisured Kashmiri populace whose

2. Also see Pollock 1989a, 1989b, 1990.
3. See Pollock 2001. Others have also challenged the static conception of Indian thought. Thus Lawrence McCrea (2008) has argued that sixteenth-to seventeenth-century Mīmāṁsā hermeneutics underwent so much change that it challenges our ideas of static philosophical systems.
4. On the distortion, also see White 2003: 16.

> "bobo" [bourgeois bohemian] profile was arguably homologous to the demographics of the twentieth and twenty-first century New Age seekers who treat "Tantric sex" as a consumer product. — White 2003: xiii

While this sort of analysis may sometimes be insightful, it also articulates a methodological prejudice that would evade the challenge of the truth claims of philosophical traditions — whether of South Asia, the West or other cultures. An unmoderated reductionism to power may itself become, ironically, a hegemonic expression of a globalized cultural system that is preoccupied with it.

Transcendental Pragmatics of Discourse Ethics

The German philosopher Karl Otto Apel has engaged the problematics of various critical and postmodern theories of culture, including Foucauldian reductions of truth to power — which he has described as "the challenge of a totalizing critique of reason" (Apel 1996). In response, he has developed a revisionist formulation of Kant's categorical imperative, which integrates considerations of biological and cultural evolution as applicable to humans in their aspect as rational animals.[5] Apel's account of what he characterizes as the *transcendental pragmatic norms of discourse ethics* has been highly influential on the communication theories of his friend Jürgen Habermas.[6]

Apel's claim, in basing his discourse ethics on a transcendental pragmatics, is that such ethics cannot be denied without "performative self-contradiction." What Apel conceives to be necessary in this sense bears much similarity to Habermas' "ideal speech situation." It comprises cooperative and egalitarian dialogue, following basic principles of logic, directed toward gaining knowledge of the truth regarding a real world — whatever that may be (Apel 1989: 280). In Apelian terms, Foucauldian and other reductions of truth to power require truth beyond power for their very cogency. Presumably scholars present reasons to accept as a matter of fact the relations of truth claims to power. This ostensible factuality would be undermined if scholars' arguments were themselves nothing but exercises of power, rhetorically manipulating readers on the basis of nothing but their own motivations for power.

Truth, Practicality and Necessity in South Asian Philosophies

I do not want to follow the Orientalist strategy of using a Western

5. For an overview of Apel's theorization in an evolutionary framework, see Apel 2001.
6. Apel further attempts to extend this discourse ethics into a global axiology covering all spheres of human action. See Apel 1991.

philosopher, Apel, to measure the value of South Asian philosophies. I also do not think that Apel's "secular humanist" framework is fully adequate for addressing the claims of Indian or other religious philosophies. Apel's belief in truth about a real world would also not be amenable to some sceptical philosophies. However, I do have sympathy for a lot of what Apel is trying to do, and hope that these ideas can be useful as a bridge to resources in South Asian thought that may offer some resolution to contemporary dilemmas.

Is there anything like a transcendental pragmatics of discursive ethics in Sanskrit philosophies? This question may lead one into some thorny debates — also sometimes with implications pertaining to Orientalism — about approaches in South Asian philosophy to theory *versus* practice, and to the nature of inferential necessity. Many other scholars have wrestled with these issues, including Bimal Krishna Matilal, Jitendra Nath Mohanty, Arindam Chakrabarti, Jonardon Ganeri and Chakravarthi Ram-Prasad.[7] While practice — including the pursuit of worldly power — is central to texts such as the *Arthaśāstra*, as well as works on medicine and other worldly arts, even the *Nyāya-Sūtra* and its commentaries situate inquiry into truth within the practical search for felicity, culminating in *apavarga*.[8] (A distinctive philosophical-hermeneutic approach, however, is seen in the Advaita Vedānta strategy of sublating Pūrva-Mīmāṁsā ritualism by the non-agential self-luminous knowledge of *ātman*.) There is also logical necessity, as deductions are found in the application step of classical syllogisms, along with supportive reasoning (*tarka*).

Scholars such as Mohanty, Ram Prasad and myself have further described some South Asian philosophical arguments as "transcendental," in an expansion of the Kantian sense of the term.[9] Recently, Dan Arnold has suggested that Sanskritic varieties of transcendental argumentation do not chiefly pertain to strict deductions of theoretical reason, but rather the performative coherence of practical reason (Arnold 2008) — a notion fairly close to what Apel has called transcendental pragmatics.

Sanskritic Discursive Ethics

South Asian discursive ethics are treated in many places. The *Mahābhārata*, various Buddhist texts such as the *Upāyahṛdaya*, the *Yogacaryābhūmiśāstra*,

7. See Chakrabarti 1997, Ganeri 2001, Mohanty 2001, and Ram Prasad 2007.

8. See *Nyāyadarśana* 1.1.1, 28; 1.1.2, 69.

9. See Mohanty 1992, Lawrence 1999 and Ram Prasad 2002.

and Vasubandhu's lost *Vādavidhi,* the *Arthaśāstra,* Caraka, and the Nyāya texts describe rules for ancient practices of public debate. These rules also provide the basic structures for debates conducted in philosophical *śāstras.*[10] I believe that many of the prescribed argumentative guidelines could be aptly characterized as transcendentally pragmatic, if that characterization is broadly conceived. These guidelines explain what is necessary for performatively coherent philosophical intercourse.

The most influential guidelines for discursive ethics in Sanskritic philosophy are the sixteen categories summarized by Gautama at *Nyāya-Sūtra* 1.1 and elaborated much further in the commentaries.[11] Various other philosophical traditions of Hinduism, Buddhism and Jainism yet further modified and built upon the Nyāya scheme in their own ways (Matilal 1998). As Abhinavagupta explains:

> The ultimate purpose in that [*śāstra*] is nothing but [explanation in terms of] the sixteen categories, such as the means of cognition [*pramāṇa*], etc. . . . When the sixteen categories are articulated [*nirūpyamāṇeṣu*], another is made to understand completely that which is to be understood.
>
> — *Īśvarapratyabhijñāvimarśinī* 2.3.17; 2.140

In South Asian discursive ethics, the influence of power is by no means thematized in the same way as it is in Marx, Nietzsche, Foucault, Said, Spivak, Inden or Pollock — but it is definitely recognized, and attempts are made to moderate it. An ancient exemplar, *The Questions of King Milinda,* which is popular in Theravāda Buddhism, describes a philosophical dialogue between the King Milinda and the monk Nāgasena. When Milinda requests a discussion with Nāgasena, the latter is willing to participate only if the former discusses as a *paṇḍit* rather than as a king. Scholars are supposed to engage in a discussion dispassionately, with a willingness to admit their errors, whereas kings inflict punishments against those who disagree with them (Rhys-Davids 1890: 46).

An important fact emphasized by Esther Solomon is that South Asian royalty often sponsored philosophical debates, and that the participants in such debates often competed for their patronage (Solomon 1976-78 (1):

---

10. For a broad historical perspective, see Solomon 1976-78. Also see the discussion of the contemporary significance of Indian traditions of public reasoning in Sen 2005.

11. The list is given in *Nyāyadarśana* 1.1.1, 28. The paradigmatic role of the Nyāya standards is demonstrated in the studies of Bimal Krishna Matilal. See particularly Matilal 1986.

22, 339, passim). Indeed the quest for patronage and status has been a central feature of academics in all cultures throughout history.

Vāda: Friendly Argument in the Pursuit of Truth

A great deal of reflection on these issues in Sanskritic discursive ethics may be found in analyses of different types of philosophical argument according to their purposes and methodologies. Such analyses are propounded in the *Caraka Saṁhitā*, the *Nyāya-Sūtra* and commentaries, and various other Hindu, Buddhist and Jaina works. The Nyāya analysis — which has parallels elsewhere, although the terminology varies — distinguishes between *vāda*, friendly argument in the pursuit of truth, conducted according to the highest standards; *jalpa*, argument in the pursuit of victory, and sometimes at the expense of truth, which may employ various deceptive or "Sophistic" rhetorical devices; and *vitaṇḍā*, argument aiming to refute the opponent's position without establishing any doctrine of one's own.

The Nyāya definition of *vāda* specifies pragmatic requirements of an honest and civil philosophical discourse. Such discourse consists in a dialogue between adherents of two contrary positions (*pakṣa* and *pratipakṣa*) on a particular topic. What could be described in Apelian terms as egalitarian, truth-oriented ethic, rather than a hegemonic one, is articulated in the specifications that the arguments in this dialogue must be based upon means of knowledge (*pramāṇa*) along with supportive reasoning (*tarka*), that they must not contradict premises (*siddhānta*) common to the parties, and that they must make use of the five steps of the Nyāya syllogism (*avayava*).[12]

Other traditions disputed the details of the Naiyāyika understanding of the syllogism, such as the number of steps, along with other aspects of the Nyāya scheme.[13] An ancient characterization of the syllogism — which was developed by the Buddhist logician Diṅnāga and reappropriated by the Nyāya and other Hindu schools — is as an "inference for the sake of others" (*parārthānumāna*). This is distinguished from the "inference for the sake of oneself" (*svārthānumāna*) one routinely and unreflexively makes in one's daily life.

Solomon observes that that it was the "social need" of intellectual

12. *Nyāyadarśana* 1.2.1. Cf. the discussion of *saṁvāda*, ibid., 4.4.47-49.

13. See the summary of the Nyāya syllogism at *Nyāyadarśana* 1.1.32. On disputes about the number of parts, see Solomon 1976-1978 (1): 356-57.

intercourse that led to the rigorous explication of the bases of reasoning in the *parārthānumāna* (Solomon 1976-78 (1): 399). Abhinavagupta clearly reflects such a view, although mistakenly attributing the term *parārthānumāna* to Gautama/Akṣapāda:

> What is the purpose with respect to the other? This [work] is for the comprehension of the other. And there is that from the inference for the sake of others. . . . It has been explained by the founder of Nyāya, Akṣapāda, that every academic text [*śāstra*] apart from *āgama* really consists of the inference for the sake of others, and [thus] brings about the complete comprehension of the other.
>
> — *Īśvarapratyabhijñāvimarśinī* 2.3.17; 2.140

Problems of Jalpa and Vitaṇḍā

The other two types of debate described by the Naiyāyikas are much more problematic and controversial among the South Asian philosophies. While not conceived in a Foucauldian manner as constructions of diverse factors of power (from the economic to the sexual), there is an understanding that they may be used for victory for the sake of personal gain. Particularly interesting in this regard is the category of *jalpa*. As Gautama explains, *jalpa* has some of the features of *vāda*, while also comprising "quibbling" (*chala*), "inappropriate rejoinders" (*jāti*) and the observation of "clinchers" (*nigrahasthāna*) in the opponents' arguments (*Nyāyadarśana* 1.2.1).

"Quibbling" (*chala*) is basically changing the meaning of expressions, improperly generalizing their meaning, and confusing literal and metaphorical meanings (*Nyāyadarśana* 1.2.10-17). For example, one might interpret the opponent's use of *nava* in the sense of "new" improperly as meaning "nine." "Inappropriate rejoinders" (*jāti*) identify invalid exceptions to the reasoning of the opponent, based upon superficial similarities and dissimilarities (*Nyāyadarśana* 1.2.18). One might argue that a new factory will not produce lower emissions because another new facility, of a different kind, did not do that. These tricks are used for the attainment of victory, even at the expense of truth.

With regard to "clinchers" (*nigrahasthāna*), all philosophical schools acknowledge that pointing out the flaws of opponents is an important part of a legitimate debate (*vāda*). My understanding is that in *jalpa* as opposed to *vāda* one might do this more than is necessary for the pursuit of truth. The Buddhist logician, Dharmakīrti, reduces the Nyāya list of twenty-four *nigrahasthāna*s to two, not properly stating the constituent of a proof (*asādhanāṅgavacana*) and not properly pointing out faults of the opponent (*adoṣodbhāvana*).[14]

Now, it must be noted that the Naiyāyikas actually allow *jalpa* and *vitaṇḍā* when one is trying to protect adherents' confidence in the true position. If one is criticized by ignorant people, and does not readily know the proper response, they say that these devices can offer protection, like thorny bushes can protect sprouting seeds (*Nyāyadarśana* 4.2.50-51).

However, such types of argument are clearly contrary to the overarching purposes and methods of the Nyāya system, oriented towards the determination of valid means of knowledge (*pramāṇa*) regarding real objects (*prameya*). And, in fact, the Naiyāyikas offer a variety of "transcendental pragmatic" considerations for the refutation of the various strategies of both *jalpa* and *vitaṇḍā*. In this they are joined by many other schools of Hindu, Buddhist and Jaina philosophy. Dharmakīrti in his *Vādanyāya* and Śāntarakṣita in his *Vipañcitārtha* commentary thereon present very strict standards. According to Dharmakīrti, debate with the aim of mere victory is never permitted.[15] Dharmakīrti's refutations of the strategies of what the Naiyāyikas call *jalpa* and *vitaṇḍā* further demonstrate the inadequacy of these devices.

For example, the Naiyāyikas explain that allegations of inconclusiveness on the basis of irrelevant similarities and differences (*jāti*) are answered by basing one's reasons on genuine concomitances with what is to be proved.[16] Dharmakīrti argues that assigning different meanings to words and concepts (*chala*) does not establish or protect the truth, and that if one pursues victory in this way, one might as well strike the opponents with fingernails, hands or weapons, or burn them. A good person should, rather, try to aid others to understand the truth through legitimate proofs and observations of their mistakes.[17] Elsewhere Dharmakīrti compares other false argumentation to singing and dancing, and offering fruits.[18]

There has been a lot of debate about the viability of *vitaṇḍā*, the effort to refute others without establishing one's own position. This is the

14. On Dharmakīrti's arguments with Nyāya, see Chinchore 1988.

15. Dharmakīrti and Śāntarakṣita, *Vādanyāya/Vipañcitārtha*, in Shastri 1972: 68-71; 107-08.

16. See the discussion beginning at *Nyāyadarśana* 5.1.3.

17. Dharmakīrti, *Vādanyāya*, in Shastri 1972: 68-71.

18. Ibid., 65-66.

approach commonly ascribed to Nāgārjuna, who indeed claimed not to have any position of his own, and even endeavoured to refute all the Nyāya categories, including *vitaṇḍā*![19] Various philosophers have propounded transcendental arguments against *vitaṇḍā* that have some analogies to Epimenides' paradox of the Cretan claiming that all Cretans are liars. The Naiyāyikas, Vatsyāyana and Uddyotakara, take this argumentation further in claiming that there are contradictions to the performance of *vitaṇḍā* even in the statement of one's purpose as demonstrating flaws in the opponent's position (cf. Jacques Derrida on deconstruction through commentaries on the works of others). Such a statement involves a variety of positions. Dharmakīrti similarly argued that there is no debate without accepting a position.[20] Scholars such as Matilal have defended Nāgārjuna's style of *vitaṇḍā* using Searle's notion of illocutionary negation. However, this takes us beyond the present subject. Whatever Nāgārjuna is doing or not doing, I think that he is trying to do it honestly, without the tricks of *jalpa,* and not for the sake of power.

Conclusion: Overcoming Fallacies in Dialogue

In attempting to make this bridge between Sanskritic protocols for philosophical argument, and contemporary culture-power analysis and discursive ethics, I do not want to commit the historical sin of anachronism that has been so devastatingly criticized by Quentin Skinner (1969). However, as Ganeri has observed, the contexts of Indian philosophies may be identified in ongoing discussions of intellectual issues rather than only immediate social circumstances (Ganeri 2008). I have been inspired by the conviction that it is important that we give South Asian philosophies a voice in relation to the kind of scholarship predominant among historical and social scientific studies of South Asia.

Though issues are thematized differently, the disparate texts to which I have referred do have their own integral approaches to conceiving the relations of intellectual pursuits of truth *versus* power or victory. And they have endeavoured, amidst all their debates about such matters, to formulate a discursive ethics that addresses the pragmatic requirements of pursuing truth by moderating rhetoric for the sake of victory. My hope has been to provide indications of how Sanskritic expressions of "counter-hegemonic" discursive ethics could be developed to encompass Foucauldian

---

19. See Nāgārjuna, *Vigrahavyāvartanī,* in Lindtner 1987: 76-86. Also see Nāgārjuna, *Vaidalyaprakaraṇa,* in Tola et al. 1995.
20. Dharmakīrti, *Vādanyāya,* in Shastri 1972: 120.

and related analyses, perhaps along the lines of Gayatri Spivak's notion of native resources to which new ethical concerns may be "stitched."[21]

My goal is neither to contribute to the formulation of an unchanging, self-contained identity for *śāstric* philosophies nor to the assimilation of them to contemporary, Western-dominated thought. Rather it is to help bring these systems forward in our pursuit of the ideal of an egalitarian dialogue aiming for truth rather than power, which cannot be denied without performative self-contradiction. Many scholars of intercultural or comparative philosophy have been converging toward this objective. In the present situation, we are talking of a dialogue of ideas about dialogue itself, and South Asia has its own important contributions to make to that.

Of course, a crucial point of contemporary power analysis is that much of what are presented as truth claims are actually systematic distortions justifying power. That certainly may be the case for traditional South Asian thought, as well as the contemporary humanities and social sciences, and this very paper. However, it would be an *ativyāpti*, "over-generalization," to say that because some theorization is just a rationalization of privilege, all theorization is that. And I would be guilty of the fault Dharmakīrti describes as *adoṣodbhāvana*, not properly pointing out faults of the opponent, to not point that out. I believe that — while facing a globalized cultural system obsessed with profit, political world order, marketing and media spin, along with the exigencies of the quest for academic status — we should strive to renew the project towards which Dharmakīrti endeavoured to contribute in his *Vādanyāya*. He explains, rather frankly, in his final verse:

> Good [people], devoted to the benefit of others, have brought life to the logic of proper philosophical discussion [*vādanyāya*]. This tears away the veil of the darkness of ignorance, which [covers] peoples' knowledge of the truth. However, poorly educated [*durvidagdha*] people are obfuscating the light of the truth. Therefore, I have made the effort to illuminate it [again].[22]

References

Apel, K.O. (1989), "The Problem of Philosophical Foundations in Light of a Transcendental Pragmatics of Language," in *After Philosophy: End or Transformation?*, ed. Kenneth

21. See Spivak 1999: 421, on the question of stitching Kant's *Third Critique* with the Bengali journal, *Chinta's* discussion of child labour in textile manufacturing.
22. Dharmakīrti, *Vādanyāya*, in Shastri 1972: 136.

Baynes, James Bohman and Thomas McCarthy, Cambridge, Massachusetts: MIT Press, pp. 250-90.

——— (1991), "A Planetary Macroethics for Humankind: The Need, the Apparent Difficulty, and the Eventual Possibility," in *Culture and Modernity: East-West Philosophic Perspectives*, ed. Eliot Deutsch, Honolulu: University of Hawaii Press, pp. 261-78.

——— (1996), "The Challenge of a Totalizing Critique of Reason and the Program of a Philosophical Theory of Rationality Types," in *Karl Otto Apel: Selected Essays, Volume Two: Ethics and the Theory of Rationality*, ed. Eduardo Mendieta. Atlantic Highlands: Humanities Press, pp. 250-74.

——— (2001), *The Response of Discourse Ethics: To the Moral Challenge of the Human Situation as Such and Especially Today*, Leuven: Peeters.

Arnold, Dan (2008), "Transcendental Arguments and Practical Reason in Indian Philosophy," in *Argumentation*, vol. 22, pp. 135-47.

Chakrabarti, A. (1997), "Rationality in Indian Philosophy," in *Companion to World Philosophy*, ed. Eliot Deutsch and Ronald Bontekoe, Oxford: Blackwell, pp. 259-78.

Chinchore, Mangala R. (1988), *Vādanyāya: The Nyāya-Buddhist Controversy*, Delhi: Satguru.

Ganeri, J. (2001), "The Motive and Method of Rational Inquiry," in *Philosophy in Classical India: The Proper Work of Reason*, London: Routledge, pp. 7-41.

——— (2008), "Contextualism in the Study of Indian Intellectual Cultures," in *Journal of Indian Philosophy*, vol. 36, pp. 551-62.

Īśvarapratyabhijñāvimarśinī: K.A. Subramania Iyer, and K.C. Pandey (eds.), (1986) *Īśvarapratyabhijñāvimarśinī of Abhinavagupta, Doctrine of Divine Recognition: Sanskrit text with Bhāskarī* (2 vols.), Delhi: Motilal Banarsidass.

Lawrence, David P. (1999), *Rediscovering God with Transcendental Argument: A Contemporary Interpretation of Monistic Kashmiri Śaiva Philosophy*, Albany: State University of New York Press.

Lindtner, Christian (1987), *Nagarjuniana: Studies in the Writings and Philosophy of Nāgārjuna*, Delhi: Motilal Banarsidass.

Matilal, Bimal K. (1986), "The Nature of Philosophical Argument," in *Perception: An Essay on Classical Indian Theories of Knowledge*, Oxford: Clarendon Press, pp. 69-93.

——— (1998), *The Character of Logic in India*, ed. Jonardon Ganeri and Heeraman Tiwari, Albany: State University of New York Press.

McCrea, Lawrence (2008), "Playing with the System: Fragmentation and Individualization in Late Pre-Colonial Mīmāṁsā," in *Journal of Indian Philosophy*, vol. 36, pp. 575-85.

Mohanty, Jitendra N. (1992), *Reason and Tradition in Indian Thought: An Essay on the Nature of Indian Philosophical Thinking*, Oxford: Clarendon Press.

——— (2001), "Theory and Practice in Indian Philosophy," in *Explorations in Philosophy: Essays by J.N. Mohanty*, Vol.1: Indian Philosophy, ed. Bina Gupta, New Delhi: Oxford University Press, pp.19-34.

Nyāyadarśana: Taranatha N. Tarkatirtha, and A. Tarkatirtha (eds.), (1985), *Nyāyadarśanam: With Vātsyāyana's Bhāṣya, Uddyotakara's Vārttika, Vācaspati Miśra's Tātparyaṭīkā and Viśvanātha's Vṛtti*, Delhi: Munshiram Manoharlal.

Pollock, Sheldon (1985), "The Theory of Practice and the Practice of Theory in Indian Intellectual History," in *Journal of the American Oriental Society*, vol. 105, pp. 499-519.

——— (1989a), "The Idea of Śāstra in Traditional India," in *Shastric Traditions in Indian Arts*, ed. Anna Libera Dallapiccola, Stuttgart: Steiner, pp. 17-26.

——— (1989b), "Playing by the Rules: Śāstra and Sanskrit Literature," in *Shastric Traditions in Indian Arts*, ed. Anna Libera Dallapiccola, Stuttgart: Steiner, pp. 301-12.

——— (1990), "From Discourse of Ritual to Discourse of Power in Sanskrit Culture," in *Journal of Ritual Studies*, vol. 4, no. 2, pp. 315-45.

——— (2001), "New Intellectuals in Seventeenth-Century India," in *Indian Economic and Social History Review*, vol. 38, no. 1, pp. 3-31.

——— (2006), *The Language of the Gods in the World of Men: Sanskrit, Culture, and Power in Premodern India*, Berkeley: University of California Press.

Ram-Prasad, Chakravarthi (2002), *Advaita Epistemology and Metaphysics: An Outline of Indian Non-Realism*, London: Routledge Curzon.

——— (2007), *Indian Philosophy and the Consequences of Knowledge: Themes in Ethics, Metaphysics and Soteriology*, Aldershot: Ashgate.

Rhys-Davids, Thomas W. (tr.), (1890), *The Questions of King Miḷinda*, in *Sacred Books of the East*, vol. 35, Oxford: Clarendon Press.

Sen, Amartya (2005), *The Argumentative Indian: Writings on Indian History, Culture and Identity*, New York: Farrar, Straus and Giroux.

Shastri, D. (ed.) (1972), *Vādanyāyaprakaraṇa of Ācārya Dharmakīrti with the Commentary Vipañcitārthā of Ācārya Śāntarakṣita and Sambandhaparīkṣā with the Commentary of Ācārya Prabhacandra*, Varanasi: Bauddha Bharati.

Skinner, Quentin (1969), "Meaning and Understanding in the History of Ideas," in *History and Theory*, vol. 8, pp. 3-53.

Solomon, Esther A. (1976-78), *Indian Dialectics: Methods of Philosophical Discussion* (3 vols.), Ahmedabad: B.J. Institute of Learning and Research.

Spivak, Gayatri C. (1999), *A Critique of Postcolonial Reason: Toward a History of the Vanishing Present*, Cambridge, Massachusetts: Harvard University Press.

Tola, Fernando and Carmen Dragonetti (eds., tr.), (1995), *Nāgārjuna's Refutation of Logic (Nyāya): Vaidalyaprakaraṇa*, Delhi: Motilal Banarsidass.

White, David G. (2003), *Kiss of the Yoginī: "Tāntric Sex" in its South Asian Contexts*, Chicago: University of Chicago Press.

15

Rāmāyaṇa Notes III
The Past Active Participle

*John Brockington**

THE contributions of Professor T.S. Rukmani to Sanskrit studies, the history of Hinduism, Indian philosophy and women's studies — as well as her prominent roles as successively Principal of Miranda House, first Chair of Hindu Studies and Indian Philosophy at the University of Durban, Westville, and head of the Department of Religion, Concordia University — are too well known to need rehearsing here. I have known her as a congenial colleague, as friendly as she is learned, for many years and also value highly her contributions to the International Association for Sanskrit Studies; so it is with great pleasure that I contribute to this felicitation volume. Since Professor Rukmani, among so much else, has organized a conference on the *Mahābhārata*, published its proceedings and written several other articles on the *Mahābhārata*, a contribution on the other Sanskrit epic, the *Rāmāyaṇa*, is not too far from her interests, I hope. In this article,[1] I continue my investigations of morphological and lexical features found in the text of the *Rāmāyaṇa*, by listing the occurrences of the past active participle formed by adding the *-vat* suffix to the past participle passive, examining its distribution within the text (which shows an increase in frequency in later stages of growth of the text),[2] and

* Centre for South Asian Studies, University of Edinburgh

1. The previous two articles in this series have also been contributions to felicitation volumes (Brockington 2009, on nominal forms which are turned into an adverbial prefix, *gati*, ending in -*ī* before √*kṛ* or √*bhū* by the *taddhita* suffix *cvi*, and Brockington 2007). All references to the *Vālmīki Rāmāyaṇa* are to the Critical Edition (*Rāmāyaṇa*: 1960-75); similarly, references to the *Mahābhārata* are to its Critical Edition (*Mahābhārata*: 1933-66).

2. For my analysis of the *Rāmāyaṇa* into stages of growth, see Brockington 1985, also Brockington 2006, which discuss the minor refinements to that analysis made in the process of preparing Brockington & Brockington 2006. The first →

commenting also on its relationship to the perfect participle, for which in theory it is a substitute.

The total of such forms in the text is only 150 but even this figure is substantially larger than the number of forms of the true perfect participle, of which there are only 46 in total; however, *vidvān* accounts for almost half of the latter total (22 out of the 46) and in reality is not felt as a participle particularly, having become a simple adjective with the meaning "wise" or "learned" (as the occurrence of *avidvān* at 1.6.8d, 14d, 13.7c, 2.47.10a and 3.35.12b and the high proportion occurring at the end of compounds demonstrates). Complete lists of the forms of both the past active participle and the perfect participle, along with their occurrences, are given at the end of this article.[3]

In a total of fourteen instances the past active participle is used with a copula, *asmi* or *asi* (once *bhavantaḥ*), as equivalent to a finite verb; there are seven occurrences in the Ayodhyā to Yuddha-Kāṇḍa: *harṣaṁ kim idam asthāne kr̥tavaty asi bāliśe* 2.8.2ab, *ratavān asmi bhāmini* 2.88.16d, *uktavān asi yat pāpaṁ* 5.20.15c, *laṅkāyām asi dr̥ṣṭavān* 6.3.5b, *sītāṁ me hr̥tavān asi* 6.16.19b, *yad uktavanto rāmasya bhavantas tan mayā śrutam* 6.26.4cd and *diṣṭyāsi darśanaṁ rāma mama tvaṁ prāptavān iha* 6.66.13ab. All except the first of these occur in passages that I consider to belong to the first stage of growth; the total involved may be too small for this to be significant but equally it may point to this usage as the earliest one in which this form occurs, especially

→ stage is the reasonably homogeneous core of the Ayodhyā to Yuddha-Kāṇḍa, the second stage comprises the material within those books which show evidence of later reworking or addition, the third stage consists of the Bāla and Uttara-Kāṇḍas, and the fourth and fifth stages comprise the *passages and Appendix I passages with good or poor manuscript support, respectively. The main argument for my analysis is contained in the second chapter (Brockington 1985: 16-61) but a convenient tabular summary may be found on p. 330. The first and second stages each comprise about 37-38 per cent of the text and the third almost 25 per cent, with the fourth and fifth stages roughly equal in length to the text.

3. In these lists I have deliberately cited the forms in the nominative singular masculine form usually, in order to distinguish those forms used exclusively in an adverbial sense which are cited with the neuter accusative *-vat* as ending. The lists were initially compiled manually many years ago (cf. Brockington 1985: 21) but have subsequently been checked against and augmented from the electronic text of the *Rāmāyaṇa* Critical Edition prepared by Muneo Tokunaga and, in the case of the past active participle, the list of verbal forms compiled by Oliver Hellwig and kindly shared with me. They ought, therefore, to be complete for the text of the Critical Edition but for the * and Appendix I passages they contain merely those forms that I happen to have noted in my readings of such passages, with varying degrees of completeness.

since most if not all of them seem to stress a continuing result of the action indicated. Nevertheless, it should be noted that the same number of instances is found in the Bāla and Uttara-Kāṇḍa, which together constitute a little under a quarter of the text. There is also just one instance anywhere in the text of its use in a verbal sense with the particle *sma*: *aṅgāram upagūhya sma pitā me nāvabuddhavān* 2.67.4cd. But in a considerable further proportion of their occurrences these forms function as finite verbs on their own (or linked with a personal pronoun); for example, in the Ayodhyā and Araṇya-Kāṇḍa: *saha mām uktavān pitā* 2.4.36d, *vacanaṁ yad ihoktavān* 2.101.2b, *yeṣām uṣitavān pūrvaṁ sakāśe sa mahāstravit* 3.10.23ab, and *saṁbhramāt tu daśagrīvas tat karma na ca buddhavān* 3.52.3cd.[4] Unlike the forms used with a copula, these forms functioning as a finite verb without a copula show an even distribution between the first and second stages (11 in the first stage and 12 in the second).

By contrast, *śrutavān* has a purely adjectival sense — "possessing/ knowing *śruti*," so "learned" — in the majority of its occurrences, at 2.94.10b, 98.35d, 4.17.23b, 5.33.13c, 6.12.1d (this a particularly clear instance, since *śrutvā* also occurs within the same verse) and probably 1.2.20b; both in this respect and also in sense it is thus comparable to *vidvān*. Only two of its occurrences, both interestingly within the episode in the Bāla-Kāṇḍa of the meeting with Rāma Jāmadagnya (at 1.74.26c and 75.2a), convey the basic meaning of "having heard," the second used as a finite verb with *asmi*.

The pattern of distribution of these forms as a whole is interesting in several respects. The largest number (44) occurs in the Uttara-Kāṇḍā, with the next largest total of 24 found in both the Bāla-Kāṇḍa and the Sundara-Kāṇḍa. This means that in terms of the stages of growth of the text the third stage — the Bāla and Uttara-Kāṇḍa combined — contains sixty-eight instances (over 45 per cent of the total in under 25 per cent of the text), whereas the first stage contains thirty-six instances (24 per cent of the total) and the second stage forty-six (just over 30 per cent), each of these two stages constituting 37-38 per cent of the text. The increase in frequency between the first and second stages of growth is, in reality, greater than these figures appear to indicate, since at least three of the

---

4. The instances in the Kiṣkindhā to Yuddha-Kāṇḍa occur at 4.12.20c (*kr̥tavān*), 31.12c (*prahitavān*), 34.5c (*prāptavān*), 51.11b (*dr̥ṣṭavantaḥ*), 60.13d (*muktavān aham*), 64.9b (*proktavān*), 5.14.11d (*prāptavān*), 31.20d (*pratigr̥hītavān*), 32.4c (*kr̥tavān*), 36.25c (*kr̥tavān*), 40.7d (*kr̥tavān*), 56.134d (*āplutavān aham*), 58.14d (*dattavān*), 15d (*pītavantau*), 65.2a (*uktavatī*), 6.31.53d (*tvaṁ hr̥tavāṁs*), 57.90b[l.v.] (*kr̥tavān*), 66.11b (*hatavān*) and 71.11d (*kr̥tavān*).

instances classified as belonging to the first stage occur in manuscripts of the Southern recension alone. These are: *evaṁ uktavatas tasya* at 3.47.5a (the northern manuscripts read *evaṁ uktvā tu vaidehī(ṁ)* instead), *hanumaty artham uktavān* at 4.43.1b (unanimous N reading: *hanūmantam uvāca ha*) and *dr̥ṣṭavanto mahad bilam* at 4.51.11b (unanimous N reading: *paśyāmo nivr̥ttaṁ bilam*); in each case the Northern reading is natural epic Sanskrit, though irregular by strict Pāṇinian standards. If, as I suspect, the Critical Edition editors' preference for the Southern recension — usually but not invariably a correct preference — has led them to choose the reading which has been emended to accord with Pāṇini, then these instances belong rather to the second stage.[5] This would have the effect of altering the totals and percentages to thirty-three (22 per cent) in the first stage and forty-nine (just over 32 per cent) in the second.

The variation in frequency between the *kāṇḍa*s of the core is at least as striking as that between its stages, with the Sundara-Kāṇḍa containing more instances (24) than the very much longer Yuddha-Kāṇḍā which contains twenty-one. This may well in part at least be the result of the differing editorial policies for each *kāṇḍa* that I have commented on elsewhere (Brockington 2006: 203-04), although it is also worth noting that there is a definite cluster of five occurrences within *sarga*s 56-58 of the Sundara-Kāṇḍa (part of a much expanded passage in which Hanumān recounts his experiences in Laṅkā; cf. Brockington 1985: 342-43). There may also be a stylistic element operative, since the polysyllabic nature of these forms in comparison with their natural equivalents of the past participle passive and the absolutive leads to a slower tempo more typical of some of the aesthetically motivated expansion of the second stage.

However, the significant difference in frequency between the first thirty-six *sarga*s of the Uttara-Kāṇḍa, Agastya's narrative of Rāvaṇa's earlier exploits (and those of Hanumān in the last two *sarga*s), which contains twenty-eight instances, and the remainder of the book, the later history of Rāma and his brothers and their families at 7.37-100, which contains sixteen, presumably has other causes. These, no doubt, lie in the

5. At least one other instance in a first stage passage also lacks any N support — *proktavān* at 4.64.9b — but the N mss have several different readings (a v.l. for 9b in D5.8-10, and substitution of either 1311* or 1315* in other mss), making the reading of the S mss the more plausible. Another three, *duṣkaraṁ kr̥tavān eṣā* at 3.12.4c, *kr̥tavān* at 5.51.10c and *uktavatī* at 5.65.2a, lack any support in the NE recension. Some instances occurring in passages of the second stage also lack much or any N support, e.g. *jitavantaḥ kr̥tārthaḥ ca* at 3.4.19a, *vegenāplutavān aham* at 5.56.134d and *tat kr̥tavān vacaḥ* at 6.71.11d. Cumulatively this evidence is undoubtedly significant.

different character of these two parts, composed in all probability at different periods.[6] It is also interesting to note that three of these occurrences are in the relatively stereotyped form *tathoktavati rāme tu* at 7.75.1a, 81.1a and 92.5a (cf. *tathoktavati deveśe* at 7.100.20a). Otherwise, there is little sign of stereotyping (as one would expect of such an infrequently occurring form).[7]

Also worth noting is the fact that certain forms are used mainly or exclusively as neuter singular accusatives in an adverbial sense; these are distributed fairly evenly across the stages (10 in the 1st stage, 12 in the 2nd, 12 in the 3rd, and at least 11 in the 4th-5th), though with a definite trend to increasing frequency. Those forms that occur more than just once or twice are: *vinītavat* (13 times in the text), *bhītavat* (4 times, the majority of them combined with a modifying prefix, *a-* or *su–*), *hr̥ṣṭavat* (4 times) and *prahr̥ṣṭavat* (5 times adverbially, twice adjectivally); the first three of these forms are the only ones occurring in the first stage, whereas *prahr̥ṣṭavat* occurs mainly in the third stage (and twice in the second). If the further seven occasional instances of adverbial use are included (*ārtavat, viparītavat, kliṣṭavat, ādiṣṭavat, saṁbhrāntavat, aśrāntavat*), well over a fifth of instances of the past active participle are so used, which is substantially higher than for other basically adjectival forms. These adverbial forms are also the only ones compounded with either *a-* (three times in the text) or *su-* (once).

As already noted, there are forty-six occurrences of the true perfect participle within the text. The highest proportion of these occurrences (14) is in the Ayodhyā-Kāṇḍa, whereas there are none at all in the Araṇya-Kāṇḍa, apart from one occurrence of *vidvān* which also accounts for five of the instances in the Ayodhyā-Kāṇḍa, and the other three core books also have few instances. The largest number of these forms in total, including *vidvān,* is found in the second stage of growth (21, over 45 per

---

6. These two parts of the Uttara-Kāṇḍa are of virtually equal extent, since the first 36 *sargas* are on average considerably longer that those in the second part. It is also worth noting that there are no less than ten past active participles in *sargas* 29-36, the last seven *sargas* of Agastya's narrative, and as many as three such forms in *sargas* 18, 75 and 81, with four in *sarga* 11.

7. The nearest to it otherwise from √*vac* are *evaṁ uktavatas tasya* at 3.47.5a (but cf. my comments above) with *evaṁ uktavato vākyaṁ* at 5.65.2a — this contrasts with the considerable number of, admittedly shorter, standard phrases formed with *uktvā* and *ukta* — and from √*kr̥* a play on cognates in *duṣkaraṁ kr̥tavaty eṣā* at 3.12.4c with *duṣkaraṁ kr̥tavān karma* at 5.1.98a and *duṣkaraṁ kr̥tavān rāmaḥ* at 7.42.14a. In reality all these are coincidental rather than deliberately constructed, except to the extent that cognates are involved.

cent), although the proportion relative to length of text is even greater for the third stage (18, over 39 per cent in under 25 per cent of the text). Excluding *vidvān* (which has become purely adjectival, lacking any verbal aspect, as noted earlier), the increase by the third stage is even more marked, with just 3 out of the 24 occurrences (12.5 per cent) in the first stage, 10 (almost 42 per cent) in the second and 11 (almost 46 per cent) in the third. It might perhaps have been expected that the perfect participle, as the grammatically more original form, would show a distribution more weighted towards the earlier stages than the past active participle, which is clearly a more popular form. Evidently, however, the perfect participle was already largely obsolete in epic Sanskrit at its earliest level and was re-introduced as part of the more ornate style and regular linguistic pattern of the second stage, carrying over into the third stage. Certainly, the observed irregularities of use or form are limited.

There are three forms in the Ayodhyā-Kāṇḍa functioning as finite verbs (*āpedivān* at 2.10.31c, *eyivān* at 2.56.17d, and *upapedivān* at 2.66.43d) and one each in the Sundara and Yuddha-Kāṇḍa (*abhipedivān* at 5.3.7d and *eyivān* at 6.47.126d); none of these forms comes from the roots given in Pāṇini 3.2.108-9 as capable of being used in a verbal sense. The only instance of lack of reduplication occurs in the compound *apriyaśaṁsivān* at 2.16.60d, on which Böhtlingk comments that we have a participle without reduplication and actually with a present or even future sense, and, quite exceptionally, compounded with its object.[8] Such a form is unparalleled in the *Rāmāyaṇa* but occasional instances (not this particular one but all from √*dṛś*) are found in the *Mahābhārata* (*Mbh.*): *pratyakṣadarśivān Mbh.* 1.54.18b, 3.36.4d (*sarva-*), 5.87.26d (*sarva-*), 7.11.1b, 62.1b, 9.28.45b, 15.26.5d (*sarva-*), *dharmārthadarśivān* 1.133.18d, 3.49.39d, 12.126.33d, *dharmadarśivān* 1.146.15d, *śāstratattvārthadarśivān* 3.83.97b, *tattvārthadarśivān* 4.26.1b, *dīrghadarśivān* 5.128.17b, 9.2.57b, *<a>rjunadarśivān* 8.27.4b,6b,10b, and *doṣadarśivān* 10.17.11b. Absence of reduplication occurs, however, in a finite form *śaṁsuḥ* at 5.51.20d (cf. *āśaṁsire Mbh.* 1.174.8a).

To sum up, the past active participle (the past participle passive + *vat/vant*) becomes more frequent in general (though never very common) by the later stages of growth of the *Rāmāyaṇa*, but certain specific usages were probably part of its language from the beginning: its functioning as a finite verb (in particular with a copula, where an emphasis on the

8. Das Partic. ohne Reduplication und zwar mit gegenwärtiger, ja eigentlich zukünftiger Bedeutung, und gegen alle Gewohnheit in Composition mit seinem Object (Böhtlingk 1887: § 802).

continuing result may be achieved by this means) and its adverbial use (although this is mainly limited to a small number of forms). Its very substantial increase in frequency by the third stage is in line with the trend to simplification of the language and a relaxing of the tautness of construction visible throughout the period of use of epic Sanskrit. In line with this is the fact that the perfect participle proper, infrequent throughout, is even less frequent in the first stage than later, since this is a somewhat recherché form compared to most participial forms. It seems to have become a little more frequent in the second and third stages as part of the influence of Pāṇinian grammar which becomes increasingly visible, although there are some irregularities in its use by Pāṇinian standards.

Past active participle (p.p.p. + vat)

āptavān	7.31.23f, 36.4d and 7.759*
avāptavān	1.1.70d, 7.33.21d and 81.23d; also 7.1173*2[l.v.]
prāptavān	1.64.11d,22d, 4.28.3c, 34.5c, 5.14.11d, 6.66.13b, 7.1.18d and 81.23a; also 7.345*1
samāptavān	1.61.26b
ārtavat (adv.)	7.42.21b (ifc), 75.11b (ifc)
viparītavat (adv.)	6.51.6b
preṣitavān	7.11.29b
kathitavān	1.8.6b, and 10.11b; also 5.418*9
prakathitavān	7.401*4[l.v.]
kṛtavān	1.17.12d, 32.20a, 47.26b (*k° asi*), 75.2b (*k° asi*), 2.8.2b (*k° asi*), 3.12.4c, 47.27a, 64.36a[l.v.], 4.12.20c, 5.1.98a, 7.69c[l.v.], 32.4c, 36.25c, 40.7d, 51.10c, 6.57.90b[l.v.], 71.11d, 7.7.35d, 23.12b, 42.14a, 63.6b, 69.5c and 72.6a; also 4.102*, 5.794*3, 1017*1, 1172*4 (loc.), 1377* (*k° asi*), 6.1083*, 1552*1, 2044*9, 7.542*, 614*3, 1455* (du.) and 1531*
kliṣṭavattaram	5.13.45b
kṣiptavān	1.55.14b
nikṣiptavān	1.74.7d (*n° asi*)
ākhyātavān	4.34.18a
gṛhītavān	5.56.106d

pratigṛhītavān	5.31.20d
chinnavān	6.3406*2
jitavān	3.4.19a and 7.18.17c; also 7.454*2
jñātavān	6.2036*2 and 7.703*
vijñaptavān	5.794*2
taptavān	1.37.5b
atṛptavat (adv.)	5.1294*2
dattavān	5.58.14d and 7.17.10b
ādiṣṭavat	2.46.58c
dṛṣṭavān	4.51.11b, 5.58.17b, 6.3.5b (*asi d°*), 7.25.38d, 30.26c and 35.12c; also 5.549*3, 628*1, 710*7, 1253*4, 6.404*, 7.1135*1
prahitavān	4.31.12c, 7.1388*
vināśitavān	1.54.27b (*v° asi*)
ānītavān	6.2049*
vinītavat (adv.)	1.53.13b, 2.14.9d, 16.2b, 33.1d, 46.6b, 78.10d, 92.2b, 4.45.5b, 53.19b, 5.30.2b, 6.99.43d, 102.30d and 7.4.10b; also 7.541*1 and 813*
pītavān	5.58.15d
āplutavān	5.56.134d
buddhavān	3.52.3d
avabuddhavān	2.67.4d and 7.1177*1
bhītavat (adv.)	5.8.10d(*su-*), 6.42.6d(*a-*), 46.14d(*a-*) and 95.6d; also 6.72*2, 1702*7 (*a-*)
vibhītavat (adv.)	5.888*3
bhuktavān	2.85.58a, 3.10.56a and 7.73.4a
saṁbhrāntavat (adv.)	7.6.12c
muktavān	4.60.13d, 7.18.17d and 29.5d
pramuktavān	7.307*
parimṛṣṭavān	7.36.3d
iṣṭavān	1.41.8b, 6.23.24b
upayuktavān	2.1950*2
ratavān	2.88.16d (*r° asmi*)

labdhavān	7.3.21a (*l*° *asmi*), 11.4d, 18.12b and 25.9c
upalabdhavān	7.75.15d
uktavān	1.71.1a, 2.4.36d, 101.2b, 108.23a, 3.47.5a, 4.43.1b, 5.20.15c (*u*° *asi*), 36.30b, 65.2a, 6.10.1b, 26.4c, 53.9a, 7.11.11a,31b, 75.1a, 81.1a, 92.5a and 100.20a; also 5.860*3 (loc.), 1163*5 (*u*° *asmi*), 6.202*1 (loc.), 3287*, 7.68*2 (pl.), 205*3 (gen.), 250*, 335* (loc.) and 1136*1[l.v.] (loc.)
proktavān	4.64.9b and 7.190*1 (*pr*° *asi*)
uṣitavān	3.10.23a
veditavān	7.35.12a
niveditavān	5.50.2c
śaptavān	1.24.10d and 47.28b
aśrāntavat	7.34.36a
śrutavān	1.2.20b, 74.26c, 75.2a (*ś*° *asmi*), 2.94.10b, 98.35d, 4.17.23b, 5.33.13c and 6.12.1d; also 4.1032*6, 5.549*3, 628*1 and 6.3486*1 (*ś*° *asmi*)
hatavān	6.66.11b; also 5.1218*2 and 6.3114*11
prahitavān	4.31.12c; also 7.1388*
hutavān	6.71.14a
hr̥tavān	1.39.26b (*h*° *asi*), 6.16.19b and 31.55d; also 5.677*4
hr̥ṣṭavat (adv.)	5.60.11b,12b, 62.5d and 7.3.15d; also 6.1244*1, 7.439*2 and 561*2
prahr̥ṣṭavān	1.49.9d, 6.91.7d (adv), 112.3d, 7.33.17d (adv.), 38.1d (adv.), 99.13d (adv.) and 100.21b (adv.); also 7.685* and 1480*2 (adv.)

Perfect participle

īyuṣaḥ	2.59.13d
eyivān	2.56.17d, 4.66.1d and 6.47.126d
apeyuṣaḥ	4.18.21b
upeyuṣaḥ	2.18.7b and 48.31b
upeyivān	1.41.9d, 57.2d and 7.95.16d
abhyupeyivān	1.68.7b

samupeyivān	1.72.1d
sameyivān	1.76.18b[l.v.]
jagmivān	6.1293*9 and 3596*11
upajagmivān	7.76.18d and 94.9d
tasthivān	7.10.6d
abhidadhyuṣī	2.14.17c
abhipedivān	5.3.7d
āpedivān	2.10.31c
upapedivān	2.66.43d
-śaṁsivān	2.16.60d (*apriya-*)
jaghnivān	7.12.19d, 13.38b and 57.16b
vijahrivāṁs	2.88.27a[l.v.]
vidvān	1.1.3c,74d, 6.8d(*a-*),14d(*a-*), 11.17b, 13.7c(*a-*), 2.2.14a(ifc), 6.23a, 47.10a(*a-*), 94.5a,29a, 3.35.12b(*a-*), 4.5.18a(ifc), 7.23d[l.v.], 12.7c(ifc), 5.16.2a(ifc), 35.12b, 6.40.27c(ifc), 51.15a(ifc), 57.13a(ifc), 59.27d(ifc) and 7.61.5c; also 1.126*2, 2.20*3 etc

References

Böhtlingk, Otto von. (1887), "Bemerkenswerthes aus Râmâjaṇa, ed. Bom. Adhj. 1-4," in *Berichte über die Verhandlungen der Königlich-Sächsischen Gesellschaft der Wissenschaften, Philologisch-Historische Klasse, Leipzig,* vol. 39, pp. 213-27.

Brockington, John (1985), *Righteous Rāma: The Evolution of an Epic*, Delhi: Oxford University Press.

——— (2006), "Some Rāmāyaṇa Textual Issues," in *India in Warsaw / Indie w Warszawie*, ed. Danuta Stasik and Anna Trynkowska, Warszawa: Elipsa, pp. 202-12.

——— (2007), "Rāmāyaṇa Notes II: terms for anger," in *Studia Indologica: Professor Satya Ranjan Banerjee Felicitation Volume*, ed. Jagat Ram Bhattacharyya, Delhi: Eastern Book Linkers, pp. 161-72.

——— (2009), "Rāmāyaṇa Notes I," in *Anantaṁ Śāstram: Indological and Linguistic Studies in Honour of Bertil Tikkanen, Studia Orientalia*, vol. 108, pp. 21–27.

Brockington, John & Mary Brockington (tr.) (2006), *Rāma the Steadfast: An Early Form of the Rāmāyaṇa*, London: Penguin Books.

Mahābhārata: 1933-66, *The Mahābhārata* (19 vols.), critically ed. Vishnu S. Sukthankar et al., Poona: Bhandarkar Oriental Research Institute.

Rāmāyaṇa: 1960-75, *The Vālmīki-Rāmāyaṇa* (7 vols.), critically ed. G.H. Bhatt and U.P. Shah, Baroda: Oriental Institute.

Part Five
Issues of Brāhmanical Intellectuals, Ascetics and Renunciants

16

Some Notes on the Difficulties in Defining Intellectual Opponents in the Mahābhārata

*Gregory Bailey**

It has long been noted that the *Mahābhārata* (*Mbh*) rarely ever mentions intellectual opponents except in the broadest of clichés. Certainly, it shows awareness of peoples who live on the fringes of society, and ethnic groups outside of the Indo-Āryan frame, *yavanas*, barbarians and the like, what might be called outcasts and outsiders.[1] But in most of its bulk it does not explicitly engage critically with the ideas of the principal socio-religious groups we, on the basis of other literary sources, might at least expect it to acknowledge. Should this be a surprise to us? Our assumptions that such an engagement should be undertaken are derived from the knowledge: (1) that the *Mbh* was composed in an highly pluralistic and rich textual environment where it may have been competing with other text genres for an audience; (2) that it operated within a social context of considerable diversity; (3) that it was aware of different ethnic groups; (4) that it looked back to a Vedic heritage in contrast to other possible heritages; (5) that it assumed the predominance of the *varṇas* and of different ascetic orders as constitutive of how society should be ordered. It is the last of these that may be of most importance for our argument, for it reflects an attempt to impose a particular view of society on what must have been a highly diverse social and linguistic environment.

On my reading of the *Mbh* the dominant social interests in the production of the Sanskrit versions of the text were delineating a particular sphere of intellectual, social and political interest, one capable of advancing their own ambitions as well providing a measure of explanatory order on

* School of Social Sciences, La Trobe University

1. On these groups see the very comprehensive recent analysis by Aloka Parasher-Sen (2006).

what must have been becoming an increasingly complex social order. Certain groups were excluded from this — the barbarians, the forest dweller, in particular — with the great majority of the population being included within it. It is my contention that the brāhmaṇa redactors of the *Mbh* had little interest in engaging with those outside of their normative arrangement for society, but that they included the Buddhists and Jainas within this arrangement. Those they criticize in the *Mbh* are the groups who are closest to them in terms of ideas and practices, even if from a twenty-first century perspective, they may appear to be dramatically different.

The *Mbh* is a "library" of texts based on the huge epic of the same name originally composed in Sanskrit, a text whose *Urfassung* we are unable to locate. Though we are still restricted to dating its origins between the years 200 BCE - CE 200, we must see these as years covering the growth of the epic, a growth in its present form, which may have been substantially complete by the time Aśvaghoṣa composed the *Buddhacarita*.[2] What is also significant about these dates is that they include the first real evidence of the *Mbh* as a tradition of knowledge and recitation recognized outside of that text itself. Here the *Jātaka* tales are very significant as is the *Buddhacarita*, the former mounting many critiques of the epic and aspects of its narrative. These have still to be researched in substantial detail. But the recognition continues in the Purāṇas where we find frequent summaries of the *Mbh* war and the plot leading up to it as well as masses of intertextual allusions. *Kāvya* also often uses the *Mbh* as a source of content for its productions. What this means is that very soon after its composition the *Mbh* was probably being recited in vernacular versions, hence the need for a Buddhist response, and that it quickly became an independent textual tradition within Sanskrit and vernacular literature, at various levels of understanding, as a source of later inspiration.

I interpret this as a sign of the success of the *Mbh* tradition in terms of the goals — transmission of a new Brāhmanical world view, synthesis of diverse cultural positions and entertainment — of its composers and transmitters, successful in its reach both to that audience which already accepted some aspects of what was communicated in the epic, and to those outside of this audience, who came to know it because they had no choice but to get to know it. This would have consisted of Buddhist and

2. See Hiltebeitel (2006).

Jaina intellectuals, and possibly more so lay devotees of both, though I tend to accept that these fell into the amorphous categories of practitioners of so-called "popular religions." The question of why intellectuals in other religions had to acquire a knowledge of it is as important as it is as difficult to answer. My immediate impulse is to argue that it was because of its immediate success as a defining text for a new highly integrated and inclusive form of society and polity resting on a religious base. This sanctioned the new form of social hierarchy that had been developing for centuries before the composition of the *Manusmṛti*, perhaps the earliest text to indicate the increasing sophistication of the caste system in early historical India and the problems associated with mixed caste.

A logical extension of this is to ask which aspect of the text would have been most accessible and which would have been taken up by people from different levels of society. I am assuming the earliest readers/hearers of the *Mbh* were not philologists in the way practised in the West and by traditional commentators, and that the recitation of the text had a different impression and purpose for them than it did have for us. In a text as vast as the *Mbh,* and the one explicitly taking upon itself the survey of all things it considers important[3], it would seem inevitable that, in addition to the huge bulk of homiletic and hortatory material it contains about Brāhmanical culture, it will have to catalogue and clear aside the opinions of objectors who might be seen as opposing some of the central propositions it advances about social structure, social roles, kingship, philosophy and the foundations of religious knowledge. This is especially so in the books dealing pedagogically and polemically with doctrinal material, encompassing books 1, 3, 5, 6, 12, 13 and 14 (in fact, most of the *Mbh* is arguably didactic in intent). To this could be added those sections in the Śalya-Parvan where Karṇa viciously attacks Śalya as being a virtual barbarian. Yet it is not always obvious where the opponents against whom polemics are being mounted might be found, let alone identified. Such is the seeming superiority of the brāhmaṇas that they may have deemed themselves not in need of naming those whom they regarded as antithetical towards their own teachings.

It is also likely, in my opinion, that the implied opponents — Jainas, Buddhists, Śaiva ascetics — may not have been anti-establishment in the ways implied in 3, 186 and 188 for instance. Indeed, the contrary is very likely. Part of the problem confronted by the brāhmaṇa intellectuals was

3. See the oft quoted 1.56.33 and much of the rest of that chapter.

the success of the institution that Buddhism had become by 200 BCE, both in material and organizational terms, and by the number of lay and royal adherents who were providing the *Saṁgha* with financial and other support. That is, a necessary condition of Buddhism's success was its capacity to integrate with those political and economic elites, and those over whom they ruled, which meant not drastically opposing the theories behind the development of new polities and the social structure that went with them and above all, of integrating themselves with the new modes of production at a localized level. It was in the interests of the Buddhists to support the material/intellectual structures from which the brāhmaṇas would eventually benefit so much, except where the brāhmaṇas attempted to skew political theory to a point where the measure of the success of a king was the extent (enumerated in 12, 56-128, esp. 12, 72-79) to which he patronized the brāhmaṇas alone in terms of work and gifts of land. The underlying assumption I make is that the brāhmaṇas were deeply concerned about the material and institutional success of Buddhism, a success that was a consequence of the *Saṁgha*'s ability to localize itself in "secular" life and no doubt to maintain a presence in the court of certain prominent kings.

Earlier Scholarship

E.W. Hopkins in his still useful book, *The Great Epic of India* devotes about five pages to what he calls "heretics" and the field of inquiry that he initially developed has not advanced much since that time (Hopkins 1978: 86-90). He mentions the three categories of *nāstika, hetuvāda* and *pāṣaṇḍa* and judiciously questions the extent to which they can be tied down to any living categories of institutional opponents such as the Buddhists and Jainas. The problem he encountered, and everybody else since, is the lack of substantive material relating to these terms in the *Mbh*. Each is seemingly a cliché that could be used when somebody wished to brush off an argument that ran counter to whatever views the brāhmaṇas were advancing at the time.

One of various examples is enough to suffice here. The context is one of several occasions when the Pāṇḍava brothers are attempting to persuade Yudhiṣṭhira that he should not become a renouncer — the favoured option for so many (defeated) kings — but should stay and rule the kingdom he has rightfully won in battle. Arjuna recounts the story of Janaka's wife attacking an ascetic lifestyle being taken on by a king — Janaka has become a Śaivite (?) ascetic — whose dhārmically sanctioned role in life is to support all the classes and ascetics who are not kings. She argues that the "Vedas and food are the never-varying fundamental substance of the strictly righteous people (*satāṁ* 12, 18, 26a) in this world." They are householders who support ascetics searching for *mokṣa*. Part of her argument involves the following passage:

> One cannot say that a man is a monk (*bhikṣukaṁ*) just from his having renounced, nor from his having a shaved head, nor from his begging. Rather, when an upright man relinquishes wealth, understand that that happy man is a monk (*bhikṣukaṁ*). O lord of the earth, that man is Absolutely Free, who, though he is unattached, goes about like someone who is attached; he has no attachments, he has untied all bonds, he is the same toward enemies and friends. The bald ones in their ochre robes are bound by many kinds of fetters (*sitā bahuvidhaiḥ pāśaiḥ*) — they travel about in order to receive gifts, piling up idle enjoyments (*parivrajanti dānārthaḥ muṇḍāḥ kāṣāyavāsasaḥ*). Lacking understanding, they abandon the three Vedas and their livelihoods (*trayīṁ ca nāma vārtāṁ*), and then they abandon their children and take up the triple staff[4] and the robe. Realize that the ochre robe on one who is not free from passion serves that person's interests; it serves as a livelihood for those bald ones who merely display the flag of Law (*dharmadhvajānāṁ muṇḍānāṁ*), in my opinion.
>
> Great king, having conquered your senses, conquer heavenly worlds by supporting holy men, whether they wear their hair piled on their heads or are bald, whether they are clad in ochre robes, antelope skins, or rags, or are naked.[5]

Hopkins is confident that 18, 32 the verse beginning "they abandon the three Vedas. . ." "refers distinctly to Buddhists," but he is not confident this judgement can be made in other like passages (Hopkins 1978: 88).

What is obvious about this passage is the number of technical terms occurring in it and the recognition it gives of the high variability of ascetic behaviour. It is the observation of somebody who has had considerable experience with ascetics, but equally knows the broad parameters of Vedic ideology in the manner it has come down in the *Mbh* and of the duties of kings in regard to this. If there is a sense of tradition in the *Mbh*, and one would expect to find it in the didactic twelfth book, this is where it would emerge.

Obviously, a sense of tradition is going to have a historical resonance attached to it, though it is arguable that the authors of Smṛti were

4. "triple staff": *triviṣṭabdhaṁ*. Patrick Olivelle has suggested to me that this designates the three sticks an ascetic uses to hold up a water pot.

5. *Mbh* 12.18.29-34. See Fitzgerald 2004: 203.

attempting to create a new form of tradition, extending what had been bequeathed to them through the various dharmaśāstric traditions and the teachings of the ascetic groups[6] being communicated as early as the old Upaniṣads. One foundation of tradition is easy to identify and it is represented here in the assertion that the ascetics Janaka's wife criticizes abandon the three Vedas, because the Vedas constitute the basis of the brāhmaṇas' lifestyle, and through them of the lifestyle they intend to have adopted by the rest of society. By this time we are surely dealing with a cliché that is found everywhere in the *Mbh*. Equally, we are told that these kinds of depraved ascetics abandon their livelihood (*vārtā*) and their children, in that sequence. Certainly, the latter is somewhat anathema for Brāhmanical householders because they are required to perform the monthly rituals for the ancestors and so must have male offspring, but none the less it was accepted. All of these could easily characterize a certain kind of Buddhist monk and this view may be strengthened by the stridently negative charge that "the ochre robe on one who is not free from passion serves that person's interests (*īhārtham iti*); it serves as a livelihood (*vr̥ttyartham iti*) for those bald ones. . . ." Clearly appearance does not replace substance, and the charge is that one *vr̥tti* is simply replacing another, but that where the true ascetic has no goal, here the sense of *artha*, used twice, invalidates the ascetic being described as the *artha* (= interest, desire) governs everything. Even here the charge could have been made of any false ascetic.[7]

What might finally lead us to assume the Buddhist monk is being addressed here is the adjective *abuddhayaḥ* to end the verse (32) that is so critical of those who abandon the Vedas and so on. If we truly are dealing with Buddhists this word may be used as a form of *śleṣa*, not unlike *sthavirabuddhayaḥ* in 3, 188, 38.[8]

Even if this passage does critique Buddhist monks, it is likely that by the time of its composition many Buddhist and Jaina monks would have become so from childhood, meaning that they were not required to abandon the Veda or a livelihood they had never practised, nor would they have abandoned children given a requirement (not always observed)

---

6. Both groups being skilled communicators, see Lubin (2005).
7. It may pay dividends to investigate how often *vr̥tti* and *vārtā* are used to designate the lifestyle of an ascetic.
8. I am dealing with this issue in detail in a forthcoming piece, "Sthavirabuddhayaḥ in the Mārkaṇḍeyasamāsya-Parvan of the *Mahābhārata*. Problems in locating critiques of Buddhism in the *Mahābhārata*."

to be celibate. This suggests an inaccurate depiction of these clichéd ascetics, but that does not matter because the goal of a passage like this is as much to affirm adherence to the Vedas and the attendant lifestyle as it is to critique those who refuse to follow this lifestyle and worse, attack its textual epistemological foundation. The point here being that the Vedas were still highly auspicious, beyond question and a source of prestige for those who claim status through connection with them. But to whom would this have applied, apart from intellectuals in several of the religions about which I am concerned here?

Clichéd Opponents

Under this heading I include the names *nāstika*, *hetuvāda* and *pāṣaṇḍa* already identified by Hopkins. However, there is a problem in placing too much weight on these terms because there are surprisingly few references to them and even where they are found it is difficult to determine what the content of the oppositional teachings they denote might be. The actual meaning of the first term implies at least a rejection of the belief of the *ātman* and probably a more general sceptical attitude, the second defines a mode of argument using logic alone, perhaps with the added implication of rejecting the Vedas as a valid source of knowledge, and the third is a general term denoting a heretic.

I am focusing mainly on *nāstika/nāstikya* in this article as it seems to be directly associated with a critique of traditional views about the efficacy of the sacrifice and the Vedas. In various forms the word occurs fifty-four times[9] in the *Mbh*, in contrast with *pāṣaṇḍa* which is found six times. It may be significant that twenty-five of these occurrences are in the twelfth book and ten in the third book. Of these fifty-four references *nāstika* itself occurs thirty-six times and *nāstikya* or "he who has the attitude of a *nāstika*" eleven times. But for all that it is difficult to place a precise content to the *nāstika*'s thought and to assign it to any but the broadest group of non-Brāhmanical ascetics. Often it seems to be used in a manner suggesting its meaning was well known without any need to define it with precision. In at least one place (12.257.4) it is used to designate one of various categories of people who support violence in the sacrifice, a direct contradiction to its use in other passages where it denotes a person opposed to the performance of sacrifices.

---

9. Here are the relevant figures: *nāstika* 36; *anāstika* 5; *nāstikya* 11; *anāstikya* 1; *nāstikatā* 1. There are several other occurrences in star passages, but they do not increase the number significantly.

A number of verses (3.247.3; 5.35.40, 39.48, 39.59, 137.7; 12.221.78) include it in lists of generally disreputable people — such as liars, the lazy, a thief and the reckless — who the king in particular should avoid. More specifically, in other passages it is associated with rejection of the Vedas (5.35.40; 7.76.4; 12.10.20, 12.4, 15.33, 162.8, 261.60; 13.107.60); the non-performance of rituals (13.105.15, 107.11; implied in 12.11.27, 12.4, 12.25, 173.46) and with ignorance of *dharma* or non-adherence to it in behaviour (3.32.1, 32.5, 198.66; 8.27.96; 12.10.20, 123.15; 13.61.38). All of these qualities apply by and large to Buddhists, Jainas and Cārvākas, but it is difficult to tie them down more specifically than that. In no sense do they apply to outcasts and debased caste groups.

Below I include glosses only of a few more extended passages that replicate the above themes, and I certainly have not exhausted the material on the *nāstika* theme in the *Mbh.* If there is a problem with the translation of *nāstika/nāstikya* in these passages, it is because I have not chosen a literal translation, but because of the breadth of content implied in the belief of the *nāstika* a specific translation is both undesirable and evades the problem of recognizing that the term might have been deliberately broad in its outlook.

Critique of the lifestyle associated with the sacrifice is immediately apparent from the following brief dialogue where Tulādhāra has suggested that agriculture be banned because of the killing of animals it involves:

> Jājāli said, "You, Tulādhāra, have advanced this teaching (*dharma*) but it will both shut the door of heaven for living beings and hinder their mode of living (*vr̥ttim*). Agriculture gives rise to food and you also live from that, merchant, and mortals too live by cattle and plants, from which the sacrifice originates. What you are preaching is the attitude of Nay-saying (*nāstikyam*), because this world will not operate (*varted*) if the mode of living (*vārtām*) is entirely abandoned."
>
> Tulādhāra said, "I will speak about the mode of living (*vr̥ttim*). I do not have the attitude of Nay-saying, brāhmaṇa. Being one who knows the sacrifice — and that is quite exceptional — I do not scorn the sacrifice."
>
> — 12.255.1-4[10]

This confession by Tulādhāra is significant in that it rests so heavily on the unquestionability of the sacrifice as the foundation of religious and even economic life.[11] It is highly rhetorical, especially in using several

10. Unless otherwise indicated these translations are my own of the Critical Edition of the *Mbh.*

11. Cf. 12.11.27 where some ascetics (possibly Ajīvikas, see vs. 7) abandon the *nāstika* way after hearing of the value to be derived from the sacrifice and the wealth it creates.

variants of the important root *vṛt*. The causal chain arising from the sacrifice is reiterated often in the *Mbh*, but it is much more complicated here because of the intrusion of non-violence as an ideological component that has penetrated into all aspects of Brāhmanical religious life. If non-violence were applied in an absolute sense the sacrifice could never be performed, hence the entire foundation of ritual and social life would be completely undermined. Thus all kinds of rationalizations are required to enable it to continue, including the use of vegetable sacrifices as Tulādhāra later goes on to assert.

On the basis of a passage like this *nāstika* is one of those broad categories designating someone who not only critiques the Vedas as the foundation for knowledge but the sacrifice as well. Both, of course, are inter-related, but from an historical perspective there had been a shift to small-scale sacrifices in the post-Vedic period, usually centred on the household. If the institution changed in practice, the ideology did not because it was so fundamental in sustaining arguments for Brāhmanical hegemony. And this is surely the point: the narrative of the *Mbh* reflects a society and economy that was highly pluralistic, one where the means of production, though primarily agrarian, were quite diverse and where statements of the kind made by Jājāli are clearly ideological in depicting a set of beliefs that were traditional in being so clearly derived from a past when they were not contested. The mere fact of the doctrine being put in the mouth of the *nāstika* is an unambiguous sign that it is now contested.

More contextually based, and extending the meaning of *nāstika* are the words of a sage Kāmānada at 123.14-18a:

> Someone who completely disregards Law and Riches and pursues (*anuvartate*) only Love destroys good judgement (*prajñānāśam*) in this life by his abandoning of Law and Riches. And the confusion (*moha*) which destroys his judgement (*prajñāpraṇāśako*) also destroys his Merit and his Riches, and from that arises Nay-saying (*nāstikatā*) and wrongdoing. And when the king does not rein in those rotten evil-doers, people are upset at that, as if there were a snake in their house. His subjects will not follow (*nānuvartate*) that king nor will the brāhmaṇas, nor the holy men, and so he comes to naught and deserves execution. Disgraced and despised, he lives a miserable life. . . . — Fitzgerald 2004: 480

Here too we find a concentration of semi-technical terms such as *prajñā*, *moha* and the three names of the *trivarga*, in a passage drawing a sharp contrast between goals of action. The *trivarga* becomes an expression of the totalistic sphere of activity of the king and the chain reaction arising from the negative influence of *moha* (12.257.4, *vimūḍhair nāstakaiḥ*), where the king becomes the epitome of the correct form of behaviour. However, the *nāstika* is not one who necessarily adopts a philosophical position, but one who narrows down his lifestyle options too much. Nor elsewhere is *moha* associated with *nāstika*s or the other two kinds of opponents mentioned earlier, and it is something both ascetics and worldly brāhmaṇas seek to overcome as the defining influence on their behaviour.

A rather extreme case where *nāstika* is used brings together some other strongly criticized modes of behaviour in a highly concentrated manner:

> I was a pedant, a rationalist, I scorned the Vedas, I was obsessed with philosophical analysis and the science of reasoning — both pointless. I asserted statements of reason and in assemblies I argued from reason. And I specifically spoke to and abused brāhmaṇas about their holy sacrifices. I was a non-believer, sceptical, a fool who considered himself wise. As a result of that I have become a jackal, brāhmaṇa.[12]

The speaker here is Indra who has taken the form of a jackal in order to persuade a Brāhmanical ascetic that he should not give up his life after having been struck by a vaiśya's chariot. His recommendation is to follow the Vedas and perform sacrifices, hardly surprising, being a theme that is repeated to the point of weariness. His birth as a jackal is a consequence, however, of leading a life that was the opposite of this.

What little could be said in his favour if anything at all? The charge of false self-attribution of intelligence (*paṇḍitamānikaḥ*) is frequently brought up in both Buddhist and Hindu texts and it could possibly be dismissed as a negative comment on self-importance. However, here it falls into a different category because it is associated with methods of argument and reasoning, on the one hand, and attacks on Brāhmanical institutions, on the other. Both of these are clearly meant to be interrelated such that the mode of argumentation (*hetuvāda, hetumat, ānvīkṣikīṁ, tarkavidyām*) leads to him being a reviler of the Vedas, a critic of the sacrifice, and from that a critic of the brāhmaṇas. This he can be because he is a *nāstika* and a sceptic, and when all this is exposed, he becomes a fool. Association of *nāstika*

12. *aham āsaṁ paṇḍitako haituko vedanindakaḥ* |
ānvīkṣikīṁ tarkavidyām anurakto nirarthikām | |
hetuvādān pravaditā vaktā saṁsatsu hetumat |
ākroṣṭā cābhivaktā ca brahmayajñeṣu vai dvijān | |
nāstikaḥ sarvaśaṅkī ca mūrkhaḥ paṇḍtamānikaḥ |
tasyeyaṁ phalanirvṛttiḥ sṛgālatvaṁ mama dvija | | — 12.173.45-47

status and scepticism go hand in hand with a refusal to accept the Vedas as being *apauruṣeya* and the sacrifice as delivering a meaningful result.

Whether or not the brāhmaṇas themselves believe in both of the latter is not necessarily beside the point in a text like the *Mbh*. Rather, it is that the social structure guaranteeing the brāhmaṇa's special status in the emergent caste hierarchy and his particular, if reciprocal, relationship with the king rests on truth being accorded to both of these institutions: Vedic knowledge and the sacrifice. Even if the empiricism associated with Buddhist thought may be adjudged as being right even by those intellectuals who were not Buddhists, it cannot be allowed to jeopardize the new system of hierarchy and obligation the brāhmaṇas were trying to consolidate in the face of the uncertainty of the political systems surrounding them, the kind of political/military instability suggested by the *Mbh* war itself. Theirs was obviously a theoretical order, grounded in social and political practice, that was placed on top of a much more fluid historical situation. As the basis of this order was the theory of sacrifice which had such a long antiquity that it could justifiably be called tradition and it was one the brāhmaṇas made great efforts to sustain even if the historical conditions which had given rise to it had long gone, such that it remained a vestige, though a vestige marked with great prestige.

Surely the *nāstika* in his rejection of this threatened the emerging dominance of the brāhmaṇa and the royal patronage he so sought after. Bear in mind the success of the *saṁgha*, both in numbers and conspicuousness by the beginning of the common era. *Vihāra*s and *stūpa*s were built where they could be seen[13] and the huge number of them recorded by archaeologists suggests the capacity of the *saṁgha* as an institution to attract and maintain financial resources. Even so, if the Buddhists (and Jainas) are *nāstika*s, would lay Buddhists living side by side with brāhmaṇas been aware of the Buddhist critique of the Vedas and the sacrifice?

A final point of interest is that there seems to be an explicit connection made between kingship and the *nāstika*. In 12.71.3 Bhīṣma warns Yudhiṣṭhira that a good king should not be a *nāstika*, but the immediate context allows us to draw no meaning from this, implying that the meaning of this word must have been so obvious to those who knew the *Mbh* that it did not need definition. Other references are 2.5.96 where *nāstikya* is one of the fourteen royal vices; 12.123.16 where it is strongly recommended

13. See most recently, Schopen (2006).

that a king restrain the *nāstika* attitude; and 13.61.38 where it is postulated that a king who is both *adharmajña* and *nāstika* will induce a lack of happiness in his subjects. To this data I would also add that two passages where there is a concentration of references to *nāstika* are addressed to kings, Dhṛtarāṣṭra (5.33-39) and Yudhiṣṭhira (12.10-15). In the first Vidura is giving advice about the foundations for the judgements kings should make, and in the second the four Pāṇḍava brothers and Draupadī are urging Yudhiṣṭhira to take on the kingship and not become a renouncer. I wonder whether this reflects a reality where certain kings were regarded as *nāstikas* even if this simply meant they offered material patronage to Buddhists and Jainas. It is not just a counter-argument against kings becoming renouncers. In my view it should be seen as an attempt to delimit the king's capacity to allocate resources.

Conclusion

In light of this all too brief survey of *nāstika* and a few other passages, what does it mean to say the *Mbh* is a text of critique? Much that we find, especially in the Śānti-Parvan, presents the opposite of normative situations, depicting the consequences when individuals fail to act in an appropriate manner, but never a sustained critique of the theoretical system underlying normative behaviour. Two points of consideration arise from this:

1. Who are the brāhmaṇas critiquing?
2. Are they critiquing other complete socio-religious traditions or ideas and practices that would occur outside of those traditions?

These questions must be asked because the whole tone of the *Mbh* is to criticize within a very large cultural framework, and it is not always easy to determine if what may seem to be a critique is really an attempt to explore alternative responses to the validity or otherwise of a particular religious/philosophical proposition. The many explorations of fate, for example, that occur throughout the 3rd, 5th and 12th books are probably the best example of this. Similar are the ongoing debates where Yudhiṣṭhira is forced to defend his desire to renounce his kingship in favour of a renunciatory life in the forest. Such debates or statements of agreement are formally defined as *vivāda* or *saṁvāda* and there are many in the *Mbh*. They are easy to distinguish from extreme attacks of the kind usually reserved for proponents or beneficiaries of *varṇasaṁkara*.

Part of the attraction of the *Mbh* is that it looks backwards as well as forwards and this requires it to assert and preserve continuities with the past and perhaps even to justify them. It is within this structure that the retention of Vedic symbols can be understood. The Vedas are the pre-eminent connection with a legendary past in which the epic action is based, even though the text is clearly moving far beyond it in ideological terms. Though it has taken on board the ascetics' practices and associated world view which seem so far distant from the Vedic ritualism, it does not allow these to be taken up as the foundation of a sustained critique of Vedic tradition. Buddhist thought consistently criticizes Vedic tradition by constantly undermining the epistemological status of the Vedas, and through that of the self-conscious class confidence it seems to attribute to the brāhmaṇas by virtue of their possession of Vedic learning. The *nāstika* is a category summarizing all of these critiques, but it must be understood as being a critique of those within the broader *Mbh* cultural system rather than those outside of it.

References

Fitzgerald, J. (tr.) (2004), *The Mahābhārata*, vol. 7, Chicago: University of Chicago Press.

Hiltebeitel, A. (2006), "Aśvaghoṣa's *Buddhacarita*: The First Known Close and Critical Reading of the Brahmanical Sanskrit Epics," in *Journal of Indian Philosophy*, vol. 34, pp. 229-86.

Hopkins, E.W. (1978/1901), *The Great Epic of India: Its Character and Origin*, Calcutta: Punthi Pustak.

Lubin, T. (2005), "The Transmission, Patronage, and Prestige of Brahmanical Piety from the Mauryas to the Guptas," in *Boundaries, Dynamics and Construction of Traditions in South Asia*, ed. Federico Squarcini, Firenze: Firenze University Press, pp. 77-103.

Parasher-Sen, A. (2006), "Naming and Social Exclusion: The Outcast and the Outsider," in *Between The Empires: Society in India 300 BCE to 400 CE*, ed. Patrick Olivelle, New York: Oxford University Press, pp. 415-55.

Schopen, Gregory (2006), "The Buddhist 'Monastery' and the Indian Garden: Aesthetics, Assimilations, and the Siting of Monastic Establishments," in *Journal of the American Oriental Society*, vol. 124, no. 4, pp. 487-505.

17

Renunciation and Celebration
Ascetics in the Temple Life of Medieval Tamil Nadu

*Leslie C. Orr**

GIVEN Prof. Rukmani's contributions to the study of renunciation in the Hindu tradition (most recently, in Rukmani 2011), it seems fitting for me to offer an essay on this topic as part of this volume in her honour. In this essay, I will focus on the history of the phenomenon of renunciation in medieval Tamil Nadu. The inscriptions engraved on the stone walls of Śaiva and Vaiṣṇava temples, in the ninth through thirteenth centuries, frequently refer to individuals and groups called *tapasyar* (or *tavasiyar*, *tapasvins*, etc.), *yogīs*, and *saṁnyāsīs*. Our understanding of what renunciation or asceticism meant to these people, and of the nature of the sectarian and institutional milieux in which they followed their religious paths, has been profoundly influenced by subsequent historical developments. In the last several centuries, the ascetic *persona* in Tamil Nadu has come to be defined with reference to one of three "schools" or "traditions" — each identified with a particular teacher, or group of teachers, from south India — the Advaita Vedānta of Śaṅkarācārya (eighth century), the Śrīvaiṣṇavism of Rāmānuja (d. 1137) and other *ācāryas* of his lineage, and the Śaiva-Siddhānta of Meykaṇṭar and his disciples, with Umāpati Śivācārya (fl. early fourteenth century) as the most prolific author of this group. Later hagiographies present each of these three teachers as being deeply involved in temple life in the Tamil country — Śaṅkara at Kāñcīpuram, Rāmānuja at Śrīraṅgam, and Umāpati at Chidambaram — and as founding, or having followers who founded, monastic establishments known as *maṭhas*.[1] We — either as scholars or as members

* Department of Religion, Concordia University

1. The earliest source to credit Śaṅkara with the establishment of *maṭhas* is Anantanadagiri's *Śaṅkaravijaya*, dating possibly from the fifteenth century. The only *maṭha* mentioned in this context is that at Śṛṅgerī, although the text suggests →

of Hindu religious communities — tend to consider the identities and activities of ascetics in the Tamil country of a thousand years ago as early representatives of the three renunciant traditions, with their disciplic successions and celibate institutions, that are known to us from recent times.

I would like to suggest that it is important for us to imagine the possibility that the nature of medieval temples and *maṭha*s was quite different from that of their modern counterparts, to try to break away from the historical modelling that the transmission of tradition imposes on the past, and to consider how medieval ascetics were imaged in the sculpture, literature, and inscriptions of their own times. In this paper, I will be basing myself primarily on inscriptional evidence of the eighth to sixteenth centuries, but I will try to bring other kinds of sources into the chronological framework that we can construct on the basis of the epigraphical material, which will both elucidate and complicate the picture we arrive at by examining the inscriptions.[2] In seeking to discern medieval patterns of renunciation, I have been repeatedly struck by the inventiveness of those ascetics and teachers who have since the earliest times capitalized on the resources available in contexts where manifold and competing perspectives and practices encountered one another. Thus, I hope that this paper will highlight the dynamic character of the complex, various and shifting definitions of the renunciant's way of life in medieval Tamil Nadu.

→ that Śaṅkara was responsible for founding the three great temples at Kanchipuram, sacred to Viṣṇu, Śiva, and the Goddess (Bader 2000: 235). *Maṭha*s as the characteristic institutions of later south Indian Śrīvaiṣṇavism and Śaiva-Siddhānta — monasteries housing a group of celibates and headed by a teacher of exalted rank — were not to come into being until the fifteenth century, despite the fact that they trace their origins back to teachers of the early medieval era (Arooran 1981; Narayanan 1990). On the south Indian *maṭha* see also: Cenkner 1983, Derrett 1974, Karashima 2010, Koppedrayer 1990, Mahalingam 1962, Rajamanikkam 1962, Sethuraman 1991, Swamy 1975, Talbot 1987, and Van Troy 1974.

2. A disclaimer may be in order here: the dates that I am providing for various texts and historical figures are almost all subject to debate. I want also to apologize for my anachronistic use of the word "Hindu" throughout this paper, which serves merely as shorthand for "Śaiva and Vaiṣṇava." The inscriptional evidence upon which I draw for this paper includes consideration of a wide range of evidence, but rests primarily on a group of about four hundred inscriptions which I have assembled especially for this paper and whose texts I have examined in detail. In the interests of intelligibility, I have in some cases altered the orthography of terms found in the Tamil inscriptions so that they are consistent with one another or so that they more closely resemble the Sanskrit terms to which they are related — although I have retained many of the variants of terms for "ascetic" found in the Tamil inscriptions. Inscriptional Tamil does not distinguish between long and short "e" or "o," so these remain unmarked in my transliterations.

Wanderers and Worshippers, Vows and Penance

We begin our exploration with the earliest evidence we have of renunciant practices in the Tamil country — which overlaps with the earliest inscriptions. These are the Tamil-Brāhmī inscriptions, dating from the second century BCE onward, found carved onto the walls or ceilings of caves in rocky hills especially in the region around the city of Madurai and in the former Pudukkoṭṭai state. The content of the inscriptions, and the context in which they are found, indicate that these caves were dwellings for Jaina ascetics, including women, and that these ascetics were the sponsors of the excavation of these shelters and the stone beds within them, as well as their recipients (Mahadevan 2003). Following the fifth century, these sites continued to serve as the dwelling places for ascetics, but were also centres for worship activities which, again, were sponsored not only by lay people but by Jaina "religious men" and "religious women." I use the terms "religious men" and "religious women" — rather than "monks" and "nuns" — because these people, although distinguishable from ordinary lay Jainas, were not represented in the Tamil inscriptions as having undergone ordination, or as being affiliated with any particular monastic order (a *saṁgha* or *gaccha*). They were instead identified with respect to a teaching lineage, and were most often referred to by terms meaning "teacher" (*kuravar* or *ācirikar* for men and *kuratti* for women) or "disciple" (*māṉākkaṉ* for men and *māṉākkiyar* for women), or with other terms meaning "honoured person" (*paṭārar* or *aṭikaḷ*) or "ascetic" (*tapasiyar* or *vairāgyar*) being occasionally applied to men. While men were invariably the disciples of male teachers, Jaina religious women identified themselves as the disciples of either male or female *gurus*.

The inscriptions of the eighth and ninth centuries from the far south of Tamil Nadu (Madurai, Kanyakumari and Tirunelveli districts), indicate that such religious men and religious women constituted fully half of the donors who set up images of *tīrthaṁkaras* and *yakṣīs* (goddesses) at Jaina sacred sites. Given the importance of the vow of non-possession for Jaina mendicants, this is rather unexpected and indicates a deviation from normative Jaina monastic practice. The site of Kalugumalai, between the cities of Madurai and Tirunelveli, is especially rich in inscriptions that indicate the prominence of religious men and women as donors. There is considerable evidence to suggest that, as in the case of the Buddhist monks and nuns further to the north whose activities Gregory Schopen has examined (Schopen 1988), the enlightened ones, and goddesses as well, were objects of devotion for members of the Jaina religious elite of the Tamil country, who not only donated the images but also arranged for lamps, bathing, festival observances and for food and other offerings to be provided for them. The term *paḷḷi*, which appears in the earliest inscriptions to denote the stone bed or, more generally, the place of residence for Jaina ascetics — or a "monastery" — comes also, by the eighth century, to signify a temple. In early medieval times, these sites in the Tamil country sacred to the Jainas were primarily of significance as places of worship, and Jaina ascetics seem to have been both sponsors and officiants.

But what do these Jainas — and especially such apparently unorthodox Jainas — have to do with the devotees and renunciants of the Śaiva or Vaiṣṇava context? In fact, they coexisted in very close proximity. At Kalugumalai, immediately adjacent to the cliff face covered with images of *tīrthaṁkaras* and *yakṣīs*, is a temple dedicated to Śiva which was excavated out of living rock in around CE 800. And although it was never completed, one can scarcely doubt that, as Richard Davis has suggested, those Śaiva adepts who were on site to ensure the ritual rectitude of its construction came into contact with their Jaina counterparts who, just a few hundred metres away and in this very period, were occupied with fashioning the rock face of Kalugumalai into an elaborate Jaina monument (Davis 1998). And not only such proximity but the Śaivas' polemics against the Jainas — especially in the works of the seventh-century poet-saints Tiruñānacampantar and Appar, which Indira Peterson (1998) has discussed — gives us the sense that the two communities, in terms of their shared practices and values, were from the Śaiva perspective sometimes a little too close for comfort. The poems of the Śaiva saints express hostility towards the Jainas, while at the same time pointing toward commonalities. Appar's description of the Śaiva devotees — "the wide world is our home;/generous householders in every town/give us food./Public halls are our only shelter . . ." (*Tēvāram* 6.312.12, trans. Peterson 1989) — suggests that these wandering Śaivas may have resembled Jaina mendicants. Nor was the Śaiva conception of the Lord as a renunciant and a teacher — perhaps seen as a model to be emulated in certain ways — so removed from the images revered by the Jainas.

The three authors of *Tēvāram* — Tiruñānacampantar, Appar, and Cuntaramūrtti, who composed their hymns to Śiva in the period of the seventh to ninth centuries — use the Tamil word *tavam* (Skt. *tapas*) in ways that reveal the tensions and ambivalence that surrounded the definition of asceticism for Śaivas who sought to distinguish themselves from Jaina ascetics. For the most part, the *Tēvāram* poets regard *tavam* very positively, as a quality of Śiva's devotees, whose *tavam* — their "austerities" or their single-minded concentration on and service of the Lord — results in their receiving a boon, or a vision of the Lord. Śiva himself is referred to by Tiruñānacampantar as *tava nīti* — the law, or truth, of *tapas* (*Tēvāram* 2.121). On the other hand, the word *tavattar* can also be used with reference to Buddhists or Jainas, whose austerities are described as unsuitable, faulty, and — most of all — fruitless.[3] That such ascetics were indeed a part of the world in which the *Tēvāram* poets lived is indicated by an eighth-century inscription from Tenimalai, in the former Pudukkoṭṭai state, celebrating the *tavam* undertaken by a Jaina ascetic, which had attracted the attention of a local chief who came into the ascetic's presence and honoured him with a gift of land.[4] It is in the ninth century that, while Jainism continued to flourish, numbers of structural stone temples dedicated to Śiva and Viṣṇu began to be constructed throughout the Tamil country — and the walls of these temples provide us with a multitude of inscriptions. I propose to provide a century-by-century review of what the inscriptions reveal about the identities and activities of ascetics, beginning with the ninth century and coming forward to the sixteenth century.

Most of the ninth-century inscriptions found in the "Hindu" context are rather terse, and record gifts of gold or livestock from various kinds of people, to support the running of perpetual lamps in the temple. But a number of inscriptions document donations intended to provide food for visitors to the temple — most often brāhmaṇas. For example, an inscription of CE 892 at the Vaikuṇṭha Perumāḷ temple in Uttaramerur, tells us of the arrangements made for feeding one thousand brāhmaṇas at the time of a festival (apparently in honour of Śiva; *SII* 6.371). Usually the numbers provided for were much more modest, and on occasion, in addition to or instead of brāhmaṇas, other sorts of people were offered food in the temple — including in a couple of cases groups of *śivayogīs*. Unlike the Jainas, Hindu ascetics do not feature as donors in this early period, and thus we do not know their names. The only hint we have of

3. Monius (2004) discusses the development of the idea of *tavam* in later Tamil Śaiva literature, showing how the critique of Jainaism continues to serve as a backdrop for the definition of *tavam* as a Śaiva ideal. See also Sivaraman (1973: 391), on the meaning of *tavam* in south Indian Śaiva-Siddhānta.

4. *IPS* 9 = *KVR* #13. See the bibliography for the abbreviations used in references to the texts of inscriptions.

the identities of the *śivayogīs* who appeared in the temples of Tamil Nadu in the ninth century comes from the qualification in one inscription (from Tiruppalatturai; *SII* 8.581) that the *śivayogīs* given food were to be knowledgeable in the Vedas (*vetamvalla*). In the few ninth-century inscriptions from Hindu temples that specify food recipients other than brāhmaṇas, we also encounter the terms *paṉmāheśvarar*, *aṭiyar*, *māṇi*, *aṭikaḷmar*, and *tavaci* or *tapasyar*.[5]

Apart from one — the *tavaci* who was provided food at Tiruvallur (in Chingleput district) who had the duty of cleaning the temple (*ARE* 1945/5) — these Hindu ascetics and devotees appear not to have had any particular role to play in the life of the temple. This contrasts with the hints we have that Jaina religious men in this period took on certain administrative responsibilities with respect to the institutions with which they were affiliated.[6] The ninth-century Jaina inscriptions also indicate that religious women were organized into communities: in two records, we find groups of women termed *koyilpiḷḷaikaḷ* — "children of the temple" — who were recipients of support. In one of these (from North Arcot district; *SII* 3.92), a donor undertook to protect, shelter and feed the "five hundred *koyilpiḷḷaikaḷ*," disciples (*māṇākkiyar*) of the lineage of a particular female teacher (*kurattiyar*), who had severed ties with the "four hundred *tapasikaḷ*" of this place — evidently their male counterparts.[7] The inscriptions of this period at shrines dedicated to Śiva and Viṣṇu do not reveal the presence of such groups of religious women. Nor, more generally, does the degree of institutionalization — of communities and lineages — indicated by the Jaina inscriptions (for example, in referring to *paḷḷis*) have any Hindu equivalent in this period — with one important exception. This exception is found in a Sanskrit record (*SII* 23.129) engraved on the walls of the temple of Kodumbalur, in Pudukkoṭṭai, which documents the foundation by the Irukkuvel chief of both the temple itself, and a *maṭha* built for a certain Mallikārjuna from Mathurā and for the fifty Kālāmukha ascetics who were his followers.

As we move into the tenth century, we begin to see more inscriptional

5. With these last two terms, there is some overlap with the Jaina context of this period, where we find provisions for feeding *aṭikaḷmar* at Aiyyampalayam in Madurai district (*SII* 14.22 = *EI* 32, 335-38), and at Kilsattamaṅgalam in North Arcot district, provision for *piccai* (Skt. *bhikṣā*) for the *tavaci*s dwelling there (*ARE* 1969/219 = *KVR* #7). On *māṇis*, see n. 13 below.

6. For example in *SII* 14.128 = *KVR* #32 and *ARE* 1969/219 = *KVR* #7.

7. There is also a ninth-century reference to a group of three hundred *koyilpiḷḷaikaḷ* from other end of Tamil Nadu, at Dalapatisamudram in Tirunelveli district (*SII* 14.40).

references to ascetics within the Hindu context, at an increasing number of different temple sites (virtually all of them Śaivite, and most of them in Coḷamaṇḍalam and Toṇḍaimaṇḍalam — i.e. the central and northern zones of Tamil Nadu), but there continue to be very few indications that these followers of the religious path found themselves incorporated into organizations of any sort, even including teaching lineages. The only two tenth-century references to *maṭha*s that I have found both indicate that those involved in such institutions, like the Kālāmukhas of Koḍumbalur in the ninth century, were not necessarily a part of the orthodox fold. So at Pallimadam (in Ramnad district; *SII* 14.88) we learn about a *maṭha* of *mahāvratikaḷ* (those undertaking great penances) associated with the memorial (*paḷḷippaṭai*) temple here; these are very likely Pāśupatas. At Tiruvorriyur (in Chingleput district), we also find *mahāvratikaḷ* being offered food in the mid-tenth century (*ARE* 1912/168); soon after, a *maṭha* was established under the leadership of a former general of the Coḷa army (*EI* 27.47; *ARE* 1912/177), perhaps also with Pāśupata connections.[8] Elsewhere, not *maṭha*s but temples provided housing and food for ascetics — referred to as *tapasyar* — for example at Kuttalam and Madurantaka (*SII* 13.386; *ARE* 1922/397). As in the ninth century, *śivayogī*s continued to be offered food, as honoured devotees. In a number of places, *śivayogī*s are described as worshipping in the temple — whether as priests or devotees, is not clear — and in one inscription from Udaiyargudi (*ARE* 1920/577) they are actually identified as brāhmaṇas, while elsewhere *śivayogī*s and brāhmaṇas are treated as distinct groups, and also differentiated from *aṭikaḷmar* (honoured devotees).

Can we imagine that the *śivayogī*s and *tapasyar* received at tenth-century temples resembled the figures of the Śaiva poet-saints that began in this same period to be made for use as processional images — the figures of

8. Although in the Āgamas, Pāśupatas are clearly distinguished from Śaivas (see, for example *Somaśambhupaddhati*), it has been argued by Hara (2002) among others, that this group was entirely orthodox and mainstream within the Śaiva fold. On the Kālāmukhas, see Lorenzen 1972.

9. The Śaiva poet-saint Māṇikkavācakar, who probably lived in the ninth century, is, rather strangely, not included in the pantheon of sixty-three Śaiva saints, the *nāyaṇmār*, celebrated in the hagiographical work the *Periya Purāṇam*, composed in the twelfth century. Images of Māṇikkavācakar, however, appear in the temples of Tamil Nadu by this time — dated by some authors (Gravely and Ramachandran 1932; Nagaswamy 1983) as early as the tenth century — and inscriptions mention his poem *Tiruvempāvai* beginning in the eleventh century (*ARE* 1912/128). Medieval images of Māṇikkavācakar usually depict him as an ascetic, and the hagiographies that circulated, apparently from the thirteenth century onward, emphasize his renunciation of worldly life when he encounters Lord Śiva and takes him as his *guru*.

Appar, Tiruñānacampantar, and Māṇikkavācakar?[9] Did the craftsmen who fashioned these images of the Śaiva saints use the appearance of their own contemporaries, the *śivayogīs* (who may have borne sacred threads, as the saints' images do) as models? Or, conversely, did the stories of the lives of these Śaiva saints that were circulating at this time emphasize their ascetic nature, influencing their depiction and also making them exemplars for the *śivayogīs*? Tenth-century inscriptions — and images — indicate that there was a place for women among Śaiva ascetics and devotees. For example, two records from the neighbourhood of Kumbakonam detail the provisions made for feeding *peṇ tapasyar* (female ascetics) or *peṇṇaṭiyarkaḷmar* (female devotees), along with their male counterparts (*SII* 13.115; *SII* 8.225).[10] Other indications of female asceticism in this period are found in the inscribed stones erected in South Arcot district that commemorated the vows — referred to as *no<u>n</u>pu* or *paraṇi* — of women identified with reference to their husbands or fathers. It seems likely that these were memorials erected by their male kinfolk to women who had undertaken severe austerities, such as a fast to death (Orr 2007).

Possibilities and Problems for the Renouncer

In the eleventh century, there continue to be at least a few inscriptional references to female ascetics; for example, in Kanyakumari district a female ascetic (*tavasiyar*) made a gift to maintain a lamp in the temple (*TAS* 6:1.9 = *ARE* 1978/250). The location of this inscription is significant, since the eleventh century marks the beginning of references to Hindu ascetics in the far south, where Jainas had earlier been dominant. By the thirteenth century the majority of inscriptional references to Hindu ascetics come from Kanyakumari, Tirunelveli, and Madurai districts, with large numbers in Ramnad district as well — all in the southern part of Tamil Nadu. Also significant is the fact that this woman is a donor, which constitutes a new role for ascetics.[11]

---

10. Very similar arrangements — and terminology — are found in tenth-century Jaina inscriptions, which document arrangements for the support of women associated with *paḷḷis* (*SII* 7.56 = *JIT* 361 from Vilappakkam, North Arcot district; Subramaniam 1958-59, 84ff = *ARE* 1962/29A = *JIT* 503 from Pallankoyil, Tanjavur district).

11. Eleventh-century examples of male ascetics acquiring wealth and making gifts to temples include inscriptions from Konerirajapuram, where a *tapasvī* attached to the temple built a shrine for the saint Candeśvara (*SII* 26.706) and from Tiruvorriyur, where one of the *tapasyar* of the temple purchased land (*ARE* 1912/229).

It is in the eleventh century that we see the first indications of asceticism in inscriptions at Vaiṣṇava temples.[12] But the art and literature of the eleventh century provide far more clues than the inscriptions about Vaiṣṇava attitudes toward renunciation. The earliest bronze images of the Vaiṣṇava saints, the Āḻvārs, appeared in the eleventh century, and the two figures most often represented are Tirumaṅgai and Nammāḻvār. If the Śaiva saints Appar, Tiruñānacampantar, and Māṇikkavācakar seem to provide models for asceticism, the Āḻvārs evidently do not — Tirumaṅgai is imaged as a kind of robber prince, and Nammāḻvār's yogic trance state, which he assumed from the very moment of his birth, according to the hagiographies, was one to which no ordinary mortal could aspire. We find Śrīvaiṣṇava models for the ascetic path in the lives not of the Āḻvārs, but of the *ācāryas*, whose renunciation is much less extreme. Nāthamuni, for example, the first in the lineage of Śrīvaiṣṇava *ācāryas*, is described in the eleventh century by his grandson Yāmuna as "the best of *yogīs*" (Neeval 1977). Yet, literary and sculptural depictions of Nāthamuni suggest that there was a range of possibilities of what it meant to be a *muni* or *yogī* within the Śrīvaiṣṇava tradition — a topic which Narayanan (1990) has explored in depth: Is Nāthamuni a renouncer or not? Is his single-minded devotion to the Āḻvārs enough to transform him as a householder into a *saṁnyāsī*? Or, was he a renunciant in loincloth, bearing a staff, as maintained by Vedāntadeśika in the fourteenth century? (Olivelle 1986 (2): 123-24).

In the eleventh century, the nascent Śrīvaiṣṇava community was deeply concerned with defining the character of *saṁnyāsa*, as attested by the eleventh-century *Yatidharmasamuccaya*. This work presents the argument of the Śrīvaiṣṇavas against those belonging to the Advaita Vedānta school. The author of this text, Yādava Prakāśa, is supposed to have been himself an Advaitin *saṁnyāsī* who "converted" and became a disciple of Rāmānuja. The form of asceticism he argues for is one that incorporates the observance of Brāhmanical ritual together with devotion to Viṣṇu. This way of life, in which the renouncer does not abandon his ritual duties or the insignia of his status as a brāhmaṇa, the sacred thread and the hair tuft, and in which he carries the triple staff (*tridaṇḍa*), was to become the model for renunciation within the Śrīvaiṣṇava community — in contrast with the tradition supposed to have been established by the Advaitin teacher

12. Inscriptions from Śrīraṅgam (*SII* 24.73) and Kāñcīpuram (*ARE* 1919/635) make reference to ascetics in the Vaiṣṇava context; at Kāñcī, there is also the mention of a *maṭha*.

Śaṅkara, where the renouncer relinquishes all marks of his Brāhmanical status and carries the single staff (*ekadaṇḍa*) (Olivelle 1986). Although the inscriptions of this period reveal very little about Vaiṣṇava asceticism, nothing at all about renunciants who may have taken the Advaitin path, and do not even use the term "*saṁnyāsī*" until the thirteenth century, Yādava's text seems to provide us with evidence of the activity of, and competition between these two ascetic groups. But, rather surprisingly, the model of *saṁnyāsa* that Yādava outlines, which comes to be normative for the Śrīvaiṣṇava tradition, is not easily reconcilable with the image of the *ācārya* that is found in the Āgamic texts. Pāñcarātra texts, which along with Vaikhānasa and Śaiva texts were circulating in south India in this period, were considered to be an essential source for the theology and ritual of Tamil Vaiṣṇavism. Yet at least some of the Pāñcarātra texts rule out *saṁnyāsa* for the *ācārya* — the teacher who was entitled to bestow initiation on others. For example, the *Paramasaṁhitā* (7.22) says that the *ācārya* must be a *gr̥hasthin*, a householder, while the *Pādmasaṁhitā* (*kriyā* 24.13) allows also for the possibility of his being a *brahmacārin* or *vānaprasthin* (Smith 1975). The Vaikhānasa and Śaiva Āgamas seem to go even further, rejecting the possibility of *vānaprastha* as a way of life for the *ācārya*. The celibate *ācārya*, therefore, can only be a life-long *brahmacārin* — and the Śaivāgamic texts that may perhaps be assigned to the eleventh or twelfth century, in fact, consider this *āśrama* is less desirable for the *ācārya* than *gr̥hastha*; in any case, *saṁnyāsa* is not an option.[13]

If the Śaivāgamas are so firm on this point, who then are the *śivayogī*s who appear in the inscriptions of the eleventh century — so often fed at festivals or in the course of the daily round of temple worship? Can they possibly be *saṁnyāsī*s? Several of the eleventh-century inscriptions (for

---

13. The earliest Śaivāgamas are silent on the subject of the *āśrama* expected of the future *ācārya* (as also is the case for *varṇa*), although there seems to be a general agreement that the best of *ācārya*s is the *gr̥hastha*, but the *brahmacārin* (whether permanent or temporary) is also acceptable; the *vānaprastha* and *yati* are excluded. Texts of the later period increasingly insist on the superiority of the status of *gr̥hastha* for the *ācārya* (Brunner 1988). For the Vaikhānasa position on this issue, see Coḷas 1996: 152-53.

    In inscriptions from the late ninth century onward (for example *SII* 2.69; *SII* 13.386), we find the term *māṇi* used apparently with reference to *brahmacārin*s who were assigned certain ritual tasks as assistants to the priest in the context of temple service; among their functions were the bringing of water for bathing the deity and holding the canopy over the deity. It is difficult to know what relationship, if any, these *māṇi*s might have had to sectarian lineages or whether they may have been considered in some way to be "junior *ācārya*s."

example, at Tiruvannamalai and Tiruppalatturai) suggest that *śivayogīs* are a subset of the category of *aṭiyar* — devotee; they continue, in other cases, to be described as Veda-knowers, and thus appear to be brāhmaṇas. Yet they are usually distinguished from those people referred to as *śivabrāhmaṇas* — as well as from *tapasyar* (ascetics) and *māheśvaras* (Śaiva devotees). Do any of these various types of people have affiliations with renunciant "orders" or with Āgamic teaching lineages?

Although the inscriptions do not allow us to answer these questions, they do point toward the emergence of some new types of institutional structures — *maṭhas* (Ta. *maṭam*). The *maṭhas* mentioned in eleventh-century inscriptions are of two kinds. One type of *maṭha* is the feeding house, which, according to the inscriptions, provided food for a variety of groups, in various combinations, including *tapasyar*, devotees, brāhmaṇas and *yogīs*. The other type of *maṭha* was centred on a teacher. Of six eleventh-century examples of such *maṭhas* from various parts of the Tamil country that I have examined, three reveal their Pāśupata associations through the name of the *maṭha* head, Lakulīśa-paṇḍita; the other three all make mention of a succession of heads, or of a disciplic lineage (*varggattār* — employing the same term that is used in the inscriptions in the case of a family lineage).[14] Are these nascent Śaiva-Siddhānta lineages? There is nothing in these eleventh-century inscriptions to indicate that this is the case.

Nor is such evidence to be found in the inscriptions of the twelfth century, when the concern with lineage or association with a particular *maṭha* on the part of the renunciant that had begun to be hinted at in the preceding century is not in evidence. In the twelfth century we find only a single reference to the lineage (*vaṁśattār*) of an ascetic (SII 7.96), and inscriptional references to *maṭhas* are almost invariably to places in which food is provided — for *śivayogīs*, *tapasvīs*, and *māheśvarar*, as well as for people termed *āṇṭārkaḷ*, and, in one case, at Tirukkoyilur, for Śrīvaiṣṇavas (*ARE* 1921/349). One of these feeding houses, at Tribhuvanai, where itinerant *śivayogīs* and *māheśvarar* were fed is named Tirunāvukkaracu *maṭha*, after the Śaiva saint Appar (*PI* 139).

Despite the undoubted fact of activity in the twelfth-century on the part of Śaiva *ācāryas* — like Aghoraśiva, who drew on the Āgamas to arrive at a theological/ritual synthesis for temple worship, and Vākica Munivar, who is regarded as an early representative of the Tamil

14. The eleventh-century inscriptions referring to heads of *maṭhas* with the name Lakulīśa are: *SII* 3.18, *SII* 22.100, and *ARE* 1927/271. Those inscriptions mentioning a succession of *maṭha* leaders are: *ARE* 1945/38, *ARE* 1963/508, and *SII* 26.694.

Siddhānta tradition (Siddhalingaiah 1979; Davis 2009) — not only are these particular historical figures off the epigraphical radar, but the institutional structures and sectarian communities within which we might today imagine these people being located seem irrelevant to the lives of ascetics as these are imaged in twelfth-century temple inscriptions. One explanation for this would be that these Tamil Siddhāntins — Aghoraśiva and Vākica Munivar — were not, in fact, renunciants. That the heads of *maṭhas* might also have been householders rather than renunciants is clearly demonstrated by the fact that a woman who appears as a donor in a twelfth-century inscription from Tiruvennainallur (*SII* 7.944) was described as the wife of a man who "did" *maṭapattiyam* — that is, he was a *maṭhādhipati* or the head of a *maṭha*.

From the twelfth-century inscriptions, we get the idea that there were indeed renunciants, especially in the case where we find them inhabiting *guhā*s (caves).[15] The inscriptions tell us that a *guhā* was maintained for *tapasyar* at Chidambaram (*ARE* 1936/3); that one was built for an ascetic doing daily worship at Tiruppugalur (*ARE* 1928/87); and that a group of people termed *āṇḍār* resided in a *guhā* at Tiruppanaiyur. It is in twelfth-century inscriptions that such *āṇḍār* start to be prominent — sometimes in association with *maṭhas* or, as we have just seen, *guhā*s. They are frequently among those offered food at festivals — where they are in several cases listed together with (and distinguished from) *śivayogī*s and/or *tapasyar*. In inscriptions of the twelfth century, as in the eleventh century, we find *tapasyar* and *śivayogī*s featuring as donors. In one case a *tapasi* buys land and donates it as *maṭappuṟam* (endowment to a *maṭha*) for feeding the *tiruvīti āṇḍār* (*āṇḍār* of the holy streets) who serve in the temple (*SII* 7.97). There is also an interesting reference to a woman described as a *paradeśī ammai* (a "pilgrim mother") who requested the Pāṇḍya king to make a donation to support offerings in a temple in Tirunelveli district (*ARE* 1928/271). At Vaiṣṇava temples, there are a few twelfth-century records relating to ascetics — at Śrīraṅgam we find *kovaṇavar* (those wearing loincloths) figuring among the temple authorities — but there is scarcely any other indication of the salience of the renunciant way of life among the Vaiṣṇavas of Tamil Nadu.

Renunciation's Intersections with Institutions

But all this changes in the thirteenth century, with the appearance of

15. In the tenth century, we also have a case of a renunciant — a former general of the Coḷa army — inhabiting a *guhā*, at Tiruvorriyur (*EI* 27.47). See also Sethuraman 1991.

images of the great Śrīvaiṣṇava teacher Rāmānuja which depict him as a *saṁnyāsī* in the Śrīvaiṣṇava style, with *tridaṇḍa* and sacred thread. Not only were such images enshrined in Vaiṣṇava temples in many parts of the Tamil country, but in the hagiographical literature that can be dated to this period Rāmānuja's *persona* as a *saṁnyāsī* was being developed and elaborated (Narayanan 1990). In thirteenth-century inscriptions engraved in temples dedicated to Viṣṇu, we also find evidence that the *saṁnyāsī* figured as an increasingly familiar personage. In inscriptions at eight different Vaiṣṇava temples we find references to provisions for feeding *saṁnyāsī*s, who are at five of these sites identified as *tridaṇḍī*s. But in at least three of these places, *ekadaṇḍī saṁnyāsī*s were offered food as well, which is quite unexpected in light of the controversy over whether an ascetic should carry a single or a triple staff that so preoccupied Yādava Prakāśa in the eleventh century and would continue to be an issue for Vedāntadeśika in the fourteenth century (Olivelle 1986). Are the *ekadaṇḍī*s that we encounter in these inscriptions ascetics belonging to Śaṅkara's Advaitin tradition, or are they Vaiṣṇavas? What about the *ekadaṇḍī saṁnyāsī*s fed at the Nelliyappar temple, dedicated to Śiva, in Tirunelveli (*ARE* 1927/72)?

Another term that is associated with Vaiṣṇava asceticism (*jīyar*) comes into prominence in thirteenth-century inscriptions. A number of Vaiṣṇava ascetics bear names which incorporate the word *jīyar* or *muni*. It is interesting, however, that most of those so named had no apparent connection with a lineage or a *maṭha*. Nor was the term or title *jīyar* exclusively Vaiṣṇava: for example, an inscription of CE 1239 from Kumaramangalam in Pudukkoṭṭai records a land grant to the Jīyar Viśveśvara Śivācārya, who is said to be graciously dwelling in the *tirumaṭam* at Tiruvanaikka, and who is clearly a Śaiva (*IPS* 196).

If, as in this case, we begin in the thirteenth century to encounter the term *śivācārya*, the *śivayogī* — rather surprisingly — has altogether vanished from the corridors of Śaiva temples. Meanwhile, individuals termed *tapasyar* are still in evidence — fulfilling a greater range of functions than in previous centuries, including reciting hymns or scriptures, performing worship, and making gifts. One of the features of such gifts, in several cases, is that the donor obtained some privilege — such as receiving consecrated food — as a consequence of his gift. *Maṭha*s and *guhā*s of the thirteenth century were frequently named for members of the *Tēvāram* trio (the Śaiva poet-saints Appar and Cuntaramūrtti — and especially Tiruñānacampantar), and *maṭha*s were also named for donors. These were often places for feeding — but also for housing — ascetics. And in several inscriptions we learn that deities were set up in *maṭhas*.

In general, the inscriptions of the thirteenth century reveal a greater and greater concern with the identities (i.e. the names) and the disciplic lineages of ascetics who appear as both donors and donees. Some such lineages seem to include women as disciples. We also encounter for the first time the term *mutaliyār* for a *maṭha* head. The main development of the thirteenth century that is of significance for our understanding of the institutional evolution of Śaiva-Siddhānta is the appearance of the Golakī and Lakṣādhyāya lineages. If there were perhaps one or two inscriptional references to these teachers and their *maṭhas* in preceding centuries, these become quite numerous in the thirteenth century. There can be no doubt that these lineages came to be allied with the Śaiva-Siddhānta teachers of the Tamil country (although exactly how remains a mystery). But did these teachers follow an ascetic way of life? We have already seen that the Śaivāgamas do not recommend that the *ācārya* be a renouncer, and I have suggested that early Tamil Siddhāntins may not have been ascetics. Indeed, Cynthia Talbot (1987) has argued that in thirteenth-century Andhra, "some members of the . . . Golakī Maṭha school abandoned the ascetic vow and became householders."[16] In the Tamil country in the thirteenth century, we find that the Golakīs, as well as other lineages, had established institutional bases in a number of temple towns, located throughout Tamil Nadu and especially in the far south.[17] Not only were many of these centres sites where numerous *maṭhas* with various teachers were concentrated, but they also served as nodes whose influence radiated to other places — either in the immediate region, or even farther afield. The town of Tiruvarur provides us with one of the most striking examples

---

16. ". . . with the advent of married *gurus*, succession to positions of power would probably have passed on hereditarily, rather than on the basis of spiritual merit or erudition. In this way, the crucial qualification for these Śaiva *gurus* would become their blood relationship with a predecessor, rather than a spiritual connection with the monastic lineage of the Golakī Maṭha" (Talbot 1987: 139).

17. The Golakī presence is in evidence beginning in the eleventh century, but becomes more prominent in the thirteenth century. Golakī centres included, in the northern part of the region, Tiruvorriyur (in Chingleput district) and Tiruvannamalai (in North Arcot district); in the Coḷa country, Chidambaram (in South Arcot), Tiruvannaikkaval (Trichy district) and Tiruvarur (in Tanjavur district — also Tiruchattimurram, near Kumbakonam); and farther south, Piranmalai (in Rāmnāḍ district), Madurai and Tirupparankunram (Madurai district), and Tirunelveli (Tirunelveli district).

of the propagation of Tamil *maṭha*-based lineages. Here, according to inscriptions from many different parts of the Tamil country, there were at least two important *maṭha*s. One of these, Tiruvarur's "northern *maṭha*," was the home of the teachers of two ascetics who were brought in the thirteenth century to Tirunelveli (over three hundred kilometres/ to the south), where they, together with nine ascetics of other lineages, including several imported from Madurai, had the responsibility of chanting "Tirujñānam" before the deity. This was arranged by the brother-in-law (himself from the Kongu country of western Tamil Nadu) of the Pāṇḍya king Maravarman Sundara II (*SII* 5.420).

The thirteenth century is the high point in terms of the sheer numbers of inscriptional references to ascetics. It is also a turning point with respect to the appearance of epigraphical evidence for the implantation of the types of institutional structures that characterized later periods — the definition of Śrīvaiṣṇava *saṁnyāsa*, and the establishment of Śaiva lineages in the Tamil country that in subsequent centuries came to be allied with Śaiva-Siddhānta *maṭha*s. In the fourteenth and fifteenth centuries, the number of inscriptions that relate to ascetics drops sharply — as the numbers of stone inscriptions generally become fewer. But we do have some hints about the consolidation of sectarian traditions (which may or may not be ascetic ones) in two records of the fourteenth and fifteenth centuries that record gifts of land to individuals of the lineage of Meykaṇṭar (*SII* 26.716; *ARE* 1936/180). Meykaṇṭar is the first of the three *ācārya*s in whose lineage Umāpati (fl. early fourteenth century) is situated.[18] Umāpati is held by tradition to provide the bridge between the Meykaṇṭar lineage to which he belonged and the non-brāhmaṇa celibate Śaiva *maṭha*s of Tiruvavaduturai and Dharmapuram which were perhaps founded in the fifteenth or sixteenth century (Siddhalingaiah 1979: 87-88, 110-19). It was also probably in the fifteenth and sixteenth centuries that the "Meykaṇṭar *śāstra*" came to be collected as a canon, and that stories of the lives of Umāpati and the other Śaiva *ācārya*s came to be written; Umāpati's hagiography stresses the encounter with his *guru*, his transformation from a householder into a *jñānī*, and the disapproval of his erstwhile colleagues among the Tillai three thousand — the brāhmaṇas of Chidambaram. Meanwhile, in the fourteenth and fifteenth centuries, we continue to find inscriptional references to Golakī and Lakṣādhyaya (and Bhikṣāṭana) *maṭha*s. Among the Vaiṣṇavas, according to the inscriptions of this period, *maṭha*s served as places for sheltering and feeding Śrīvaiṣṇavas and *saṁnyāsī*s (at

18. On Umāpati, his hagiography, and his connection with the Meykaṇṭar lineage, see Goodall 2000, Janaki 1996, Pechilis Prentiss 2001, and Siddhalingaiah 1979.

Kattumannarkoyil and Tirukurunkudi - *ARE* 1920/529; *ARE* 1960/355) and *māmunikaḥ* — great *munis* — (at Alvar Tirunagari - *SII* 26.489).

The sixteenth century is the last period where stone inscriptions are of much use for our project. Increasingly copperplates and other kinds of records, not literally attached to temples, are our sources for following the renunciant and tracing the development of the *maṭha* as an institution. For example, at the Śaṅkarācārya *maṭha* in Kāñcīpuram there is a Sanskrit copperplate grant, dated CE 1506, which records the gift of the ruler of Vijayanagara to Guru Mahādeva Sarasvatī, disciple of Sadāśiva Sarasvatī, described as a *paramahaṁsa parivrājakācārya*, a teacher of Advaita, and a *tapasvin* (*EI* 14.17). We should note here the Śaiva flavour of these *gurus'* names. For the Vaiṣṇavas, a sixteenth-century record from Kāñcīpuram (*SITI* 346 CE 1521) records a land grant to Caṭakopa Jīyar, disciple of Parivrājakācārya Nārāyaṇa Jīyar, for conducting festivals and making offerings. Here we see an overlap with the *parivrājakācārya* terminology found in the context of the Śaṅkarācārya *maṭha* which evidently points toward renunciation; *jīyar*, however, seems by this time to have become a term applied exclusively to Vaiṣṇava ascetics. And although it seems impossible to trace the development of the non-brāhmaṇa celibate Śaiva *maṭhas* which flourish today, or their possible connections with the Golakī *maṭhas* (which are still mentioned in sixteenth-century inscriptions), there is a very interesting Śaiva record from Tiruvanaikka (on a slab near what is today the dilapidated *maṭha*) (*ARE* 1937/135; see Derrett 1974). Dated in CE 1584, it is an order from the temple to Candraśekharaguru Uṭaiyar commanding him to become a householder (*gr̥hasthin*) Pāśupata — while formerly, the Pāśupata-*vratam* and rights of worship and other privileges were the entitlement of heads of the *maṭha* in succession from *guru* to disciple, now these privileges were to be enjoyed by his descendants in succession from father to son. So the definition of — or the necessity for — renunciation continued to be negotiable.

Reflections on Medieval Tamil Renunciation

When I first began to try to discern a pattern in the various manifestations of renunciation in Tamil Nadu, I came up with the word "intermediate." We have Jaina religious men and women who inhabited cave-retreats, who were *gurus* and disciples of *gurus*, but who — evidently from the earliest times in Tamil Nadu — had not renounced wealth and who served as patrons of religious establishments and places of worship. We have women described as *tapasyar* who were welcomed as honoured devotees in Hindu temples and women who, as Hindu householders, practised severe austerities. We have *śivayogīs* who must have been engaged in some form of *yoga*, but who were also described as Veda-knowing and who perhaps retained the marks of brāhmaṇa status while clad in a loin-cloth. And we have Vaiṣṇava *saṁnyāsīs*, who certainly appeared in this fashion, incorporating *gṛhastha* observances into *saṁnyāsa*, and becoming not only heads of *maṭhas* but temple patrons.

But the word "intermediate" is not quite right. Mediation implies resolution, and I think we do not find anything very fixed and final in this picture — even from a synchronic perspective. We see, instead, composites, experiments, and *continua* of possibilities. I am not suggesting that a particular individual would have had a range of choices, various alternatives for how to be a Jaina religious, how to be a female renunciant, how to be a *śivayogī*, how to be a Vaiṣṇava *saṁnyāsī*. But any particular model that presented itself to the prospective renunciant itself contained juxtaposed elements which were not so easily reconcilable with one another. People within these communities had a lot of work to do in order to create consistency, order, meaning — and to determine the correct way, among a number of possibilities, of following the renunciant path.

A flag is raised — we begin to suspect definitional difficulties and tensions among competing elements within the community — when the polemics directed outward get heated. That the Jainas spent so much effort — for example in the Tamil text *Nīlakēci* — condemning the Buddhists for their laxity in the matter of eating practices, could well be a mark of their concern about deviation from Jaina norms in their own mode of life. That the *Tēvāram* poets — and in later centuries Nampiyāṇṭār Nampi and Cēkkiḻar — come down so heavily on the Jainas suggests a self-conscious effort to craft a kind of Śaiva *yoga*, a Śaiva *tapas*, which did not spill over into what were perceived as the excessive ascetic practices of the Jainas. Similarly, among the Vaiṣṇavas . . . why do they go on and on about the *tridaṇḍa* and the *ekadaṇḍa*? Why does Vedāntadeśika say that the mere sight of Vedāntins pollutes and that conversing with them leads to hell? Is it because the Advaita ways of thought and behaviour were, in fact, very much present among the Śrīvaiṣṇavas?

In this polemical literature, and among the renunciants themselves, we see something going on that resembles the work of the philosophers — as is typified, for example, in the figures whom I invoked at the beginning of this paper: Śaṅkara, Rāmānuja and Umāpati. To take the case of Śaṅkara's *Brahmasūtra-Bhāṣya*, here it is clear that the effort is to reconcile Śruti and Smṛti, using various principles of interpretation, as well as to provide a new creative synthesis that makes sense of these disparate elements. I would suggest that it is not only great philosophers but also those who as individuals made it their business to craft an ascetic way of life who were also engaged in this work of synthesis. For such people, the renunciants of medieval Tamil Nadu — often functioning outside of established institutions — it was in their very activities, embodied *personas*, and self-presentation that precisely the same kind of incorporation, imagination and inventiveness was expressed.

References

PRIMARY SOURCES

Inscriptions

ARE *Annual Reports on (South Indian) Epigraphy*, Delhi: Manager of Publications, 1887 ff. Transcripts of the inscriptions abstracted in the *ARE* have been graciously made available to me at the office of the Chief Epigraphist, Archaeological Survey of India, Mysore.

EI *Epigraphia Indica*, Calcutta/Delhi: Director General, Archaeological Survey of India, 1892ff.

IPS *Inscriptions (Texts) of the Pudukkottai State arranged according to Dynasties*, Pudukkottai, 1929.

JIT *Jaina Inscriptions in Tamil Nadu (A Topographical List)*, A. Ekambaranathan and C.K. Sivaprakasam, Madras: Research Foundation for Jainology, 1987.

KVR K.V. Ramesh, "Jaina Epigraphs in Tamil," appendix to *Jaina Literature in Tamil*, A. Chakravarti, New Delhi: Bhāratīya Jñānapīṭha, 1974.

PI *Pondicherry Inscriptions/Putucceri manilak kalvettukkal.* Compiled by Bahour S. Kuppusamy, and ed. G. Vijayavenugopal, Pondicherry: ὸcole française d'extrême-orient/Institut français de Pondichéry, 2006.

SII *South Indian Inscriptions*, vols. 1-26, Delhi: Director-General, Archaeological Survey of India, 1891-1990.

SITI *South Indian Temple Inscriptions*, ed. T.N. Subrahmaniam, Madras: Government Oriental Manuscripts Library, 1953-57.

TAM *Tiruvannamalai: A Śaiva Sacred Complex of South India*, vols. 1.1 and 1.2: *Inscriptions*, Introduction, ed. and tr. P.R. Srinivasan, Institut français de Pondichéry, 1990.

TAS *Travancore Archaeological Series*, vols. 1-8. Trivandrum, 1910-38.

Texts in Sanskrit and Tamil

Somaśambhupaddhati, 4 vols., ed. and tr. Hélène Brunner-Lachaux, Pondicherry: Institut français d'Indologie, 1963-1998.

Tēvāram, Tamil text, ed. T.V. Gopal Iyer, 3 vols. Pondichéry: Institut français d'Indologie, 1984-91. Selected poems translated into English by Indira Viswanathan Peterson, in her *Poems to Śiva: The Hymns of the Tamil Saints*, Princeton: Princeton University Press, 1989.

Yatidharmasamuccaya, tr. P. Olivelle, 1995, *Rules and Regulations of Brahmanical Asceticism:*

Yatidharmasamuccaya of Yadava Prakaśa, Albany: State University of New York Press.

SECONDARY SOURCES

Arooran, K.N. (1981), "The Changing Role of Three Śaiva Maths in Tanjore District from the Beginning of the 20th Century," in *Changing South Asia: Religion and Society*, vol. 1, ed. K. Ballhatchet and D. Taylor, London: SOAS.

Bader, Jonathan (2000), *Conquest of the Four Quarters: Traditional Accounts of the Life of Śaṅkara*, New Delhi: Aditya Prakashan.

Brunner, Hélène (1988), "L'*ācārya* śivaïte: du *guru* au *gurukkal*," in *Bulletin d'études indiennes*, vol. 6, pp. 145-76.

Cenkner, William (1983), *A Tradition of Teachers: Śaṅkara and the Jagadgurus Today*, Delhi: Motilal Banarsidass.

Colas, Gérard (1996), *Viṣṇu, ses images et ses feux: Les métamorphoses du dieu chez les vaikhānasa*, Paris: Presses de l'òcole française d'Extrẹme-Orient.

Davis, R.H. (1998), "The Case of the Disappearing Jainas: Retelling the Śaiva-Jaina Encounter in Medieval South India," in *Open Boundaries: Jaina Communities and Cultures in Indian History*, ed. John E. Cort, Albany: State University of New York Press.

———, (2009) *A Priest's Guide for the Great Festival: Aghoraśiva's Mahotsavavidhi*, New York: Oxford University Press.

Derrett, J. Duncan M. (1974), "Modes of Sannyasis and the Reform of a South Indian Matha Carried out in 1584," in *Journal of the American Oriental Society*, vol. 94, pp. 65-72.

Goodall, D. (2006), "Initiation et délivrance selon le Śaiva Siddhānta," in *Rites hindous : transferts et transformations*, ed. Gérard Colas and Gilles Tarabout, Paris: Editions de l'EHESS, pp. 93-116.

Gravely, Frederic H. & T.N. Ramachandran (1932), *Catalogue of Hindu Metal Images in the Government Museum*, Madras: Government Museum.

Hara, Minoru (2002), *Paśupata Studies*, ed. by Jun Takashima, Wien: Sammlung de Nobili, Institut fur Sudasien-, Tibet- and Buddhismuskunde/Delhi: Motilal Banarsidass.

Janaki, S.S. (ed.) (1996), *Sri Umāpati Śivācārya: His Life, Works and Contribution to Śaivism*, Chennai: Kuppaswami Sastri Research Institute.

Karashima, N., Y. Subbarayalu and P. Shanmugam (2010), "Mathas and Medieval Religious Movements in Tamil Nadu: An Epigraphical Study," in *Indian Historical Review*, vol. 37, pp. 217-34.

Koppedrayer, Kathleen I. (1990), *The Sacred Presence of the Guru: The Velala Images of Tiruvavatuturai, Dharmapuram, and Tirupanantal*, PhD diss., Hamilton: McMaster University.

Lorenzen, David N. (1972), *The Kapalikas and Kalamukhas*, Berkeley: University of California Press.

Mahadevan, Iravatham (2003), *Early Tamil Epigraphy: From the Earliest Times to the Sixth Century* CE, Chennai: Cre-A and Cambridge MA: Harvard University Press.

Mahalingam, T.V. (1962), "The Golaki Matha," in *Essays in Philosophy Presented to Dr. T.M.P. Mahadevan on his Fiftieth Birthday*, ed. C.T.K. Chari, Madras: Ganesh & Co.

Monius, Anne E. (2004), "Love, Violence, and the Aesthetics of Disgust: Śaivas and Jainas in Medieval South India," in *Journal of Indian Philosophy*, vol. 32, nos. 2-3, pp. 113-72.

Nagaswamy, R. (1983), *Masterpieces of Early South Indian Bronzes*, New Delhi: National Museum.

Narayanan, V. (1990), "'Renunciation' in Saffron and White Robes," in *Monastic Life in the Christian and Hindu Traditions: A Comparative Study*, ed. Austin B. Creel and Vasudha Narayanan, Lewiston, NY: Edwin Mellen Press.

Neeval, Walter G. Jr. (1977), *Yamuna's Vedanta and Pancaratra: Integrating the Classical and the Popular*, Missoula, Montana: Scholar's Press.

Olivelle, Patrick (1986), *Renunciation in Hinduism: A Medieval Debate*, 2 vols., Vienna: Indologisches Seminar der Universitat Wien.

Orr, Leslie C. (2007), "Domesticity and Difference/Women and Men: Religious Life in Medieval Tamil Nadu," in *Women's Lives, Women's Rituals in the Hindu Tradition*, ed. Tracy Pintchman, New York: Oxford University Press.

Pechilis Prentiss, Karen (2001), "On the Making of a Canon: Historicity and Experience in the Tamil Śiva-*bhakti* Canon and Translation of the *Tirumuṟaikantapurāṇam;* attributed to Umāpati Civācāriyar," in *International Journal of Hindu Studies*, vol. 5, no. 1, pp. 1-44.

Peterson, I.V. (1998) "Śramaṇas against the Tamil Way: Jainas as Others in Tamil Śaiva Literature," in *Open Boundaries: Jaina Communities and Cultures in Indian History*, ed. John E. Cort. Albany: State University of New York.

Rajamanikkam, M. (1962), "The Tamil Śaiva Maṭhas under the Coḷas," in *Essays in Philosophy Presented to Dr. T.M.P. Mahadevan on his Fiftieth Birthday*, ed. C.T.K. Chari. Madras: Ganesh & Co.

Rukmani, Trichur S. (2011), *Saṁnyāsin in the Hindu Tradition: Changing Perspectives*, New Delhi: D.K. Printworld.

Schopen, Gregory (1988), "On Monks, Nuns and 'Vulgar' Practices: The Introduction of the Image Cult into Indian Buddhism," in *Artibus Asiae*, vol. 49, nos. 1-2, pp. 153-68.

Sethuraman, N. (1991), "Crusade against Guhai (Monastery)," in *Journal of the Epigraphical Society of India (Purabhilekha Patrika)*, vol. 17, pp. 29-37.

Siddhalingaiah, T.B. (1979), *Origin and Development of Śaiva Siddhānta Upto 14th Century*, Madurai: Nepolean Press.

Sivaraman, Krishna (1973), *Śaivism in Philosophical Perspective: A Study of the Formative Concepts, Problems and Methods of Śaiva Siddhānta*, Delhi: Motilal Banarsidass.

Smith, H. Daniel (1975), *A Descriptive Bibliography of the Printed Texts of the Pāñcarātrāgama*, 2 vols., Baroda: Oriental Institute.

Subramaniam, T.N. (1958-59), "Paḷḷaṅkōvil Framentary Jainaa Copperplate Grant of Early Cōḷa Period," in *Transactions of the Archaeological Society of South India*, pp. 84-110.

Swamy, B.G.L. (1972), "The Four Śaivite Samayācāryas of the Tamil Country in Epigraphy," in *Journal of Indian History*, vol. 50, no. 1, pp. 95-128.

———, (1975) "The Golaki School of Śaivism in the Tamil Country," in *Journal of Indian History*, vol. 53, no. 2, pp. 167-209.

Talbot, C. (1987), "Golakī Maṭha Inscriptions from Andhra Pradesh: A Study of a Śaiva Monastic Lineage," in *Bajapeya (K.D. Bajpai Felicitation Volume)*, ed. A.M. Shastri and R.K. Sharma, Delhi: Agam Kala Prakashan.

Van Troy, Joseph (1974), "The Social Structure of the Śaiva-Siddhāntika Ascetics (700-1300)," in *Indica*, vol. 11, pp. 77-86.

Part Six

Issues in Contemporary Hinduism

Environment, Non-Violence, Gender, Faith and Syncretism

18

Hinduism and the Environment
Then and Now

*Georges A. James**

Hindu Environmental Ethics

SINCE the emergence of the sub-field in the study of religion known as Religion and Ecology scholars have been examining the religious or spiritual traditions of the world for the insight they might offer towards the development of an environmental ethic. Some scholars have found neglected insights in texts from the great religious traditions that support the environment. Others have argued that religious traditions have supported the exploitation and neglect of nature. In the case of the Hindu religious tradition scholars such as Ranchor Prime, O.P. Dwivedi, Christopher Chapple, and others have argued that the attitude of the Hindu religious tradition to nature has been a positive one (Prime 1996; Dwivedi 1997; Chapple et al. 2000). Others have argued that the other-worldly attitude of Hindu religious thought is in large part responsible for the condition of India's environment today (Passmore 1974; Callicott 1997; Nelson 1998).

Today, scholars occupied with the relationship of India's religious traditions to her environmental problems are less inclined to discuss India's disposition towards nature in terms of a single moral outlook. They recognize that like others the Hindu religious tradition is as rich in diversity as it is in age, and that it would be misleading to depict the entire tradition as either eco-friendly or environmentally destructive. Scholars today are more occupied with specific periods, figures, and schools of thought within the tradition and specific problems in which environmental issues are at stake. The objective is to see the manner in

* Department of Philosophy & Religious Studies, University of North Texas

which religious perspectives in various periods and in the thought of various individuals have informed, empowered, and motivated action in support of the environment, or on the other hand supported acquiescence to its destruction or neglect. Scholars are also interested in the environmental significance of the broad contours of thought and practice that have emerged as the Hindu religious tradition has negotiated new religious, social, and political realities. The Hindu religious tradition is appropriately characterized as very old, very diverse, and very much alive. It might be argued that as a living tradition, it has been and remains engaged with the environment as it has dealt with other challenges in its past. The environmental ethic of the Hindu religious tradition is to be seen not so much in a single philosophical or religious viewpoint as in the attitude towards nature reflected in the contours of the tradition as a whole.

Nature in Ancient and Medieval Hinduism

Discussions of nature in the broad contours of Hindu thought and practice and their relevance to the environment issues today have been undertaken by a number of scholars (Narayanan 2001: 170-206; James 2004: 341-80). It is necessary here only to touch upon a few of the most important highlights. From the very earliest sources of Indian civilization, a strong interest and a deep appreciation for nature is evident. The remains of the Indus Valley Civilization (2800-1800 BCE) include small, mostly square steatite seals (1½ to 3 inches across) depicting trees, water, and a goddess figure, standing in close relation with one another. Some of them appear to depict the Earth as a mother giving birth to a tree. Others depict scenes composed of animals, trees, and human beings, which experts interpret as revealing the common rhythm in human, animal, and vegetative life (Darian 1978: 42-47). In the *Ṛgveda* (composed 1800-800 BCE), hymns of praise and adoration are directed to a number of the phenomena of nature depicted as deities. The *Ṛgveda* and other ancient collections lavish praise on such rivers as the Yamunā, the Sarasvatī, the Indus, and the Ganges. They regard all rivers as sacred, and the deification of the great rivers of India continues in hymns, prayers, and poems composed throughout the tradition. On the banks of such rivers today, we still find ancient temples in which a deep piety toward the great rivers of India is expressed.

While an ethic of regard for nature can be inferred from the remains of the Indus Valley Civilization and from the Vedas, it is in the Śāstras or writings concerned with *dharma* or moral virtue and with *artha* or economic and political well-being, that the most explicit guidance concerning the treatment of the natural world is to be found. One of the most important sources relating to these material values is the *Arthaśāstra* (*c.* 300 BCE, Radhakrishnan et al. 1957: 193). The attention of this authority to matters of environmental concern is indicated by specific fines for such offences as disposing of dust on roads, urinating, or defecating near a well, or pond, or inappropriately disposing of a dead animal. A striking example of concern for forest resources is the schedule of sanctions this document imposes upon those who destroy trees, groves, or forests. For the cutting of the tender sprouts of fruit trees, flowering trees, or shade trees in parks near a city, it recommends a fine of six *paṇa*s. For the cutting of the minor branches of such trees, the fine is twelve *paṇa*s, and for the cutting of the large branches of such trees, the fine is twenty-four *paṇa*s. For the cutting of the trunk of such trees, the fine is forty-eight to ninety-six *paṇa*s, and for the felling of such trees, the fine is 200–500 *paṇa*s. For trees that mark boundaries or are worshipped, the sanctions are doubled. While we cannot know with certainty the ancient value of a *paṇa*, it is significant that offenses that result in damage to forest resources were taken seriously enough that a fine would have been imposed. Another ancient legal document, the *Manusmr̥ti* (*c.* 100 BCE), widely considered the most influential of the ancient treatments of *dharma* or duty, states specifically that impure objects like urine, faeces, spit, or anything that contains blood or poison is never to be disposed of in water (*Manusmr̥ti* 4.56, cited by Narayanan 2001: 188).

In the *Matsya Purāṇa* (composed fifth to tenth century CE) the Goddess Pārvatī plants an *aśoka* tree and cares for it. As the tree prospers the other deities and sages observe her attention to this tree and begin to question her. Pārvatī replies that a person who digs a well in a place where water is scarce lives in heaven for as many years as there are drops of water in the well. She states that a large reservoir is worth ten wells, and that one son is like ten reservoirs. She then goes on to say that one tree is equal to ten sons. The same Purāṇa describes a festival for the planting of trees, indicating that in the context in which the Purāṇas were originally written the planting of trees was an activity that had strong religious support. Another document of the period, the *Viṣṇu Dharmottara*, states that one who plants a single tree will never fall into hell (Narayanan 2001: 187-88).

Regard for nature can also be seen in the veneration for the various features of the landscape that are not always preserved in documentary form. In various parts of India today sacred groves are dedicated to a deity that is understood to reside within it. Sacred groves are ancient natural sanctuaries wherein living creatures and vegetation are protected. Even when they are not designated as sacred groves, forests have had a deep significance for Indian culture. Forests were the dwelling of teachers whose forest hermitages were set apart. Near such places no animal or tree was to be harmed. There even kings were forbidden to hunt. In ancient times, the shade of a tree was the proper place for a disciple to receive spiritual instruction from his *guru*. Today, India stands at the end of a very long and considered tradition in which nature is celebrated, protected, and valued.

Hindu Values and Regard for Nature Today

Given what can only be called a remarkable history of adoration, veneration, and care for nature, the question arises as to why it is that these values have not prevented the exploitation and destruction of nature that has led to India's present environmental crisis. In one respect, the question might be interpreted as an audacious one, analogous perhaps to question why the values of humility, compassion, and non-violence embedded in the Christian faith, and in European civilization, did not prevent the holocaust of European Jewry? Is it the case that human beings, when they are faced with a choice between long-standing values and political complicity or expediency, will inevitably abandon their values? Audacious or not, such questions demand an answer. In the case of Indian values and the crisis of the environment, scholars have drawn attention to a number of historical factors that have prevented the application of traditional Hindu religious ideas from informing environmental policy. Among these, there is one whose influence has sometimes been seen to be so momentous as to render all others insignificant. It has been argued that colonialism so marginalized the traditions of veneration and care for nature that under the British Raj the lands, forests, and waterways of India could be exploited with impunity (Shiva 1989: 61-67). It is not the case that the British did not value the Indian landscape. But the value of nature that motivated their action was largely the material and commercial value of nature. The forest of Malabar and then of the Himalayas were valuable to the British not because of their intrinsic worth but for their value in the burgeoning ship building industry in England and in the expanding railway system of India, the objective of which was to extend the reach of commerce.

The effective attitude of the British to the religious and literary traditions of India can perhaps be summarized in the view of Lord Thomas

Macaulay, the English architect of the British educational system in India. In his famous "Education Minute," a speech he made to the Supreme Council of the British Government in India in 1935, he argued for the teaching of English language and literature in India, and the rejection of literature in Sanskrit and Arabic. While his main point was that Sanskrit and Arabic would be useless to a new generation of young people living in an increasingly British India, his speech reflects an attitude to the traditions of Ancient India that dismisses any literary, historical, scientific, or ethical merit to be found therein. He argues here "that a single shelf of a good European library is worth the whole native literature of India and Arabia," that the historical information to be collected from all the books written in the Sanskrit language is less valuable than the content of a common English school book (Prime 1996: 79n).

While Macaulay articulated his views about the merit of British education in 1935, the educational system he endorsed had already been in place in India for a considerable period of time. Born in 1869, the youngest son of a one-time prime minister of a small princely state in what is today the Indian state of Gujarat, Mohandas K. Gandhi was educated in the prevailing British system. He states that his father had little religious training. His mother was devout but not intellectually sophisticated (Gandhi 1948: 12-14). Gandhi's own first encounter with the wisdom of ancient India occurred, when in his late teens, he travelled to London to study law. There, in the search for a vegetarian restaurant to satisfy the promise to his mother that he would not consume meat, he found himself in the company of a circle of vegetarian friends who invited him to give a talk on what they considered the central document of the Hindu faith, the *Bhagavad-Gītā*. His promise to his mother thus led him, in the course of time, to examine those philosophical, literary, and religious traditions of India that to the British educational system was a waste of time. During his years in South Africa he came to reject the image of an upwardly mobile British lawyer to recover the ideals and values he had found in the Hindu religious tradition. Later in India, he would say that it was not the British that he rejected but British civilization. The traditions of India, he would argue, are second to none in the world (Gandhi 1938b: 52-55). And, with his recovery of these ancient ideals he also came to re-examine the contemporary relevance of the philosophy of nature embedded in the Hindu religious tradition.

While Gandhi was an eclectic thinker, the central features of Gandhi's thought reveal a strong environmental ethic, grounded in the religious thought of India. T.N. Khoshoo has found the basis for many of Gandhi's famous eleven vows of life in the *yama*s and *niyama*s of the *Yoga-Sūtras* of Patañjali (Khoshoo 1995). In 1948, only shortly before his assassination, Gandhi stated that while the Indian National Congress had won political freedom, her economic, social, and moral freedom was yet to be attained. For the achievement of these, his focus was upon rural and especially village development. He argued that in the simplicity of her villages India could fully realize the virtues of truth and non-violence. In the village setting, attending to real and not artificial needs, the human person could achieve true *svadeśī*, or self-reliance, by means of true *swarāj*, or self-mastery. In the ideal village, he said, people would not live in ignorance, darkness, or filth. Rather free, intelligent, and independent women and men would dwell neither in luxury nor want (Gandhi 1976: 217). Gandhi conceived of the future of India as a republic of independent, self-reliant villages, living in harmony with their natural surroundings. When asked whether an independent India would achieve the standard of living of Britain, Gandhi replied that it took half the resources of the planet to achieve the prosperity that Britain now enjoys. He then rhetorically inquired, "How many planets will a country like India require!" On another occasion he suggested that if India were to follow Britain's example of industrial development and economic exploitation "it would strip the world bare like locusts." He believed that the self-reliant village living in co-operation with nature would be the heart of a self-reliant and truly independent India. Gandhi's future life would be a protest against the supposed needs of a consumer society and its unreasonable demands on the biosphere. "The world," he said, "has enough for everybody's need, but not enough for one person's greed" (Khoshoo 1995: 65-69; Guha 2000: 22).

Undoubtedly, there were among Europeans, more positive attitudes towards the traditions of India than we find in the thought of Thomas Macaulay. Max Müller's massive collection of the *Sacred Books of the East*, for instance, placed some of the most important works of oriental literature in the libraries of Western Europe. Yet the attitude expressed in the thought of Macaulay is the one that held sway in terms of its impact upon environmental policy. Clearly, with the proliferation through education of Western history, science, philosophy, and literature, the significance of nature in the ancient traditions of India (the injunction, for instance, in the *Arthaśāstra* against the cutting of trees) was of little interest. The possibility of the implementation of the values embedded in the writings of Ancient India into policy and law was and would have been much less so.

But the historical reality of colonialism cannot be taken as the sole explanation of India's present environmental problems. Environmentalists in India have pointed out that since Independence India's forest cover has been denuded at a faster pace than it had been before Independence, her soil has been more depleted of nutrients, and her waterways have become more polluted than at any time during the colonial period (Agarwal et al. 1985: 394-7; Gadgil et al. 1995). Moreover, as many environmentalists in India have pointed out, the colonial rulers themselves had environmental concerns. In 1864, the colonial government in India invited a German Botanist named Dietrich Brandis to head the newly established Indian Forest Service. Brandis was a friend and correspondent of the American environmentalist George Perkins March whose book *Man and Nature: Or, Physical Geography as Modified by Human Action*, of the same year became, as Lewis Mumford once remarked, the "fountainhead of the conservation movement." According to Ramachandra Guha, the Indian Forest Service which Brandis headed for almost twenty years, has been one of the most influential institutions in the history of conservation. While the British attitude towards nature in India was one of exploitation they wanted the supply of nature to continue. Thus, the objective of "sustained yield" stood on the belief that scientists could accurately estimate an annual increment of such renewable resources as wood and water, fish and wildlife. "Scientists prescribed that utilization stayed within this increment, thus maintaining nature's capital and ensuring a yield capable of being 'sustained' in the long run" (Guha 2000: 25-26). Thus, while the objective of the Forest Service was the preservation of a viable supply of revenue producing species, and while conservation measures emerged only after the forest industry was well established, conservation was not outside the concerns of the Forest Service.

Yet the environmentalism of the colonial period reveals another distinctive feature of the colonial attitude towards nature. Brandis shared with his American colleague a deep concern with the pace of deforestation but also an abiding faith in the power of science to reverse it. It was scientific expertise that was capable of reversing the damage that had already been done and it was scientific expertise that would prevent further harm. But the apparent objectivity of science concealed the context in which that science was deployed. The science to which environmentalists of the colonial period were committed was a science occupied with forestry in the economic context of an industry committed to the wealth of the empire, not with the good of the country, and least of all with the welfare of the forest dwellers. The long-term effect of colonialism was not simply the damage done to nature especially by way of deforestation but the proliferation of an understanding of nature as commodity and a faith in the capability of science to limit the impact of exploitation through effective management, management that usually discounted the needs of the forest people. With independence, the national government did not recover the regard for nature that Gandhi found among the values of Indian civilization but appropriated and continued the natural resource management policies of the British, their optimism about science, and their philosophy of nature. By the turn of the twentieth century, the Indian Forest Department came to control a little over one-fifth of the land area of India. It was by far the largest landholder in the nation, a status, as Guha points out, that it enjoys to this day (Guha 2000: 26). With political independence, the National Forest Department and its philosophy of nature remained in place. But now the objective was not the wealth of the empire but the development of the nation, a change that utilized power concentrated among the economically advantaged at the expense of the poor and disenfranchised. Gandhi's vision of an India of self-governing, self-reliant villages was gradually supplanted by a vision of industrial development that required capital from abroad and the further exploitation of nature. A philosophy of nature focused on her material and commercial value dismissed the religious and spiritual significance of nature expressed in the Hindu religious tradition.

There are, as I have said, a number of factors that have prevented the implementation of Hindu religious values to matters of environmental concern. While some scholars have focused on the impact and legacy of colonialism, another factor and one that is especially troubling today, is the growing influence of the Hindu religious right. With Independence, India was constituted as a secular state, meaning at least that the individual has the right, expressed in Article 25 (1) of the Indian Constitution "freely to profess, practise and propagate religion." Yet the understanding and motivation for secularism differs significantly among those who have used the term. In the context of contemporary Indian juridical discourse, the term is perhaps minimally defined as a "non-theocratic, non-communal state that seeks to embody equality for all citizens regardless of religious affiliation" (Stephens 2004: 327). For Gandhi, the responsibility of a secular government was to have equal regard for all faiths in its jurisdiction and to treat all religions equally. Such equality, to him, was the sacred purpose of the secular state. Nehru agreed with Gandhi's concern for the equal treatment of all religions, but he did so because he believed that minimizing the role of religion in Indian political life was an effective way to maximize the development of India as a modern country. For some, the Constitution of India as a secular state was itself an obstacle to the implementation of Hindu values into the sphere of public policy. In accordance with this view, religion is a private and personal commitment that serves no purpose in the political arena. The implementation of environmental values found in the Hindu religious tradition would tend to favour one religion over another. The difficulty with this position is that it fails to recognize the environmental values that are shared across religious lines.

The Constitution of India as a secular state, however, has by no means silenced the voices of those who believed that with a Hindu majority, India should have been constituted, and should yet become, a Hindu nation. In the context of secular politics, those who remain most committed to the idea of India as a Hindu nation, what is called the Sangh Parivar, or "family of organizations," are those who most passionately express the concern for the Hindu religious tradition. Today, the recovery of the religious regard for nature in Hinduism seems to have become a preoccupation of the religious right. Recognizing the neglect of her religious and spiritual traditions as a moral failing, the religious right has addressed this neglect by promoting Hindu values, including those pertaining to nature, while vilifying their secularizing opponents and with them the adherents of other religious traditions. British Scholar Emma Mawdsley explains that this family of organizations includes the political wing, Bharatiya Janata Party (BJP) founded in 1980, which from 1998 until 2004 was the main party of the central government of India. It includes the Rashtriya Swayamsevak Sangh (RSS), or the National Organization of Volunteers, a cultural organization founded in 1925 for the protection of "national religion and culture," and that among other things promotes paramilitary and martial arts training for the building of character. It also includes the Vishva Hindu Parishad (VHP), or World Hindu Council set up in 1964 to "protect, develop and spread Hindu values," and to bring together the diverse elements of Hindu belief and practice. She explains that the core ideology of the Sangh has been that of "Hindutva," meaning Hindu-ness, but she indicates that it has come more recently to refer to the narrow agenda of Hindu nationalism. "Essentially, Hindutva represents a 'blood and soil' vision of the sacred land of Hindustan for the Hindus" (Mawdsley 2005: 7-8).

Because it conflates traditional Hindu values, especially those pertaining to nature, with Hindu nationalism, the Sangh Parivar has often presented an obstacle to genuine engagement with traditional values concerning nature. In cases such as the recent protest against a proposed ship canal, called the Sethusamudram Project, in the Palk Strait between India and Sri Lanka the religious right co-opted a critical environmental issue to promote a Hindu nationalist agenda (for this example I am indebted to Bidisha Kumar). In the protest against the Tehri Dam the perceived relationship of environmental activism to the religious right tended to discredit the environmental movement. Without doubt, there are many efforts towards environmental protection and restoration inspired and motivated by the Hindu scriptures and Hindu religious ideas that have not been taken over by Hindu nationalism. Nevertheless, the ways in which the religious right has engaged with environmental issues to support its communal agenda have often rendered the environmental insights of the Hindu religious tradition ineffective. In this context enthusiasm for religion can itself present a barrier to the application of environmental values rooted in the Hindu religious tradition to real environmental issues. What can be done?

Gandhi's View of Religion

The understanding of religion that Gandhi advanced points the way to a recognition of shared environmental values that overlap religious traditions and that could be implemented to support environmental issues without promoting a communalist political agenda. Among the eleven vows of life that Gandhi formulated was one called *sarvadharma sambhāva.* It is often assumed that this vow simply affirms "the equality of all religions." Gandhi, however, was by no means arguing that all religions are the same. Rather, he was arguing that one ought to have equal regard for all religions. His claim was that I ought to have the same regard for my neighbour's religion as I would desire that my neighbour should have for mine.

In his many references to religion, Gandhi uses the term in two distinctive ways. On the one hand, he uses the word to designate those traditions that are referred to by such terms as Judaism, Christianity, Hinduism, Buddhism, Jainism, Islam and others. On the other hand, he refers to religion as that reality to which each of these great religions directs its adherents. In one place in his publication the *Young India,* he makes clear just what he means:

> Let me explain what I mean by religion. It is not the Hindu religion, which I certainly prize above all other religions, but the religion which transcends Hinduism, which changes one's very nature, which binds

> one indissolubly to the truth within and which ever purifies. It is the permanent element in human nature which counts no cost too great in order to find full expression and which leaves the soul utterly restless until it has found itself, known its Maker and appreciated the true correspondence between the Maker and itself. — Gandhi 1920

Religions, according to Gandhi, "are different roads converging to the same point." For him it does not matter that we take different roads, so long as we reach the goal. He states, moreover, that "if a man reaches the heart of his own religion, he has reached the heart of the others too." For Gandhi the different religions are like beautiful flowers from the same garden or different branches of the same majestic tree. "Therefore," says Gandhi, "they are all equally true" (Gandhi 1958: 54).

At the same time, he adds that, being received and interpreted through human instruments, religions are also equally imperfect, because "everything that the human hand touches, by reason of the very fact that human beings are imperfect, becomes imperfect" (Gandhi 1927). He declares that all religions are imperfect because all people are imperfect, and states that the Vedas, the Koran, and the Bible are therefore, the imperfect word of God. Moreover, he continues, "imperfect beings that we are, swayed to and fro by a multitude of passions, it is impossible for us even to understand this word of God in its fullness" (Gandhi 1937a). For this reason, he believes it is no business of his to criticize the scriptures of other faiths, or to point out their defects, though he sees it as a duty to observe and correct the defects of his own religion (Gandhi 1937b). The need of the moment, he says, is not the emergence of one religion but for mutual respect among the devotees of the different religions. "Any attempt to root out traditions, effects of heredity, climate and other surroundings is not only bound to fail but is a sacrilege. The soul of religion is one, but it is encased in a multitude of forms" (Gandhi 1925). Gandhi holds, in fact, that it is God who created the different faiths just as he has created the votaries of those faiths. He believes that if this claim is taken seriously it will be impossible even secretly to harbour the thought that his neighbour's faith is inferior to his or that he should give up his faith to embrace mine. On the contrary, "As a true and loyal friend, I can only wish and pray that he may live and grow perfect in his own faith" (Gandhi 1934b). Says Gandhi:

> I believe in the fundamental truth of all the great religions of the world. I believe that they are all God-given, and I believe that they were necessary for the people to whom these religions were revealed. And I believe that,

> if only we could all of us read the scriptures of the different faiths from the standpoint of the followers of those faiths, we should find that they were at the bottom all one and were helpful to one another.
>
> — Gandhi 1934a

Different religions, according to Gandhi, can be helpful to one another. This insight, as engaging as it is, would perhaps be a hard-sell to persons who would entertain no distinction between the essence of religion and its observable forms, who believe that their own religion is the correct one, and that all the others are simply wrong. Nevertheless, it is never quite correct to judge the merit of an insight by the difficulty of persuading a convinced opponent. It is often said that communal conflict is rooted not in ideas but in prejudice towards the religious identity of persons. Clearly, so long as the environmental insights of the Hindu religious tradition are no more than the pretext to announce the superiority of one religious tradition over another, they cannot be an effective means to address environmental issues. A critical step towards the implementation of traditional Hindu values to issues of environmental concern must be a recognition of the environmental insights that are shared by other religious traditions. The best strategy for dealing with such prejudice is a strategy of genuine religious encounter. It was Gandhi's view that if I am to respect my neighbour's religion as I would have them respect my own, it is necessary for me to know something about my neighbour's religion. For him it is a matter of paramount importance that I become acquainted with the views and practices of other faiths. "If we are to respect other's religions as we would have them respect our own, a friendly study of the world's religions is a sacred duty" (Gandhi 1962: 15). By exploring the environmental insights of other religious traditions one can discover environmental insights that are supportive of the environmental insights of one's own religious tradition. By examining, recognizing, and celebrating the environmental insights of other religious traditions we can hope to work effectively to apply the environmental insights of all religious traditions to contemporary environmental issues.

References

Agarwal, Anil & Sunita Narain (eds.) (1985), *India: The State of the Environment 1984-85: The Second Citizens' Report*, New Delhi: Centre for Science and Environment.

Callicott, J. Baird (1997), *Earth's Insights: A Multicultural Survey of Ecological Ethics from the Mediterranean Basin to the Australian Outback*, Berkeley CA: University of California Press.

Chapple, Christopher K. and M. Evelyn Tucker (eds.) (2000), *Hinduism and Ecology: The Intersection of Earth, Sky, and Water*, New Delhi: Oxford University Press.

Darian, Steven G. (1978), *The Ganges in Myth and History*, Honolulu: University of Hawaii Press.

Dwivedi, O.P. (1997), "Vedic Heritage for Environmental Stewardship," in *Worldviews: Environment, Culture and Religion*, vol. 1, no. 1, pp. 25-36.

Gadgil, Madhav & Ramachandra Guha (1995), *Ecology and Equity: The Use and Abuse of Nature in Contemporary India*, New Delhi: Penguin Books.

Gandhi, Mohandas K. (1920), *Young India*, 12 May.

———, (1925) *Young India*, 25 September.

———, (1927) *Young India*, 22 September.

———, (1928) *Young India*, 6 December.

———, (1934a) *Harijan*, 16 February.

———, (1934b) *Harijan*, 20 April.

———, (1937a) *Harijan*, 30 January.

———, (1937b) *Harijan*, 13 March.

———, (1938a) *Harijan*, 14 May.

———, (1938b) *Hind Swaraj or Indian Home Rule*, Ahmedabad: Navajivan Publishing House.

———, (1948) *Autobiography: The Story of My Experiments with Truth*, tr. Mahadev Desai, Washington D.C.: Public Affairs Press.

———, (1958) *All Men Are Brothers: Life and Thoughts of Mahatma Gandhi as Told in his Own Words*, ed. Krishna Kripalani, New York: Columbia University Press.

———, (1962) *All Religions are True*, Bombay: Pearl Publications.

———, (1976) *Collected Works of Mahatma Gandhi*, vol. LXIV, New Delhi: Publications Division, Ministry of Information and Broadcasting.

Guha, Ramachandra (2000), *Environmentalism: A Global History*, New York: Longman.

James, George A. (2004), "The Environment and Environmental Movements in Hinduism," in *Contemporary Hinduism: Ritual, Culture, and Practice*, ed. Robin Rinehart, Santa Barbara CA: ABC CLIO.

Khoshoo, Triloki N. (1995), *Mahatma Gandhi: An Apostle of Applied Human Ecology*, New Delhi: Tata Energy Research Institute.

Mawdsley, Emma (2005), "The Abuse of Religion and Ecology: The Vishva Hindu Parishad and Tehri Dam," in *Worldviews: Environment, Culture and Religion*, vol. 8, no. 2, pp. 1-24.

Narayanan, Vasudha (2001), "Water, Wood, and Wisdom: Ecological Perspectives from the Hindu Traditions," in *Daedalus*, vol. 130, no. 4, pp.179-206.

Nelson, Lance (1998), "The Dualism of Nondualism: Advaita Vedanta and the Irrelevance of Nature," in *Purifying the Earthly Body of God: Religion and Ecology in Hindu India*, ed. Lance Nelson, Albany NY: SUNY Press.

Passmore, John (1974), *Man's Responsibility for Nature: Ecological Problems and Western Traditions*, London: Gerald Duckworth.

Prime, Ranchor (1996), *Hinduism and Ecology: Seeds of Truth*, New Delhi: Motilal Banarsidass.

Radhakrishnan, Sarvepalli and Charles A. Moore (eds.) (1957), *A Sourcebook in Indian Philosophy*, Princeton NJ: Princeton University Press.

Ramachandran, R. (2007), "Myth vs. Science," in *Frontline*, vol. 24, no. 19 (22 September - 5 October).

Shiva, Vandana (1989), *Staying Alive: Women, Ecology and Development*, London: Zed Books.

Stephens, Robert J. (2004), "Hinduism in Independent India: Fundamentalism and Secularism," in *Contemporary Hinduism: Ritual, Culture and Practice*, ed. Robin Rinehart, Santa Barbara CA: ABC CLIO.

19

Earth, Water and Dhārmic Ecology
Perspectives from the Svādhyāya Practitioners

*Pankaj Jain**

Introduction

THIS is an article about the *svādhyāyīs*, *svādhyāya* practitioners, in the Indian states of Gujarat and Maharashtra. The Svādhyāya movement arose in the mid-twentieth century in Gujarat as a new religious movement led by its founder the late Pandurang Shastri Athavale. In my research, I discovered that there is no category of "environmentalism" in the "way of life" of *svādhyāyīs* living in the villages. Following Weightman and Pandey (1978), I argue that the concept of *dharma* can be successfully applied as an overarching term for the sustainability of the ecology, environmental ethics, and the religious lives of *svādhyāyīs*. *Dharma* synthesizes their way of life with environmental ethics based on its multidimensional interpretations.

Svādhyāya's Dhārmic Ecology

Having heard about the *svādhyāya*, I called their office in Mumbai to visit one of such sites in summer of 2006 during my trip to India. Soon, I found myself on my way to Valsad in Gujarat. I arrived at the home of a Svādhyāya volunteer, Maheshbhai,[1] who took me to the water harvesting site managed by local *svādhyāyīs*. All of them showed warmth and enthusiasm to welcome me and explain about their various activities and ideologies of the Svādhyāya movement. As the caretakers of the water harvesting site began explaining about the way they perceive the nature and the vision of their *guru* Athavale, I began asking questions related to

* Department of Anthropology, Department of Philosophy and Religion Studies, University of North Texas

1. In this article, I have used pseudonyms except for the well-known personalities.

environmentalism. What I present below is based on my several such interviews with Svādhyāya followers. I have also extracted relevant information from the vernacular literature of *svādhyāya* that is based on the video-recorded discourses of Athavale.

Svādhyāya is one of the least known new religious movements that arose in the mid-twentieth century in the western states of India. Although this movement now has some presence in several Western countries such as the United States, Canada, and the UK, it has not received the attention of scholars of Hinduism, except few introductory articles.[2] Before I begin introducing the ecological work of Svādhyāya, it is important to mention that their environmental significance is denied by the *svādhyāyīs*. In fact, one of the *svādhyāyīs* was taken aback when I told him about my topic of research. In his own words:

> You might misrepresent *Svādhyāya* if you choose to research it from ecological perspective. *Svādhyāya* and its activities are only about our devotion to the Almighty; ecology is not our concern. Environmental problems are due to industrialization and the solution lies beyond Svādhyāya's activities. *Svādhyāyīs* are not environmentalists!

Based on my observations of *svādhyāya*'s several activities, I tend to agree with him. Athavale has repeatedly emphasized that the main goal of *svādhyāya* is to transform the human society based on the Upaniṣadic concept of "Indwelling God." According to him, since the Almighty resides in everybody, one should develop a sense of *spiritual* self-respect[3] for oneself irrespective of *materialistic* prestige or possessions. In addition to one's own dignity, the concept of "Indwelling God" also helps transcend the divisions of class, caste, and religion and Athavale exhorted his followers to develop the Svādhyāya community based on the idea of "brotherhood of humans under the fatherhood of God." Activities of Svādhyāya are woven around this main principle, which in turn are also aimed at the Indian cultural renaissance.

---

2. Between 1994 and 1996, some observers and scholars have visited the Svādhyāya villages. Their observations were compiled in an edited volume by Srivastava (1998). This is a helpful introduction of the movement. In addition, I have provided some other scholarly articles in the references above, see: Dharampal-Frick (2001), James (2005), Little (1995), Paranjape (2005), Rukmani (1999), Sharma (1999), and Unterberger et al. (1990). After completing this article, I also came to know that Ananta Giri has published a monograph on self-development and social transformation brought about by Svādhyāya, see Giri (2009).
3. Since 1990s, this became the theme of celebration for the Athavale's birthday, which is celebrated as "Human Dignity Day" around the world by his followers.

Although environmentalism is neither the means nor the goal of Svādhyāya's activities, natural resources such as the earth, the water, the trees, and the cattle are revered and nurtured by *svādhyāyīs* based on this understanding. Environmentalism does come out as an important by-product of its multi-faceted activities and this was noted by a 1992 conference in Montreal where Svādhyāya was invited to present its ecological philosophy and work.[4] I argue that a multivalent term like *dharma* can comprehend and describe this kaleidoscopic phenomenon and the way it relates to ecology. Svādhyāya followers do not regard environmentalism as their main duty, their *dharma*. Alternatively, from the outside, one can regard their *dharma*, their cultural practices, as ecologically sustainable as I show below. I also want to note that my observations are based on their activities in the rural parts of India since the urban and the diaspora *svādhyāyīs* do not have such ecological projects yet.

Svādhyāya's Earth Dharma

Let me now describe Athavale's thoughts on *bhūmi pūjana* that I have termed as the "earth *dharma*." Athavale has inspired tens of millions of *svādhyāyīs* to recite this verse every morning:[5]

> *samudravasane devī, parvata stanamaṇḍale* |
> *viṣṇupatni! namastubhyaṁ pādasparśaṁ kṣamasva me* |
> (O ocean-clad Goddess Earth, with mountains as your nurturing-breasts. O wife of Viṣṇu! I bow to you and ask for forgiveness as I touch you with my feet).[6]

Explaining this verse, he teaches that the Earth is the mother of every

---

4. This conference, "Living with the Earth: Cross-cultural Perspectives on Sustainable Development, Indigenous and Alternative Practices," took place on 30 April – 3 May 1992. It was organized by the Intercultural Institute of Montreal, Canada. A three-page report titled "Presentation by Dīdī (the current leader of the movement) on the Svādhyāya Movement" was written by Robert Vachon in the proceedings of the conference. An interview with Dīdī was subsequently broadcast nationwide by the Canadian Broadcasting Corporation in a one-hour radio programme called Ideas.
5. Traditional Indians have been reciting these verses in addition to some other as part of their *prātaḥ smaraṇa*, remembering the divine as one wakes up in the morning. Athavale has included some of the traditional Sanskrit verses in his foundational Svādhyāya *prayoga* called *trikāla sandhyā*, chanting of verses thrice a day, in the morning, before the lunch time, and at the bedtime.
6. In Indian culture, it is one of the most disrespectful gestures to touch someone with feet. It is common to see someone accidentally touching a person or a book or food with feet and immediately asking for forgiveness.

creature, providing shelter to all living creatures and dead substances. She takes care of everyone by feeding her love-nectar. There is such a great attraction of her that one gets satisfaction only after returning to her after taking a flight into the sky. This motherly attraction is appropriately named as gravitation by scientists. Only someone with *gravity* can *attract* someone else. Mother Earth possesses this gravity based on her unique qualities such as patience, forgiveness, tolerance, and humility. Continuing his ethical teaching combining both the earth and the ocean, Athavale cites the above verse and calls the ocean as her clothes. Just as humans cover most of their bodies with clothes, the majority of earth is also covered with ocean. Just as the ocean maintains its humility by not crossing its boundaries, humans should also observe humility in wearing clothes and should not wear them with obscenity. Mother Earth is a living testimony of kindness. She gives all the precious jewels to its children. She also nurtures her children with her mountains. Since the Sanskrit word *pāyas* means both water and milk, mountains are compared with the nurturing-breasts and are referred as *payodhara*, i.e. carriers of *pāyas*. The rivers originated from the mountains nurture the humans just as mothers feed their babies with their milk.

We find some stories in the Purāṇas, in which rivers were full of milk. Mountains also carry numerous herbs and vegetables to cure and nourish humans. Mother earth's kindness, tolerance, and mercy are also evident by the process of farming. We dig the earth but get water in return to quench our thirst; we plough the land but get grain in return to satisfy our hunger. Indeed, mother earth is the best teacher to teach benevolence in return for malevolence! She tolerates all our mischief, we run on it, attack her with our feet, build skyscrapers on it, but she tolerates our entire burden with a smile! Hence, it is our gratitude and humaneness that we express by bowing to her. Since mother Earth is the wife of Viṣṇu, he is our father. Although the mother serves us, she is not for exploitation; rather she is to be revered. Our perspective towards the earth should be of reverence in addition to consumption. As long as we do not understand that only god is the owner of the earth, not humans, we cannot become true children of her. Today, we have started exploiting the earth only for our selfish and egoistic reasons and hence she is becoming barren.

There is a story in the *Bhāgavata Purāṇa* 5.25.1 that Śeṣanāga, the great serpent, had stationed the earth on its head. Athavale explains that a human who does not revere mother earth or Viṣṇu is indeed a burden on the earth. Mother Earth has kept its treasure open for us in the form of numerous minerals such as gold, silver, iron, copper, etc. We should cultivate proper emotions to accept her gifts as a divine *prasāda* and should revere her gratefully. Athavale notes other Sanskrit verses from the *Skanda Purāṇa* such as *vasundharā puṇyavatī ca tena!* (By whom mother earth becomes auspicious). He differentiates great sages and holy men by whose touch mother earth becomes sacred, and exhorts *svādhyāyīs* to try to follow such great people. One can become a true child of mother earth by cultivating great virtues and qualities following the great people. When brāhmaṇas change their sacred thread, they touch the sand to their forehead and recite *mr̥ttike hanme pāpam,* "Sand! Remove my sins." Athavale also quotes Khalil Gibran, "In the heart of the earth, a poem originated and she cultivated trees and gardens in her leisure. We cleared them to maintain our hollowness" (my translation). The earth also has a special fragrance. In the *Bhagavad-Gītā,* Kr̥ṣṇa says *puṇyo gandhaḥ pr̥thivyām ca!* (7.9), which is literally translated as "the fragrance in the earth is auspicious." Mother Earth is warm in the summer and when the rainwater falls upon it, it spreads a unique fragrance.

According to Athavale, mother earth has different fragrances in different seasons. Like the earthen fragrance, our lives should also be fragrant with good virtues and qualities. In the *R̥gveda,* Śrisūktam's second *mantra* reveres the earth with several adjectives. The first adjective given to the earth is *gandhavatī,* i.e. fragrant. The second one is *durādharṣā,* i.e. that which cannot be taken away by anyone. The land is for everyone and no single person can own or carry it away. The third one is *nityapuṣṭām,* i.e. ever nourishing. Mother earth not only nourishes our bodies with different kinds of food, but it also nourishes our minds and hearts. Indian farmers have such reverence for the earth that after ploughing they do not even allow wearing shoes into their farms. Mother earth is ever nourishing for such people who respect and revere it. Mother earth nourishes people living close to it in villages and forests by her "breathings." People in cities have become aloof from her and therefore they do not get her proper nourishment. The next adjective for the earth is *kariṣiṇim,* i.e. that which has abundant dry cowdung. This has an implicit appreciation for cows. Even the Vedas mention cowdung as a natural fertilizer. The next adjective for the earth is *īśvarī,* meaning capable and magnificent. Capable and efficient people should protect the beauty and grandeur of mother earth.

Athavale's reverential discourses about mother earth took a constructive shape when his followers launched several projects related to the groundwater. In a country like India, where life is dependent on rainfall in large parts of the country, a lot of work is being done to raise public awareness of rainwater harvesting. Centres have been set up in places like Meerut and Chennai. According to the Centre for Science and Environment at New Delhi:

> Our ancestors harvested rain just as naturally as they tilled the ground to grow crops. We lost touch with these local solutions. Now, as the taps dry up, more and more people are reviving this age-old system and practising it very successfully. Water has been harvested in India since antiquity, with our ancestors perfecting the art of water management. Many water harvesting structures and water conveyance systems specific to the eco-regions and culture had been developed.[7]

Although various Indian organizations have started harvesting the rainwater, Svādhyāya's work in this regard is different because of its underlying inspiration based on devotional reverence for the water and for the earth (Sharma 2000). While inaugurating one of the tree-temples, Athavale had once said, "If you quench the thirst of Mother Earth, she will quench yours." This "earth *dharma*" became the driving force for Svādhyāya, especially after three successive droughts between 1985-87 in the Saurashtra region of Gujarat. Some *svādhyāyī* villages started trying out well-recharged experiments. The first such experiment was done at Chokli village, and by 1992 it started taking the shape of a movement and all the nearby farmers began collecting as much rainfall as they could on their fields and in the village and canalized it to a recharged source. Between 1992 and 1996, 99,355 wells were recharged (*bhūgarbha jala sañcaya*) and 554 *nirmala nīra*s (farm ponds for recharge) were built.[8] According to K.K. Khakkhar at the Saurashtra University, the water recharge activities by Svādhyāya have resulted in approximately Rs. 39 million of more income. According to Tushar Shah (Shah 2003), *svādhyāyī*s built over 1,25,000 wells and over 1,000 farm ponds during 1997. Shah believes that if half a million wells in Saurashtra are recharged, the region can solve its irrigation as well as drinking water problem; and at the rate at which the movement is growing, it would not be surprising if this target has been met. The Svādhyāya "water ethic" is, "rain falling on your roof stays in your house; rain falling in your field, stays in your field; rain falling in your village, stays in your village." By 1993-94, the

---

7. http://www.rainwaterharvesting.org/ (viewed on 29 January 2007).
8. http://laetusinpraesens.org/docs/indiaoz.php (viewed on 5 June 2007).

well recharge movement had begun spreading to other parts of Gujarat, notably Sabarkantha, Mehsana, and Panchamahal districts. Shah laments that the mainstream discourse has largely ignored the impact of Svādhyāya work:

> Many dismiss it as a religious, sectarian affair; others see these successes as inimitable and donors are lukewarm to it because the movement accepts neither external funding nor can they be catalyzed by funding support; and scholars are stymied by it because it does not fit into the normal linear logic pattern. All in all, then, the larger implications and lessons that the Svādhyāya movement offers in mobilizing masses for regenerating natural resources are more or less lost. — Shah 2003: 20

I agree with Shah on his frustration. Svādhyāya's work does demonstrate a great potential to mobilize the community at the grassroot level by invoking the cultural and dhārmic paradigms. On the one hand, we have community of religious scholars in the West often struggling to connect ecological concerns with their respective communities. On the other hand, we have examples such as Svādhyāya, which have silently recharged ecological resources based on the religious inspiration of its practitioners. N.R. Sheth also expresses similar observations (Sheth 2002:14):

> Some friends and I observed in June 1994 an outstanding effort in recharging of water resources in a village where a project of constructing a simple check-dam to impound waters flowing in a rivulet was in the final stage of completion. A group of young men constituting the local unit of the Svādhyāya youth centre had conceived and undertaken this project to store the rivulet water in a tank created within it by means of the dam. The stones and soil dug out to make the tank were used to build a 100-m long dam. The main purpose of this project was to preserve water in the river tank to raise the water table for wells in the neighbouring villages. The entire project was executed by an extremely innovative deployment of collective labours. Over a thousand men and women from villages around the dam site had offered their time and energy for the purpose in the spirit of *śramabhakti* (devotional labour). Typically, the males worked on the dam site for about six hours from 7:30 in the evening after they had finished work on their own farms. The females worked during the day in neighbourhood groups. The people had followed this pattern of work for nine months when we visited the place and they were expecting to finish the work within a week. Barring small amounts of money spent on explosives to break stone, no cash expenditure was involved in this work. Had the project been executed in a conventional manner, it would have cost around Rs. 4,00,000. A visitor

to a *nirmala nīra* work-site cannot fail to be moved by the picnic-like social atmosphere as well as a crusader-like spirit exuded by the volunteers in spite of very hard physical labour they perform at a time when they normally relax or sleep. The social bonding of love and goodwill which is created among Svādhyāyīs as well as between them and others is truly remarkable.

Having witnessed several Svādhyāya festival celebrations and other gatherings, I can certainly agree with Sharma's observations. One of the most remarkable features of this work is its consistent denial of any outside financial, political, or social help. It has continued to depend solely on the devotional inspiration of its own volunteers. According to Jitendrabhai, a senior *svādhyāyī*, who has supervised several *nirmala nīra* projects in Gujarat in his volunteer work for Svādhyāya for more than two decades, it is important to note the dhārmic perspective in *nirmala nīra prayoga*:[9]

> In the morning, we ask for her forgiveness since we touch her with our feet as we wake up. We bow to her and call her as the wife of Viṣṇu, thus, the earth is our divine mother. Just as *Śivaliṅga* is worshipped by pouring clean water on it, *nirmala nīra* is also our way to worship the earth with clean water. It is an *abhiṣeka,* ritual of sprinkling, done for mother earth. In this *prayoga,* water is cleaned in different stages using sand, brick-powder, and coal and this clean water is stored in the wells and ponds. Water enters the wells through the small holes and splinters in their walls. Existing ponds are also deepened in this *prayoga.* People work together to deepen the wells that also deepens their mutual relationships.[10]

Recalling the visit of Magsaysay Award winner water conservationist Rajendra Singh to the *nirmala nīra prayoga*s, Jitendrabhai continued:

> Rajendra Singh was amazed to see that most of the *nirmala nīra* ponds and wells were built by *svādhyāyī* people working not in their own villages but in different villages completely selflessly. Thousands of people are motivated to build ponds and wells for other villages because these *prayoga*s are not for selfish reasons. They are not merely out of the necessity of water but they are essentially tokens of gratitude for mother earth. While Rajendra Singh's Tarun Bharat Sangh had to work hard to motivate people of the same village to build ponds for themselves, *svādhyāyī*s of one village worked for other villages selflessly with great motivation. Everybody brings his or her own food and shares it with

9. *Prayoga* is the word in Indian languages Sanskrit, Gujarati, Marathi, and Hindi which means "experiment" and is used widely in several Svādhyāya activities.

10. Personal communication, July 2006.

> others. This working and sharing with each other builds and develops relationships among all castes and classes of the village. Muslims work together with Hindus, Harijans work together with brāhmaṇas. Muslims recite their Qurān verses while Hindus recite Sanskrit verses at the time of regular prayers. After the Gujarat riots, Muslims of Lunāwādā village in Anand district had told the district collector that only *svādhyāyī*s should be trusted to deliver the government aid to the Muslim victims of the riots since most other Hindus had turned against Muslims. Earlier farmers used to quarrel if water from neighbouring farms would enter their own farms but after working together in Svādhyāya *prayoga*s they now welcome water drained out from neighbouring farms to come to their farms. This reflects increased cooperation and unity in the farmers. In another example, farmers of Maganpura village share each other's losses if anybody's cotton crops fail to yield sufficiently. Another benefit of Svādhyāya *prayoga*s that villagers experienced is that the water tables of all nearby wells increased.

The above ideas expressed by a lay *svādhyāyī* clearly show the zeal and the spirit of the Svādhyāya work. While communal tensions have been flared up several times in Gujarat, *svādhyāyī*s show a different glimpse from this state. In addition, most people would be surprised to note the selfless enthusiasm of *svādhyāyī*s. Their motive is not just to do the utilitarian work for the village or even to protect the ecological resources of the village. Rather, the underlying objective of *svādhyāyī*s is to bring about constructive social manifestation of their spiritual understanding towards the divine that is dwelling in them, in their village society, and the village ecology. Indeed, Jitendrabhai succinctly summarized this in his own words:

> In ancient times, Indian sages also were aware about agriculture and ecological resources. For instance, Kaśyapa is referred as "father of Indian soil." Similarly, Pārāśara is attributed of having written *Kṛṣi Pārāśara*, a Sanskrit text for agriculture. Similarly, several community leaders and wealthy people had build water tanks called bāvaḍī in many villages and towns with Hindu idols near them. However, Svādhyāya *prayoga*s are based on *karma-yoga*, not *karma-kāṇḍa*. *Nirmala nīra prayoga*s do not have any ritualistic idol worship. They are *prayoga*s for implementing devotion in one's behaviour instead of limiting it into rituals. This openness invites people of all castes, sects, and religions to come and work together.

Another similar experiment is called *śoṣa khaḍḍā* (soak pit); this is meant to absorb the sewage water of individual houses outside the house. Sewage water and sanitation is a big problem in Indian villages and cities alike. Drainage is neither built properly nor kept clean by local municipal officers. Svādhyāya has devised a novel *prayoga* for this problem. *Śoṣa khaḍḍā*, absorbing pit, is built outside the house in which the water that was originally taken from the earth for use by people is returned to the earth after household use. This avoids the accumulation of dirty water in the villages that prevents the spread of diseases like malaria and cholera. Villagers are told that just as temple of God is kept clean for worshipping in it, every house and every village is also temple of omnipresent God and hence should be kept clean. When somebody falls in the dirty water, God inside that person also suffers with him or her. Therefore, dirty water should not be let accumulate in surrounding neighbourhoods of a village. Near every *śoṣa khaḍḍā, tulasī* plant is also planted. On the rooftop, clean water is made available for the birds. In this way, every family tries to practise reverence for house, village, plants, and birds.

Overall, *svādhyāyīs*' attitude towards the water and the earth shows their long-standing relationships with their ecology which is revitalized by the thoughts and teachings of Athavale. I now present the agricultural work undertaken by *svādhyāyīs*, that is one of the most widespread experiments in Gujarat and Maharashtra, because most of the followers come from the farming communities.

Yogeśvara Kṛṣi[11]

According to Athavale, agriculture includes four components: trust on neighbour, love for animals, faith in God, and respect for nature. Obviously, the second and the fourth components affect ecology directly even though the main activity is about growing grains and not about growing big trees. On festival days such as *akṣaya tṛtīyā* and *dhanateras*, oxen used in *Yogeśvara Kṛṣi* are bathed and beautifully decorated and their procession is arranged in the entire village.[12] Ladies smear the foreheads of their husbands and oxen with red *tilaka* and welcome them. Later, the farms are tilled together where all the oxen participate. Often, the response is so overwhelming that more number of oxen turn up at a particular piece of land, than the required number for farming. Thus, this experiment

11. Information in this section is based on my interviews with several *svādhyāyīs*.
12. Ann G. Gold (2001: 128-29) has observed that such celebration of cattle is linked with the collective management of rainmaking and fertility themes. It also helps develop appropriate harmonies among people and between people and the environment.

also develops unity, harmony, and goodwill in the entire village. A related experiment, *Śrīdarśanam*, involves twenty villages. Twenty people come from different villages and live together periodically on monthly and yearly basis. For every twenty people, one cow also lives with them for their dairy needs. This cow is dearly cared for by these twenty people. Since this cow is treated reverentially by the people participating in this devotional experiment, their attitude becomes reverential for their own personal domestic animals also when they return home for performing their routine farming. Thus, in this mechanical age of tractors and other machines, the relationship of farmers with their farm-animals is strengthened and revitalized. *Yogeśvara Kṛṣi* also inspires farmers to develop respect and love for nature. One of their slogans is *hariyālī mein hari*, literally "God in greenery." One of the *svādhyāyī* volunteers explained:

> One who goes to farms just for work is a farmer, but one who goes to enjoy and respect greenery, goes with reverence and gratitude for God. This reverential perspective inspires to make the entire world green.[13]

Another volunteer explained that they cannot avoid the bare minimum violence required during the harvest but they try to avoid harming the nearby plants, trees, and bushes. Moreover, the earlier use of pesticides is now replaced with the herbal powders that are sprinkled on the crops. Vermiculture compost has also been taken up by the villagers on a large scale (Sinha 1998). The products generated from this devotional farming are treated as the *prasāda* from God. This helps develop the understanding that nature is not just for anybody's consumption or exploitation but it is for reverence since it is a creation by God. Similarly, the inherent love for animals in farmers is strengthened by such experiments. To recount an example from *Yogeśvara Kṛṣi*, a *svādhyāyī* narrated this incident from Timberwa village in Vadodara district of Gujarat. *svādhyāyī*s go to offer their efficiency at *Śrīdarśanam* periodically, as I noted above. When one of them got his turn, his wife was extremely sick and his crop was ready to be cut. He was in a dilemma whether to go or not. Eventually, the couple decided that the husband should give priority to "god's work" and wife stayed alone at home in her sick condition. When the husband came back, he found that his farming needs were already taken care of. Later, they discovered that other *svādhyāyī*s had secretly helped the couple by neatly collecting their crops in their warehouse. These secret helpers once had criminal records but now with Svādhyāya experiments, they were so

13. Personal communication with Jitubhai (January 2007).

deeply transformed that they were secretly helping others with the feeling of divine unity.

It is important to note the Svādhyāya agricultural experiments are different from purely "natural farming" pioneered by Masanobu Fukuoka in Japan in 1940s (Fukuoka 1978). Although natural farming is also being promoted by Mohan Shankar Deshpande[14] and other Indians, Svādhyāya's approach is different from them. In the latter case, there is no mention of *Kṛśipārāśara*, the ancient Sanskrit text about farming. Unlike natural farming or *Ṛṣi Kṛṣi*, *svādhyāyī*s do not hesitate in tilling the ground or using natural fertilizers. Rather than rejecting the commonly used tools and methods of agriculture, Svādhyāya approach is simply to bring about the ethical, spiritual and social transformation of the farmers (and of the rest of the society). This transformation seeks to develop a familial interrelationship among the farmers of a small village and a reverential perspective towards the mother earth.

Anil Agarwal (Chapple and Tucker 2000: 165-79) has mentioned that Hindu beliefs, values, and practices, built on a "utilitarian conservationism," rather than "protectionist conservationism," could play an important role in restoring a balance between environmental conservation and economic growth. Svādhyāya experiments do not fall in either category. In fact, when I interviewed some of the people who were involved in the first such experiment of tree temples in Gujarat, they vehemently denied both utilitarian and protectionist motives behind their experiments and underscored the devotional motive instead, as I noted above.

Concurring with Haberman's theoretical framework and his observations from fieldwork on the banks of the Yamunā (Haberman 2006), these Svādhyāya experiments are Indian counterparts of what could be called "environmental activism." Similar to Haberman's examples, Svādhyāya experiments are inspired by Indic traditions. I visited one tree-temple in Valsad in Gujarat in 2006 where local *svādhyāyī*s had told me that *vṛkṣamandira*s inspired the farmers to grow more trees even in their personal farms. They also started using more organic and traditional fertilizers, such as earthworms. Their perspective towards trees was changed from exploitative to reverential. When I asked them about the practical challenges or difficulties related to Svādhyāya *prayoga*s, they noted several challenges. The biggest challenge is to be able to sustain the transformation based on the Svādhyāya's teachings. Without the

14. http://www.rishi-krishi.com/index.htm (viewed on 20 January 2007).

dhārmic perspective, the work can become "mechanical" or can take the form of another "religious ritual." If the tree-temples fail to inspire people to develop an ethos, develop a bonding with the trees, or if *svādhyāyīs* stop practising this ethics in their daily life, then the work can take a "religious" shape based on the devotional faith on the words of Athavale. That would reduce the dhārmic work into another religious ritual as has happened with some rituals in both India and elsewhere. Another challenge is to take these *prayogas* and replicate them at a bigger level. So far, these have remained smaller local role models at the district level rather than projects at the regional or national level. They also confessed that the number of volunteers available to work at different tree-temples varies according to the intensity and depth of Svādhyāya's thoughts in the surrounding villages. Since the spread of Svādhyāya is not uniform across the different villages and towns of Gujarat and Maharashtra, the number of volunteers working at such *prayogas* is also not uniform. Noted environmentalist Anupam Mishra aptly remarked (Mishra 1993):

> Even without involving the environmentalists, people are bringing out miracles at the grass-root level. Upon seeing them, we should humbly accept them. Even if they may not fit our measuring scale, may be our measuring scale itself may be inappropriate. A work that has already reached millions belongs to the people. Media reports only political parties but it cannot represent the people.

Athavale developed several more *prayogas* to fructify his mission for socio-spiritual transformation based on dhārmic philosophy of "Indwelling God." I have described only some of them that relate to natural resources such as the trees, the cows, and the earth. These *prayogas* do not label themselves as "environmental projects" and yet they have succeeded in sustaining natural resources in thousands of Indian villages. Like any other such work, the challenge now is to maintain them and to develop new such *prayogas* especially now that Athavale has passed away. To my knowledge, the current leadership has not developed new ecological *prayogas*. However, it seems focused to strengthen the existing *prayogas* by inspiring more villagers to join the movement. I agree with Ramachandra Guha's remark that there was no environmentalism before industrialization; there were only the elements of an environmental sensibility. The traditional societies did not transcend their locality to offer any systematic vision of reorganizing nature (Guha 2006: 6).

The Svādhyāya followers also show similar sensibilities in their local *prayogas* in the villages. This sensibility in turn is inspired by their cosmology that is based on the texts, myths, and legends derived from the dhārmic traditions. We do see a reflection of textual reverence for nature in the behaviour of *svādhyāyīs*. Whether this behaviour will take a generic ecological ethos across the time-space limitation is yet to be seen. It is still a nascent movement with the charisma of the founder still fresh in the memories of its followers. Will they become environmentalists that are more active in the new century in the absence of Athavale? Svādhyāya is also emerging as a movement spread around the globe. When *svādhyāyīs* migrate to different parts of the world, will they connect their environmental sensibility to respond to the problems of climate change?

Conclusion

Overall, we can conclude that the dhārmic ecological work done by Athavale and his followers can be compared with ecological work done by environmental NGOs. However, for the *svādhyāyīs*, their work is simply a reflection of their *kṛtibhakti,* activity inspired by their devotion to the divinity inherent in themselves and in nature around them. For Athavale's followers, trees and plants merely symbolize the divine force that works as a connecting force between the human society and nature. As *svādhyāyīs* told me: *"To be is to be related."* By developing reverential relationships with the trees, cows, and other ecological resources, *svādhyāyīs* strive to develop their dharmic teachings into practice.

Athavale often cited the definition of *dharma* in the *Mahābhārata* as one that *sustains* both the personal order and the cosmic order.[15] *Svādhyāyīs*, like many other Hindu communities, use *dharma* interchangeably to describe their ethos as it relates to their religion and natural order. For them, the distinction between the religious ethos and the ecological order is negligible since they describe them with the common term *dharma* or *dharam*. Several scholars have noted this trend in Indians. Ann Gold's observations from her fieldwork in Rajasthan are especially helpful. She describes the villagers who relate their moral actions with the ecological outcomes (Gold and Gujar 2002). Frederick Smith records similar trends in ethnosociology of Marriott and Inden (Smith 2006: 586). Smith also cites Arjun Appadurai, "South Asians do not separate the moral from natural order, act from actor, person from collectivity, and everyday life from the realm of the transcendent." Smith concludes, "The distinction between mind and body, humanity and nature, essence, idea, quality, and deity, would be (largely) one of degree rather than of kind."

15. *dhāraṇād dharma ity āhur dharmeṣa vidhṛtāḥ prajāḥ* |
yat syād dhāraṇasaṁyuktaṁ sa dharma iti niścayaḥ | | — *Mahābhārata* 12.110.11

Dharma as "virtue ethics" has served as a role model for Indians for several millennia (Matilal 2002). From my research with the *svādhyāyīs*, I found that their inspirations were the Hindu epic heroes and their *guru* whom they see as role-models practising *dharma* to attain the *mokṣa*. In several of the discourses of Athavale, I found him exhorting his followers to follow the ideal of Arjuna, the warrior of the *Mahābhārata* who preferred the path of the *pravṛtti* (action) instead of *nivṛtti* (renunciation). Athavale repeatedly stressed that only actions done with a devotional motive can be considered dhārmic actions leading to *mokṣa*. He correlated the motive of the action with the potential for *mokṣa*. Based on my case study of *svādhyāyīs*, an ethical framework based on *dharma* and *karma* that is also integrated with *mokṣa*, can serve as an important step to develop comprehensive Hindu environmental ethics.

Several authors, such as T.S. Rukmani, George A. James, Vasudha Narayanan, and O.P. Dwivedi have shown theoretical and textual references from Indian texts to show ecological reverence (Chapple and Tucker 2000). These textual references have also been the part of the world view or cosmology of Hindus from last several millennia as I noted in the lives of the *svādhyāyīs*. They follow the texts by revering the natural resources such as the trees and the earth. Their relationship with nature not only includes revering it, but it inspires them to restore, protect, and conserve it. However, considerations of Hindu *dharma* must extend from mental textual constructs to daily experiences by the body in its immediate cosmic environment where the world is imagined as a transparent unity. As the stream of sensory experience is constantly flowing, *dharma* only has the appearance of permanence. While the *dharma* texts show that *dharma* boundaries are fixed and absolute, the flow of bodily experience, upon which such boundary conditions are superimposed, is constantly changing. The ambiguity that results is often better reflected in the myths of the Epics and Purāṇas than in the *dharma* texts themselves. Thus, Hindu *dharma* manifestations at the level of bodily perception (house walls, field boundaries, rivers, etc.) are important for the study of Indian culture.

I have found such patterns in my case study. By participating in different activities related to ecology, the practitioners of traditional communities such as the *svādhyāyīs* not only undergo somatic experiences but also these experiences help them to "relive" the lives of Vedic sages and other mythical figures such as Arjuna. This is the embodied imagination or the "ecological mind" where perceptions, self-perception, and symbolic ideas resonate together. This is the level at which *dharma* means something to them before it has acquired its extremely diverse lexical meanings and social functions. It connects the practitioners with the experiences of their *gurus* and their natural surroundings.

Marriott has suggested (Marriott 1990) that *dharma* can be an *ethnosociological* category to study and analyze the Indic world that frequently transgresses the world of religion, environmental ethics, and human social order, as is evident from my case studies of *svādhyāyīs*. *Svādhyāyīs*, like other Hindus, use *dharma* to mean both their religious practices and their social duties. Thus, I suggest that the *dharma* can function as a bridge between the ecological notions and environmental ethics of local Hindu communities and the ecological message related to the planet Earth. The word *dharma* can be effectively used to translate the ecological awareness to reach out to the local communities of Hindus based on its meanings related to the duties, ecological order, sustenance, virtues, righteousness, and religion.

References

Chapple, Christopher K. and M. Evelyn Tucker (eds.) (2000), *Hinduism and Ecology: The Intersection of Earth, Sky, and Water*, Cambridge: Harvard University Press.

Dharampal-Frick, G. (2001), "Svādhyāya and the 'Stream' of Religious Revitalisation," in *Charisma and Canon: Essays on the Religious History of the Indian Subcontinent*, ed. Vasudha Dalmia, Angelika Malinar and Martin Christof, New Delhi: Oxford University Press.

Fukuoka, Masanobu (1978), *The One-Straw Revolution*, Pennsylvania: Rodale Press.

Giri, Ananta K. (2009), *Self-Development and Social Transformations: The Vision and Practice of the Self-Study Mobilization of svādhyāya*, Lanham: Lexington Books.

Gold, A.G. (2001), "Story, Ritual, and Environment in Rajasthan," in *Sacred Landscapes and Cultural Politics: Planting a Tree*, ed. Philip P. Arnold and Ann G. Gold, Aldershot: Ashgate.

Gold, Ann G. & Bhoju Ram Gujar (2002), *In the Time of Trees and Sorrows: Nature, Power, and Memory in Rajasthan*, London: Duke University Press.

Guha, Ramachandra (2006), *How Much Should a Person Consume? Environmentalism in India and the United States*, Berkeley: University of California.

Haberman, David L. (2006), *River of Love in an Age of Pollution: The Yamuna River of Northern India*, Berkeley: University of California Press.

James, G.A. (2005), "Athavale and Svādhyāya," in *The Encyclopedia of Religion and Nature*. ed. Bron Taylor, New York: Thoemmes Continuum.

Little, J.T. (1995), "Video Vachana, *svādhyāya* and Sacred Tapes," in *Media and the Transformation of Religion in South Asia*, ed. Lawrence A. Babb and Susan S. Wadley, Philadelphia: University of Pennsylvania Press.

Marriott, McKim (ed.) (1990), *India Through Hindu Categories*, New Delhi: Sage Publications.

Matilal, Bimal K. (2002), *Ethics and Epics: Philosophy, Culture, and Religion*, ed. Jonardon Ganeri, Oxford/ New York: Oxford University Press.

Mishra, Anupam (1993), *Aaj Bhi Khare Hain Talab*, Delhi: Gandhi Peace Foundation.

Paranjape, M. (ed.) (2005), *Dharma and Development: The Future of Survival*, Delhi: Samvad India Foundation.

Rukmani, Trichur S. (1999), *Turmoil, Hope, and the Svādhyāya*, Montreal: CASA Conference.

Shah, Tushar (2003), *Management of Natural Resources*, Mumbai: Sir Dorabji Tata Trust.

Sharma, Devinder (2000), "Shedding Tears Over Failed Watersheds," in *Business Line* 14 June, 2000.

Sharma, Sudhirendar (1999), *Food Security through Rainwater Catchment*, New Delhi: UNDP–World Bank Water Sanitation Program.

Sheth, N.R. (2002), "A Spiritual Approach to Social Transformation," in *The Other Gujarat*, ed. Takashi Shinoda, Mumbai: Popular Prakashan.

Sinha, B.K. (1998), "The Answers Within," in *Down To Earth* (May 1998).

Smith, Frederick M. (2006), *The Self Possessed: Deity and Spirit Possession in South Asian Literature and Civilization*, New York: Columbia University Press.

Srivastava, Raj K. (1998), *Vital Connections: Self, Society, and God: Perspectives on Svādhyāya*, New York: Weatherhill Publications.

Unterberger, Betty M. & Rekha R. Sharma (1990), "Shri Pandurang Vaijnath Athavale Shastri and the Svādhyāya Movement in India," in the *Journal of Third World Studies* 7, pp. 116-32.

Weightman, S. & S.M. Pandey, (1978), "The Semantic Fields of Dharma and Kartavya in Modern Hindi," in *The Concept of Duty in South Asia*, ed. Wendy D. O'Flaherty and J, Duncan M. Derrett, Columbia: South Asia Books for the School of Oriental and Africa Studies.

20

Technology, Violence and Non-Violence
A Gandhian Type of Response

*Carl Olson**

AMONG the features that characterize the twentieth and twenty-first centuries, technology and violence are prominent. The rapid advances in technology are nothing short of astounding in diverse fields like medicine, science, business, manufacturing, communications, energy, and the military. Computer developments have only enhanced these already impressive advances in so many fields. In retrospect, technological advances have been connected at times with violence against human beings and other animals on earth. Contemporary technology enables sovereign states or politically motivated individuals to destroy more systematically people and things. Whether it is high explosives carried on a person or placed on an airplane, whether it is smart bombs launched from many miles away from its intended target or a hand-held missile launcher, whether it is ethnic cleansing or a so-called holocaust, whether it is the killing of insects or decimation of entire species of animals, whether it is chemical or nuclear pollution, the past century serves as a reminder at how proficient states, political groups, or individuals have become at destroying others. If the last 120 years can be remembered for its many technological breakthroughs in various areas and its voracious and rampant violence unmatched in any other period of historical time, we have to be concerned with what this new century might bring in destructive potential.

It is also possible to isolate social violence that is built into the social order and that is associated with everyday life. The former assumes many forms and dynamics, while the violence of everyday life is also multiple and "the outcome of the interaction of changing cultural representations,

---

* Philosophy and Religious Studies Department, Allegheny College

social experience, and individual subjectivity" (Kleinman 2000: 238). Social violence is inflicted on people by extreme poverty, high disease rates, unemployment, homelessness, lack of education, hunger, thirst, bodily pain, and death. As parts of the social structure, hierarchy and inequality tend to normalize violence, which gives authority to culture. As a consequence of this feature of culture, Kleinman explains that

> Violence, thus, is crucial to culture processes of routinization, legitimation, essentialism, normalization, and simplification through which the social world orders the flow of experience within and between body selves.
> — Kleinman 2000: 238

According to its ordinary usage, the term "violence" is used to describe a situation, action, or person. It possesses an evaluative component by those using the term that implies approval or disapproval or judgements about its motives or intentions. Its descriptive nature and evaluative aspect are often inextricably intertwined. Violence can be directed toward humans, non-human animals, structures, and the natural world, although it is typically inflicted by one individual upon another without the consent of the other. Of course, violence can also be inflicted upon oneself in cases of suicide or asceticism for example. Although violence can be inflicted accidentally upon another, it is usually a deliberate or predictable harming, injury, mutilating, or killing. This intentional aspect of the nature of violence stands in direct contrast to ordinary human activity in which violence is most often absent as an intentional aim. In this sense, violence is aberrant and stands out from normal, social inter-reactions and relationships, which is partly why the media, for instance, calls attention to it and probably why it arouses our curiosity and prurient interest.

As we look ahead to unfolding events of this new century, does the apparent connection between technological advances and the increase of violence represent an apocalyptic future for citizens of the earth? Or, are there some guidelines or sage advice that we can use to break the apparent connection between proliferating violence and advances in technology? Can we use developments and thinking in the twentieth century to learn how to cope in this new century? Or, are we condemned to be swept away by violence and technology? In order to respond to such questions, this paper proposes to look at two Western philosophers — more specifically Martin Heidegger and Jacques Derrida — and what they inform us about technology and to apply some of the insights of Mahatma Gandhi on non-violence to our problematic connection between technology and violence.

In his 1955 essay entitled "The Question Concerning Technology," Martin Heidegger suggests some problems connected with technology that focus on its efficiency, its violence, its use of human beings, its power to level and abolish, and its destructiveness. A decision to reflect on the problematic nature of technology involves violence, according to Heidegger, and writing about the relationship of technology and violence is also to engage in violence according to Jacques Derrida. Is there a less violent way to deal with the violence associated with technology? If thinking and writing involve violence to some extent, there does not seem to be a path out of this dilemma. Acknowledging this situation, this paper proposes to examine a Gandhian response to the various problems raised by Heidegger in his essay on technology, in order to discern if there is not a way to suggest that it is possible for technology to become more non-violent. If non-violence presupposes truth and serves as a means to truth, and if violence can only be removed by a strength that derives from truth, these kinds of Gandhian guidelines can help us to re-think the violence associated with technology in order to make some modest suggestions for making it less prone to violence.

Reflections of Heidegger

In his essay on technology, Heidegger invites the reader to engage in a philosophical experiment by questioning the nature of technology with the aim of discerning its essence. Moreover, the reader is invited to undertake a way. This way is a path of thinking, questioning, and reflecting upon what shows itself, and it proceeds through language. Heidegger's aim is for the reader to enter into a free relationship with technology in order to discover its essence. By endeavouring to find the essence of technology, we must not be misled or confused by any identification of its essence with technology itself (Heidegger 1959: 13). Being common in prior philosophy to connect the essence of something to what it is, Heidegger suggests that we are motivated to seek the essence of technology because we are in bondage to it, a philosophical stance that suggests that gaining knowledge of it frees us from our chains to it.

As the notion of technology is now commonly understood, it is both a means to some end and a human activity, which represents its instrumental nature. This type of definition does not, however, reveal its essence (Heidegger 1959: 15). If one questions the instrumental nature of technology along with its means and ends, the questioner arrives at causality, which enables it to bring itself forth and reveal itself. Therefore, the question of technology concerns revealing and concealing in which the coming to presence of truth comes to pass (Heidegger 1959: 41). This implies that for Heidegger technology is not a mere instrument or a means; it is rather a way of revealing the truth. What comes to be within this revealing process used to be called *techné*. By reviewing the Greek word *techné*, Heidegger calls attention to the term in its relation to the skilful work of a craftsman, arts of mind, and the fine arts. He finds that there is not only something poetic about it, but it is also connected to the Greek notion of *epistémé* because both terms share a knowing that opens up, brings something forth (*hervor-bringen*), and reveals (Heidegger 1959: 20). By means of his craft, the cobbler, for instance, reveals leather. The process of revealing takes what one intends to create and gathers it together in advance. As a prior gathering together and bringing forth, *techné* does not represent the manufacturing of something because the process of manufacturing something uses an instrumental method to create or reproduce something.

By serving as a mode of revealing, technology itself comes to presence within a locus of unconcealment, a place where truth (*alétheia*) occurs. The older technology embodied in the Greek term *techné* shares with modern technology the process of revealing, but the modern version is devoid of the poetic sense. Modern technology unlocks the secrets of nature, it transforms nature, stores nature, distributes it, and challenges nature with an unreasonable demand that nature gives us its energy (Heidegger 1959: 22). This suggests neither that modern technology loses its power to reveal nor that humans have any control over the process of revealment. Heidegger thinks that an instrumental definition of technology is untenable because it implies some foundational metaphysical or religious explanation.

Not only does Heidegger connect the essence of modern technology with Western metaphysics (Heidegger 1959: 80, 99; 1963), he refers to contemporary science, a form of knowing, as the genuine heir of metaphysics (Heidegger 1963: 195). Technology, science and metaphysics share a similar drive towards total control. If science represents controlled observation of nature, technology is controlled exploitation. Science and technology absorb humans, things and nature (Heidegger 1963: 79, 236). With the assault of science and technology, presence ceases to reign (Heidegger 1963: 100). None the less, technology still represents a mode of disclosure of the truth despite its exploitative tendency.

What Heidegger wants from us is a response to the challenge given by modern technology that gathers us into a process of ordering the real that reveals itself. In order to respond properly, we must avoid defining the essence of technology as some kind of mental representation that transforms it into an object. Moreover, if technology exhibits its presence as nothing more than a cause-effect coherence for a representational mode of thinking, it will lose its mysteriousness. A representational mode of thinking assumes a correspondence between appearance and reality and is supported by a metaphysical edifice (Olson 2000; 2002). In order to retain its mysterious nature, overcome the representational mode of thinking, and respond to the challenge of modern technology, Heidegger thinks that it is possible to gather together, reveal, order, and stand in what he calls "*Ge-stell*" (enframing). Werner Marx explains that "Gestell" usually means something like the frame of a piece of furniture. When the term is hyphenated it indicates a "style," the way, the logos, the essence of technology, particularly the provocative positing that occurs between man and Being (Marx 1971: 176).

Enframing can be called the essence of technology, but not in the sense that it represents a genus or *essentia*. Enframing endures as the essence of technology, but it is not something that we can grasp by means of the representational mode of thinking. In fact, technology itself demands us to think in another way and to rethink the meaning of essence (Heidegger 1959: 37). Enframing makes a claim upon humans to which they fail to respond and understand in what sense they exist in the sense of standing out from their essence. This is a dangerous situation because humans do not encounter their genuine essence. They rather appoint themselves dominion over the earth, and manifest the delusional belief that they encounter only themselves (Heidegger 1959: 35). The danger to human beings is not technology as such, but it is humans themselves that are problematic and threaten themselves.

This does not suggest that Heidegger is unconcerned about a modern technology that attacks and transforms nature in order that it remains available for use and further development. By identifying the essence of technology as "*Ge-stell,*" Heidegger wants to call attention to a complete system of ordering in which all human beings are caught, stored, and ceaselessly switched around, a situation that renders human goals and purposes devoid of independent content. This implies that human actions lack any significance beyond what they accomplish in a purely efficient manner. Thus, it is difficult to discern what confers worth on any course of action in contrast to the old world of the craftsperson in which his/her work possesses value.

And as technology, which serves to glorify the might of human beings, utilizes the earth as raw material, human beings become human material to be used and are transformed into a mere instrument of technology. Within the context of the unlimited productivity of technology, the person stands in danger of losing his/her self (Heidegger 1963: 270). No longer existing as *Dasein* (literally, being-there), the person exists as something ready-at-hand like a piece of equipment.

Another danger of technology, which is the epitome of subjectivism, is its tendency to reverse a person's relation to being. If an individual is a shepherd of being for Heidegger, technology deludes one into thinking that one can become the uncontested master of all beings and no longer a servant of being. This kind of total subjectivity is one in which one assumes that one is an absolute subject and master of all things and represents a genuine threat of death to one's essence and ontic life. From Heidegger's perspective, there is a tendency within technology to negate death because it assumes that what is real is what can be measured, manipulated and controlled. Any attempt to control death, to view it as something negative, or to be avoided derives from the negation of death by technology, which suggests that death becomes something negative and empty (Heidegger 1963: 279). Heidegger wants us to think death positively by thinking about it in relation to being. Therefore, embodied within the essence of technology is the ontological threat of death not in the sense of a killing-machine, but as a powerful imposition of the human will upon everything (Heidegger 1963: 271). This inner urge to dominate and the illusion of one's absolute power represent the real danger of death, a kind of absolute subjectivity and will-to-power.

There are additional dangers associated with technology and what we assume that it can empower us to do. It threatens our entrance into the "Open," which constitutes us in our being (Heidegger 1963: 277). This departure from the "Open" becomes irreversible when one remains on the subject-object level with its representational mode of thinking, which does not allow us to witness the richness of Being. Representational thinking gives us a one-dimensional view of Being. Although it gives us the power to dominate and exploit other beings, the representational thinking common to technology transforms other beings into indistinctive and uniform entities (Heidegger 1959: 96; 1963: 237). By being able to control others by means of technology and our subjectivism, we transform the world into a picture (*Weltbild*) that we can conquer and control (Heidegger 1963: 87). We can behold the picture like a photograph, and we can propose the world and make it submit to us because it ceases to have any sense without the subjective person. By departing from the "Open" and treating the world as a picture, *Dasein* forgets the mystery of Being and stands in errance, an attitude enhanced by technology.

Dasein finds itself in a fallen condition in which it attempts to use and control beings, is forgetful of the mystery of Being, is disinterested in beings except to exploit them, and sinks into subjective thinking. If we become a slave to technology, we become a captive to merely representative thinking, distracted, unable to hear the call of Being, and unable to witness the wonders of the simple.

Heidegger proposes that we extricate ourselves from the level of representational thinking to a more profound and interior level that he identifies with foundational thinking, which represents a reversal of consciousness that allows us to witness the immanence of objects. In short, Heidegger follows the poetic voice of the German poet Rilke and his call to re-collect (*Er-innerung*). This is a type of thinking that is pre-subjective, non-representational, pre-logical, and pre-rational. By means of a re-collection upon things, we witness the coming to presence of a presentation of objects as they reveal themselves. In this way we attend to Being as it comes to presence in things and recall its mystery. As one retreats from the representational mode of thinking into foundational thought or re-collection, one extricates oneself from errance and overcomes the subjective attitude of technology. Heidegger thinks that re-collection can be achieved by poetry because language represents the primary means of access to Being.

Reflections of Derrida

The vision of Heidegger of a fallen individual absorbed by technology is similar to the view of Derrida, although there is a different spirit in the latter's work because he is reacting against the philosophy of Heidegger. Derrida perceives persons and events as being more decentred: "The age is off its hinges. Everything beginning with time, seems out of kilter, unjust, dis-adjusted" (Derrida 1994: 77). The unfolding of events in this postmodern era upsets any *telos* of history to such an extent that what is occurring does not happen within time but rather to time. Thus, everything is disjointed. During this decentred and disjointed time, it is possible to observe that "never have violence, inequality, exclusion, famine, and thus economic oppression affected as many human beings in the history of the earth and of humanity" (Derrida 1994: 85). Whatever common features exist between the philosophical visions of Heidegger and Derrida there are serious differences between them. Derrida wants to upset and undermine, for instance, Heidegger's conception of technology by inviting one to think about technology in another way. Derrida wants us to think technology devoid of the initial appearance of Being. Since the so-called "first" can never be the initial appearance of Being in any absolute sense because the initial arrival in any chronological or logical order is posterior to a prior moment, there cannot be an order, logos, or metaphysics. Derrida differentiates his non-position from that of Heidegger:

> If I take my "departure" from the destination and the destiny or destining of Being (*Das Schicken im Geshick des Seins*), no one can dream of them *forbidding me to speak* of the "post," except on the condition of making of this word the element of an image, of a figure, of a trope, a post card of Being in some way. — Derrida 1987b: 65

By making remarks in Heidegger's text, Derrida cuts into his text and performs an act of castration. Why does Derrida think that this process of castration is necessary? Since *logos* itself is phallocentric, Derrida castrates or clips it by means of moving through a text by means of deconstruction. Moreover, Derrida thinks that it is misguided to connect the complete history of Being with its destination because "as soon there is, there is différance. . ." (Derrida 1987b: 66). Derrida uses the notion of *différance* as a neologism, which suggests that he wants to stress difference in his philosophy in a very special sense.

Since Derrida wants to capture the sense of "differing" as spacing and temporalizing and to indicate the sameness that is non-identical, he uses the neologism *différance* to indicate a necessarily finite movement that precedes and structures all opposition. The *ance* ending of *différance,* marked by a silent "*a,*" suggests that it is not simply a word or a concept; it is neither existence nor essence, and is neither active nor passive because the perceiving subject is similarly constituted (Derrida 1973: 66). *Différance,* a necessarily finite movement, is what precedes and structures all opposition. In other words, it originates before all differences, and represents the play of differences. It is impossible for it to be exposed because it cannot reveal itself in the present moment and never produces presence itself, whose structure is constituted by difference and deferment (Derrida 1973: 134).

Referring to Heidegger's discussion of *techné*, Derrida claims that it represents a metaphysical and technical "determination of the envoi or of the destinality (*Geschick*) of Being" (Derrida 1987a: 192). But Derrida denies that it comes into presence. If we view *techné* as *différance*, it does not arrive into presence, and it does not arrive as language, poetry, or song (Derrida 1987a: 192). From Derrida's perspective, Heidegger is involved in a metaphysic of presence that presupposes sameness.

Derrida alters Heidegger's connection of forgetfulness with Being. The latter thinker connects forgetfulness with a "mediation and the departure of the *logos* from itself" (Derrida 1976: 37). If we conceive of the computer as a machine invented to resemble human memory in part to cope with forgetfulness, this kind of archival technology is a kind of prosthetic device that serves to supplement an open system like the mind, language, writing, or technology. The contemporary computer is a supplement to the mind or ultimately forgetfulness. Since the computer or other forms of technology are closed systems of epistemology, Derrida wants to not only challenge such things, but he also wants to attack and undermine such closed systems.

If we use the computer as a metaphor for technology, what Derrida objects to is the way the computer relativizes the difference between the mind, a living system, and the computer, a mechanical and mathematical system. In order words, the simulation of human processes of memory tends to challenge and radically blur the line of demarcation generally accepted between the natural and the artificial. Derrida does not object to the supplemental and simulation aspects of the computer. What Derrida wants to criticize is the closed epistemological system of which it is captured by the Western thought and its representational mode of thinking.

Since computers are a new form of technology in at least a relative sense, their inauguration is accompanied by violence. This is a non-anthropological violence because such violence "precedes and transcends the instance of the human or the subjective" (Johnson 1993: 73). Violence precedes necessarily the constitution of any new space, as the space of its possibility. Derrida refers to several forms of violence that are evident with difference, classification, application of appellations, and even writing (Derrida 1976: 110). We find with writing a connection with violence and *techné*. Derrida explains:

> Writing, here, is *techné* as the relation between life and death, between present and representation, between the two apparatuses. It opens up the question of technics: of the apparatus in general and of the analogy between the psychical apparatus and the nonpsychical apparatus.
>
> — Derrida 1978: 228

Derrida envisions a primordial violence prior to any form of technology. This silent and absolute violence must not be confused with ordinary violence. The violence envisioned by Derrida is not even the opposite of non-violence. From Derrida's perspective, Heidegger's notion of Being, time, the presence of the present, and the coming to presence are all marked with violence (Derrida 1978: 133, 147). Thus, Derrida tends to envision an entire economy of violence.

Within this economy, violence circulates and is exchanged, but most significantly it defers the advent of a menace of an even greater and totally annihilating violence. As the possibility of an even greater violence is deferred, violence distributes itself in acts of lesser violence. By constantly distributing itself and defusing the advent of a primordial form, violence manifests the same non-structure as *différance*. Since violence resembles *différance* and happens within a pluralistic context of decisions, violence persists as traces of the primordial violence. Does this mean that non-violence is impossible? Derrida responds to such a question by stating that "every philosophy of non-violence can only choose the lesser violence within an *economy of violence*" (Derrida 1978: 313, note 21). Derrida's position suggests that technology can only be established in an act of violence that merely antedates an even more primordial violence.

It is evident that violence is closely linked with technology in Derrida's philosophy, whereas it was emphatically implied in the philosophy of Heidegger because of the way that technology absorbs the individual. Does a champion of non-violence like Gandhi have anything useful to say to these two Western philosophers? Is there a way to apply some of the principles of Gandhian non-violence in such a way as to ameliorate the violence associated with technology? If what Heidegger strongly suggests and Derrida makes emphatically clear about the connection between technology and violence, is it possible for technology to become more non-violent? Before attempting to address these questions, it seems wise to review Gandhi's notions of violence and non-violence.

Reflections of Gandhi

Gandhi has some important things to say about technology and violence. From the beginning of his career, Gandhi was suspicious of technology because it represents a threat to humans due to its tendency to absorb, displace, and de-humanize beings (Gandhi 1986-87: 3, 517). This does not mean that Gandhi was opposed to all technology, although he affirms opposition to its misuse and its concentration of power in the hands of the few at the expense of the many (Gandhi 1986-87: 3, 525). He does advocate simple village types of technology like the practice of *khādī* (homespun cotton). During his lifetime, the simple technology of the spinning wheel represented a symbol of simplicity and economic freedom, even though it is an all-together different question as to whether or not *khādī* represents a viable and realistic economic policy. The practice of activities like *khādī* does suggest that Gandhi wants individuals to be self-reliant (*svadeśī*) and self-dependent because self-reliance is the only legitimate means to *swarāj* (self-rule), a notion connected to self-determination (*swarājya*). From Gandhi's political perspective, these connected notions can be manifested as self-rule and national self-dependence. Self-determination (*swarājya*) and self-reliance (*svadeśī*) are both based on non-violence (*ahiṁsā*). In agreement with Gandhi, Heidegger and Derrida can accept this emphasis on self-reliance and self-determination. Since technology is potentially or actually violent according to either Heidegger or Derrida, it is significant to ask: What is wrong with violence from the perspective of Gandhi?

For Gandhi, one violent act leads to another (Gandhi 1986-87: 1, 350). If this is true, violence contributes to a potential cycle of violence. There is also a tendency for violence to concentrate power in the hands of the few. Oftentimes, this concentration of power in the hands of a select few leads to suffering and degradation for many others. In short, violence is evil. Gandhi does not conceive of the nature of humans as being inherently violent, although Gandhi does make a distinction when he writes "Man as animal is violent, but as Spirit is non-violent" (Gandhi 1955: 61). Moreover, the adoption and practice of non-violence distinguishes humans from other animals (Gandhi 1986-87: 2, 240).

It is a false impression to assume that non-violence is a device of the weak because it is rather a weapon of strength (Gandhi 1986-87: 3, 509). In fact, Gandhi argues that the roots of *ahiṁsā* spring from fearlessness. This implies that one must be willing to suffer and even be prepared to die. From this position of strength, Gandhi enumerates five axioms of the creed of non-violence. Firstly, it implies self-purification, which Gandhi means in a spiritual, moral, and ethical sense because it involves rigorous ethical discipline and taking of vows. The strength of non-violence is associated with the ability of the person practising it, and it is not dependent on the will of the person. A central axiom of non-violence for Gandhi is that it is always superior to violence. If non-violence can never fail, there is no such thing as defeat for someone practising non-violence.

Any apparent failure can be traced to the moral inadequacy of the practitioner. Finally, the last axiom claims that the ultimate end of non-violence is victory (Gandhi 1986-87: 2, 321-22). In a sense, adhering to and practising non-violence is equivalent to knowing the truth and acting on it.

Non-violence is synonymous with non-injury and harmlessness. It represents the renunciation of the will to kill and the intention to harm any living thing. It includes the abstention from hostile thought, word, and deed. There are two forms of non-violence for Gandhi. On the one hand, the negative form of non-violence is related to non-injury of any living being and requires deliberate self-suffering. On the other hand, the positive form of non-violence involves love and charity, and it includes truth and fearlessness (Gandhi 1986-87: 2, 212-13). Although Gandhi admits that non-violence is the law of his life and should guide all our actions, he does not adhere to this law in a rigid manner because he did allow for exceptions to the law. These exceptions of the law of non-violence are grouped into three headings: exceptions with respect to maintaining the safety of one's person; giving relief from excruciating pain and suffering; and offering protection to those dependent upon one's care (Jordens 1998: 228).

These kinds of exceptions are connected to Gandhi's wish not to turn non-violence into some kind of fetish. Gandhi endorses the destruction, for instance, of disease carrying rodents and insects. Glyn Richards captures the spirit of Gandhi's position by explaining that "He accepts then the necessity to permit the destruction of some forms of life, while at the same time holding onto a firm belief in the essential unity of all life and the principle of non-violence" (Richards 1982: 66). Gandhi does not advocate a radical kind of non-violence that seeks to exempt from violence all living things such as the Jaina path of religion, which shapes his philosophy of non-violence to a large extent.

Non-violence is not merely a religious, social, or political theory. It is a path of life that one can follow and practise in one's everyday mode of existence. Writing in an autobiographical manner, Gandhi affirms:

> Non-violence for me is not a mere experiment. It is part of my life and the whole of the creed of *satyāgraha*, non-cooperation, civil disobedience, and the like are necessary deductions from the fundamental proposition that non-violence is the law of life for human beings. For me it is both a means and an end and I am more than ever convinced that in the complex situation that faces India, there is no other way of gaining real freedom.

> In applying my mind to the present situation I must, therefore, test everything in terms of non-violence. — Gandhi 1986-87: 2, 320

Furthermore, this path of non-violence includes the following elements: non-attachment; suffering; and endless patience. When one lives it and practises it, one's intention is not to coerce others into adopting it; it is rather intended to convert them to the path and practice of non-violence. This way of life implies a willingness to treat all beings as one's self.

Living a non-violent life presupposes truth (*satya*), and it is also the means to the truth. Margaret Chatterjee argues that "It is an ontological conception of Truth, rooted in the Indian tradition which provides the ground for Gandhi's non-violent theory of action" (1983: 74). Certainly, Gandhi views truth and non-violence as intertwined. Gandhi acknowledges that it is even more difficult to attain truth than it is to practise non-violence. He also thinks that the pursuit of truth gives us the humility necessary to accept the need for non-violence. And conversely the pursuit of non-violence indicates that violence is rooted in fear that can be eradicated by the strength that derives from truth. It is also possible to promote truth by practising non-violence.

It is not merely enough to live a life of non-violence, however laudable such a lifestyle might be for oneself and others, in accordance with the truth; it is also necessary to recognize that non-violence is a genuine power in the sense of being a moral force for good. Writing to a publication in New York City in 1924, Gandhi writes the following message:

> My study and experience of non-violence have proved to me that it is the greatest force in the world. It is the surest method of discovering the truth and it is the quickest because there is no other. It works silently, almost imperceptibly, but none the less surely. It is the one constructive process of Nature in the midst of incessant destruction going on about us. I hold it to be a superstition to believe that it can work only in private life. There is no department of life public or private to which that force cannot be applied. But this non-violence is impossible with complete self-effacement. — Gandhi 1986-87: 2, 306

As exemplified by such a statement, non-violence assumes a quasi-metaphysical status for Gandhi, even though it retains its pragmatic aspect to accomplish positive goals of a person, society, or nation. At the same time, Gandhi's great faith in non-violence is tied to the moral preparation and status of the practitioner. Even though he demonstrates his faith in his method, way of life, and its power, Gandhi did not think it wise to impose non-violence upon others because such a force works best by means of persuasion and conversion (Gandhi 1986-87: 2, 233, 264-65).

Technology and Non-violence

If Heidegger is correct in his assessment of the ability of technology to absorb and enslave a person, or if Derrida is right to claim that there is a primordial violence at the root of technology, they both agree that it is desirable to be freed from such possibilities. In contrast to Heidegger and Derrida, Gandhi perceives non-violence as the means to liberation (*mokṣa*), which he also connects with the realization of the truth. From Gandhi's perspective, non-violence possesses the potential to overcome the violence associated with either that recognized by Heidegger or Derrida.

However, a question that needs to be asked at this point is the following: Can we apply non-violence to technology and its violence — whether primordial or derivative — successfully? Even though there are instances when the violence associated with technology is justified, technology does not necessarily preclude using non-violence as a guideline with respect to the application of technology. Therefore, with respect to non-violence, it is not impractical or impossible to use it as a guideline for the development of technology. There are a few items that can be used to measure whether an application of non-violence is impracticable or impossible.

If we adhere to a basic Gandhian tenet not to introduce non-violence unless it is a response to violence, we can certainly apply it to an understanding of technology based on the philosophies of both Heidegger and Derrida because of their suggestions about violence and its association with technology. If external circumstances render non-violent techniques inadvisable, unworkable, or unlikely to succeed, non-violent applications should not be introduced into the application of technology. This is especially true if the perceived change leads to a less beneficial state than the present one. It is not possible to introduce a non-violent feature into technology if the agents lack certain characteristics necessary for success like courage, willingness to suffer, respect, ability to act from principle rather than expediency, being devoid of violent feelings, and embodying love. We can connect technology to non-violence only if the method is performed openly and without secrecy following guidelines established by Gandhi. It is also important to allow for criticism by others and self-correction.

Besides allowing for this type of external criticism and internal correction, Gandhi offers two types of tests that one can employ to measure oneself and the application of non-violence. Gandhi uses violence as a litmus test to measure religions: "We should understand that the less violence a religion permits, the more is the truth contained in it" (Gandhi 1986-87: 1, 303). This type of test of a religion can also be applied to technology. Thus, if a form of technology causes less violence than another form, the form producing the least amount of violence is to be preferred over the other. This type of test assumes, of course, that there is a viable choice between two competing types of technology. It is possible to grasp this type of test as an external type of measurement. A more internal type of measurement is the following type of test:

> Indeed the acid test of non-violence is that one thinks, speaks and acts non-violently, even when there is the gravest provocation to be violent. There is no merit in being non-violent to the good and the gentle. Non-violence is the mightiest force in the world capable of resisting the greatest imaginable temptation. — Gandhi 1986-87: 2, 357

From a critical perspective, Karl H. Potter thinks that Gandhi assumes that the internal and external factors of non-violence depend on the moral character of the agent (Potter 1971: 105). Although Potter is probably correct with his observation, any philosophy begins with some presuppositions as Heidegger makes clear in the early part of *Sein und Zeit* by dismissing the possibility that a thinker can develop a purely presuppositionless philosophy.

Certainly, Derrida agrees with the spirit of Heidegger's conviction about a presuppositionless philosophy and applying it to technology with respect to the impossibility of having a technology that is completely free of violence. The sweeping presence of violence before the emergence of technology from Derrida's perspective corresponds to the very wide scope of Gandhi's understanding of non-violence. According to Gandhi, non-violence includes much more than a prohibition against physical forms of violence or killing because it extends to include violence associated with speech and thought, which Gandhi refers to as the "acid test of non-violence" (Gandhi 1986-87: 2, 357).

Such a test is probably more difficult to apply to technology. It is highly likely that Heidegger and Derrida could counter Gandhi's emphasis on non-violence by stating that its complete application would make life impossible. In other words, the positions of Heidegger and Derrida strongly imply that violence necessarily accompanies technology. From Gandhi's perspective, such criticism is aptly countered by indicating that non-violence is an ideal and could even be considered a far distant goal for which one should strive, even though it is not totally attainable within our embodied condition. The really important thing is that Gandhi's notion of non-violence can serve as a pragmatic way of testing any technology. And if its actuality or potentiality for inflicting or promoting violence is high, it can be rejected or altered to make it less lethal and more non-harmful as possible.

And as Gandhi asserts, since violence is a destructive energy and non-violence is a creative energy (Gandhi 1986-87: 2, 216), the latter is preferable to the former. Although Heidegger agrees with the spirit of Gandhi's position, he wants to stress that representation is a form of violence because it forces objects into constant presence to the subject. By means of conceiving something, one represents it in such a way as to attack it. This assault mode of presencing is rooted in logic and metaphysics and leads to a more universal violence. Thinking and poetry must regain non-violence. This non-violent mode of thinking envisioned by Heidegger is releasement (*Gelassenheit*), a letting be (Heidegger 1966: 73-74). Releasement allows one to dwell within the world, not as its master, but as its servant, a position embraced by the spirit of Gandhi's philosophy of non-violence. In contrast, Derrida's radical scepticism and conviction about a primordial violence seems to exclude his possible agreement with Gandhi or Heidegger at this point. Certainly, the three thinkers are resigned to the fact of and prevalence of violence and its connection in some respect to technology.

For the sake of examining another possibility with respect to the relationship between technology and non-violence, it can be asked of a postmodern thinker such as Derrida: Is non-violence a secret hidden within technology? If one states that one possesses a secret, it ceases to be a secret by being divulged and negated. Any divulgence that one possesses a secret spills it and divides it against itself. Therefore, a pure secret is impossible and cannot appear (Derrida 1987a: 558). From the perspective of Derrida, the secret about non-violence is that there is no secret. In other words, there is no secret non-violence in itself that can serve as a transcendental signified or function as an object of intuition by which one can gain extratextual access to it (Derrida 1992: 67; 1995: 29).

Concluding Reflections

By using Gandhian guidelines for non-violence in a pragmatic way, it is possible to begin to recognize a path from the violence connected to technology in Heidegger's sense of enframing (*Ge-stell*). These Gandhian guidelines can help us to begin to accomplish the turning (*die Kehre*), a basic transformation of disclosure from a mode of absorption to a renewed revealment of truth, from the violence associated with technology. It seems that Gandhi's guidelines for non-violence would be difficult to apply to Derrida's grasping of the relationship between technology and violence because as soon as non-violence is applied to technology it loses its sameness and becomes a play of differences and never comes into presence. And since Derrida envisions a technology without the appearance of Being, without *logos*, and without metaphysics, he suggests that the best situation within which we can find ourselves is one of less violence within an economy of violence. Although non-violence is impossible for Derrida due to the economy of violence that exchanges and circulates violence, the postmodernist can agree with the spirit of Gandhi's guidelines to the extent of creating less violence. These are useful lessons to keep in mind with respect to the potential success of using Gandhi's guidelines for the application of non-violence to technology.

Another lesson that one can draw from the three thinkers considered in this essay is that they are not advocating a simple rejection of technology. None of them denigrate technology. They agree that we cannot exit from technology, escape it, or leap beyond it. Neither are any of these possibilities necessarily desirable. Each thinker wants us to see the violence and other dangers associated with technology, find a way to deal with these problematic aspects of technology, overcome these problems, render technology less violent, and use technology in a non-violent way. Overall, they invite us to reflect on the relationship between technology and violence.

Even though Gandhi does not address the issue himself, if technology manifests for Heidegger the supreme form of controlled representation (Heidegger 1963: 80, 91-92), the German philosopher and the French philosopher invite us to find another mode of thinking and a way to become less violent, even though Derrida thinks that non-violence is impossible. This invitation to reflect on the relationship between violence and technology encourages us to find another paradigm of thinking and being. If what enframing (*Ge-stell*) of technology suggests is how we represent, arrange, organize, and mobilize the universe for some human purpose in a violent way, we need, then, to ponder other possibilities that might be more non-violent.

References

Chatterjee, Margaret (1983), *Gandhi's Religious Thought*, Houndmills: Macmillan.

Derrida, Jacques (1973), *Speech and Phenomena and Other Essays on Husserl's Theory of Signs*, tr. David B. Allison, Evanston: Northwestern University Press.

——— (1976), *Of Grammatology*, tr. Gayatri C. Spivak, Baltimore/London: John Hopkins University Press.

——— (1978), *Writing and Difference*, tr. Alan Bass, Chicago: University of Chicago Press.

——— (1987a), *Psyché: Inventions de l'autre*, Paris: Galilée.

——— (1987b), *The Postcard: From Socrates to Freud and Beyond*, tr. Alan Bass, Chicago: University of Chicago Press.

——— (1992), "'Passions': An Oblique Offering," in *Derrida: A Critical Reader*, ed. and tr. David Wood, Oxford/Cambridge: Blackwell, pp. 5-35.

——— (1994), *Specters of Marx: The State of the Debt, the Work of Mourning, and the New International*, tr. Peggy Kamuf, New York/London: Routledge.

——— (1995), *On the Name*, ed. Thomas Dutoit, Stanford: Stanford University Press.

Gandhi, Mohandas K. (1955), *My Religion*, Ahmedabad: Navajivan Publishing House.

——— (1986-87), *The Moral and Political Writings of Mahatma Gandhi* (3 vols.), ed. Raghavan Iyer, Oxford: Clarendon Press.

Heidegger, Martin (1959), *Vorträge und Aufsätze*, Tübingen: Verlag Günther Neske Pfulligen.

——— (1963), *Holzwege*, Franfurt am Main: Victtorio Klostermann.

——— (1966), *Discourse on Thinking*, tr. John M. Anderson and E. Hans Freund, New York: Harper & Row Publishers.

Johnson, Christopher (1993), *System and Writing in the Philosophy of Jacques Derrida*, Cambridge: Cambridge University Press.

Jordens, Joseph Teresa Florent (1998), *Gandhi's Religion: A Homespun Shawl*, Houndmills: Macmillan Press Ltd.

Kleinman, A. (2000), "The Violence of Everyday Life: The Multiple Forms and Dynamics of Social Violence," in *Violence and Subjectivity*, ed. Veena Das et al., Berkeley: University of California Press, pp. 226-41.

Marx, Werner (1971), *Heidegger and the Traditions*, tr. Theodore Kisiel and Mary Greene, Evanston: Northwestern University Press.

Olson, Carl (2000), *Zen and the Art of Postmodern Philosophy: Two Paths of Liberation from the Representational Mode of Thinking*, Albany: State University of New York Press.

——— (2002), *Indian Philosophers and Postmodern Thinkers: Dialogues on the Margins of Culture*, Delhi: Oxford University Press.

Potter, K.H. (1971), "Explorations in Gandhi's Theory of Non-violence," in *The Meanings of Gandhi*, ed. Paul F. Power, Honolulu: University Press of Hawaii, pp. 91-117.

Richards, Glyns. (1982), *The Philosophy of Gandhi: A Study of his Basic Ideas*, London: Curzon Press.

21

Reviewing Hinduism
Religion, Violence and Non-violence

*Madhav M. Deshpande**

MOST religious traditions do not present us with unequivocal answers to complicated issues. If Jesus asks us to turn the other cheek to the offender, how could we explain the Crusades? If the great Mahatma Gandhi, practising non-violence right up to his death, was the ideal Hindu who derived his philosophy of non-violence from the *Bhagavad-Gītā*, how do we account for the fact that Nathuram Godse, an educated brāhmaṇa who shot Mahatma Gandhi, cites the same *Bhagavad-Gītā* as the text where he sought his justification to carry out his "necessary" violence without remorse?

Since the 11 September 2001 events, the televised discussions involving theologians of various faiths have tried to point toward religious faith as a source of reassurance in a difficult time like the present. We are asked to pray to god to protect us and offer us peace and security through his grace and compassion. However, the question of where the evil comes from has largely remained unanswered in these discussions. No theologian would accept god as the source of the evil we faced on 11 September 2001. Where did it come from? Is there some other source, besides god? Do we then inevitably land into some sort of perennial dualism of god *versus* satan? How come god did not stop this evil? If He did not know it was coming, then what happens to his omniscience? If he knew it was coming, but did not wish to prevent it, then what happens to his compassion and love? Is this a cruel god, who allows for inequality and cruelty to occur in the world of his own creation? If he knew the evil was coming, did wish to stop it, but could not, then what happens to his omnipotence? Or was this punishment from god, as some have suggested? These issues have been debated for centuries among philosophers.

* The Department of Asian Languages and Cultures, The University of Michigan

John Mackie, in his "Evil and Omnipotence," presents this dilemma as follows:

> I think, however, that a more telling criticism can be made by way of the traditional problem of evil. Here it can be shown, not that religious beliefs lack rational support, but that they are positively irrational, that the several parts of the essential theological doctrine are inconsistent with one another. . . . In its simplest form the problem is this: God is omnipotent; God is wholly good; yet evil exists. There seems to be some contradiction between these three propositions, so that if any two of them were true the third would be false. But at the same time all three are essential parts of most theological positions; the theologian, it seems, at once *must* adhere and *cannot consistently* adhere to all three. — Mackie 1971: 92-93

The dilemma thus pointed out by John Mackie is not unique to any particular religious tradition. It is common to them all. In Indian philosophical systems, the classical *darśana*s, this becomes a major point of debate between Jainas and Buddhists on the one hand and the Hindu philosophical systems on the other. In several prominent texts from the Jaina and Buddhist traditions, essentially Mackie's position is advocated in rejecting the concept of *Īśvara* (= god). The Hindu traditions on the other hand try to defend god against these arguments. The famous *Brahma-Sūtra* of Bādarāyaṇa[1] (*sūtra* 2.1.34: *vaiṣamya-nairghr̥ṇye na sāpekṣatvāt* . . .) says that one cannot point to inequality and evil in the world and then use that as an argument to prove that god must be unequal and cruel, because god's decisions in dispensing rewards are contingent (*sāpekṣa*) upon people's own prior good and bad *karma*. God, then, is not a free agent, but He is like a judge who must abide by the evidence of people's good or bad *karma*. The philosophical debate takes many turns and twists. The atheists, the Jainas and the Buddhists, are not convinced of this argument. They would rather rely solely on the law of *karma* to account for good and bad events in the world and dispense with god completely. On the other hand, the theory of *karma* leads to an inevitable regress *ad infinitum* in search for causes. *Karma* and *saṁsāra* (transmigration through endless series of births and deaths) must then be a beginningless (*anādi*) process. Seeking any beginning becomes problematic, because one is then not able to point to a cause for good or evil. Not only the Jainas and the Buddhists, Bādarāyaṇa, the author of the *Brahma-Sūtra*, is himself forced to admit that a beginningless god needs to rely on a beginningless series of *karma*

1. References to the *Brahma-Sūtra* and the commentary by Śaṅkara (*Brahmasūtrabhāṣya*) are from Acharya 1948.

(*sūtra* 2.1.35: *na karmāvibhāgād iti cen nānāditvāt*). The great Śaṅkarācārya comments on this *sūtra*:

> This (inequality and cruelty found in the world) would be a problem (for maintaining the doctrine of *Īśvara*) if the transmigratory existence had a beginning. However, in the beginningless transmigratory existence, in a continuum of cause-effect chains like seed and sprout, there is no contradiction in emergence of unequal *karma* and creation.

This is certainly no great argument for god's omnipotence, and, in admitting the unequal *karma* and its consequences to be beginningless, one has essentially admitted to the permanent presence of good and evil, without being able to resolve the question of their origin. But, while the atheistic traditions are willing to live without god, the theists are euphoric about god and his abilities. One of the best descriptions of the god of theism is to be found at the very beginning of Rāmānuja's commentary on the *Bhagavad-Gītā*:

> Now, the Consort of Śrī, whose proper form, antagonistic to all that is evil and solely comprising all that is good, is nothing but knowledge and bliss; the ocean of innumerable beautiful qualities, such as boundless and supreme knowledge, power, force, sovereignty, fortitude, mastery, etc. qualities proper to his nature; the treasury of numberless properties, such as brilliance, beauty, comeliness, youthfulness, etc. which are in accord with his pleasure and which are unimaginable, divine and miraculous, impeccable and incomparable; whose divine shape is adorned with manifold and maniform endless, wonderful, eternal, irreproachable, immeasurable divine ornaments and equipped with innumerable weapons which, being worthy of their bearer, are of inconceivable power, eternal, impeccable and incomparable; whose perfections, glory and lordship, being essentially in accordance with his will, are eternal and unrivaled. — van Buitenen 1968: 45-46

God of Rāmānuja is omnipotent, omnipresent, and omniscient. He is "antagonistic to all that is evil and solely comprising all that is good." God is not responsible for evil. On the contrary, He is antagonistic to all that is evil. On the other hand, everything that ensues from god is good. But then again where does evil come from? For Rāmānuja, it cannot come from god. But then there is no satan in his universe. It comes from the beginningless *karma* of individuals, and god is there to rescue the devotees faced with evil, fully armed with appropriate weapons of "inconceivable power, eternal, impeccable and incomparable." While one may not agree with Rāmānuja's explanation of the origin of evil, one can certainly find reassurance in the power of god to help his devotees. The selectivity of that power may be a problem for the logician, but not for the devotee who is at the core of religious belief and experience.

But is this faith in god's power leading us, at least some of us, to usurp that power in god's name and to perpetrate violence in god's name? The temple mount in Jerusalem is a battleground. The temple/mosque in Ayodhyā is a battleground. The Babri mosque in Ayodhyā was torn down by a riotous Hindu mob in 1992 to make space for a temple to Rāma. Those who want to build the Rāma temple in Ayodhyā are willing to use violence in the name of god to build it, and those who want to stop the construction of that temple are also willing to use violence in the name of god. In the name of god, hundreds of innocent Hindus and Muslims have been victimized. It almost seems like we are not willing to wait to let god take his turn to protect us. Before he can protect us, we want to protect our god from their god. Mahatma Gandhi may have preached that *Īśvara* and Allāh are just two names for the same god. But in Ayodhyā, there is no willingness to let Rāma and Allāh coexist. These are the facts. Longfellow said: "God is in his heaven and all is right with the world." We cannot be sure, though we desperately want to believe, that god is in his heaven, but we can be sure that all is not right with the world.

Is religion itself a problem that sometimes causes evil or is religion a solution to evil? All the arguments given by Bertrand Russell in his thought-provoking essay "Why I am not a Christian" (Russell 1957) need to be taken seriously. But the title of that book may as well have been "Why I am not a Hindu," or "Why I am not a Muslim," or "Why I am not a Jew." All the same arguments would still be relevant. Religion, like race, nationalism, and other ideologies, unites and divides at the same time and it does so with equal force. Referring to the recent Hindu-Muslim riots in Gujarat, the land of Mahatma Gandhi — India's apostle of peace — Salman Rushdie agonizes over its cause in an article (Slaughter in the Name of God) published in the *Washington Post* on 7 March 2002. He reaches a shocking conclusion:

> The political discourse matters, and explains a good deal. But there is something beneath it, something we don't want to look in the face: namely, that in India, as elsewhere in our darkening world, religion is the poison in the blood. Where religion intervenes, mere innocence is no excuse. Yet we go on skating around this issue, speaking of religion in the fashionable language of "respect." What is there to respect in any of this, or in any of the crimes now being committed almost daily around

> the world in religion's name? How well, with what fatal results, religion erects totems, and how willing we are to kill for them! And when we've done it often enough, the deadening of affect that results makes it easier to do it again. So India's problem turns out to be the world's problem. What happened in India has happened in god's name. The problem's name is god.

I am not sure I would use the same wording as Rushdie. I am not sure that god is the problem. We are looking in the wrong direction. It is our conception of god, for which we alone are responsible, that is the source of the problem. It is not so much that god creates man in his image. It is man who creates god in his own image. That is the source of our problems. We need to take responsibility for the mythologies that we construct. We need to look in the mirror and find the culprit.

In the ancient Hindu literature and mythology, these issues are addressed and resolved to the satisfaction of the believers in diverse ways. While the theological debate discussed earlier tries to absolve god from being the source of evil, other texts and traditions are not so reticent about admitting that both good and evil originate from the same unitary original principle. Here, I would like to briefly discuss the question of the origin of the so-called demonic *asura*s. The ancient Vedic literature is replete with stories of competition between the good *deva*s and the demonic *asura*s. The *deva*s are good by definition and the *asura*s evil by definition. However, in their perpetual competition and struggle, sometimes the *asura*s win, sometimes the *deva*s win. It goes without saying that we want the *deva*s to win. But why are the *asura*s there to begin with? Well, when Prajāpati created the world, he created both, the *deva*s as well as the *asura*s. They are both called *prājāpatya*, "sons of Prajāpati" in Vedic literature (cf. *Chāndogya Upaniṣad* 1.2.1: *devāsurā ha vai yatra saṁyetire, ubhaye prājāpatyāḥ*). Why were the *asura*s evil, if their brothers, the *deva*s, are good? Were the *asura*s always evil?

The Purāṇic mythology provides some interesting stories that shed light on ancient conceptions. Here I would like to discuss the mythical account of the famous event of Śiva burning and destroying the three cities of *asura*s. Here is the version from the *Śivamahāpurāṇa* (Pandeya 1963). This Purāṇa (*Rudrasaṁhitā, Yuddhakhaṇḍa, adhyāya* 2) describes how the *deva*s are being dominated by the demon Tārakāsura and his son Maya from the city of Tripura. The gods approach Brahmā for advice. Brahmā says that since the *asura*s are also his own creation and *since righteousness is on the increase in the city of Tripura* (*Rudrasaṁhitā, Yuddhakhaṇḍa,* *adhyāya* 2, verse 9), he cannot help the *devas*, but that they should approach Śiva who may be able to help them. The gods then approach and praise Śiva and request his help. However, Śiva explains his own dilemma (*Rudrasaṁhitā, Yuddhakhaṇḍa, adhyāya* 3):

> This overlord of Tripura is at this time meritorious. He who has merit (*puṇya*) should not be killed at any time. O gods! I realize all the great difficulties of the gods. Those powerful *daityas* cannot be killed either by *devas* or *asuras*. All the sons of Tāraka, including Maya, are meritorious (*puṇyavantaḥ*). . . . Becoming harsh in battle, how can I knowingly betray my friends? . . . Those *daityas* are my devotees. How can they be killed by me, O gods?

Śiva's dilemma is critical for our understanding. The *daityas* are not primordially immoral or unrighteous in this account. They are in fact devoted to Śiva and are meritorious (*puṇyavantaḥ*). However, from the point of view of the *devas*, the *daityas* must be defeated, because they represent the "other." As the story progresses, Śiva asks the *devas* to go to Viṣṇu to find a solution. Viṣṇu first plots to push the *daityas* away from the path of righteousness by luring them into the religion of the Jainas (*Rudrasaṁhitā, Yuddhakhaṇḍa, adhyāya* 4). After the *daityas* are lured away to anti-Vedic Jainism, they are then destroyed by Śiva. The message of the story is not a clear moral victory of the *devas* over the *daityas*/*asuras*. It is a message of unchallenged survival of the *devas* by defeating and eliminating the "other." There is no alternative of bringing the *daityas* over to moral and righteous behaviour. By the admission of the *Śivamahāpurāṇa*, they were indeed already moral and righteous, and devotees of Śiva, and yet they had to be destroyed (cf. parallel in *Viṣṇu Purāṇa*,[2] 3.17.39-40). The *asuras* must be at least defeated and contained, if not destroyed and eliminated, for the *devas* to live in their own self-assured self-domination. This mythological message is quite compatible with the requests of the Ṛgvedic Āryas to their gods to defeat and destroy the *dāsa varṇa*.

This Purāṇic account gives us some important clues. Neither the *devas* nor the *asuras* are evil in their original state. However, the very division between *deva* and *asura* suggests a prototypical rivalry between the two groups for domination over the entire domain. It is the element of rivalry (*spardhā*) between the two groups that naturally leads each group to view the other group with suspicion and as potentially evil. At the same time, the dilemma of the *devas* in our story is very important for our

2. See Gupta 1990.

understanding. They would like to eliminate the *asuras*, even when the *asuras* are not evil, for the simple reason that they cannot tolerate being dominated by them. However, Brahmā and Śiva have qualms about destroying the *asuras* who are not evil and are following the path of *dharma*. Viṣṇu, on the other hand, devises a scheme to push the *asuras* away from the good Vedic *dharma* and goads them into following the adhārmic non-Vedic ways of the Jainas. Now that the *asuras* are following the non-Vedic path, evil by definition, Śiva feels no guilt in destroying the *asuras*. The story points to the guilt one feels in destroying one's "good" rival. In order for the rival to be destroyed without guilt or remorse, the rival must be designated evil. He must be demonized. In the ancient Sanskrit literature, it is typically the *bhrātṛvya* "brother's son, nephew" who emerges as one's mortal enemy, because he has an equal and opposing claim to one's inheritance.

The story points to a deeper sociological message. Each group or individual has a right of survival. If individuals or groups can learn to co-exist without encroaching upon each other's domains, there is no rivalry. However, such is often not the case. It was not the case with the *devas* and the *asuras*. It was not the case with the Kauravas and the Pāṇḍavas. With desire for total domination on the part of an individual or a group, the other necessarily becomes a rival and an intruder, and must be demonized before being destroyed without remorse. In the story narrated above, Viṣṇu emerges as the true god of survival and preservation of his chosen party. In order to achieve the survival and preservation of the *devas*, Viṣṇu is willing and able to take recourse to any and all means at his disposal. It is the end that justifies the means.

This notion of the end justifying the means is illustrated on a vast scale in the great epic of *Mahābhārata*. But first a warning sounded by R.C. Zaehner about misinterpreting a text like the *Bhagavad-Gītā*. In his thought-provoking book, *Our Savage God*, Zaehner begins his Introduction with these words (Zaehner 1974: 9-10):

> It [= this book] was, I suppose, triggered off by a letter I received from an American professor which included an offprint of his, along with a typescript of an article he had written about the *Bhagavad-Gītā* which pointed out how dangerous this most highly esteemed of all the Hindu sacred books could be if literally interpreted. As witness for the prosecution he produced, among others, the sinister figure of Charles Manson who was responsible for the Sharon Tate murders which shocked the world in 1969. What was so peculiarly horrifying about these murders

> was that neither Manson nor his youthful accomplices, most of whom came from respectable middle-class homes, showed the slightest remorse at what they had done. How was this possible?

Referring to *The Family* by Ed Sanders and *Witness to Evil* by George Bishop, Zaehner points out that

> It was not only drugs that launched Charles Manson on his murderous career but also some experience of what he took to be "enlightenment" as preached by the religions of Indian origin. Could it, then, be that mystical experience or at least some types of it could lead not to a "holy indifference" but to a diabolic insensitivity which was experienced as being beyond good and evil? After all, there are plenty of texts, whether Hindu, Zen, Buddhist or Taoist, which speak of a timeless state of being which transcends good and evil, right and wrong, and all the opposites and contradictions which bedevil our human life, and it is very easy to misinterpret them.

Yes, indeed, it is very easy to misinterpret these texts. If the term *dharmayuddha*, "a lawful combat" refers to the combatants following the rules for a fair combat, then the Mahābhārata war was indeed not a *dharmayuddha*, "a lawful combat," because, in most combats, the rules of fair combat were wilfully violated, by far most frequently by the Pāṇḍavas at the instigation of Kr̥ṣṇa. On the face of it, Kr̥ṣṇa is the incarnation of God Viṣṇu, and if he violates himself or causes others to violate rules of fair battle, what kind of dhārmic message may we derive from the *Mahābhārata*? Is there another way of looking at the same situation? This is the principle that the end justifies the means. If one's end is justifiable, good, noble, then one is permitted freedom in the use of one's means. In the case of the *Mahābhārata*, the first proposition, "if one's end is dhārmically determined," is the primary motif emphasized by the text.

While we have no historical evidence to know for sure what actually happened in the Mahābhārata War and who actually said what to whom, the text of the *Mahābhārata* as we have it has a primary mythical frame of reference. The *deva*s and the *asura*s of the Vedic mythology, perpetually in conflict with each other, incarnate on earth as Pāṇḍavas ("sons" of the Vedic gods Yama, Vāyu, Indra, and the two Aśvins) and their evil cousins, the Kauravas. Viṣṇu, the classical god of survival and preservation, incarnates as Kr̥ṣṇa, also a cousin of the Pāṇḍavas. As the *deva*s and the *asura*s are sons of the same creator god Prajāpati, so too the Kauravas and the Pāṇḍavas are members of the same family. They are equal, and yet opposite. Both have a claim on the whole kingdom. The Pāṇḍavas believe, evidently rightfully, that the whole kingdom belongs to them, as it belonged to their father, king Pāṇḍu. The Kauravas believe that it rightfully belongs to them, because their father, Dhṛtarāṣṭra, was older than Pāṇḍu, and should have inherited the kingdom, which he was denied by the family because of his blindness. I do not wish to recount the whole story. However, it is clear that the author of the *Mahābhārata* is on the side of the Pāṇḍavas and believes that their claim was the lawful claim. The Pāṇḍavas, the good guys, are willing to settle for five towns, but the Kauravas will yield no territory to them. This is the basic dhārmic conflict outlined by the text.

Kṛṣṇa's role as god of preservation is very critical. It is his cosmic obligation to ensure that the world will be ruled by the righteous, and not by the unrighteous. That sounds fair as an ideal expectation from god. As part of that cosmic, divine obligation, Kṛṣṇa must make sure that the righteous Pāṇḍavas win the battle, and that the earth is no longer ruled by the evil Kauravas. As this divine obligation plays out on the battlefield of Kurukṣetra, it receives a temporary setback when Arjuna is overwhelmed by a sense of the impending slaughter of immense proportion and declines to proceed with the combat. Let us listen to the reasons given by Arjuna for not fighting:

> Filled with infinite pity, desponding, this he said: Having seen this, my own people, O Kṛṣṇa, desiring to fight, approaching (*BG* 1.28), my limbs sink down and my mouth dries up, and my body trembles, and my hair stands on end (*BG* 1.29). Gāṇḍīva, my bow, falls from my hand, and my skin burns, and I am unable to remain as I am, and my mind seems to ramble (*BG* 1.30). And I perceive inauspicious omens, O Kṛṣṇa, and I foresee misfortune in destroying my own people in battle (*BG* 1.31). Teachers, fathers, sons, and also grandfathers, maternal uncles, fathers-in-law, grandsons, brothers-in-law, thus kinsmen (*BG* 1.34). I do not desire to kill them who are bent on killing, O Slayer of Madhu, even for the sovereignty of the three worlds, how then for the earth (*BG* 1.35)? What joy to us should it be to strike down the sons of Dhṛtarāṣṭra, O agitator of men? Evil thus should cling to us having killed these aggressors (*BG* 1.36). Therefore we are not justified in killing the sons of Dhṛtarāṣṭra, our own kinsmen. How, having killed our own people, should we be happy, O Kṛṣṇa (*BG* 1.37)? Even if they do not perceive, those whose thoughts are overpowered by greed, the wrong caused by destruction of family, and the crime of treachery to friend (*BG* 1.38). Why should we not know enough to turn back, through discernment, from this evil, the wrong caused by destruction of family, O agitator of men (*BG* 1.39)? Alas! Alas! We are resolved to do a great evil, which is to be

> intent on killing our own people, through greed for royal pleasures (*BG* 1.45). If the armed sons of Dhṛtarāṣṭra should kill me in battle, while I was unresisting and unarmed, this would be to me a greater happiness (*BG* 1.46). Thus having spoken, in battle, Arjuna sat down upon the seat of the chariot, throwing down both arrow and bow, with a heart overcome by sorrow (*BG* 1.47).

Arjuna does not know at this point in the story that Kṛṣṇa is god. He does not consult him before formulating his decision not to fight. One may say that he has made his decision not to fight of his free will. Is this a decision of a wise man, or that of an ignorant man? If we look at Kṛṣṇa's response, we get the answer that the *Bhagavad-Gītā* would like us to adopt:

> The Blessed Lord spoke: Whence this timidity of thine, come to thee in time of danger, not acceptable in an Aryan, not leading to heaven, causing disgrace, O Arjuna — *BG* 2.2
>
> Do not become a coward, son of Pṛthā, this, in thee, is not suitable. Abandoning base faint heartedness, stand up! O Scorcher of the Foe. — *BG* 2.3
>
> Thou hast mourned the not-to-be-mourned and yet thou speakest words as if with wisdom; for the dead and for the not dead, the *paṇḍit*s do not mourn. — *BG* 2.11

As far as Kṛṣṇa, as god, is concerned, Arjuna's ignorant free will has landed him into false wisdom. What is true wisdom, then? "For the dead and for the not dead, the *paṇḍit*s do not mourn." This is indeed followed by verses explaining that the real soul of man is eternal and cannot die even when the body must die. No one can prevent the death of the body, and no one can kill the eternal soul. After a long explication of this doctrine, Kṛṣṇa concludes with the following words:

> These bodies inhabited by the eternal, the indestructible, the immeasurable embodied one, are said to come to an end. Therefore Fight, Descendant of Bharata. — *BG* 2.18

This is indeed a problematic argument, and no wonder R.C. Zaehner and others were worried about the *Bhagavad-Gītā* being misunderstood by murderers like Charles Manson. Professor Zaehner wonders that we can nod approval at the Zen doctrine of "all is one," Heraclitus' "justice is strife," the Scripture's "Do not fear those who kill the body," or the *Kaṭha Upaniṣad*, "The killer does not kill and the killed is not killed" — and yet express surprise and revulsion at the Manson murders. Zaehner contends that we have not so much *mis*-interpreted Eastern and Western classics as we have *under*-interpreted them (text on the cover of Zaehner's book *Our Savage God*). Zaehner argues:

> This is not a joking matter. There is no manner of harm in the innocent frolics of the Hare Kṛṣṇa boys and girls: they are simply imitating their god who, they think, plays games with them as Kṛṣṇa himself did with the milkmaids; but His Divine Grace Bhaktivedanta Swami would do well to remind them that the same God is the terrible God of Time who will devour you in the end whether you like it or not.
>
> — Zaehner 1974: 295

I do believe that Zaehner has *under*-interpreted the *Bhagavad-Gītā*. It is true that the argument in *BG* 2.18 cited above is logically inconsistent and insufficient. It is like saying: "Since the grass is green, therefore snow must be white." Even if the souls are eternal and bodies are perishable, it may follow that one should not mourn the death of a body, But It Does Not Follow That One Should Therefore Go and Kill those Bodies in Battle. Zaehner fails to point out that Arjuna is not convinced by this argument, and clearly it takes a lot more effort and many qualitatively different arguments on the part of Kṛṣṇa to bring Arjuna around. But this argument is not one of those. The best arguments as to why Arjuna must go and fight do not consist of the fact that souls are eternal. They consist of the explanation of why god incarnates on earth from time to time:

> Whenever a decrease of righteousness occurs, O descendant of Bharata, and there is a rising up of unrighteousness, then I give forth myself, for the protection of the good and the destruction of evil doers; for the sake of establishing righteousness, I come into being from age to age.
>
> — *BG* 4.7-8

Man is an incarnation of god, and god is placing his own example and his own purposes before man to be emulated by man. There is supposed to be a moral purpose to Arjuna's battle. By declining to fight a dhārmically necessary battle, Arjuna would be defeating the divine purpose in his very existence. His battle has a larger purpose than just killing his enemies and regaining his kingdom. That purpose is clearly stated as "the protection of the good and the destruction of the evil doers." This is god's plan for man, and to the extent man carries out this moral purpose in his battle against evil, the violence involved in the battle itself need not deter one's participation in such a just and necessary battle. This seems to be the message of the *Bhagavad-Gītā*, and it should not be difficult to see how the understanding of Charles Manson is not what was intended by the text.

However, there is a dilemma as to the question of one's free will. It was Arjuna's initial decision not to fight the battle that was born out of his own free will, and yet, at least for the author of the *Bhagavad-Gītā*, it turned out to be the free will of an ignorant man, ignorant of god and his purposes. What happens at the end of the *Bhagavad-Gītā* is most interesting. In the 18th chapter of the *Bhagavad-Gītā*, Kṛṣṇa is making his closing arguments. He has already shown his cosmic form to Arjuna, who is already convinced of Kṛṣṇa's divinity. Arjuna that emerges from his experience of Kṛṣṇa's cosmic godhood is a person completely transformed by that experience. But Kṛṣṇa is taking no chances. In his stick and carrot approach, he says to Arjuna:

> Thinking of Me, thou shalt pass over all difficulties, through my grace; but if, through egotism, though wilt not listen, then thou shalt perish.
>
> — *BG* 18.58

> If, taking refuge in egotism, thou thinkest "I shall not fight," thus, vain will be this, thy resolve. Thine own nature will command thee.
>
> — *BG* 18.59

> The Lord abides in the heart of all beings, Arjuna, causing all beings to move by His incomprehensible power, as if fixed on a machine.
>
> — *BG* 18.61

> Thus to thee by Me has been expounded the knowledge that is more secret than the secret. Having reflected on this fully, do as thou desirest.
>
> — *BG* 18.63

On the face of it, it may seem that god is returning to man his free will: "Do thou as thou desirest." But if man were to exercise his free will, contrary to god's will, then god says: "thou shalt perish." This message is not lost on Arjuna, who has by this time completely surrendered himself to god. In spite of Kṛṣṇa's words, "do as thou desirest," Arjuna responds:

> Delusion is lost and wisdom gained, through thy grace, by me, O unchanging one. I stand with doubt dispelled. I shall do thy command.
>
> — *BG* 18.73

Certainly, it seems to me that the *Bhagavad-Gītā* wants us to believe that the wise use of one's free will is to opt to carry out the will of god, because any attempt to do contrary will be in vain. What sort of freedom is this? Is this the freedom of a slave to do what his master asks him to do?

Did Arjuna have any freedom? Do we have any freedom? This is an important question. The commentaries on the *Bhagavad-Gītā* would like us to believe that we do have the freedom to accept or not to accept god's words. Arjuna listens to Kṛṣṇa's words and chooses to accept and follow them. But Dhṛtarāṣṭra who also listens to Kṛṣṇa's words through the reportage of Sañjaya remains unswayed by them. So, the *Mahābhārata* does inform us that we do have a choice to make. Either we go with Arjuna, or we go with Dhṛtarāṣṭra. That is our choice. So there is scope for free will after all.

The other arena where we have free will is to not just listen to the words of a scriptural text in a slavish way, but to use our god-given intelligence to make sense of the scriptures within a bigger context of one's common sense, rationality, and a personal sense of what is right. The meaning does not reside in the words of the text. Each reader recreates it for himself or herself in light of his or her total awareness and understanding. The Indian tradition is not unaware of the fact that texts are diverse and interpretations contradict each other. One of the commonly cited verse (of unclear origin) says:

vedāḥ pramāṇaṁ, śrutayo vibhinnāḥ
naiko munir yasya vacaḥ pramāṇam |

dharmasya tattvaṁ nihitaṁ guhāyāṁ
mahājano yena gataḥ sa panthāḥ | |

> The Vedas are said to be authoritative, but Vedic statements are diverse. There is not a single sage whose words can be authoritative [because sages contradict each other]. The true secret of righteousness is hidden in a cave. [Therefore], what the leading people follow is the path [to be followed].

There is an obligation for every person to make sense of his or her received religious tradition. If one chooses to act simply as a follower and give up one's prerogative to think for oneself, even then one has the obligation to choose who to follow and how far to go in following one's chosen leader. To the extent one abdicates this responsibility and follows someone else blindly, one is perhaps acting in an irresponsible way. If we were to ask Arjuna why he decided to follow Kṛṣṇa, there would be some interesting answers. Initially, Kṛṣṇa is merely his relative and friend. Ultimately, Arjuna comes to recognize Kṛṣṇa as god. However, if we look at the questions asked by Arjuna from time to time, it is clear that Arjuna is not walking into a blind alley. He uses his freedom to question Kṛṣṇa, raises doubts about answers given by him, and finally asks for an experiential verification of his claim to godhood. It is Arjuna's responsibility to ensure that the person he has chosen to follow is indeed who he says he is. He has to make sure that Kṛṣṇa is god rather than a demon in disguise. It has to be the responsibility of Arjuna to make that choice in a conscious knowledgeable way.

In the story of the *Mahābhārata*, the plot may inform us that Kṛṣṇa sent a reluctant Arjuna back into the battle. What moral message does the *Mahābhārata* impart to us? That depends on what baggage we bring with us when we read the *Mahābhārata*. For example, the whole context of war and the idea of sending Arjuna back to fight the battle was irrelevant to the understanding of the great Śaṅkarācārya. For him, the *Bhagavad-Gītā* begins with Arjuna's delusion and sorrow (*śokamohau*) and ends with the removal of that delusion and sorrow. Whatever else Arjuna does is not part of the message of the *Bhagavad-Gītā* for Śaṅkarācārya. This is how the relevance of the *Mahābhārata* appears to a brāhmaṇa ascetic. Consider the case of Mahatma Gandhi. In his autobiography, Gandhi says:

> About the same time I met a good Christian from Manchester in a vegetarian boarding house. He talked to me about Christianity. . . . He said, "Do please read the Bible." I began reading it, but could not possibly read through the Old Testament. . . . But the New Testament produced a different impression, especially the Sermon on the Mount which went straight to my heart. I compared it with the *Gītā*. The verses, "But I say unto you, that ye resist not evil: but whosoever shall smite thee on thy right cheek, turn to him the other also," delighted me beyond measure. My young mind tried to unify the teaching of the *Gītā*, the Light of Asia and the Sermon on the Mount. That renunciation was the highest form of religion appealed to me greatly. — Gandhi 1951: 41-43

This vividly gives us the context in which Gandhi was reading the *Bhagavad-Gītā*. He was not going to allow the massive description of the gory war in the *Mahābhārata* to sway his mind. Non-violence must remain the goal, even at the cost of reading the *Bhagavad-Gītā* allegorically. In his *Anāsaktiyoga* (speech on 24 June 1929), Gandhi says:

> Even in 1888-89, when I first became acquainted with the *Gītā*, I felt that it was not a historical work, but that, under the guise of physical warfare, it described the duel that perpetually went on in the hearts of the mankind. . . . This preliminary intuition became more confirmed on a closer study of religion and the *Gītā*. A study of the *Mahābhārata* gave it added confirmation. I do not regard the *Mahābhārata* as a historical work in the accepted sense. . . . The persons therein described may be historical, but the author of the *Mahābhārata* has used them merely to drive home his religious theme.

> The author of the *Mahābhārata* has not established the necessity of physical warfare; on the contrary, he has proved its futility. He has made the victors shed tears of sorrow and repentance, and has left them nothing but a legacy of misery.
> — Desai 1946: 123-24

On the other hand, Lokamanya B.G. Tilak took a more literalist approach to the *Bhagavad-Gītā*. For him, the purpose of the *Bhagavad-Gītā* is not just to remove the delusion and sorrow in Arjuna's mind, but it must include, first and foremost, the need to send him back to fight. This fight must be fought in order to save the dhārmic order, even if it involves violence in the process. Tilak uses this argument to justify the use of violence against the British colonial rule, if necessary, as part of what he saw as the legitimate and just struggle for freedom. Inspired by Tilak, several nationalist young men carried out attacks on British officials, and when sentenced to death, proudly and calmly walked to the gallows with copies of the *Bhagavad-Gītā* in their hands.

The religious texts do not automatically produce decisive messages for us by themselves. And even if they were to contain some intrinsic messages, a Mahatma Gandhi, with a free mind of his own, was not willing to cast his lot with Arjuna and engage in violence. V.R. Shinde, a leader of the untouchables, reported what Tilak said: "If a God were to tolerate untouchability, I would not recognize him as God at all" (Bapat 1925: 204). It is such personalities in the Hindu tradition that show the independence left to individuals in making sense of their own religious traditions while responding to their contemporary and emerging circumstances. Religious understandings are not stagnant waters. They are rather like flowing rivers that change their course depending upon the lay of the land.

References

Acharya, Narayan R. (ed.) (1948), *Brahmasūtrabhāṣya of Śaṅkara*, 3rd edn., Bombay: Nirnaya Sagar Press.

Bapat, S.V. (ed.) (1925), *Lokamānya Ṭiḷak yāñcyā Āṭhavaṇī va Ākhyāyikā*, vol. 2, Pune: Keśava Rāvajī Gondhaḷekar.

Desai, Mahadev (ed.) (1946), *The Gospel of Selfless Action or the Gītā according to Gandhi*, Ahmedabad: Navajivan Publishing House.

Gandhi, Mohandas K. (1951), *Autobiography* (abridged), Bombay: Hind Kitabs Limited.

Gupta, Munilal (ed. tr.) (1990), "Viṣṇupurāṇa," in *Śrī Banārasīdevī Cūḍīvāla Dharmagranthamālā*, no. 1. Gorakhpur: Gita Press.

Mackie, J. (1971), "Evil and Omnipotence," in *The Philosophy of Religion*, ed. Basil Mitchell, London: Oxford University Press.

Pandeya, Ramateja S. (ed.) (1963), *Śivamahāpurāṇa*, Banaras: Paṇḍita Pustakālaya.

Russell, Bertrand (1957), *Why I am not a Christian, and Other Essays on Religion and Related Subjects*, ed. Paul Edwards, New York: Simon and Schuster.

van Buitenen, J.A.B. (tr.) (1968), *Rāmānuja on the Bhagavadgītā*, Delhi: Motilal Banarsidass.

Zaehner, Robert C. (1974), *Our Savage God*, New York: Sheed and Ward.

22

The Role of Government Education in the Lives of Females in Rural Chhattisgarh

*Ramdas Lamb**

I FIRST had the good fortune to meet Professor T.S. Rukmani when she was a speaker at the University of Hawai'i East West Philosophers' Conference in 2000. After listening to a captivating discussion by her, I invited her to speak in a UH mysticism course I was teaching at the time. Her wisdom and graciousness left an indelible impression on me and many of the students. Since that time, I have come to consider her as one of my academic *gurus* and inspirations. Her ability to blend traditional Indian and Western approaches to understanding philosophy and life is a gift she has bestowed on the academic community over the years. I have also come to utilize her as an inspirational example and role model for the rural Indian students with whom I have been working for the last three decades. During that time, one of the issues on which I have focused has been the way contemporary rural education impacts females from poor, especially Scheduled Caste (SC) families in the way they conceive themselves and their relationships to their families, their traditional culture, Hinduism, and the caste-based society in which they live.

Religious and cultural beliefs and practices are integral to the lives of most Hindus, especially the rural poor. Similar to what is found in many societies, those at the bottom of the socio-economic ladder are usually the ones who depend most on the divine and on their religious traditions for security, stability, and a sense of meaning in their lives. Integral to these is a Hindu concept known as *dharma*. The term has had slight variations of meaning throughout the millennia, but its collective roots

---

* Department of Religion, University of Hawai'i at Manoa

are found in common values from all the spiritual and religious traditions of India. Because it is grounded in a deeply personal and inner understanding of one's own moral being and duties as an individual, it can transcend limited external categories in its application. At the same time these duties and responsibilities are embedded in a social order and network as they relate to the existing value system of the culture and society in which people live. *Dharma*, then, has both a personal and individual dimension as well as social and relational one. For the purpose of this study, the concept of *dharma* will be used as it applies to the lives of rural Hindu girls and women. This essay will look at the development of academic education in government schools in the rural areas of the central Indian state of Chhattisgarh, what role it plays in the life of low-caste and poor female students, and how it affects their traditional understanding of and relationship to religion and *dharma* in the changing world in which they live. This is important since the way the current generation of youth relates to their religious and cultural traditions can reveal much about the future of both traditional *dharma* and society in India.[1]

The first section of the essay will address issues surrounding rural education in the Chhattisgarh region prior to its becoming a separate state (November, 2000): the second will look at the educational changes that have occurred from its statehood to present day; the third will discuss the current situation and the problems girls face in getting a quality education that is relevant to their rural lives and their understanding of *dharma*. The definitions provided here are for clarification purposes. The term "Scheduled Caste" ("SC" or "Anusucit Jāti") is the government designation for those who were previously labelled as "Untouchable" in the traditional social hierarchy. Today, when speaking specifically of Hindus from that caste group, the term "Harijan" is also one with which many in the region self-identify, while a significant number of those who are not Hindu use "Dalit" on occasion instead. However, nearly three-quarters of the SCs in rural Chhattisgarh belong to the Satnāmī sub-caste (*jāti*), as have been most of the rural students with whom I worked and whom I have studied. Since they have been the primary focus of my research and they generally prefer their *jāti* name for identity, "SC" and "Satnāmī" will be the caste and sub-caste labels most used herein.

---

1. Although there is a large portion of the population of Chhattisgarh that is composed of STs who also have limited education, the research from which this study is drawn has been primarily limited to SC female students.

Education from the British to Statehood

The British government introduced academic education to India and promoted it while the country was a part of its empire. Its focus, however, was the Westernization and indoctrination of urban upper-caste individuals to act as bureaucrats and government servants as well as intermediaries between the colonial government and the masses. The purpose of education was essentially to train people in ways that would directly benefit the government. Education for individual development and growth was not seen as relevant and rural education was largely ignored as having minimal functional value. The British did come to realize that the urban Indian females had great intellectual potential, and by the mid-1800s there were girls' schools all over India. Yet, even those established by Indians utilized the Western educational model and focused on upper-caste urban students. Traditional methods of learning were not seen to have substantive worth and were essentially ignored. After gaining Independence in 1947, the Indian government began to increase and expand the focus on education in its words and rules, although monetary allocations clearly fell short of the rhetoric. The methodologies adopted remained Western in style and primarily relevant to urban youth, while ignoring most rural lifestyles and needs. By the mid-1950s, laws were enacted to provide various forms of monetary assistance to encourage at least a rudimentary education for SC and ST (Scheduled Tribe) girls, most of whom lived in villages. However, due to the physical and bureaucratic chasm between the political centres of Delhi, the various state capitals where policies were being made, and the villages where most of the SCs and STs reside, a significant portion of what was allotted for rural schools and students never seemed to reach its expressed destination. Additionally, state level officials whose task it was to determine what policies were given attention, what forms of educational assistance were ultimately provided, and what schools received that assistance have always tended to see the needs in the cities where they reside as having greater priority, and this has typically resulted in rural needs being treated as of secondary importance. As a consequence, the per capita spending by both central and state governments was overwhelmingly for the benefit of urban students. This was the case for the bulk of the programmes specifically targeting girls and SC students as well.

From the mid-1950s until November 2000, Chhattisgarh constituted the eastern portion of the state of Madhya Pradesh (MP). It contained the highest percentage of rural people (close to 80 per cent), low-castes, tribes, and illiteracy of all the regions in the state. Nevertheless, the MP government's emphasis was, like with the British and the central governments, on urban education. Rural schools continued to be given relatively little attention, especially in Chhattisgarh, so they had to function with a bare bones budget. Students had to either purchase their own books or go without; they were mandated to wear uniforms (costing as much as a week's wages) in order to attend school; and they had to pay tuition fee as well. Although monetary assistance was technically available, families would typically have to pay all these costs up front with the hope that government reimbursement would come sometime during the academic year. Since most rural poor have no bank accounts or any significant amount of cash on hand, the combination of these costs was more than many could afford. Consequently, a large percentage of children from poorer families simply never went to school. At best, some families might send a son to school for a primary education, but even they would likely stop attending after fifth or sixth grade.

Money was not the only obstacle that limited the participation of Satnāmī girls. Caste prejudice was a widely prevalent factor as well. While most caste Hindu teachers did not bring prejudice into the classroom, some did, and the general environment in the schools clearly reflected the existing social hierarchy and the low status afforded to Satnāmīs. Most found a less than supportive environment that was not at all conducive to learning, so they did not focus on what they were being taught and told. This fed a typical assumption by many in the educational system that SC students were not as intelligent as caste Hindu students and therefore less likely to succeed. Ample research done on the dynamics of teaching reveals that such preconceived notions by teachers have a strong effect on the ability of students viewed as inferior, to be treated equally or to succeed. In addition, when lunch would be served at some rural schools, SC students would have to sit separate from others and were fed last. Tales of various forms of outright prejudice were frequently heard within their communities and they functioned to further discourage SC parents from sending their children to school. In such situations, whenever any condition arises that discourages education, girls are generally the first to be its victims.

Another disincentive for SC girls to go to school under the MP government was the overall lack of rural SC teachers anywhere in the state, except in some rural primary schools. Even amongst them, there were almost no females. Although some of the more intellectually driven

SC teachers had received the education necessary to teach higher grades, few were ever able to move up in the system. Existing caste prejudices, the cost of higher education, and the amount of monetary bribe that was often necessary to secure a position all functioned to keep most away from even considering entry into the process. As a consequence, only a very small number of SC teachers had higher educational aspirations. For SC youth, then, there were very few role models within the system to inspire them, and even fewer educated family members.

For those SC students who did continue in school and reached higher secondary grades (roughly equivalent to high school in the US), prejudice became a more apparent part of their academic experiences. Some would be suspected of cheating if they did well, for no other reason than their caste status. Even when their accomplishments were accepted, teachers might attempt to dissuade them from thoughts of going to college or into teaching, explaining to them the difficulties and expenses involved. Others would straightforward make statements to the effect that people of "your community (i.e. sub-caste)" do not possess the required abilities and funding sources for such pursuits. In interviews over the years I have conducted with teachers, many of those who acknowledged saying such things claimed that they were simply "warning" SC and other Satnāmī students of the difficulties of seeking further education and therefore providing an honest assessment of the situation so that such students would not waste their time and money attempting something at which they would likely fail.[2] Thus, very few SCs even considered college or teaching as within their realm of possibility. The impression left in the minds of many was that there was no real place for them in government education, which was meant for caste Hindus by caste Hindus.

This belief seemed to be validated when the caste Hindu leaders in at least several villages in the region with significant SC populations prevented planned government schools from being built in their villages while they sent their own children to schools in nearby towns or larger villages. Other leaders would make it difficult if not impossible for SC students get the necessary paperwork to be able to register in existing schools. As a consequence, when I first visited rural Chhattisgarh in the 1970s, there was a significant number of Satnāmī youth who were not attending school or who had dropped out by sixth grade, the highest

2. I began including interviews with teachers of various castes in the region as a part of my overall research on education in the mid-1980s. A variety of sentiments similar to those here were fairly apparent and commonplace among a significant number of caste Hindu teachers at the time.

grade level in most village schools at the time. Only about 30 per cent of Satnāmī boys and about 15 per cent of Satnāmī girls attended school with any regularity, while the numbers of caste Hindu youth attending schools in the region were more than double that. The more I got to know members of the Satnāmī community, the more it became apparent that there was a great deal of untapped potential and a desire for education among the youth, but the lack of faith and opportunity in the existing educational system prevented it from being realized.

Another factor that limited educational possibilities and was quite prevalent until after Chhattisgarh statehood was the lack of experienced teachers in rural schools. Similar to what has happened in many countries including America, new and inexperienced teachers are usually placed in rural or outlying schools. As soon as they gain seniority or some clout, many seek a school closer to their homes or urban schools where teaching materials are more readily available and where students tend to be more in tune with the methods of education the teachers have learned. This resulted in a relative lack of experienced teachers in many rural schools, since most sought to move as soon as they got the opportunity. This also led to very little consistency of teachers and teaching in rural schools in comparison to urban schools.

Statehood to Present Day

When Chhattisgarh became its own state in November 2000, most of the rural schools still only went as high as fifth or sixth grade, trailed far behind their urban counterparts in funding and supplies, remained largely understaffed, had very few female or SC teachers, and continued to attract only a small percentage of Satnāmī youth. Fortunately, many in the new state government understood some of the more obvious problems and the need for good rural schools, and they began to overhaul the policies and practices of the previous state government. In 2001, the legislature instituted a new approach to education with rural schools as one of the primary areas of focus. It showed genuine interest in correcting the problems of the past, but its understanding of the situation was limited by the information it received from rural teachers. The state had put forth a goal of all school-aged girls becoming registered for school, and it assigned teachers the task of collecting the necessary data for tracking progress toward this end. To be done properly, teachers would have to visit all the households in the villages served by their particular school. Due to time, caste restrictions and prejudices, and other restraints, however, a significant percentage of teachers never actually performed the task. Instead, they might simply ask existing female students if they had any friends their age not in school. Even if names were given, many teachers did little more than tell their students to inform the friends they were supposed to register for school. Rarely was there sufficient follow-up, which would have included meeting with the girls' parents to try to encourage the family to send their daughters to school. Yet, principals had to submit reports of their school's progress in meeting the government's goal of full participation of girls in attending school. The route many principals found easiest to take was to provide the government with an inflated percentage figure to a level that would minimize bureaucratic interference or inquiry. The situation continues to the present day. Although the state government's estimates of school-aged girls attendance in urban areas may be relatively accurate, it still largely overestimates the number of rural girls in school. This is especially the case with respect to SC and ST girls, less than half of whom attend with any regularity in many areas.

In attempting to get all SC and ST female students in school, a variety of government programmes have been instituted. Included in those introduced since the statehood are funds to provide girls with free tuition and books up to the tenth grade. In addition, an annual monetary stipend of Rs. 250-500[3] is given to those registered in first through eighth grade, while those in higher secondary school receive Rs. 500-750. In both situations, the money is given near the end of the school year with the actual amount supposedly based on the percentage of school attendance. Lack of accurate record-keeping by many teachers results in "favoured" students tending to receive full allotments, while others may not. Several years ago, an additional Rs. 500 was made available to girls from families who do "unclean jobs," such as street sweepers or those who deal with dead bodies, animal or human. Since 2009, SC and ST students are given free tuition, although many end up having to pay "extra charges" that local village councils have imposed in order to be allowed to attend. While the government funding programmes do inspire more Satnāmī parents to register their daughters, it does not guarantee that those registered will actually attend school on any regular basis. Some girls will register in order to be in line for the money but not actually start going until well into the school year, knowing that record-keeping is haphazard at best.

3. At the time of writing this (Fall, 2010), the monetary exchange rate for US $1 is approximately Rs. 45.

Since statehood, the Chhattisgarh government has also taken steps to increase the number of SC and ST teachers in rural schools, both to meet central government fixed quotas on hiring and also so that they can serve as role models and inspire more participation in schools by students from their respective communities. At the time it became a state, approximately 10 per cent of the teachers were Satnāmī, about half their percentage in the overall population, and almost all were male and confined to teaching in primary schools. The new government began to change the situation by actively seeking out Satnāmīs, other SCs, and females to become teachers. The numbers gradually began to grow as more and more gained the requisite education. Currently, the percentage of rural female Satnāmī teachers has risen to nearly 16 per cent, and the overall number of female teachers in the state is nearly 40 per cent.[4] This has created an environment where more and more female Satnāmī students have role models they can look up to for inspiration. While the percentage of Satnāmī girls who attend school regularly is still not more than half of those who are of school-age, the percentage of those who are in school and are now considering teaching as a career has increased significantly. Nevertheless, there are still obstacles that limit many from regularly attending school, and until these are minimized the percentage of girls who do attend will likely stay close to the current levels. In fact, there are signs that the percentage may even go down somewhat.

The lack of any significant increase in regular school attendance during the last few years can be traced to several factors. One of the most obvious is that many SC families still know little or nothing about the current government cash assistance for their daughters. Teachers have been given the task of informing qualified students of monies available to them, but most have not stayed current with rules, guidelines, and availability of funds. Also, until the last few years, the vast majority of the teachers in the region have been from upper-caste families, and many have not been happy about the prospect of SC and ST females being given special treatment over boys or students from their own caste. This situation has possibly helped facilitate the lack of sufficient information about assistance being made available to students. Even when SC and ST students learn about available money, they have to travel to a nearby town to receive it from a designated bank. On occasion, they get turned away for various reasons, such as not having proper paper-work, not having the correct

4. A majority of the remaining female teachers are from ST and are hired to teach in the various tribal schools that the state is pushing to have built.

signatures from teachers, showing up at the wrong time, etc. By the time they return, which might be a week or so later, they may be told that it is too late to receive the money. On more than a few occasions when the alloted funds were not provided, some have also been told they still have to sign that they received the money or their names will be permanently struck off from the list of recipients for future payments.

All Teachers are not Equal

There is no shortage of individuals in Chhattisgarh who are qualified to teach. For many, the profession is a career choice borne out of a genuine desire to help improve the lives of their community through education. For others, it is little more than a way to secure government employment that offers a secure position, relatively good pay, the ability to do relatively minimal work, and a good pension. However, the aggregate (combination of both legal and illegal) costs involved in becoming a government school teacher is extremely difficult for all but those who are most determined and who have access to sufficient monetary resources. Those who do extremely well in entrance exams can usually get admitted without a bribe but still have to pay for room and board, books, exams, and whatever other expenses arise. The costs even at a small town college for the two years it takes to become qualified to teach primary school can be as high as Rs. 10,000 in addition to any room and board costs, which can add an additional Rs. 20,000 to the bill. For the three years required to become a higher secondary school teacher, the overall expenses today get as high as Rs. 25,000, independent of any additional room and board expenses. After all this, at least 20 per cent of primary school teachers currently have to pay a bribe of Rs. 50,000-75,000 to actually secure a position, while at least 25 per cent of higher secondary school teachers currently working have had to pay twice that amount for their jobs. The aggregate cost to get a teaching degree and position is far beyond what the vast majority of rural Satnāmīs can afford. It must be acknowledged here that bribes have become necessary to secure almost any form of government employment in the region today. If one wants to enter one of the more lucrative fields like medicine, engineering, or law, the aggregate costs for the requisite education and securing of employment can be more than two million rupees (approximately $45,000 at current rates). Less than 2 per cent of Satnāmīs can even dream about securing such a job. Within this environment, only those considered wealthy by village standards will seriously consider supporting a daughter's wish to pursue higher education. Even they would rather spend the money on a son, who will remain with the family after marriage, while the daughter will become a part of her husband's family.

Government mandated syllabus and curriculum for schools also serve as disincentives for girls. These are provided by the state government and are expected to be followed closely. Yet, because they are created for urban schools and urban life, they do not take into consideration the realities of village existence, the local farming calendar, or rural life. Since most politicians who enact and oversee the implementation of education laws have an upper caste, upper class, urban background and world experience, they have little or no understanding of village life, nor can they empathize with the kind of problems that villagers, low-castes, and female students face in obtaining quality education. The many good teachers who want to adapt to the educational process to meet the needs of their students' lives are usually hampered by regulations and by officials who have a difficult time allowing anything that is not "by the book." If teachers become too "creative" in their approach, they are likely to raise the ire of an official and will likely be transferred to a different school. As a result, it is not uncommon to find an inordinate number of teachers who have simply lost interest in their vocation and now just pass the time waiting for retirement.

For this and other reasons, as many as 25 per cent of rural teachers are absent on a regular basis in some schools, and it can even reach above 50 per cent in some schools. Situations like this are most often found where principals or district administrators are in the habit of accepting bribes from teachers. In exchange, the latter are able to miss school almost whenever they wish and are not held accountable. As an example, a teacher in one of the schools not far from my adopted village has missed nearly all his classes for the last two years. Due to his political connections and payoffs, he has not been fired, nor can the school hire someone to replace him. As a consequence, students in far too many classes get a partial education at best, and a significant number never know when or if any of their teachers will show up on any given day. Without regularity in teacher attendance, there is a lack of adult supervision as well, and it is not uncommon for village mothers to become reticent about sending their post-pubescent daughters into such a situation for a variety of reasons, especially since higher secondary schools can be as many as fifteen kilometres. away from a student's home village.

Dharma, Traditional Education, and the Academic Curriculum

Whenever there is discussion about education in academia today, the focus is almost always on that which occurs in institutions that heavily rely on methods commonly found in the Western style schools. Traditional forms of education that have predated academic learning in every culture throughout history are often seen as inferior relative to contemporary needs. Yet, understanding the difference between the academic and traditional methods helps one to understand some of the challenges that confront rural girls and their families with regard to the girls' participation in government schools. Among these challenges, two seem to be the most significant. The first is the predominance of the Western model of education in which each student learns as an individual rather than collectively. The second is the avoidance of discussing any aspect of traditional culture and values that may be considered "religious."

Traditional education for village youth in India has long centred around the home and family for girls and various aspects of farming for boys. By the time children would typically reach about six years of age, they would begin the process of learning chores and tasks that they would likely have to know and use throughout their lives. The traditional learning processes for boys and girls in the region were, and still are, quite different. Young boys learn from their fathers, uncles, or older brothers how to perform farm chores, whether on their own family's own land or as share croppers or farm labourers on others' land. They watch as the older males undertake various farm-related activities, then are expected to attempt the same themselves, starting with the more simple tasks and progressing to the more physically difficult and time-consuming projects. They typically work alone although in the proximity of other males. For the most part, whatever conversation that occurs is related to the tasks at hand. The boys' success is generally rated on their ability to satisfactorily accomplish the tasks they undertake. Girls, on the other hand, learn from the older females in their homes, such as mothers, aunts, older sisters, or grandmothers. The skills acquired are those they will need to manage a home and rear a family as wife and mother. They typically learn alongside and in conjunction with the older women as they do various chores and gain various skills. They almost always work jointly in a group environment. They often converse about the chores, but also about events occurring in the family and the village, difficulties that arise in relating to others in the family or neighbourhood, etc. The success of the girls is determined by how well they learn to function with, and relate to, the older women in performing the various chores and duties.

In the academic approach to education, the learning process is individually oriented and thus more closely reflects the way boys are taught farming. Instruction is given, and students are expected to work alone to complete their assignments. Group learning is not a common practice nor is it encouraged. This presents a definite challenge to girls who have been raised to work with others in order to accomplish tasks. Many feel unfamiliar and uncomfortable learning under those circumstances, and this may lead them to prefer home and the company of their mothers and the other females instead of school. In addition, the curriculum taught in government schools is not geared toward the obvious needs of rural girls. When academic education was first introduced into rural areas during the latter part of the British rule, most villagers saw little or no use for it, especially for girls. The curriculum seemed to lack any practical value for their youth. It was geared far more toward those who looked to have a career outside the village in business or as a government employee. Since Indian Independence, the basic curriculum has not changed substantially. Nevertheless, during the last decade or so more and more village boys have started considering careers outside the village or one involved in some field other than farming. For them, securing an academic education has become more meaningful. Even if the actual subjects taught are not necessarily seen as relevant, becoming literate, educated, and possibly obtaining a degree of some sort are all seen as valuable steps toward their career goals.

The academic curriculum continues to offer relatively little for girls. There remains nothing of substance being taught that most villagers see as necessary or even useful for a girl who is destined to be a stay-at-home wife and mother. Only those who have a definite interest in a career outside the home pursue their academic education with any resolve. The remainder who attend school may do so simply to see and spend time with friends and to be able to get a respite from home chores. Currently, the vast majority of rural girls who do go to school, especially from the poorer families, stop by or prior to the last grade available in their home village. Nowadays, this is usually either sixth or eighth grade. Within a few years, a girl will enter puberty and traditionally this makes her of marriageable age. The Indian government has banned marriage prior to the age to eighteen, but the law seldom influences rural parents' decision on when to arrange their daughter's marriage. If they are having difficulty affording to keep a daughter in school, or if she lacks interest in what they are being taught, or if no practical value is seen from her attendance, then parents are likely to pull their daughter out of school the first time a decent marriage offer is made.[5]

The second challenge that has a negative impact on girls attending school is the lack of any inclusion of *dharma* or other forms of value education, in what is being taught. After Independence, the government wanted to make sure it was impartial with respect to religion so it passed rules that prohibit the teaching of any single religion in government schools. This has come to be interpreted by many school officials and teachers as being an outright ban on any discussion of religion, or on any discussion of *dharma*, except in its criticism. While the purpose was ostensibly to restrict any form of religious proselytization in schools, the result has been, as with similar restrictions in the US, to essentially limit any form of discussion of issues associated with religion. What typically gets left out in the process is not only religious beliefs and practices, but also discussion of values, morals, and ethics.

In schools, students are told that academic education is necessary, and that it will furnish them with the knowledge they need to live and prosper in the rapidly changing world. The lack of any positive discussion of *dharma*, values, character, and associated elements leads a significant number of students to believe that these are not that important or relevant in the world of today. They are also told by more and more teachers that religious beliefs and traditional concepts of *dharma* are *rūḍhī*. This latter term literally means "conventional" or "conservative," but nowadays it carries a negative connotation as referring to something based in ignorance and narrow-mindedness. The inference is that religion and *dharma* are for the uneducated and backward. Consequently, such an attitude from teachers leads more and more students to think of their religious and cultural traditions and even their parents in a dismissive and even negative way. If traditional morality is presented as something that only old and uneducated people follow, then it is obviously not going to be something that girls are inspired to learn, and this sets up tension between what many are taught at home *versus* what they are taught in school. Mothers often complain that their daughters who attend school regularly seem

5. In Chhattisgarh, the fathers and other male family members of marriageable boys search for a potential bride. Tradition forbids girls' families from initiating any contact. Thus, girls parents who are not financially secure have a tendency to accept for their daughter any decent marriage offer that will not cost them too much. In other regions of India, it may be the girls' father who does the search.

less likely to value long-held religious and cultural traditions, tend to be less interested in helping their mothers in home chores, show less respect to their elders, and seem more interested in their physical appearances with respect to clothing, etc. In short, many mothers see government schooling as tending to make their daughters less interested in traditional *dharma* and the things that their mothers know, value, and want to teach them. When more traditional, and often poorer, parents come to understand what their daughters' are being taught and told, this becomes yet another reason to be hesitant about sending the girls to school, so many do not. The girls who do continue to attend are either from higher caste and educated families or those who have less concern with their cultural and religious traditions.

Conclusion

In the introduction to her volume entitled *Hindu Diaspora*, Professor Rukmani notes that as lifestyles and environments change, so do religious and cultural traditions (Rukmani 2001: xi). This clearly describes the process occurring with rural Satnāmīs and their daughters. Since mothers are seen as the traditional "abodes" and disseminators of *dharma* (as defined), the changes and influences that girls are being exposed to in schools will have a definite influence on the way they understand and refashion *dharma* for themselves as they grow up and become mothers. It will then become reflected in how they teach their own children. The practice of religion is more of an ongoing developmental process than simply a duplication and replication of the past. Although change is integral and expected, the rate and manner of change has increased a great deal in the last half century and especially in the last decade. Witnessing what the present generation of youth is undergoing can provide clues as to what form *dharma* will likely take as they become adults, and whether it will remain an integral part of their consciousness. As the government continues to push the present brand of academic education, it will continue to be a challenge for rural peoples to hold on to many of their cultural traditions. While the letting go of some of these is good, such as those that promote caste and gender prejudice, others serve important functions in helping provide a sense of place and security for the poor the way traditional culture and *dharma* have long done in India.

Because females are almost always more closely associated with traditional culture, its demise tends to affect them the greatest. When education does little more than challenge and denigrate existing forms as outdated without providing useful alternatives, then girls and all youth are left with few useful tools to craft the future. The inclusion of discussions about *dharma*, character, and their relevance in society would benefit students. In an article entitled "Social, Emotional, Ethical, and Academic Education" in the Harvard Educational Review, Jonathan Cohen emphasizes the view that when properly undertaken, education places a priority on social, emotional, and ethical competencies, as well as on academic learning. Character education is integral to the process (Cohen 2006: 210-13). The addition of collective learning by motivated teachers with the ability to apply the curriculum relative to the needs of the students would also help to bring about a more relevant style of education for rural girls. Finally, if government corruption could be diminished and higher education made more affordable for the masses, the number of educated females in the country would increase exponentially, as would their presence in the workforce and intellectual realms helping the country solve its many problems. With the right tools to awaken all that potential, being a village Satnāmī girl would no longer mean the stifling of intelligence, the voiceless acceptance of an inferior social status, and the likelihood of remaining poor. When quality education becomes available at the village level, it will provide poor students, both girls and boys, creative ways of negotiating their relationship to the changing society and world in which they live. In addition, there will be opportunities for many rural girls to follow in the footsteps of Prof. Rukmani in adding rich and unique insight to a world often in need of it.

References

Cohen, Jonathan (2006), "Social, Emotional, Ethical, and Academic Education: Creating a Climate for Learning, Participation in Democracy and Well-Being," in *Harvard Educational Review*, vol. 76, no. 2, pp. 201-37.

Johnson, Anna D. (2006), "The Effects of Early Education on Children in Poverty," in *Education and Poverty in an International Context*, Society for International Education, pp. 14-18.

Rukmani, Trichur S. (ed.) (2001), *Hindu Diaspora*, Delhi: Munshiram Manoharlal.

23

On Being Hindu

Some Autobiographical Reflections

*Acharya Vidyasagar V.V. Raman**

My Parental Roots

LIKE most Hindus, I am a Hindu because both my parents were, and as far as I can tell, my grandparents and their parents too. In fact, they were all practising Tamil brāhmaṇas of the Iyer sub-division: to be more exact, of the *Aṣṭasahasram* variety. Although I learnt this from my father, I gained a deeper historical perspective on this and other matters from an English book (Thurston and Rangachari 1909). I mention this fact explicitly because many Neo-Hindus who have gathered much knowledge and information about their tradition from the Western scholars seldom acknowledge how they themselves have also benefited from the labours of Western Indologists about whom they have some legitimate generic grievances.

Traditionally, the only way one became a Hindu, more exactly, a brāhmaṇa, kṣatriya, vaiśya, or śūdra, was by virtue of one's birth and lineage. As luck or *karma* or whatever unfathomable determining factor would have it, I was born into a brāhmaṇa family, which cast me as a Brāhmin, with the associated advantages.

Today, anyone who wishes to become a Hindu is welcome. There are quite a few who do this through the Ārya Samāj, the Ramakrishna Mission, or the ISKCON, for example. Some of them even become *ācārya*s who preach and spread the religion. Most converts to Hinduism are from the Christian or Jewish faith. They embrace Hinduism voluntarily and wholeheartedly, with few rituals and no monetary or other inducements. They are not assigned a caste: thus at a great advantage, devoid of feelings of superiority, and not assigned an inherited status of inferiority.

---

* Emeritus Professor Physics and Humanities, Rochester Institute of Technology

My father was religious in the best sense of the term: adhering to the canonical rites prescribed by caste and custom, performing the routine rituals assiduously, doing *pūjās* to family deities, and reciting various *sahasranāmams* on a regular basis: all of which I learned to do also. He initiated his sons into the spiritual phase of life through the *upanayanam* ceremony, and encouraged me to learn by rote Sanskrit chants like *puruṣa-sūktam, rudram,* and *chamakam*. I learnt from my father that this last invocation to Śiva (who is regarded here as another aspect of Viṣṇu) is the foremost principle in the Śaiva tradition. It is here that the five-syllabic *mantra "namaḥ śivāya"* occurs, as it does in the Tamil *Śiva Purāṇam*.[1] When I first heard these at a tender age, and participated in the annual feasts and festivals associated with the tradition, I had little incentive to inquire into their historical bases. The picture of a thousand-headed universal Person with a thousand eyes and a thousand feet struck me by its sheer majesty, and invoked in me a reverence for the Splendour of the Cosmos. There is a magic in this which fascinated me.

My father also instilled in me a deep love for the Tamil language whose genius is known to few outside of the Tamil tradition. He guided me through *Tirukkural* and *Kamba Rāmāyaṇam*.[2] Then there was my mother who, like most Hindu mothers, made me aware of many a legend from the Itihāsas and Purāṇas. I recall vividly her narration of the story of Prahlāda and Hiraṇyakaśipu, as she had seen it performed on stage in her village near Tirunelveli. We had *bhajanas* at home every Thursday evening in which a diverse group of people participated. From those sessions I learned to experience the joy in devotional music, sung in Sanskrit and Tamil, and occasionally in Bengali and Marathi also. For the first decade and a half of my life Hinduism was primarily cultural and spiritual affiliation. It was deeply rooted in my life, from engaging in *toppikaraṇam*[3]

1. Many years later I wrote an English translation of the Tamil *Śiva Purāṇam* with short commentaries: *Sivapuranam, A Mystic Poem by Manikkavasakar: English Rendering, Meanings, and Explanatory Reflections*, Xlibris, 2012.

2. Later in life, I founded *The Rochester Tamil Sangam* where I initiated Tamil classes for children, and discussions on the *Kural*. In this context, I published a word-by-word translation with core ideas of the first book of *Tirukkural*, Chennai: Manimekalai Prasuram, 2000.

3. *Toppikkaraṇam* is a simple exercise in which one holds the left earlobe with the right hand and the right earlobe with the left hand, and does several sit-ups, usually in front of an icon of Lord Gaṇeśa in a worship mode. I used to do this prior to going to school on exam days. A couple of years ago I happened to see on TV news that some doctors and schools in California are recommending this to their patients and to young children as a beneficial exercise, calling it *super-brain yoga*.

to reciting *yā-kundetu tuṣāra-hāra-dhavalā*[4] at school.

I was about fourteen when a *swāmijī* from the Divine Life Society of Rishikesh came to our home in Kolkata and initiated some of us youngsters into Yoga. I managed to learn a few *āsanas*. I remember in particular *padmāsana* and *prāṇāyāma* as also *śīrsāsana* which I practised by posturing myself vertically upside down while leaning against a wall. At the end of this short course, as I was reflecting on my yogic efforts, it occurred to me that it should be possible to meditate on the divine without engaging in uncommon and sometimes difficult postures, whatever their esoteric significance and physical benefits might be. So I worked out a system of my own: I spend ten minutes every morning, focusing my wandering mind on a specific number, and at the end of it I promise myself to do an act of kindness or say something pleasant to somebody, and to bring a smile on a face in the course of the day. I have managed to do this for more than sixty years now. I am well aware that this has no link whatever to the spiritual discipline of Yoga, but it was Yoga that led me to it. I have been immensely enriched by it.

Moving Beyond

My father was imbued in Hindu orthopraxis, but he was also an enlightened scholar. He belonged to a generation in India where this was not uncommon. The people of that generation were anti-British to the core, yet did not suffer from colonial hang-ups. They were faithful to their tradition without feeling culturally insecure or looking down upon others. They did not brag about their superiority nor derive paltry satisfaction from bad-mouthing Christians, Muslims, Americans, or the West. My father inspired me to read the masterpieces of English literature, from Christopher Marlow and William Shakespeare to William Makepeace Thackeray and Charles Dickens and yes, even Thomas Babington Macaulay of whose literary essays not many of his ardent Indian critics know.

To broaden my outlook, I was sent for a couple of years to a Jesuit school: St Lawrence High School in Calcutta. Here I studied Latin under Father MacDonald, and learned the Lord's prayer in that language. I was not required to do this, but I did it for the fun of it. Latin led me to the discovery of the similarities in sounds between *agni* and *ignis*, *rājā* and *rex*, *mātā* and *mater*: words which don't at all sound like *neruppu*, *aracan* or

4. This *śloka* is one of the most beautiful invocations to Sarasvatī, the Hindu Goddess of Learning. To this day I pay this homage to Sarasvatī whom I have always regarded as my favourite divine representation.

tāi, the corresponding words in pure Tamil. It struck me that Sanskrit and some European languages must belong to the same linguistic family. So, the now derided Aryan Invasion Theory sounded reasonable to me.[5] I really don't resonate with the cultural patriotism that argues that Tamil belongs to the same linguistic group as Sanskrit.[6] English has many words of French and Latin derivation, which doesn't make English a Romance language. I don't think recognizing Tamil as part of another Indian language family has to affect the unity of Hinduism or the integrity of India as a nation.

Literature and philosophy have always held great interest for me. So over the years I continued to study other languages beyond Sanskrit and Hindi, Tamil and Bengali which were part of me as a Tamil Hindu in Kolkata in pre-Independent India. Over the years, I studied several other languages, because I wanted to enjoy poetry in various languages.

On Macaulayites

There are valid reasons for regretting the introduction of English into the Indian educational system. Anglo-indoctrination has created a class of Hindus who have lost touch with their own roots, between whom and the vast majority of their compatriots, there is even today a gaping intellectual chasm. This is the predicament of many English-educated Indians (and English-educated citizens of other former non-Western British colonies as well) today. On the one hand, they want to kick out from the very core of their being the British (and the French and the Dutch, and the Portuguese, etc.) and everything the exploiting colonizers have left behind. There is a growing body of literature in the non-Western world that argues about, condemns and bashes, the West in books, articles, and internet postings, often for justifiable reasons. Yet, these authors are more at ease in discourse with fellow English-educated intellectuals than with millions of their own non-English-educated compatriots. This is not a happy situation.

Though I too detest the British colonialists of earlier generations for the terrible things they did, I am glad their intervention in India saved

5. I am *not arguing* for the Aryan Invasion Theory. I am merely mentioning how the linguistic similarity made the Aryan Invasion Theory reasonable to me at one time.

6. The idea of Draviḍian languages was introduced by Robert Caldwell in 1856. He has been severely chastised for proposing this with evil intentions. Unfortunately, prior to him no Hindu scholar seems to have investigated from linguistic perspectives the origin of Indian languages.

me from having to pay servile obeisance to a descendant of Bahadhur Shah. I am very grateful too for parliamentary democracy and the penal code in India, initiated by Macaulay. I am not speaking for all Indians, but perhaps for at least some when I say I am glad my world views have been moulded by the thinkers of the European Enlightenment, though there have certainly been enlightened thinkers in ancient India too. I also feel more fulfilled because I have derived aesthetic delights not only from Kamban, Kālidāsa, Tagore and Bharathiyar, but also from Shakespeare and Shelley; not only from Khajurāho and Mahābalipuram but also from Rubens and the Sistine Chapel. I have been immeasurably enriched by the physics of Galileo and Newton, and by the equations of Einstein and Dirac also. No, we certainly did not need humiliating British colonialism for all this: this much I know. No, the British did not have in mind my aesthetic, scientific or intellectual thrills when they inflicted their grammar and vocabulary on India: this too I know. But I have personally benefited immensely from Macaulay's victory in the 1835 debate which introduced English as a medium of instruction in Indian education. If his motives were malicious, so much the worse for him. The road to (my) heaven was paved with (his) bad intentions. As with Gandhi, Sri Aurobindo, Tagore, and others, my love for Hinduism has not diminished because of this.

Later Developments and Reactions

At college I was drawn to mathematics and physics. Delving into these subjects as also my assimilation of literatures of European languages had a significant impact on how I came to regard the world and Hinduism. I began to discover the historical and analytical dimensions of Hinduism, beyond the experiential. When I read Sri Aurobindo's *Essays on the Gita* it impressed me more as philosophy than religion, and his *Sāvitrī* struck me as lofty poetry rather than spirituality. I am not suggesting there is no religion and spirituality in the sage-poet's works. I am confessing that my study of physics transformed my reactions to these. These changes have sharpened, metamorphosed, and deepened my own vision of Hinduism.

Vedic hymns have esoteric meanings, incomprehensible at the superficial level. Their oral transmission from generation to generation is among the marvels of cultural continuity. Passages from Vedic *mantra*s continue to resound in Hindu sacraments. Aside from rote recitations of a few famous hymns, I have only read Sanskrit selections from the Vedas. I have heard itinerant *swāmī*s refer to them. When I plodded through Griffith's translation, I did not find it to be half as fulfilling as the passages when chanted: the sacred *mantra*s have a sonorous dignity when enunciated by *paṇḍits* trained in Sanskrit diction. From Griffith I discovered that, contrary to my earlier impression, Vedic poetry contains more than religious invocations to ethereal deities. The mystic humility of the Nāsadīya-Sūkta moved me, and I recast it in English.[7]

Like Mahatma Gandhi and thousands of modern Hindus, I became familiar with the *Bhagavad-Gītā* through English. I have read passages from the *Gītā* in different translations, from Tamil and Hindi to Italian and French, and listened to it on tape countless times. I gathered from the *Gītā* many insights into human psychology and the human potential. I used to keep notes on my reactions to various *śloka*s of the immortal work, and in 1998, I published a book (Raman 1998) in which I reflected on select nuggets from that multifaceted classic.

When I first listened to the *Rāmāyaṇa* and the *Mahābhārata*, like most Hindus, I took them as historical accounts. But my views began to change.

---

7. Not even nothing existed then,
No air yet, and no heaven.
Who encased and kept it where?
Was water in the darkness there?
Neither deathlessness nor decay,
Nor the rhythm of night and day:
The self-existent, with breath sans air:
That, and that alone was there.
Darkness was in darkness found.
Like lightless water all around.
One emerged, with nothing on.
It was from *tapas* that this was born.
In it did Desire, its way did find:
The primordial seed born of mind.
Sages know deep in the heart:
What exists is kin to what does not.
Across the void the cord was thrown,
The place of every thing was known.
Seed-sowers and powers now came by,
Impulse below and force on high.
Who really knows, and who can swear,
How creation arose, when or where!
Even gods came after creation's day,
Who really knows, who can truly say?
When and how did creation start?
Did He do it?
Or did He not?
Only He up there knows, maybe.
Or perhaps, not even He.

Upon carefully reading them in their entirety, I came to regard them as magnificent poetry, weaved together by writers from the hearsay of ancient anecdotes. They have become sacred history: a respectable blend of myth, magic, and inspiring narrative that links people of Hindu heritage through an intangible cultural network.

The *Rāmāyaṇa* and the *Mahābhārata* impress me as the Iliad and the Odyssey which speak of Achilles and Agamemnon, Menelaus and Helen, except that I resonate more heartily with Rāma and Sītā, Kṛṣṇa and Draupadī. The *Gītā* is like the Ten Commandments or the Sermon on the Mount: beacons of insightful ethical guideposts in the rough and tumble of life where we are tossed into unexpected situations and interact with people of different backgrounds and values; but the *Gītā* touches me more deeply than the ethical dimensions of the Bible.

Learned scholars have presented their conclusions as to the precise date when Rāma was born and when the Kurukṣetra battle began, though the traditional view is that the *avatāra*s of Rāma and Kṛṣṇa appeared in different *yuga*s lasting hundreds of thousands of years. From my perspective, the importance of the epics lies in the values they convey: truthfulness, steadfastness, righteousness, subjugation of evil, keeping the promised word, and the like, as also in the wealth of information they provide on ancient Indic culture.[8] To me, Rāma and Kṛṣṇa are heroes in the mythic sense, divine principles portrayed in flesh and blood.

As to the Purāṇas, they too contain nuggets of wisdom here and there, but their fantasy components don't resonate with my epistemological framework. I respect those whom these impress very differently, though I am not persuaded that Purāṇic legends were part of the world such as I understand it. They are as much (or as little) interesting to me as Hesiod's *Theogony*.

The eminent scholar Arvind Sharma said,

> Although the standard position within Hinduism doubtless equates Śruti with revelation and Smṛti with tradition, virtually every phase of the history of Hinduism provides some evidence that the term revelation was either actually or tentatively extended to include what we call tradition. The earliest piece of evidence comes from the Upaniṣads themselves, wherein no distinction is drawn between the Vedas and the Itihāsas, Purāṇas and so on. . . . — Sharma 1991: 75

With me, even Śruti (revelation) is transformed into Smṛti (tradition).

8. My perspectives on this may be seen from my book, *Bālakāṇḍa: Rāmāyaṇa as Literature and Cultural History* (Raman 1998).

Reflection on the Dichotomy

The tension between scholarship and tradition is a cultural manifestation of the conflict between the head and the heart. The beliefs of traditionalists have often been challenged by inquiring minds, resulting in newer understandings. The conquests of the mind in matters spiritual tend to upset the joyful heart resting on unquestioning faith and emotion. Whether one should accept the persuasive evidence of facts and the logic of reasoned arguments, or respond to the tantalizing call of faith that promises emotional comfort and spiritual delights, is the delicate dilemma that many have to face. Some make a decisive choice, and plead for their own preference as the right one to make. Wisdom probably lies in recognizing that there is no right or wrong choice here because one is as human as the other.

This dichotomy of human inclinations illustrates what is known in physics as the principle of complementarity, by which ultimate reality consists of mutually complementing features. In this view, there are two kinds of truths, small and great ones. A small truth is one whose contrary is clearly false.[9] That milk is white is a small truth, because to say that milk is black is clearly false. But a great truth is one whose contrary is no less true. To say that religions have done much good is as true a statement as that religions have done much harm.

When we are experiencing one side of a coin, we cannot perceive the other. But it would be a grave error to imagine that a coin has but one face. For the analytical scholar to maintain that the spiritual dimension is without significance would be as partial a vision as that of the religious devotee who does not wake up to the fact that *bhajanas*, like the *salah/namāz* and the Lord's Prayer, are symbols and instruments that have evolved over the ages.

I have been able to delight in the spiritual fountain of the epics because I grew up in the tradition. But it has been equally possible and no less satisfying, to look into them as creations of gifted poets. The charm of an Aesop Fable lies not so much in the actions and conversations of the animals, as, and even more so, in the morals they spell out.

On Attitudes to Doctrines and Folk Beliefs

I envision Brahmā as a metaphor for whatever gave rise to the Cosmos,

9. As Niels Bohr put it, "Two sorts of truth: trivialities, where opposites are obviously absurd, and profound truths, recognized by the fact that the opposite is also a profound truth" (Bohr 1967: 328).

Viṣṇu as the totality of the physical laws that enable the world to function the way it does, and Śiva as the principle that will heave a final sigh on all existence. Invoking them with hymns and attending to them with floral offerings are for me the aesthetic-spiritual dimensions of our culture.

As to *karma*: the notion that our current status is the result of our previous actions is an enlightened way of considering the human condition, as reasonable an explanation as any for the uneven distribution of fortunes and misfortunes. It is a wiser approach than pointing the finger at a merciless god when disaster strikes. It is also an incentive to behave for ensuring a better future. Yet, I have difficulty with reincarnation. In the rigid framework of rationality to which I am constrained, I am unable to subscribe to this notion wholeheartedly. To the question, "Do you believe in re-incarnation," all I can say is, "I might have in a previous incarnation."

I am agnostic about any postmortem state. There may or may not be one, but I doubt that those who talk about it or about god with cocksure confidence do so on the basis of direct knowledge. Declarations on these subjects rest generally on the sacred writings of one's religious affiliation, reinforced by cultural conditioning.

Taking purifying baths after an eclipse, avoiding certain days for initiating matrimony and travel, and promising temple-gods half a month's salary if a favour were granted are among the beliefs which are meaningful to many, but not to me.

On Casteism

In my view, the most objectionable aspect of Hindu society is birth-based hierarchical categorization of people.[10] Casteism (whether as *varṇāśrama* or as *jāti*) was probably useful for trade and craft specialization. Similar systems existed in other societies, giving rise to family names like Smith, Charpentier, and Schubert. There were feudal-serf systems and master-slave designations as well. I have read many explanations and justifications for the caste system by Western commentators and upper caste Hindus. I don't know of any śūdra or Dalit scholar offering apologetics for it.

10. *Varṇa* (literally "colour") may not have been, in essence, very different from the white and black classifications in other societies. But it has also been pointed out that the root meaning of the word is *appearance* or *inner quality*. Thus, when it says in the *Bhagavad-Gītā* (XVIII: 41): *brāhmaṇa-kṣatriya-viśāṁ śūdrāṇām ca parantapa, karmāṇi pravibhaktāni svabhāva-prabhavaiḥ gunaiḥ*, it is suggested that the classification is based on work (*karma*) and inner qualities (*svabhāva* and *guṇa*). *Jāti*, on the other hand, is simply a classification based on ancestral professions. No matter what, casteism is casteism, and is anachronistic.

As a lad, I used to see how *dhobīs* (washermen), *mocīs* (cobblers), and *jāmedārs* (sweepers) were treated as impure. That seemed normal to me at one time. Then I saw the play *Nandanār Caritram*.[11] This is the story of the *pariah* Nandanār who was an ardent devotee of Naṭarāja of Chidabaram. The lowly serf who was bonded to a Veda-chanting brāhmaṇa (*Vediar*) was derided by the master for even expressing a desire to go on pilgrimage to Chidabaram for a *darśana* of Naṭarāja. Eventually, through a miracle in the fields where Nandanār toiled, the brāhmaṇa realised that the *pariah* was no ordinary man. Now with full permission, Nandanār went to Chidabaram and became one with Naṭarāja.

This play was a transformative experience for me. It made me aware that there is something unrighteous and terribly unjust in the way Hindu society has been treating the lower castes. I began to see casteism as anachronistic, unconscionable and unacceptable. I felt guilty that millions of my brothers and sisters were denied the privileges given to me.[12]

I have no idea what prompted my ancestors to casteism. The theory that the upper castes were the invading Aryans and the lowest ones were the indigenous people is so uncomfortable that it is now discarded. Whatever the origin, many poets and saints of the tradition have condemned casteism. But I haven't heard many venerable leaders of our times — *ācāryas*, *swāmījīs*, or *bābās* — speak out against this social scourge and spiritual embarrassment which continues to slur many sections of Hindu society. Hindu spokespeople become defensive and clumsily apologetic when this matter is brought out to the world. Some have claimed, without batting an eye, that the system was instituted by the conniving British. It is sometimes argued that the religion-sanctioned marginalization of one's own people such as one sees in Hinduism has parallels in other societies, which is very true; but I really don't care about the dirty linen in other people's closets. I am confident that change will occur in this matter in the next few decades, if not earlier.

At the investiture of my *yajñopavītam* my uncle whispered the sacred *gāyatrī mantra* and my *gotram* into my ear. This made me feel good. My

11. The nineteenth century Tamil poet Gopalakrishna Bharati wrote this in the format of a *kathākālakṣepam*, an art-form that combines music, narration, and humour.

12. For several years now I have been an enthusiastic supporter of a group called Navyaśāstra, founded by Jayashree Gopal and Vikram Masson, whose goal is to eliminate caste hierarchy from Hindu mind-set and practice, and bring the religion back to its legitimate glory. The group is not looked upon favourably by some traditional groups.

negative reaction to the caste system arises from the denial of an articulated lineage to girls and to children of other castes. As long as all castes are treated with equal dignity, I see nothing wrong in the system. I like to imagine a chastened Hinduism where all Hindus will be regarded as equal, and every Hindu will have the freedom to enter a temple, and have spiritual initiation with a sacred thread.

On the occasion of the inauguration of Mayor William Johnson of Rochester, NY in 1994, I was asked to offer a prayer from the Hindu tradition. In that context, inspired by Hindu visions, I composed the following:

> A wholesome society has people with diverse interests and talents:
> There are those who study, meditate, and reflect: the thinking ones.
> There are those who manage and govern: the administering ones.
> There are those who engage in commerce: the trading ones.
> There are those who work and produce: the labouring ones.
> None is more important, and none any less.
> None is more exalted, and none too lowly,
> For all are essential for the well-being of society.
> May each person follow the path of one's own talent and inclination.
> May knowledge and wisdom come to those that strive for it.
> May caring and compassion come to those that make the laws.
> May fairness and honesty be with those who trade.
> May commitment and just recompense be part of those that labour.
> May there be appreciation for one other's contribution.
> May there be respect for each other's work and profession.
> May all act in accordance with the laws of the country.
> May the laws of the country be fair and just.
> May justice always prevail.
> May our children grow under the guidance of caring parents.
> May our young people have respect for teachers and elders.
> May there be unconditional love in every family.
> May there be joy and harmony in the community.
> May there be happiness in the whole world.
> May there be peace, peace, and peace in the world.

Existential Angst and Hindutva

Terrorist attacks, new epidemics, collapse of financial systems, drastic changes in weather patterns and such are lurking in the background of our conscious existence these days. Aside from these, there is a fear in the hearts of many Hindus that our religion is vilified by outsiders with ill-will towards us. The religion is also callously ignored by many of our own.

There are valid reasons for some of these feelings. True, there have been writings and pronouncements by non-Hindu scholars who display a superficial and mistaken understanding of Hinduism, or who are intentionally portraying Hindu culture in a negative light.[13] The resurgence of Islam on the world scene has had unhappy impacts within India. Many Westernized Hindus discard their traditional culture. All this has led to frustration in a growing number of Hindus *vis-à-vis* the preservation of our culture and religion within Hinduism's own land. The Partition of India was heart-wrenching for millions. Beyond that, there are provisions in the Indian Constitution which are said to be more favourable to non-Hindus. Then again, Christian missionaries from other faith-systems have been successful in drawing away many Hindus into their folds. Hindus who are angered by this don't seem to recognize that part of the blame must go to casteism. Rightly or wrongly, *ādivāsī*s and Dalits feel that they would acquire dignity if they became Christian, Muslim, or Buddhist.

The secular Hindu establishment seems to do little to present the lore and wisdom of India in an historical framework. Children graduate from high-schools in India without being exposed to the Vedas and the Upaniṣads, the *Mahābhārata*, the *Rāmāyaṇa*, and the *Bhagavad-Gītā* in any systematic way. Nor do they learn about Tirumūlar, Tiruvalluvar, Guru Nānak, Mahāvīra, Patañjali or Kālidāsa as intellectual giants of the tradition. This blatant negligence of a people's cultural history in the education of its young, combined with protests when *Vande Mātaram* is sung in public places, adds to the legitimate existential Angst that many Hindus feel.

As I see it, the Hindutva movement, though associated with politics and religious conservatives, is an effort on the part of Hindus devoted to their culture to affirm and reclaim their civilization within India. Culturally speaking, India is as much Hindu as the West is Judeo-Christian, China is Confucian, Japan is Shinto and Buddhist, Israel is Judaic, and most Arab nations, Iran, Indonesia, Malaysia, and Turkey are Islamic. This in no way implies that Muslims, Christians, Jews, Sikhs, Jainas, Buddhists, Parsees, Baha'is, atheists and others shouldn't enjoy equal rights under the laws of India. And they do. But to deny the incontrovertible fact that Indic culture has been nourished for three millennia by Vedic visions and Upaniṣadic world views and the grand epics would be a reckless and offensive repudiation of India's cultural and spiritual past and present, a travesty of history.

13. See, in this context, Ramaswamy et al. (2007).

One inevitable, if unfortunate, consequence of all this is that many Hindus are beginning to emulate their adversaries in the denigration of other religions. Hindus generally respect all faiths. In fact, this is what makes Hindus unique as a religious group. Even now most Hindus show reverence for the places of worship and the sacred symbols of Christianity and Islam. But the historical victimization of Hindus, accentuated by recent experiences has instigated many otherwise decent and tolerant Hindus to bad-mouth these religions in internet messages and articles.

This is not the Hinduism I learned at home, nor the one preached by the likes of Sri Ramakrishna, Swami Vivekananda, Ramana Maharshi, or Sri Aurobindo. That vintage Hinduism seems to have vanished like the glory days of genuine patriots and uncorrupt politicians who selflessly served *Bhārat Mātā*. Today, hate and abuse have replaced understanding and reverence, the essential messages of the Hinduism of my youthful days. The loss of a moral high ground is fine, some say, because tolerance is what landed us on the receiving end in history, and it is about time we launch systematic abusive retaliation.

Then again, though the Hindu Diaspora is doing quite well and is held in high esteem for its professionalism, intelligence, and hardwork, many Hindus feel they are insufficiently recognized. They feel that Hinduism gets only passing notice, or is mentioned only through negative references to caste, inscrutable representations of the divine, and barely clad god-men dipping periodically in sacred waters. Many Hindus in the West, though they may not themselves feel at home in certain authentically Hindu milieu in India, resent such portrayals.

Concluding Thoughts

Unlike many of my co-religionists, I will not say I am *proud* to be a Hindu, because that word smacks of a cultural high-ground on which I am not comfortable to put myself. However, I consider myself to be extremely fortunate to have been born as a Hindu, and this for several reasons. There is no other religion I am aware of that gives its members as much freedom of thought and practice as modern Hinduism does. One can find among Hindus ardent believers in astrology and numerology, but also sceptics and agnostics. There are charismatic spokespersons for god and miracle-performing *guru*s who tell people what to do and what not to, but also atheists and rationalists. There is no vested authority who can decree who is a Hindu and who is not. Some venerable personages declare that those who don't subscribe to their version of Kṛṣṇa or believe in their sacred Purāṇa, have no right to talk about sacred works. But there are no saintly *swāmīs* who have the power to penalize whomsoever they deem and denounce as errant Hindus. If a Hindu chooses to abandon his/her religion, no man or monster can call for that person's execution. Hinduism is too civilized to make apostasy a capital crime. Efforts to define a Hindu and to subject Hindus to claustrophobic doctrinal fetters have not succeeded thus far, and hopefully never will.

I feel comfortable and fulfilled with mainstream Hinduism's core belief which I refer to as the spirituality thesis: beneath and beyond the physical world of matter and energy there exists an intangible substratum that spans the stretch of space and has been there even prior to the first tick of time. This insubstantial entity is the spiritual throb of the Cosmos. Then there is the related cryptic truth (*mahāvākya*): *tat tvam asi* (That thou art). That is to say, each one of us is a spark from that divine fire, a fleeting photon from the galactic core as it were, and we are all groping in our various ways to get a glimpse of the unfathomable mystery. This is a vision sublime and majestic in scope, for it paints our finitude on an infinite canvass.

This elevating vision can shape the attitudes and behaviour of those who take this as more than a quotable insight. It instills in me respect and reverence for fellow-humans, for the cosmic fire is smouldering in each one of us. If this to be so, how can one in good conscience treat another human being as inferior or wretched or unworthy of respect? This is one of the paradoxes in Hindu society which I have never been able to resolve.

Over two centuries ago, when European Enlightenment thinkers articulated the principle of religious tolerance, they were unwittingly echoing an ancient Vedic view: There is but one Truth (referred to as god), and That Truth is described in different ways. This affirmation of multiple approaches to the Divine is the most significant contribution of Hindu insights to humanity. Per this message of Hinduism, god can be seen in the Star of David as in the Christian Cross, in the contemplation of the Buddha as in the Crescent of Islam, in the *Ādi Granth* of the Sikhs as in the abstract sound of the sacred *auṁ* of the Hindus, and in yet other modes too.

Ultimate Truth, the quintessence of the Cosmic Whole, is infinite, and appears to finite minds only as hazy insights. Every view of the Divine, whether from revelation or through speculation, whether from reading or by reflection, is partial. It is narrow self-righteousness to claim that one view of god is the only right one. Our picture is never accurate, let alone complete. This uniquely Hindu insight may be called *poly-odosism* (from the Greek *odos:* path) or *bahu-mārga* in Sanskrit and *palavazhigal* in

Tamil: the doctrine of many paths to individual and group spiritual fulfilment. This, and this alone, can save civilization from the religious conflicts that disfigure human history. Fighting with one another in the name of god is the most disgraceful insult to god's name.

When I read Bertrand Russell's book entitled *Why I am Not a Christian* (1957), I noted in my journal that I should write a book entitled, *Why I am Still a Hindu*. However, others have plagiarized Russell's title before I could. In 1987, Hans Küng wrote a book called *Why I am still a Christian* (2006). In 1995, Ibn Warraq published *Why I am not a Muslim* (1995), and the following year we saw Kancha Ilaiah's *Why I am not a Hindu* (1996). Here, I have reflected on the ways in which I consider myself to be still a Hindu.

Mine is one of millions of voices that sing the song of Hinduism. My experiences have been abundant and awesome through the pleasing poetry and profound philosophy, magnificent music and colourful dances that have emerged in the Hindu world. Kabīr and Kamban, Śaṅkara and Rāmānuja, Śrī Caitanya and Saint Thyāgarāja, Bharata Nāṭyam and Maṇipurī dance are but some of the countless cultural manifestations of Hinduism that have made my life extraordinarily rich. I feel blessed to be part of this tradition for, while offering me many fulfilling visions of the abstract beyond, it also allows me to reflect on the same from my own limited perspectives.

I am well aware of the threats, real and imagined that Hinduism is facing in our own times. Yet I feel confident that in the course of this century, Hinduism will grow to become a stronger and sounder religion, with as yet unimagined visions and world views. It has the potential to serve as a beacon in this complex world of ours.

Auṁ śāntiḥ, śāntiḥ, śāntiḥ!

References

Bohr, H.H. (1967), "My Father," in *Niels Bohr: His Life and Work as Seen by His Friends and Colleagues*, ed. Stefan Rozental, Amsterdam: North-Holland.

Ilaiah, Kancha (1996), *Why I am not a Hindu: A Śūdra Critique of Hindutva Philosophy, Culture and Political Economy*, Calcutta: Samya.

Küng, Hans (2006), *Why I am Still a Christian*, New York: Continuum Publishers.

Raman, Varadaraja, V. (1998), *Bālakāṇḍa: Rāmāyaṇa as Literature and Cultural History*, Mumbai: Popular Prakashan.

——— (1999), *Nuggets from the Gītā*, Mumbai: Bharati Vidya Bhavan.

Ramaswamy et al. (2007), *Invading the Sacred: An Analysis of Hinduism Studies in America*, New Delhi: Rupa & Co.

Russell, Bertrand (1957), *Why I am Not a Christian and other Essays on Religion and Related Subjects*, ed. Paul Edwards, New York: Touchstone edition.

Sharma, Arvind (1991), *A Hindu Perspective on the Philosophy of Religion*, New York: St. Martin's Press.

Thurston, Edgar & K. Rangachari (1909), *Castes and Tribes of Southern India*, Madras: Government Press.

Warraq, Ibn (1995), *Why I am not a Muslim*, New York: Prometheus Books.

24

Ẓiyāratu Darśanam
A South Indian Pilgrimage Beyond the Boundaries

*Afsar Mohammad**

Introduction

"EVEN if I can afford to go to Mecca, our family always prefers to visit Gūgūḍu for the blessings of the local *pīr* (saint) Kuḷḷāyappa. It's our family tradition to make this *ẓiyāratu darśanam* each year," said seventy-year old Hussain. In 2007, when I met him in Gūgūḍu, he announced that he was on his fiftieth pilgrimage to Gūgūḍu during the month of Muharram. A small businessman in a town close to Kadapa in Andhra Pradesh, Hussain along with his family members travels to Gūgūḍu every year to pay his respects to the local *pīr*. In his younger years, Hussain used to save money for this annual trip, which even then he designated a *hajj*. Although he is now rich enough to visit Mecca each year, he prefers Gūgūḍu to Mecca. Hussain explained to me that

> In terms of *aslī Islam* (True or proper Islam), the *hajj* and *ẓiyāratu darśanam* may not be same. Although religiously it's very important to make the *hajj*, our family tradition is confined to *ẓiyāratu darśanam* and our Mecca is here in Gūgūḍu.

Another pilgrim, Lakṣmamma, who came from a nearby village in Karnataka, expressed similar devotional sentiments saying that she had been making this pilgrimage — *ẓiyāratu darśanam* — since she was fourteen years old. Now sixty-five years old Lakṣmamma remembers her first visit to Gūgūḍu.

> It is as fresh as yesterday. Actually it was not our family tradition to make this pilgrimage. At that point, my family joined with another family

* South Asia Institute, The University of Texas at Austin

> who made an annual pilgrimage to Gūgūḍu. After that first experience of pilgrimage, I got married into a good family. My mother started believing that it was only because of the pilgrimage we had made to Gūgūḍu and now annual visits became a crucial part of our family tradition and the ritual standards of Kuḷḷāyappa have found a prominent place in our domestic shrine too.

Besides Hussain and Lakṣmamma, thousands of pilgrims who visit Gūgūḍu during the month of Muharram, use similar vocabulary and ideas to describe their annual pilgrimage.

Though Lakṣmamma never uses the term *tīrtha* explicitly, her interpretations explain that Gūgūḍu is a "crossing place" or "ford" and that to her Gūgūḍu is the one and only centre of her devotional life. As we can see, her perception is different from Hussain's though she uses similar religious vocabulary most of the time. Focusing on similar pilgrim narratives of Lakṣmamma's and Hussain's, but different perceptions of the pilgrimage, this paper endeavours to capture the idea of a blended pilgrimage performed by Muslims and non-Muslims, who use the same term *ẓiyāratu darśanam* to describe this rich experience.

Despite their different family and religious backgrounds, both Hussain and Lakṣmamma use the same religious vocabulary and articulate their ardent devotion for the local *pīr* Kuḷḷāyappa who supposedly made Gūgūḍu his home several centuries ago. However, when they visit the *pīr*-house in Gūgūḍu during the month of Muharram, they observe a different set of rituals. Hussain's family observes normal Islamic practices such as reciting the *fātehā* and performing water rituals such as gifting the juice-pots and food rituals such as *kandūrī* on the seventh day of Muharram,[1] while Lakṣmamma's family performs non-Muslim practices such as observing *pradakṣiṇā* (walking around the fire-pit), *porlu dandālu* (rolling wet bodies around the ritual standards) and performing *pūjā*, what they call *fātehā pūjā*" to the ritual standards.

For thousands of pilgrims who visit Gūgūḍu, the month of Muharram is the holiest month to make such a pilgrimage. Muharram is the first month of the Islamic calendar. In the history of Islam, Muharram is important for its remembrance of the martyrdom at Karbalā, a place in present-day Iraq where the martyrs shed their last blood to protect their community. Muslims everywhere in the world perform the rituals of this memory by installing the ritual standards of the martyrs of Karbalā and

1. For the importance of the food ritual called *kandūri*, see Bowen 1993: 229-50.

telling their stories.[2] However, here is a different story in Gūgūḍu. In the local story of Karbalā, it is narrated that the battle was to protect local religious practices and the devotional community that resides in Gūgūḍu. Whereas many places celebrate Muharram to memorialize the martyrdom of Karbalā, devotees from many villages from the three south Indian states — Andhra, Tamil Nadu and Karnataka — visit Gūgūḍu to remember the martyrs and pay their respects to them. In 2007, it was estimated that nearly 300,000 pilgrims visited this small place to pay their respects to the local *pīr* Kuḷḷāyappa.

The story of this local *pīr* Kuḷḷāyappa arriving in Gūgūḍu itself marks an end of a religious journey that happened several hundred years ago. At least one of several stories about the *pīr* narrates that this *pīr* called Kuḷḷāyappa — a term that literally means "a lord with a cap," or as Muslims call him "Topi wala sahib," — was a Muslim traveller travelling south India spreading the Sūfī message. While continuing on his way, the messenger was invited by the villagers of Gūgūḍu. Convinced that this place would become the centre of devotion, he decided to settle there. Many Muslims believe that "as one crucial pilgrimage came to an end here, the public event of Muharram is also a celebration of that pilgrimage." As we can observe from multiple pilgrim narratives, this story of pilgrimage authenticates such a local manifestation of the *hajj*. On the other hand, this aspect of highlighting the local also complicates

2. As familiarly known, Karbalā is within the geographical boundaries of present-day Iraq. Nevertheless, Karbalā is more than a place as it symbolically refers to the entire of Shi'i history and the gradual enactments of Muharram events. An intensely powerful and definitive Karbalā represents, as David Pinault put it, "an overriding paradigm of persecution, exclusion and suffering." Michael Fischer in his *Iran: From Religious Dispute to Revolution*, used the key term 'Karbalā paradigm' specifically to comprehend the interactions between Karbalā and the modern Islamic world. Specifically, in the post-1980s turbulent times, the traditional mourning of the Karbalā martyrdom has been replaced "with active witnessing through political demonstration" in Iran and to a certain extent, in Lebanon. In turn, this also led to the revival of Shi'a Islam as a theological force rather than a political tool. These studies explain the breadth of the idea of Karbalā that has manifested in varied ways in political and religious arena thus providing a lens to envision many Karbalās. Korom has rightly pointed out that, "The Karbalā paradigm is a force as vital and potent today as it was during the first few centuries after the original event; it is one without parallel in human history." For more on the theme of Karbalā, see Pinault (2001) and Fischer (1980). For a detailed discussion on these aspects, see Fischer and Abedi (1990). For more on the revival of Shi'i Islam in the post-Iranian Revolution period, see Nasr (2006). For more on the dramatic aspect of Muharram performances in Iran, Trinidad and south India, see Chelkowski (1979); Korom (2003); and Sharif (1921).

the usually perceived hierarchical order in the making of the Islamic community, *umma* (Eickelman and Piscatori 1990: 13). Muslim devotees who travel to Gūgūḍu also talk about the local notion of *umma* and call themselves a community of pilgrims for Kuḷḷāyappa. However, this *umma* has no religious boundaries as it consists of both Muslim and Hindu groups. These devotees consider this kind of journey a pilgrimage and so call it a *ẓiyāratu darśanam*, a term that combines the idea of *ẓiyārat* — a visit to the shrines as explained in any Islamic tradition and *darśanam* — a visit to any Hindu temple. What makes these pilgrims combine these two different pilgrimage traditions? And what elements do they borrow from each discrete religious tradition in producing this local term? These are two major questions that this paper endeavours to explore.

The term *ẓiyārat* is used in the context of a pilgrimage to sites associated with the prophet Muhammad, his companions, or other venerated figures in Islamic history, such as Shi'a *imāms* or Sūfī saints. Several studies on the idea of *ẓiyārat* discuss the prominence of *ẓiyārat* within the Islamic tradition (Werbner 2003: 259). Most of these studies highlight *ẓiyārat* as a lesser pilgrimage as understood and experienced by Muslim communities. Similarly, many studies on the idea of *tīrtha* and pilgrimage in Hinduism focus on Hindu-related pilgrim sites.[3] The pilgrim site in Gūgūḍu deifies these boundaries and the pilgrims who visit Gūgūḍu participate in a devotional world that clearly contests any dividing lines. However, this paper argues that these pilgrims are aware of their religious differences while participating in this shared pilgrimage, yet they respect each other's practices and interpretations as they journey to the abode of their *pīr* or an *avatāra* of their family deity. I will present this argument with evidence from various groups of pilgrims and their stories of pilgrimages.

As familiarly known, the *hajj* is an ultimate obligation that can be fulfilled only in Mecca. Scholars such as Bianchi have observed that

> journeys to other sacred places are mere "visits" (*ẓiyāra*) that can never substitute for a *hajj* no matter how many times they are repeated. No combination of *ẓiyāra* can equal a *hajj*, even if their destinations include the prophet's mosque in Medina, the tombs of the most venerated imāms in Iraq and Iran, or the final resting places of the thousands of saints and martyrs all across Asia and Africa. — Bianchi 2004: 40

3. As Diana Eck puts it appropriately, "The understanding of India's 'sacred' places may be enlarged and enriched by seeing them, not as destinations, but as fords, where caste and sex, sins, sickness, and death, and even *saṁsāra* itself, may be transcended in the crossing" (Eck 1981).

Yet the truth is there are many Muslim families that visit Gūgūḍu each year and never hesitate to call their *ẓiyāra* a *hajj*. In addition, for Shi'a Muslims *ẓiyārat* is a "religious merit that is considered equal to a thousand pilgrimages to Mecca" (Wayne 2003: 651). My evidence from Gūgūḍu demonstrates that this is true not only for Shi'a Muslims, but also for non-Muslims. In essence, the pilgrimage to Gūgūḍu acquires the significance of an obligatory ritual for several reasons that include personal and family too. In the next section, I will narrate both Muslim and non-Muslim pilgrim narratives.

Pilgrim Narratives: Four Major Groups

For many devotees who visit Gūgūḍu each year, the visitation serves various purposes including business. So it is not surprising that they narrate their stories of these experiences in various ways, which however are generally of four types. They describe their experiences as: (1) pilgrims who visit Gūgūḍu as a family tradition; (2) pilgrims who connect their pilgrimage to a larger network of Sūfī Islam and Vaiṣṇavism; (3) pilgrims who revisit Gūgūḍu as a kind of home-coming; and finally (4) as pilgrims who also visit Gūgūḍu for business purposes. For many pilgrims, this pilgrimage is not a personal journey or something that is separate or distinct from their ordinary family life. Since family tradition still remains the centre of this pilgrimage, most of the pilgrims' experiences are deeply rooted in their family history.

PILGRIMAGE AS A FAMILY TRADITION

Born into a Muslim sub-caste of cotton-carders called *dudekula*, Kullayamma visits Gūgūḍu not only in the month of Muharram, but throughout the year particularly on Thursdays or Fridays, notably before every major family event such as a marriage, but also in connection with children's education and health issues. But she calls her family's visit during the month of Muharram a *ẓiyāratu darśanam*, thereby specifying it as an annual pilgrimage. The other visits that she and her family perform outside the month of Muharram are, as she described it, "regular visits that Hindus perform on an everyday basis for performing *pūjā*." She explains that because as a Muslim she cannot keep the icon of the *pīr* in her domestic shrine and perform daily worship or *fāteḥā*, she prefers visiting the *pīr* at least once a month. Non-Muslims call this kind of daily worship *fāteḥā pūjā*, again a blended term.

Explaining the differences between regular but occasional visits and the major annual pilgrimage, she said,

> Each visit has its own purpose and we cannot call each visit a *ẓiyāratu darśanam*. For our family, *ẓiyāratu* has very specific meaning when we visit all the sacred graves in Gūgūḍu and pay our respects and perform *fātehā* for each grave. *Ẓiyāratu darśanam* is nothing less than the *hajj* for our family. Since we cannot go all the way to Mecca to perform the ultimate ritual *hajj*, we visit Gūgūḍu and ask for the intercession of the *pīr*. During the annual *ziyāratu darśanam*, we stay in Gūgūḍu for at least three days until the tenth day when the last rites called *Śahādat* are performed for the *pīrs*. We believe attending these last rites is the real purpose of performing *ziyāratu darśanam* in the month of Muharram.

Many Muslim or non-Muslim families make this clear distinction between regular visits and the annual pilgrimage. Muslim families often perceive this practice of pilgrimage as the fulfilment of the fifth pillar of Islam — the *hajj*. For at least five centuries, the pilgrimage to Gūgūḍu has been an integral part of their religious life. Kullayamma was not sure when exactly her ancestors had begun this practice of pilgrimage, but she confidently asserted that not even a single generation of their family had failed to perform this pilgrimage. According to Kullayamma, "Our family can't even imagine the failure of this practice. Though we have failed to attend a few monthly visits, the pilgrimage during the month of Muharram and our stay in Gūgūḍu on the tenth day is an obligation. That is what we actually call the pilgrimage — our *hajj*." For Kullayamma and her family, the pilgrimage to Gūgūḍu is an affordable *hajj*.

While some Muslims use the term *hajj* at least once when describing their annual pilgrimage, non-Muslim pilgrims barely know the term. However, they consistently use the term *ẓiyāratu darśanam* or *ẓāratu darśanam*.

Many studies on pilgrimage hold that an act of pilgrimage is an "exceptional" event and that it represents a separation from everyday mundane activities. Many pilgrims' stories, including Hussain's and Lakṣmamma's, question this usual understanding of pilgrimage and inform us that pilgrimage is an extension of everyday life with an emphasis on religiosity.

SŪFĪ AND VAIṢṆAVA CONNECTIONS

Gūgūḍu is part of a network of several popular and geographically close shrines such as Penukoṇḍa, and Guntakal which are also well known for their Sūfī practices. Interestingly, Gūgūḍu is surrounded by several Vaiṣṇava sites such as Kadiri, sites well known for their Narasiṁha cult, a popular tradition of Vaiṣṇava in Andhra. Thousands of devotees from

Karnataka and Tamil Nadu visit these places as pilgrims. From the British gazetteers, we learn that these places have a history of pilgrimage that stretches back several hundred years (Francis 1905: 147-48). Pilgrims who visit Gūgūḍu commonly continue on their pilgrimage to Penukoṇḍa and then Guntakal too. The aspect of family tradition further deepens when these pilgrims connect their visit to Gūgūḍu to a larger network of Sūfī sites within this region. Several of these Muslim families also visit nearby Sūfī sites such as the Baba Fakruddin shrine in Penukoṇḍa, the Mastan Vali Dargāh in Guntakal and the Amin Pīr Dargāh in Kadapa. They plan to spend at least one night at each shrine to perform the rituals of *ẓiyārat* and finally to spend three to ten days in Gūgūḍu. However, I have observed that while non-Muslims definitely visit most of these Sūfī sites, Muslims barely consider Vaiṣṇava sites to be worth visiting.

For pilgrims such as Khaja Basha, visiting Gūgūḍu is an opportunity to visit other Sūfī sites around Gūgūḍu. Two days before the seventh day of Muharram, Khaja Basha arrives in Gūgūḍu and sets up his food stall on the main road of the Pīr-house. He has been visiting Gūgūḍu for at least ten years to sell food items such as sweets and snacks. Khaja Basha's family in Karnataka lives on the profits from this food business. But coming to Gūgūḍu is not just a business affair for him. Khaja is familiar with some of the foundational ideas of Sufism and he is a practising Muslim, praying five times a day and keeping a month-long fast in the holy month of Ramadan. Often in his conversations, Khaja referred to the names of various Sūfī sites and Sūfī saints too.

> To be honest, I never feel at home in Gūgūḍu. But when I perform rituals for the *pīr* and participate in the final rites of the *pīr*, I feel the *pīr* is an intimate friend (*walī*). Many of these illiterate villagers consider the *pīr* as their god, but god is god (*dēvuḍu*), none can be equal with god. If you visit my food stall in Gūgūḍu, you can see the *ṣahādā* which says "There is no god but Allah, and Muhammad is the messenger of Allah." Kuḷḷāyappa for me is only a *pīr*, but none the less an influential *pīr* in my life. Earlier, we used to go to Ajmer to perform the *ẓiyārat* for Khaja Moinuddin Chisti.[4] My father used to visit Ajmer each year and our family bears the name of Khaja as our middle name. For every occasion, it was our family tradition to visit Ajmer or perform food rituals in the name of Khaja. When I came to Gūgūḍu by chance ten years ago, my family tradition took a new turn and I began participating in the rituals

4. The shrine of Khaja Moinuddin Chishti is a popular pilgrim centre in the religious life of south Indian Muslim life. Each year thousands of Muslims from south India travel to Ajmer to pay respects to Khaja, see Currie (2006).

> of *Tōpi walī sāhib*. Gradually, my food business also took a new turn and during every Muharram we opened a store here for three days. That way, we began to believe that *Tōpi walī sāhib* has shown us a way of livelihood too. In a way, my livelihood and piety are connected. If you ask which comes first, it's difficult. But our family has a long tradition of piety and after turning to *Tōpi walī sāhib* we stuck there. Gūgūḍu is a busy place in the month of Muharram just like any pilgrim place, tens of thousands of devotees visit this place and so it's good for our business too.

Mastan and his family are long-time pilgrims to Gūgūḍu from Bellari during the month of Muharram. Fifty-five-year-old Mastan who now teaches at a primary school in the nearby village of the state of Karnataka started visiting the *pīr* in Gūgūḍu in 1980. Mastan said:

> I was 28 when I made the first *ẓiyāratu* to Gūgūḍu. Since then, Gūgūḍu has become part of our life and rituals, thanks to our everyday prayers at our domestic shrine. When we arrive in Gūgūḍu, we do not feel as if we are outsiders, but we feel as if we are at our home. We feel the constant presence of the *pīr* here at every step. We know that here was the place where the *pīr* walked and was martyred for the *umma* (community).

When I asked him to explain the term *umma*, he said:

> *Umma* is primarily a devotional community that has a faith in the Prophet and venerates the heirs of the Prophet. We perform Muharram in our village: every village does it. But coming to Gūgūḍu is like *ẓiyārat* and *hajj* for our family.

Pointing at the special bus by which he along with seventy devotees of different caste groups had travelled to Gūgūḍu, he said,

> When we come here, we feel that we are meeting a big *umma* of devotees. You've seen them throughout the journey. This is the most crucial journey we make every year during Muharram for the *pīr*.

When Khaja Basha's family visits Gūgūḍu, they travel to Penukoṇḍa and Guntakal to visit local Sūfī shrines as well. But their allegiance remains with *Tōpi walī sāhib*. He said:

> We visit many places, actually. It's not unusual for Muslims to visit several pilgrim places and shrines to perform various rituals. But when we come to Gūgūḍu and visit the *pīr*, we feel this is our family tradition.

Muslims narrate their stories of pilgrimage in a clear pattern that attributes a Sūfī identity to the *pīr* and very often they describe their pilgrimage as an obligatory *hajj*. In practice, they participate in a shared or blended mode of pilgrimage which combines both Muslim and non-Muslim practices. For instance, many Muslim families observe some non-Muslim practices such as rolling the wet bodies — a ritual in which after bathing in the local holy pond, the devotees roll around the ritual standards during the tenth day procession.

Vaiṣṇava Tīrtha

In contrast to Khaja Basha, Tirumala makes an obligatory pilgrimage every year from a town called Proddatur in the district of Kadapa and includes Gūgūḍu among his list of Vaiṣṇava sites. Tirumala is an elementary school teacher and belongs to Śrī Vaiṣṇava sect. He also uses the same term *ẓiyāratu darśanam* for his pilgrimage while using a few Vaiṣṇava terms to describe it. When they visit the *pīr*-house in Gūgūḍu, Tirumala and his family participate in a night-long session of *bhajana*, a collective singing activity. Some of these hymns telling about the experience of pilgrimage and their total surrender to the *pīr*, an act they call *prapatti*.[5] One of the popular hymns usually sung during these *bhajana*s connects various Viṣṇu-related sacred sites in the state of Andhra Pradesh:

> With intense devotion, and surrendering totally
> They prostrate their bodies and stretch their hands towards his feet
> Coming from Kambam, Garudadri and Kadiri
> Never tired of chanting *din govindaa*
> They utter every word for Kuḷḷāyappa
> . . . . only Kuḷḷāyappa
> And their acts culminate in Kuḷḷāyappa
> . . . . only Kuḷḷāyappa.

This hymn not only tells about passionate devotion to the *pīr* Kuḷḷāyappa, but also provides an itinerary of a Vaiṣṇava pilgrimage in Andhra. Kambam, Garudadri and Kadiri are three major Vaiṣṇava sites that have a profound impact on local religious life. By providing this extensive itinerary, local Vaiṣṇavas connect the *pīr* tradition to their community history too.

For Tirumala and many other Vaiṣṇava pilgrims, visiting Gūgūḍu is also an opportunity to extend their itinerary to these Vaiṣṇava sites. During one of our conversations in Gūgūḍu, Tirumala explained the importance to his family of visiting Kuḷḷāyappa. In his words, "visiting the *pīr* is a transformative experience and it guarantees and renews the grace of the

5. For a better understanding of the Vaiṣṇava idea of *prapatti*, see Raman (2007).

pīr." Previously, Tirumala's grandparents used to visit big Vaiṣṇava sites in India. Since his father's generation their family has stopped visiting other Vaiṣṇava places thus confirming their commitment to the *pīr*. Visiting Gūgūḍu has now become their new family tradition. He said,

> *Darśanam* is not just *darśanam*, for a moment's eye contact with the deity or one-time prostration before the deity. Our pilgrimage to Gūgūḍu involves many things as well, although *darśanam* is obviously one of them. The worship for the *pīr* has now become a family tradition for us. We also visit Gūgūḍu when it is not Muharram. Our family is very traditional and when we start something new or perform any family event, it's an imperative for us to make a gift to the *pīr* first.

However, like other pilgrims, Tirumala's family also makes a distinction between regular visits and the annual pilgrimage.

During my conversations with these devotees, I learned some of their experiences including a few miraculous stories about the *pīr*. Some pilgrims connect the teachings of the *pīr* with some of Śaiva teachings. Seventy-year-old Lakṣmamma, one of the pilgrims, belongs to the Liṅgāyat caste in Karnataka. She has been travelling to Gūgūḍu since her twentieth year when she was first introduced to a Śaiva saint named Tikkayya Swāmi whose shrine is located in Nārpala, a town close to Gūgūḍu.

> Devotion means reciting the hymns sung by Tikkayya Swāmi to me when I was a child. But it was during my twentieth year that I realized the importance of making a pilgrimage. Actually the pilgrimage stories of Tikkayya Swāmi made me realize this. Though originally from Karnataka, Tikkayya Swāmi was supposedly a great pilgrim, and visited Gūgūḍu and was blessed by the *pīr*. When I heard the *pīr*'s name from Tikkayya Swāmi, I turned to Kuḷḷāyappa too. When I recite the hymns of Tikkayya Swāmi, though they're for Śiva, they also teach me about the *pīr*. Specifically, the idea of *niyyatu* and *śuddhi* are the same for me. Tikkaya Swāmi's hymns are about the importance of purity of mind and pure intention. When I realized this connection between Tikkayya Swāmi's devotion for both Śiva and the *pīr*, I began to understand his hymns more. Now I also began to understand why Tikkayya Swāmi, though he travelled to hundreds of places, settled close to Kuḷḷāyappa."

For Lakṣmamma, the shrine of Tikkayya Swāmi at Nārpala and the shrine of Kuḷḷāyappa at Gūgūḍu are as local as her native village, Chellikeri, in Karnataka. As she explained, for her coming to Gūgūḍu is like visiting a *tīrtha*. For her, devotion is not about land or space. She said:

> Wandering saints and *faqīrs* never lived in only one place, though their death in one place might be mere chance. We visit Gūgūḍu or Nārpala to remember their last moments and deaths. Wherever these saints resided, that's my home too. That's what I learn from wandering saints such as Tikkayya Swāmi who never settled at a single place, but settled at Nārpala only to die a few days later. Just like Tikkayya Swāmi, Kuḷḷāyappa was also a wandering saint, but was martyred at Gūgūḍu.

In saying this, her emphasis was on the practices of Jaṅgama Śaivas who were supposedly on a constant pilgrimage.[6]

THE HOME-COMING

For a few pilgrims, the annual pilgrimage is an occasion for a family reunion in the presence of their family deity Kuḷḷāyappa. At least a small percentage of these pilgrims are natives of neighbouring villages of Gūgūḍu who migrated to far-off places in search of work, usually as a result of drought and migration. As a result, the population of many villages in the Anantapuram district has been decreasing gradually since the late nineteenth century.[7] Before 1880, Rāyalasīmā including Anantapuram and Kaḍapa districts were famous for their handlooms and the British gazetteers estimate that there were more than 11,000 looms operating there in the early 1880s. The areas around Gūgūḍu were well known for silk-handloom work too. By the 1880s, the market for handloom-woven products was undergoing widespread changes as the colonial British government encouraged merchant-trading, which uprooted the caste-based handloom production of woven goods. This in turn destabilized the rural areas, and urban centres became crucial in the production process. Thousands of villagers who used to live by handloom-weaving migrated to urban centres and when the market began to move towards mechanization, they completely lost their livelihoods. The constant drought and famine affected the lives of rural agricultural societies as well. As two of the most important sources of work in the rural economy came to an end, both agricultural f artisan groups suffered big losses and

6. For more on Jaṅgama Śaivas, see Ramanujan 1973: 20-22. Although locally Śaivism is really a minor sect among the pilgrims to Gūgūḍu, non-Muslims particularly from Karnataka try to find a connection between Śaivism and the teachings of Kuḷḷāyappa.

7. For a study of drought and migration in Anantapuram, see Sainath (1996). According to the gazetteer of Anantapur published in 1908, "the district has suffered constantly from famines, owing to the lightness of the rainfall . . . in the famine of 1876-7, 137, 347 persons were at one time in receipt of relief — more than 18 per cent of the total population" (Francis 1905).

they were forced to migrate to new places to take up new professions. The family of sixty-year-old Yusuf Basha was one of them. His ancestors were handloom weavers and they were forced to leave that profession and turn to petty jobs to earn their livelihoods.

Yusuf Basha himself, however, has interesting rags to riches story. When his family lost their only source of income through the decline of handloom work, they almost became beggars in their own village. He said:

> Economically, our family sank to the lowest depths. Literally, we had to beg for each meal. Then, I made a decision to become involved in the scrap business, selling used metals. This business actually grew so fast that we migrated to Goa after ten years and are now settled in Goa.

Each year during the month of Muharram he and his family visit Gūgūḍu and actively participate in rituals of Gūgūḍu such as *kandūrī*. Yusuf's family also helps to fund the maintenance of the local mosque, and thus they also help to promote localized Islam in Gūgūḍu. Yusuf's family is devout and they sincerely believe that their *imān* in the *pīr* saved them in their hard times. "Only *imān* saved us. Whatever our condition was, wherever we were we never missed a single *namāẓ* and we never fail to remember *Tōpi walī sāhib*."

Yusuf's family can now actually easily afford to go to Mecca for the *hajj*, but they sincerely believe that coming to Gūgūḍu is their *hajj*. Yusuf's wife said:

> This is our annual *hajj* since *Tōpi walī Sāhib* is our family *pīr*. In our family, we all perform regular *namāẓ* and our men go to mosques. This idea of making a choice between the mosque and the *pīr*-house never existed before. As pure Muslims, we do both.

She repeatedly emphasized that they are "pure" (*aslī*) Muslims.

PILGRIMAGE AND BUSINESS

Pilgrim centres are not mere devotional spaces; particularly, in a village context, these places also become immensely profitable business centres. At the beginning of this paper, I narrated the story of Kullayamma for whom this annual pilgrimage has become a family tradition. One specific reason that made this a family tradition is that their family belongs to *dudekula*, a cotton-carder's community and a sub-caste of Muslims. Cotton-carders live on making cotton bedsheets and mattresses. After they have accumulated some money, some of them also take to textile business and sell readymade garments. For Kullayamma's husband Maulana, it's also an opportunity to earn some money by selling his readymade dresses. In Karnataka, his entire family lives on the meagre income from this store. Like Maulana, several of these Muslims are small traders who sell food items such as sweets, readymade dresses, toys and the framed pictures of the local *pīr* Kuḷḷāyappa. They start arriving in Gūgūḍu one day before the first day of the month of Muharram and set up their business stalls. In spite of current tensions between "proper" Muslim practices known as *Aslī Islām* (true Islam) and *pīr* practices, these traders also participate in everyday prayer at the local mosque.

Hussain has a small food store that sells sweets in his hometown. He visits Gūgūḍu each year not only to perform his *hajj* but also to earn some money by selling his products. Non-Muslim devotees also usually set up temporary food carts and earn money by selling their food items. Most important, each year one circus company stays in this village for a week and plays three shows a day attracting large audiences. Surrounding this circus tent, we can also see number of soft drink and snack stalls. A few of them come to Gūgūḍu only to sell their products, but most of them combine this opportunity with earning some religious merit too. However, the idea of *ẓiyāratu darśanam* still preoccupies them. Narayanappa, one of the toy-sellers who visit Gūgūḍu every year said,

> Since it's our livelihood and we just live on day-to-day earnings, we cannot afford to close our business for an entire ten days. Instead, we found this middle way where we can deal with both worlds — the material and the *pīr* ritual. And I don't think they're separate anyhow. It doesn't mean that we are coming here just for money. We make money so that we can make this pilgrimage. We save money throughout the year and make this pilgrimage.

Most of these comments made by my informants reiterate the idea that the act of pilgrimage is an extension of my informant's everyday lives.

Conclusion

Shared sacred spaces are not uncommon in South Asia.[8] Most of the Muslim shrines such as *dargāhs* (tomb shrines) are popular for the shared rituals and devotional practices that take place there. Several studies focus on the significance of the space and highlight the efficacy of the shrines.[9] Although shrines are believed to have a peculiar power, it is also important to understand how pilgrims and devotees make sense of that power.

8. More on sacred spaces in India, see Sikand (2003).
9. For a recent study on *dargāhs*, see Bigelow (2010).

Specifically, the particular act of pilgrimage and the involvement of the pilgrims who consider this act to be a religious obligation provide new meanings to the efficacy of these shared spaces by telling stories with an open religious mind. In essence, the lived and shared experiences of the pilgrims empower the shrine by interweaving their family and community histories with the story of the shrine.

In addition, several studies on Sūfī shrines and saints reiterate the syncretic traditions of the specific shrines. Most of these studies focus on similarities in the pattern of devotion rather than on differences. In Gūgūḍu, we can see that various caste and religious groups are aware of their different identities and even when they visit the local sacred shrines they stick to their differences. Naming their pilgrimage as *ẓiyāratu darśanam* makes explicit this difference, but at the same time it also reveals the ability of the pilgrims to blend those differences conveniently. As we can observe in Gūgūḍu, these differences still work, but they work in a different way in which they begin to learn to respect their differences. Daniel has observed in his study that pilgrimage is a process towards a perfect knowledge that helps a person to connect self and other. Daniel points out that,

> the pilgrimage itself is a ritual, a *karmam* — a very powerful and efficacious *karmam* at that — that seeks to generate this kind of knowing experience, which is expected to help the pilgrim to eventually obtain perfect knowledge, or *vidyā*. — Daniel 1984: 237

However, knowledge and *karmam* are also redefined and reconfigured by local devotees and pilgrims. As one pilgrim in Gūgūḍu told me,

> Knowing the difference is knowledge and knowingly erasing the difference is the lesson we learn from this pilgrim to Kuḷḷāyappa. We come here as different persons, different communities, we pray and talk to the *pīr* in different languages, but the essence of our words remains the same. We are same, but different. We are different, but the same.

References

Bianchi, R. Robert (2004), *Guests of God: Pilgrimage and Politics in the Islamic World*, Oxford: Oxford University Press.

Bigelow, Anna (2010), *Sharing the Sacred: Practicing Pluralism in Muslim North India*, Oxford: Oxford University Press.

Blackburn, Stuart et al. (2003), *South Asian Folklore: An Encyclopedia*, New York: Routledge.

Bowen, John (1983), *Muslims through Discourse: Religion and Ritual in Gayo Society*, Princeton: Princeton University Press.

Chelkowski, P.J. (ed.) (1979), *Tazi'yeh : Ritual and Drama in Iran*, New York: New York University Press.

Currie, P.M. (2006), *The Shrine and Cult of Mu'īn al-Dīn Chishtī of Ajmer*, Delhi: Oxford University Press.

Daniel, E. Valentine (1984), *Fluid Signs: Being a Person the Tamil Way*, Berkeley: University of California Press.

Eck, Diana L. (1981), "India's 'Tirthas': 'Crossings' in Sacred Geography," in *History of Religions*, vol. 20, no. 4, pp. 322-44.

Eickelman, Dale F. and James Piscatori (eds) (1990), *Muslim Travellers: Pilgrimage, Migration, and the Religious Imagination*, Berkeley: University of California Press.

Fischer, Michael (1980), *Iran: From Religious Dispute to Revolution*, Cambridge: Harvard University Press.

Fischer, Michael & Mehdi Abedi (1990), *Debating Muslims: Cultural Dialogues in Postmodernity and Tradition*, Madison: University of Wisconsin Press.

Francis, W. (1905), *Madras District Gazetteers: Anantapur*, Madras: Addison and Co.

Korom, Frank. J. (2003), *Hosay Trinidad, Muharram Performances in an Indo-Caribbean Diaspora*, Philadelphia: University of Pennsylvania Press.

Nasr, Vali Reja Seyyed (2006), *The Shia Revival: How conflicts within Islam Shape the Future*, New York: Norton.

Pinault, David (2001), *The Shiites: Rituals and Popular Piety in a Muslim Community*, New York: Palgrave.

Raman, Srilata (2007), *Self-surrender (prapatti) to God in Srivaishnavism: Tamil Cats or Sanskrit Monkeys?* Hoboken: Taylor and Francis.

Ramanujan, Attipat Krishnaswami (1973), *Speaking of Siva*, Harmondsworth: Penguin.

Sainath, Palagummi (1996), *Everybody Loves a Good Drought: Stories from India's Poorest Districts*, New York: Penguin Books.

Sharif, Ja'far (1921), *Islam in India or the Qanun-i-Islam*, tr. G.A. Herklots, Oxford: Oxford University Press.

Sikand, Yoginder (2003), *Sacred Spaces: Exploring Tradition of Shared Faith in India*, New Delhi: Penguin Books.

Wayne, Husted R. (2003), "Ziyarat," in *South Asian Folklore: An Encyclopaedia: Afghanistan, Bangladesh, India, Nepal, Pakistan, Sri Lanka*, ed. Margaret A. Mills, Peter J. Claus and Sarah Diamond, New York: Routledge.

Werbner, Pnina (2003), *Pilgrims of Love: The Anthropology of a Global Sufi Cult*, Bloomington: Indiana University Press.

Contributors

ASHOK AKLUJKAR is Professor Emeritus in the Department of Asian Studies at the University of British Columbia. There he taught courses in Sanskrit language and in the related mythological and philosophical literatures (occasionally also in Indian belles lettres in general) from 1969 to 2006. His published research is mostly in the areas of Sanskrit linguistic tradition and poetics. He has been a visiting professor at Hamburg, Harvard, Rome, Kyoto, Paris, Oxford and Marburg.

GREGORY BAILEY, formerly reader in Sanskrit, is an Honorary Research Fellow in the Program in Asian Studies, La Trobe University, Melbourne. He has published translations and studies of the *Gaṇeśa Purāṇa*, Bhartṛhari's *Śatakatrayam* and books on the god Brahmā, early Buddhism and many articles on Sanskrit literature. At present he is working on social, literary and economic aspects of the relationship between early Buddhism and the *Mahābhārata*.

JOHN BROCKINGTON is Emeritus Professor of Sanskrit at the University of Edinburgh, U.K., Secretary General of the International Association of Sanskrit Studies, and the author or editor of several books and numerous articles, mainly on the Sanskrit epics and the history of Hinduism.

CHRISTOPHER KEY CHAPPLE is Doshi Professor of Indic and Comparative Theology at Loyola Marymount University in Los Angeles. He has published more than a dozen books, including *Reconciling Yogas: Haribhadra's Collection of Views on Yoga* (2003) and *Yoga and the Luminous: Patañjali's Spiritual Path to Freedom* (2008, winner of the Gandhi Prize for Dharma Studies), and several edited volumes on religion and ecology. He serves as editor of the journal *Worldviews: Global Religions, Culture, and Ecology* (Brill) and is on the advisory boards for the *Forum on Religion and Ecology* (Yale) and the *Ahimsa Center* (Pomona).

MADHAV M. DESHPANDE was originally trained in Sanskrit Studies in Pune, India. With a Master's degree in Sanskrit from the University of Pune (1968), Deshpande came to Philadelphia and received his Ph.D. degree from the University of Pennsylvania in 1972. From 1972, Deshpande has served as Professor of Sanskrit and Linguistics at the University of Michigan in Ann Arbor. He has published over fifteen books and more than a hundred research papers relating to the areas of Sanskrit linguistics, Indian languages, cultures, and philosophy.

JONATHAN DUQUETTE is currently a Visiting Researcher at the Asien-Afrika-Institut from the Universität Hamburg, Germany. He received his Ph.D. in Religious Studies with Prof. Trichur S. Rukmani as his supervisor and has also been her research assistant for several years. His research interests include Advaita Vedānta, Indian Buddhism, Sanskrit commentarial literature and the interaction between natural sciences and philosophy of religion. He has published articles in *Philosophy East and West*, *Journal of Indian Philosophy*, *Numen* and *Zygon: Journal of Religion and Science*. He lives in Germany with his wife Aslihan and their son Emil-Jivan.

JOHN GRIMES received his B.A. in Religious Studies from the University of California at Santa Barbara and his M.A. and Ph.D. in Indian Philosophy from the University of Madras. He has taught at Universities in the United States, Canada, Singapore and India. He has published several books, including *Ramana Maharshi: The Crown Jewel of Advaita* (2010), *The Vivekacūḍāmaṇi of Śaṅkarācārya Bhagavatpāda* (2004) and *A Concise Dictionary of Indian Philosophy* (1996). He currently spends his time writing and travelling between California and Chennai.

EDELTRAUD HARZER teaches courses in Sanskrit, Indian Philosophy, Indian Epics, the Art of the Body in India, and the Culture of Food in India in Department of Asian Studies of the University of Texas at Austin since 1998. Among several awards, was a fellowship from the National Endowment for the Humanities. She has published in scholarly journals and has written articles for Encyclopedias. Her book *The Yuktidīpikā: A Reconstruction of Sāṅkhya Methods of Knowing* pieces together the little known epistemology of Sāṁkhya in the context of the second half philosophical debate of the first millennia CE.

BARBARA A. HOLDREGE is Professor of Religious Studies and Chair of the South Asian Studies Committee at the University of California, Santa Barbara. Her research and teaching interests as a comparative historian of religions focus on historical and textual studies of Hindu and Jewish traditions and also engage broader theoretical issues arising out of critical interrogation of analytical categories such as the body, space, scripture, and ritual. Her current research is concerned with Hindu discourses of the body and constructions of sacred space in South Asia. Her publications include *Veda and Torah: Transcending the Textuality of Scripture*; *Bhakti and Embodiment: Fashioning Divine Bodies and Devotional Bodies in Kṛṣṇa Bhakti*; and two edited volumes, *Ritual and Power* and *Refiguring the Body: Embodiment in South Asian Religions*.

PANKAJ JAIN is an Assistant Professor at the Departments of Anthropology and of Philosophy and Religion Studies, University of North Texas. He is the author of *Dharma and Ecology of Hindu Communities: Sustenance and Sustainability* (Ashgate 2011) and has also published articles in journals such as *Religious Studies Review*, *Worldviews*, *Religion Compass*, *Journal of Vaishnava Studies*, *Union Seminary Quarterly Review*, and the *Journal of Visual Anthropology*. He also contributes to the Huffington Post, Washington Post's forum *On Faith*, and Patheos.com.

GEORGE A. JAMES is Associate Professor of Philosophy and Religion Studies at the University of North Texas. For the past twenty years he has been researching in the areas of comparative environmental philosophy and environmental movements in India. He has recently completed a monograph concerning the activism and environmental philosophy of the Indian environmentalist Sunderlal Bahuguna.

P. PRATAP KUMAR is Professor of Hindu Studies and Indian Philosophy and Comparative Religions in the School of Religion and Theology, University of KwaZulu Natal, South Africa. In addition to several scholarly essays and articles, his publications include *The Goddess Lakshmi in South Indian Vaishnavism* (1997); *Hindus in South Africa: Their Traditions and Beliefs* (2000); *Methods and Theories in the Study of Religions: Perspectives from the Study of Hinduism and other Indian Religions* (2004); *Religious Pluralism and the Diaspora*, edited by P. Pratap Kumar (2006). He was also one of the editors of the Numen Book Series of the International Association for the History of Religions, published by Brill.

RAMDAS LAMB is currently an Associate Professor in the Religion Department at the University of Hawai'i. He was a Hindu monk for nearly ten years before pursuing an academic career. For more than thirty years, he has been working to help educate village youth in Central India, for which he founded the Sahayog Foundation (www.sahayogfoundation.org).

GERALD JAMES LARSON is Tagore Professor Emeritus, Indiana University, Bloomington, and Professor Emeritus, Religious Studies, UC Santa Barbara. He is also currently serving as Research Professor, University of California, Irvine. He is the author or editor of some twelve books and well over one hundred scholarly articles on cross-cultural philosophy of religion, history of religions, classical Sanskrit and South Asian history and culture. His recent books include *India's Agony over Religion* (1995, 1997), *Changing Myths and Images* (1997), and *Religion and Personal Law in Secular India: A Call to Judgment* (2002).

DAVID PETER LAWRENCE received his Ph.D. from the University of Chicago, and is Associate Professor in the Department of Philosophy and Religion at the University of North Dakota. His publications include the books *Rediscovering God with Transcendental Argument* (1999) and *The Teachings of the Odd-Eyed One* (2008).

AFSAR MOHAMMAD has achieved his Ph.D. on the shared devotional practices of Hinduism and Islam in south India from the University of Wisconsin–Madison. Currently, he is a lecturer at the University of Texas at Austin. He is teaching South Asian religion courses along with the Telugu language. Afsar has recently published two publications in the *Oxford Journal of Hindu Studies*, and in the edited volume of *Transfer and Spaces* published by Harroswitz, Germany. He is a well-known poet and literary theorist in Telugu and won *Bhasha Saraswatee Samman*, a prestigious literary award from the Government of India in 2007.

CARL OLSON teaches at Allegheny College. Besides numerous essays in journals, books and encyclopedias, he has published 15 books on subjects such as Hinduism, Buddhism, comparative philosophy, and method and theory in the study of religion. Professor Olson has been appointed to following positions: Holder of the National Endowment for the Humanities Chair, 1991-94; Holder of the Teacher-Scholar Chair in the Humanities, 2000-03; Visiting Fellowship at Clare Hall, University of Cambridge, 2002; and elected Life Member of Clare Hall, University of Cambridge, 2002.

LESLIE C. ORR is an Associate Professor in the Department of Religion at Concordia University, Montreal, Canada. Her research interests include the religious and social history of medieval Tamil Nadu; temple architecture, iconography and epigraphy; the interaction of Hinduism, Buddhism, Jainism, and Islam; the history of south Indian Śaivism; and colonial archaeology. She is the author of the book *Donors, Devotees and Daughters of God: Temple Women in Medieval Tamilnadu* (2000) and numerous articles.

VARADARAJA V. RAMAN is Emeritus Professor of Physics and Humanities at the Rochester Institute of Technology. He has authored articles and books on the philosophical, historical, and cultural aspects of science, and on aspects of Indic culture. He is in the editorial boards of the *Encyclopedia of Hinduism*, *Zygon: Journal of Religion and Science*, and *Theology and Science*. Currently, he is President of IRAS: Institute on Religion in an Age of Science.

K. RAMASUBRAMANIAN holds a Ph.D. in theoretical physics from the University of Madras. His areas of research include non-linear dynamics, Indian astronomy and mathematics as well as Indian philosophy. He has authored several books and articles in the area of Indian astronomy and mathematics. For completing a rigorous course in Advaita Vedānta he was honoured with the coveted title *Vidvat Pravara* in 2003. He was also conferred in 2008, the prestigious *Maharshi Badarayan Vyas Samman* by the President of India, in recognition of his outstanding contribution towards the synergy between tradition and modernity. Currently he is Associate Professor at the Cell for Indian Science and Technology in Sanskrit at IIT Bombay (India).

DANIEL RAVEH is a lecturer at the Department of Philosophy, Tel Aviv University. He works in the fields of Indian and comparative philosophy. His book *Exploring the Yogasūtra: Philosophy and Translation* is forthcoming with Continuum Press. He is co-editor of *Contrary Thinking: Selected Essays of Daya Krishna*, forthcoming with Oxford University Press.

FREDERICK M. SMITH is Professor of Sanskrit and Classical Indian Religions at the University of Iowa. His interests have been in Vedic ritual, deity and spirit possession in South Asia, the philosophical and religious teachings of the early sixteenth-century North Indian Vaiṣṇava leader Vallabhācārya, and the *Mahābhārata*. His most recent book is *The Self Possessed: Deity and Spirit Possession in South Asian Literature and Civilization* (2006), and is in the final stages of translation of the last five books of the *Mahābhārata* for the University of Chicago Press.

VIDYASANKAR SUNDARESAN is a chemical engineer working as a Lead Technologist at GE Power and Water. He is an independent scholar of Indian philosophy who maintains a website on Advaita Vedānta (www.advaita-vedanta.org/avhp) and has contributed papers to journals such as *Philosophy East and West*.

STHANESHWAR TIMALSINA (Ph.D. Martin Luther University, Halle, Germany) is an Associate Professor in the Department of Religious Studies at San Diego State University. He works mainly in the areas of Indian religions and philosophies. Two of his books, *Seeing and Appearance* (2006) and

Consciousness in Indian Philosophy (2009), explore the Advaita Vedānta philosophy of consciousness. He has published number of essays in Tantric studies. He is currently working on a book, *Language of Images*, that examines meaning and visualization of Tantric images.

IAN WHICHER received his Ph.D. from the University of Cambridge. He is a Professor and Head of the Department of Religion at the University of Manitoba and specializes in the Yoga tradition. He is the author of several books and articles including *The Integrity of the Yoga Darśana*, and co-editor of *Yoga: The Indian Tradition*.

Appointments and Publications

Professional Appointments

Lecturer in Sanskrit, Kamala Nehru College, Jodhpur, Rajasthan, India (1962).

Lecturer and Senior Lecturer in Sanskrit, Indraprastha College, University of Delhi, New Delhi, India (1964-81).

Post-Doctoral Fellow, Department of Indian Studies, University of Toronto, Toronto, Canada (1972-73).

Director, Non-collegiate Women's Education Board, University of Delhi, New Delhi, India (1981-82).

Principal, Miranda House, University of Delhi, New Delhi, India (1982-93).

Professor, Department of Hindu Studies and Indian Philosophy, University of Durban, Westville, South Africa (1993-95).

Professor and Chair (of Hindu Studies), Department of Religion, Concordia University, Montreal, Canada (1996-present).

Adjunct Professor, Hindu University of America, Orlando, USA (2002-present).

Visiting Professor, Shivdasani Fellow, Oxford University Hindu Studies Centre, Oxford University, UK (April-June 2006).

Adjunct Professor, Faculty of Theology and Sciences of Religions, University of Montreal, Montreal, Canada (2006-11).

Visiting Professor, Jawaharlal Nehru University, New Delhi, India (April-August 2007).

Visiting Professor, Madras University, Chennai, India (April-August 2007).

List of Publications

1971 *A Critical Study of the Bhāgavata Purāṇa*, Varanasi: Chowkhamba Sanskrit Series, 1971.

1978 "The Theory of Knowledge in the Yoga System" *Ganganatha Jha Kendriya Sanskrit Vidyapeetha*, vol. 34, 1978, pp. 83-90.

1978 "Vijñānabhikṣu on Bhava-Pratyaya and Upāya-Pratyaya Yogīs in Yoga-sūtras" *Journal of Indian Philosophy*, vol. 5, no. 4, 1978, pp. 311-17.

1980 "*Vikalpa* as Defined by Vijñānabhikṣu in the *Yogavārttika*", *Journal of Indian Philosophy*, vol. 8, no. 4, 1980, pp. 385-92.

1981-89 *Yogavārttika of Vijñānabhikṣu's*, Delhi: Munshiram Manoharlal, 4 vols., 1981-89.

1981 "Patañjali's *Yogasūtras*: A Synthesis of Many Yogic Traditions", *Annals of the Bhandarkar Oriental Research Institute*, vol. 62, 1981, pp. 213-18.

1984 "*Samprajñāta samādhi* in the Pātañjala Yoga System : Difference in Interpretation between Vācaspati Miśra and Vijñānabhikṣu", *Ganganatha Jha Kendriya Sanskrit Vidyapeetha*, vol. 11, 1984, pp. 47-57.

1985 "*Sphoṭa* and the Pātañjala *Yogasūtras*", *Śodha-prabhā* (*Dr. Rajendra Prasad Birth Centenary Volume*), Part four (Philosophy), 1985, pp. 103-08.

1986 "Avidyā in the System of Yoga and an Analysis of the Negation in it", *Adyar Library Bulletin*, Golden Jubilee Volume, vol. 50, 1986, pp. 526-34.

1987 "Patañjali's Prajñā and Bhartṛhari's Pratibhā: A Comparative Study" *Indian Philosophical Quarterly*, vol. 14, no. 1, 1987, pp. 81-90.

1988 *Religious Consciousness and Life Worlds* (editor), Shimla: Indian Institute of Advanced Study, 1988.

1988 "Vijñānabhikṣu's Double Reflection Theory of Knowledge in the Yoga System", *Journal of Indian Philosophy*, vol. 16, no. 4, 1988, pp. 367-75.

1989 "Moral Dilemmas in the Mahābhārata", in *Moral Dilemmas in the Mahābhārata*, ed. B.K. Matilal, Shimla: Indian Institute of Advanced Study, 1989, pp. 20-34.

1990 "Women in the *Bhāgavata Purāṇa*", in *Purāṇa and National Integration*, ed. P. Kumar, Delhi: Nag Publishers, 1990, pp. 1-11.

1991 *Śaṅkara: The Man and his Philosophy*, Shimla: Indian Institute of Advanced Study, 1991.

1991 "Kālidāsa and Shakespeare: A Study in Contrast", in *Kulshreshta Commemoration Volume*, ed. S. Kulashreshta and S. Narang, Delhi: Eastern Book Linkers, pp. 216-20.

1992 "Upaniṣadic Philosophy and the *Pañcakoṣa* Concept Compared with Recent Humanistic Psychology in the West", in *Philosophy, Grammar and Indology* (Essays in honour of Professor Gustav Roth), ed. H.S. Prasad, Delhi: Indian Books Centre, 1992, pp. 383-88.

1992 "Quality of Life and the *puruṣārthas*", in *Quality of Life*, ed. A. Dutta and M.M. Agrawal, Shimla: Indian Institute of Advanced Study, 1992, pp. 195-206.

1992 "The Problem of the Authorship of the Yogasūtra-bhāṣya-vivaraṇam", *Journal of Indian Philosophy*, vol. 20, no. 4, 1992, pp. 419-23.

1993 "Siddhis in the Bhāgavata Purāṇa and the Yogasūtras: A Comparison", in *Researches in Indian and Buddhist Philosophy* (Essays in Honour of Prof. Alex Wayman), ed. R.K. Sharma, Delhi: Motilal Banarsidass, 1993, pp. 217-25.

1993 "Folk Traditions Related to the Mahābhārata in South India", in *The Mahābhārata in the Tribal and Folk Traditions of India*, ed. K.S. Singh, Shimla: Indian Institute of Advanced Study, 1993, pp. 184-96.

1993 "Śaṅkara's Views on Yoga in the Light of the Authorship of the Yogasūtra-bhāṣya-vivaraṇa", *Journal of Indian Philosophy*, vol. 21, no. 4, 1993, pp. 395-404.

1994 *Śaṅkarācārya*, Delhi: Publications Division, Government of India, 1994 (reprinted in 2000).

1994 "The Concept of Jīvanmukti in the Advaita-Vedānta and Sāṁkhya-Yoga Traditions", In *Pandit N.R. Bhatt Felicitation Volume*, ed. P.-S. Filliozat, S.P. Narang and C.P. Bhatta, Delhi: Motilal Banarsidass, 1994, pp. 311-17.

1994 "Vitaṇḍa in the Khaṇḍanakhaṇḍa-khādya", *Adyar Library Bulletin*, vol. 48, 1994, pp. 1-13.

1995 "Environmental Ethics as Enshrined in Sanskrit Sources",*Nidan*, Journal of the Department of Hindu Studies and Indian Philosophy, University of Durban (Westville), vol. 7, 1995, pp. 30-41.

1995 "Bhakti, the Bhāgavata Purāṇa and the Empowerment of Women", *Journal for the Study of Religion in South Africa*, vol. 8, no. 1, 1995, pp. 55-70.

1997 "Tension between Vyutthāna and Nirodha in the Yoga-Sūtras", *Journal of Indian Philosophy*, vol. 25, no. 6, 1997, pp. 613-28.

1998 "Saṁnyāsa and Some Indian Reform Movements in the 18th, 19th and 20th centuries", *Adyar Library Bulletin*, vol. 62, 1998, pp. 23-50.

1998 "The Yogasūtrabhāṣyavivaraṇa Is Not a Work of Śaṅkarācārya the Author of the Brahmasūtrabhāṣya", *Journal of Indian Philosophy*, vol. 26, no. 3, 1998, pp. 263-74.

1998 "Critique of 'Om' Based on the Upaniṣads: tasya vācakaḥ praṇavaḥ (Yogasūtra I. 27)", *Journal of the Institute of Asian Studies*, vol. 15, no. 2, 1998, pp. 101-12.

1998 "Sannyāsa, Śaṅkara and the Bhagavadgītā", *Journal of Studies on Ancient India*, World Association for the Study of World Religions, 1998, pp. 8-23.

1998 "Mahātma Gandhi and Women", *Journal of Gender in World Religions*, McGill University, December 1998, pp. 1-27.

1999 "Sāṅkhya and Yoga: Where They Do Not Speak in One Voice", *Asiatische Studien (Études Asiatiques)*, vol. 53, no. 3, 1999, pp. 733-53.

2000 "Literary Foundations for an Ecological Aesthetic: Dharma, Āyurveda, the Arts, and Abhijñāna-śākuntalam", in *Hinduism and Ecology: The Intersection of Earth, Sky and Water*, ed. C. Chapple and M.E. Tucker, Cambridge: Harvard University Press for the Center for the Study of World Religions, 2000, pp. 101-27.

2000 "Vedānta and the Bhakti Traditions" in *Facets of Indian Culture*, ed. P.C. Muraleemadhavan, New Delhi: Bharatiya Book Corporation, 2000, pp. 125-47.

2000 "*Jīvanmukti* in *Sāṁkhya-Yoga:* Is it Ontic or Epistemic?" In *Quest for Excellence*, ed. D.P. Chattopadhyaya, Delhi: Richa Prakashan, 2000, pp. 148-53.

2000 "Turmoil, Hope and the Swādhyāyamaṇḍali", in *South Asia between Turmoil and Hope*, ed. H. Johnston et al., Montreal: Canadian Asian Studies Association and Shastri Indo Canadian Institute, 2000, pp. 223-37.

2000 "Indian Theories of Self", in *Concise Routledge Encyclopedia of Philosophy*, London/New York: Routledge, p. 812.

2001 *Yogasūtra-bhāṣyavivaraṇa*, Delhi: Munshiram Manoharlal, 2 vols., 2001.

2001 *Yogasūtras of Patañjali with the Commentary of Vyāsa*, Montreal: Chair in Hindu Studies, Concordia University, 2001.

2001 *Hindu Diaspora: Global Perspectives* (ed.), Jointly published by the Chair in Hindu Studies (Montreal, Concordia University), 1999 and Munshiram Manoharlal (Delhi), 2001.

2001 "Prakṛti as material and efficient cause in the Yogasūtra", *Adyar Library Bulletin*, vol. 65, 2001, pp. 57-71.

2001 Review of David Gordon White's (ed.) *Tantra in Practice*, *Religiologiques*, vol. 24, 2001, pp. 284-88.

2002 "The Epics and the Purāṇas Supplement the Vedas", *Annals of the Bhandarkar Oriental Research Institute*, vol. 82, 2002, pp. 125-41.

2003 "Perception in Yoga", in *Perception: East and West*, ed. V.N. Jha, Delhi: Srisatguru Publications, 2003, pp. 1-10.

2003 "The Problematic of Karma and Karmajñāna-samuccaya in the Bhagavadgītābhāṣya of Śaṅkarācārya", in *Paramparā: Essays in Honour of R. Balasubramanian*, ed. S. Rao and G. Mishra, Delhi: Indian Council for Philosophical Research, 2003, pp. 191-211.

2003 "Gandhi and Tagore", in *Indian Critiques of Gandhi*, ed. H. Coward, New York: SUNY, 2003, pp. 107-28.

2003 "Consciousness Theories in the Six Āstikadarśanas", *Studies in Humanities and Social Sciences: Journal of Inter-University Centre*, IIAS, vol. 10, no. 1, 2003, pp. 22-34.

2003 "Dr. Richard De Smet and Śaṅkara's Advaita Vedānta", *Hindu-Christian Studies Bulletin*, vol. 16, 2003, pp. 12-21.

2003 "Prajñā in the Yogasūtra", *Adyar Library Bulletin*, vol. 67, 2003, pp. 75-89.

2004 Review of Bradley Malkovsky's The Role of Divine Grace in the Soteriology of Śaṅkarācārya, *Journal of the American Oriental Society*, vol. 124, no. 4, pp. 813-16.

2005 *The Mahābhārata: What is Not Here is Nowhere Else* (ed.), Delhi: Munshiram Manoharlal, 2005.

2005 "Dharmaputra in the Context of Rājadharma and Āpaddharma in the Śāntiparvan", in *The Mahābhārata: What is Not Here is Nowhere Else*, ed. T.S. Rukmani, Delhi: Munshiram Manoharlal, 2005, pp. 179-93.

2005 "Revisiting the Jīvanmukti Question in Context of the Sāṁkhyasūtra", in *Theory and Practice of Yoga: Essays in Honour of Gerald James Larson*, ed. K. Jacobsen, Leiden/Boston: Brill, 2005, pp. 61-74.

2005 "Hindu Saṁnyāsins: Changing Perspectives", in *Encyclopedia of Indian Wisdom* (Felicitation Volume for Prof. Satyavrat Sastry, ed. R.K. Sharma, Delhi: Bharatiya Vidya Prakashan, 2005.

2006 "Yoga in Śaṅkara's Advaita Vedānta", *Annals of the Bhandarkar Oriental Research Institute*, vol. 87, 2006, pp. 123-34.

2007 "Vijñānabhikṣu: A Maverick Philosopher", *Journal of Indian Council of Philosophical Research*, vol. 24, no. 4, 2007, pp. 131-43.

2007 "Dharmamegha-samādhi in the Yogasūtras of Patañjali: A Critique", *Philosophy East and West*, vol. 57, no. 2, 2007, pp. 131-39.

2007 "Ethics in Śaṅkara's Advaita Vedānta", *The Voice of Śaṅkara*, vol. 32, nos. 1-2, 2007, pp. 59-76.

2008 "Value Ethics in the Early Upaniṣads: A Hermeneutic Approach", in *Hermeneutics and Hindu Thought: Toward a Fusion of Horizons*, ed. R.D. Sharma and A. Sharma, Springer Science+Business Media, 2008, pp. 151-68.

2008 "*Yogavārtttika* of *Vijñānabhikṣu:* A Summary" and "Yogasūtrabhāṣyavivaraṇa of Śaṅkara: A Summary", in *The Encyclopedia of Indian Philosophies – Yoga: India's Philosophy of Meditation* (vol.XII), ed. G.J. Larson and R.S. Bhattacharya, Delhi: Motilal Banarsidass, 2008, pp. 239-60 and pp. 295-320 (respectively).

2008 "Philosophical Hermeneutics within a Darśana (Philosophical School)", *The Journal of Hindu Studies*, vol. 1, nos. 1-2, 2008, pp. 120-37.

2008 "Methodological Approaches to Hindu-Christian Studies: Some Thoughts", *Journal of Hindu-Christian Studies*, vol. 21, 2008, pp. 43-47.

2009 "Ahiṁsā versus Hiṁsā in the Context of Hinduism", in *Wisdom Indologica: Prof. A.C. Sarangi Felicitation Volume*, ed. R. Dash, New Delhi: Pratibha Prakashan, 2009, pp. 300-12.

2009 "Rethinking Gender based on Sanskrit Texts", *Annals of the Bhandarkar Oriental Research Institute*, vol. 90, 2009, pp. 177-94.

2009 "Women Characters in the Mahābhārata in the Context of Dharma", in *The*

Journal of Oriental Research, Madras (for Dr. V. Raghavan Birth Centenary Commemoration Volume), ed. V. Kameshvari et al., Chennai: Kuppuswamy Sastri Research Institute, 2009-2010, pp. 112-32.

2010 "*Saṁnyāsins* in a Temple Context", in *Archaeology and Text: The Temple in South Asia*, ed. H. Prabha Ray, Oxford: Oxford University Press, 2010, pp. 296-311.

2010 "Mind and Consciousness in Indian philosophy" and "Jīvanmukti in Indian Philosophy", in *Encyclopedia of Hinduism*, Netherlands: Brill/Reidel Publication, 2010.

2011 *Saṁnyāsins in the Hindu Tradition: Changing Perspectives*, Delhi: D.K. Printworld, 2011.

2011 "Vijñānabhikṣu: The Sāṁkhya-Yoga-Vedāntācārya", *Journal of Indian Council for Philosophical Research*, vol. 27, no. 3, 204 pp. 21-38.

2011 "Reconciliation of mukti for Śisupāla in the Bhāgavata Purāṇā: A Critique", in *Fourteenth World Sanskrit Conference Proceedings*, ed. N. Sheth, forthcoming.

2011 "Sāṁkhya-Yoga", in *The Oxford Handbook of World Philosophy*, ed. W. Edelglass and J. Garfield, New York: Oxford University Press, 2011, pp. 127-37.

2012 "How Much Adhikāra Does a Commentator Have to Interpret a Śāstra Text", in *Modern Perspectives in Vedanta: Proceedings of the 20th International Congress of Vedanta, December 28-31, 2011*, JNU, New Delhi, 2012, pp. 84-96.

2012 "Intellectual Freedom in Ancient India", *Journal of Rashtriya Sanskrit Sansthan Saṁskṛtavimarśaḥ*, World Sanskrit Conference Special, vol. 6, 2012, pp. 183-97.

2013 "Vijñānabhikṣu's Approach to the Īśvara Concept in Patañjali's Yogasūtras", *Hindu-Christian Bulletin*, forthcoming.

Index

361, 394-408 *passim*, 413, 420, 429
ego/egoity, 53, 58, 60, 65, 83, 85, 105, 107, 109, 120, 160
Eliade, Mircea, 48n3, 55n18, 64, 236, 245
embodiment, 48, 61, 63, 94, 155, 157-59, 161, 166, 168-69, 171-72, 174, 243, 442
emptiness, 18, 21
energy, 25, 72, 211, 220, 254, 349, 360, 363, 375, 422
environment/environmentalism, 3, 329-30, 335, 340-41, 343, 348, 352n12, 355, 357-58
environmental ethics, 10, 329-30, 333, 343-45, 357-58, 447
evil, 12, 239, 242, 301, 370, 378-86, 388, 391-92, 412n6, 415

Foucault, Michel, 269, 273
freedom, 5, 12-13, 23, 26-29, 48, 51-52, 56n19, 60, 63-64, 68n4, 69, 93, 111, 140, 161, 233, 236-37, 241-46, 334, 370-71, 385, 389-90, 392, 419, 421, 440, 450
free will, 12, 387-90 *passim*

Gandhi, Mohandas Karamchand, 12, 233, 245, 333-41 *passim*, 361, 369-77 *passim*, 378, 381, 391-92, 413-14, 448-49
Gauḍapāda (Vedānta), 103, 112, 119-20, 123n1, 245
Gauḍīya-Vaiṣṇavism, 7, 155-75 *passim*
Gautama (Nyāya), 230, 273, 275
Ghosh, Aurobindo, 233, 245
god/God, 5-6, 12, 36, 40-41, 65, 74, 77-95 *passim*, 105-06, 115, 159-60, 174, 212, 270, 279, 339, 341, 344, 346, 352-53, 355, 359, 378-82, 384-93, 417, 421, 422-23, 431, 438-40, 443
goddess/Goddess, 219-20, 224-25, 227, 307n1, 308, 330-31, 345, 411n4, 442
Godhead, 157-63, 172
guṇa, 8, 20, 25-27, 38n19, 50-54, 57-58, 71, 74-75, 158, 239-42, 244-45
guru, 40n23, 41, 55, 101, 106-07, 116, 143, 145, 202n36, 203, 308, 312n9, 319n16, 320-21, 324, 332, 343, 357-58, 394, 420-21

Habermas, Jürgen, 271
Hacker, Paul, xvi, 40n24, 45, 123n1, 135, 138, 174
hagiography, 306, 312n9, 314, 318, 320
hajj, 425, 427-30, 432, 436-37
Haribhadra, 23, 29, 440
Harivaṁśa, 251-52, 255n12, 265
Hauer, Jakob Wilhelm, 27, 29, 65, 245
Hegel, Georg Wilhelm Friedrich, 90-92, 95
Heidegger, Martin, 11-12, 65, 361-70, 373-77
Helārāja, 198, 208-09, 212n2, 218, 225-26, 231
hermeneutics, 250, 268, 270n3, 449
Hindu diaspora, xvii, 268, 345, 407-08, 421, 448
Hinduism, xiv-xv, xvii-xviii, 3, 13, 45-46, 63, 67n3, 68n4, 76, 156,